U.S. SUPREME COURT, 1975

Standing, left to right: Lewis F. Powell, Jr., Thurgood Marshall, Harry A. Blackmun, William H. Rehnquist

Seated, left to right: Potter Stewart, William O. Douglas, Chief Justice Warren E. Burger, William J. Brennan, Byron R. White

American

CHARLES E. MERRILL PUBLISHING COMPANY
A Bell & Howell Company
Columbus, Ohio

Constitutional Law
Text and Cases

Albert B. Saye

The University of Georgia

MERRILL POLITICAL SCIENCE SERIES

Under the Editorship of
John C. Wahlke

Department of Political Science
University of Iowa

Published by
Charles E. Merrill Publishing Company
A Bell & Howell Company
Columbus, Ohio 43216

This book was set in Times Roman and Optima.
The production editor was Linda Gambaiani.
The cover was designed by Will Chenoweth.

ISBN: 0–675–08746–5

Library of Congress Catalog Card Number: 74–33811

1   2   3   4   5   6   7   8—82   81   80   79   78   77   76   75

Printed in the United States of America

Preface

This book is designed as a text for courses in American constitutional law. It consists primarily of a selection of cases designed to show how the Supreme Court has interpreted the Constitution of the United States. Emphasis is on recent cases; hence, there are separate chapters on freedom of religion, freedom of speech, equal protection of law, and criminal procedure. Cases to July 25, 1974, are included. The first chapter contains material on the organization and operation of the federal courts and introduces the subject of judicial review. The proper place of the judiciary in our constitutional system remains a subject of interest throughout the text and explains the inclusion of many of the concurring and dissenting opinions.

The opinions of the Supreme Court are quoted from the official United States Reports. The headnotes are not always quotations.

Portions of this text were published by Callaghan & Company in 1965. I express appreciation to Rae S. Smith and other members of that company for pleasant relations. My indebtedness to Noel T. Dowling and other authors in the field is great. I am also indebted to Olive Hall Shadgett for help in editing the manuscript and to Joan Burns for typing it. Suggestions for corrections or revisions of the text will be welcomed.

A.B.S.

To Ruth

Contents

TABLE OF CASES   xv

Part I. Governmental Powers

CHAPTER 1.   THE JUDICIARY

  A. Introduction   5

  B. Judicial Review   15

  C. Evaluation of Judicial Review   29

  D. Congressional Control over Judiciary   38
     Ex parte McCardle

  E. Law Applied   41
     Erie Railroad Co. v. *Tompkins*
     Texas v. *New Jersey*

  F. Equity   48

  G. Suits against States   48
     Ex parte Young

CHAPTER 2. THE PRESIDENT

  A. Introduction   53

  B. Enforcement of Laws   56
     In re Neagle
     Youngstown Sheet & Tube Co. v. *Sawyer*
     United States v. *Nixon*

C. Foreign Relations   **64**
    United States v. *Curtiss-Wright Export Corp.*
    United States v. *Belmont*
    Kent v. *Dulles*

D. Military Powers   **70**
    The Prize Cases
    Korematsu v. *United States*

E. Appointments and Removals   **74**
    Wiener v. *United States*

F. Pardons   **77**
    Ex parte Grossman

CHAPTER 3. THE CONGRESS

A. Introduction   **81**
    McCulloch v. *Maryland*

B. Regulation of Commerce   **93**
    Gibbons v. *Ogden*
    The Shreveport Rate Case
    Hammer v. *Dagenhart*
    United States v. *Darby*
    Heart of Atlanta Motel, Inc. v. *United States*

C. Fiscal Powers   **108**
    Hylton v. *United States*
    Veazie Bank v. *Fenno*
    Bailey v. *Drexel Furniture Co.*
    Charles C. Steward Machine Co. v. *Davis*

D. Protection of Civil Rights   **115**
    Katzenbach v. *Morgan*
    Oregon v. *Mitchell*
    Jones v. *Alfred H. Mayer Co.*

CHAPTER 4. THE STATES

A. Introduction   **123**

B. Regulation of Commerce   **125**
    Cooley v. *Board of Wardens*
    Leisy v. *Hardin*
    Finch & Co. v. *McKittrick*
    South Carolina State Highway Dept. v. *Barnwell*
    Hood & Sons v. *Du Mond*
    Guss v. *Utah Labor Board*

C. Taxation of Commerce   **141**
    Brown v. *Maryland*
    Kosydar v. *National Cash Register Co.*
    Best & Co. v. *Maxwell*
    Henneford v. *Silas Mason Co.*
    Braniff Airways v. *Nebraska*
    General Motors v. *Washington*
    Evco v. *Jones*

CHAPTER 5. INTERGOVERNMENTAL RELATIONS

A.	Taxation	**163**
B.	Regulations	**168**
C.	State and National Courts	**169**
D.	Rendition	**172**
E.	Full Faith and Credit	**173**
F.	Interstate Agreements	**173**

Part II. Civil Rights

CHAPTER 6. THE ORIGINAL CONSTITUTION

A.	Introduction	**179**
B.	Writ of Habeas Corpus *Duncan* v. *Kahanamoku*	**179**
C.	Bill of Attainder *United States* v. *Lovett*	**184**
D.	Ex Post Facto Laws *Calder* v. *Bull*	**186**
E.	The Contract Clause *Fletcher* v. *Peck* *Charles River Bridge* v. *Warren Bridge* *Stone* v. *Mississippi* *Home Building and Loan Ass'n* v. *Blaisdell*	**188**
F.	Trial by Jury (Treated in chapter 12)	**198**
G.	Treason	**198**
H.	Religious Tests	**200**

CHAPTER 7. THE BILL OF RIGHTS AND THE FOURTEENTH AMENDMENT

A.	Introduction	**201**
B.	Scope of Application *Barron* v. *Baltimore* *Adamson* v. *California*	**202**
C.	The "State Action" Concept *Civil Rights Cases* *Shelley* v. *Kraemer* *Williams* v. *United States* *Pennsylvania* v. *Board of Trusts* *Bell* v. *Maryland* *Evans* v. *Abney*	**208**

CHAPTER 8. FREEDOM OF RELIGION

A. Introduction   227

B. Free Exercise of Religion   234
    Reynolds v. *United States*
    Pierce v. *Society of Sisters*
    West Virginia Board of Education v. *Barnette*
    Wisconsin v. *Yoder*

C. Establishment of Religion   242
    Everson v. *Board of Education*
    Zorach v. *Clauson*
    School District of Abington v. *Schempp*
    Committee for Public Education v. *Nyquist*

CHAPTER 9. FREEDOM OF SPEECH AND ASSOCIATION

Section 1. Seditious Speech

Introduction   253
    Schenck v. *United States*
    Gitlow v. *New York*
    Yates v. *United States*
    Lamont v. *Postmaster General*

Section 2. Special Problems Relating to Speech

A. Obscenity   263
    Roth v. *United States*
    Miller v. *California*

B. Libel   271
    New York Times Co. v. *Sullivan*

C. Fighting Words   274
    Chaplinsky v. *New Hampshire*

D. Contempt of Court   276
    Craig v. *Harney*

E. Previous Restraint   280
    Near v. *Minnesota*
    Lovell v. *City of Griffin*
    New York Times Co. v. *United States*

F. Regulation of Media   287
    Columbia Broadcasting System v. *Democratic National Committee*

Section 3. Special Problems Relating to Speech and Association

A. Forced Disclosure   292
    NAACP v. *Alabama*
    Barenblatt v. *United States*
    Branzburg v. *Hayes*

B. Loyalty and Security 306

C. Students and Government Employees 310
Healy v. *James*
U.S. Civil Service Comm'n v. *Letter Carriers*

D. Soldiers 316
Parker v. *Levy*

E. Prisoners 318
Procunier v. *Martinez*

Section 4. Time, Place, and Manner of Expression

A. Symbolic Speech 322
Smith v. *Goguen*

B. Pickets and Handbills 326

C. Unwilling Audience 328
Terminiello v. *Chicago*

D. Parades and Demonstrations 332
Colten v. *Kentucky*

CHAPTER 10. DUE PROCESS OF LAW

A. Procedure 339
Cleveland Board of Education v. *LaFleur*
Arnett v. *Kennedy*

B. Substance 353
Lochner v. *New York*
Coppage v. *Kansas*
West Coast Hotel Co. v. *Parrish*
Griswold et al. v. *Connecticut*

CHAPTER 11. EQUAL PROTECTION

Introduction 365

Section 1. Traditional Analysis

A. Background 367
Lindsley v. *Natural Carbonic Gas Co.*

B. Recent Cases 369
Lehnhausen v. *Lake Shore Auto Parts Co.*
San Antonio Independent School District v. *Rodriguez*

Section 2. Suspect Classifications

A. Race 377
Plessy v. *Ferguson*
Brown v. *Board of Education*
Loving v. *Virginia*

B. Alienage   389
    Takahashi v. *Fish and Game Commission*

C. Illegitimacy   391
    Weber v. *Aetna Casualty & Surety Co.*

D. Sex (?)   394
    Frontiero v. *Richardson*

Section 3. Classifications Affecting Fundamental Rights

A. Voting Rights   398
    Reynolds v. *Sims*
    Harper v. *Virginia Board of Elections*
    Lubin v. *Panish*
    Dunn v. *Blumstein*
    Kusper v. *Pontikes*
    Kramer v. *Union Free School District*

B. Access to Courts   416
    Griffin v. *Illinois*

C. Travel   419
    Shapiro v. *Thompson*

D. Privacy (?)   423

CHAPTER 12. CRIMINAL PROCEDURE

A. Searches and Seizures   425
    Mapp v. *Ohio*
    Adams v. *Williams*

B. Counsel   442
    Powell v. *Alabama*

C. Self-Incrimination   445
    Miranda v. *Arizona*
    California v. *Byers*

D. Trial by Jury   457
    United States v. *Barnett*

E. Trial by News Media   463
    Sheppard v. *Maxwell*

F. Double Jeopardy   467
    United States v. *Tateo*

G. Miscellaneous   474
    Furman v. *Georgia*

CHAPTER 13. CITIZENSHIP

A. Acquisition of Citizenship   479

B. Loss of Citizenship   480
    Afroyim v. *Rusk*

C. Privileges and Immunities 482
    Slaughterhouse Cases
    Corfield v. *Coryell*

APPENDIXES

A   Supreme Court Justices 489
B   Constitution of the United States 492

INDEX

505

Table of Cases

References are to pages. Cases reported are in **boldface;** cases discussed at length in the notes or in the introductory essays are indicated by boldface page numbers.

Abate v. *Mundt,* **403**
Abbate v. *U.S.,* 468
Abington School District v. Schempp, 247
Ableman v. *Booth,* **171**
Abrams v. *U.S.,* 260
Accardi v. *Shaughnessy,* 61
Adair v. *U.S.,* 357
Adams v. Williams, 439
Adams Mfg. Co. v. *Storen,* 161
Adamson v. California, 203
Adderley v. *Florida,* **334**
Adickes v. *Kress Co.,* 215
Adkins v. *Children's Hospital,* 28, 33, 358
Aetna Life Ins. Co. v. *Haworth,* 19, 25
Affiliated Ute Citizens v. *U.S.,* 52
Afroyim v. Rusk, 480
A. G. Spalding & Bros. v. *Edwards,* 146
Aguilar v. *Texas,* 426
Air Pollution Variance Bd. v. *Western Alfalfa Corp.,* 428
Alabama v. *King & Boozer,* 166
Albertson v. *Subversive Activities Control Bd.,* 296, 455

Alderman v. *U.S.,* **430**
Alexander v. *Holmes County Bd. of Ed.,* 383
Alexander v. *Louisiana,* 388
Alicia, The, 35
Allee v. *Medrano,* 171
Allen v. *Illinois,* 477
Almeida-Sanchez v. *U.S.,* **426**
Altman & Co. v. *U.S.,* 67
Amalgamated Food Employees Union v. *Logan Valley Plaza,* 327
American Communications Ass'n. v. *Douds,* 294, **306**
American Federation of Musicians v. *Wittstein,* 402
American Ins. Co. v. *Canter,* 13
American Party of Texas v. *White,* 406
Anderson v. *Dunn,* 85
Anderson v. *Martin,* 387
Apodaca v. *Oregon,* 458
Aptheker v. *Secretary of State,* 309, 485
Argersinger v. *Hamlin,* 442
Arnett v. Kennedy, 344
Ashe v. *Swenson,* **468**
Ashton v. *Cameron Co. Water Imp. Dist.,* 37
Astol Calero-Toledo v. *Pearson Yacht Co.,* 353
Atlantic Coast Line R. Co. v. *Phillips,* **193**
Avery v. *Midland County,* 402

Baggett v. *Bullitt,* 307
Bailey v. Drexel Furniture Co., 111
Bailey v. *Richardson,* 310
Baird v. *State Bar of Arizona,* 307
Bakelite Corp., Ex parte, 14
Baker v. *Carr,* 25, 29, 399, 400
Baldwin v. *Franks,* 35
Baldwin v. *Seelig,* 136
Banco Nacional de Cuba v. *Farr,* 68
Banco Nacional de Cuba v. *Sabbatino,* **46**
Bantam Books, Inc. v. *Sullivan,* 285
Barenblatt v. U.S., 296
Barron v. Baltimore, 202
Barrows v. *Jackson,* 24
Bartkus v. *Illinois,* 468
Bates v. *Little Rock,* 296
Beck v. *Ohio,* 427
Bell v. *Burson,* 342, 346
Bell v. Maryland, 217
Bellis v. *United States,* 446
Benton v. *Maryland,* 207, 467

Berger v. *U.S.,* 61
Berman v. *Parker,* 360
Best & Co. v. Maxwell, 148
Better Austin v. *Keefe,* 328
Betts v. *Brady,* 442
Bibb v. *Navajo Freight Lines,* 135
Billie Sol Estes v. *Texas,* **464**
Bivens v. *Six Unknown Agents,* 8, **46,** 426, **437**
Blackledge v. *Perry,* **471**
Blount v. *Rizzi,* 283
Board of Education v. *Allen,* 229
Board of Regents v. *Roth,* 345
Bode v. *Barrett,* 155
Bolling v. *Sharpe,* 381
Bollman, Ex parte, 199
Bonelli Cattle Co. v. *Arizona,* 48
Bonham's Case, 350
Booth v. *U.S.,* 36
Bowman v. *Chicago & N.W. Railway Co.,* 129, 130
Boyd v. *Blue Ridge Rural Elec. Coop. Inc.,* 46
Boyd v. *U.S.,* 423, 434
Boyle v. *Landry,* 26
Boynton v. *Virginia,* 107, 389
Bradford v. *Roberts,* **229**
Brandenburg v. *Ohio,* 256
Braniff Airways v. Nebraska, 153
Branzburg v. Hayes, 301
Branzburg v. *Meigs,* 304
Braunfeld v. *Brown,* 241
Breard v. *Alexandria,* 150, 332
Bridges v. *California,* 276, 278
Brig Aurora v. *U.S.,* 83
Brooks v. *U.S.,* 106
Brotherhood of Locomotive Engineers v. *Chicago R.I. & P. R. Co.,* 141
Brown v. Bd. of Education, 91, **379, 381**
Brown v. Maryland, 129, **141,** 144
Brown v. *Walker,* 79
Brush v. *Commissioner of Internal Revenue,* 165
Bryant v. *Zimmerman,* 295
Buchanan v. *Warley,* 220
Bugajewitz v. *Adams,* 188
Bullock v. *Carter,* 406
Burbank v. *Lockheed Air Terminal,* 135, 141
Burnet v. *Coronado Oil and Gas Co.,* 165
Burton v. *Wilmington Parking Authority,* 221
Butts v. *Merchants' & Miners' Co.,* 36
Byrne v. *Karalexis,* 264

Cady v. *Dombrowski,* 427
Cafeteria Workers v. *McElroy,* 310, 346
Calder v. Bull, 186
California v. Byers, 454
California v. *LaRue,* 133
Callan v. *Wilson,* 35
Camara v. *Municipal Court,* 428
Campbell v. *Hussey,* 140
Cantwell v. *Connecticut,* 227, **332**
Capitol Greyhound Lines v. *Brice,* 155
Cardwell v. *Lewis,* **427**
Cargo of the Brig Aurora v. *U.S.,* 83
Carmichael v. *Southern Coal Co.,* 370
Carrington v. *Rash,* 342
Carrol v. *U.S.,* **426**
Carson v. *Roane-Anderson Co.,* 167
Carter v. *Carter Coal Co.,* 37
Case v. *Bowles,* 168
Chaffin v. *Stynchcombe,* 477
Champion v. *Ames,* 99
Chandler v. *Judicial Council,* 14
Chaplinsky v. New Hampshire, 274
Charles C. Steward Machine Co. v. Davis, 113
Charles River Bridge v. Warren Bridge, 192
Cheff v. *Schnackenberg,* 460
Chicago B. & Q. R. Co. v. *Chicago,* 207
Chicago v. *Willett Co.,* 155
Chimel v. *California,* **429**
Choate v. *Trapp,* 36
Choctaw O. & G. R. Co. v. *Harrison,* 166
Cities Service Co. v. *Peerless Co.,* 138
Citizens to Preserve Overton Park v. *Volpe,* 340
Civil Rights Cases, 90, 106, 120, **208**
Clark Distilling Co. v. *Western Maryland R. Co.,* 131
Clearfield Trust Co. v. *U.S.,* 47
Cleveland v. *U.S.,* 167
Cleveland Bd. of Education v. LaFleur, 340
Cochran v. *Bd. of Education,* 229
Coe v. *Errol,* 146, 147
Cohen v. *California,* **275**
Cole v. *Richardson,* **307**
Cole v. *Young,* 77, 310
Coleman v. *Alabama,* 442
Coleman v. *Miller,* 29
Colgate v. *Harvey,* 485
Collector v. Day, 163
Collins v. *Hardyman,* 216

Collins v. Yosemite Park Co., 132
Collonade Catering Corp. v. U.S., 428
Colo. Anti-Discrimination Comm. v. Continental Air Lines, Inc., 127
Colten v. Kentucky, 335
Columbia Broadcasting System v. Democratic Nat'l Committee, 287
Committee for Public Ed. v. Nyquist, 248
Communist Party v. Control Board, **295**
Communist Party of Indiana v. Whitcomb, **308**
Confiscation Cases, 61
Connally v. General Constr. Co., 340
Connecticut General Life Ins. Co. v. Johnson, 368
Connell v. Higginbotham, 307
Cook v. Pennsylvania, 130
Cooley v. Board of Wardens, 125, 133
Coolidge v. New Hampshire, 429, 441
Cooper v. Aaron, 11, 28
Coppage v. Kansas, 33, 356
Corfield v. Coryell, 485
Cornell v. Coyne, 146
Corning Glass Works v. Brennan, 397
Cox v. Louisiana, 334, 337
Cox v. New Hampshire, 228
Coyle v. Oklahoma, 36
Craig v. Harney, 276
Craig v. Hecht, 278
Cramer v. U.S., **200**
Cramp v. Board of Public Instruction, 308
Crampton v. Zabriskie, 24
Crandall v. Nevada, 483
Cummings v. Missouri, 184

DaCosta v. Laird, 72
Damon v. Brodhead, **168**
Dandridge v. Williams, 374
Dartmouth College v. Woodward, **192**
Dean Milk Co. v. City of Madison, 135
DeFunis v. Odegard, **21**
Dennis v. U.S., **256**
Dept. of Revenue v. Beam Distillers, 132
Dept. of Treasury v. Ingram-Richardson Mfg. Co., 161
Desist v. U.S., 477
Detroit v. Murray Corp., 167
Dobbins v. Commissioners of Erie County, 163, 165
D'Oench, Duhme & Co. v. F.D.I.C., 47
Donnelly v. DeChristoforo, 443
Donovan v. City of Dallas, **171**
Douglas v. California, **419**

Downum v. *U.S.,* 471, **473**
Dred Scott v. *Sandford,* 32
Dreuding v. *Devlin,* 408
Dukes v. *Warden,* 452
Duncan v. Kahanamoku, 181
Duncan v. *Louisiana,* 207, **458**
Duncan v. *Missouri,* 188
Dunn v. Blumstein, 407
Dutton v. *Evans,* 202

Eakin v. *Raub,* **30**
Eaton v. *Price,* 11
Edwards v. *California,* 128
Edwards v. *South Carolina,* 333
Eisener v. *Macomber,* 36
Eisenstadt v. *Baird,* 424
Elfbrandt v. *Russell,* 307
Eli Lilly & Co. v. *Sav-on-Drugs,* 150
El Paso v. *Simmons,* 189
Employers' Liability Cases, 36
Empressa Siderurgica v. *Merced County,* 147
Engel v. *Vitale,* 230, 247
England v. *Louisiana,* 170
Epperson v. *Arkansas,* 230
Erie R. Co. v. *New York,* 140
Erie R. Co. v. Tompkins, 41, 47
Escobedo v. *Illinois,* 442, 451
Esteban v. *Illinois,* 442, 451
Esteban v. *Central Missouri State College,* 313
Evans v. Abney, 221
Evans v. *Cornman,* 169, 411
Evans v. *Gore,* 36
Evans v. *Newton,* 224
Evansville Vanderburgh Airport Authority v. *Delta Airlines, Inc.,* 155
Evco v. Jones, 160
Everson v. Board of Education, 242

Fairbank v. *U.S.,* 35
Falchetti v. *Pennsylvania R. Co.,* 43
Fay v. *Noia,* 172
Federal Power Comm'n v. *Hope Natural Gas Co.,* 353
Federal Trade Commission v. *Mandel Bros.,* 106
Ferguson v. *Scrupa,* 360
Finch & Co. v. McKittrick, 131
First National Bank v. *Maine,* 360
First Nat'l City Bank v. *Banco Nacional de Cuba,* 48
Fiske v. *Kansas,* 207

Flast v. *Cohen,* **24,** 27
Flemming v. *Nestor,* 188
Fletcher v. Peck, 190
Flint v. *Stone Tracy Co.,* 167
Flood v. *Kuhn,* 46
Fortson v. *Dorsey,* 402
Fox Film Corp. v. *Doyal,* 166
Frank v. *U.S.,* 459
Freedman v. *Maryland,* 283
Freeman v. *Hewit,* 152
Frontiero v. Richardson, 394
Frothingham v. *Mellon,* 24, 27
Fry Roofing Co. v. *Wood,* 161
Fuentes v. *Shevin,* 346, 352
Fujii v. *California,* 391
Fuller v. *Oregon,* 443
Furman v. Georgia, 207, **474**

Garland, Ex parte, 185
Garner v. *Louisiana,* **333**
Gault, In re, 477
Geduldig v. *Aiello,* 343
Geer v. *Connecticut,* 128
Gelbard v. *U.S.,* 280
General Motors v. Washington, 156
General Trading Co. v. *Tax Comm'n,* 153
Georgia v. *Rachel,* 170
Gerende v. *Election Board,* 306
Gertz v. *Welsh, Inc.,* **271**
Gibbons v. Ogden, 93, 101, 123
Gibson v. *Florida Legislative Investigation Committee,* **301,** 446
Gibson v. *Mississippi,* 188
Gideon v. *Wainwright,* 207, 442
Gillespie v. *Oklahoma,* 166
Gillette v. *U.S.,* 241
Gilmore v. *Montgomery,* **224**
Ginsberg v. *New York,* 264, 267
Ginzburg v. *U.S.,* 267
Gitlow v. New York, 255, 258
Glidden Co. v. *Zdanok,* 14, 40
Goesaert v. *Cleary,* 369
Goldberg v. *Kelly,* 346
Gold Clause Cases, 190
Goldstein v. *Calif.,* 141
Gompers v. *Buck Stove & Range Co.,* 281
Gooding v. *Wilson,* **275**
Gordon v. *Lance,* 414

Gordon v. *U.S.,* 35
Gori v. *U.S.,* 474
Goss v. *Bd. of Education of Knoxville,* 382
Graham v. *Richardson,* 391, **487**
Gravel v. *U.S.,* 83
Graves v. *New York ex rel. O'Keefe,* 164
Grayned v. *City of Rockford,* 338
Grayson v. *Harris,* 162
Great A. & P. Tea Co. v. *Grosjean,* 368
Green v. *County School Bd.,* 383
Green v. *U.S.,* **461, 469**
Greene v. *McElroy,* 310
Greiner v. *Lewellyn,* 167
Griffin v. *Breckenridge,* **216**
Griffin v. Illinois, 416
Griffin v. *Prince Edward County,* 382
Griffiths, In Re, 391
Griggs v. *Duke Power Co.,* **122,** 389
Griswold v. Connecticut, 361, 428
Grossman, Ex parte, 77
Grosso v. *U.S.,* 37
Grovey v. *Townsend,* 386
Grubbs v. *General Electric,* 9
Guaranty Trust Co. v. *New York,* 46
Guinn v. *U.S.,* 386
Guss v. Utah Labor Board, 138
Gut v. *Minnesota,* 188
Gwin, White & Prince, Inc. v. *Henneford,* 161

Hadley v. *Junior College District,* **402**
Hall v. *DeCuir,* **127**
Hall, In re, 40
Hamilton v. *Regents,* 231
Hamling v. *U.S.,* 267
Hamm v. *City of Rock Hill,* 220
Hammer v. Dagenhart, 88, 98, 101, 112
Hampton & Co. v. *U.S.,* 83
Hannegan v. *Esquire, Inc.,* 263
Harper v. Virginia Bd. of Elections, 403
Harris v. *Battle,* 21
Harris v. *New York,* **451**
Haupt v. *U.S.,* **200**
Hawker v. *New York,* 188
Hayburn's Case, 21
Healy v. James, 225, 310, 320
Heart of Atlanta Motel v. U.S., 103
Heff, Matter of, 36

Heiner v. Donnan, 36
Heller v. New York, 284
Helvering v. Davis, 88
Helvering v. Gerhardt, 164
Henderson v. Mayor of New York, 130
Henneford v. Silas Mason Co., 150
Hepburn v. Griswold, 35
Heublein v. S.C. Tax Comm'n, 133, 162
Hill v. Wallace, 36
Hinderlider v. LaPlata River Co., 47
Hipolite Egg Co. v. U.S., 99
Hirabayashi v. U.S., 73
Hodges v. U.S., 36
Hoffa v. U.S., 430
Hoffman v. U.S., 446
Hoke v. U.S., 99
Holmes v. City of Atlanta, 389
Home Building & Loan Ass'n v. Blaisdell, 196
Hood & Sons v. Du Mond, 135
Hoover & Allison Co. v. Evatt, 144
Hopkins Federal Savings & Loan Ass'n. v. Cleary, 36
Hostetter v. Idlewild Liquor Corp., 132
Houston, E. & W. Texas Ry. Co. v. U.S., 96
Hudson Distributors, Inc. v. Eli Lilly, 107
Hudson Water Co. v. McCarter, 128
Humble Pipe Line Co. v. Waggoner, 167
Humphrey's Executor v. U.S., **75,** 84
Hunt v. McNair, 230
Huron Portland Cement Co. v. City of Detroit, 135
Hylton v. U.S., 108

Illinois v. Somerville, **470**
Indian Motorcycle Co. v. U.S., 167
Internat'l Brotherhood of Teamsters v. Vogt, 327
Irvin v. Dowd, **463**
Irvine v. Calif., 438

Jackson, Ex parte, 285
Jackson v. Denno, 448
Jackson v. Mayes, 277
James v. Bowman, 36
James v. Dravo Contracting Co., 166
James v. Strange, 443
Jefferson v. Hackney, 374
Jencks v. U.S., 477
Jenkins v. Georgia, **270**
Jenkins v. McKeithen, 301

Jenness v. *Fortson*, 406
Jimenez v. *Weinberger*, 37
Johnson v. *Maryland*, 168
Johnson v. *Mississippi*, 477
Johnson v. *Virginia*, 389
Joint Anti-Fascist Refugee Committee v. *McGrath*, 310
Jones v. Alfred H. Mayer Co., 119
Jones v. *Meehan*, 35
Joseph Burstyn, Inc. v. *Wilson*, 283
Joy Oil Co. v. *State Tax Comm'n*, 148
Justices v. *Murray*, 35

Kahn v. *Shevin*, **397**
Kastigar v. *U.S.*, **447**
Katz v. *U.S.*, 423, **430**
Katzenbach v. *McClung*, **107**
Katzenbach v. Morgan, 115, 232
Kawakita v. *U.S.*, **200, 481**
Kedroff v. *St. Nicholas Cathedral*, **232**
Keller v. *Potomac Electric Co.*, 36
Keller v. *U.S.*, 36
Kennedy v. *Mendoza-Martinez*, 37
Kent v. Dulles, 68, 485
Kentucky v. *Dennison*, 172
Kern-Limerick, Inc. v. *Scurlock*, 166
Kewanee Oil Co. v. *Bicron Corp.*, 141
Keyes v. *Denver*, **385**
Keyishian v. *Board of Regents*, 307
Kilbourn v. *Thompson*, 86, 300
Kingsley Books, Inc. v. *Brown*, 283
Kinsella v. *Singelton*, 37
Kirby v. *Illinois*, 443
Kirby v. *U.S.*, 35
Kirkpatrick v. *Preisler*, 403
Kleindienst v. *Mandel*, 309
Klopfer v. *North Carolina*, 207
Knickerbocker Ice Co. v. *Stewart*, 36
Knote v. *U.S.*, 79
Korematsu v. U.S., 72
Kosydar v. National Cash Register Co., 144
Kotch v. *River Port Pilots Comms.*, 404
Kovacs v. *Cooper*, 332
Kramer v. Union Free School District, 414
Kusper v. Pontikes, 411

Labine v. *Vincent*, 392
Laird v. *Tatum*, 26

Lake Carriers Ass'n v. *MacMullan,* 170
Lamont v. Postmaster General, 262
Larson v. *Domestic & Foreign Commerce Corp.,* 52
Lassiter v. *Northampton Election Bd.,* 115, 415
Law Students Civil Rights Research Council, Inc. v. *Wadmond,* 307
Leary v. *U.S.,* 39
Lee v. *U.S.,* 431
Lee v. *Washington,* 389
Lefkowitz v. *Turley,* 445, **447**
Legal Tender Cases, 88, 165
Lego v. *Twomey,* **452**
Lehman v. *Shaker Heights,* 332
Lehnhausen v. Lake Shore Auto Parts Co., 369
Leisy v. Hardin, 128
Lemon v. *Kurtzman,* 27, **229,** 257
Levy v. *Louisiana,* 392
Lewis v. *City of New Orleans,* **276**
Lewis v. *U.S.,* 430
License Cases, 131
Lincoln Federal Labor Union v. *Northwestern Iron & Metal Co.,* **360**
Lindsey v. *Normet,* **419**
Lindsley v. Natural Carbonic Gas Co., 367
Liner v. *Jafco,* 21, 22
Lloyd A. Fry Roofing Co. v. *Wood,* 161
Lloyd Corp. v. *Tanner,* **327**
Lochner v. New York, 34, 354
Lombard v. *Louisiana,* 220
Long v. *Rockwood,* 166
Looker v. *Maynard,* 195
Lopez v. *U.S.,* 431
Lottery Case, 106
Louisiana v. *U.S.,* 387
Louisville Joint Stock Land Bank v. *Radford,* 36
Lovell v. City of Griffin, 284
Loving v. Virginia, 387
Lubin v. Panish, 405
Lucas v. *Forty-Fourth General Assembly of Colorado,* 400, **401**
Lynch v. *Household Finance Corp.,* **369**
Lynch v. *U.S.,* 36

Madden v. *Kentucky,* 370, 485
Mahan v. *Howell,* 403
Mallett v. *North Carolina,* 188
Malloy v. *Hogan,* 207, 445
Mapp v. Ohio, 207, 426, 433
Marbury v. Madison, 15
Marchetti v. *U.S.,* 113, 455

Marsh v. *Alabama*, 327
Marston v. *Lewis*, 411
Martin v. *Hunter's Lessee*, 33, 169
Martin v. *Mott*, 317
Martin v. *Struthers*, 228, **331**
Maryland v. *Baltimore Radio Show*, 276
Maryland v. *Wirtz*, **168**
Maryland and Va. Eldership v. *Church of God at Sharpsburg, Inc.*, 233
Maryland Casualty Co. v. *Pacific Coal & Oil Co.*, 20
Mason v. *Missouri*, 416
Massachusetts v. *Laird*, 72
Massachusetts v. *Mellon*, **23**
Mayberry v. *Pennsylvania*, 477
Mayer v. *Chicago*, 419
Mayo v. *U.S.*, 166
Mayor of Baltimore v. *Dawson*, 388
McCardle, Ex parte, 38
McClannahan v. *State Tax Comm'n of Arizona*, 166
McCollum v. *Board of Education*, 230, 244
McCray v. *Illinois*, 427
McCulloch v. Maryland, 91
McGoldrick v. *Berwind-White Coal Min. Co.*, 152
McGowan v. *Maryland*, **230**
McGrain v. *Daugherty*, 86
McKeiver v. *Pennsylvania*, 477
McLaughlin v. *Florida*, 388
McLaurin v. *Okla. State Regents*, 380
McLeod v. *Dilworth Co.*, 152
Memoirs v. *Massachusetts*, 264
Memorial Hospital v. *Maricopa*, 423
Mescalero Apache Tribe v. *Jones*, 168
Metcalf v. *Mitchell*, 166
Metropolitan Bd. of Excise v. *Barrie*, 195
Meyer v. *Nebraska*, 236
Miami Herald Pub. Co. v. *Tornillo*, **291**
Michigan v. *Tucker*, **452**
Miles v. *Graham*, 36
Milk Control Board v. *Eisenburg*, 137
Miller v. *Arkansas*, **168**
Miller v. California, 268
Miller v. *Schoene*, 360
Miller Brothers Co. v. *Maryland*, 153
Milligan, Ex parte, **181**
Milliken v. *Bradley*, **384**
Milton v. *Wainwright*, **443**
Milwaukee Pub. Co. v. *Burleson*, 263

Minersville School Dist. v. *Gobitis,* 237
Minnesota v. *Blasius,* 156
Minor v. *Happersett,* 416
Minor v. *U.S.,* 113
Mintz v. *Baldwin,* 131
Miranda v. Arizona, 34, 41, **448,** 453
Mishkin v. *New York,* 267
Missouri v. *Holland,* 88
Missouri v. *Illinois,* 23
Missouri ex rel. Gaines v. *Canada,* 382
Missouri Employees v. *Missouri,* 52
Mitchell v. *W. T. Grant Co.,* 352
Mitchum v. *Foster,* 171
Monogahela Nav. Co. v. *U.S.,* 35
Monroe v. *Pape,* **214**
Moore v. *Dempsey,* 171
Moore v. *Mead's Fine Bread Co.,* 107
Moose Lodge No. 107 v. *Irvis,* 224
Mora v. *McNamara,* 72
Morey v. *Doud,* 369
Morgan v. *Virginia,* 127, 389
Morrissey v. *Brewer,* 352, **477**
Motor Coach Employees v. *Lockridge,* 141
Mulford v. *Smith,* 88
Munn v. *Illinois,* 124, 353
Murdock v. *Pennsylvania,* 150, 228, **285**
Murphy v. *Waterfront Commission,* **446,** 454
Muskrat v. *U.S.,* 19, 21
Myers v. *U.S.,* **75**

NAACP v. Alabama, **292,** 366
NAACP v. *Button,* 273
Nader v. *Bork,* **77**
Naim v. *Naim,* 387
Napier v. *Atlantic Coast Line R. Co.,* 140
Nardone v. *U.S.,* 430
Nashville, C. & St. L. Ry. v. *Wallace,* 20
Nat'l. Bellas Hess v. *Dept. of Revenue,* 153
NLRB v. *Jones & Laughlin Steel Corp.,* 88, **102**
National Life Ins. Co. v. *U.S.,* 36
Neagle, In re, 56
Near v. Minnesota, 280
Nebbia v. *New York,* 360
Nelson v. *Sears, Roebuck & Co.,* 153
New Orleans City Parks Imp. Ass'n v. *Detiege,* 389
New York v. *Miln,* **124**

New York v. *O'Neill,* 172
New York v. *U.S.,* 165
New York Times Co. v. Sullivan, 263, 271, **272**
New York Times Co. v. U.S., 285
Newberry v. *U.S.,* 36
Nichols v. *Coolidge,* 36
Nixon v. *Herndon,* 91, 386
Nixon v. *Sirica,* 85
Norfolk & W. R. Co. v. *Missouri,* 156
Norman v. *B. & O. R. Co.,* 190
Norris v. *Alabama,* 338
North Carolina v. *Pearce,* 469
North Carolina v. *Rice,* 21, 22
North Dakota State Bd. of Pharmacy v. *Snyders Drug Stores, Inc.,* 360
Northwest Airlines v. *Minnesota,* 155, 158
Northwestern Mut. Life Ins. Co. v. *Wisconsin,* 166
Northwestern States Portland Cement Co. v. *Minnesota,* 158, 162
Norton v. *Shelby County,* 27
Norton Co. v. *Dept. of Revenue,* 159
Norwood v. *Harrison,* 224
Noto v. *U.S.,* 308

O'Brien v. *Brown,* **29**
O'Callahan v. *Parker,* **459**
Offutt Housing Co. v. *Sarpy County,* **168**
Ohio v. *Wyandotte,* 12
Oil Workers Unions v. *Missouri,* 21
Oklahoma Press Pub. Co. v. *Walling,* 445
Oklahoma Tax Comm'n v. *Texas Co.,* 166
Oliver, In re, 207
Olmstead v. *U.S.,* 423, 430
Oregon v. Mitchell, 117
Organization for a Better Austin v. *Keefe,* 285, 328
Osborn v. *Bank of the U.S.,* 165
Osborn v. *Ozlin,* 487
Ott v. *Miss. Barge Line Co.,* 156

Pacific Tel Co. v. *Tax Commission,* 137
Palermo v. *U.S.,* 477
Palko v. *Connecticut,* 204
Palmer v. *Thompson,* **223**
Panama Refining Co. v. *Ryan,* 84
Panhandle Eastern Pipe Line Co. v. *Michigan,* 128
Panhandle Oil Co. v. *Mississippi,* 166
Parden v. *Terminal Railway,* 52
Paris Adult Theatre I v. *Slayton,* **270**

Parker v. *Brown,* 138
Parker v. Levy, 316
Parsons v. *Bedford,* 460
Passenger Cases, 144, 420
Patterson v. *Colorado,* 258
Patton v. *U.S.,* 458
Pell v. *Procunier,* 321
Pennekamp v. *Florida,* 276
Pennsylvania v. Board of Trusts, 216
Pennsylvania v. *Nelson,* 256
Pennsylvania v. *New York,* 45
Pennsylvania Coal Co. v. *Mahon,* **359**
People v. *Defore,* 438
Perez v. *Brownell,* 480
Perez v. *Ledesma,* 48
Pernell v. *Southern Realty,* 460
Perry v. *Sinderman,* 345
Perry v. *U.S.,* 190
Peters v. *Hobby,* 310
Peters v. *Kiff,* 388
Peters v. *N.Y.,* 441
Peterson v. *Greenville,* 220
Phoenix v. *Kolodziejski,* 414
Pickering v. *Bd. of Education,* 348
Pierce v. Society of Sisters, 235, 239, 251
Pittsburgh v. *Alco Parking Corp.,* 354
Pittsburgh Press Co. v. *Human Relations Comm'n,* 291
Plessy v. Ferguson, 377, 380
Plumley v. *Massachusetts,* 131
Poe v. *Ullman,* 363
Pointer v. *Texas,* 207
Polar Co. v. *Andrews,* 138, 164
Pollock v. *Farmers' Loan & Trust Co.,* 88, 165
Pope v. *Williams,* 411, 416
Portland Ry. Light & Power Co. v. *R. R. Comm'n,* 162
Powell v. Alabama, 444
Powell v. *McCormack,* 21, 22, 29, 83
Presbyterian Church in the U.S. v. *Hull Church,* **233**
Prince v. *Massachusetts,* 228
Prize Cases, 70
Procunier v. Martinez, 318
Prudential Ins. Co. v. *Benjamin,* 131
Public Service Commission v. *Benjamin,* 131
Public Service Commission v. *Wycoff Co.,* 20
Public Utilities Commission of R.I. v. *Attleboro Steam & Electric Co.,* 137
Public Utilities Commission v. *Pollak,* 288, 332
Pullman's Palace Car Co. v. *Pa.,* 156

Quaker City Cab Co. v. *Pa.*, 370
Quick Bear v. *Leupp*, 229
Quirin, Ex parte, 11, 459

Radovich v. *National Football League*, 107
Rahrer, In re, 131
Railroad Retirement Board v. *Alton R.*, 36
Railway Express Agency v. *N.Y.*, 369
Railway Express Agency v. *Va.*, 156
Rassmussen v. *U.S.*, 36
Ray v. *Blair*, 54
Reconstruction Finance Corp. v. *Beaver County*, 167
Red Lion Broadcasting Co. v. *FCC*, 288
Reed v. *Reed*, 395
Regina v. *Burns*, 254
Regina v. *Hicklin*, 266
Reichart v. *Felps*, 35
Reid v. *Covert*, 89, 459
Reitman v. *Mulkey*, **223**
Relford v. *Commandant*, 459
Reynolds v. Sims, 34, 398
Reynolds v. U.S., 234
Richardson v. *Belcher*, 374
Richardson v. *Ramirez*, 414
Richfield Oil Corp. v. *State Bd. of Equalization*, 147
Rickert Rice Mills v. *Fontenot*, 37
Roaden v. *Kentucky*, 284
Robbins v. *Shelby County*, 130, 149
Robinson v. *California*, 207
Roberts v. *Boston*, 378
Roe v. *Wade*, 23, 364, **423**
Rogers v. *Bellei*, 481
Rosario v. *Rockefeller*, 412, 414
Rosenberg v. *U.S.*, 11
Rosenbloom v. *Metromedia*, 271
Ross v. *Bernhard*, 460
Ross v. *Oregon*, 188
Roth v. U.S., 264
Roudebush v. *Hartke*, 29
Rowan v. *U.S. Post Office Dept.*, **267**

S. v. *D.*, 26
Saia v. *New York*, 332
St. Pierre v. *U.S.*, 21
Salsburg v. *Maryland*, 382
Salyer Land Co. v. *Tulane Basin Water District*, 403
San Antonio Independent School District v. Rodriguez, 366, 371

Santa Clara County v. *Southern Pacific Rr.,* 368
Sarnoff v. *Shultz,* 72
Savin, In re, 461
Scales v. *U.S.,* 308
Schaefer v. *U.S.,* 260, 279
Schechter Poultry Corp. v. *U.S.,* 84
Schenck v. U.S., 255, **257**
Scheuer v. *Rhodes,* 52
Schilb v. *Kuebel,* 419
Schiro v. *Bynum,* 389
Schlesinger v. *Reservist Committee,* 27
Schmerber v. *California,* 456
Schneckloth v. *Bustamonte,* 172, 426
Schneider v. *Irvington,* 300
School District of Abington v. Schempp, 34, **247**
Schware v. *Bd. of Bar Examiners,* 308
Schwegmann v. *Calvert Distillers Corp.,* 107
Screws v. *U.S.,* 213
Seagram & Sons v. *Hostetter,* 133
Secretary of Navy v. *Avrech,* 318
Securities & Exchange Comm'n v. *Ralston Purina Co.,* 106
Selective Draft Law Cases, 231
Service v. *Dulles,* 77, 310
Shadwick v. *City of Tampa,* 426
Shapiro v. Thompson, 373, **419**
Shelley v. Kraemer, 211, 219, 222
Shelton v. *Tucker,* 296, 306, 312, 341
Sheppard v. Maxwell, 465
Sherbert v. *Verner,* **228**
Shreveport Rate Case, 96
Shuttlesworth v. *Birmingham Bd. of Ed.,* 382
Sibron v. *New York,* 21, 22, 441
Sierra Club v. *Morton,* 26
Silverthorne Lumber Co. v. *U.S.,* 435
Simons v. *Miami Beach First Nat'l Bank,* 173
Singer v. *U.S.,* 460
Sioux City Bridge Co. v. *Dakota County,* 368
Skinner v. *Oklahoma,* 341, 366
Slaughterhouse Cases, 89, 210, 365, **482**
Sligh v. *Kirkwood,* 128
Sloan v. *Lemon,* 252
Smith v. *Allwright,* 91, 386
Smith v. *California,* 267
Smith v. Goguen, 322
Smith v. *U.S.,* 446
Smyth v. *Ames,* 353
Sniadach v. *Family Finance Corp.,* 339, 346

Sonzinsky v. *U.S.*, 112
South Carolina v. *U.S.*, 164
South Carolina State Highway Dept. v. Barnwell, 133
Southern Pacific Co. v. *Arizona,* 127
Southern Pacific Co. v. *Kentucky,* 156
Southern Pacific Terminal Co. v. *ICC,* 21, 23
Spalding & Bros. v. *Edwards,* 36
Spector Motor Service, Inc. v. *O'Conner,* 155, 158
Speiser v. *Randall,* 306
Spence v. *Washington,* 326
Spevak v. *Klein,* 446
Spinelli v. *U.S.,* 426
Standard Oil Co. of Calif. v. *Johnson,* 166
Standard Oil Co. v. *Peck,* 155
Stanley v. *Georgia,* 267, 423
Stanley v. *Illinois,* 342
State v. *Gibson,* 378
State v. *Van Duyne,* 467
State Athletic Commission v. *Dorsey,* 389
State Board of Equalization v. *Young's Market Co.,* 132
State Freight Tax Case, 129
State Tax Commission v. *Aldrich,* 360
Steffel v. *Thompson,* 20
Stephenson v. *Binford,* 197
Steward Mach. Co. v. Davis, 88, **113**
Stinson v. *Atlantic Coast Line R. Co.,* 28
Stolar, In re, 307
Stone v. Mississippi, 194
Storer v. *Brown,* 406
Strauder v. *West Virginia,* 210, 388
Strawbridge v. *Curtiss,* 8
Stromberg v. *California,* 324
Sturges v. *Crowninshield,* 197
Sugarman v. *Dougall,* 391
Super Tire Engineering Company v. *McCorkle,* **20**
Swann v. *Charlotte-Mecklenburg Bd. of Ed.,* 384
Sweatt v. *Painter,* 382
Sweezy v. *New Hampshire,* 294, 366
Swift v. *Tyson,* **42**

Takahashi v. Fish and Game Commission, 389, 487
Talley v. *California,* **327**
Tate v. *Short,* 419
Terminiello v. Chicago, 328
Terry v. *Adams,* 386
Terry v. *Ohio,* 423, **427,** 440
Texas v. New Jersey, 44

Textile Workers v. *Lincoln Mills*, 47
Thames & Mersey Mar. Ins. Co. v. *U.S.*, 36
Thomas v. *Collins*, 285
Thompson v. *Utah*, 188
Thornhill v. *Alabama*, 326
Tidal Oil Co. v. *Flanagan*, 189
Tillman v. *Wheaton-Haven Recreation Asso.*, 122
Tilton v. *Richardson*, **230**
Time Film Corp. v. *Chicago*, 283
Tinker v. *Des Moines School District*, 311, 319
Toomer v. *Witsell*, **487**
Torcaso v. *Watkins*, 200
Tot v. *U.S.*, 340
Toth v. *Quarles*, 316
Townsend v. *Sain*, 41, 172
Toyota v. *U.S.*, 389
Trade-Mark Cases, 35
Trafficante v. *Metropolitan Life Ins. Co.*, **26**
Trop v. *Dulles*, 37
Truax v. *Raich*, 289
Trusler v. *Crooks*, 36
Trustees of Dartmouth College v. *Woodward*, **192,** 194
Tumey v. *Ohio*, 339
Twining v. *New Jersey*, 206

Ullmann v. *U.S.*, 446
Underhill v. *Hernandez*, 66
Ungar v. *Sarafite*, 463
Union Pacific R. Co. v. *Botsford*, 423
United Air Lines v. *Mahin*, 153
United Public Workers v. *Mitchell*, 25
U.S. v. *Ball*, 473, 474
U.S. v. *Baltimore & Ohio R. Co.*, 107, 165
U.S. v. Barnett, 460
U.S. v. Belmont, 66
U.S. v. *Biswell*, 428
U.S. v. *Boyd*, 168
U.S. v. *Brewster*, **82**
U.S. v. *Brown*, **185**
U.S. v. *Burr*, 63
U.S. v. *Butler*, 88
U.S. v. *Caldwell*, 302
U.S. v. *California*, 168
U.S. v. *Cardiff*, 37
U.S. v. *Carolene Products Co.*, 253
U.S. v. *Causby*, 360
U.S. v. *Classic*, 213

U.S. v. *Cohen Grocery Co.,* 213
U.S. v. *Constantine,* 36
U.S. v. *Coolidge,* 474
U.S. v. *Cox,* 61
U.S. v. Curtiss-Wright, 64
U.S. v. Darby, 100
U.S. v. *Detroit,* 167
U.S. v. *Dewitt,* 35
U.S. v. *E. C. Knight Co.,* 87
U.S. v. *Edwards,* **427**
U.S. v. *Evans,* 36
U.S. v. *Fox,* 35
U.S. v. *Giordano,* **432**
U.S. v. *Guest,* **215,** 420
U.S. v. *Harris,* 35
U.S. v. *Hvoslef,* 36
U.S. v. *Jackson,* 37
U.S. v. *Jorn,* **469**
U.S. v. *Kahn,* 431
U.S. v. *Kahriger,* **112**
U.S. v. *Klein,* 35
U.S. v. *Kordel,* 446
U.S. v. *Lanza,* 468
U.S. v. *Laub,* 485
U.S. v. Lovett, 184
U.S. v. *Matlock,* 426
U.S. v. *Miss. Tax Comm'n,* 132
U.S. v. *Montgomery County Bd. of Ed.,* 383
U.S. v. *Moreland,* 36
U.S. v. Nixon, 60
U.S. v. *O'Brien,* 325
U.S. v. *Paramount Pictures, Inc.,* 289
U.S. v. *Perez,* 470
U.S. v. *Phosphate Export Assn.,* 23
U.S. v. *Pink,* 68
U.S. v. *Reese,* 35
U.S. v. *Richardson,* **26**
U.S. v. *Robel,* 308, 309
U.S. v. *Robinson,* 429
U.S. v. *Romano,* 37
U.S. v. *Sanchez,* 112
U.S. v. *Seeger,* 231
U.S. v. *SCRAP,* 27
U.S. v. *Shauver,* 88
U.S. v. Tateo, 472
U.S. v. *Thirty-Seven Photographs,* 267
U.S. v. *U.S. District Ct.,* **431**

U.S. v. *Van Leeuwen,* **428**
U.S. v. *W. T. Grant Co.,* 23
U.S. v. *Wade,* 442, 456
U.S. v. *White,* **430,** 445
U.S. v. *Witkovich,* 298
U.S. v. *Women's Sportswear,* 107
U.S. v. *Wong Kim Ark,* **479**
U.S. Civil Service Comm'n v. Letter Carriers, 314
U.S. Dept. of Ag. v. *Moreno,* 37
U.S. Dept. of Ag. v. *Murry,* 342
U.S. ex rel. Toth v. *Quarles,* 459
U.S. Plywood Corp. v. *City of Algoma,* 144
Untermeyer v. *Anderson,* 36

Van Brocklin v. *Tennessee,* 163, 167
Veazie Bank v. Fenno, 110
Vermont v. *New York,* 12
Village of Belle Terre v. *Boraas,* 364
Virginia, Ex parte, 212
Virginia v. *Rives,* 212
Virginia v. *Tennessee,* 174
Virginia State Bd. of Elections v. *Hamm,* 389
Vitarelli v. *Seaton,* 77, 310
Vlandis v. *Kline,* 342, 343

Wabash, St. L. & P. Ry. Co. v. *Illinois,* 124, 130
Wagner v. *City of Covington,* 150
Waller v. *Florida,* 468
Walton v. *Missouri,* 150
Walz v. *New York,* 229
Washington v. *Dawson,* 36
Washington v. *McGrath,* 310
Washington v. *Texas,* 207
Watkins v. *U.S.,* 298, 301
Weber v. Aetna Casualty, 391
Weeds, Inc. v. *U.S.,* 36
Weeks v. *U.S.,* 106, 425, 435
Wells v. *Edwards,* 403
Welsh v. *U.S.,* 28, **231**
Werner Mach. Co. v. *Director of Taxation,* 167
West Coast Hotel Co. v. Parrish, 28, **358**
West Virginia v. *Sims,* **174**
West Virginia Bd. of Education v. Barnette, 228, **237**
Western Live Stock v. *Bureau of Revenue,* 157
Western Union Tel. Co. v. *Mass.,* 156
Western Union Tel. Co. v. *Texas,* 166
Weston v. *Charleston,* 165

Wheeling Steel Corp. v. *Glander,*
White River Co. v. *Arkansas,* 370
Whiteley v. *Warden,* 426
Whitney v. *California,* 308
Wickard v. *Filburn,* **103**
Wieman v. *Updegraff,* 306
Wiener v. U.S., 74
Willcutts v. *Bunn,* 167
William E. Arnold Co. v. *Carpenters District Council,* 141
Williams v. *Florida,* **458**
Williams v. *Mississippi,* 386
Williams v. *North Carolina,* 173
Williams v. *Rhodes,* 308, 406
Williams v. U.S., 212, 429
Williamson v. *Lee Optical Co.,* 360
Willie Mae Weber v. *Aetna,* **391**
Willson v. *Black Bird Creek Marsh Co.,* 123, 133
Wilson v. *Girard,* 11
Winship, In re, 477
Winters v. *New York,* 213
Wisconsin v. *J. C. Penney Co.,* 157
Wisconsin v. Yoder, 238
Witherspoon v. *Illinois,* **477**
Wolf v. *Colorado,* 434
Wolff v. *McDonnell,* 321
Wong Wing v. *U.S.,* 35
Wood v. *Georgia,* 276
Woodruff v. *Parham,* 144
Worthen Co. v. *Kavanaugh,* 189
Wyman v. *James,* **428**

Yakus v. *U.S.,* 40
Yates v. U.S., 260, 308
Yick Wo v. *Hopkins,* 404
Young, Ex parte, 48
Younger v. *Harris,* 171
Youngstown Sheet & Tube Co. v. *Bowers,* 144
Youngstown Sheet & Tube Co. v. Sawyer, 58, 84

Zemel v. *Rusk,* 485
Zenger Case, 255
Zorach v. Clauson, 244
Zucht v. *King,* 11
Zwickler v. *Koota,* 20, 340

American Constitutional Law

Part I

Governmental

Powers

Chapter 1

The Judiciary

A. INTRODUCTION

"The judicial power of the United States shall be vested in one supreme court, and in such inferior courts as the Congress may from time to time ordain and establish," states Article III of the Constitution of the United States. Congress is thus given full control over the structure of the judiciary, with the exception of the constitutional provision for one Supreme Court. The number of justices on the Supreme Court is left to the control of Congress.

The second sentence in Article III reads: "The judges, both of the supreme and inferior courts, shall hold their offices during good behavior, and shall, at stated times, receive for their services, a compensation, which shall not be diminished during their continuance in office." Could a more meaningful sentence be written to assure the independence of the judiciary? These two sentences forming Section 1 of the judiciary article constitute an excellent illustration of the way in which the Constitution combines elasticity in detail with definiteness in principle, a quality for which it is famous. The names of the lower federal courts, the number of courts, and other details on structure and organization have been changed by Congress many times, but Congress has rarely sought to interfere with the independence of the judges. An attempt to remove Justice Samuel Chase through impeachment failed during the administration of President Jefferson, and no justice of the Supreme Court has ever been removed in that way. In our entire history, only four judges of lower federal courts have been removed by impeachment.[1]

---

1. For details, see the *Congressional Directory,* 91st Congress, 1st sess. (Washington, D.C., 1971), p. 363.

Section 2 of Article III defines the extent of the federal judicial power. "The judicial power shall extend to all cases, in law and equity, arising under this constitution, the laws of the United States, and treaties made or which shall be made, under their authority." These are subject-matter cases. The federal judicial power extends to them because their decision involves the correct application of federal law. The Constitution then proceeds to list cases to which the federal judicial power will extend because of the parties to the litigation, regardless of the subject-matter involved. Thus, the federal judicial power extends "to all cases affecting ambassadors, other public ministers and consuls; to all cases of admiralty and maritime jurisdiction; to controversies to which the United States shall be a party; to controversies between two or more states, between a state and citizens of another state, between citizens of different states, between citizens of the same state claiming lands under grants of different states, and between a state, or the citizens thereof, and foreign states, citizens or subjects."

Judicial systems usually contain a hierarchy of courts with a large number of lower courts where trials are held and a few higher courts to which appeals may be carried to correct errors made by the lower courts. A court is said to have original jurisdiction if certain types of cases may originate in it and be tried there without having previously been heard in another court. For example, a United States district court has original jurisdiction and may hear a case brought by *A* against *B* for an alleged violation of *A*'s copyright. Original jurisdiction is contrasted to appellate jurisdiction, the latter signifying jurisdiction to reexamine cases already decided by a lower court and to correct errors made by the lower court.

Article III provides that "In all cases affecting ambassadors, other public ministers and consuls, and those in which a state shall be party, the supreme court shall have original jurisdiction. In all the other cases before mentioned, the supreme court shall have appellate jurisdiction, both as to law and fact, with such exceptions, and under such regulations as the Congress shall make."

The Federal Courts

The principal courts of the United States are the ninety-one district courts, the eleven courts of appeals, and the Supreme Court. Specialized courts include the Court of Claims, the Customs Court, territorial courts, and the courts of the District of Columbia.

Evolution of federal judiciary. The Judiciary Act of 1789 provided for three grades of courts: thirteen district courts, three circuit courts, and one Supreme Court. The district courts were principally admiralty courts. There was one judge for each. The circuit courts were the principal trial courts and they had a limited appellate jurisdiction over the district courts. They had no separate judges; each was presided over by two justices of the Supreme Court and a district judge. The Supreme Court consisted of a chief justice and five associate justices. The Judiciary Act of 1801 increased the number of circuit courts to six and created sixteen circuit judgeships, thus relieving the justices of the Supreme Court of the duty of circuit riding. But an act of 1802 abolished these circuit judgeships and reestablished circuit riding. The number of district and circuit courts was increased from year to year, and in 1869 Congress again authorized separate circuit judges to relieve the Supreme Court justices of part of their circuit-riding duty. Thereafter the practice of circuit riding gradually withered away.

The increased volume of the Supreme Court's work led in 1891 to the creation of nine circuit courts of appeals. The circuit courts continued, but in 1911 they were abolished and their jurisdiction transferred to the district courts. See Felix Frankfurter and J. M. Landis, *The Business of the Supreme Court* (New York, 1927), and Dwight F. Henderson, *Courts for a New Nation* (Washington, D.C., 1971). In 1948 the name circuit court of appeals was changed to court of appeals.

The District Courts

There is at least one district court in each of the fifty states, and the more populous states are divided into two, three, or four districts. These courts are normally presided over by one judge, but many districts have several judges who hold court simultaneously.

These are the principal trial courts, and they have original jurisdiction in a wide variety of cases. All prosecutions for crimes against the United States are tried in the district courts. The civil jurisdiction of these courts is defined in Title 28 of the United States Code in twenty-nine numbered subsections, of which the following are the most important:

Section 1331. Federal Questions.

The district courts shall have original jurisdiction of all civil actions wherein the matter in controversy exceeds the sum or value of $10,000, exclusive of interest and costs, and arises under the Constitution, laws or treaties of the United States.

Section 1332. Diversity of Citizenship.

The district courts shall have original jurisdiction of all actions where the matter in controversy exceeds the sum or value of $10,000, exclusive of interest and costs, and is between:

(1) Citizens of different states;

(2) Citizens of a state, and foreign states or citizens or subjects thereof; and

(3) Citizens of different states and in which foreign states or citizens or subjects thereof are additional parties. . . .

Section 1343. Civil Rights and Elective Franchise.

The district courts shall have original jurisdiction of any civil action authorized by law to be commenced by any person: . . .

(3) To redress the deprivation, under color of any state law, statute, ordinance, regulation, custom or usage, of any right, privilege or immunity secured by the Constitution of the United States or by any Act of Congress providing for equal rights of citizens or of all persons within the jurisdiction of the United States;

(4) To recover damages or to secure equitable or other relief under any Act of Congress providing for the protection of civil rights, including the right to vote. . . .

Section 1345. United States as Plaintiff.

Except as otherwise provided by Act of Congress, the district courts shall have original jurisdiction of all civil actions, suits or proceedings commenced by the United

States, or by any agency or officer thereof expressly authorized to sue by Act of Congress.

In many cases state and federal courts have concurrent jurisdiction, but Congress has given the federal courts exclusive jurisdiction of prosecutions for crimes against the United States, admiralty cases, bankruptcy cases, patent and copyright cases, actions against foreign consuls and vice-consuls, and claims against the United States.

Federal questions.   Traditionally the general statute giving the district courts jurisdiction in cases "arising under" federal law has been so strictly construed that relatively few cases have gotten into the courts under it. See Ernest J. London, "Federal Question Jurisdiction—A Snare and a Delusion," 57 Mich L Rev 835 (1959). In 1971, however, the Supreme Court held that an illegal search and seizure provided the basis for a suit for damages as a suit arising under the Constitution. See *Bivens* v. *Six Unknown Agents,* 403 US 388. There are dozens of statutes giving the federal courts jurisdiction over specific types of cases such as patent, copyright, and trademark cases. Most of these specific statutes require no specific amount to be in controversy; hence, not all cases in the district courts involve amounts in excess of $10,000.

Diversity of citizenship.   Presumably on the ground that the courts of a state would be partial to a citizen of that state, Article III of the Constitution provides that the judicial power of the United States shall extend "to controversies . . . between citizens of different States; between citizens of the same State claiming lands under grants of different States, and between a State, or the citizens thereof, and foreign States, citizens, or subjects." Section 1332 of Title 28 of the United States Code vesting this jurisdiction in the district courts is quoted above. In the early case of *Strawbridge* v. *Curtiss,* 3 Cranch 267 (1806), Chief Justice Marshall held that "where the interest is joint, each of the persons concerned in that interest must be competent to sue, or liable to be sued," to bring a case within the jurisdiction of the federal courts based on diversity of citizenship. The rule denying jurisdiction to a federal court in a suit in which a party plaintiff and a party defendant have a common citizenship became the established rule. It is not followed in interpleader cases, however. Charles A. Wright, *Handbook of the Law of Federal Courts* (St. Paul, 1970), p. 72.

Corporations are not ordinarily regarded as citizens, but for purposes of jurisdiction the presumption is followed that all shareholders of a corporation are citizens of the state of incorporation. An act of 1958 provides that a corporation shall be deemed a citizen of both the state in which it has its principal place of business and of any state in which it is incorporated. National banking associations are by statute "deemed citizens" of the states in which they are respectively located.

The presumption holding all shareholders in a corporation to be citizens of the same state is not applied to members of a partnership, labor union, or any kind of association other than a corporation. In some instances, however, federal jurisdiction is acquired by bringing a class action for or against members of such an association and naming as parties only representatives who have the requisite diversity of citizenship.

Removal from state courts.   If a civil action over which the United States district courts have original jurisdiction is brought in a state court, the defendant may have the case removed to the United States district court of the district where the action is pending. The general statute on removal is 28 USC § 1441. In addition, see sections 1442 through 1450 and *Grubbs* v. *General Electric Credit Corp.,* 405 US 699 (1972), for more specific provisions applicable to particular types of cases. There are also statutes providing for the removal of specific criminal cases, notably prosecutions against federal officers for designated acts and prosecutions in certain civil rights cases.

The procedure for removal is for the defendant to file with the proper United States district court a petition for removal. The petition must be accompanied by a full record of the case and, if a civil case, by a bond with surety conditioned that the defendant will pay all costs incurred by reason of the removal proceedings should it be determined that the case was improperly removed. The removal petition in a civil action must be filed within twenty days after receipt by the defendant of the pleading setting forth the plaintiff's claim. A petition for the removal of a criminal prosecution may be filed at any time before trial.

Three-judge cases.   District courts are ordinarily presided over by a single judge, but for designated types of cases there are statutes requiring three judges. Notable among these statutes are those governing suits to enjoin enforcement of a state statute or order of a state administrative tribunal and suits to enjoin enforcement of an act of Congress claimed to be unconstitutional. 28 USC § 2281 and § 2282. The district judge to whom an application for such an injunction is made notifies the chief judge of the circuit who assigns two other judges, one of whom must be a circuit judge, to sit on the case. Appeals from the decision of a three-judge district court are made directly to the Supreme Court.

Courts of Appeals

The United States is divided into ten circuits with a court of appeals for each, and there is a court of appeals for the District of Columbia. These are intermediate courts, designed to prevent the Supreme Court from having an excess of appellate work. They have no original jurisdiction other than that involved in their power to enforce orders of a number of administrative agencies, such as the Interstate Commerce Commission. They have jurisdiction to review all final decisions in the district courts except in the few instances where a direct review may be had in the Supreme Court. A court of appeals must have at least three judges, two of whom constitute a quorum.

The Supreme Court

"The judicial power of the United States shall be vested in one supreme court, and in such inferior courts as the Congress may from time to time ordain and establish," states the Constitution. The number of justices on the Supreme Court is fixed by act of Congress. As noted above, the Judiciary Act of 1789 provided for six justices. Subsequent acts increased the number of justices, an act of 1863 placing the number at ten. In 1869 the number was fixed at nine, and no further change has been made. A list of the justices is given in Appendix A.

Procedure.   The Supreme Court is principally an appellate court; hence it relies heavily upon printed records in the conduct of its business. Oral arguments, usually limited to one hour for each side, are used, however, and are significant. The justices ask questions of the attorneys presenting a case during the public, oral arguments. Assuring his audience that there had been "no change in the method of work in the last fifty years," and so far as he was able to determine, the Court's habits of work had undergone "little or no change from the beginning," Mr. Justice Stone presented the following description of the work of the Court before the Annual Meeting of the American Bar Association in 1928:

> Every Saturday [now Friday] the Court sits in conference, meeting at noon, just when the call of golf is most alluring. At the sessions during the week the Judges have heard arguments in cases on the merits. The time of argument . . . is limited so as to make impracticable decisions from the Bench in most cases. During the spacious hours of leisure before the Court sits at twelve, and after it adjourns at half past four, the Judges have had opportunity to examine the records in the argued and submitted cases, and to examine the petitions and briefs upon current applications for *certiorari.* They have also received and examined the papers in the miscellaneous motions affecting the cases which have been docketed. On the day before the conference each Judge receives a list giving the cases which will be taken up at the conference, and the order in which they will be considered. This list usually includes every cause which is ready for final disposition, including the cases argued the day before the conference, and all pending motions and applications for *certiorari.*
>
> At conference each case is presented for discussion by the Chief Justice, usually by a brief statement of the facts, the questions of law involved and with such suggestions for their disposition as he may think appropriate. No cases have been assigned to any particular Judge in advance of the conference. Each justice is prepared to discuss the case at length and to give his views as to the proper solution of the questions presented. In Mr. Justice Holmes's pungent phrase, each must be ready to "recite" on the case. Each Judge is requested by the Chief Justice, in the order of seniority, to give his views and the conslusions which he has reached. The discussion is of the freest character and at its end, after full opportunity has been given for each member of the Court to be heard and for the asking and answering of questions, the vote is taken and recorded in the reverse order of the discussion, the youngest in point of service voting first.
>
> On the same evening, after the conclusion of the conference, each member of the Court receives at his home a memorandum from the Chief Justice advising him of the assignment of cases for opinions. Opinions are written for the most part in recess, and as they are written they are printed and circulated among the justices, who make suggestions for their correction and revision. At the next succeeding conference these suggestions are brought before the full conference and accepted or rejected as the case may be. On the following Monday the opinion is announced by the writer as the opinion of the Court.
>
> In the preparation of opinions it has been from the beginning the practice to state the case fully in the opinion. This practice gives a clarity and focus to the opinion not otherwise attainable and has added in no small degree to the prestige and influence of the court.[2]

---

2. Justice H. F. Stone, "Fifty Years of Work of the United States Supreme Court," *Report of the American Bar Association* LIII (July 1928): 259–81. Compare Tom C. Clark, "The Decisional Process of the Supreme Court," *Cornell Law Quarterly* L (Spring 1965): 390.

Terms and sessions. The Supreme Court has but one regular term. It begins on the first Monday in October and lasts until the following May or June. On rare occasions the Court convenes during its summer recess for a special term to hear a case of great public concern. For illustrations, see *Ex parte Quirin,* 317 US 1; *Rosenberg* v. *United States,* 346 US 273; *Wilson* v. *Girard,* 354 US 524; *Cooper* v. *Aaron,* 358 US 1. The Court usually hears arguments for a two-week period and then recesses for two weeks, alternately, during its regular term. Decisions and orders of the Court are announced at 10:00 A.M., usually on Mondays or Tuesdays.

The Revised Rules of the Supreme Court of June 15, 1970, are found in Title 28 of the United States Code Annotated. Six justices constitute a quorum, and four must agree before a decision can be rendered. If all nine justices participate, a decision may be reached by a five-to-four division. A justice who disagrees with the decision of the majority may enter in the record a dissenting opinion. A justice who agrees with the majority decision, but disagrees with the reasoning whereby the decision was reached, may write a concurring opinion. Despite a concurrence of a majority of the justices in the decision that appears first in the United States Reports, which presumably represents the decision of the Court, in some cases, notably in recent years, it is difficult to ascertain any reasoning as that of a majority of the Court, each justice being inclined to write at length his own opinion.

Certiorari and appeal. Prior to 1928 there were four technical methods of bringing cases before the Supreme Court for review: writ of error, appeal, *certiorari,* and certificate. A *writ of error* is a common law process issued from an appellate court to a lower court to bring up a case for a review limited to questions of law. This writ is still widely used in the state courts, but in 1928 Congress abolished the writ for the federal courts, leaving three forms for bringing cases to the Supreme Court for review. An *appeal* is a procedure which brings up a case for a review of both the law and the facts. A right of appeal is provided by statute in designated cases. *Certiorari* is a form of review issued in the discretion of the appellate court. A litigant may petition the appellate court to issue the writ to bring up his case, but the court has full discretion in granting or denying the petition. *Certificate* is a form used by a court of appeals to submit specific questions concerning which it has doubt to the Supreme Court. The Supreme Court may answer the questions, or it may order the court of appeals to send up the entire case in which the questions arose to the Supreme Court for decision.

Most cases reach the Supreme Court by certiorari or by appeal. Other than technical points, there is in practice little significant difference between the two. While there is a theoretical right of appeal in certain cases designated by statute, Rule 15 of the Court limits the application of this right to cases involving a "substantial" federal question. *Zucht* v. *King,* 260 US 174 (1922). The justices spend much time in conference deciding which cases they will review. A vote of four justices is necessary to bring up a case either by certiorari or by appeal. See the statements on procedure in *Eaton* v. *Price,* 360 US 246 (1959).

Jurisdiction. "In all cases affecting ambassadors, other public ministers and consuls, and those in which a state shall be a party, the Supreme Court shall have original jurisdiction." In practice, the word *shall* in this sentence has been interpreted as meaning *may,* and the fact that the Supreme Court has original jurisdiction in the cases enumerated has not meant that the jurisdiction would be exclusive. Thus Congress has given the district courts concurrent original jurisdiction in suits *commenced by* ambassadors or other public ministers and in most suits to which a state is a party. Congress cannot add to the original jurisdiction of the Supreme Court as defined in the Constitution, but it is free to give concurrent jurisdiction to lower federal courts in any of the cases where the Supreme Court has original jurisdiction.

Under the Judicial Code, the Supreme Court is given original and exclusive jurisdiction of: "(1) All controversies between two or more states; and (2) All actions or proceedings against ambassadors or other public ministers of foreign states or their domestics or domestic servants, not inconsistent with the law of nations." The Supreme Court is given original but not exclusive jurisdiction of: "(1) All actions or proceedings brought by ambassadors or other public ministers of foreign states or to which consuls or vice consuls of foreign states are parties; (2) All controversies between the United States and a state; and (3) All actions or proceedings by a State against the citizens of another State or against aliens." 28 USC § 1251. If a suit is one in which the Supreme Court has original but not exclusive jurisdiction, the right to commence the suit must be obtained from the Court, and every step in the case proceeds upon special motion and leave. Explaining its lack of expertise for exercising original jurisdiction in cases involving fact-finding in complicated situations and the necessity of devoting most of its time to "those matters of federal law and national import as to which we are the primary overseers," in 1971 the Court declined to permit Ohio to file a bill of complaint invoking its original jurisdiction against Michigan, Delaware, and Canadian companies alleged to be polluting Lake Erie. *Ohio* v. *Wyandotte Chemicals Corp. et al.,* 401 US 493 (1971). Compare *Vermont* v. *New York,* 406 US 186 (1972).

The appellate jurisdiction of the Supreme Court extends to both state courts and the lower federal courts. Review of state cases is limited to final decisions of the highest state court that can pass upon a case. Ordinarily a case originating in a state court must go through the hierarchy of state courts to the state supreme court before it can be appealed to the United States Supreme Court.

As defined by act of Congress (28 USC § 1257), final decisions rendered by the highest state court in which a decision can be had may be reviewed by the United States Supreme Court as follows:

> (1) By appeal, where is drawn in question the validity of a treaty or statute of the United States and the decision is against its validity. (2) By appeal, where is drawn in question the validity of a statute of any state on the ground of its being repugnant to the Constitution, treaties or laws of the United States, and the decision is in favor of its validity. (3) By writ of certiorari, where the validity of a treaty or statute of the United States is drawn in question on the ground of its being repugnant to the Constitution, treaties or laws of the United States, or where any title, right, privilege or immunity is especially set up or claimed under the Constitution, treaties or statutes of, or commission held or authority exercised under, the United States.

If appealed, cases originating in a United States district court are ordinarily taken to the court of appeals of the circuit. However, a decision of a district court holding an act of Congress void may be appealed directly to the Supreme Court if the United States or any of its agencies or officers is a party in the proceeding. The Judicial Code also gives the Supreme Court the right to review directly the decisions of district courts in specific types of civil cases of general public importance required to be heard originally in a special sitting of three judges. Among these are (1) equity suits brought by the United States under specified acts (e.g. the Sherman Act, the Interstate Commerce Act, and the Communications Act), wherein the attorney general files a certificate of public importance; (2) actions wherein an injunction is sought to restrain enforcement of certain orders of the Interstate Commerce Commission; (3) actions seeking to restrain enforcement of an act of Congress for alleged unconstitutionality; and (4) actions seeking to restrain enforcement of a state statute or order of a state administrative agency for alleged unconstitutionality. Direct appeal to the Supreme Court is also permitted from certain types of decisions in criminal cases, e.g., a decision setting aside an indictment where such decision is based upon the invalidity or construction of the statute upon which the indictment is founded. 18 USC § 3731.

The only case in which there is a right of appeal to the Supreme Court from a court of appeals is a case in which the court of appeals has declared a state or federal statute void. Most cases that go to the Supreme Court from the courts of appeals are brought up by certiorari. The Supreme Court has the right to call up from a court of appeals any case, civil or criminal, either before or after judgment in the court of appeals, but few cases are called up before a decision has been reached by the court of appeals.

Title 28 of the United States Code, sec. 1254, provides for review by the Supreme Court over the court of appeals as follows:

(1) By writ of *certiorari* granted upon the petition of any party to any civil or criminal case, before or after rendition of judgment or decree;

(2) By appeal by a party relying on a State statute held by a court of appeals to be invalid as repugnant to the Constitution, treaties or laws of the United States, but such appeal shall preclude review by writ of certiorari at the instance of such appellant, and the review on appeal shall be restricted to the Federal questions presented;

(3) By certification at any time by a court of appeals of any question of law in any civil or criminal case as to which instructions are desired, and upon such certification the Supreme Court may give binding instructions or require the entire record to be sent up for decision of the entire matter in controversy.

Specialized Courts

The principal courts of the United States with specialized jurisdiction are the Court of Claims, the Customs Court, the Court of Customs and Patent Appeals, territorial courts, and courts of the District of Columbia.

Legislative courts. The concept of "legislative courts" was introduced by Chief Justice Marshall in *American Insurance Co.* v. *Canter,* 1 Peters 511 (1828). Marshall held that the provisions of Article III did not limit the powers of Congress in establishing courts in the territories. These courts were designed to be temporary, and life tenure for their judges would be inappropriate. They were legislative courts created under the power of Congress in Article I to govern the territories. In subsequent cases the term legislative courts was used to sustain acts conferring administrative duties on a number of courts in the District of Columbia. An expanded review of legislative courts was given in *Ex parte Bakelite Corporation,* 279 US 438 (1929). As explained in that case, "various matters, arising between the government and others . . . from their nature do not require judicial determination and yet are susceptible of it. The mode of determining matters of this class is completely within congressional control. Congress may reserve to itself the power to decide, may delegate that power to executive officers, or may commit it to judicial tribunals." Examples are claims against the government and questions arising in the administration of customs and revenue laws.

While in earlier cases they had been classified as legislative courts, in 1962 the Court of Claims and the Court of Customs and Patent Appeals were held to be constitutional courts whose judges could be assigned to hear criminal cases in district courts. *Glidden Company* v. *Zdanok,* 370 US 530 (1962).

Administrative Unification

Congress has enacted a number of measures designed to unify the administration of the federal courts. Various conferences of judges are authorized at which administrative problems are discussed and recommendations formulated. Statutory provisions authorize the temporary transfer of circuit and district judges. The director of the Administrative Office of the United States Courts, appointed by the Supreme Court, supervises clerical personnel, collects data for reports, provides supplies, and directs administrative matters in general. See 28 USC 601 and the annual Report of the Director, Administrative Office of the United States Courts.

An example of an exceptional use of power is seen in the 1965 action of the Judicial Council of the Tenth Circuit. The Council held that Judge Chandler of the Western District Court of Oklahoma was "unable or unwilling to discharge efficiently the duties of his office" and ordered that, until further action by the Council, Judge Chandler "take no action whatsoever in any case or proceeding now or hereafter pending" in his court. He appealed the order but received no relief from the Supreme Court. See *Chandler* v. *Judicial Council,* 382 US 1002 (1966) and 398 US 74 (1970).

Proposed Changes

As chairman of the Federal Judicial Center, in 1971 Chief Justice Burger appointed a seven-member group to study the case load of the Supreme Court. Its members were Paul A. Freund, Alexander M. Bickel, Peter D. Ehrenkaft, Russell D. Niles, Bernard G. Segal, Robert L. Stern, and Charles A. Wright. The report of this group recommended (1) several jurisdictional and procedural reforms, including substitution of certiorari for appeal in all cases to be considered by the Supreme Court, and (2) the creation by statute of a new National Court of Appeals. This new court would screen petitions for review by the Supreme Court, send the "review-worthy" cases to that Court, and decide the others itself. The proposal for the new intermediate court of appeals met formidable opposition. See "The National Court of Appeals: Composition, Constitutionality, and Desirability," 41 *Fordham Law Review* 863 (May 1972).

B. JUDICIAL REVIEW

Marbury v. Madison

1 Cranch 137, 2 L Ed 60 (1803)

An act of Congress repugnant to the Constitution is not law. The 13th section of the Judiciary Act is inoperative, so far as it attempts to grant to this court power to issue writs of mandamus in classes of cases of original jurisdiction not conferred by the Constitution on this court.

[The Jeffersonian-Republicans defeated the Federalists in the election of 1800, but the term of President Adams did not expire until March 4 of the following year. In the meanwhile, Congress created a number of new judgeships, among them several new justices of the peace for the District of Columbia. William Marbury was appointed justice of the peace by President Adams, and his appointment was confirmed by the Senate on March 3, 1801. John Marshall, who continued to serve as Secretary of State under President Adams after he was appointed as Chief Justice, failed to deliver Marbury's commission, although it was signed by the President and sealed. James Madison became Secretary of State under Jefferson, and Marbury instituted a suit in the Supreme Court to force Madison to deliver to him his commission.]

Afterwards, on the 24th February, the following opinion of the court was delivered by the CHIEF JUSTICE [John Marshall]. . . .

It is then the opinion of the court,

1st. That by signing the commission of Mr. Marbury, the President of the United States appointed him a justice of peace for the county of Washington, in the District of Columbia; and that the seal of the United States, affixed thereto by the secretary of state, is conclusive testimony of the verity of the signature, and of the completion of the appointment; and that the appointment conferred on him a legal right to the office for the space of five years.

2dly. That, having this legal title to the office, he has a consequent right to the commission; a refusal to deliver which is a plain violation of that right, for which the laws of his country afford him a remedy.

It remains to be inquired whether,

3rdly. He is entitled to the remedy for which he applies. This depends on,

1st. The nature of the writ applied for; and,

2dly. The power of this court.

1st. The nature of the writ.

Blackstone, in the 3d volume of his Commentaries, page 110, defines a *mandamus* to be "a command issuing in the king's name from the court of king's bench, and directed to any person, corporation, or inferior court of judicature within the king's dominions, requiring them to do some particular thing therein specified, which appertains to their office and duty, and which the court of king's bench has previously determined, or at least supposes, to be consonant to right and justice. . . ."

This, then, is a plain case for a *mandamus,* either to deliver the commission, or a copy of it from the record; and it only remains to be inquired,

Whether it can issue from this court.

The act to establish the judical courts of the United States authorizes the supreme court "to issue writs of *mandamus,* in cases warranted by the principles and usages of law, to any courts appointed, or persons holding office, under the authority of the United States."

The secretary of state, being a person holding an office under the authority of the United States, is precisely within the letter of the description; and if this court is not authorized to issue a writ of *mandamus* to such an officer, it must be because the law is unconstitutional, and therefore absolutely incapable of conferring the authority, and assigning the duties which its words purport to confer and assign.

The constitution vests the whole judicial power of the United States in one supreme court, and such inferior courts as congress shall, from time to time, ordain and establish. This power is expressly extended to all cases arising under the laws of the United States; and consequently, in some form may be exercised over the present case, because the right claimed is given by a law of the United States.

In the distribution of this power it is declared that "the supreme court shall have original jurisdiction in all cases affecting ambassadors, other public ministers and consuls, and those in which a State shall be a party. In all other cases, the supreme court shall have appellate jurisdiction."

It has been insisted, at the bar, that as the original grant of jurisdiction, to the supreme and inferior courts, is general, and the clause, assigning original jurisdiction to the supreme court contains no negative or restrictive words, the power remains to the legislature to assign original jurisdiction to that court in other cases than those specified in the article which has been recited; provided those cases belong to the judicial power of the United States.

If it had been intended to leave it in the discretion of the legislature to apportion the judicial power between the supreme and inferior courts according to the will of that body, it would certainly have been useless to have proceeded further than to have defined the judicial power, and the tribunals in which it should be vested. The subsequent part of the section is mere surplusage, is entirely without meaning, if such is to be the construction. If congress remains at liberty to give this court appellate jurisdiction, where the constitution has declared their jurisdiction shall be original; and original jurisdiction where the constitution has declared it shall be appellate; the distribution of jurisdiction, made in the constitution, is form without substance.

Affirmative words are often, in their operation, negative of other objects than those affirmed; and in this case, a negative or exclusive sense must be given to them, or they have no operation at all.

It cannot be presumed that any clause in the Constitution is intended to be without effect; and, therefore, such a construction is inadmissible, unless the words require it. . . .

To enable this court, then, to issue a *mandamus,* it must be shown to be an exercise of appellate jurisdiction, or to be necessary to enable them to exercise appellate jurisdiction.

It has been stated at the bar that the appellate jurisdiction may be exercised in a variety of forms, and that if it be the will of the legislature that a *mandamus* should be used for that purpose, that will must be obeyed. This is true, yet the jurisdiction must be appellate, not original.

It is the essential criterion of appellate jurisdiction, that it revises and corrects the proceedings in a cause already instituted, and does not create that cause. Although, therefore, a *mandamus* may be directed to courts, yet to issue such a writ to an officer for the delivery of a paper, is in effect the same as to sustain an original action for that paper, and, therefore, seems not to belong to appellate, but to original jurisdiction. Neither is it necessary in such a case as this, to enable the court to exercise its appellate jurisdiction.

The authority, therefore, given to the supreme court, by the act establishing the judicial courts of the United States, to issue writs of *mandamus* to public officers, appears not to be warranted by the constitution; and it becomes necessary to inquire whether a jurisdiction so conferred can be exercised.

The question, whether an act repugnant to the constitution can become the law of the land, is a question deeply interesting to the United States; but, happily, not of an intricacy proportioned to its interest. It seems only necessary to recognize certain principles, supposed to have been long and well established to decide it.

That the people have an original right to establish, for their future government, such principles as, in their opinion, shall most conduce to their own happiness, is the basis on which the whole American fabric has been erected. The exercise of this original right is a very great exertion; nor can it, nor ought it, to be frequently repeated. The principles, therefore, so established, are deemed fundamental. And as the authority from which they proceed is supreme, and can seldom act, they are designed to be permanent.

This original and supreme will organizes the government, and assigns to different departments their respective powers. It may either stop here, or establish certain limits not to be transcended by those departments.

The government of the United States is of the latter description. The powers of the legislature are defined and limited; and that those limits may not be mistaken, or forgotten, the constitution is written. To what purpose are powers limited, and to what purpose is that limitation committed to writing, if these limits may, at any time, be passed by those intended to be restrained? The distinction between a government with limited and unlimited powers is abolished, if those limits do not confine the persons on whom they are imposed, and if acts prohibited and acts allowed, are of equal obligation. It is a proposition too plain to be contested, that the constitution controls any legislative act repugnant to it; or, that the legislature may alter the constitution by an ordinary act.

Between these alternatives there is no middle ground. The constitution is either a superior paramount law, unchangeable by ordinary means, or it is on a level with ordinary legislative acts, and, like other acts, is alterable when the legislature shall please to alter it.

If the former part of the alternative be true, then a legislative act contrary to the constitution, is not law; if the latter part be true, then written constitutions are absurd attempts, on the part of the people, to limit a power in its own nature illimitable.

Certainly all those who have framed written constitutions contemplate them as forming the fundamental and paramount law of the nation, and consequently, the theory of every such government must be, that an act of the legislature, repugnant to the constitution, is void.

This theory is essentially attached to a written constitution, and is consequently to be considered, by this court, as one of the fundamental principles of our society. It is not, therefore, to be lost sight of in the further consideration of this subject.

If an act of the legislature, repugnant to the constitution, is void, does it, notwithstanding its invalidity, bind the courts, and oblige them to give it effect? Or, in other words, though it be not law, does it constitute a rule as operative as if it was a law? This would be to overthrow in fact what was established in theory; and would seem, at first view, an absurdity too gross to be insisted on. It shall, however, receive a more attentive consideration.

It is emphatically the province and duty of the judicial department to say what the law is. Those who apply the rule to particular cases, must of necessity expound and interpret that rule. If two laws conflict with each other, the courts must decide on the operation of each.

So if a law be in opposition to the constitution; if both the law and the constitution apply to a particular case, so that the court must either decide that case conformably to the law, disregarding the constitution; or conformably to the constitution, disregarding the law; the court must determine which of these conflicting rules governs the case. This is of the very essence of judicial duty.

If, then, the courts are to regard the constitution, and the constitution is superior to any ordinary act of the legislature, the constitution, and not such ordinary act, must govern the case to which they both apply. . . .

The judicial power of the United States is extended to all cases arising under the constitution.

Could it be the intention of those who gave this power, to say that in using it the constitution should not be looked into? That a case arising under the constitution should be decided without examining the instrument under which it arises?

This is too extravagant to be maintained.

In some cases, then, the constitution must be looked into by the judges. And if they can open it at all, what part of it are they forbidden to read or to obey?

There are many other parts of the constitution which serve to illustrate this subject.

It is declared that "no tax or duty shall be laid on articles exported from any State." Suppose a duty on the export of cotton, of tobacco, or of flour; and a suit instituted to recover it. Ought judgment to be rendered in such a case? Ought judges to close their eyes on the constitution, and only see the law? . . .

Why does a judge swear to discharge his duties agreeably to the constitution of the United States, if that constitution forms no rule for his government—if it is closed upon him, and cannot be inspected by him? If such be the real state of things, this is worse than solemn mockery. To prescribe, or to take this oath, becomes equally a crime.

It is also not entirely unworthy of observation, that in declaring what shall be the supreme law of the land, the constitution itself is first mentioned; and not the laws of the United States generally, but those only which shall be made in pursuance of the constitution, have that rank.

Thus, the particular phraseology of the constitution of the United States confirms and strengthens the principle, supposed to be essential to all written constitutions, that

a law repugnant to the constitution is void; and that courts, as well as other departments, are bound by that instrument.

The rule must be discharged.

Related Topics

1. *Advisory opinions.* "In 1793, by direction of the President, Secretary of State
Jefferson addressed to the Justices of the Supreme Court a communication soliciting
their views upon the question whether their advice to the Executive would be available in the solution of important questions of the construction of treaties, laws of
nations and laws of the land, which the Secretary said were often presented under
circumstances which 'do not give a cognizance of them to the tribunals of the
country.' The answer to the question was postponed until the subsequent sitting of
the Supreme Court, when Chief Justice Jay and his associates answered to President
Washington that, 'in consideration of the lines of separation drawn by the Constitution
between the three departments of government, and being judges of a court of last
resort, afforded strong arguments against the propriety of extrajudicially deciding the
questions alluded to. . . .'" *Muskrat* v. *United States,* 219 US 346. The Court still
holds to this precedent and refuses to give advisory opinions.

For a case or controversy to be decided by the judiciary, it must be presented in
an appropriate form and under appropriate circumstances. No rigid, mechanical test
can be given to determine when it is appropriate for the judiciary to act upon a
controversy, for this is a matter admitting of judicial discretion.

2. *Declaratory judgments.* While the federal courts do not render advisory opinions (as do the courts of Colorado, Massachusetts, and several other states), they do
render declaratory judgments. An advisory opinion is advice by the judiciary to the
executive or to the legislature on a hypothetical question. By contrast, a declaratory
judgment grows out of an adjudication of an actual controversy between adverse
parties and differs from an ordinary judgment primarily in that it involves no compulsory process.

In 1934 Congress passed the Federal Declaratory Judgment Act, which reads as
follows:

> In a case of actual controversy within its jurisdiction, except with respect to Federal
> taxes, any court of the United States, upon the filing of an appropriate pleading, may
> declare the rights and other legal relations of any interested party seeking such declara-
> tion, whether or not further relief is or could be sought. Any such declaration shall
> have the force and effect of a final judgment or decree and shall be reviewable as
> such. . . . 28 USC § 2201.

The constitutionality of this Act was upheld in *Aetna Life Ins. Co.* v. *Haworth,* 300
US 227 (1937). In that case there was a controversy between Haworth and an
insurance company as to whether a policy covering disability had expired because
of Haworth's failure to pay premiums. Haworth had presented claims to the company
based upon disability. The company denied liability. Haworth persisted in presenting
claims but failed to institute a suit. Thereupon the company sought a declaratory

judgment determining with finality that Haworth's policy was void, alleging that it was compelled to maintain reserves to cover Haworth's claim as long as it was in controversy and that it might lose the benefit of evidence through the death of witnesses if the controversy remained open. The Supreme Court held this to be an appropriate case for a declaratory judgment. Compare *Nashville, C. & St. L. Ry.* v. *Wallace,* 288 US 249 (1933), and *Public Service Commission* v. *Wycoff Co.,* 344 US 237 (1952). *Steffel* v. *Thompson,* 415 US 452 (1974), held that "Congress plainly intended declaratory relief to act as an alternative to the strong medicine of the injunction and to be utilized to test the constitutionality of state criminal statutes in cases where injunctive relief would be unavailable. . . ."

3. *Cases and controversies.*   "The judicial power shall extend to . . . cases . . . [and] controversies . . .," states Article III, and argument over the scope of "cases and controversies" never ceases. This was, of course, the background issue in the cases cited above under "advisory opinions" and "declaratory judgments." In recent years the Supreme Court has tended to broaden the scope of the cases and controverises concept. This is illustrated by the decision in *Super Tire Engineering Company* v. *McCorkle,* 416 US 115 (1974).

The Company contended that it was contrary to the federal labor policy under the Labor Management Relations Act for New Jersey to make welfare payments to striking workers. It sought both a declaratory judgment and injunctive relief. At the hearing on the company's motion for a preliminary injunction, counsel for the union contended that "this entire matter . . . has been mooted" because "these employees voted to return to work tomorrow morning." The district court rejected the union's argument and proceeded to the merits of the dispute. On appeal, the Court of Appeals for the Third Circuit reversed the district court. The Supreme Court then reversed the court of appeals. A portion of the record follows:

> MR. JUSTICE BLACKMUN delivered the opinion of the Court.
> . . . The question presented is whether a "case" or "controversy" still exists, within the meaning of Art. III, § 2, of the Constitution, and of the Declaratory Judgment Act, 28 USC §§ 2201–2202. . . .
> The petitioners here have sought, from the very beginning, *declaratory* relief as well as an injunction. Clearly, the District Court had "the duty to decide the appropriateness and the merits of the declaratory request irrespective of its conclusion as to the propriety of the issuance of the injunction." *Zwickler* v. *Koota,* 380 US 241, 254 (1967); *Roe* v. *Wade,* 410 US 113, 166 (1973); *Steffel* v. *Thompson,* 415 US 452,   (1974). Thus, even though the case for an injunction dissolved with the subsequent settlement of the strike and the strikers' return to work, the parties to the principal controversy, that is, the corporate petitioners and the New Jersey officials, may still retain sufficient interests and injury as to justify the award of declaratory relief. The question is "whether the facts alleged, under all the circumstances, show that there is a substantial controversy, between parties having adverse legal interests, of sufficient immediacy and reality to warrant the issuance of a declaratory judgment." *Maryland Casualty Co.* v. *Pacific Coal & Oil Co.,* 312 US 270, 273 (1941). And since this case involves governmental action, we must ponder the broader consideration whether the short-term nature of that action makes the issues presented here "capable of repetition, yet evading review," so that petitioners are adversely

affected by government "without a chance of redress." *Southern Pac. Terminal Co. v. Interstate Commerce Comm'n,* 219 US 498, 515 (1911).

A. We hold that the facts here provide full and complete satisfaction of the requirement of the Constitution's Art. III, § 2, and the Declaratory Judgment Act, that a case or controversy exist between the parties. Unlike the situations that prevailed in *Oil Workers Unions v. Missouri,* 361 US 363 (1960), on which the Court of Appeals' majority chiefly relied, and in *Harris v. Battle,* 348 US 803 (1954), the challenged governmental activity in the present case is not contingent, has not evaporated or disappeared, and, by its continuing and brooding presence, casts what may well be a substantial adverse effect on the interests of the petitioning parties. . . .

A strike that lasts six weeks, as this one did, may seem long, but its termination, like pregnancy at nine months and elections spaced at year-long or biennial intervals, should not preclude challenge to state policies that have had their impact and that continue in force, unabated and unreviewed. The judiciary must not close the door to the resolution of the important questions these concrete disputes present.

The judgment of the Court of Appeals is reversed and the case is remanded for further proceedings on the merits of the controversy.

It is so ordered.

Mr. Justice Stewart, with whom The Chief Justice, Mr. Justice Powell, and Mr. Justice Rehnquist join, dissenting.

The Court today reverses the Court of Appeals and holds that this case is not moot, despite the fact that the underlying labor dispute that gave rise to the petitioners' claims ended even before the parties made their initial appearance in the District Court. I think this holding ignores the limitations placed upon the federal judiciary by Article III of the Constitution and disregards the clear teachings of prior cases. Accordingly, I dissent.

This Court has repeatedly recognized that the inability of the federal judiciary "to review moot cases derives from the requirement of Article III of the Constitution under which the exercise of judicial power depends on the existence of a case or controversy." *Liner v. Jafco, Inc.,* 375 US 301, 306, n. 3. See also *North Carolina v. Rice,* 404 US 244, 246; *Powell v. McCormack,* 395 US 486, 496 n. 7; *Sibron v. New York,* 392 US 40, 50 n. 8. Since Article III courts are precluded from issuing advisory opinions, *Hayburn's Case,* 2 Dall. 409; *Muskrat v. United States,* 219 US 346, it necessarily follows that they are impotent "to decide questions that cannot affect the rights of litigants in the case before them." *North Carolina v. Rice, supra,* at 246; *St. Pierre v. United States,* 319 US 41, 42. . . .

In short, I think that this case is completely controlled by *Harris* [v. *Battle,* 348 US 803] and *Oil Workers* [*Union v. Missouri,* 361 US 363]. The doctrine of mootness is already a difficult and complex one, and I think that the Court today muddies the waters further by straining unnecessarily to distinguish and limit some of the few clear precedents available to us.

For these reasons I would affirm the judgment of the Court of Appeals.

In *DeFunis v. Odegaard,* 416 US 312 (1974), the Court gave a *per curiam* decision reading as follows:

In 1971 the petitioner, Marco DeFunis, applied for admission as a first-year student at the University of Washington Law School, a state-operated institution. The size of the incoming first-year class was to be limited to 150 persons, and the Law School received some 1,600 applications for these 150 places. DeFunis was eventually notified that he had been denied admission. He thereupon commenced this suit in a Washington trial court, contending that the procedures and criteria employed by the Law School Admissions Committee invidiously discriminated against him on account of his race in violation of the Equal Protection Clause of the Fourteenth Amendment to the United States Constitution.

DeFunis brought the suit on behalf of himself alone, and not as the representative of any class, against the various respondents, who are officers, faculty members, and members of the Board of Regents of the University of Washington. He asked the trial court to issue a mandatory injunction commanding the respondents to admit him as a member of the first-year class entering in September of 1971, on the ground that the Law School admissions policy had resulted in the unconstitutional denial of his application for admission. The trial court agreed with his claim and granted the requested relief. DeFunis was, accordingly, admitted to the Law School and began his legal studies there in the fall of 1971. On appeal, the Washington Supreme Court reversed the judgment of the trial court and held that the Law School admissions policy did not violate the Constitution. By this time DeFunis was in his second year at the Law School.

He then petitioned this Court for a writ of *certiorari,* and Mr. Justice Douglas, as Circuit Justice, stayed the judgment of the Washington Supreme Court pending the "final disposition of the case by this Court." By virtue of this stay, DeFunis has remained in law school, and was in the first term of his third and final year when this Court first considered his *certiorari* petition in the fall of 1973. Because of our concern that DeFunis' third-year standing in the Law School might have rendered this case moot, we requested the parties to brief the question of mootness before we acted on the petition. In response, both sides contended that the case was not moot. The respondents indicated that, if the decision of the Washington Supreme Court were permitted to stand, the petitioner could complete the term for which he was then enrolled but would have to apply to the faculty for permission to continue in the school before he could register for another term.

We granted the petition for *certiorari* on November 19, 1973. 414 US 1038.The case was in due course orally argued on February 26, 1974.

In response to questions raised from the bench during the oral argument, counsel for the petitioner has informed the Court that DeFunis has now registered "for his final quarter in law school." Counsel for the respondents have made clear that the Law School will not in any way seek to abrogate this registration. In light of DeFunis' recent registration for the last quarter of his final law school year, and the Law School's assurance that his registration is fully effective, the insistent question again arises whether this case is not moot, and to that question we now turn.

The starting point for analysis is the familiar proposition "that federal courts are without power to decide questions that cannot affect the rights of the litigants before them." *North Carolina* v. *Rice,* 404 US 244, 246 (1971). The inability of the federal judiciary "to review moot cases derives from the requirement of Art. III of the Constitution under which the exercise of judicial power depends on the existence of a case or controversy." *Liner* v. *Jafco, Inc.,* 375 US 301, 306, n. 3 (1964); see also *Powell* v. *McCormack,* 395 US 486, 496, n. 7 (1969); *Sibron* v. *New York,* 392 US 40, 50, n. 8 (1968). Although as a matter of Washington state law it appears that this case would be saved from mootness by "the great public interest in the continuing issues raised by this appeal" . . ., the fact remains that under Art. III "[e]ven in cases arising in the state courts, the question of mootness is a federal one which a federal court must resolve before it assumes jurisdiction." . . .

There is a line of decisions in this Court standing for the proposition that the "voluntary cessation of allegedly illegal conduct does not deprive the tribunal of power to hear and determine the case, *i.e.,* does not make the case moot." *United States* v. *W. T. Grant Co.,* 345 US 629, 632 (1953); . . . *United States* v. *Phosphate Export Assn.,* 393 US 199, 202–203 (1968). These decisions and the doctrine they reflect would be quite relevant if the question of mootness here had arisen by reason of a unilateral change in the *admissions procedures* of the Law School. For it was the admissions procedures that were the target of this litigation, and a voluntary cessation of the admissions practices complained of could make this case moot only if it could be said with assurance "that there is no reasonable expectation that the wrong will be repeated." *United States* v. *W. T. Grant Co., supra,* at 633. Otherwise, "[t]he defendant is free to return to his old ways," *id.,* at 632, and this fact would be enough to prevent mootness because of the "public interest in having the legality of the practices settled." *Id.,* at 632. But mootness in the present case depends not at all upon a "voluntary cessation" of the admissions practices that were the subject of this litigation. It depends, instead, upon the simple fact that DeFunis is now in the final quarter of the final year of his course of study, and the settled and unchallenged policy of the Law School to permit him to complete the term for which he is now enrolled.

It might also be suggested that this case presents a question that is "capable of repetition, yet evading review," *Southern Pacific Terminal Co.* v. *ICC,* 219 US 498, 515 (1911); *Roe* v. *Wade,* 410 US 113, 125 (1973), and is thus amenable to federal adjudication even though it might otherwise be considered moot. But DeFunis will never again be required to run the gauntlet of the Law School's admission process, and so the question is certainly not "capable of repetition" so far as he is concerned. . . .

Because the petitioner will complete his law school studies at the end of the term for which he has now registered regardless of any decision this Court might reach on the merits of this litigation, we conclude that the Court cannot, consistently with the limitations of Art. III of the Constitution, consider the substantive constitutional issues tendered by the parties. Accordingly, the judgment of the Supreme Court of Washington is vacated, and the cause is remanded for such proceedings as by that Court may be deemed appropriate.

It is so ordered.

Mr. Justice Douglas, dissenting.

I agree with . . . Justice[s] Brennan [White and Marshall] that this case is not moot, and because of the significance of the issues raised I think it is important to reach the merits. . . .

4. *Standing to sue.* In *Massachusetts* v. *Melon,* 262 US 447 (1923), the Court held that the state of Massachusetts could not, as the representative of its citizens, bring a suit to restrain enforcement of the Maternity Act passed by Congress in 1921 on the ground that Congress lacked power to pass the act. "It cannot be conceded that a State, as parens patriae, may institute judicial proceedings to protect citizens of the United States from the operation of the statutes thereof. While the State, under some circumstances, may sue in that capacity for the protection of its citizens (*Missouri* v. *Illinois,* 180 US 208, 241), it is no part of its duty or power to enforce their rights in respect of their relations with the federal government. In that field it is the United States, and not the state, which represents them as parens patriae, when such repre-

sentation becomes appropriate; and to the former, and not to the latter, they must look for such protective measures as flow from that status," wrote Justice Sutherland.

In the companion case of *Frothingham* v. *Mellon,* the Court stated: "The attack upon the statute in the *Frothingham* case is, generally, the same, but this plaintiff alleges in addition that she is a taxpayer of the United States; and her contention, though not clear, seems to be that the effect of the appropriations complained of will be to increase the burden of future taxation and thereby take her property without due process of law. . . . The interest of a taxpayer of a municipality in the application of its moneys is direct and immediate and the remedy by injunction to prevent their misuse is not inappropriate. It is upheld by a large number of state cases and is the rule of this Court. *Crampton* v. *Zabriskie,* 101 US 601, 609. Nevertheless, there are decisions to the contrary. See, for example, *Miller* v. *Grandy,* 13 Mich 540, 550. The reasons which support the extension of the equitable remedy to a single taxpayer in such cases are based upon the peculiar relation of the corporate taxpayer to the corporation, which is not without some resemblance to that subsisting between stockholder and private corporation. IV Dillon *Municipal Corporations,* 5th Ed, § 1580 *et seq.* But the relation of a taxpayer of the United States to the Federal Government is very different. His interest in the moneys of the Treasury—partly realized from taxation and partly from other sources—is shared with millions of others; is comparatively minute and indeterminable; and the effect upon future taxation, of any payment out of the funds, so remote, fluctuating and uncertain, that no basis is afforded for an appeal to the preventive powers of a court of equity."

Flast v. *Cohen,* 392 US 83 (1968), created an exception to the rule of the *Frothingham* case. Flast and others, resting their standing to maintain the action solely on their status as federal taxpayers, sought to enjoin Cohen and other officials in charge of administering the Elementary and Secondary Education Act of 1965 from approving the expenditure of federal funds for use in purchasing instructional materials for use in religious and sectarian schools. In the majority opinion holding that the taxpayers had standing to sue, Chief Justice Warren wrote:

> . . . [T]he judicial power of federal courts is constitutionally restricted to "cases" and "controversies." As is so often the situation in constitutional adjudication, those two words have an iceberg quality, containing beneath their surface simplicity submerged complexities which go to the very heart of our constitutional form of government. Embodied in the words "cases" and "controversies" are two complementary but somewhat different limitations. In part those words limit the business of federal courts to questions presented in an adversary context and in a form historically viewed as capable of resolution through the judicial process. And in part those words define the role assigned to the judiciary in a tripartite allocation of power to assure that the federal courts will not intrude into areas committed to the other branches of government. Justiciability is the term of art employed to give expression of this dual limitation placed upon federal courts by the case and controversy doctrine.
>
> Justiciability is itself a concept of uncertain meaning and scope. . . . [T]hat doctrine has become a blend of constitutional requirements and policy considerations. And a policy limitation is "not always clearly distinguished from the constitutional limitation." *Barrows* v. *Jackson,* 346 US 249, 255 (1953). . . .
>
> Standing is an aspect of justiciability and, as such, the problem of standing is surrounded by the same complexities and vagaries that inhere in justiciability. . . .

Some of the complexities peculiar to standing problems result because standing "serves, on occasion, as a shorthand expression for all the various elements of justiciability." In addition, there are at work in the standing doctrine the many subtle pressures which tend to cause policy considerations to blend into constitutional limitations.

Despite the complexities and uncertainties, some meaningful form can be given to the jurisdictional limitations placed on federal court power by the concept of standing. The fundamental aspect of standing is that it focuses on the party seeking to get his complaint before a federal court and not on the issues he wishes to have adjudicated. The "gist of the question of standing" is whether the party seeking relief has "alleged such a personal stake in the outcome of the controversy as to assure that concrete adverseness which sharpens the presentation of issues upon which the court so largely depends for illumination of difficult constitutional questions." *Baker* v. *Carr,* 369 US 186, 204 (1962). In other words, when standing is placed in issue in a case, the question is whether the person whose standing is challenged is a proper party to request an adjudication of a particular issue and not whether the issue itself is justiciable. Thus, a party may have standing in a particular case, but the federal court may nevertheless decline to pass on the merits of the case because, for example, it presents a political question. A proper party is demanded so that federal courts will not be asked to decide "ill-defined controversies over constitutional issues." *United Public Workers* v. *Mitchell,* 330 US 75, 90 (1947), or a case which is of "a hypothetical or abstract character." *Aetna Life Insurance Co.* v. *Haworth,* 300 US 227, 240 (1937). So stated, the standing requirement is closely related to, although more general than, the rule that federal courts will not entertain friendly suits, . . . or those which are feigned or collusive in nature. . . .

The various rules of standing applied by federal courts have not been developed in the abstract. Rather, they have been fashioned with specific reference to the status asserted by the party whose standing is challenged and to the type of question he wishes to have adjudicated. We have noted that, in deciding the question of standing, it is not relevant that the substantive issues in the litigation might be nonjusticiable. However, our decisions establish that, in ruling on standing, it is both appropriate and necessary to look to the substantive issues for another purpose, namely, to determine whether there is a logical nexus between the status asserted and the claim sought to be adjudicated. . . . Such inquiries into the nexus between the status asserted by the litigant and the claim he presents are essential to assure that he is a proper and appropriate party to invoke federal judicial power. Thus, our point of reference in this case is the standing of individuals who assert only the status of federal taxpayers and who challenge the constitutionality of a federal spending program. Whether such individuals have standing to maintain that form of action turns on whether they can demonstrate the necessary stake as taxpayers in the outcome of the litigation to satisfy Article III requirements.

The nexus demanded of federal taxpayers has two aspects to it. First, the taxpayer must establish a logical link between that status and the type of legislative enactment attacked. . . . Secondly, the taxpayer must establish a nexus between that status and the precise nature of the constitutional infringement alleged. Under this requirement, the taxpayer must show that the challenged enactment exceeds specific constitutional limitations imposed upon the exercise of the congressional taxing and spending power and not simply that the enactment is generally beyond the powers delegated to Congress by Art. I, § 8. When both nexuses are established, the litigant will have shown a taxpayer's stake in the outcome of the controversy and will be a proper and appropriate party to invoke a federal court's jurisdiction.

The taxpayer-appellants in this case have satisfied both nexuses to support their claim of standing under the test we announce today. Their constitutional challenge is made to an exercise by Congress of its power under Art. I, § 8, to spend for the general welfare, and the challenged program involves a substantial expenditure of federal tax funds. In addition, appellants have alleged that the challenged expenditures violate the Establishment and Free Exercise Clauses of the First Amendment. Our history vividly illustrates that one of the specific evils feared by those who drafted the Establishment Clause and fought for its adoption was that the taxing and spending power would be used to favor one religion over another or to support religion in general. . . . [T]hat clause of the First Amendment operates as a specific constitutional limitation upon the exercise by Congress of the taxing and spending power conferred by Art. I, § 8.

The allegations of the taxpayer in *Frothingham* v. *Mellon, supra,* were quite different from those made in this case, and the result in *Frothingham* is consistent with the test of taxpayer standing announced today. The taxpayer in *Frothingham* attacked a federal spending program and she, therefore, established the first nexus required. However, she lacked standing because her constitutional attack was not based on an allegation that Congress, in enacting the Maternity Act of 1921, had breached a specific limitation upon its taxing and spending power. . . .

. . . Whether the Constitution contains other specific limitations can be determined only in the contest of future cases. However, whenever such specific limitations are found, we believe a taxpayer will have a clear stake as a taxpayer in assuring that they are not breached by Congress. Consequently, we hold that a taxpayer will have standing consistent with Article III to invoke federal judicial power when he alleges that congressional action under the taxing and spending clause is in derogation of those constitutional provisions which operate to restrict the exercise of the taxing and spending power. . . .

In *Boyle* v. *Landry,* 401 US 77 (1971), *Sierra Club* v. *Morton,* 405 US 727 (1972), *Laird* v. *Tatum,* 408 US 1 (1972), and *S.* v. *D.,* 411 US 614 (1973), the Court enforced strictly the requirement of standing. By contrast, in *Trafficante* v. *Metropolitan Life Ins. Co.,* 409 US 205 (1972), influenced by statutory construction, the Court was lenient in regard to standing. The Civil Rights Act of 1968 authorizes civil suits by "any person who claims to have been injured by a discriminatory housing practice." Paul J. Trafficante and another tenant of an apartment complex filed suit for damages, claiming that the owner had discriminated against nonwhites by such practices as manipulating the waiting list for apartments. The injuries asserted were "loss of the social benefits of living in an integrated community; . . . professional advantages which would have accrued . . . ; [and] embarrassment. . . . " The Court held that it could give vitality to the Act of 1968 "only by a generous construction which gives standing to sue to all in the same housing unit who are injured by racial discrimination in the management. . . . " "The role of 'private attorneys general' is not uncommon in modern legislative programs," wrote Justice Douglas. Compare *United States* v. *SCRAP,* 412 US 669 (1973).

In 1974 the Court reverted to the traditional concept of standing. *United States* v. *Richardson,* 418 US 166 (1974), held that a taxpayer as such had no standing to challenge the constitutionality of the provision of the act which permits the Central Intelligence Agency to account for its expenditures "solely on the certificate of the Director." Chief Justice Burger wrote:

It can be argued that if respondent is not permitted to litigate this issue, no one can do so. In a very real sense, the absence of any particular individual or class to litigate these claims gives support to the argument that the subject matter is committed to the surveillance of Congress, and ultimately to the political process. Any other conclusion would mean that the Founding Fathers intended to set up something in the nature of an Athenian democracy or a New England town meeting to oversee the conduct of the National Government by means of lawsuits in federal courts. The Constitution created a *representative* Government with the representatives directly responsible to their constituents at stated periods of two, four, and six years. . . .

Concurring, Justice Powell wrote:

I join the opinion of the Court because I am in accord with most of its analysis, particularly insofar as it relies on traditional barriers against federal taxpayer or citizen standing. And I agree that *Flast* v. *Cohen,* 392 US 83 (1968), which set the boundaries for the arguments of the parties before us, is the most directly relevant precedent and quite correctly absorbs a major portion of the Court's attention. I write solely to indicate that I would go further than the Court and would lay to rest the approach undertaken in *Flast.* I would not overrule *Flast* on its facts, because it is now settled that federal taxpayer standing exists in Establishment Clause cases. I would not, however, perpetuate the doctrinal confusion inherent in the *Flast* two-part "nexus" test. . . .

Justices Brennan, Douglas, Marshall, and Stewart dissented.

Schlesinger v. *Reservist Committee to Stop the War,* 418 US 208 (1974), was a class action challenging the Reserve membership of some members of Congress. The Court held that being citizens and taxpayers gave the petitioners no standing to sue. Justices Brennan, Douglas, and Marshall dissented. Justice Stewart, however, concurred, writing:

I agree with the Court that the respondents lack standing to sue either as citizens or taxpayers in this case. Here, unlike *United States* v. *Richardson, post,* at   , the respondents do not allege that the petitioners have refused to perform an affirmative duty imposed upon them by the Constitution. Nor can there be taxpayer standing under *Flast* v. *Cohen,* 392 US 83, since there is simply no challenge to an exercise of the taxing and spending power.

The Court's judgment in this case is wholly consistent with *United States* v. *SCRAP,* 412 US 669. Standing is not today found wanting because an injury has been suffered by many, but rather because *none* of the respondents has alleged the sort of direct, palpable injury required for standing under Art. III. Like the plaintiff in *Frothingham* v. *Mellon,* 262 US 447, the respondents seek only to air what we described in *Flast* as "generalized grievances about the conduct of government." 392 US, at 106. Our prior cases make clear that such abstract allegations cannot suffice to confer Art. III standing, and I therefore join the opinion and judgment of the Court.

5. *Effect of an unconstitutional statute.* There are a variety of theories on the effect of an unconstitutional statute. Under the *void ab initio* theory, such a statute is "in legal contemplation, as inoperative as though it had never been passed." Field, J., in *Norton* v. *Shelby County,* 118 US 425 (1886). By contrast, the existence of such a statute is sometimes considered an operative fact. Thus, in *Lemon* v. *Kurtzman,* 411

US 193 (1973), the Court refused to enjoin payment of $24 million set aside by Pennsylvania to compensate sectarian schools for services rendered prior to the date the Pennsylvania statute authorizing payment for the services was held to be unconstitutional. The decision emphasized the broad discretion of the trial court in shaping equity decrees.

In 1923 the Supreme Court held the minimum wage law for the District of Columbia to be void. *Adkins* v. *Children's Hospital,* 261 US 525. In 1937 in a case dealing with a state law the Court announced that " the case of *Adkins* v. *Children's Hospital, supra,* should be, and it is, overruled." *West Coast Hotel Co.* v. *Parrish,* 300 US 379. The minimum wage statute for the District remained on the statute books; and following the decision in the *Parrish* case, the attorney general informed the president that the statute "is now a valid act of Congress and may be administered in accordance with its terms." 39 *Opinions of the Attorney General* 22 (1937). On the general subject, see O. P. Field, *The Effect of an Unconstitutional Statute* (Minneapolis, 1935).

6. *Separability.*   The fact that a part of a statute is declared invalid does not necessarily mean that the whole of the statute is void. This depends upon the relation of the void part to other parts and upon the judiciary's interpretation of whether the legislature meant for the parts to be independent of each other. This problem leads into the controversial realm of rules of construction. See the opinion of Justice Harlan in *Welch* v. *United States,* 398 US 33 (1970).

7. *Enforcement of Supreme Court decisions.*   Even though a subject of recurrent criticism, the Supreme Court has enjoyed enough respect throughout our history to have most of its decisions enforced without serious opposition. The Court can enter judgment and award execution, or remand a case with specific directions to enter judgment. See 28 USCA, § 2106 and 9 USCA §§ 547, 549, and 672. In the last analysis, however, the judiciary is dependent upon the political branches of the government and popular support. President Washington called out troops to enforce the law and stamp out the "whiskey rebellion" in western Pennsylvania in 1794, and President Eisenhower used troops to prevent defiance of federal judicial decrees in Arkansas in 1957. See *Cooper* v. *Aaron,* 358 US 1 (1958).

When the Supreme Court reverses a state court, typical phraseology used in concluding its opinion is as follows: "The judgment is reversed and the cause is remanded for further proceedings not inconsistent with this opinion." The "mandate" may be more specific, e.g., "The judgment of the Supreme Court of Alabama is therefore reversed and the cause is remanded for consideration of any grounds not disposed of on the first appeal; and, if none has merit, with instructions to reinstate the judgment entered by the jury verdict of June 12, 1953, awarding the petitioner damages of $46,000." *Stinson* v. *Atlantic Coast Line R. Co.,* 355 US 62 (1957).

8. *Impact of Supreme Court decisions.*   One of the many criteria used by judges in determining the meaning of the Constitution or in deciding whether a statute or practice is to be held constitutional or declared void is the "consequence of the decision." The justices of the Supreme Court have long been aware of this factor, and there has in fact been a "balancing of interests" throughout the Court's history. In

recent years a number of systematic studies on the relationship between judicial decisions and social change have been undertaken by political scientists. See Theodore L. Becker, *The Impact of Supreme Court Decisions* (New York, 1969) and Stephen Wasby, *The Impact of the Supreme Court of the United States* (Homewood, Ill., 1970).

9. *Political questions.*   The courts sometimes label an issue as political in nature and refuse to pass judgment upon it. Thus, in *Coleman* v. *Miller,* 307 US 433 (1939), the Supreme Court held that the question of whether the legislature of Kansas could in 1937 validly ratify the Child Labor Amendment proposed by Congress in 1924 to be "political and not justiciable."

For many years questions concerning the geographic distribution of representation in legislative bodies were considered to be political. This line of decisions was reversed by *Baker* v. *Carr,* 369 US 186 (1962).

In *Powell* v. *McCormack,* 395 US 486 (1969), the Court held that the House of Representatives was "without power" to exclude Adam Clayton Powell from its membership.

Roudebush v. *Hartke,* 405 US 15 (1972), held that an Indiana recount of the votes in a race for the United States Senate did not usurp power vested in the Senate.

In *O'Brien* v. *Brown,* decided July 8, 1972, by a six-to-three vote, the Supreme Court decided against judicial intervention in contests over the selection of delegates to the Democratic National Convention. The party's credentials committee had voted to bar the seating of 151 persons who ran in a California primary as part of a 271-person slate pledged to the candidacy of George McGovern. The credentials committee had held the California "winner-take-all" practice to be a violation of national party rules. The Court of Appeals of the District of Columbia held that the credentials committee was in fact creating a new rule and applying it retroactively, in violation of due process of law. The Supreme Court reversed, holding that "in light of the availability of the convention as a forum" where McGovern might yet prevail, the lack of precedent to support convention-eve intervention, and "the large public interest in allowing the political process to function free from judicial supervision," the intervention by the court of appeals was inappropriate.

10. *Judicial review abroad.*   In no other country does the judiciary play so exalted a part in the making of national policy as does the Supreme Court of the United States of America; yet a limited amount of judicial review is to be found in Australia, Austria, Argentina, Brazil, Canada, Colombia, India, Ireland, Italy, Japan, Mexico, Norway, Switzerland, and West Germany. See Joseph Tannenhaus, "Judicial Review," *International Encyclopedia of the Social Sciences* 8 (1968): 303–6.

C. EVALUATION OF JUDICIAL REVIEW

Introduction

The power of the courts to invalidate legislative and executive acts found in conflict with the Constitution is firmly established as a part of the American system of government, but argument over the extent to which this judicial power should be used and the wisdom of specific decisions never ceases. See Raoul Berger, *Congress* v. *The Supreme Court* (Cambridge, Mass., 1969).

Eakin v. *Raub,* 12 Sergt. and Rowle 330 (Pennsylvania Supreme Court, 1825), contains the classic rebuttal of Marshall's argument in *Marbury* v. *Madison.* In a dissenting opinion Justice Gibson begins by pointing out that at common law the English judges had no power to pass upon the validity of statutes and that no express grant of such power is found in the Constitution. Continuing, he says:

> The constitution and the right of the legislature to pass the act, may be in collision. But is that a legitimate subject for judicial determination? If it be, the judiciary must be a peculiar organ, to revise the proceedings of the legislature, and to correct its mistakes; and in what part of the constitution are we to look for this proud preeminence? Viewing the matter in the opposite direction, what would be thought of an act of assembly in which it should be declared that the supreme court had, in a particular case, put a wrong construction on the constitution of the United States, and that the judgment should therefore be reversed? It would doubtless be thought a usurpation of judicial power. But it is by no means clear, that to declare a law void which has been enacted according to the forms prescribed in the constitution, is not a usurpation of legislative power. . . .
>
> The oath to support the constitution is not peculiar to the judges, but is taken indiscriminately by every officer of the government. . . .
>
> In the business of government a recurrence to first principles answers the end of an observation at sea with a view to correct the dead reckoning; and for this purpose, a written constitution is an instrument of inestimable value. It is of inestimable value, also, in rendering its first principles familiar to the mass of people; for, after all, there is no effectual guard against legislative usurpation but public opinion, the force of which, in this country is inconceivably great. . . .
>
> [T]he judiciary is not infallible; and an error by it would admit of no remedy but a more distinct expression of the public will, through the extraordinary medium of a convention; whereas, an error by the legislature admits of a remedy by an exertion of the same will, in the ordinary exercise of the right of suffrage,—a mode better calculated to attain the end, without popular excitement. It may be said, the people would probably not notice an error of their representatives. But they would as probably do so, as notice an error of the judiciary; and, besides, it is a postulate in the theory of our government, and the very basis of the superstructure, that the people are wise, virtuous, and competent to manage their own affairs; and if they are not so, in fact, still every question of this sort must be determined according to the principles of the Constitution, as it came from the hands of the framers, and the existence of a defect which was not foreseen, would not justify those who administer the government, in applying a corrective in practice, which can be provided only by convention. . . .

The argument by Justice Gibson is appealing, but is it as persuasive as that of Chief Justice Marshall?

Historical Background

A basic element of the theory upon which judicial review rests is as old as the history of political thought—namely, the distinction between true law and arbitrary force. In early Greece the Sophists argued that "Man is the measure of all things" and that the only basis on which law rests is human convention. Fire burns in Greece and in Persia, but no such universal quality is associated with law. Laws differ from city to city and from time to time. They represent merely the will of those in control of power at a given time and place, argued the Sophists.

Plato's *Republic* was written with the view of combatting the sophistic skepticism that threatened the very foundation or organized society. The influence of his writing has never subsided. His view on the relation of law and justice is clearly reflected in the writings of the Roman statesman Cicero who said: "There is in fact a true law— namely, right reason—which is in accordance with nature, applies to all men, and is unchangeable and eternal. . . . To invalidate this law by human legislation is never morally right, nor is it permissible ever to restrict its operation, and to annul it wholly is impossible. Neither the senate nor the people can absolve us from our obligation to obey this law, and it requires no Sextus Aelius to expound and interpret it. It will not lay down one rule at Rome and another at Athens, nor will it be one rule today and another tomorrow. But there will be one law, eternal and unchangeable, binding at all times upon all peoples; and there will be, as it were, one common master and ruler of men, namely God, who is the author of this law, its interpreter, and its sponsor. The man who will not obey it will abandon his better self, and, in denying the true nature of a man, will thereby suffer the severest of penalities, though he has escaped all the other consequences which men call punishment."[3]

Statements of this kind may not be proved scientifically, but there is something within our makeup that tells us they are true. "We hold these truths to be self-evident, that all men are created equal; that they are endowed by their Creator with certain unalienable rights; that among these are life, liberty, and the pursuit of happiness," wrote Thomas Jefferson in the American Declaration of Independence.

In Dr. Bonham's Case in 1610, Sir Edward Coke wrote that "it appears in our books, that in many cases the common law will control Acts of Parliament, and sometimes adjudge them to be utterly void: for when an Act of Parliament is against common right and reason, or repugnant, or impossible to be performed, the common law will control it, and adjudge such Act to be void."[4] But Coke cited no precedents, and there are no examples of the courts of England invalidating an act of Parliament. Judicial review is an American innovation.

In the history of colonial America, written charters granted to trading companies, proprietors, and colonies played a significant role. Statutes enacted by colonial legislatures were sometimes vetoed by the British Privy Council because of alleged conflict with charter provisions. In this practice we have a precedent for the concept of a hierarchy of laws, with governmental machinery for enforcing the higher law. The higher law involved was not, however, the higher law of the Ciceronean natural-law concept.

Within a few months of the Declaration of Independence in 1776, each one of the American states adopted a written constitution embodying its fundamental law. In the *Marbury* case, Chief Justice Marshall held the theory of judicial review to be "essentially attached to a written constitution." This, however, remains the debatable point.

---

3. George H. Sabine and Stanley B. Smith, *On the Commonwealth, Marcus Tullius Cicero* (Columbus, Ohio, 1929), p. 215.

4. Arthur E. Sutherland, *Constitutionalism in America* (New York, 1965), p. 1.

Basic Issue

The basic issue involved in the debate over judicial review is *who is to decide* constitutional issues. Marshall's argument in the *Marbury* case boils down to three fundamental points: (1) the people have established the Constitution as the supreme law; (2) a statute in conflict with the Constitution is void; and (3) the judges are the highest authority on the question of the validity of statutes. Few people have ever questioned points (1) and (2), but point (3) has always been a subject of debate.

American Experience

The practice of judicial review has been in operation in the United States for more than a century and a half. This experience should be of help in evaluating the practice.

The early period, 1789–1860. In the period prior to the Civil War, the Supreme Court invalidated acts of Congress in only two cases. The *Marbury* case of 1803 was significant primarily for its enunciation of a theory of judicial review. The office which William Marbury sought was relatively insignificant, the term for which he had been appointed was more than half over, and the Court issued no award or process in its decision. In a sense the "Opinion of the Court" was more of a political essay than the decision of a case. Thomas Jefferson denounced the "gratuitous opinion" by Marshall and denied it to be law. "The Constitution intended that the three great branches of the government should be co-ordinate, and independent of each other," explained Jefferson. "As to acts, therefore, which are to be done by either, it has given no control to another branch. . . . Where different branches have to act in their respective lines, finally and without appeal, under any law, they may give to it different and opposite constructions. . . . From these different constructions of the same act by different branches, less mischief arises than from giving to any one of them a control over the others."[5]

Never again during the thirty-four years that John Marshall served as chief justice did the Supreme Court declare an act of Congress void. In the celebrated case of *McCulloch* v. *Maryland,* 4 Wheaton 316 (1819), Marshall wrote: "We admit, as all must admit, that the powers of the government are limited, and that its limits are not to be transcended. But we think the sound construction of the Constitution must allow to the national legislature that discretion, with respect to the means by which the powers it confers are to be carried into execution, which will enable that body to perform the high duties assigned to it, in the manner most beneficial to the people. Let the end be legitimate, let it be within the scope of the Constitution, and all means which are appropriate, which are plainly adapted to that end, which are not prohibited, but consist with the letter and spirit of the Constitution, are constitutional. . . ."

Dred Scott v. *Sanford,* 19 Howard 393 (1857), was the other case before the Civil War in which the Supreme Court held void an act of Congress. Speaking for the majority of the justices, Chief Justice Taney held void the Compromise of 1850 and all other legislation limiting the right of citizens of the United States to carry slaves into the territories. By this decision which backed the proslavery interests, the Court hoped

---

5. Paul Leicester Ford, ed., *The Works of Thomas Jefferson* (New York, 1906), vol. X, pp. 395–96.

to put an end to the principal political issue of the day. Abraham Lincoln expressed the contempt felt by most citizens for the *Dred Scott* decision when he said in his First Inaugural Address: "The candid citizen must confess that if the policy of the government, upon vital questions affecting the whole people, is to be irrevocably fixed by decisions of the Supreme Court, the instant they are made, in ordinary litigation between parties in personal actions, the people will have ceased to be their own rulers, having to that extent practically resigned the government into the hands of that tribunal."

In the early years of our national history when state's rights fervor was strong, the Supreme Court had some difficulty in establishing its right to reverse a decision of the highest court of a state. (See *Martin* v. *Hunter's Lessee,* 1 Wheaton 304 (1816).) *Fletcher* v. *Peck* (1810) was the first case in which the Court held void a state law. Prior to 1861 there were thirty-five cases, most of them arising under the contract or the commerce clause, in which a state law or a municipal ordinance was held void.

The middle period, 1861–1937. In an essay published in 1914 which has become classic, Edward S. Corwin explained that the protection of vested property rights was "the basic doctrine of American constitutional law."[6] In our early history the clause of the Constitution used most frequently in advancing this basic doctrine was the clause in Article I prohibiting any state from "impairing the obligation of contracts." In the middle period from 1861 to 1937 when in 75 cases acts of Congress and in 464 cases state laws were declared to be unconstitutional, the Supreme Court relied most heavily upon the "due process of law" clauses of the Fifth and Fourteenth amendments. A laissez-faire philosophy regarding economics predominated on the Court, and no "socialistic legislation" was permitted to stand. Unfortunately, this philosophy was espoused by the Court in the era of the demise of the frontier and the emergence of an industrial nation, thus creating a social lag. Illustrative of the Court at its worst are *Coppage* v. *Kansas,* 236 US 1 (1915), which struck down a state statute prohibiting yellow-dog contracts, and *Adkins* v. *Children's Hospital,* 261 US 525 (1923), which struck down an act of Congress prescribing minimum wages for women in the District of Columbia.

The most notable dissents to decisions of this type were those by Oliver Wendell Holmes, Jr., a justice of the United States Supreme Court from 1902 to 1932. When in 1905 the Court struck down a New York statute limiting employment in bakers' shops to sixty hours per week, Holmes dissented as follows:

> This case is decided upon an economic theory which a large part of the country does not entertain. If it were a question whether I agreed with that theory, I should desire to study it further and long before making up my mind. But I do not conceive that to be my duty, because I strongly believe that my agreement or disagreement has nothing to do with the right of a majority to embody their opinions in law. . . . Some of these laws embody convictions or prejudices which judges are likely to share. Some may not. But a constitution is not intended to embody a particular economic theory, whether of paternalism and the organic relation of the citizen to the State or of *laissez faire.* It is made for people of fundamentally differing views, and the accident of our

---

6. Edward S. Corwin, "The Basic Doctrine of American Constitutional Law," *Michigan Law Review* 12: 247.

finding certain opinions natural and familiar or novel and even shocking ought not to conclude our judgment upon the question whether statutes embodying them conflict with the Constitution of the United States.[7]

President Franklin D. Roosevelt was greatly irritated when the "nine old men" on the Supreme Court invalidated key measures in his New Deal program, including the National Industrial Recovery Act and the Agricultural Adjustment Act. In a dramatic move on February 5, 1937, he asked Congress to increase the membership of the Court to fifteen. The avowed objective of thus packing the Court was to overcome its ultra-conservative philosophy. There was already a five-to-four division among the justices on a number of key issues, and, during the weeks that the president's packing plan was under study by Congress, Justice Owen J. Roberts changed his mind and began voting to sustain social legislation. In addition, Justice Van Devanter, an arch-conservative, announced that he would retire. The need for packing the Court disappeared, and the packing proposal was rejected by Congress. But the president won in the end. By 1941 eight of the nine Justices on the Supreme Court were Roosevelt appointees. A revolution in constitutional interpretation was well under way.[8]

Recent decades.   In the thirty-seven-year period from 1937 to 1974 the Supreme Court held void acts of Congress in 27 cases and state statutes and municipal ordinances in more than 200 cases. The general trend in constitutional interpretation was from right to left, from conservatism to liberalism. Emphasis shifted from liberty to equality, from a protection of property rights to the protection of minority groups.

The Court practically abandoned judicial review of economic legislation. After 1937, few economic measures enacted by Congress were held void, and the Court displayed a tolerant attitude toward economic regulations enacted by the states. In this area the judicial neutralism advocated by Justice Holmes came to a dominant position. But, as the figures above indicate, the Court by no means abandoned judicial review. It simply turned its attention to different areas.

In the period before 1937 the Supreme Court used tradition and precedent as its guide. It sought to preserve practices of the past, to maintain the *status quo.* What guide did the Court use after 1937 when its attention turned from economic to social matters?

To single out characteristics that accurately describe the Court's leading decisions of the past four decades is difficult, but even a fumbling attempt may be helpful. Protection of minority groups suggests itself as a label. Numerous cases dealt with Jehovah's Witnesses, atheists, blacks, Communists, and persons accused of crime. The scope of the First and Fourteenth amendments was expanded enormously, and equal protection became the dominant note in the law.

The Court assumed the role of formulator of new policy rather than the conservator of an established one, and it sometimes made sudden and sweeping changes in the law. Decisions like (1) *School District of Abington* v. *Schempp* (1963) that prohibited prayers in the public schools, (2) *Reynolds* v. *Sims* (1964) that required representation on a population basis in both houses of state legislatures, and (3) *Miranda* v. *Arizona*

---

7. *Lochner* v. *New York,* 198 US 45 (1905).
8. Edward S. Corwin, *Constitution Revolution Ltd.* (Claremont, Calif., 1941).

(1966) that drastically altered the rules of evidence in criminal procedure aroused storms of protest. By 1969, the year in which Chief Justice Warren retired, the legislatures of thirty-three states had petitioned Congress to call a constitutional convention.[9] Under the leadership of Chief Justice Burger, the Court began to modify the extreme positions taken by the Warren Court.

Conclusion. If one views the work of the Supreme Court as a whole, it appears to have been least successful when it abandoned judicial restraint and sought to enforce economic or social policies based primarily upon the personal preferences of the justices. Under our constitutional system, some participation by the judiciary in the formulation of public policy is inevitable, but many question the wisdom of having the Supreme Court seek to elevate to the status of constitutional law policies not rooted in the traditions of our people and upon which there is no widespread consensus.

Statutes invalidated. The total number of cases to date (July, 1974) in which acts of Congress have been invalidated is 106. These cases are as follows:

1. *Marbury* v. *Madison,* 1 Cranch 137 (1803)
2. *Dred Scott* v. *Sandford,* 19 How 393 (1857)
3. *Gordon* v. *United States,* 2 Wall 561 (1865)
4. *Ex parte Garland,* 4 Wall 333 (1867)
5. *Reichart* v. *Felps,* 6 Wall 160 (1868)
6. *The Alicia,* 7 Wall 571 (1869)
7. *Hepburn* v. *Griswold,* 8 Wall 603 (1870)
8. *United States* v. *DeWitt,* 9 Wall 41 (1870)
9. *The Justices* v. *Murray,* 9 Wall 274 (1870)
10. *The Collector* v. *Day,* 11 Wall 113 (1871)
11. *United States* v. *Klein,* 13 Wall 128 (1872)
12. *United States* v. *Baltimore & Ohio Ry.,* 17 Wall 322 (1873)
13. *United States* v. *Reese,* 92 US 214 (1876)
14. *United States* v. *Fox,* 95 US 670 (1878)
15. *Trade-Mark Cases,* 100 US 82 (1879)
16. *United States* v. *Harris,* 106 US 629 (1883)
17. *Civil Rights Cases,* 109 US 3 (1883)
18. *Boyd* v. *United States,* 116 US 616 (1886)
19. *Baldwin* v. *Franks,* 120 US 678 (1887)
20. *Callan* v. *Wilson,* 127 US 540 (1888)
21. *Monongahela Nav. Co.* v. *United States,* 148 US 312 (1893)
22. *Pollock* v. *Farmers' L. & T. Co.,* 157 US 429 (1895)
23. Same—Rehearing, 158 US 601 (1895)
24. *Wong Wing* v. *United States,* 163 US 288 (1896)
25. *Kirby* v. *United States,* 174 US 47 (1899)
26. *Jones* v. *Meehan,* 175 US 1 (1899)
27. *Fairbank* v. *United States,* 181 US 283 (1901)

9. *Congressional Quarterly,* 1 August 1969, p. 1372. In August, 1958, the Conference of Chief Justices (of the supreme courts of the fifty states) adopted a resolution calling upon the United States Supreme Court to "depart from politics and return to the law." "Report of the Committee on Federal State Relationships," *The Conference of Chief Justices,* August, 1958, p. 14.

28. *James* v. *Bowman,* 190 US 127 (1903)
29. *Matter of Heff,* 197 US 488 (1905)
30. *Rassmussen* v. *United States,* 197 US 516 (1905)
31. *Hodges* v. *United States,* 203 US 1 (1906)
32. *Employers' Liability Cases,* 207 US 463 (1908)
33. *Adair* v. *United States,* 208 US 161 (1908)
34. *Keller* v. *United States,* 213 US 138 (1909)
35. *United States* v. *Evans,* 213 US 297 (1909)
36. *Muskrat* v. *United States,* 219 US 346 (1911)
37. *Coyle* v. *Oklahoma,* 221 US 559 (1911)
38. *Choate* v. *Trapp,* 224 US 665 (1912)
39. *Butts* v. *Merchants' & Miners' Co.,* 230 US 126 (1913)
40. *United States* v. *Hvoslef,* 237 US 1 (1915)
41. *Thames & Mersey Mar. Ins. Co.* v. *United States,* 237 US 19 (1915)
42. *Hammer* v. *Dagenhart,* 247 US 251 (1918)
43. *Knickerbocker Ice Co.* v. *Stewart,* 253 US 149 (1920)
44. *Eisner* v. *Macomber,* 252 US 189 (1920)
45. *Evans* v. *Gore,* 253 US 245 (1920)
46. *United States* v. *Cohen Grocery Co.,* 255 US 81 (1921)
47. *Weeds, Inc.* v. *United States,* 255 US 109 (1921)
48. *Newberry* v. *United States,* 256 US 232 (1921)
49. *United States* v. *Moreland,* 258 US 433 (1922)
50. *Bailey* v. *Drexel Furniture Co.,* 259 US 20 (1922)
51. *Hill* v. *Wallace,* 259 US 44 (1922)
52. *Keller* v. *Potomac Electric Co.,* 261 US 428 (1923)
53. *Adkins* v. *Children's Hospital,* 261 US 525 (1923)
54. *Spalding & Bros.* v. *Edwards,* 262 US 66 (1923)
55. *Washington* v. *Dawson,* 264 US 219 (1924)
56. *Miles* v. *Graham,* 268 US 501 (1925)
57. *Trusler* v. *Crooks,* 269 US 475 (1926)
58. *Myers* v. *United States,* 272 US 52 (1926)
59. *Nichols* v. *Coolidge,* 274 US 531 (1927)
60. *Untermeyer* v. *Anderson,* 276 US 440 (1928)
61. *National Life Ins. Co.* v. *United States,* 277 US 508 (1928)
62. *Indian Motorcycle Co.* v. *United States,* 283 US 570 (1931)
63. *Heiner* v. *Donnan,* 285 US 312 (1932)
64. *Burnet* v. *Coronado Oil and Gas Co.,* 285 US 393 (1932)
65. *Booth* v. *United States,* 291 US 339 (1934)
66. *Lynch* v. *United States,* 292 US 571 (1934)
67. *Panama Refining Co.* v. *Ryan et al.,* 293 US 388 (1935)
68. *Perry* v. *United States,* 294 US 330 (1935)
69. *Railroad Retirement Board* v. *Alton R. R.,* 295 US 330 (1935)
70. *Schechter Poultry Corp.* v. *United States,* 295 US 495 (1935)
71. *Louisville Joint Stock Land Bank* v. *Radford,* 295 US 555 (1935)
72. *United States* v. *Constantine,* 296 US 287 (1935)
73. *Hopkins Federal Savings and Loan Ass'n.* v. *Cleary,* 295 US 315 (1935)

74. *United States* v. *Butler,* 297 US 1 (1936)
75. *Rickert Rice Mills* v. *Fontenot,* 297 US 110 (1936)
76. *Carter* v. *Carter Coal Co.,* 298 US 238 (1936)
77. *Ashton* v. *Cameron Co. Water Imp. Dist.,* 298 US 513 (1936)
78. *Tot* v. *United States,* 319 US 463 (1943)
79. *United States* v. *Lovett,* 328 US 303 (1946)
80. *United States* v. *Cardiff,* 344 US 174 (1952)
81. *Bolling* v. *Sharpe,* 347 US 497 (1954)
82. *U.S. ex rel. Toth* v. *Quarles,* 350 US 11 (1955)
83. *Reid* v. *Covert,* 354 US 1 (1957)
84. *Trop* v. *Dulles,* 356 US 86 (1958)
85. *Kinsella* v. *Singleton,* 361 US 234 (1960)
86. *Kennedy* v. *Mendoza-Martinez,* 372 US 144 (1963)
87. *Schneider* v. *Rusk,* 377 US 163 (1964)
88. *Aptheker* v. *Secretary of State,* 378 US 500 (1964)
89. *Lamont* v. *Postmaster General,* 381 US 301 (1965)
90. *United States* v. *Brown,* 381 US 437 (1965)
91. *Albertson* v. *Subversive Activities Control Board,* 382 US 70 (1965)
92. *United States* v. *Romano,* 382 US 136 (1965)
93. *Afroyin* v. *Rusk,* 387 US 253 (1967)
94. *United States* v. *Robel,* 389 US 258 (1967)
95. *Marchetti* v. *United States,* 390 US 62 (1968)
96. *Grosso* v. *United States,* 390 US 62 (1968)
97. *Haynes* v. *United States,* 390 US 85 (1968)
98. *United States* v. *Jackson,* 390 US 570 (1968)
99. *Shapiro* v. *Thompson,* 394 US 618 (1969)
100. *Leary* v. *United States,* 395 US 6 (1969)
101. *Oregon* v. *Mitchell,* 400 US 112 (1970)
102. *Blount* v. *Rizzi,* 400 US 410 (1971)
103. *Tilton* v. *Richardson,* 403 US 672 (1971)
104. *U.S. Dept. of Agriculture* v. *Murry,* 413 US 508 (1973)
105. *U.S. Dept. of Agriculture* v. *Moreno,* 413 US 528 (1973)
106. *Jimenez* v. *Weinberger,* 417 US 628 (1974).

More than 800 state laws and municipal ordinances have been held void by the United States Supreme Court. The need for judicial review in this area is today generally accepted. It is interesting to observe, however, that the most prominent scholar of the Supreme Court's history emphasizes that during the nineteenth century the chief conflicts were "over the Court's decisions restricting the limits of State authority and not over those restricting the limits of Congressional power." Charles Warren, *The Supreme Court in United States History* (Boston, 1922), vol. I., p. 5.

For a list of the cases in which a state statute or a municipal ordinance has been declared void, see Norman J. Small, ed., *The Constitution of the United States of America,* Sen. Doc. 39, 88th Cong., 1st sess., p. 1403. See also Wilfred C. Gilbert, *Provision of Federal Law Held Unconstitutional by the Supreme Court of the United States* (Washington, D.C., 1936).

D. CONGRESSIONAL CONTROL OVER JUDICIARY

Ex parte McCardle

7 Wallace 506, 19 L Ed 264 (1869)

The appellate jurisdiction of this court is conferred by the Constitution, and not derived from Acts of Congress; but is conferred "with such exceptions, and under such regulations, as Congress may make;" and, therefore, Acts of Congress affirming such jurisdiction have always been construed as excepting from it all cases not expressly described and provided for.

Appeal from the Circuit Court for the Southern District of Mississippi.
The case was this:
The Constitution of the United States ordains as follows:

"§ 1. The judicial power of the United States shall be vested *in one Supreme Court,* and in such inferior courts as the Congress may from time to time ordain and establish.
"§ 2. The judicial power shall extend to all cases in law and equity arising *under this Constitution, the laws of the United States,*" etc.

And in these last cases the Constitution ordains that,

"The Supreme Court shall have appellate jurisdiction, both as to law and fact, *with such exceptions and under such regulations, as the Congress shall make.*"

With these constitutional provisions in existence, Congress, on the 5th February, 1867, by "An act to amend an act to establish the judicial courts of the United States, approved September 24, 1789," provided that the several courts of the United States, and the several justices and judges of such courts, within their respective jurisdiction, in addition to the authority already conferred by law, should have power to grant writs of *habeas corpus* in all cases where any person may be restrained of his or her liberty in violation of the Constitution, or of any treaty or law of the United States. And that, from the final decision of any judge, justice, or court inferior to the Circuit Court, appeal might be taken to the Circuit Court of the United States for the district in which the cause was heard, and *from the judgment of the said Circuit Court to the Supreme Court of the United States.*

This statute being in force, one McCardle, alleging unlawful restraint by military force, preferred a petition in the court below, for the writ of *habeas corpus.*

The writ was issued, and a return was made by the military commander, admitting the restraint, but denying that it was unlawful.

It appeared that the petitioner was not in the military service of the United States, but was held in custody by military authority for trial before a military commission, upon charges founded upon the publication of articles alleged to be incendiary and libelous, in a newspaper of which he was editor. The custody was alleged to be under the authority of certain acts of Congress.

Upon the hearing, the petitioner was remanded to the military custody; but, upon his prayer, an appeal was allowed him to this court, and upon filing the usual appeal-bond, for costs, he was admitted to bail upon recognizance, with sureties, conditioned for his future appearance in the Circuit Court, to abide by and perform the final judgment of this court. The appeal was taken under the above-mentioned act of February 5, 1867.

A motion to dismiss this appeal was made at the last term, and, after argument, was denied.

Subsequently, on the 2d, 3d, 4th, and 9th March, the case was argued very thoroughly and ably upon the merits, and was taken under advisement. While it was thus held, and before conference in regard to the decision proper to be made, an act was passed by Congress, returned with objections by the President, and, on the 27th March, repassed by the constitutional majority, the second section of which was as follows:

> "*And be it further enacted,* That so much of the act approved February 5, 1867, entitled 'An act to amend an act to establish the judicial courts of the United States, approved September 24, 1789,' as authorized an appeal from the judgment of the Circuit Court to the Supreme Court of the United States, or the exercise of any such jurisdiction by said Supreme Court, on appeals which have been, or may hereafter be taken, be, and the same is hereby repealed." . . .

The CHIEF JUSTICE [Chase] delivered the opinion of the court.

The first question necessarily is that of jurisdiction; for, if the act of March, 1868, takes away the jurisdiction defined by the act of February, 1867, it is useless, if not improper, to enter into any discussion of other questions.

It is quite true, as was argued by the counsel for the petitioner, that the appellate jurisdiction of this court is not derived from acts of Congress. It is, strictly speaking, conferred by the Constitution. But it is conferred "with such exceptions and under such regulations as Congress shall make."

It is unnecessary to consider whether, if Congress had made no exceptions and no regulations, this court might not have exercised general appellate jurisdiction under rules prescribed by itself. For among the earliest acts of the first Congress, at its first session, was the act of September 24, 1789, to establish the judicial courts of the United States. That act provided for the organization of this court, and prescribed regulations for the exercise of its jurisdiction. . . .

The principle that the affirmation of appellate jurisdiction implies the negation of all such jurisdiction not affirmed having been thus established, it was an almost necessary consequence that acts of Congress, providing for the exercise of jurisdiction, should come to be spoken of as acts granting jurisdiction, and not as acts making exceptions to the constitutional grant of it.

The exception to appellate jurisdiction in the case before us, however, is not an inference from the affirmation of other appellate jurisdiction. It is made in terms. The provision of the act of 1867, affirming the appellate jurisdiction of this court in cases of *habeas corpus* is expressly repealed. It is hardly possible to imagine a plainer instance of positive exception. . . .

[T]he general rule, supported by the best elementary writers, is, that "when an act of the legislature is repealed, it must be considered, except as to transactions past and closed, as if it never existed." . . .

It is quite clear, therefore, that this court cannot proceed to pronounce judgment in this case, for it has no longer jurisdiction of the appeal; and judicial duty is not less fitly performed by declining ungranted jurisdiction than in exercising firmly that which the Constitution and the laws confer.

Counsel seem to have supposed, if effect be given to the repealing act in question, that the whole appellate power of the court, in cases of *habeas corpus,* is denied. But this is an error. The act of 1868 does not except from that jurisdiction any cases but appeals from Circuit Courts under the act of 1867. It does not affect the jurisdiction which was previously exercised.

The appeal of the petitioner in this case must be dismissed for want of jurisdiction.

Notes

1. *Validity of McCardle rule.* An exception to the rule that Congress can withdraw jurisdiction from a federal court in a case already before it was made in *United States* v. *Klein,* 13 Wallace 128 (1872). The congressional act declared void was found to be an attempt to interfere with both the judicial power and the pardoning power of the president. Justice Harlan commented upon this exception in *Glidden Company* v. *Zdanok,* 370 US 530 (1961) as follows:

> Congress has consistently with [Article III] withdrawn the jurisdiction of this Court to proceed with a case then *sub judice,* Ex parte McCardle, 7 Wall. 506; its power can be no less when dealing with an inferior federal court, *In re Hall,* 167 US 38, 42. . . .
>
> The authority is not, of course, unlimited. In 1870, Congress purported to withdraw jurisdiction from the Court of Claims and from this Court on appeal over cases seeking indemnification for property captured during the Civil War, so far as eligibility therefore might be predicated upon an amnesty awarded by the President, as both courts had previously held that it might. Despite *Ex parte McCardle, supra,* the Court refused to apply the statute to a case in which the claimant had already been adjudged entitled to recover by the Court of Claims, calling it an unconstitutional attempt to invade the judicial province by prescribing a rule of decision in a pending case. *United States* v. *Klein,* 13 Wall 128. . . .

2. *Emergency Price Control Act.* Under the Emergency Price Control Act of 1942, prices established by the administrator were reviewable in the Emergency Court of Appeals, and upon certiorari from this specialized court, by the Supreme Court. The Act provided that no temporary injunction could be issued against enforcement of its provisions until the Emergency Court of Appeals had dealt with the complaint, and that no trial court should examine the validity of any regulation or price schedule in any criminal prosecution instituted under the Act. In *Yakus* v. *United States,* 321 US 414 (1944), the Supreme Court sustained the constitutionality of the Act. Justice Roberts dissented on the ground that Congress could not confer jurisdiction on the trial courts to enforce an act and regulations thereunder and at the same time deny to these courts jurisdiction or power to consider the validity of the regulations for which enforcement was sought.

3. *Power to issue writs.* At the outset of our national history, Congress asserted an authority to regulate the issuance of writs by the federal courts. Sections 13 and 14 of the Judiciary Act of 1789 dealt with specific kinds of writs, and also authorized all United States courts "to issue writs of *scire facias, habeas corpus,* and all other writs not specifically provided for by statute, which may be necessary for the exercise of their respective jurisdictions, and agreeable to the principles and usages of law." In numerous instances Congress has restricted the use of certain writs, notably in suits of equity. Examples are the act of 1793 (1 State 333, 28 USCA § 1651) restricting the use of injunctions to stay proceedings in state courts; the act of 1867 (14 Stat 475, 28 USCA § 3653(a)) prohibiting the use of injunctions to restrain the collection of taxes; and in the act of 1942 (56 Stat 31, Sec. 204; 506 USCA § 924) limiting the use of injunctions in cases arising under the Emergency Price Control Act. All acts of Congress restricting the issuance of writs by the courts have been sustained.

4. *Amendment to Habeas Corpus Act in 1966.* By this amendment Congress sought to curtail the existensive use of the writ under guidelines set by the Court in *Townsend* v. *Sain,* 372 US 290 (1963).

5. *Omnibus Crime Control Act of 1968.* By this act, Congress sought to modify the guidelines for criminal procedure enunciated by the Court in *Miranda* v. *Arizona,* 384 US 436 (1966).

E. LAW APPLIED

Erie Railroad Co. v. Tompkins

304 US 64, 58 S Ct 817, 82 L Ed 1188 (1937)

There is no federal general common law. Except in matters goverened by the Federal Constitution or by Acts of Congress, the law to be applied in any case is the law of the state.

MR. JUSTICE BRANDEIS delivered the opinion of the Court.

The question for decision is whether the oft-challenged doctrine of *Swift* v. *Tyson* shall now be disapproved.

Tompkins, a citizen of Pennsylvania, was injured on a dark night by a passing freight train of the Erie Railroad Company while walking along its right of way at Hughestown in that State. He claimed that the accident occurred through negligence in the operation, or maintenance, of the train; that he was rightfully on the premises as licensee because on a commonly used beaten footpath which ran for a short distance alongside the tracks; and that he was struck by something which looked like a door projecting from one of the moving cars. To enforce that claim he brought an action in the federal court for southern New York, which had jurisdiction because the company is a corporation of that State. It denied liability; and the case was tried by a jury.

The Erie insisted that its duty to Tompkins was no greater than that owed to a trespasser. It contended, among other things, that its duty to Tompkins, and hence its liability, should be determined in accordance with the Pennsylvania law; that under the law of Pennsylvania, as declared by its highest court, persons who use pathways along the railroad right of way—that is a longtitudinal pathway as distinguished from a crossing—are to be deemed trespassers; and that the railroad is not liable for injuries to undiscovered trespassers resulting from its negligence, unless it be wanton or wilful. Tomkins denied that any such rule had been established by the decisions of the Pennsylvania courts; and contended that, since there was no statute of the State on the subject, the railroad's duty and liability is to be determined in federal courts as a matter of general law.

The trial judge refused to rule that the applicable law precluded recovery. The jury brought in a verdict of $30,000; and the judgment entered thereon was affirmed by the Circuit Court of Appeals, which held . . . that it was unnecessary to consider whether the law of Pennsylvania was as contended, because the question was one not of local, but of general, law and that "upon questions of general law the federal courts are free, in the absence of a local statute, to exercise their independent judgment as to what the law is; and it is well settled that the question of the responsibility of a railroad for injuries caused by its servants is one of general law. . . . Where the public has made open and notorious use of a railroad right of way for a long period of time and without objection, the company owes to persons on such permissive pathway a duty of care in the operation of its trains. . . . It is likewise generally recognized law that a jury may find that negligence exists toward a pedestrian using a permissive path on the railroad right of way if he is hit by some object projecting from the side of the train."

The Erie had contended that application of the Pennsylvania rule was required, among other things, by § 34 of the Federal Judiciary Act of September 24, 1789, c 20, 28 USC § 725, which provides:

> "The laws of the several States, except where the Constitution, treaties, or statutes of the United States otherwise require or provide, shall be regarded as rules of decision in trials at common law, in the courts of the United States, in cases where they apply."

Because of the importance of the question whether the federal court was free to disregard the alleged rule of the Pennsylvania common law, we granted *certiorari*.

First.   *Swift* v. *Tyson,* 16 Pet 1, 18, held that federal courts exercising jurisdiction on the ground of diversity of citizenship need not, in matters of general jurisprudence, apply the unwritten law of the State as declared by its highest court; that they are free to exercise an independent judgment as to what the common law of the State is—or should be; and that, as there stated by Mr. Justice Story: "The true interpretation of the thirty-fourth section limited its application to state laws strictly local, that is to say, to the positive statutes of the state, and the construction thereof adopted by the local tribunals, and to rights and titles to things having a permanent locality, such as the rights and titles to real estate, and other matters immovable and intraterritorial in their nature and character. It never has been supposed by us, that the section did apply, or was intended to apply, to questions of a more general nature, not at all dependent upon local statues or local usages of a fixed and permanent operation, as, for example, to the construction of ordinary contracts or other written instruments, and especially to questions of general commercial law, where the state tribunals are called upon to perform the like functions as ourselves, that is, to ascertain upon general reasoning and legal analogies, what is the true exposition of the contract or instrument, or what is the just rule furnished by the principles of commercial law to govern the case."

Second. Experience in applying the doctrine of *Swift* v. *Tyson* had revealed its defects, political and social; and the benefits expected to flow from the rule did not accrue. Persistence of state courts in their own opinions on questions of common law prevented uniformity; and the impossibility of discovering a satisfactory line of demarcation between the province of general law and that of local law developed a new well of uncertainties. . . .

Third. Except in matters governed by the Federal Constitution or by Acts of Congress, the law to be applied in any case is the law of the State. And whether the law of the State shall be declared by its Legislature in a statute or by its highest court in a decision is not a matter of federal concern. There is no federal general common law. Congress has no power to declare substantive rules of common law applicable in a State whether they be local in their nature or "general," be they commercial law or a part of the law of torts. And no clause in the Constitution purports to confer such a power upon the federal courts. . . .

The fallacy underlying the rule declared in *Swift* v. *Tyson* is made clear by Mr. Justice Holmes. The doctrine rests upon the assumption that there is "a transcendental body of law outside of any particular State but obligatory within it unless and until changed by statute"; that federal courts have the power to use their judgment as to what the rules of common law are; and that in the federal courts "the parties are entitled to an independent judgment on matters of general law":

> "but law in the sense in which courts speak of it today does not exist without some definite authority behind it. The common law so far as it is enforced in a State, whether called common law or not, is not the common law generally but the law of that State existing by the authority of that State without regard to what it may have been in England or anywhere else. . . .
>
> "The authority and only authority is the State, and if that be so, the voice adopted by the State as its own [whether it be of its Legislature or of its Supreme Court] should utter the last word."

Thus the doctrine of *Swift* v. *Tyson* is, as Mr. Justice Holmes said, "an unconstitutional assumption of powers by courts of the United States which no lapse of time or respectable array of opinion should make us hesitate to correct." In disapproving that doctrine we do not hold unconstitutional § 34 of the Federal Judiciary Act of 1789 or any other act of Congress. We merely declare that in applying the doctrine this Court and the lower courts have invaded rights which in our opinion are reserved by the Constitution to the several States.

Fourth. The defendant contended that by the common law of Pennsylvania as declared by its highest court in *Falchetti* v. *Pennsylvania R. Co.,* 307 Pa 203, 160 A 859, the only duty owed to the plaintiff was to refrain from wilful or wanton injury. The plaintiff denied that such is the Pennsylvania law. In support of their respective contentions the parties discussed and cited many decisions of the Supreme Court of the State. The Circuit Court of Appeals ruled that the question of liability is one of general law; and on that ground declined to decide the issue of state law. As we hold this was error, the judgment is reversed and the case remanded to it for further proceedings in conformity with our opinion.

Reversed.

[The concurring opinions of JUSTICES BUTLER and REED are omitted.]

Texas v. New Jersey

379 US 674, 85 S Ct 626, 13 L Ed2d 596 (1965)

In the absence of a federal statute governing the subject, the Supreme Court will adopt and apply a rule to settle a dispute between states over the power of escheat.

MR. JUSTICE BLACK delivered the opinion of the Court.

Invoking this Court's original jurisdiction under Art III, § 2, of the Constitution, Texas brought this action against New Jersey, Pennsylvania, and the Sun Oil Company for an injunction and declaration of rights to settle a controversy as to which State has jurisdiction to take title to a certain abandoned intangible personal property through escheat, a procedure with ancient origins whereby a sovereign may acquire title to abandoned property if after a number of years no rightful owner appears. The property in question here consists of various small debts totaling $26,461.65 which the Sun Oil Company for periods of approximately seven to 40 years prior to the bringing of this action has owed to approximately 1,730 small creditors who have never appeared to collect them. The amounts owed, most of them resulting from failure of creditors to claim or cash checks, are either evidenced on the books of Sun's two Texas offices or are owing to persons whose last known address was in Texas, or both. Texas says that this intangible property should be treated as situated in Texas, so as to permit that State to escheat it. New Jersey claimed the right to escheat the same property because Sun is incorporated in New Jersey. Pennsylvania claimed power to escheat part or all of the same property on the ground that Sun's principal business offices were in that State. Sun has disclaimed any interest in the property for itself, and asks only to be protected from the possibility of double liability. . . .

With respect to tangible property, real or personal, it has always been the unquestioned rule in all jurisdictions that only the State in which the property is located may escheat. But intangible property, such as a debt which a person is entitled to collect, is not physical matter which can be located on a map. The creditor may live in one State, the debtor in another, and matters may be further complicated if, as in the case before us, the debtor is a corporation which has connections with many States and the creditor is a person who may have had connections with several others and whose present address is unknown. Since the States separately are without constitutional power to provide a rule to settle this interstate controversy and since there is no applicable federal statute, it becomes our responsibility in the exercise of our original jurisdiction to adopt a rule which will settle the question of which State will be allowed to escheat this intangible property.

Four different possible rules are urged upon us by the respective States which are parties to this case. . . . We think the rule proposed by the Master, based on the one suggested by Florida, is [the fairest available].

The rule Florida suggests is that since a debt is property of the creditor, not of the debtor, fairness among the States requires that the right and power to escheat the debt should be accorded to the State of the creditor's last known address as shown by the debtor's books and records. Such a solution would be in line with one group of cases dealing with intangible property for other purposes in other areas of the law. Adoption of such a rule involves a factual issue simple and easy to resolve, and leaves no legal issue to be decided. It takes account of the fact that if the creditor instead of perhaps leaving behind an uncashed check had negotiated the check and left behind the cash, this State would have been the sole possible escheat claimant; in other words, the rule recognizes that the debt was an asset of the creditor. The rule recommended by the Master will tend to distribute escheats among the States in the proportion of the commercial activities of their residents. And by using a standard of last known address, rather than technical legal concepts of residence and domicile, administration and application of escheat laws should be simplified. It may well be that some addresses left by vanished creditors will be in States other than those in which they lived at the time the obligation arose or at the time of the escheat. But such situations probably will be the exception, and any errors thus created, if indeed they could be called errors, probably will tend to a large extent to cancel each other out. We therefore hold that each item of property in question in this case is subject to escheat only by the State of the last known address of the creditor, as shown by the debtor's books and records. . . .

We realize that this case could have been resolved otherwise, for the issue here is not controlled by statutory or constitutional provisions or by past decisions, nor is it entirely one of logic. It is fundamentally a question of ease of administration and of equity. We believe that the rule we adopt is the fairest, is easy to apply, and in the long run will be the most generally acceptable to all the States.

The parties may submit a proposed decree applying the principle announced in this opinion.

It is so ordered.

Mr. Justice Stewart, dissenting.

I adhere to the view that only the State of the debtor's incorporation has power to escheat intangible property when the whereabouts of the creditor are unknown. . . .

Notes

1. *Pennsylvania* v. *New York,* 407 US 206 (1972), dealt with the escheat of unclaimed funds paid to Western Union Telegraph Co. for the purchase of money orders. The decision placed the right of escheat in the state shown by the company's records to be the payee's address, but where the record showed no address, in the company's domiciliary state. Three justices dissented.

2. *Flood* v. *Kuhn,* 407 US 258 (1972), held that baseball, unlike other interstate professional sports, was not subject to the antitrust laws. This aberration, long acquiesced to by Congress, was given the benefit of *stare decisis.*

3. *Bivens* v. *Six Unknown Federal Narcotics Agents,* 403 US 388 (1971), held that even though Congress had failed to create a cause of action for monetary damages against a federal officer who makes an unlawful search and seizure, the federal courts could imply authority for such suits from the Fourth Amendment.

For the majority, Justice Brennan wrote:

> Of course, the Fourth Amendment does not in so many words provide for its enforcement by an award of monetary damages for the consequences of its violation. But it is . . . well settled that where legal rights have been invaded, and a federal statute provides for a general right to sue for such invasion, federal courts may use any available remedy to make good the wrong done. . . . The present case involves no special factors counselling hesitation in the absence of affirmative action by Congress. . . . [W]e have here no explicit congressional declaration that persons injured by a federal officer's violation of the Fourth Amendment may not recover monetary damages from the agents, but must instead be remitted to another remedy, equally effective in the view of Congress.

Chief Justice Burger, Justice Black, and Justice Blackmun each wrote a dissenting opinion. Black stated: "There can be no doubt that Congress could create a federal cause of action for damages for an unreasonable search in violation of the Fourth Amendment. Although Congress has created such a federal cause of action against *state* officials acting under color of state law, it has never created such a cause of action against federal officials. . . . [T]he point of this case and the fatal weakness in the Court's judgment is that neither Congress nor New York has enacted legislation creating such a right of action. . . . The task of evaluating the pros and cons of creating judicial remedies for particular wrongs is a matter for Congress and the legislatures of the States. Congress has not provided that any federal court can entertain a suit against a federal officer for violation of Fourth Amendment rights occurring in the performance of his duties. A strong inference can be drawn from creation of such actions against state officials that Congress does not desire to permit such suits against federal officials."

4. *Guaranty Trust Co.* v. *New York,* 326 US 99 (1945), held that in a suit in equity in a federal court because of diversity of citizenship, a state statute of limitations which would be applicable in a state court must be applied. The principle emphasized in the decision was that the outcome of the case should be the same, whether tried in a federal or state court.

5. In *Boyd* v. *Blue Ridge Rural Electric Cooperative, Inc.,* 356 US 525 (1958), the federal courts refused to follow a South Carolina decision making it the province of the judge rather than the jury to pass upon certain defenses. The Supreme Court found "a strong federal policy against allowing state rules to disrupt the judge-jury relationship in federal courts."

6. *Banco Nacional de Cuba* v. *Sabbatino,* 376 US 398 (1964), marked a significant limitation to the application of international law. The factual background was as follows: An American commodity broker, Whitlock & Co., contracted to purchase

Cuban sugar from C.A.V., a corporation organized under Cuban law but owned principally by United States residents. In August, 1960, while the sugar was being loaded in a ship, the Cuban government issued a decree nationalizing all assets of C.A.V. To secure shipment, Whitlock & Co. signed a new contract agreeing to pay the Cuban government for the sugar. The sugar was delivered to Whitlock & Co. Both C.A.V. and the Cuban government claimed the right to payment. By order of the New York Supreme Court, Whitlock & Co. transferred the fund which it held to pay for the sugar to a court appointed receiver, Sabbatino. Cuba instituted the present case in a United States district court. That court ruled against Cuba's claim to the fund in question on the ground that the expropriation of the sugar by the Cuban government without compensation was a violation of international law. The court of appeals affirmed. The Supreme Court reversed.

The opinion of the Court, by Justice Harlan, followed the "act of state" doctrine which "precludes the courts of this country from inquiring into the validity of the public acts a recognized foreign sovereign power committed within its own territory." As applied here, the courts of the United States would not examine the validity of the expropriation of property in Cuba, even though it was alleged that the expropriation violated international law. The basic thought underlying the decision is that the executive branch of the government through negotiation is better adapted to deal with compensation for expropriations than is the judiciary through deciding individual cases. In dissenting, Justice White stated: "I do not believe that the act of state doctrine, as judicially fashioned in this Court, and the reasons underlying it, require American courts to decide cases in disregard of international law and of the rights of litigants to a full determination on the merits. . . ."

Since the lower federal courts had taken jurisdiction of the case on the basis of diversity of citizenship, the question of what law to apply was involved. On this subject Justice Harlan wrote:

> However, we are constrained to make it clear that an issue concerned with a basic choice regarding the competence and function of the Judiciary and the National Executive in ordering our relationships with other members of the international community must be treated exclusively as an aspect of federal law. It seems fair to assume that the Court did not have rules like the act of state doctrine in mind when it decided *Erie R. Co.* v. *Tompkins*. . . . We are not without other precedent for a determination that federal law governs; there are enclaves of federal judge-made law which bind the States. A national body of federal-court-built law has been held to have been contemplated by § 301 of the Labor Management Relations Act, *Textile Workers* v. *Lincoln Mills,* 353 US 448. Principles formulated by federal judicial law have been thought by this Court to be necessary to protect uniquely federal interests, *D'Oench, Duhme & Co.* v. *Federal Deposit Ins. Corp.,* 315 US 447; *Clearfield Trust Co.* v. *United States,* 318 US 363. Of course the federal interest guarded in all these cases is one the ultimate statement of which is derived from a federal statute. Perhaps more directly in point are the bodies of law applied between States over boundaries and in regard to the apportionment of interstate waters.
>
> In *Hinderlider* v. *La Plata River Co.,* 304 US 92, 110, in an opinion handed down the same day as Erie and by the same author, Mr. Justice Brandeis, the Court declared, "For whether the water of an interstate stream must be apportioned between the two States is a question of federal common law upon which neither the statutes nor the decisions of either State can be conclusive." . . .

For all practical purposes, the decision in *Sabbatino* was overruled by subsequent congressional enactments. The act of state doctrine was not applied in *First National City Bank* v. *Banco Nacional de Cuba,* 406 US 759 (1972).

7. *Bonelli Cattle Co.* v. *Arizona,* 414 US 313 (1974), held that title to land formerly a part of the Colorado River bed but surfaced by a reclamation project was governed by federal common law.

F. EQUITY

The Constitution provides that the judicial power shall extend to cases "in law and equity." Cases not fully covered by law are described as cases in equity. The two types of cases are best explained in terms of English history. By the fourteenth century the common law courts had become so rigid in their forms and procedures that it was sometimes necessary to appeal to the King to intervene and administer justice if a case involved unusual features. The King ordinarily acted through his secretary, the Chancellor, in such cases. In this way the Court of Chancery came into being.

Whereas the common law courts only awarded monetary damages in civil cases, the Court of Chancery could act upon the person and require the specific performance of contracts. The chancellor could also render preventive justice by issuing injunctions restraining a person from committing a threatened act which would cause irreparable injury. Separate systems of courts for cases in law and for suits in equity were maintained in England until passage of the Judicature Act of 1873 which unified the courts into one system.

Some of the states in the United States originally maintained separate courts of equity, but the trend has been toward a merger of law and equity. The United States has never maintained separate courts of equity. From the outset, judges of the constitutional courts of the United States have exercised equity powers.

The following texts offer a brief introduction to equity: William Q. deFuniak, *Handbook of Modern Equity* (Boston, 1956); William F. Walsh, *A Treatise on Equity* (Chicago, 1930); and Garn H. Webb, *Equity* (New York, 1970). On the current status of equity jurisdiction, see *Perez* v. *Ledesma,* 401 US 82 (1971).

G. SUITS AGAINST STATES

Ex Parte Young

209 US 123, 28 S Ct 441, 52 L Ed 714 (1908)

The Eleventh Amendment does not prohibit a suit to restrain a state officer from enforcing an unconstitutional statute.

[In 1907 the state of Minnesota passed legislation reducing freight and passenger rates to be charged by railroads in that state. The acts provided severe penalties against railroads and their officials who wilfully disobeyed their provisions. Stockholders in the Northern Pacific Railway Company brought suit to restrain the railroad from complying with the rates prescribed by the state and to enjoin Edward T. Young, as attorney general of Minnesota, from instituting any proceeding to enforce the penalties prescribed in the acts. The United States Circuit Court granted temporary injunctions. In violation of the injunction against him, Attorney General Young petitioned a state court for a writ of mandamus directing the railway to comply with the new rates. The circuit court adjudged Young to be in contempt. He applied to the United States Supreme Court for writs of habeas corpus and *certiorari.]*

MR. JUSTICE PECKHAM . . . delivered the opinion of the court. . . .

Jurisdiction is given to the Circuit Court in suits involving the requisite amount, arising under the Constitution or laws of the United States . . . , and the question really to be determined under this objection is whether the acts of the legislature and the orders of the railroad commission, if enforced, would take property without due process of law, and although that question might incidentally involve a question of fact, its solution nevertheless is one which raises a Federal question. . . .

Another Federal question is the alleged unconstitutionality of these acts because of the enormous penalties denounced for their violation, which prevent the railway company, as alleged, or any of its servants or employes, from resorting to the courts for the purpose of determining the validity of such acts. The contention is urged by the complainants in the suit that the company is denied the equal protection of the laws and its property is liable to be taken without due process of law, because it is only allowed a hearing upon the claim of the unconstitutionality of the acts and orders in question, at the risk, if mistaken, of being subjected to such enormous penalties, resulting in the possible confiscation of its whole property, that rather than take such risks the company would obey the laws, although such obedience might also result in the end (though by a slower process) in such confiscation. . . .

We conclude that the Circuit Court had jurisdiction in the case before it, because it involved the decision of Federal questions arising under the Constitution of the United States.

Coming to the inquiry regarding the alleged invalidity of these acts, we take up the contention that they are invalid on their face on account of the penalties. For disobedience to the freight act the officers, directors, agents and employees of the company are made guilty of a misdemeanor, and upon conviction each may be punished by imprisonment in the county jail for a period not exceeding ninety days. Each violation would be a separate offense, and therefore, might result in imprisonment of the various agents of the company who would dare disobey for a term of ninety days each for each offense. Disobedience to the passenger rate act renders the party guilty of a felony and subject to a fine not exceeding five thousand dollars or imprisonment in the state prison for a period not exceeding five years, or both fine and imprisonment. The sale of each ticket above the price permitted by the act would be a violation thereof. It would be difficult, if not impossible, for the company to obtain officers, agents or employees willing to carry on its affairs except in obedience to the act and orders in question. The company itself would also, in case of disobedience, be liable to the immense fines provided for in violating orders of the Commission. The company, in order to test the validity of the acts, must find some agent or employee to disobey them at the risk stated. The necessary effect and result of such legislation must be to preclude a resort to the courts (either state or Federal) for the purpose of testing its validity. The officers and employees could not be expected to disobey any of the provisions of the acts or orders at the risk of such fines and penalties being imposed upon them, in case the court should decide that the law was valid. The result would be a denial of any hearing to the company. . . .

If the law be such as to make the decision of the legislature or of a commission conclusive as to the sufficiency of the rates, this court has held such a law to be unconstitutional. . . . A law which indirectly accomplishes a like result by imposing such conditions upon the right to appeal for judicial relief as works an abandonment of the right rather than face the conditions upon which it is offered or may be obtained, is also unconstitutional. . . .

We have, therefore, upon this record the case of an unconstitutional act of the state legislature and an intention by the Attorney General of the State to endeavor to enforce its provisions, to the injury of the company, in compelling it, at great expense, to defend legal proceedings of a complicated and unusual character, and involving questions of vast importance to all employees and officers of the company, as well as to the company itself. The question that arises is whether there is a remedy that the parties interested may resort to, by going into a Federal court of equity, in a case involving a violation of the Federal Constitution, and obtaining a judicial investigation of the problem, and pending its solution obtain freedom from suits, civil or criminal, by a temporary injunction, and if the question be finally decided favorably to the contention of the company, a permanent injunction restraining all such actions or proceedings.

This inquiry necessitates an examination of the most material and important objection made to the jurisdiction of the Circuit Court, the objection being that the suit is, in effect, one against the State of Minnesota, and that the injunction issued against the Attorney General illegally prohibits state action, either criminal or civil, to enforce obedience to the statutes of the State. This objection is to be considered with reference to the Eleventh and Fourteenth Amendments to the Federal Constitution. The Eleventh Amendment prohibits the commencement or prosecution of any suit against one of the United States by citizens of another State or citizens or subjects of any foreign State. The Fourteenth Amendment provides that no State shall deprive any person of life, liberty or property without due process of law, nor shall it deny to any person within its jurisdiction the equal protection of the laws. . . .

The various authorities we have referred to furnish ample justification for the assertion that individuals, who, as officers of the State, are clothed with some duty in regard to the enforcement of the laws of the State, and who threaten and are about to commence proceedings, either of a civil or criminal nature, to enforce against parties affected an unconstitutional act, violating the Federal Constitution, may be enjoined by a Federal court of equity from such action. . . .

It is also argued that the only proceeding which the Attorney General could take to enforce the statute, so far as his office is concerned, was one by *mandamus,* which would be commenced by the State in its sovereign and governmental character, and that the right to bring such action is a necessary attribute of a sovereign government. It is contended that the complainants do not complain and they care nothing about any action which Mr. Young might take or bring as an ordinary individual, but that he was complained of as an officer, to whose discretion is confided the use of the name of the

State of Minnesota so far as litigation is concerned, and that when or how he shall use it is a matter resting in his discretion and cannot be controlled by any court.

The answer to all this is the same as made in every case where an official claims to be acting under the authority of the State. The act to be enforced is alleged to be unconstitutional, and if it be so, the use of the name of the State to enforce an unconstitutional act to the injury of complainants is a proceeding without the authority of and one which does not affect the State in its sovereign or governmental capacity. It is simply an illegal act upon the part of a state official in attempting by the use of the name of the State to enforce a legislative enactment which is void because unconstitutional. If the act which the state Attorney General seeks to enforce be a violation of the Federal Constitution, the officer in proceeding under such enactment comes into conflict with the superior authority of that Constitution, and he is in that case stripped of his official or representative character and is subjected in his person to the consequences of his individual conduct. The State has no power to impart to him any immunity from responsibility to the supreme authority of the United States. . . . It would be an injury to complainant to harass it with a multiplicity of suits or litigation generally in an endeavor to enforce penalties under an unconstitutional enactment, and to prevent it ought to be within the jurisdiction of a court of equity. If the question of unconstitutionality with reference, at least, to the Federal Constitution be first raised in a Federal court that court, as we think is shown by the authorities cited hereafter, has the right to decide it to the exclusion of all other courts. . . .

There is nothing in the case before us that ought properly to breed hostility to the customary operation of Federal courts of justice in cases of this character.

The rule to show cause is discharged and the petition for writs of habeas corpus and *certiorari* is dismissed.

So ordered.

MR. JUSTICE HARLAN, dissenting. . . .

It is to be observed that when the State was in effect prohibited by the order of the Federal court from appearing in its own courts, there was no danger, absolutely none whatever, from anything that the Attorney General had ever done or proposed to do, that the property of the railway company would be confiscated and its officers and agents imprisoned, beyond the power of that company to stay any wrong done *by bringing to this court, in regular order, any final judgment of the state court, in the mandamus suit, which may have been in derogation of a Federal right.* When the Attorney General instituted the *mandamus* proceeding in the state court against the railway company there was in force, it must not be forgotten, an order of injunction by the Federal court which prevented that company from obeying the state law. There was consequently no danger from that direction. Besides, the *mandamus* proceeding was not instituted for the recovery of any of the penalties prescribed by the state law, and therefore no judgment in that case could operate directly upon the property of the railway company or upon the persons of its officers or agents. The Attorney General in his response to the rule against him assured the Federal court that he did not contemplate any proceeding whatever against the railway company except the one in *mandamus.* Suppose the *mandamus* case had been finally decided in the state court, the way was open for the railway company to preserve any question it made as to its rights under the Constitution, and, in the event of a decision adverse to it in that court, at once to carry the case to the highest court of Minnesota and thence by a writ of error bring it to this court. That course would have served to determine every question of constitutional law raised by the suit in the Federal court in an orderly way without trampling upon the State, and without interfering, in the meantime, with the operation of the railway property in the accustomed way. Instead of adopting that course—so manifestly consistent with the dignity and authority of both the Federal and state judicial tribunals—the Federal court practically closed the state courts against the State itself when it adjudged that the Attorney General, without regard to the wishes of the Governor of Minnesota, and without reference to his duties as prescribed by the laws of that State, should stand in the custody of the Marshal, unless he dismissed the *mandamus* suit. . . .

Notes

1. *Statutory limitation on Ex parte Young doctrine.*   Congress has limited the application of the *Ex parte Young* doctrine by a statute requiring a three-judge district court to issue an injunction restraining execution of a state statute (28 USC § 2281), by the Johnson Act of 1934 (28 USC § 1342) governing injunctions against state rate-making agencies, and by the Tax Injunction Act of 1927 (28 USC § 1341).

2. *Parden* v. *Terminal Railway,* 377 US 184 (1964), held that a railroad owned by Alabama was subject to suit in a federal court under the Federal Employers' Liability Act. The Court adopted the theory that by engaging in interstate commerce by the operation of a railroad, Alabama impliedly consented to be sued. Compare *Missouri Employees* v. *Missouri,* 411 US 279 (1973).

3. *Scheuer* v. *Rhodes,* 416 US 232 (1974), held that the district court erred in dismissing on Eleventh Amendment grounds a suit for damages against the Governor of Ohio and members of the Ohio National Guard who, acting under color of state law, allegedly recklessly caused the death of several Kent State University students. The immunity of executive officers "is qualified, not absolute," explained the Court, and Congress included within the scope of the Civil Rights Act of 1870 the "[m]isuse of power possessed by virtue of state law and made possible only because the wrongdoer is clothed with the authority of state law."

4. *Suits against the United States.*   The United States is not subject to suit without its consent. Congress has given the Court of Claims jurisdiction of a variety of claims against the United States. See 28 USC §§ 1491–1506. Since 1946 the district courts have been given concurrent jurisdiction in some of these cases and exclusive jurisdiction in others. See 28 USC § 1346. A summary of the case law in the field is found in *Larson* v. *Domestic and Foreign Commerce Corp.,* 337 US 682, 69 S Ct 1457, 93 L Ed 1628 (1949). See also *Affiliated Ute Citizens* v. *United States,* 406 US 128 (1972).

Chapter 2

The President

A. INTRODUCTION

"The executive power shall be vested in a President of the United States of America" states Section I of Article II of the Constitution. It then proceeds to set forth provisions on the election of the President by an electoral college.

Election

In the Federal Convention of 1787 there was strong sentiment for electing the executive by the legislature. James Madison recorded in his *Journal* that Roger Sherman of Connecticut "said he considered the Executive magistracy as nothing more than an institution for carrying the will of the Legislature into effect, that the person or persons ought to be appointed by and accountable to the Legislature only, which was the depository of the supreme will of the Society. As they were the best judges of the business which ought to be done by the Executive department, and consequently of the number necessary from time to time for doing it, he wished the number might not be fixed but that the legislature should be at liberty to appoint one or more as experience might dictate." By contrast, James Wilson of Pennsylvania "preferred a single magistrate, as giving more energy and dispatch and responsibility to the office." Wilson was "in favor of an appointment by the people. He wished to derive not only both branches of the Legislature from the people, without the intervention of the State Legislatures, but the Executive also; in order to make them as independent as possible of each other, as well as of the States."

The provision for a single executive elected by an electoral college was a compromise accepted in the closing days of the convention. Every delegate knew that George Washington, the father of the new nation, would be first chief executive, and this contributed to the acceptance of the single-executive provision. The compromise provided for the election of "the president" by an electoral college.

53

In the electoral college each state was to receive a number of electors equal to the number of senators and representatives to which it was entitled in Congress. These electors were to be chosen in each state in such manner as the legislature thereof should direct. By 1836 popular election of presidential electors had been introduced in all of the states except one. (South Carolina's legislature continued to name the state's presidential electors until after the Civil War.) In our early history, some states provided for the election of one presidential elector from each congressional district and two from the state at large. The trend, however, was toward the election of electors on a general ticket, with each political party sponsoring a full slate of electors and the winning party taking all of the state's electoral votes.

Under this winner-take-all system of electing presidential electors in the states, the candidate for president receiving a majority of the popular votes in the nation as a whole may not be elected. Rutherford B. Hayes in 1876 and Benjamin Harrison in 1888 received fewer popular votes than their opponents. They are our only "minority presidents" in the sense of presidents receiving fewer popular votes than their opponents. We have, however, had twelve other instances of presidents being elected by a plurality but not a majority of the popular votes, as follows: Polk (1844), Taylor (1848), Buchanan (1856), Lincoln (1860), Garfield (1880), Cleveland (1884 and 1892), Wilson (1912 and 1916), Truman (1948), Kennedy (1960), and Nixon (1968). John Quincy Adams, elected president by the House of Representatives in 1824 when no candidate received a majority of the electoral votes, had received fewer popular votes and fewer electoral votes than Andrew Jackson.

Another defect of the electoral college as it now works is the matter of unpledged electors. In most of the elections since 1948 one or more persons elected to the electoral college as a Democrat or Republican has refused to vote for the presidential nominee of his party. For example, in 1968 an elector in North Carolina chosen as a Republican cast his electoral vote for George C. Wallace. A partial solution to this problem may be found in the use of party loyalty pledges. In *Ray* v. *Blair,* 343 US 214 (1952), the Supreme Court held that "the Twelfth Amendment does not bar a political party from requiring the pledge to support the nominee of the National Convention."

Election of the President has already been the subject of five constitutional amendments (No. 12 in 1804, No. 20 in 1933, No. 22 in 1951, No. 23 in 1961, and No. 25 in 1967), and there is widespread sentiment for further amendment. On September 18, 1969, the House of Representatives passed a resolution for a constitutional amendment (H. J. Res. 681) that would abolish the electoral college and substitute direct popular election of the President. Under its terms, the candidate receiving the largest popular vote, provided it be 40 percent of the total, would be elected president. If no candidate received 40 percent, a runoff election would be held between the two candidates with the highest votes. In the Senate there was strong support for continuing the electoral college, but requiring that its members be chosen by districts within the states. Born of compromise in the Federal Convention of 1787, Section I of Article II is easily the winner as the most amended section of the Constitution, and it remains highly controversial.

Powers

In the debate in the Federal Convention over the method of selecting the "national executive" and the comparative merits of single and plural executive, "Mr. Madison thought it would be proper, before a choice should be made between a unity and a plurality in the Executive, to fix the extent of the Executive authority." This is the subject matter of Sections 2 and 3 of Article II which read as follows:

> The President shall be commander in chief of the army and navy of the United States, and of the militia of the several states, when called into the actual service of the United States; he may require the opinion, in writing, of the principal officer in each of the executive departments, upon any subject relating to the duties of their respective offices, and he shall have power to grant reprieves and pardons for offenses against the United States, except in cases of impeachment.
>
> He shall have power, by and with the advice and consent of the Senate, to make treaties, provided two-thirds of the Senators present concur; and he shall nominate, and by and with the advice and consent of the Senate, shall appoint ambassadors, other public ministers and consuls, judges of the supreme court, and all other officers of the United States, whose appointments are not herein otherwise provided for, and which shall be established by law. But the Congress may by law vest the appointment of such inferior officers, as they think proper, in the President alone, in the courts of law, or in the heads of departments.
>
> The President shall have power to fill up all vacancies that may happen during the recess of the Senate, by granting commissions which shall expire at the end of their next session.
>
> He shall from time to time give to the Congress information of the state of the union, and recommend to their consideration such measures as he shall judge necessary and expedient; he may, on extraordinary occasions, convene both houses, or either of them, and in case of disagreement between them with respect to the time of adjournment, he may adjourn them to such time as he shall think proper; he shall receive ambassadors and other public ministers; he shall take care that the laws be faithfully executed, and shall commission all the officers of the United States.

In addition to these specific powers, it is well to repeat and emphasize the opening sentence in Article II: "The executive power shall be vested in a President of the United States of America." As written in 1787, the Constitution reflects a competition between the concept of an executive subordinate to a supreme legislative power and the concept of an executive autonomous and self-directing within a broad range of power. The struggle between these competing concepts has surfaced time and time again in our national history. It is most evident when we have the anomaly of a Republican president and a Democratic Congress, or vice versa. Consider, for example, the tension between President Nixon and the 73d Congress.[1] In the struggle for power between the president and the Congress, through the years the president has in general been the winner. As Professor Corwin puts it, "Taken by and large, the history of the presidency is a history of aggrandizement, but the story is a highly discontinuous one."[2]

Strong presidents like Abraham Lincoln have found in the undefined "executive power" a vast reservoir of strength. Theodore Roosevelt advanced a "stewardship theory" of presidential power as follows:

> My view was that every executive officer, and above all every executive officer in high position, was a steward of the people bound actively and affirmatively to do all he

---

1. See *Watergate: Chronology of a Crisis* (Washington, D.C., 1973).
2. Edward S. Corwin, *The President: Office and Powers* (New York, 1957), p. 29.

could for the people, and not to content himself with the negative merit of keeping his talents undamaged in a napkin. I declined to adopt the view that what was imperatively necessary for the Nation could not be done by the President unless he could find some specific authorization to do it. My belief was that it was not only his right but his duty to do anything that the needs of the Nation demanded unless such action was forbidden by the Constitution or by the laws.[3]

The complexity of government in modern industrial nations has usually led to a concentration of power in the executive, and the United States is no exception to this general practice. Congress is not qualified to prescribe detailed freight rates for inter-state carriers nor to assign permits for broadcasting to radio and television stations. It has only prescribed that freight rates be "fair and reasonable" and that licenses for broadcasting be granted in accord with the "public convenience, interest, or necessity." Power to prescribe detailed regulations in these and numerous other areas has been vested either in the president or in independent regulatory commissions within the executive branch of the government.

Bibliography. The power of the president as head of a victorious political party is reflected hardly at all in casebooks on constitutional law. His power as symbolic head of the nation is reflected only tangentially. Cases serve best to illustrate specific powers of the president. The cases that follow may stimulate the alert student to read some broad-based books on the presidency, such as James D. Barber, *The Presidential Character: Predicting Performance in the White House* (Englewood Cliffs, N.J., 1973); Wilfred E. Binkley, *The Man in the White House* (New York, 1964); Edward S. Corwin, *The President: Office and Power* (New York, 1957); Louis Fisher, *The President and Congress* (New York, 1973); Neal R. Pierce, *The People's President* (New York, 1968); and Clinton L. Rossiter, *The American Presidency* (New York, 1966). A vivid account of the debates in the Federal Convention is found in Catherine D. Bowen, *Miracle at Philadelphia* (Boston, 1966).

B. ENFORCEMENT OF LAWS

In re Neagle

135 US 1, 10 S Ct 658, 34 L Ed 55 (1890)

The power of the president to see that the laws be faithfully executed is not confined to technical provisions expressly stated in statutes.

[David S. Terry, dissatisfied with a judgment in a case in a United States circuit court in California over which Justice Stephen J. Field, a justice of the Supreme Court, presided, threatened to kill Justice Field. David Neagle, a United States marshal, was

3. *Autobiography* (New York, 1919), p. 388.

assigned by the attorney general to accompany and protect Justice Field. Terry and his wife boarded a train on which Justice Field was traveling. The train stopped at Lathrop, California, for breakfast. In the dining room, Terry made an assault upon Justice Field, and Neagle shot and killed Terry. Neagle was arrested by California authorities and held on a charge of murder. The United States circuit court in California, on habeas corpus, ordered that Neagle be discharged from custody. From that order, an appeal was taken to the Supreme Court.]

MR. JUSTICE MILLER delivered the opinion of the Court. . . .

We have no doubt that Mr. Justice Field when attacked by Terry was engaged in the discharge of his duties as Circuit Justice of the Ninth Circuit, and was entitled to all the protection under those circumstances which the law could give him.

It is urged, however, that there exists no statute authorizing any such protection as that which Neagle was instructed to give Judge Field in the present case, and indeed no protection whatever against a vindictive or malicious assault growing out of the faithful discharge of his official duties; and that the language of section 753 of the Revised Statutes, that the party seeking the benefit of the writ of *habeas corpus* must in this connection show that he is "in custody for an act done or omitted in pursuance of a law of the United States," makes it necessary that upon this occasion it should be shown that the act for which Neagle is imprisoned was done by virtue of an act of Congress. It is not supposed that any special act of Congress exists which authorizes the marshals or deputy marshals of the United States in express terms to accompany the judges of the Supreme Court through their circuits, and act as a bodyguard to them, to defend them against malicious assaults against their persons. . . . But we are of opinion that this view of the statute is an unwarranted restriction of the meaning of a law designed to extend in a liberal manner the benefit of the writ of *habeas corpus* to persons imprisoned for the performance of their duty. And we are satisfied that if it was the duty of Neagle, under the circumstances, a duty which could only arise under the laws of the United States, to defend Mr. Justice Field from a murderous attack upon him, he brings himself within the meaning of the section we have recited. . . .

In the view we take of the Constitution of the United States, any obligation fairly and properly inferable from that instrument, or any duty of the marshal to be derived from the general scope of his duties under the laws of the United States, is "a law" within the meaning of this phrase. . . .

The Constitution, section 3, Article 2, declares that the President "shall take care that the laws be faithfully executed," . . .

Is this duty limited to the enforcement of acts of Congress or of treaties of the United States according to their *express* terms, or does it include the rights, duties and obligations growing out of the Constitution itself, our international relations, and all the protection implied by the nature of the government under the Constitution? . . .

We cannot doubt the power of the President to take measures for the protection of a judge of one of the courts of the United States, who, while in the discharge of the duties of his office, is threatened with a personal attack which may probably result in his death, and we think it clear that where this protection is to be afforded through the civil power, the Department of Justice is the proper one to set in motion the necessary means of protection. The correspondence [produced in evidence] between the marshal of the Northern District of California, and the Attorney General, and the District

Attorney of the United States for that district, although prescribing no very specific mode of affording this protection by the Attorney General, is sufficient, we think, to warrant the marshal in taking the steps which he did take, in making the provisions which he did make, for the protection and defence of Mr. Justice Field. . . .

We therefore affirm the judgment of the Circuit Court authorizing his discharge from the custody of the sheriff of San Joaquin County.

[CHIEF JUSTICE FULLER and JUSTICE LAMAR dissented.]

Youngstown Sheet & Tube Co. v. Sawyer

343 US 579, 72 S Ct 863, 96 L Ed 1153 (1952)

The order of the president directing the secretary of commerce to seize and operate the steel mills was not authorized by the Constitution or laws of the United States.

MR. JUSTICE BLACK delivered the opinion of the Court.

We are asked to decide whether the President was acting within his constitutional power when he issued an order directing the Secretary of Commerce to take possession of and operate most of the Nation's steel mills. . . . The issue emerges here from the following series of events:

In the latter part of 1951, a dispute arose between the steel companies and their employees over terms and conditions that should be included in new collective bargaining agreements. Long-continued conferences failed to resolve the dispute. On December 18, 1951, the employees' representative, United Steelworkers of America, C.I.O., gave notice of an intention to strike when the existing bargaining agreements expired on December 31. The Federal Mediation and Conciliation Service then intervened in an effort to get labor and management to agree. This failing, the President on December 22, 1951, referred the dispute to the Federal Wage Stabilization Board to investigate and make recommendations for fair and equitable terms of settlement. This Board's report resulted in no settlement. On April 4, 1952, the Union gave notice of a nation-wide strike called to begin at 12:01 A.M. April 9. The indispensability of steel as a component of substantially all weapons and other war materials led the President to believe that the proposed work stoppage would immediately jeopardize our national defense and that governmental seizure of the steel mills was necessary in order to assure the continued availability of steel. Reciting these considerations for his action, the President, a few hours before the strike was to begin, issued Executive Order 10340. . . . The order directed the Secretary of Commerce to take possession of most of the steel mills and keep them running. The Secretary immediately issued his own possessory orders, calling upon the presidents of the various seized companies to serve as operating managers for the United States. They were directed to carry on their activities in accordance with regulations and directions of the Secretary. The next morning the President sent a message to Congress reporting his action. . . . Twelve days later he sent a second message. . . . Congress has taken no action.

Obeying the Secretary's orders under protest, the companies brought proceedings against him in the District Court. Their complaints charged that the seizure was not authorized by an act of Congress or by any constitutional provisions. The District Court was asked to declare the orders of the President and the Secretary invalid and to issue preliminary and permanent injunctions restraining their enforcement. Opposing the motion for preliminary injunction, the United States asserted that a strike disrupting steel production for even a brief period would so endanger the well-being and safety of the Nation that the President had "inherent power" to do what he had done—power "supported by the Constitution, by historical precedent, and by court decisions." The Government also contended that in any event no preliminary injunction should be issued because the companies had made no showing that their available legal remedies were inadequate or that their injuries from seizure would be irreparable. Holding against the Government on all points, the District Court on April 30 issued a preliminary injunction restraining the Secretary from "continuing the seizure and possession of the plants . . . and from acting under the purported authority of Executive Order No. 10340." . . . On the same day the Court of Appeals stayed the District Court's injunction. . . . Deeming it best that the issues raised be promptly decided by this Court, we granted *certiorari* on May 3 and set the cause for argument on May 12. . . .

The President's power, if any, to issue the order must stem either from an act of Congress or from the Constitution itself. There is no statute that expressly authorizes the President to take possession of property as he did here. Nor is there any act of Congress to which our attention has been directed from which such a power can fairly be implied. Indeed, we do not understand the Government to rely on statutory authorization for this seizure. . . .

Moreover, the use of the seizure technique to solve labor disputes in order to prevent work stoppages was not only unauthorized by any congressional enactment; prior to this controversy, Congress had refused to adopt that method of settling labor disputes. When the Taft-Hartley Act was under consideration in 1947, Congress rejected an amendment which would have authorized such governmental seizures in cases of emergency. Apparently it was thought that the technique of seizure, like that of compulsory arbitration, would interfere with the process of collective bargaining. Consequently, the plan Congress adopted in that Act did not provide for seizure under any circumstances. Instead, the plan sought to bring about settlements by use of the customary devices of mediation, conciliation, investigation by boards of inquiry, and public reports. In some instances temporary injunctions were authorized to provide cooling-off periods. All this failing, unions were left free to strike after a secret vote by employees as to whether they wished to accept their employers' final settlement offer.

It is clear that if the President had authority to issue the order he did, it must be found in some provision of the Constitution. And it is not claimed that express constitutional language grants this power to the President. The contention is that presidential power should be implied from the aggregate of his power under the Constitution. Particular reliance is placed on provisions in Article II which say that "The Executive Power shall be vested in a President . . . "; that "he shall take care that the Laws be faithfully executed"; and that he "shall be Commander in Chief of the Army and Navy of the United States."

The order cannot properly be sustained as an exercise of the President's military power as Commander in Chief of the Armed Forces. The Government attempts to do so by citing a number of cases upholding broad powers in military commanders engaged in day-to-day fighting in a theater of war. Such cases need not concern us here. Even though "theater of war" be an expanding concept, we cannot with faithfulness to our constitutional system hold that the Commander in Chief of the Armed Forces has the ultimate power as such to take possession of private property in order to keep labor disputes from stopping production. This is a job for the Nation's lawmakers, not for its military authorities.

Nor can the seizure order be sustained because of the several constitutional provisions that grant executive power to the President. In the framework of our Constitution, the President's power to see that the laws are faithfully executed refutes the idea that he is to be a lawmaker. The Constitution limits his functions in the lawmaking process to the recommending of laws he thinks wise and the vetoing of laws he thinks bad. And the Constitution is neither silent nor equivocal about who shall make laws which the President is to execute. The first section of the first article says that "All legislative powers herein granted shall be vested in a Congress of the United States. ... "

The President's order does not direct that a congressional policy be executed in a manner prescribed by Congress—it directs that a presidential policy be executed in a manner prescribed by the President. . . .

The Founders of this Nation entrusted the lawmaking power to the Congress alone in both good and bad times. It would do no good to recall the historical events, the fears of power and the hopes for freedom that lay behind their choice. Such a review would but confirm our holding that this seizure order cannot stand.

The judgment of the District Court is

Affirmed.

[The concurring and dissenting opinions are omitted here. The opinion by JUSTICE FRANKFURTER contains a wealth of historical data on presidential seizures. He concurred in the decision here holding seizure to be illegal primarily because Congress had recently debated and rejected this method of dealing with labor disputes.]

United States v. Nixon

417 US 683 , 94 S Ct 2098, 41 L Ed 1039

Neither the doctrine of separation of powers nor the need for confidentiality of high level communications, without more, can sustain an absolute, unqualified presidential privilege of immunity from judicial process under all circumstances.

MR. CHIEF JUSTICE BURGER delivered the opinion of the Court.

These cases present for review the denial of a motion, filed on behalf of the President of the United States, in the case of *United States* v. *Mitchell et al.* (D.C. Crim. No.

74-110), to quash a third-party subpoena duces tecum issued by the U.S. District Court for the District of Columbia, pursuant to Fed. Rule Crim. Proc. 17 (c). The subpoena directed the President to produce certain tape recordings and documents relating to his conversations with aides and advisers. The court rejected the President's claims of absolute executive privilege, of lack of jurisdiction, and of failure to satisfy the requirements of Rule 17 (c). The President appealed to the Court of Appeals. We granted the United States' petition for *certiorari* before judgment, and also the President's responsive cross-petition for *certiorari* before judgment, because of the public importance of the issues presented and the need for their prompt resolution. . . .

In the District Court, the President's counsel argued that the court lacked jurisdiction to issue the subpoena because the matter was an intrabranch dispute between a subordinate and superior officer of the Executive Branch and hence not subject to judicial resolution. . . . Since the Executive Branch has exclusive authority and absolute discretion to decide whether to prosecute a case, *Confiscation Cases,* 7 Wall 454 (1869), *United States* v. *Cox,* 342 F. 2d 167, 171 (CA5) cert. denied, 381 US 935 (1965), it is contended that a President's decision is final in determining what evidence is to be used in a given criminal case. Although his counsel concedes the President has delegated certain specific powers to the Special Prosecutor, he has not "waived nor delegated to the special prosecutor the President's duty to claim privilege as to all materials . . . which fall within the President's inherent authority to refuse to disclose to any executive officer." Brief for the President 47. The Special Prosecutor's demand for the items therefore presents, in the view of the President's counsel, a political question under *Baker* v. *Carr,* 369 US 186 (1962), since it involves a "textually demonstrable" grant of power under Art. II.

The mere assertion of a claim of an "intrabranch dispute," without more, has never operated to defeat federal jurisdiction; justiciability does not depend on such a surface inquiry. . . .

Our starting point is the nature of the proceeding for which the evidence is sought —here a pending criminal prosecution. It is a judicial proceeding in a federal court alleging violation of federal laws and is brought in the name of the United States as sovereign. *Berger* v. *United States,* 296 US 78, 88 (1935). Under the authority of Art. II, §2, Congress has vested in the Attorney General the power to conduct the criminal litigation of the U.S. Government. 28 USC 516. It has also vested in him the power to appoint subordinate officers to assist him in the discharge of his duties. 28 USC 509, 510, 515, 533. Acting pursuant to those statutes, the Attorney General has delegated the authority to represent the United States in these particular matters to a Special Prosecutor with unique authority and tenure. The regulation gives the Special Prosecutor explicit power to contest the invocation of executive privilege in the process of seeking evidence deemed relevant to the performance of these specially delegated duties. 38 Fed. Reg. 30739.

So long as this regulation is extant it has the force of law. . . .

Here, as in *Accardi* [v. *Shaughnessy,* 347 US 260], it is theoretically possible for the Attorney General to amend or revoke the regulation defining the Special Prosecutor's authority. But he has not done so. So long as this regulation remains in force the Executive Branch is bound by it, and indeed the United States as the sovereign composed of the three branches is bound to respect and to enforce it. Moreover, the delegation of authority to the Special Prosecutor in this case is not an ordinary delegation by the Attorney General to a subordinate officer: with the authorization of the President, the Acting Attorney General provided in the regulation that the Special Prosecutor was not to be removed without the "consensus" of eight designated leaders of Congress. . . .

In light of the uniqueness of the setting in which the conflict arises, the fact that both parties are officers of the Executive Branch cannot be viewed as a barrier to justiciability. It would be inconsistent with the applicable law and regulation, and the unique facts of this case, to conclude other than that the Special Prosecutor has standing to bring this action and that a justiciable controversy is presented for decision. . . .

Having determined that the requirements of Rule 17 (c) were satisfied, we turn to the claim that the subpoena should be quashed because it demands "confidential conversations between a President and his close advisors that it would be inconsistent with the public interest to produce." App. 48a. The first contention is a broad claim that the separation of powers doctrine precludes judicial review of a President's claim of privilege. The second contention is that if he does not prevail on the claim of absolute privilege, the court should hold as a matter of constitutional law that the privilege prevails over the subpoena duces tecum. . . .

However, neither the doctrine of separation of powers, nor the need for confidentiality of high level communications, without more, can sustain an absolute, unqualified presidential privilege of immunity from judicial process under all circumstances. The President's need for complete candor and objectivity from advisers calls for great deference from the courts. However, when the privilege depends solely on the broad, undifferentiated claim of public interest in the confidentiality of such conversations, a confrontation with other values arises. Absent a claim of need to protect military, diplomatic or sensitive national security secrets, we find it difficult to accept the argument that even the very important interest in confidentiality of presidential communications is significantly diminished by production of such material for in camera inspection with all the protection that a district court will be obliged to provide. . . .

In this case we must weigh the importance of the general privilege of confidentiality of presidential communications in performance of his responsibilities against the inroads of such a privilege on the fair administration of criminal justice. The interest in preserving confidentiality is weighty indeed and entitled to great respect. However, we cannot conclude that advisers will be moved to temper the candor of their remarks by the infrequent occasions of disclosure because of the possibility that such conversations will be called for in the context of a criminal prosecution. . . .

We conclude that when the ground for asserting privilege as to subpoenaed materials sought for use in a criminal trial is based only on the generalized interest in confidentiality, it cannot prevail over the fundamental demands of due process of law in the fair administration of criminal justice. The generalized assertion of privilege must yield to the demonstrated, specific need for evidence in a pending criminal trial.

We have earlier determined that the District Court did not err in authorizing the issuance of the subpoena. If a President concludes that compliance with a subpoena would be injurious to the public interest he may properly, as was done here, invoke a claim of privilege on the return of the subpoena. Upon receiving a claim of privilege from the Chief Executive, it became the further duty of the District Court to treat the subpoenaed material as presumptively privilege and to require the Special Prosecutor to demonstrate that the presidential material was "essential to the justice of the [pending criminal] case." *United States* v. *Burr, supra,* at 192. Here the District Court treated the material as presumptively privileged, proceeded to find that the Special Prosecutor had made a sufficient showing to rebut the presumption and ordered an *in camera* examination of the subpoenaed material. On the basis of our examination of the record we are unable to conclude that the District Court erred in ordering the inspection. Accordingly we affirm the order of the District Court that subpoenaed materials be transmitted to that court. We now turn to the important question of the District Court's responsibilities in conducting the *in camera* examination of presidential materials or communications delivered under the compulsion of the subpoena duces tecum.

Enforcement of the subpoena *duces tecum* was stayed pending this Court's resolution of the issues raised by the petitions for *certiorari.* Those issues now having been disposed of, the matter of implementation will rest with the District Court. "[T]he guard, furnished to [President] to protect him from being harassed by vexatious and unnecessary subpoenas, is to be looked for in the conduct of the [district] court after the subpoenas have been issued; not in any circumstances which is to precede their being issued." *United States* v. *Burr, supra,* at 34. Statements meeting the test of admissibility and relevance must be isolated; all other material must be excised. At this stage the District Court is not limited to representations of the Special Prosecutor as to the evidence sought by the subpoena; the material will be available to the District Court. It is elementary that *in camera* inspection of evidence is always a procedure calling for scrupulous protection against any release or publication of material not found by the court, at that stage, probably admissible in evidence and relevant to the issues of the trial for which it is sought. That being true of an ordinary situation, it is obvious that the District Court has a very heavy responsibility to see to it that presidential conversations, which are either not relevant or not admissible, are accorded that high degree of respect due the President of the United States. . . .

A President's communications and activities encompass a vastly wider range of sensitive material than would be true of any "ordinary individual." It is therefore necessary in the public interest to afford presidential confidentiality the greatest protection consistent with the fair administration of justice. The need for confidentiality even as to idle conversations with associates in which casual reference might be made concerning political leaders within the country or foreign statesmen is too obvious to call for further treatment. We have no doubt that the District Judge will at all times accord to presidential records that high degree of deference suggested in *United States* v. *Burr, supra,* and will discharge his responsibility to see to it that until released to the Special Prosecutor no *in camera* material is revealed to anyone. This burden applies with even greater force to excised material; once the decision is made to excise, the material is restored to its privileged status and should be returned under seal to its lawful custodian.

Since this matter came before the court during the pendency of a criminal prosecution, and on representations that time is of the essence, the mandate shall issue forthwith.

Affirmed.

MR. JUSTICE REHNQUIST took no part in the consideration or decision of these cases.

C. FOREIGN RELATIONS

United States v. Curtiss-Wright Export Corp.

299 US 304, 57 S Ct 216, 81 L Ed 255 (1936)

In view of the delicacy of foreign relations and of the power peculiar to the president in this regard, congressional legislation which is to be made effective in the international field must often accord to him a degree of discretion and freedom which would not be admissible were domestic affairs alone involved.

[The Curtiss-Wright Export Corporation was indicted for selling machine guns to Bolivia in violation of a presidential proclamation prohibiting the sale of munitions of war to the countries engaged in the Chaco conflict. By a joint resolution Congress had authorized the president to issue the proclamation involved if he found that such a limitation on the sale of munitions would contribute toward the reestablishment of peace. Curtiss-Wright challenged the validity of the joint resolution on the ground that it delegated legislative power to the president.]

Mr. Justice Sutherland delivered the opinion of the Court. . . .

Whether, if the Joint Resolution had related solely to internal affairs, it would be open to the challenge that it constituted an unlawful delegation of legislative power to the Executive, we find it unnecessary to determine. The whole aim of the resolution is to affect a situation entirely external to the United States, and falling within the category of foreign affairs. The determination which we are called to make, therefore, is whether the Joint Resolution, as applied to that situation, is vulnerable to attack under the rule that forbids a delegation of the lawmaking power. In other words, assuming (but not deciding) that the challenged delegation, if it were confined to internal affairs, would be invalid, may it nevertheless be sustained on the ground that its exclusive aim is to afford a remedy for a hurtful condition within foreign territory?

It will contribute to the elucidation of the question if we first consider the differences between the powers of the federal government in respect of foreign or external affairs and those in respect of domestic or internal affairs. That there are differences between them, and that these differences are fundamental may not be doubted.

The two classes of powers are different, both in respect of their origin and their nature. The broad statement that the federal government can exercise no powers except those specifically enumerated in the Constitution, and such implied powers as are necessary and proper to carry into effect the enumerated powers, is categorically true only in respect of our internal affairs. In that field, the primary purpose of the Constitution was to carve from the general mass of legislative powers *then possessed by the states* such portions as it was thought desirable to vest in the federal government, leaving those not included in the enumeration, still in the states. . . . That this doctrine applies only to powers which the states had is self-evident. And since the states severally never possessed international powers, such powers could not have been carved from the mass of state powers but obviously were transmitted to the United States from some other source. During the Colonial period, those powers were possessed exclusively by and were entirely under the control of the Crown. By the Declaration of Independence, "the Representatives of the United States of America" declared the United (not the several)

Colonies to be free and independent states, and as such to have "full Power to levy War, conclude Peace, contract Alliances, establish Commerce and to do all other Acts and Things which Independent States may of right do."

As a result of the separation from Great Britain by the colonies, acting as a unit, the powers of external sovereignty passed from the Crown not to the colonies severally, but to the colonies in their collective and corporate capacity as the United States of America. . . .

As a member of the family of nations, the right and power of the United States in that field are equal to the right and power of the other members of the international family. . . .

Not only, as we have shown, is the federal power over external affairs in origin and essential character different from that over internal affairs, but participation in the exercise of the power is significantly limited. In this vast external realm, with its important, complicated, delicate and manifold problems, the President alone has the power to speak or listen as a representative of the nation. He *makes* treaties with the advice and consent of the Senate; but he alone negotiates. Into the field of negotiation the Senate cannot intrude; and Congress itself is powerless to invade it. As Marshall said in his great argument of March 7, 1800, in the House of Representatives, "The President is the sole organ of the nation in its external relations, and its sole representative with foreign nations." Annals, 6th Cong, col 613. . . .

It is quite apparent that if, in the maintenance of our international relations, embarrassment—perhaps serious embarrassment—is to be avoided and success for our aims achieved, congressional legislation which is to be made effective through negotiation and inquiry within the international field must often accord to the President a degree of discretion and freedom from statutory restriction which would not be admissible were domestic affairs alone involved. Moreover, he, not Congress, has the better opportunity of knowing the conditions which prevail in foreign countries, and especially is this true in time of war. . . .

The judgment of the court below must be reversed and the cause remanded for further proceedings in accordance with the foregoing opinion.

It is so ordered.

MR. JUSTICE MCREYNOLDS does not agree. He is of opinion that the court below reached the right conclusion and its judgment ought to be affirmed.

MR. JUSTICE STONE took no part in the consideration or decision of this case.

United States v. Belmont

301 US 324, 57 S Ct 758, 81 L Ed 1134 (1937)

In the settlement and assignment of claims between the United States and the Soviet government, the president had authority to speak as the sole organ of the government.

MR. JUSTICE SUTHERLAND delivered the opinion of the Court.

This is an action at law brought by petitioner against respondents in a federal district court to recover a sum of money deposited by a Russian corporation (Petrograd Metal Works) with August Belmont, a private banker doing business in New York City under the name of August Belmont & Co. August Belmont died in 1924; and respondents are the duly-appointed executors of his will. A motion to dismiss the complaint for failure to state facts sufficient to constitute a cause of action was sustained by the district court, and its judgment was affirmed by the court below. . . . The facts alleged, so far as necessary to be stated, follow.

The corporation had deposited with Belmont, prior to 1918, the sum of money which petitioner seeks to recover. In 1918, the Soviet Government duly enacted a decree by which it dissolved, terminated and liquidated the corporation (together with others), and nationalized and appropriated all of its property and assets of every kind and wherever situated, including the deposit account with Belmont. As a result, the deposit became the property of the Soviet Government, and so remained until November 16, 1933, at which time the Soviet Government released and assigned to petitioner all amounts due to that government from American nationals, including the deposit account of the corporation with Belmont. Respondents failed and refused to pay the amount upon demand duly made by petitioner.

The assignment was effected by an exchange of diplomatic correspondence between the Soviet Government and the United States. The purpose was to bring about a final settlement of the claims and counterclaims between the Soviet Government and the United States; and it was agreed that the Soviet Government would take no steps to enforce claims against American nationals; but all such claims were released and assigned to the United States, with the understanding that the Soviet Government was to be duly notified of all amounts realized by the United States from such release and assignment. The assignment and requirement for notice are parts of the larger plan to bring about a settlement of the rival claims of the high contracting parties. The continuing and definite interest of the Soviet Government in the collection of assigned claims is evident; and the case, therefore, presents a question of public concern, the determination of which well might involve the good faith of the United States in the eyes of a foreign government. The court below held that the assignment thus effected embraced the claim here in question; and with that we agree.

That court, however, took the view that the situs of the bank deposit was within the State of New York; that in no sense could it be regarded as an intangible property right within Soviet territory; and that the nationalization decree, if enforced, would put into effect an act of confiscation. And it held that a judgment for the United States could not be had, because, in view of that result, it would be contrary to the controlling public policy of the State of New York. The further contention is made by respondents that the public policy of the United States would likewise be infringed by such a judgment. The two questions thus presented are the only ones necessary to be considered.

First. We do not pause to inquire whether in fact there was any policy of the State of New York to be infringed, since we are of opinion that no state policy can prevail against the international compact here involved.

This court has held, *Underhill* v. *Hernandez,* 168 US 250, that every sovereign state must recognize the independence of every other sovereign state; and that the courts of one will not sit in judgment upon the acts of the government of another, done within its own territory. . . .

We take judicial notice of the fact that coincident with the assignment set forth in the complaint, the President recognized the Soviet Government, and normal diplomatic relations were established between that government and the Government of the United States, followed by an exchange of ambassadors. The effect of this was to validate, so far as this country is concerned, all acts of the Soviet Government here involved from the commencement of its existence. The recognition, establishment of diplomatic relations, the assignment, and agreements with respect thereto, were all parts of one transaction, resulting in an international compact between the two governments. That the negotiations, acceptance of the assignment and agreements and understandings in respect thereof were within the competence of the President may not be doubted. Governmental power over internal affairs is distributed between the national government and the several states. Governmental power over external affairs is not distributed, but is vested exclusively in the national government. And in respect of what was done here, the Executive had authority to speak as the sole organ of that government. The assignment and the agreements in connection therewith did not, as in the case of treaties, as that term is used in the treaty-making clause of the Consitution (Art II, § 2), require the advice and consent of the Senate.

A treaty signifies "a compact made between two or more independent nations with a view to the public welfare." *Altman & Co.* v. *United States,* 224 US 583, 600. But an international compact, as this was, is not always a treaty which requires the participation of the Senate. There are many such compacts, of which a protocol, a *modus vivendi,* a postal convention, and agreements like that now under consideration are illustrations. See 5 Moore, Int Law Digest, 210–221. The distinction was pointed out by this court in the *Altman* case, *supra,* which arose under § 3 of the Tariff Act of 1897, authorizing the President to conclude commercial agreements with foreign countries in certain specified matters. We held that although this might not be a treaty requiring ratification by the Senate, it was a compact negotiated and proclaimed under the authority of the President, and as such was a "treaty" within the meaning of the Circuit Court of Appeals Act, the construction of which might be reviewed upon direct appeal to this court.

Plainly, the external powers of the United States are to be exercised without regard to state laws or policies. The supremacy of a treaty in this respect has been recognized from the beginning. . . .

Second. The public policy of the United States relied upon as a bar to the action is that declared by the Constitution, namely, that private property shall not be taken without just compensation. But the answer is that our Constitution, laws and policies have no extraterritorial operation, unless in respect of our own citizens. . . . What another country has done in the way of taking over property of its nationals, and especially of its corporations, is not a matter for judicial consideration here. Such nationals must look to their own government for any redress to which they may be entitled. So far as the record shows, only the rights of the Russian corporation have been affected by what has been done; and it will be time enough to consider the rights of our nationals when, if ever, by proper judicial proceeding, it shall be made to appear that they are so affected as to entitle them to judicial relief. The substantive right to the moneys, as now disclosed, became vested in the Soviet Government as the successor to the corporation; and this right that government has passed to the United States. It does not appear that respondents have any interest in the matter beyond that of a custodian. Thus far no question under the Fifth Amendment is involved.

It results that the complaint states a cause of action and that the judgment of the court below to the contrary is erroneous. In so holding, we deal only with the case as now presented and with the parties now before us. We do not consider the status of adverse claims, if there be any, of others not parties to this action. And nothing we have said is to be construed as foreclosing the assertion of any such claim to the fund involved, by intervention or other appropriate proceeding. We decide only that the complaint alleges facts sufficient to constitute a cause of action against the respondents.

Judgment reversed.

[The concurring opinion by JUSTICE STONE is omitted.]

Note

Compare the decisions in *United States* v. *Pink,* 315 US 203 (1942), *Banco Nacional de Cuba* v. *Sabbatino,* 376 US 398 (1964), and *Banco Nacional de Cuba* v. *Farr,* 243 F Supp 957 (1965).

Kent v. Dulles

357 US 116, 78 S Ct 1113, 2 L Ed2d 1204 (1958)

The secretary of state denied passports to petitioners because of their alleged Communistic beliefs and associations and their refusal to file affidavits concerning present or past membership in the Communist party. *Held:* The secretary was not authorized to deny the passports.

MR. JUSTICE DOUGLAS delivered the opinion of the Court.

This case concerns two applications for passports, denied by the Secretary of State. One was by Rockwell Kent who desired to visit England and attend a meeting of an organization known as the "World Council of Peace" in Helsinki, Finland. The Director of the Passport Office informed Kent that issuance of a passport was precluded by § 51.135 of the Regulations promulgated by the Secretary of State on two grounds: (1) that he was a Communist and (2) that he had had "a consistent and prolonged adherence to the Communist Party line." The letter of denial specified in some detail the facts on which those conclusions were based. Kent was also advised of his right to an informal hearing under § 51.137 of the Regulations. But he was also told that whether or not a hearing was requested it would be necessary, before a passport would be issued, to submit an affidavit as to whether he was then or ever had been a Communist. Kent did not ask for a hearing but filed a new passport application listing several European countries he desired to visit. When advised that a hearing was still available to him, his attorney replied that Kent took the position that the requirement of an affidavit concerning Communist Party membership "is unlawful and that for that reason and as a matter of conscience," he would not supply one. He did, however, have a hearing at which the principal evidence against him was from his book, "It's Me O Lord," which Kent agreed was accurate. He again refused to submit the affidavit, maintaining that any matters unrelated to the question of his citizenship were irrelevant to the Department's consideration of his application. The Department advised him that no further consideration of his application would be given until he satisfied the requirements of the Regulations.

Thereupon Kent sued in the District Court for declaratory relief. The District Court granted summary judgment for respondent. On appeal the case of Kent was heard with that of Dr. Walter Briehl, a psychiatrist. When Briehl applied for a passport, the Director of the Passport Office asked him to supply the affidavit covering membership in the Communist Party. Briehl, like Kent, refused. . . .

Briehl filed his complaint in the District Court which held that his case was indistinguishable from Kent's and dismissed the complaint.

The Court of Appeals heard the two cases *en banc* and affirmed the District Court by a divided vote. . . . The cases are here on writ of *certiorari.* . . .

A passport not only is of great value—indeed necessary—abroad; it is also an aid in establishing citizenship for purposes of re-entry into the United States. . . . But throughout most of our history—until indeed quite recently—a passport, though a great convenience in foreign travel, was not a legal requirement for leaving or entering the United States. . . . Apart from minor exceptions to be noted, it was first made a requirement by § 215 of the Act of June 27, 1952, 66 Stat 190, 8 USC § 1185, which states that, after a prescribed proclamation by the President, it is "unlawful for any citizen of the United States to depart from or enter, or attempt to depart from or enter, the United States unless he bears a valid passport." And the Proclamation necessary to make the restrictions of this Act applicable and in force has been made. . . .

The right to travel is a part of the "liberty" of which the citizen cannot be deprived without due process of law under the Fifth Amendment. So much is conceded by the Solicitor General. In Anglo-Saxon law that right was emerging at least as early as the Magna Carta. Chafee, Three Human Rights in the Constitution of 1787 (1956), 171–181, 187 et seq., shows how deeply engrained in our history this freedom of movement is. Freedom of movement across frontiers in either direction, and inside frontiers as well, was a part of our heritage. Travel abroad, like travel within the country, may be necessary for a livelihood. It may be as close to the heart of the individual as the choice of what he eats, or wears, or reads. Freedom of movement is basic in our scheme of values. . . .

The difficulty is that while the power of the Secretary of State over the issuance of passports is expressed in broad terms, it was apparently long exercised quite narrowly. So far as material here, the cases of refusal of passports generally fell into two categories. First, questions pertinent to the citizenship of the applicant and his allegiance to the United States had to be resolved by the Secretary, for the command of Congress was that "No passport shall be granted or issued to or verified for any other persons than those owing allegiance, whether citizens or not, to the United States." 32 Stat 386, 22 USC § 212. Second, was the question whether the applicant was participating in illegal conduct, trying to escape the toils of the law, promoting passport frauds, or otherwise engaging in conduct which would violate the laws of the United States. . . .

We . . . hesitate to impute to Congress, when in 1952 it made a passport necessary for foreign travel and left its issuance to the discretion of the Secretary of State, a purpose to give him unbridled discretion to grant or withhold a passport from a citizen for any substantive reason he may choose. . . .

Thus we do not reach the question of constitutionality. We only conclude that § 1185 and § 211a do not delegate to the Secretary the kind of authority exercised here.

To repeat, we deal here with a constitutional right of the citizen, a right which we must assume Congress will be faithful to respect. We would be faced with important constitutional questions were we to hold that Congress by § 1185 and § 211a had given the Secretary authority to withhold passports to citizens because of their beliefs or associations. Congress has made no such provision in explicit terms; and absent one, the Secretary may not employ that standard to restrict the citizens' right of free movement.

Reversed.

MR. JUSTICE CLARK, with whom MR. JUSTICE BURTON, MR. JUSTICE HARLAN, and MR. JUSTICE WHITTAKER concur, dissenting.

On August 28, 1952, acting under authority vested by Executive Order No. 7856, 22 CFR § 51.77, the Secretary of State issued the regulations in question, § 51.142 of which provides that a passport applicant may be required to make a statement under oath "with respect to present or past membership in the Communist Party." 22 CFR § 51.142. Since 1917, the Congress has required that every passport application "contain a true recital of each and every matter of fact which may be required by . . . any rules" of the Secretary of State, and that requirement must be satisfied "[b]efore a passport is issued to any person." 40 Stat 227, 22 USC § 213. In the context of that background, the Secretary asked for, and petitioners refused to file, affidavits stating whether they then were or ever had been members of the Communist Party. Thereupon the Secretary refused to further consider petitioners' applications until such time as they filed the required affidavits.

The Secretary's action clearly must be held authorized by Congress if the requested information is relevant to any ground upon which the Secretary might properly refuse to issue a passport. The Court purports today to preclude the existence of such a ground by holding that the Secretary has not been authorized to deny a passport to a Communist whose travel abroad would be inimical to our national security. . . .

D. MILITARY POWERS

The Prize Cases

2 Black 635, 17 L Ed 459 (1863)

The proclamation of blockade by the president is of itself conclusive evidence that a state of war exists.

[On April 27 and 30, 1861, President Lincoln proclaimed a blockade of southern ports. Four merchant vessels and their cargo seized by public ships of the United States while entering or leaving southern ports were condemned as prizes in United States district courts. Their owners appealed from the decrees of condemnation.]

M R. J USTICE G RIER. There are certain propositions of law which must necessarily affect the ultimate decision of these cases, and many others, which it will be proper to discuss and decide before we notice the special facts peculiar to each.

The right of prize and capture has its origin in the *"jus belli,"* and is governed and adjudged under the law of nations. To legitimate the capture of a neutral vessel or property on the high seas, a war must exist *de facto,* and the neutral must have a knowledge or notice of the intention of one of the parties belligerent to use this mode of coercion against a port, city, or territory, in possession of the other. . . .

As a civil war is never publicly proclaimed, *eo nomine* against insurgents, its actual existence is a fact in our domestic history which the Court is bound to notice and to know. . . .

By the Constitution, Congress alone has the power to declare a national or foreign war. It cannot declare war against a State, or any number of States, by virtue of any clause in the Constitution. The Constitution confers on the President the whole Executive power. He is bound to take care that the laws be faithfully executed. He is Commander-in-chief of the Army and Navy of the United States, and of the militia of the several States when called into the actual service of the United States. He has no power to initiate or declare a war either against a foreign nation or a domestic State. But by the Acts of Congress of February 28th 1795, and 3d of March, 1807, he is authorized to call out the militia and use the military and naval forces of the United States in case of invasion by foreign nations, and to suppress insurrection against the government of a State or of the United States.

If a war be made by invasion of a foreign nation, the President is not only authorized but bound to resist force by force. He does not initiate the war, but is bound to accept the challenge without waiting for any special legislative authority. And whether the hostile party be a foreign invader, or States organized in rebellion, it is none the less a war, although the declaration of it be *"unilateral. . . ."*

The battles of Palo Alto and Resaca de la Palma had been fought before the passage of the Act of Congress of May 13th, 1846, which recognized *"a state of war as existing by the act of the Republic of Mexico."* This act not only provided for the future prosecution of the war, but was itself a vindication and ratification of the Act of the President in accepting the challenge without a previous formal declaration of war by Congress.

This greatest of civil wars was not gradually developed by popular commotion, tumultuous assemblies, or local unorganized insurrections. However long may have been its previous conception, it nevertheless sprung forth suddenly from the parent brain, a Minerva in the full panoply of *war.* The President was bound to meet it in the shape it presented itself, without waiting for Congress to baptize it with a name; and no name given to it by him or them could change the fact. . . .

Whether the President in fulfilling his duties, as Commander-in-chief, in suppressing an insurrection, has met with such armed hostile resistance, and a civil war of such alarming proportions as will compel him to accord to them the character of belligerents, is a question to be decided *by him,* and this Court must be governed by the decisions and acts of the political department of the Government to which this power was entrusted. "He must determine what degree of force the crisis demands." The proclamation of blockade is itself official and conclusive evidence to the Court that a state of war existed which demanded and authorized a recourse to such a measure under the circumstances peculiar to the case. . . .

The decree below is affirmed with costs. . . .

MR. JUSTICE NELSON, dissenting. . . .

Upon the whole, after the most careful consideration of this case which the pressure of other duties has admitted, I am compelled to the conclusion that no civil war existed between this Government and the States in insurrection till recognized by the Act of Congress 13th of July, 1861; that the President does not possess the power under the Constitution to declare war or recognize its existence within the meaning of the law of nations, which carries with it belligerent rights, and thus change the country and all its citizens from a state of peace to a state of war; that this power belongs exclusively to the Congress of the United States, and, consequently, that the President had no power to set on foot a blockade under the law of nations, and that the capture of the vessel and cargo in this case, and in all cases before us in which the capture occurred before the 13th of July, 1861, for breach of blockade, or as enemies' property, are illegal and void, and that the decrees of condemnation should be reversed and the vessel and cargo restored.

MR. CHIEF JUSTICE TANEY, MR. JUSTICE CATRON and MR. JUSTICE CLIFFORD, concurred in the dissenting opinion of MR. JUSTICE NELSON.

Note

Vietnam.   Repeated attempts to have the federal courts pass upon the legality and constitutionality of the United States military action in Vietnam have failed. See *Mora* v. *McNamara*, 389 US 934 (1967), *Massachusetts* v. *Laird,* 400 US 886 (1970), *DaCosta* v. *Laird,* 405 US 479 (1972), and *Sarnoff* v. *Shultz,* 409 US 929 (1972).

Korematsu v. United States

323 US 214, 65 S Ct 173, 89 L Ed 194 (1944)

The exclusion of persons of Japanese ancestry from designated areas during World War II is held to have been justified by military danger.

MR. JUSTICE BLACK delivered the opinion of the Court.

The petitioner, an American citizen of Japanese descent, was convicted in a federal district court for remaining in San Leandro, California, a "Military Area," contrary to Civilian Exclusion Order No. 34 of the Commanding General of the Western Command, U.S. Army, which directed that after May 9, 1942, all persons of Japanese ancestry should be excluded from that area. No question was raised as to petitioner's loyalty to the United States. The Circuit Court of Appeals affirmed, and the importance of the constitutional question involved caused us to grant *certiorari.*

It should be noted, to begin with, that all legal restrictions which curtail the civil rights of a single racial group are immediately suspect. That is not to say that all such restrictions are unconstitutional. It is to say that courts must subject them to the most rigid scrutiny. Pressing public necessity may sometimes justify the existence of such restrictions; racial antagonism never can.

In the instant case prosecution of the petitioner was begun by information charging violation of an Act of Congress, of March 21, 1942, 56 Stat 173, which provides that ". . . whoever shall enter, remain in, leave, or commit any act in any military zone prescribed, under the authority of an Executive Order of the President, by the Secretary of War, or by any military commander designated by the Secretary of War, contrary to the restrictions applicable to any such area or zone or contrary to the order of the Secretary of War or any such military commander, shall, if it appears that he knew or should have known of the existence and extent of the restrictions or order and that his act was in violation thereof, be guilty of a misdemeanor and upon conviction shall be liable to a fine of not to exceed $5,000 or to imprisonment for not more than one year, or both, for each offense."

Exclusion Order No. 34, which the petitioner knowingly and admittedly violated, was one of a number of military orders and proclamations, all of which were substantially based upon Executive Order No. 9066, 7 Fed Reg 1407. That order, issued after we were at war with Japan, declared that "the successful prosecution of the war requires every possible protection against espionage and against sabotage to national-defense material, national-defense premises, and national-defense utilities. . . ."

One of the series of orders and proclamations, a curfew order, which like the exclusion order here was promulgated pursuant to Executive Order 9066, subjected all persons of Japanese ancestry in prescribed West Coast military areas to remain in their residences from 8 P.M. to 6 A.M. As in the case with the exclusion order here, that prior curfew order was designed as a "protection against espionage and against sabotage." In *Hirabayashi* v. *United States,* 320 US 81, we sustained a conviction obtained for violation of the curfew order. The *Hirabayashi* conviction and this one thus rest on the same 1942 Congressional Act and the same basic executive and military orders, all of which orders were aimed at the twin dangers of espionage and sabotage.

The 1942 Act was attacked in the *Hirabayashi* case as an unconstitutional delegation of power; it was contended that the curfew order and other orders on which it rested were beyond the war powers of the Congress, the military authorities and of the President, as Commander in Chief of the Army; and finally that to apply the curfew order against none but citizens of Japanese ancestry amounted to a constitutionally prohibited discrimination solely on account of race. To these questions we gave the serious consideration which their importance justified. We upheld the curfew order as an exercise of the power of the government to take steps necessary to prevent espionage and sabotage in an area threatened by Japanese attack.

In the light of the principles we announced in the *Hirabayashi* case, we are unable to conclude that it was beyond the war power of Congress and the Executive to exclude those of Japanese ancestry from the West Coast war area at the time they did. True, exclusion from the area in which one's home is located is a far greater deprivation than constant confinement to the home from 8 P.M. to 6 A.M. Nothing short of apprehension by the proper military authorities of the gravest imminent danger to the public safety can constitutionally justify either. But exclusion from a threatened area, no less than curfew, has a definite and close relationship to the prevention of espionage and sabotage.

Here, as in the *Hirabayashi* case, ". . . we cannot reject as unfounded the judgment of the military authorites and of Congress that there were disloyal members of that population, whose number and strength could not be precisely and quickly ascertained. We cannot say that the war-making branches of the Government did not have ground for believing that in a critical hour such persons could not readily be isolated and separately dealt with, and constituted a menace to the national defense and safety, which demanded that prompt and adequate measures be taken to guard against it."

Like curfew, exclusion of those of Japanese origin was deemed necessary because of the presence of an unascertained number of disloyal members of the group, most of whom we have no doubt were loyal to this country. . . .

To cast this case into outlines of racial prejudice, without reference to the real military dangers which were presented, merely confuses the issue. Korematsu was not excluded from the Military Area because of hostility to him or his race. He *was* excluded because we are at war with the Japanese Empire, because the properly constituted military authorities feared an invasion of our West Coast and felt constrained to take proper security measures, because they decided that the military urgency of the situation demanded that all citizens of Japanese ancestry be segregated from the West Coast temporarily, and finally, because Congress, reposing its confidence in this time of war in our military leaders—as inevitably it must—determined that they should have the power to do just this. There was evidence of disloyalty on the part of some, the military authorities considered that the need for action was great, and time was short. We cannot—by availing ourselves of the calm perspective of hindsight—now say that at that time these actions were unjustified.

Affirmed.

[The concurring opinion of JUSTICE FRANKFURTER and the dissenting opinion of JUSTICES ROBERTS, MURPHY, and JACKSON are omitted here.]

E. APPOINTMENTS AND REMOVALS

Wiener v. United States

357 US 349, 78 S Ct 1275, 2 L Ed2d 1377 (1958)

The power of the president to remove an officer depends on the nature of the functions involved.

MR. JUSTICE FRANKFURTER delivered the opinion of the Court.

This is a suit for back pay, based on petitioner's alleged illegal removal as a member of the War Claims Commission. The facts are not in dispute. By the War Claims Act of 1948 . . . Congress established that Commission with "jurisdiction to receive and adjudicate according to law" . . . claims for compensating internees, prisoners of war, and religious organizations . . . who suffered personal injury or property damage at the hands of the enemy in connection with World War II. The Commission was to be composed of three persons, at least two of whom were to be members of the bar, to be appointed by the President, by and with the advice and consent of the Senate. The Commission was to wind up its affairs not later than three years after the expiration of the time for filing claims, orginally limited to two years but extended by successive legislation . . . to March 31, 1952. . . . This limit on the Commission's life was the mode by which the tenure of the Commissioners was defined, and Congress made no provision for removal of a Commissioner.

Having been duly nominated by President Truman, the petitioner was confirmed on June 2, 1950, and took office on June 8, following. On his refusal to heed a request for his resignation, he was, on December 10, 1953, removed by President Eisenhower in the following terms: "I regard it as in the national interest to complete the administration of the War Claims Act of 1948, as amended, with personnel of my own selection." The following day, the President made recess appointments to the Commission, including petitioner's post. After Congress assembled, the President, on February 15, 1954, sent the names of the new appointees to the Senate. The Senate had not confirmed these nominations when the Commission was abolished, July 1, 1954, by Reorganization Plan No. 1 of 1954, 68 Stat 1279, issued pursuant to the Reorganization Act of 1949, 63 Stat 203. Thereupon, petitioner brought this proceeding in the Court of Claims for recovery of his salary as a War Claims Commissioner from December 10, 1953, the day of his removal by the President, to June 30, 1954, the last day of the Commission's existence. A divided Court of Claims dismissed the petition. . . . We brought the case here . . . because it presents a variant of the constitutional issue decided in *Humphrey's Executor* v. *United States,* 295 US 602.

Controversy pertaining to the scope and limits of the President's power of removal fills a thick chapter of our political history. The long stretches of its history, beginning with the very first Congress, with early echoes in the Reports of this Court, were laboriously traversed in *Myers* v. *United States,* 272 US 52, and need not be retraced. President Roosevelt's reliance upon the pronouncements of the Court in that case in removing a member of the Federal Trade Commission on the ground that "the aims and purposes of the Administration with respect to the work of the Commission can be carried out most effectively with personnel of my own selection" reflected contemporaneous professional opinion regarding the significance of the *Myers* decision. Speaking through a Chief Justice, who himself had been President, the Court did not restrict itself to the immediate issue before it, the President's inherent power to remove a postmaster, obviously an executive official. As of set purpose and not by way of parenthetic casualness, the Court announced that the President had inherent constitutional power of removal also of officials who have "duties of a quasi-judicial character . . . whose decisions after hearing affect interests of individuals, the discharge of which the President can not in a particular case properly influence or control." *Myers* v. *United States, supra,* at 135. This view of presidential power was deemed to flow from his "constitutional duty of seeing that the laws be faithfully executed." Ibid.

The assumption was short-lived that the *Myers* case recognized the President's inherent constitutional power to remove officials, no matter what the relation of the executive to the discharge of their duties and no matter what restrictions Congress may have imposed regarding the nature of their tenure. The versatility of circumstances often mocks a natural desire for definitiveness. Within less than ten years a unanimous Court, in *Humphrey's Executor* v. *United States,* 295 US 602, narrowly confined the scope of the *Myers* decision to include only "all purely executive officers." 295 US, at 628. The Court explicitly "disapproved" the expressions in *Myers* supporting the

President's inherent constitutional power to remove members of quasi-judicial bodies. 295 US, at 626–627. Congress had given members of the Federal Trade Commission a seven-year term and also provided for the removal of a Commissioner by the President for inefficiency, neglect of duty or malfeasance in office. In the present case, Congress provided for a tenure defined by the relatively short period of time during which the War Claims Commission was to operate—that is, it was to wind up not later than three years after the expiration of the time for filing of claims. But nothing was said in the Act about removal.

This is another instance in which the most appropriate legal significance must be drawn from congressional failure of explicitness. Necessarily this is a problem in probabilities. We start with one certainty. The problem of the Presdent's power to remove members of agencies entrusted with duties of the kind with which the War Claims Commission was charged was within the lively knowledge of Congress. Few contests between Congress and the President have so recurringly had the attention of Congress as that pertaining to the power of removal. Not the least significant aspect of the *Myers* case is that on the Court's special invitation Senator George Wharton Pepper, of Pennsylvania, presented the position of Congress at the bar of this Court.

Humphrey's case was a *cause celebre*—and not least in the Halls of Congress. And what is the essence of the decision in Humphrey's case? It drew a sharp line of cleavage between officials who were part of the Executive establishment and were thus removable by virtue of the President's constitutional powers, and those who are members of a body "to exercise its judgment without the leave or hindrance of any other official or any department of the government," 295 US, at 625–626, as to whom a power of removal exists only if Congress may fairly be said to have conferred it. This sharp differentiation derives from the difference in functions between those who are part of the Executive establishment and those whose tasks require absolute freedom from Executive interference. "For it is quite evident," again to quote Humphrey's Executor, "that one who holds his office only during the pleasure of another, cannot be depended upon to maintain an attitude of independence against the latter's will." 295 US, at 629.

Thus, the most reliable factor for drawing an inference regarding the President's power of removal in our case is the nature of the function that Congress vested in the War Claims Commission. What were the duties that Congress confided to this Commission? And can the inference fairly be drawn from the failure of Congress to provide for removal that these Commissioners were to remain in office at the will of the President? For such is the assertion of power on which petitioner's removal must rest. The ground of President Eisenhower's removal of petitioner was precisely the same as President Roosevelt's removal of Humphrey. Both Presidents desired to have Commissioners, one on the Federal Trade Commission, the other on the War Claims Commission, "of my own selection." They wanted these Commissioners to be their men. The terms of removal in the two cases are identical and express the assumption that the agencies of which the two Commissioners were members were subject in the discharge of their duties to the control of the Executive. An analysis of the Federal Trade Commission Act left this Court in no doubt that such was not the concept of Congress in creating the Federal Trade Commission. The terms of the War Claims Act of 1948 leave no doubt that such was not the conception of Congress regarding the War Claims Commission.

The history of this legislation emphatically underlines this fact. . . .

If, as one must take for granted, the War Claims Act precluded the President from influencing the Commission in passing on a particular claim, *a fortiori* must it be inferred that Congress did not wish to have hang over the Commission the Damocles' sword of removal by the President for no reason other than that he preferred to have on that Commission men of his own choosing.

For such is this case. We have not a removal for cause involving the rectitude of a member of an adjudicatory body, nor even a suspensory removal until the Senate could act upon it by confirming the appointment of a new Commissioner or otherwise dealing with the matter. Judging the matter in all the nakedness in which it is presented, namely, the claim that the President could remove a member of an adjudicatory body like the War Claims Commission merely because he wanted his own appointees on such a Commission, we are compelled to conclude that no such power is given to the President directly by the Constitution, and none is impliedly conferred upon him by statute simply because Congress said nothing about it. The philosophy of *Humphrey's Executor,* in its explicit language as well as its implications, precludes such a claim.

The judgment is

Reversed.

Note

Nader v. *Bork,* 42 Law Week 2262 (1973), held that Acting Attorney General Bork acted illegally in removing Special Prosecutor Cox upon the request of President Nixon. District Judge Gesell based his decision upon the view that Bork had failed to follow a regulation formulated by Richardson, his predecessor as attorney general. Gesell ignored the precedents relating to the removal power of the president. He relied upon a line of cases dealing with the removal of subordinates as security risks by department heads, including *Cole* v. *Young,* 351 US 536 (1955), *Service* v. *Dulles,* 354 US 363 (1957), and *Vitarelli* v. *Seaton,* 359 US 535 (1959).

F. PARDONS

Ex parte Grossman

267 US 87, 45 S Ct 332, 69 L Ed 527 (1925)

The president's power to pardon offenses against the United States extends to criminal contempts.

MR. CHIEF JUSTICE TAFT delivered the opinion of the Court.

This is an original petition in this Court for a writ of *habeas corpus* by Philip Grossman against Ritchie V. Graham, Superintendent of the Chicago House of Correction, Cook County, Illionis. The respondent has answered the rule to show cause. The facts are not in dispute.

On November 24, 1920, the United States filed a bill in equity against Philip Grossman in the District Court of the United States for the Northern District of Illinois, under Section 22, of the National Prohibition Act . . ., averring that Grossman was maintaining a nuisance at his place of business in Chicago by sales of liquor in violation of the Act and asking an injuction to abate the same. Two days later the District Judge granted a temporary order. January 11, 1921, an information was filed against Grossman, charging that, after the restraining order had been served on him, he had sold to several persons liquor to be drunk on his premises. He was arrested, tried, found guilty of contempt and sentenced to imprisonment in the Chicago House of Correction for one year and to pay a fine of $1,000 to the United States and costs. The decree was affirmed by the Circuit Court of Appeals, 280 Fed 683. In December, 1923, the President issued a pardon in which he commuted the sentence of Grossman to the fine of $1,000 on condition that the fine be paid. The pardon was accepted, the fine was paid and the defendant was released. In May, 1924, however, the District Court committed Grossman to the Chicago House of Correction to serve the sentence notwithstanding the pardon. . . . The only question raised by the pleadings herein is that of the power of the President to grant the pardon.

Special counsel, employed by the Department of Justice, appear for the respondent to uphold the legality of the detention. The Attorney General of the United States, as *amicus curiae,* maintains the validity and effectiveness of the President's action. The petitioner, by his counsel, urges his discharge from imprisonment.

Article II, Section 2, clause one, of the Constitution, dealing with the powers and duties of the President, closes with these words:

"... and he shall have power to grant Reprieves and Pardons for Offenses against the United States, except in Cases of Impeachment."

The argument for the respondent is that the President's power extends only to offenses against the United States and a contempt of Court is not such an offense, that offenses against the United States are not common law offenses but can only be created by legislative act, that the President's pardoning power is more limited than that of the King of England at common law, which was a broad prerogative and included contempts against his courts chiefly because the judges thereof were his agents and acted in his name; that the context of the Constitution shows that the word "offenses" is used in that instrument only to include crimes and misdemeanors triable by jury and not contempts of the dignity and authority of the federal courts, and that to construe the pardon clause to include contempts of the court would be to violate the fundamental principle of the Constitution in the division of powers between the Legislative, Executive and Judicial branches, and to take from the federal courts their independence and the essential means of protecting their dignity and authority.

The language of the Constitution cannot be interpreted safely except by reference to the common law and to British institutions as they were when the instrument was framed and adopted. . . .

The King of England before our Revolution in the exercise of his prerogative, had always exercised the power to pardon contempts of court, just as he did ordinary crimes and misdemeanors and as he has done to the present day. In the mind of a common law lawyer of the eighteenth century the word pardon included within its scope the ending by the King's grace of the punishment of such derelictions, whether it was imposed by the court without a jury or upon indictment, for both forms of trial for contempts were had. . . .

[The history of the clause shows] that the words "for offenses against the United States" were inserted by a Committee on Style, presumably to make clear that the pardon of the President was to operate upon offenses against the United States as distinguished from offenses against the States. It cannot be supposed that the Committee on Revision by adding these words, or the Convention by accepting them, intended *sub silentio* to narrow the scope of a pardon from one at common law or to confer any different power in this regard on our Executive from that which the members of the Convention had seen exercised before the Revolution.

Nor is there any substance in the contention that there is any substantial difference in this matter between the executive power of pardon in our Government and the King's prerogative. . . .

The power of a court to protect itself and its usefulness by punishing contemnors is of course necessary, but it is one exercised without the restraining influence of a jury and without many of the guarantees which the Bill of Rights offers to protect the individual against unjust conviction. Is it unreasonable to provide for the possibility that the personal element may sometimes enter into a summary judgment pronounced by a judge who thinks his authority is flouted or denied? May it not be fairly said that in order to avoid possible mistake, undue prejudice or needless severity, the chance of pardon should exist at least as much in favor of a person convicted by a judge without a jury as in favor of one convicted in a jury trial?

The rule is made absolute and the petitioner is discharged.

Note

Amnesty. "Although the Constitution vests in the President 'power to grant reprieves and pardons . . .,' this power has never been held to take from Congress the power to pass acts of general amnesty. . . . The distinction between amnesty and pardon is of no practical importance. It is said in *Knote* v. *United States,* 95 US 149, 152, 'the Constitution does not use the word "amnesty," and, except that the term is generally applied where pardon is extended to whole classes or communities, instead of individuals, the distinction between them is one rather of philological interest than of legal importance. ' " *Brown* v. *Walker,* 161 US 591 (1896).

Chapter 3

The Congress

A. INTRODUCTION

"All legislative powers herein granted shall be vested in a Congress of the United States, which shall consist of a Senate and House of Representatives" states the opening sentence of Article I of the Constitution. The framers undoubtedly considered the legislature as the first branch of government. They provided for it in the first article and gave more space to this article than to the other six articles combined. In the shifting of power through the years, the president and the Supreme Court have expanded their power at the expense of Congress, but the separation of powers into three branches of government remains a distinctive feature of the American constitutional system, with the Congress a vital unit of the government in substance as well as form.

Under modern practice, the president takes the lead in initiating the major legislative programs, but the Congress rejects some proposals, modifies others, and gives legitimacy to the proposals that it enacts into law. Congress also exercises a continuous supervision and restraint upon the executive. Every department and agency of government must look to Congress for the appropriation of funds with which to operate, and members of the standing committees of both the House and Senate become experts in chosen fields, capable of effectively scrutinizing requests for funds.

Congress is vested not only with legislative powers but also with extensive nonlegislative powers, including the power to investigate, to approve or disapprove appointments to superior offices, to ratify or disapprove treaties, and to impeach both executive and judicial officers. This is a part of the system of checks and balances associated with the separation-of-powers theory underlying our Constitution.

Separation of Powers

The three most important principles of the American constitutional system are (1) limited government, (2) federalism, and (3) the separation of powers. In a way, federalism and the separation of powers are but means designed by the framers of the Constitution to insure the principle of limited government. The Constitution attempts to keep governmental power under control by dividing it up on a geographic basis between the nation and the states and by conditioning the exercise of power at the national level by a separation of power between the legislative, executive, and judicial branches. The principle of the separation of powers, dating back to Polybius, was popularized in modern times by Montesquieu's famous book, *Spirit of the Laws,* published in 1748. The writings of Montesquieu and of John Locke were highly regarded by the founding fathers in America.

In contrast to the British system of selecting the cabinet from members of Parliament, the American system requires a separation of personnel. "No senator or representative shall, during the time for which he was elected, be appointed to any civil office under the authority of the United States, which shall have been created, or the emoluments whereof shall have been encreased during such time; and no person holding any office under the United States, shall be a member of either house during his continuance in office," states Article I.

In common with the British system, the United States Constitution contains several provisions designed specifically to protect the legislature and its members from interference by the executive and judiciary. Article I states that "Each house shall be the judge of the elections, returns, and qualifications of its own members. . . . Each house may determine the rules of its proceedings . . . and for any speech or debate in either house, they [senators and representatives] shall not be questioned in any other place." Similar provisions in the English Bill of Rights of 1689 marked a victory for the House of Commons in its long struggle with the Tudor and Stuart monarchs for legislative independence.

United States v. *Brewster,* 408 US 501 (1972), held that the Speech or Debate Clause did not bar prosecution of a United States senator for solicitation and acceptance of a bribe. For the majority, the chief justice wrote:

> . . . A legislative act has consistently been defined as an act generally done in Congress in relation to the business before it. In sum, the Speech or Debate Clause prohibits inquiry only into those things generally said or done in the House in the performance of official duties and the motivation for those acts.
>
> It is well known, of course, that Members of the Congress engage in many activities other than the purely legislative activities protected by the Speech and Debate Clause. These include a wide range of legitimate "errands" performed for constituents, the making of appointments with government agencies, assistance in securing government contracts, preparing so-called "news letters" to constituents, news releases, speeches delivered outside the Congress. The range of these related activities has grown over the years. They are performed in part because they have come to be expected by constituents and because they are a means of developing continuing support for future elections. Although these are entirely legitimate activities, they are political in nature rather than legislative, in the sense that term has been used by the Court in prior cases.

But it has never been seriously contended that these political matters, however appropriate, have the protection afforded by the Speech or Debate Clause. . . .

Gravel v. *United States,* 408 US 606 (1972), held that the Speech or Debate Clause applied to a Senator's aide insofar as the aide's conduct was a legislative act. But the clause "does not extend immunity to the Senator's aide from testifying before the grand jury about the alleged arrangement for private publication of the Pentagon Papers, as such publication had no connection with the legislative process."

In *Powell* v. *McCormack,* 395 US 486 (1969) the Court gave little heed to the constitutional clause making each house "the judge of the elections, returns, and qualifications of its own members." The Court itself held that "since Adam Clayton Powell, Jr., was duly elected by the voters of the 18th Congressional District of New York and was not ineligible to serve under any provision of the Constitution, the House was without power to exclude him from its membership."

Flexibility in principle. As already indicated, the division of power between the executive, legislative, and judicial branches of government is not marked by a straight, unwavering line. It was never intended that the three branches of government should constitute watertight compartments. As James Madison expressed it in No. 47 of *The Federalist,* when Montesquieu said: " 'There can be no liberty where the legislative and executive powers are united in the same person, or body of magistrates,' or, 'if the power of judging be not separated from the legislative and executive powers,' he did not mean that these departments ought to have no *partial agency* in, or no *control* over, the acts of each other. His meaning, as his own words import, and still more conclusively as illustrated by the example in his eye, can amount to no more than this, that where the *whole* power of one department is exercised by the same hands which possess the *whole* power of another department, the fundamental principles of a free constitution are subverted."

Delegation of Power

Delegatus non potest delegare (a delegate cannot delegate) was a maxim of the common law, applied primarily in agency cases. An agent holding delegated power could not delegate this power to another unless specifically authorized to do so by his principal. Should a similar rule prevent the legislature of a state from delegating legislative power to the executive or to administrative agencies?

State courts in America have applied such a rule from time to time with varying degrees of flexibility, but the rule has had slight application in the federal courts. By an Act of June 4, 1794, Congress authorized the president to proclaim embargoes against foreign vessels "whenever, in his opinion, the public safety shall so require." This practice, continued in subsequent statutes, was upheld by the Supreme Court in *Cargo of the Brig Aurora* v. *United States,* 7 Cranch 382 (1813); but delegation of quasilegislative power by Congress was used sparingly for the first hundred years. It was the rise of an industrial society and the necessity of extensive governmental regulations in complex areas that led to an extensive delegation of power. In addition to giving the president wide discretion to act on many matters, e.g., the right to vary tariffs, *Hampton & Co.* v. *United States,* 276 US 394 (1928), Congress began in 1887 to create independent agencies charged with the responsibility both of making rules to govern specialized areas and to adjudicate violations of these rules. Congress has prescribed standards for the guidance of these agencies, but the standards have been very broad, leaving much discretion to the agency. Thus, the Interstate Commerce Commission of 1887 is authorized to prescribe "fair and reasonable" transportation rates for interstate commerce; the Federal Trade Commission of 1915 is authorized to prevent "unfair methods of competition in commerce"; and the Federal Communications Commission of 1934 is authorized to grant licenses and regulate broadcasting stations in the light of "public convenience, interest, or necessity."

The independent regulatory commissions have been subjected to more scrutiny by the judiciary in the exercise of their quasijudicial function of adjudicating violations of rules than in their quasilegislative function of making rules. The due process clause of the Constitution is interpreted to require notice and hearing to interested parties before their rights can be adjudicated. There was a vast field of judge-made law on fair play in procedure before the enactment of the Administrative Procedures Act of 1946. However, it is well to emphasize that this judge-made law was based on the due process concept of fair play rather than on the concept of an unconstitutional delegation of power.

In 1935 the Supreme Court held the National Industrial Recovery Act void as an unconstitutional delegation of legislative power to the president. (See *Panama Refining Co.* v. *Ryan,* 293 US 388, and *Schechter Poultry Corporation* v. *United States,* 295 US 495.) This, however, is the only act of Congress ever held void on this basis. *Youngstown Sheet & Tube Co.* v. *Sawyer* (p. 58) and *Humphrey's Executor* v. *United States* (p. 75) mark important limitations on presidential power growing out of the separation of powers doctrine, but in neither of these cases was a delegation of power involved.

Investigations

The Constitution contains no specific clause authorizing Congress to conduct investigations, but this traditional legislative power, first used in 1792 by the House to inquire into the causes of the St. Clair military disaster, has been used throughout our history. In his classic study *Congressional Government* (Boston, 1895, p. 303), Woodrow Wilson wrote: "The informing function of Congress should be preferred even to its legislative function." Through investigations Congress obtains information as a basis for legislation and determines how the laws it has enacted are being enforced. The legislatures of the several states also conduct investigations.

In Great Britain, investigations are conducted by royal commissions composed of persons with special competence in the subject field concerned. American legislatures occasionally authorize an investigation of this type, but, in general, they rely upon their own members to conduct investigations, feeling that the people's chosen representatives are the best "experts" to unearth facts. Each standing committee of the national Senate and House has the duty to "exercise continuous watchfulness of the execution by the administrative agencies concerned of any law, the subject matter of which is within the jurisdiction of such committee," and a number of the standing committees have authority by subpoena to require the attendance of witnesses and the production of records. In addition to investigations by the standing committees and their subcommittees, special committees are created for a particular investigation by both houses of Congress from time to time, and occasionally the two houses create a joint committee for a special investigation.

The power of Congress to investigate is supported by its power to punish for contempt of its authority. This power was recognized by the Supreme Court in *Anderson* v. *Dunn,* 6 Wheaton 204 (1821). The House of Representatives by resolution had ordered the arrest of Anderson for attempting to bribe one of its members. His arrest and imprisonment was by the sergeant-at-arms of the House. In 1857 Congress passed a statute providing that "contumacy in a witness called to testify in a matter properly under consideration by either House, and deliberately refusing to answer questions pertinent thereto, shall be a misdemeanor against the United States." 2 USC 192.

Congressional committees of investigation are limited by the terms of the resolutions creating them, including the amount of money appropriated for their use. They are also limited (1) by the immunity of the president and, by his order, other executive officials, and (2) by the imposition of restraints by the courts through their enforcement of the separation of powers principle and the constitutional provisions on self-incrimination and on free speech and assembly.

Immunity of executive officers. In the famous *Marbury* v. *Madison* case, Mr. Lincoln, a former acting secretary of state, when called as a witness by the Court, said that he would reveal any information that came to him as a "ministerial officer" but, as to facts which came to him "in the capacity of an agent to the President," he was not bound to answer. The Court said "if he thought that any thing was communicated to him in confidence he was not bound to disclose it."

President Jefferson refused to be bound by the subpoena *duces tecum* issued by Chief Justice Marshall in the trial of Aaron Burr. He reserved "the necessary right of the President of the US to decide, independently of all other authority, what papers, coming to him as President, the public interests permit to be communicated, & to whom. . . ." Would not the independence of the president be lost "if the several courts could bandy him from pillar to post, keep him constantly trudging from north to south & east to west, and withdraw him entirely from his constitutional duties?" Albert J. Beveridge, *The Life of John Marshall* (Boston, 1919), vol. III, pp. 430–69.

From the Burr trial of 1807 to the year 1973, no subpoena was issued to the president. But during the Watergate episode of 1973 Special Prosecutor Cox secured from the District Court of the District of Columbia a subpoena ordering President Nixon to submit certain records for in camera inspection to determine if they contained information pertinent to a grand jury investigation. The Court of Appeals of the District sustained the district court, ruling in *Nixon* v. *Sirica,* 42 Law Week 2211, as follows: "We acknowledge that wholesale access to executive deliberations and documents would cripple the Executive as a co-equal branch. But this is an argument for recognizing Executive privilege and for according it great weight, not for making the Executive the judge of its own privilege." Dissenting, Judge Wilkey wrote: "The critical issue on which I part company with my five colleagues is, in the shortest terms, Who decides?" Compare *United States* v. *Nixon,* p. 60.

On February 6, 1974, the House of Representatives "*Resolved,* That the Committee on the Judiciary . . . is authorized and directed to investigate fully and completely whether sufficient grounds exist for the House of Representatives to exercise its constitutional power to impeach Richard M. Nixon, President of the United States of America. . . . For the purpose of making such investigation, the committee is authorized to require . . . by subpoena or otherwise . . . the attendance and testimony of any person . . . and . . . the production of such things . . . as it deems necessary to such investigation." H. Res. 803 (1974). Confrontation between the House Committee on the Judiciary and President Nixon appeared imminent.

While cases dealing with subpoenas by the courts to the president are few, there are many examples of refusal by the president to supply information requested by a committee of one of the houses of Congress. In 1825 President Monroe declined to comply with a request by the House of Representatives for papers lest their publication do an injustice to a naval officer still at sea. The doctrine that executive officers cannot be forced to divulge information when the president thinks divulgence would be against the public interest is well established. Having set up a Loyalty Review Board in the executive branch of the government, on March 15, 1949, President Truman issued a general order forbidding any executive department or agency to furnish information concerning the loyalty of its members to any committee of Congress. And in 1954, during the controversy between the Army and Senator McCarthy, President Eisenhower instructed members of the Department of the Army not to testify before the Senate's Permanent Subcommittee on Investigations concerning communications between executive employees. There are no cases of executive officers being subpoenaed to testify before a congressional committee when restrained from testifying by orders of the president. See Edward S. Corwin, *The President: Office and Powers* (New York, 1957), pp. 110–18.

Judicially enforced restraints. In *Kilbourn* v. *Thompson,* 103 US 168 (1881), the Supreme Court ordered the release of a person held in prison for alleged contempt in refusing to testify before a committee of the House of Representatives investigating the bankruptcy of Jay Cook & Company, in which the United States had funds deposited. The committee was delving into a private real estate pool forming part of the company's financial structure. The basis of the decision was that the investigation related to "a matter wherein relief or redress could be had only in a judicial proceeding" instead of to legislation and was hence beyond the scope of congressional power. However, the line of division between what does and what does not relate to matters within the scope of congressional power is by no means clear, and in most of the cases involving investigations prior to 1957 congressional power was sustained. Notable among these was *McGrain* v. *Daugherty,* 273 US 135 (1927). A Senate committee was investigating scandals in naval oil releases and other matters under President Harding's administration. Mally S. Daugherty, brother of the attorney general, was cited for contempt in refusing to testify. In sustaining his conviction the Court held: "It is quite true that the resolution directing the investigation does not in terms avow that it is intended to be in aid of legislation. . . . Plainly [however] the subject was one on which legislation could be had and would be materially aided by the information which the investigation was calculated to elicit."

Limitations upon the power of Congress to investigate based upon the First Amendment are discussed in chapter 9, sec. 3; limitations growing out of the self-incrimination clause of the Fifth Amendment are in chapter 12, sec. C.

Federalism

Following the Declaration of Independence, the former British colonies in America became, to a large extent, sovereign states. They were joined together in a loose union under the Articles of Confederation before the Revolutionary War was over, but the national government thus created was weak and ineffective, lacking the power to levy taxes or to regulate commerce. The Federal Convention of 1787 was called to remedy these defects. The Constitution of the United States which it wrote strengthened the national government, but it by no means made the states creatures of the national government.

In the federal union established by the Constitution, the powers of government are divided between the national government and the state governments. The Constitution lists in Article I, Section 8, the powers of Congress: "The Congress shall have power to lay and collect taxes. . . . To borrow money. . . . To regulate commerce with foreign nations and among the several states. . . ." and so on. This enumeration closes with the broad delegation of power "To make all laws which shall be necessary and proper for carrying into execution the foregoing powers. . . ." The powers not delegated to the national government were reserved to the states.

The proper division of power between the national government and the state governments has been a topic of debate throughout our history. Charles A. Beard labeled the persistent difference of opinion on this subject as "the orthodox theory of American party difference." That the controversy over states' rights versus centralized government should have spilled over into the judiciary is not suprising, for, as Alexis de Tocqueville wrote in his *Democracy in America* in 1834, "Scarcely any political question arises in the United States that is not resolved, sooner or later, into a judicial question."

As chief justice of the United States from 1801 to 1835, John Marshall made the most of his opportunity to strengthen the powers of the national government. His ability to articulate basic principles was exceptional, and his opinions are quoted with approval to this day. His masterful statement in *McCulloch* v. *Maryland* is presented in this chapter.

Regulation of Commerce

The controversy over states' rights was waged in the courts most frequently under the commerce clause. The power conferred by the Constitution upon Congress to regulate commerce is sometimes described as a two-edged sword. It operates in a positive way to sustain congressional legislation and in a negative way to cut down state regulations that burden interstate commerce. The section in this chapter on commerce opens with *Gibbons* v. *Ogden,* a case in which a state act in conflict with a congressional regulation is held to be void, but the other cases included deal with the positive aspect of congressional power over commerce. The negative aspect is developed more fully in chapter 4.

Throughout most of our history the Supreme Court has sustained whatever regulations of commerce Congress has adopted, but in *United States* v. *E. C. Knight Co.,* 156 US 1 (1895), it held that the Sherman Antitrust Act could not be applied to manufacturing. Judicial pronouncement that manufacturing was subject to state and not national control reached its most dogmatic statement in *Hammer* v. *Dagenhart* (1918) and continued as a factor in our law until 1937. However, in *National Labor Relations Board* v. *Jones & Laughlin Steel Corporation,* 301 US 1 (1937), the Court recognized that "interstate commerce . . . is a practical concept" and that one of "the plainest facts of our national life" is that conditions affecting manufacturing necessarily affect commerce. Since 1937 no act of Congress regulating commerce has been invalidated by the judiciary.

Fiscal Powers

The Constitution vests broad fiscal powers in Congress. One of the few specific limitations upon its taxing powers is the provision that "No capitation or other direct tax shall be laid, unless in proportion to the census or enumeration hereinbefore directed to be taken." A "direct tax" is frequently defined as a tax of which the incidence, or burden, falls on the person upon whom the tax is laid and cannot be easily shifted to another as can an indirect tax such as a stamp tax, which is ultimately shifted to the consumer. Notable examples of direct taxes are taxes on land and buildings. But what of an income tax? The ruling by the Court in *Pollock* v. *Farmers' Loan and Trust Co.,* 158 US 601 (1895), that an income tax was a direct tax that would have to be apportioned among the states led to the adoption of the Sixteenth Amendment in 1913.

The power of Congress to appropriate funds for such purposes as it deems necessary for the general welfare has not been a serious problem in adjudication. The decision in *United States* v. *Butler,* 297 US 1 (1936), holding void the Agricultural Adjustment Act of 1933 with its program of parity payments to farmers, marked a temporary departure from the mainstream of judicial opinion in this area. A revised Agricultural Adjustment Act was sustained in *Mulford* v. *Smith,* 307 US 38 (1939). Leading cases sustaining the Social Security Act of 1935 are *Steward Machine Co.* v. *Davis,* 301 US 548 (1937) and *Helvering* v. *Davis,* 301 US 619 (1937).

An area of uncertainty regarding the fiscal powers of Congress lies in the possible conflict between fiscal regulations and individual rights, particularly the right against self-incrimination. Recent cases on this subject are presented in chapter 12.

Treaties

The "elastic clause" relied upon by Chief Justice Marshall in the *McCulloch* case vests Congress with power to make all laws necessary and proper for carrying into execution not only the powers enumerated but also "all other powers vested by this Constitution in the Government of the United States, or in any department or officer thereof." Article II authorizes the president to make treaties, "by and with the advice and consent of the Senate. . . ."

Missouri v. *Holland,* 252 US 416 (1920), raised the question of whether the United States could acquire power through a treaty which it could not exercise in the absence of the treaty. In an earlier case, *United States* v. *Shauver,* 214 Fed. 154, a district court had held void a congressional act designed to protect migratory birds. The basis of the decision had been that migratory birds were owned by the states, and not subject to control by Congress. The decision was not reviewed by the Supreme Court.

Subsequently, the United States entered a treaty with Great Britain under the terms of which the United States and Canada were to enforce closed seasons and other protections for migratory birds. Congress then passed the Migratory Bird Treaty Act of 1918. The state of Missouri sought to restrain Holland, a United States game warden, from enforcing the act.

In the opinion of the Court sustaining the act, Justice Holmes wrote: "Acts of Congress are the supreme law of the land only when made in pursuance of the Constitution, while treaties are declared to be so when made under the authority of the United States. It is open to question whether the authority of the United States means more than the formal acts prescribed to make the convention." Despite Holmes' warning that "We do not mean to imply that there are no qualifications to the treaty power," his opinion gave rise to speculation that treaties could be made that violate the Constitution. In 1953 Senator Bricker sponsored an amendment which would have specifically subordinated treaties and executive agreements to the Constitution. Interest in such an amendment subsided in 1957 when *Reid* v. *Covert,* 354 US 1, held that treaties were subordinate to the Constitution. "The reason treaties were not limited to those made in 'pursuance' of the Constitution was so that agreements made by the United States under the Articles of Confederation . . . would remain in effect" wrote Justice Black.

Protection of Civil Rights

The term "civil rights" is sometimes used to designate rights of individuals secured by the Constitution against encroachment by the government. For example, the First Amendment provides that "Congress shall make no law respecting an establishment of religion, or prohibiting the free exercise thereof"; and the Fourteenth Amendment provides that "No State shall make or enforce any law which shall abridge the privileges or immunities of citizens of the United States. . . ." At other times the term "civil rights" is used to designate rights of individuals, particularly members of minority ethnic groups, protected by the government against abuse by other individuals. For example, the Civil Rights Act of 1964 provided that all persons shall be entitled to equal services in public accommodations without discrimination because of race. Both aspects of the subject are covered extensively in Part II of this text. However, a few cases illustrating the power of Congress to pass legislation protecting civil rights are included in this chapter.

While not designated as civil-rights acts, Congress has long used its delegated powers, particularly the commerce power, to protect individuals against damage from other individuals. The White Slave Act, the Federal Kidnaping Act, the Fair Labor Standards Act, and the Pure Food and Drug Act are familiar examples. But it is legislation to protect members of minority ethnic groups, particularly blacks, that has been the subject of most controversy and litigation.

The Civil War was followed by the enactment of the Thirteenth, Fourteenth, and Fifteenth Amendments to the Constitution. Each of these articles of amendment has a concluding paragraph reading as follows: "Congress shall have power to enforce this Article by appropriate legislation."

In the *Slaughterhouse Cases* of 1872, the first case in which the Supreme Court dealt with the post–Civil War amendments, Justice Miller wrote: "We repeat, then, in the light of this recapitulation of events, almost too recent to be called history, but which are familiar to us all; and on the most casual examination of the language of these amendments, no one can fail to be impressed with the one pervading purpose found in them all, lying at the foundation of each, and without which none of them would have been even suggested; we mean the freedom of the slave race, the security and firm establishment of that freedom, and the protection of the newly-made freeman and citizen from the oppressions of those who had formerly exercised unlimited dominion over him. It is true that only the fifteenth amendment, in terms, mentions the negro by speaking of his color and his slavery. But it is just as true that each of the other articles was addressed to the grievances of that race, and designed to remedy them as the fifteenth."

Civil rights acts.   In the decade following the Civil War, Congress passed four major civil rights acts. An act of 1866 (14 Stat 27) declared all persons born in the United States to be citizens thereof, entitled to the right "to make and enforce contracts . . . and to full and equal benefit of all laws . . . for the security of person and property, as is enjoyed by white citizens. . . ." An act of 1870 (16 Stat 140) was designed primarily to implement the voting right established by the Fifteenth Amendment, but it contained a section making it a felony for two or more persons to conspire to "oppress, threaten, or intimidate any citizen with the intent to prevent or hinder his free exercise and enjoyment of any right or privilege granted or secured to him by the Constitution or laws of the United States. . . ." An Act of 1871 (17 Stat 13), popularly known as the Ku Klux Klan Act, authorized civil actions for the recovery of damages and also criminal penalties against "two or more persons . . . [who] go in disguise on the highways or on the premises of another, for the purpose of depriving . . . any person or class of persons of the equal protection of the laws, or of equal privileges and immunities under the laws. . . ." An Act of 1875 (18 Stat 335) sought to admit blacks to "public accommodations." It provided that "all persons within the jurisdiction of the United States shall be entitled to the full and equal enjoyment of the accommodations, advantages, facilities, and privileges of inns, public conveyances on land or water, theatres, and other places of public amusement; subject only to the conditions and limitations established by law, and applicable alike to citizens of every race and color, regardless of any previous condition of servitude."

Most of this legislation was emasculated by the Supreme Court within a few years after its enactment. In the *Civil Rights Cases* of 1883 the Court held that the prohibitions of the Fourteenth Amendment applied to state action only and not to discrimination by one individual against another individual, even in public accommodations. Moreover, the Court held that the legislation authorized by Congress to enforce the Fourteenth Amendment "is not *direct* legislation on the matters respecting which the States are prohibited from making or enforcing certain laws . . . but is *corrective* legislation, such as may be necessary or proper for counteracting and redressing the effect of such laws or acts." Fragments of these early civil rights laws in effect in 1974 are given in chapter 7, pages 208–25.

For almost a century after this case, Congress passed no major new civil rights acts. The effectiveness of the Thirteenth, Fourteenth, and Fifteenth Amendments was confined largely to such force as the judiciary saw fit to apply to the constitutional provisions as self-executing, unaided by statute.

In *Nixon* v. *Herndon,* 272 US 536 (1927), the Supreme Court held void a Texas statute providing that "in no event shall a Negro be eligible to participate in a Democratic primary election." Attempts by Texas and other southern states to preserve the Democratic white primary by repealing all laws regulating primaries were foiled by the Court. "State action" was given an expanded concept. In 1944 in *Smith* v. *Allwright* the Court held primaries to be an integral part of the election process and subject to the Fourteenth Amendment's prohibition against racial discrimination. Four years later in *Shelley* v. *Kraemer,* the Court held that the enforcement by a state court of a private contract containing a racial covenant on occupancy of property was state action, prohibited by the Fourteenth Amendment. By 1957, the date of the first civil rights act of the twentieth century, the Court was well on its way toward formulating a broad range of judge-made law on civil rights, including the rule against racial discrimination in public schools established in *Brown* v. *Board of Education* (1954).

In the thirteen-year period from 1957 to 1970, Congress passed six major civil rights acts. The acts of 1957, 1960, 1965, and 1970 were largely voter rights acts. The act of 1964 was the public accommodations act, and the act of 1968 was the open housing act. Cases explaining the major portions of these acts are included in section D of this chapter.

McCulloch v. Maryland

4 Wheaton 316, 4 L Ed 570 (1819)

The act incorporating the Bank of the United States is a law made in pursuance of the Constitution. The law of Maryland imposing a tax on the operations of the bank is unconstitutional.

[Establishment of the Bank of the United States was a matter of political controversy, and the Bank was opposed in some regions. In 1818 the state of Maryland sought to tax the Bank by enacting a statute requiring that all bank notes issued by any bank in Maryland, except banks chartered by Maryland, should be issued on stamped paper to be purchased from Maryland. James McCulloch, cashier of the Baltimore branch of the Bank of the United States, issued bank notes that were not on the stamped paper, and Maryland brought and won an action for debt against him in the state courts. The case went to the United States Supreme Court by writ of error.]

MARSHALL, C. J., delivered the opinion of the court. . . .

The first question made in the cause is, has congress power to incorporate a bank? . . .

Although, among the enumerated powers of government, we do not find the word "bank," or "incorporation," we find the great powers to lay and collect taxes; to borrow money; to regulate commerce; to declare and conduct a war; and to raise and support armies and navies. The sword and the purse, all the external relations, and no inconsiderable portion of the industry of the nation, are intrusted to its government. It can never

[handwritten margin note: Inherent powers]

be pretended that these vast powers draw after them others of inferior importance, merely because they are inferior. Such an idea can never be advanced. But it may, with great reason, be contended, that a government, intrusted with such ample powers, on the due execution of which the happiness and prosperity of the nation so vitally depends, must also be intrusted with ample means for their execution. . . .

But the constitution of the United States has not left the right of congress to employ the necessary means, for the execution of the powers conferred on the government, to general reasoning. To its enumeration of powers is added that of making "all laws which shall be necessary and proper, for carrying into execution the foregoing powers, and all other powers vested by this constitution, in the government of the United States, or in any department thereof." . . .

To employ the means necessary to an end, is generally understood as employing any means calculated to produce the end, and not as being confined to those single means, without which the end would be entirely unattainable. Such is the character of human language, that no word conveys to the mind, in all situations, one single definite idea; and nothing is more common than to use words in a figurative sense. Almost all compositions contain words, which, taken in their rigorous sense, would convey a meaning different from that which is obviously intended. . . .

We admit, as all must admit, that the powers of the government are limited, and that its limits are not to be transcended. But we think the sound construction of the constitution must allow to the national legislature that discretion, with respect to the means by which the powers it confers are to be carried into execution, which will enable that body to perform the high duties assigned to it, in the manner most beneficial to the people. Let the end be legitimate, let it be within the scope of the constitution, and all means which are appropriate, which are plainly adapted to that end, which are not prohibited, but consist with the letter and spirit of the constitution, are constitutional. . . .

After the most deliberate consideration, it is the unanimous and decided opinion of this court that the act to incorporate the Bank of the United States is a law made in pursuance of the constitution, and is a part of the supreme law of the land. . . .

It being the opinion of the court that the act incorporating the bank is constitutional, and that the power of establishing a branch in the State of Maryland might be properly exercised by the bank itself, we proceed to inquire:—

2. Whether the State of Maryland may, without violating the constitution, tax that branch? . . .

[handwritten margin note: power to tax power to destroy / is power useless]

That the power to tax involves the power to destroy; that the power to destroy may defeat and render useless the power to create; that there is a plain repugnance, in conferring on one government a power to control the constitutional measures of another, which other, with respect to those very measures, is declared to be supreme over that which exerts the control, are propositions not to be denied. But all inconsistencies are to be reconciled by the magic of the word confidence. Taxation, it is said, does not necessarily and unavoidably destroy. To carry it to the excess of destruction would be an abuse, to presume which, would banish that confidence which is essential to all government.

But is this a case of confidence? Would the people of any one State trust those of another with a power to control the most insignificant operations of their state government? We know they would not. Why, then, should we suppose that the people of any one State should be willing to trust those of another with a power to control the operations of a government to which they have confided their most important and most valuable interest? In the legislature of the Union alone are all represented. The legislature of the Union alone, therefore, can be trusted by the people with the power of controlling measures which concern all, in the confidence that it will not be abused. This, then, is not a case of confidence, and we must consider it as it really is. . . .

If the States may tax one instrument employed by the government in the execution of its powers they may tax any and every other instrument. They may tax the mail; they may tax the mint; they may tax patent rights; they may tax the papers of the customhouse; they may tax judicial process; they may tax all the means employed by the government, to an excess which would defeat all the ends of government. This was not intended by the American people. They did not design to make their government dependent on the States. . . .

It has also been insisted, that, as the power of taxation in the general and state governments is acknowledged to be concurrent, every argument which would sustain the right of the general government to tax banks chartered by the States, will equally sustain the right of the States to tax banks chartered by the general government.

But the two cases are not on the same reason. The people of all the States have created the general government, and have conferred upon it the general power of taxation. The people of all the States, and the States themselves, are represented in congress, and, by their representatives, exercise this power. When they tax the chartered institutions of the States, they tax their constituents; and these taxes must be uniform. But, when a State taxes the operations of the government of the United States, it acts upon institutions created, not by their own constituents, but by people over whom they claim no control. It acts upon the measures of a government created by others as well as themselves, for the benefit of others in common with themselves. The difference is that which always exists, and always must exist, between the action of the whole on a part, and the action of a part on the whole; between the laws of a government declared to be supreme, and those of a government which, when in opposition to those laws, is not supreme. . . .

[The judgment of the Court of Appeals of Maryland against McCulloch was reversed.]

B. REGULATION OF COMMERCE

Gibbons v. Ogden

9 Wheaton 1, 6 L Ed 23 (1824)

Commerce among the states does not stop at the external boundary line of each state but may be introduced into the interior. A state regulation in conflict with a congressional regulation of interstate commerce is void.

[In recognition of advancements made by them in steam navigation, in 1808 the New York legislature granted to Robert L. Livingston and Robert Fulton the exclusive right to operate steamboats in New York for a period of thirty years. Under an assignment from Livingston and Fulton, Aaron Ogden operated a steamboat line between Elizabethtown, New Jersey, and New York City. Thomas Gibbons opened a steamboat line in competition to Ogden, and Ogden obtained an injunction from the New York Court of Chancery restraining Gibbons from operating his steamboats. The New York Court for the Correction of Errors sustained the injunction. Gibbons, who held a coasting license from the United States, appealed this decree to the Supreme Court of the United States.]

CHIEF JUSTICE MARSHALL delivered the opinion of the Court. . . .

The appellant contends that this decree is erroneous, because the laws which purport to give the exclusive privilege it sustains, are repugnant to the constitution and laws of the United States.

They are said to be repugnant:

1. To that clause in the constitution which authorizes Congress to regulate commerce. . . .

To what commerce does this power extend? The constitution informs us, to commerce "with foreign nations, and among the several states, and with the Indian tribes."

It has, we believe, been universally admitted that these words comprehend every species of commercial intercourse between the United States and foreign nations. No sort of trade can be carried on between this country and any other, to which this power does not extend. It has been truly said, that commerce, as the word is used in the constitution, is a unit, every part of which is indicated by the term.

If this be the admitted meaning of the word, in its application to foreign nations, it must carry the same meaning throughout the sentence, and remain a unit, unless there be some plain intelligible cause which alters it.

The subject to which the power is next applied is to commerce "among the several states." The word "among" means intermingled with. A thing which is among others, is intermingled with them. Commerce among the states cannot stop at the external boundary line of each state, but may be introduced into the interior.

It is not intended to say that these words comprehend that commerce which is completely internal, which is carried on between man and man in a state, or between different parts of the same state, and which does not extend to or affect other states. Such a power would be inconvenient, and is certainly unnecessary. . . .

We are now arrived at the inquiry, what is this power?

It is the power to regulate; that is, to prescribe the rule by which commerce is to be governed. This power, like all others vested in Congress, is complete in itself, may be exercised to its utmost extent, and acknowledges no limitations, other than are prescribed in the constitution. These are expressed in plain terms, and do not affect the questions which arise in this case, or which have been discussed at the bar. If, as has always been understood, the sovereignty of Congress, though limited to specified objects, is plenary as to those objects, the power over commerce with foreign nations, and among the several States, is vested in Congress as absolutely as it would be in a single government, having in its constitution the same restrictions on the exercise of the power as are found in the constitution of the United States. The wisdom and the discretion of Congress, their identity with the people, and the influence which their constituents possess at elections, are, in this, as in many other instances, as that, for example, of declaring war, the sole restraints on which they have relied, to secure them from its abuse. They are the restraints on which the people must often rely solely, in all representative governments. . . .

But it has been urged with great earnestness, that although the power of Congress to regulate commerce with foreign nations, and among the several states, be coextensive with the subject itself, and have no other limits than are prescribed in the constitution, yet the states may severally exercise the same power within their respective jurisdictions. In support of this argument, it is said that they possessed it as an inseparable attribute of sovereignty, before the formation of the constitution, and still retain it, except so far as they have surrendered it by that instrument; that this principle results from the nature of the government, and is secured by the tenth amendment; that an affirmative grant of power is not exclusive, unless in its own nature it be such that the continued exercise of it by the former possessor is inconsistent with the grant, and that this is not of that description.

The appellant, conceding these postulates, except the last, contends that full power to regulate a particular subject, implies the whole power, and leaves no residuum; that a grant of the whole is incompatible with the existence of a right in another to any part of it. . . .

It has been contended by the counsel for the appellant, that, as the word "to regulate" implies in its nature, full power over the thing to be regulated, it excludes, necessarily, the action of all others that would perform the same operation on the same thing. That regulation is designed for the entire result, applying to those parts which remain as they were, as well as to those which are altered. It produces a uniform whole, which is as much disturbed and deranged by changing what the regulating power designs to leave untouched, as that on which it has operated.

There is great force in this argument, and the court is not satisfied that it has been refuted.

Since, however, in exercising the power of regulating their own purely internal affairs, whether of trading or police, the states may sometimes enact laws, the validity of which depends on their interfering with, and being contrary to, an act of Congress passed in pursuance of the constitution, the court will enter upon the inquiry, whether the laws of New York, as expounded by the highest tribunal of that state, have, in their application to this case, come into collision with an act of Congress, and deprived a citizen of a right to which that act entitles him. . . .

This act demonstrates the opinion of Congress that steamboats may be enrolled and licensed, in common with vessels using sails. They are, of course, entitled to the same privileges, and can no more be restrained from navigating waters, and entering ports which are free to such vessels, than if they were wafted on their voyage by the winds, instead of being propelled by the agency of fire. The one element may be as legitimately used as the other, for every commercial purpose authorized by the laws of the Union; and the act of a state inhibiting the use of either to any vessel having a license under the act of Congress, comes, we think, in direct collision with that act. . . .

[The concurring opinion of JUSTICE JOHNSON is omitted.]

DECREE. . . . This Court is therefore of opinion, that the decree of the Court of New York for the Trial of Impeachments and the Correction of Errors, affirming the decree of the Chancellor of that State, which perpetually enjoins the said Thomas Gibbons, the appellant, from navigating the waters of the State of New York with the steamboats the Stoudinger and the Bellona, by steam or fire, is erroneous, and ought to be reversed, and the same is hereby reversed and annulled. And this Court doth further direct, order and decree, that the bill of the said Aaron Ogden be dismissed, and the same is hereby dismissed accordingly.

The Shreveport Rate Case

[*Houston, E.&W. Texas Ry. Co.* v. *United States*]

234 US 342, 34 S Ct 833, 58 L Ed2d 1341 (1914)

> Whenever the interstate and intrastate transactions of carriers are so related that the government of the one involves the control of the other, Congress is entitled to prescribe the final and dominant role.

MR. JUSTICE HUGHES delivered the opinion of the Court.

These suits were brought in the Commerce Court by the Houston, East & West Texas Railway Company and the Houston & Shreveport Railroad Company, and by the Texas & Pacific Railway Company, respectively, to set aside an order of the Interstate Commerce Commission, dated March 11, 1912, upon the ground that it exceeded the Commission's authority. . . . The petitions were dismissed. 205 F. 380.

The order of the Interstate Commerce Commission was made in a proceeding initiated in March, 1911, by the Railroad Commission of Louisiana. The complaint was that the appellants, and other interstate carriers, maintained unreasonable rates from Shreveport, Louisiana, to various points in Texas, and further, that these carriers, in the adjustment of rates over their respective lines, unjustly discriminated in favor of traffic within the state of Texas, and against similar traffic between Louisiana and Texas. . . .

The gravamen of the complaint, said the Interstate Commerce Commission, was that the carriers made rates out of Dallas and other Texas points into eastern Texas which were much lower than those which they extended into Texas from Shreveport. The situation may be briefly described: Shreveport, Louisiana, is about 40 miles from the Texas state line, and 231 miles from Houston, Texas, on the line of the Houston, East & West Texas and Houston & Shreveport Companies (which are affiliated in interest); it is 189 miles from Dallas, Texas, on the line of the Texas & Pacific. Shreveport competes with both cities for the trade of the intervening territory. The rates on these lines from Dallas and Houston, respectively, eastward to intermediate points in Texas, were much less, according to distance, than from Shreveport westward to the same points. It is undisputed that the difference was substantial, and injuriously affected the commerce of Shreveport. It appeared, for example, that a rate of 60 cents carried first-class traffic a distance of 160 miles to the eastward from Dallas, while the same rate would carry the same class of traffic only 55 miles into Texas from Shreveport. . . .

The Interstate Commerce Commission found that the interstate class rates out of Shreveport to named Texas points were unreasonable, and it established maximum class rates for this traffic. These rates, we understand, were substantially the same as the class rates fixed by the Railroad Commission of Texas, and charged by the carriers, for transportation for similar distances in that state. The Interstate Commerce Commission also found that the carriers maintained "higher rates from Shreveport to points in Texas" than were in force "from cities in Texas to such points under substantially similar conditions and circumstances," and that thereby "an unlawful and undue preference and advantage" was given to the Texas cities, and a "discrimination" that was "undue and unlawful" was effected against Shreveport. In order to correct this discrimination, the carriers were directed to desist from charging higher rates for the transportation of any commodity from Shreveport to Dallas and Houston, respectively, and intermediate points, than were contemporaneously charged for the carriage of such commodity from Dallas and Houston toward Shreveport for equal distances, as the Commission found that relation of rates to be reasonable. . . . The report states that under this order it will be the duty of the companies "to duly and justly equalize the terms and conditions" upon which they will extend "transportation to traffic of a similar character, moving into Texas from Shreveport, with that moving wholly within Texas," but that, in effecting such equalization, the class scale rates as prescribed shall not be exceeded. . . .

The point of the objection to the order is that, as the discrimination found by the Commission to be unjust arises out of the relation of intrastate rates, maintained under state authority, to interstate rates that have been upheld as reasonable, its correction was beyond the Commission's power. Manifestly the order might be complied with, and the discrimination avoided, either by reducing the interstate rate from Shreveport to the level of the competing intrastate rates, or by raising these intrastate rates to the level of the interstate rates, or by such reduction in the one case and increase in the other as would result in equality. . . . The invalidity of the order in this aspect is challenged upon two grounds:

(1) That Congress is important to control the intrastate charges of an interstate carrier even to the extent necessary to prevent injurious discrimination against interstate traffic; and

(2) That, if it be assumed that Congress has this power, still it has not been exercised and hence the action of the Commission exceeded the limits of the authority which has been conferred upon it. . . .

Congress is empowered to regulate,—that is, to provide the law for the government of interstate commerce; to enact "all appropriate legislation" for its "protection and advancement." . . . Whenever the interstate and intrastate transactions of carriers are so related that the government of the one involves the control of the other, it is Congress, and not the State, that is entitled to prescribe the final and dominant rule, for otherwise Congress would be denied the exercise of its constitutional authority, and the State, and not the Nation, would be supreme within the national field. . . .

. . . The use of the instrument of interstate commerce in a discriminatory manner so as to inflict injury upon that commerce, or some part thereof, furnishes abundant ground for Federal intervention. Nor can the attempted exercise of state authority alter the matter, where Congress has acted, for a State may not authorize the carrier to do that which Congress is entitled to forbid and has forbidden. . . .

It is also clear that, in removing the injurious discriminations against interstate traffic arising from the relation of intrastate to interstate rates, Congress is not bound to reduce the latter below what it may deem to be a proper standard, fair to the carrier and to the public. Otherwise, it could prevent the injury to interstate commerce only by the sacrifice of its judgment as to interstate rates. Congress is entitled to maintain its own standard as to these rates, and to forbid any discriminatory action by interstate carriers which will obstruct the freedom of movement of interstate traffic over their lines in accordance with the terms it establishes.

Having this power, Congress could provide for its execution through the aid of a subordinate body; and we conclude that the order of the Commission now in question cannot be held invalid upon the ground that it exceeded the authority which Congress could lawfully confer. . . .

Affirmed.

Mr. Justice Lurton and Mr. Justice Pitney dissent.

Hammer v. Dagenhart

247 US 251, 38 S Ct 529, 62 L Ed 1101 (1918)

The manufacture of goods is not commerce, nor does the fact that they are intended for, and are afterwards shipped in interstate commerce make their production a part of that commerce subject to the control of Congress.

Mr. Justice Day delivered the opinion of the Court.

A bill was filed in the United States District Court for the Western District of North Carolina by a father in his own behalf and as next friend of his two minor sons, one under the age of fourteen years and the other between the ages of fourteen and sixteen years, employees in a cotton mill at Charlotte, North Carolina, to enjoin the enforcement of the act of Congress intended to prevent interstate commerce in the products of child labor.

The District Court held the act unconstitutional and entered a decree enjoining its enforcement. This appeal brings the case here. . . .

The controlling question for decision is: Is it within the authority of Congress in regulating commerce among the States to prohibit the transportation in interstate commerce of manufactured goods, the product of a factory in which, within thirty days prior to their removal therefrom, children under the age of fourteen have been employed or permitted to work, or children between the ages of fourteen and sixteen years have been employed or permitted to work more than eight hours in any day, or more than six days in any week, or after the hour of 7 o'clock P.M. or before the hour of 6 o'clock A.M.?

The power essential to the passage of this act, the Government contends, is found in the commerce clause of the Constitution which authorizes Congress to regulate commerce with foreign nations and among the States.

In *Gibbons* v. *Ogden* . . . Chief Justice Marshall, speaking for this court, and defining the extent and nature of the commerce power, said, "It is the power to regulate; that is, to prescribe the rule by which commerce is to be governed." In other words, the power is one to control the means by which commerce is carried on, which is directly the contrary of the assumed right to forbid commerce from moving and thus destroy it as to particular commodities. But it is insisted that adjudged cases in this court establish the doctrine that the power to regulate given to Congress incidentally includes the authority to prohibit the movement of ordinary commodities and therefore that the subject is not open for discussion. The cases demonstrate the contrary. They rest upon the character of the particular subjects dealt with and the fact that the scope of governmental authority, state or national, possessed over them is such that the authority to prohibit is as to them but the exertion of the power to regulate.

The first of these cases is *Champion* v. *Ames,* 188 US 321, the so-called Lottery Case, in which it was held that Congress might pass a law having the effect to keep the channels of commerce free from use in the transportation of tickets used in the promotion of lottery schemes. In *Hipolite Egg Co.* v. *United States,* 220 US 45, this court sustained the power of Congress to pass the Pure Food and Drug Act which prohibited the introduction into the States by means of interstate commerce of impure foods and drugs. In *Hoke* v. *United States,* 227 US 308, this court sustained the constitutionality of the so-called "White Slave Traffic Act" whereby the transportation of a woman in interstate commerce for the purpose of prostitution was forbidden. . . .

In each of these instances the use of interstate transportation was necessary to the accomplishment of harmful results. In other words, although the power over interstate transportation was to regulate, that could only be accomplished by prohibiting the use of the facilities of interstate commerce to effect the evil intended.

This element is wanting in the present case. The thing intended to be accomplished by this statute is the denial of the facilities of interstate commerce to those manufacturers in the States who employ children within the prohibited ages. The act in its effect does not regulate transportation among the States, but aims to standardize the ages at which children may be employed in mining and manufacturing within the States. The goods shipped are of themselves harmless. The act permits them to be freely shipped after thirty days from the time of their removal from the factory. When offered for shipment, and before transportation begins, the labor of their production is over, and the mere fact that they were intended for interstate commerce transportation does not make their production subject to federal control under the commerce power. . . .

It is further contended that the authority of Congress may be exerted to control interstate commerce in the shipment of child-made goods because of the effect of the circulation of such goods in other States where the evil of this class of labor has been recognized by local legislation, and the right to thus employ child labor has been more rigorously restrained than in the State of production. In other words, that the unfair competition, thus engendered, may be controlled by closing the channels of interstate commerce to manufacturers in those States where the local laws do not meet what Congress deems to be the more just standard of other States.

There is no power vested in Congress to require the States to exercise their police power so as to prevent possible unfair competition. Many causes may cooperate to give one State, by reason of local laws or conditions, an economic advantage over others. The Commerce Clause was not intended to give to Congress a general authority to equalize such conditions. . . .

The grant of authority over a purely federal matter was not intended to destroy the local power always existing and carefully reserved to the States in the Tenth Amendment to the Constitution. . . .

For these reasons we hold that this law exceeds the constitutional authority of Congress. It follows that the decree of the District Court must be

Affirmed.

[The dissenting opinion of JUSTICE HOLMES, in which JUSTICES McKENNA, BRANDEIS, and CLARKE joined, is omitted.]

United States v. Darby

312 US 100, 61 S Ct 451, 85 L Ed 609 (1941)

The Fair Labor Standards Act of 1938 governing the production of goods for interstate commerce is within the commerce power of Congress.

MR. JUSTICE STONE delivered the opinion of the Court.

The two principal questions raised by the record in this case are, *first,* whether Congress has constitutional power to prohibit the shipment in interstate commerce of lumber manufactured by employees whose wages are less than a prescribed minimum or whose weekly hours of labor at that wage are greater than a prescribed maximum, and, *second,* whether it has power to prohibit the employment of workmen in the production of goods "for interstate commerce" at other than prescribed wages and hours. A subsidiary question is whether in connection with such prohibitions Congress can require the employer subject to them to keep records showing the hours worked each day and week by each of his employees including those engaged "in the production and manufacture of goods to-wit, lumber, for 'interstate commerce.' "

Appellee [Fred W. Darby] demurred to an indictment found in the district court for southern Georgia charging him with violation of . . . the Fair Labor Standards Act of 1938. . . . The district court sustained the demurrer and quashed the indictment and the case comes here on direct appeal. . . .

The Fair Labor Standards Act set up a comprehensive legislative scheme for preventing the shipment in interstate commerce of certain products and commodities produced in the United States under labor conditions as respects wages and hours which fail to conform to standards set up by the Act. Its purpose . . . is to exclude from interstate commerce goods produced for the commerce and to prevent their production for interstate commerce, under conditions detrimental to the maintenance of the minimum standards of living necessary for health and general well-being; and to prevent the use of interstate commerce as the means of competition in the distribution of goods so produced, and as the means of spreading and perpetuating such substandard labor conditions among the workers of the several states. . . .

The indictment charges that appellee is engaged, in the State of Georgia, in the business of acquiring raw materials, which he manufactures into finished lumber with the intent, when manufactured, to ship it in interstate commerce to customers outside the state, and that he does in fact so ship a large part of the lumber so produced. There are numerous counts charging appellee with the shipment in interstate commerce from

Georgia to points outside the state of lumber in the production of which, for interstate commerce, appellee has employed workmen at less than the prescribed minimum wage or more than the prescribed maximum hours without payment to them of any wage for overtime. Other counts charge the employment by appellee of workmen in the production of lumber for interstate commerce at wages of less than 25 cents an hour or for more than the maximum hours per week without payment to them of the prescribed overtime wage. Still another count charges appellee with failure to keep records showing the hours worked each day a week by each of his employees. . . .

The demurrer, so far as now relevant to the appeal, challenged the validity of the Fair Labor Standards Act under the Commerce Clause and the Fifth and Tenth Amendments. The district court quashed the indictment in its entirety upon the broad grounds that the Act, which it interpreted as a regulation of manufacture within the states, is unconstitutional. . . .

While manufacture is not of itself interstate commerce the shipment of manufactured goods interstate is such commerce and the prohibition of such shipment by Congress is indubitably a regulation of the commerce. . . .

The power of Congress over interstate commerce "is complete in itself, may be exercised to its utmost extent, acknowledges no limitations other than are prescribed in the Constitution." *Gibbons* v. *Ogden, supra* (9 Wheaton 1, 6 L Ed 23). That power can neither be enlarged nor diminished by the exercise or nonexercise of state power. . . . Congress, following its own conception of public policy concerning the restrictions which may appropriately be imposed on interstate commerce, is free to exclude from the commerce articles whose use in the states for which they are destined it may conceive to be injurious to the public health, morals or welfare, even though the state has not sought to regulate their use. . . .

The motive and purpose of a regulation of interstate commerce are matters for the legislative judgment upon the exercise of which the Constitution places no restriction and over which the courts are given no control. . . .

In the more than a century which has elapsed since the decision of *Gibbons* v. *Ogden,* these principles of constitutional interpretation have been so long and repeatedly recognized by this Court as applicable to the Commerce Clause that there would be little occasion for repeating them now were it not for the decision of this Court twenty-two years ago in *Hammer* v. *Dagenhart.* . . .

Hammer v. *Dagenhart* has not been followed. The distinction on which the decision was rested that Congressional power to prohibit interstate commerce is limited to articles which in themselves have some harmful or deleterious property—a distinction which was novel when made and unsupported by any provision of the Constitution—has long since been abandoned. . . .

The conclusion is inescapable that *Hammer* v. *Dagenhart* was a departure from the principles which have prevailed in the interpretation of the Commerce Clause both before and since the decision and that such vitality, as a precedent, as it then had has long since been exhausted. It should be and now is overruled.

Validity of the wage and hour requirements. Section 15 (a) (2) and §§ 6 and 7 require employers to conform to the wage and hour provisions with respect to all employees engaged in the production of goods for interstate commerce. As appellee's employees are not alleged to be "engaged in interstate commerce" the validity of the prohibition turns on the question whether the employment, under other than the prescribed labor standards, of employees engaged in the production of goods for interstate commerce is so related to the commerce and so affects it as to be within the reach of the power of Congress to regulate it. . . .

The power of Congress over interstate commerce is not confined to the regulation of commerce among the states. It extends to those activities intrastate which so affect interstate commerce or the exercise of the power of Congress over it as to make regulation of them appropriate means to the attainment of a legitimate end, the exercise of the granted power of Congress to regulate interstate commerce. . . .

Congress, having by the present Act adopted the policy of excluding from interstate commerce all goods produced for the commerce which do not conform to the specified labor standards, it may choose the means reasonably adapted to the attainment of the permitted end, even though they involve control of intrastate activities. . . .

Congress, to attain its objective in the suppression of nationwide competition in interstate commerce by goods produced under substandard labor conditions, has made no distinction as to the volume or amount of shipments in the commerce or of production for commerce by any particular shipper or producer. It recognized that in present day industry, competition by a small part may affect the whole and that the total effect of the competition of many small producers may be great. . . .

Validity of the requirement of records of wages and hours. . . . These requirements are incidental to those for the prescribed wages and hours, and hence validity of the former turns on validity of the latter. Since, as we have held, Congress may require production for interstate commerce to conform to those conditions, it may require the employer, as a means of enforcing the valid law, to keep a record showing whether he has in fact complied with it. The requirement for records even of the intrastate transaction is an appropriate means to the legitimate end. . . .

Reversed.

Notes

1. *National Labor Relations Board* v. *Jones and Laughlin Steel Corporation,* 301 US 1 (1937). In sustaining the power of Congress to control labor relations, Chief Justice Hughes wrote:

Giving full weight to respondent's contention with respect to a break in the complete continuity of the "stream of commerce" by reason of respondent's manufacturing operations, the fact remains that the stoppage of those operations by industrial strife would have a most serious effect upon interstate commerce. In view of respondent's far-flung activities, it is idle to say that the effect would be indirect or remote. It is obvious that it would be immediate and might be catastrophic. We are asked to shut our eyes to the plainest facts of our national life and to deal with the question of direct and indirect effects in an intellectual vacuum. Because there may be but indirect and remote effects upon interstate commerce in connection with a host of local enterprises throughout the country, it does not follow that other industrial activities do not have such a close and intimate relation to interstate commerce as to make the presence of industrial strife a matter of the most urgent national concern. When industries organize themselves on a national scale, making their relation to interstate commerce the dominant factor in their activities, how can it be maintained that their industrial labor relations constitute a forbidden field into which Congress may not enter when it is necessary to protect interstate commerce from the paralyzing consequences of industrial war? We have often said that interstate commerce itself is a practical conception. It is equally true that interferences with that commerce must be appraised by a judgment that does not ignore actual experience.

Experience has abundantly demonstrated that the recognition of the right of employees to self-organization and to have representatives of their own choosing for the purpose of collective bargaining is often an essential condition of industrial peace. Refusal to confer and negotiate has been one of the most prolific causes of strife. This is such an outstanding fact in the history of labor disturbances that it is a proper subject of judicial notice and requires no citation of instances. . . .

2. *Wickard* v. *Filburn,* 317 US 111 (1942). Wickard "operated a small farm in Montgomery County, Ohio, maintaining a herd of dairy cattle, selling milk, raising poultry, and selling poultry and eggs. It has been his practice to raise a small acreage of winter wheat, sown in the Fall and harvested in the following July; to sell a portion of the crop; to feed part to poultry and livestock on the farm, some of which is sold; to use some in making flour for home consumption; and to keep the rest for the following seeding. . . . "

In sustaining the application of the Agricultural Adjustment Act of 1938 to Filburn's farm operation, Justice Jackson wrote:

Whether the subject of the regulation in question was "production," "consumption," or "marketing" is, therefore, not material for purposes of deciding the question of federal power before us. That an activity is of local character may help in a doubtful case to determine whether Congress intended to reach it. The same consideration might help in determining whether in the absence of Congressional action it would be permissible for the state to exert its power on the subject matter, even though in so doing it to some degree affected interstate commerce. But even if appellee's activity be local and thought it may not be regarded as commerce, it may still, whatever its nature, be reached by Congress if it exerts a substantial economic effect on interstate commerce and this irrespective of whether such effect is what might at some earlier time have been defined as "direct" or "indirect."

That appellee's own contribution to the demand for wheat may be trivial by itself is not enough to remove him from the scope of the federal regulation where, as here, his contribution, taken together with that of many others similarly situated, is far from trivial.

Heart of Atlanta Motel, Inc. v. United States

379 US 241, 85 S Ct 348, 13 L Ed2d 258 (1964)

The public accommodation provisions of the Civil Rights Act of 1964 constitute a valid exercise of the power of Congress to regulate interstate commerce.

MR. JUSTICE CLARK delivered the opinion of the Court.

This is a declaratory judgment action, 28 USC § 2201 and § 2202, attacking the constitutionality of Title II of the Civil Rights Act of 1964, 78 Stat 241. In addition to declaratory relief the complaint sought an injunction restraining the enforcement of the Act and damages against respondents based on allegedly resulting injury in the event compliance was required. Appellee counterclaimed for enforcement under § 206 (a) of the Act and asked for a three-judge district court under § 206 (b). A three-judge court, empaneled under § 206 (b) as well as 28 USC § 2282, sustained the validity of the Act and issued a permanent injunction on appellee's counterclaim restraining appellant from continuing to violate the Act which remains in effect on order of MR. JUSTICE BLACK, 85 Sup Ct 1. We affirm the judgment.

1. The Factual Background and Contentions of the Parties

The case comes here on admissions and stipulated facts. Appellant owns and operates the Heart of Atlanta Motel which has 216 rooms available to transient guests. The motel is located on Courtland Street, two blocks from downtown Peachtree Street. It is readily accessible to interstate highways 75 and 85 and state highways 23 and 41. Appellant solicits patronage from outside the State of Georgia through various national advertising media, including magazines of national circulation; it maintains over 50 billboards and highway signs within the State, soliciting patronage for the motel; it accepts convention trade from outside Georgia and approximately 75% of its registered guests are from out of State. Prior to passage of the Act the motel had followed a practice of refusing to rent rooms to Negroes, and it alleged that it intended to continue to do so. In an effort to perpetuate that policy this suit was filed.

The appellant contends that Congress in passing this Act exceeded its power to regulate commerce under Art I, § 8, cl 3, of the Constitution of the United States; that the Act violates the Fifth Amendment because appellant is deprived of the right to choose its customers and operate its business as it wishes, resulting in a taking of its liberty and property without due process of law and a taking of its property without just compensation; and, finally, that by requiring appellant to rent available rooms to Negroes against its will, Congress is subjecting it to involuntary servitude in contravention of the Thirteenth Amendment.

The appellees counter that the unavailability to Negroes of adequate accommodations interferes significantly with interstate travel, and that Congress, under the Commerce Clause, has power to remove such obstructions and restraints; that the Fifth Amendment does not forbid reasonable regulation and that consequential damage does not constitute a "taking" within the meaning of that amendment; that the Thirteenth Amendment claim fails because it is entirely frivolous to say that an amendment directed to the abolition of human bondage and the removal of widespread disabilities associated with slavery places discrimination in public accommodations beyond the reach of both federal and state law. . . .

2. The History of the Act [Omitted here.]

The Act [of 1964] as finally adopted was most comprehensive, undertaking to prevent through peaceful and voluntary settlement discrimination in voting, as well as in places of accommodation and public facilities, federally secured programs and in employment. Since Title II is the only portion under attack here, we confine our consideration to those public accommodation provisions.

3. Title II of the Act

This Title is divided into seven sections beginning with § 201 (a) which provides that:

All persons shall be entitled to the full and equal enjoyment of the goods, services, facilities, privileges, advantages, and accommodations of any place of public accommodation, as defined in this section, without discrimination or segregation on the ground of race, color, religion, or national origin.

There are listed in § 201 (b) four classes of business establishments, each of which "serves the public" and "is a place of public accommodation" within the meaning of § 201 (a) "if its operations affect commerce, or if discrimination or segregation by it is supported by State action." The covered establishments are:

(1) any inn, hotel, motel, or other establishment which provides lodging to transient guests, other than an establishment located within a building which contains not more than five rooms for rent or hire and which is actually occupied by the proprietor of such establishment as his residence;

(2) any restaurant, cafeteria ... [not here involved];

(3) any motion picture house ... [not here involved];

(4) any establishment ... which is physically located within the premises of any establishment otherwise covered by this subsection, or ... within the premises of which is physically located any such covered establishment ... [not here involved].

Section 201 (c) defines the phrase "affect commerce" as applied to the above establishments. It first declares that "any inn, hotel, motel, or other establishment which provides lodging to transient guests" affects commerce *per se*. Restaurants, cafeterias, etc., in the second class affect commerce only if they serve or offer to serve interstate travelers or if a substantial portion of the food which they serve or products which they sell have "moved in commerce." Motion picture houses and other places listed in class three affect commerce if they customarily present films, performances, etc., "which move in commerce." And the establishments listed in class four affect commerce if they are within, or include within their own premises, an establishment "the operations of which affect commerce." Private clubs are excepted under certain conditions. See § 201 (e).

Section 201 (d) declares that "discrimination or segregation" is supported by state action when carried on under color of any law, statute, ordinance, regulation or any custom or usage required or enforced by officials of the State or any of its subdivisions.

In addition, § 202 affirmatively declares that all persons "shall be entitled to be free, at any establishment or place, from discrimination or segregation of any kind on the ground of race, color, religion, or national origin, if such discrimination or segregation is or purports to be required by any law, statute, ordinance, regulation, rule, or order of a State or any agency or political subdivision thereof."

Finally § 203 prohibits the withholding or denial, etc., of any right or privilege secured by § 201 and § 202 or the intimidation, threatening or coercion of any person with the purpose of interfering with any such right or the punishing, etc., of any person for exercising or attempting to exercise any such right.

The remaining sections of the Title are remedial ones for violations of any of the previous sections. Remedies are limited to civil actions for preventive relief.

4. Application of Title II to Heart of Atlanta Motel

It is admitted that the operation of the motel brings it within the provisions of § 201 (a) of the Act and that appellant refused to provide lodging for transient Negroes because of their race or color and that it intends to continue that policy unless restrained.

The sole question posed is, therefore, the constitutionality of the Civil Rights Act of 1964 as applied to these facts. The legislative history of the Act indicates that Congress based the Act on § 5 and the Equal Protection Clause of the Fourteenth Amendment as well as its power to regulate interstate commerce under Art I, § 8, cl 3 of the Constitution.

5. The Civil Rights Cases, 109 US 3 (1883), and their application

In light of our ground for decision, it might be well at the outset to discuss the *Civil Rights Cases, supra,* which declared provisions of the Civil Rights Act of 1875 unconstitutional. 18 Stat 335, 336. We think that decision inapposite, and without precedential value in determining the constitutionality of the present Act. Unlike Title II of the present legislation, the 1875 Act broadly proscribed discrimination in "inns, public conveyances on land or water, theaters, and other public places of amusement," without limiting the categories of affected businesses to those impinging upon interstate commerce. In contrast, the applicability of Title II is carefully limited to enterprises having a direct and substantial relation to the interstate flow of goods and people, except where state action is involved. Further, the fact that certain kinds of businesses may not in 1875 have been sufficiently involved in interstate commerce to warrant bringing them within the ambit of the commerce power is not necessarily dispositive of the same question today.

6. The Basis of Congressional Action

While the Act as adopted carried no congressional findings, the record of its passage through each house is replete with evidence of the burdens that discrimination by race or color places upon interstate commerce. . . . We shall not burden this opinion with further details since the voluminous testimony presents overwhelming evidence that discrimination by hotels and motels impedes interstate travel.

7. The Power of Congress Over Interstate Travel

The power of Congress to deal with these obstructions depends on the meaning of the Commerce Clause.

The same interest in protecting interstate commerce which led Congress to deal with segregation in interstate carriers and the white slave traffic has prompted it to extend the exercise of its power to gambling, *Lottery Case,* 188 US 321 (1903); to criminal enterprises, *Brooks* v. *United States,* 267 US 432 (1925); to deceptive practices in the sale of products, *Federal Trade Comm'n* v. *Mandel Bros., Inc.,* 359 US 385 (1959); to fraudulent security transactions, *Securities and Exchange Comm'n* v. *Ralston Purina Co.,* 346 US 119 (1953); to misbranding of drugs, *Weeks* v. *United States,* 245 US 618 (1918); to wages and hours, *United States* v. *Darby,* 312 US 100 (1941); to members of labor unions, *Labor Board* v. *Jones & Laughlin Steel Corp.,* 301 US 1 (1937); to crop control, *Wickard* v. *Filburn*, 317 US 111 (1942); to discrimination against shippers, *United States* v. *Baltimore & Ohio R. Co.*, 333 US 169 (1948); to the protection of small business from injurious price cutting, *Moore* v. *Mead's Fine Bread Co.*, 348 US 115 (1954); to resale price maintenance, *Hudson Distributors, Inc.* v. *Eli Lilly & Co.*, 377 US 386 (1964); *Schwegmann* v. *Calvert Distillers Corp.*, 341 US 384 (1951); to professional football, *Radovich* v. *National Football League*, 352 US 445 (1957); and to racial discrimination by owners and managers of terminal restaurants, *Boynton* v. *Virginia*, 364 US 454 (1960).

That Congress was legislating against moral wrongs in many of these areas rendered its enactments no less valid. In framing Title II of this Act Congress was also dealing with what is considered a moral problem. But that fact does not detract from the overwhelming evidence of the disruptive effect that racial discrimination has had on commercial intercourse. It was this burden which empowered Congress to enact appropriate legislation, and, given this basis for the exercise of its power, Congress was not restricted by the fact that the particular obstruction to interstate commerce with which it was dealing was also deemed a moral and social wrong.

It is said that the operation of the motel here is of a purely local character. But, assuming this to be true, "if it is interstate commerce that feels the pinch, it does not matter how local the operation that applies the squeeze." *United States* v. *Women's Sportswear Mfrs. Ass'n*, 336 US 460, 464 (1949). . . . Thus the power of Congress to promote interstate commerce also includes the power to regulate the local incidents thereof, including local activities in both the States of origin and destination, which might have a substantial and harmful effect upon that commerce. One need only examine the evidence which we have discussed above to see that Congress may—as it has—prohibit racial discrimination by motels serving travelers, however "local" their operations may appear.

Nor does the Act deprive appellant of liberty or property under the Fifth Amendment. The commerce power invoked here by the Congress is a specific and plenary one authorized by the Constitution itself. The only questions are: (1) whether Congress had a rational basis for finding that racial discrimination by motels affected commerce, and (2) if it had such a basis, whether the means it selected to eliminate that evil are reasonable and appropriate. If they are, appellant has no "right" to select its guests as it sees fit, free from governmental regulation. . . .

We find no merit in the remainder of appellant's contentions, including that of "involuntary servitude." As we have seen, 32 States prohibit racial discrimination in public accommodations. These laws but codify the common-law innkeeper rule which long predated the Thirteenth Amendment. It is difficult to believe that the Amendment was intended to abrogate this principle. . . .

Affirmed.

[JUSTICES DOUGLAS, BLACK, and GOLDBERG wrote concurring opinions.]

Note

Katzenbach v. *McClung*, 379 US 294, 85 S Ct 377, 13 L Ed2d 290 (1964). This case was decided on the same date as the *Heart of Atlanta Motel* case. Ollie

McClung operated a family-owned restaurant in Birmingham, Alabama, "specializing in barbecued meats and homemade pies, with a seating capacity of 220 customers. It is located on a state highway 11 blocks from an interstate one and a somewhat greater distance from railroad and bus stations. The restaurant caters to a family and white-collar trade with a take-out service for Negroes. It employs 36 persons, two-thirds of whom are Negroes." The Court concerned itself with the application of the Civil Rights Act of 1964 to restaurants which serve food a substantial portion of which has moved in commerce.

McClung argued that Congress had attempted to legislate a conclusive presumption that a restaurant affects interstate commerce if it serves food a substantial portion of which has moved in commerce. The Court noted that in hearings before Congress there was "an impressive array of testimony that discrimination in restaurants had a highly restrictive effect upon interstate travel by Negroes. . . . Likewise, it was said, that discrimination deterred professional, as well as skilled, people from moving into areas where such practices occurred and thereby caused industry to be reluctant to establish there." "Of course," concluded the Court, "the mere fact that Congress has said when particular activity shall be deemed to affect commerce does not preclude further examination by this Court. But when we find that the legislators, in light of the facts and testimony before them, have a rational basis for finding a chosen regulatory scheme necessary to the protection of commerce, our investigation is at an end."

C. FISCAL POWERS

Hylton v. United States

3 Dallas 171, 1 L Ed 556 (1796)

A tax on carriages is not a direct tax and is not required by the Constitution to be laid according to the census.

CHASE, J. By the case stated, only one question is submitted to the opinion of this court:—Whether the law of congress of the 5th of June, 1794 . . . entitled, "An act to lay duties upon carriages for the conveyance of persons," is unconstitutional and void?

The great object of the constitution was to give congress a power to lay taxes adequate to the exigencies of government; but they were to observe two rules in imposing them, namely, the rule of uniformity when they laid duties, imposts, or excises; and the rule of apportionment, according to the census, when they laid any direct tax.

If there are any other species of taxes that are not direct, and not included within the words duties, imposts, or excises, they may be laid by the rule of uniformity or not, as congress shall think proper and reasonable. If the framers of the constitution did not comtemplate other taxes than direct taxes, and duties, imposts, and excises, there is great inaccuracy in their language. If these four species of taxes were all that were meditated, the general power to lay taxes was unnecessary. If it was intended that congress should have authority to lay only one of the four above enumerated, to wit, direct taxes by the rule of apportionment, and the other three by the rule of uniformity, the expressions would have run thus: "Congress shall have power to lay and collect direct taxes and duties, imposts, and excises; the first shall be laid according to the census, and the three last shall be uniform throughout the United States." The power in the eighth section of the first article to lay and collect taxes, included a power to lay direct taxes (whether capitation, or any other) and also duties, imposts, and excises, and every other species or kind of tax whatsoever, and called by any other name. Duties, imposts, and excises were enumerated, after the general term taxes, only for the purpose of declaring that they were to be laid by the rule of uniformity. I consider the constitution to stand in this manner,—a general power is given to congress to lay and collect taxes of every kind or nature without any restraint, except only on exports; but two rules are prescribed for their government, namely, uniformity and apportionment; three kinds of taxes, to wit, duties, imposts, and excises by the first rule, and capitation or other direct taxes by the second rule.

I believe some taxes may be both direct and indirect at the same time. If so, would congress be prohibited from laying such a tax because it is partly a direct tax?

The constitution evidently contemplated no taxes as direct taxes, but only such as congress could lay in proportion to the census. The rule of apportionment is only to be adopted in such cases where it can reasonably apply; and the subject taxed must ever determine the application of the rule.

If it is proposed to tax any specific article by the rule of apportionment, and it would evidently create great inequality and injustice, it is unreasonable to say that the constitution intended such tax should be laid by that rule.

It appears to me that a tax on carriages cannot be laid by the rule of apportionment, without very great inequality and injustice. For example, suppose two States equal in census, to pay eighty thousand dollars each, by a tax on carriages of eight dollars on every carriage, and in one State there are one hundred carriages, and in the other one thousand. The owners of carriages in one State would pay ten times the tax of owners in the other. A, in one State, would pay for his carriage eight dollars; but B, in the other State, would pay for his carriage, eighty dollars. . . .

I think an annual tax on carriages for the conveyance of persons, may be considered as within the power granted to congress to lay duties. The term duty, is the most comprehensive next to the generical term *tax;* and practically in Great Britain (whence we take our general ideas of taxes, duties, imposts, excises, customs, etc.) embraces taxes on stamps, tolls for passage, etc., and is not confined to taxes on importation only.

It seems to me that a tax on expense is an indirect tax; and I think an annual tax on a carriage for the conveyance of persons is of that kind; because a carriage is a consumable commodity, and such annual tax on it is on the expense of the owner.

I am inclined to think, but of this I do not give a judicial opinion, that the direct taxes contemplated by the constitution, are only two, to wit, a capitation or poll tax, simply without regard to property, profession, or any other circumstance; and a tax on land. I doubt whether a tax, by a general assessment of personal property, within the United States, is included within the term direct tax.

As I do not think the tax on carriages is a direct tax, it is unnecessary at this time for me to determine whether this court constitutionally possesses the power to declare an act of congress void, on the ground of its being made contrary to, and in violation of, the constitution; but if the court have such power, I am free to declare, that I will never exercise it but in a very clear case.

I am for affirming the judgment of the circuit court. . . .

[The opinions of the other JUSTICES, delivered *seriatim,* are omitted here.]
By the Court. Let the judgment of the Circuit Court be affirmed.

Veazie Bank v. Fenno

8 Wallace 533, 19 L Ed 482 (1869)

Congress having undertaken to provide a currency for the whole country may constitutionally secure the benefit of it to the people by appropriate legislation, and to that end may restrain the circulation of any notes not issued under its own authority.

[In the period before the Civil War, the principal monetary media in the United States were gold and silver coins and notes issued by state-chartered banks. In 1863 Congress authorized national banking associations, and in 1866 it levied a tax of 10 percent on all notes other than National bank notes used for circulation by any bank. The Veazie Bank, chartered by the State of Maine, paid the tax under protest and sued Fenno, collector of Internal Revenue, to recover the amount paid. The judges of the Circuit Court of the District of Maine were "opposed in opinion" and certified the question of the constitutionality of the tax to the Supreme Court.]

The CHIEF JUSTICE [CHASE] delivered the opinion of the Court. . . .

It cannot be doubted that under the Constitution the power to provide a circulation of coin is given to Congress. And it is settled by the uniform practice of the government and by repeated decisions, that Congress may constitutionally authorize the emission of bills of credit. It is not important here, to decide whether the quality of legal tender, in payment of debts, can be constitutionally imparted to these bills; it is enough to say, that there can be no question of the power of the government to emit them; to make them receivable in payment of debts to itself; to fit them for use by those who see fit to use them in all the transactions of commerce; to provide for their redemption; to make them a currency, uniform in value and description, and convenient and useful for circulation. These powers, until recently, were only partially and occasionally exercised. Lately, however, they have been called into full activity, and Congress has undertaken to supply a currency for the entire country.

The methods adopted for the supply of this currency were briefly explained in the first part of this opinion. It now consists of coin, of United States notes, and of the notes of the National banks. Both descriptions of notes may be properly described as bills of credit, for both are furnished by the government; both are issued on the credit of the government; and the government is responsible for the redemption of both; primarily as to the first description, and immediately upon default of the bank, as to the second. When these bills shall be made convertible into coin, at the will of the holder, this currency will, perhaps, satisfy the wants of the community, in respect to a circulating medium, as perfectly as any mixed currency that can be devised.

Having thus, in the exercise of undisputed constitutional powers, undertaken to provide a currency for the whole country, it cannot be questioned that Congress may, constitutionally, secure the benefit of it to the people by appropriate legislation. To this end, Congress has denied the quality of legal tender to foreign coins, and has provided by law against the imposition of counterfeit and base coin on the community. To the same end, Congress may restrain, by suitable enactments, the circulation as money of any notes not issued under its own authority. Without this power, indeed, its attempts to secure a sound and uniform currency for the country must be futile.

Viewed in this light, as well as in the other light of a duty on contracts or property, we cannot doubt the constitutionality of the tax under consideration.

The three questions certified from the Circuit Court of the District of Maine must, therefore, be answered

Affirmatively.

[MR. JUSTICE NELSON, with whom concurred MR. JUSTICE DAVIS, dissented.]

Bailey v. Drexel Furniture Co.

259 US 20, 42 S Ct 449, 66 L Ed2d 817 (1922)

An act which shows on its face that it is a penalty upon the employment of child labor cannot be sustained as a valid exercise of the power to tax.

MR. CHIEF JUSTICE TAFT delivered the opinion of the Court.

This case presents the question of the constitutional validity of the Child Labor Tax Law. . . .

The law is attacked on the ground that it is a regulation of the employment of child labor in the states—an exclusively state function under the federal Constitution and within the reservations of the Tenth Amendment. It is defended on the ground that it is a mere excise tax levied by the Congress of the United States under its broad power of taxation conferred by section 8, article 1, of the federal Constitution. . . .

The difference between a tax and a penalty is sometimes difficult to define, and yet the consequences of the distinction in the required method of their collection often are important. Where the sovereign enacting the law has power to impose both tax and penalty, the difference between revenue production and mere regulation may be immaterial, but not so when one sovereign can impose a tax only, and the power of regulation rests in another. Taxes are occasionally imposed in the discretion of the Legislature on proper subjects with the primary motive of obtaining revenue from them and with the incidental motive of discouraging them by making their continuance onerous. They do not lose their character as taxes because of the incidental motive. But there comes a time in the extension of the penalizing features of the so-called tax when it loses its character as such and becomes a mere penalty, with the characteristics of regulation and punishment. Such is the case in the law before us. Although Congress does not invalidate the contract of employment or expressly declare that the employment within the mentioned ages is illegal, it does exhibit its intent practically to achieve the latter result by adopting the criteria of wrongdoing and imposing its principal consequence on those who transgress its standard.

The case before us cannot be distinguished from that of *Hammer* v. *Dagenhart,* 247 US 251. Congress there enacted a law to prohibit transportation in interstate commerce of goods made at a factory in which there was employment of children within the same ages and for the same number of hours a day and days in a week as are penalized by the act in this case. . . .

In the case at the bar, Congress in the name of a tax which on the face of the act is a penalty seeks to do the same thing, and the effort must be equally futile. . . .

For the reasons given, we must hold the Child Labor Tax Law invalid and the judgment of the District Court is

Affirmed.

Mr. Justice Clarke, dissents.

Note

Subsequent development.   The judicially created "tax penalty" doctrine had a checkered career from 1922 to 1936. It was abandoned in 1937 and has only appeared occasionally in dissenting opinions since that date. *Sonzinsky* v. *United States,* 300 US 506 (1937), sustained a special excise tax on the transfer of sawed-off shotguns or rifles; *United States* v. *Sanchez,* 340 US 42 (1950), sustained a special tax on the transfer of marijuana; and *United States* v. *Kahriger,* 345 US 22 (1953), sustained a tax on persons engaged in the business of accepting wagers.

In the 1953 case, Kahriger argued that "Congress, under the pretense of exercising its power to tax has attempted to penalize illegal interstate gambling through the regulatory features of the Act and has thus infringed the police power which is reserved to the States." Rejecting this argument, in the opinion of the Court Justice Reed wrote:

> Appellee would have us say that, because there is legislative history indicating a congressional motive to suppress wagering, this tax is not a proper exercise of the taxing power.
>   It is conceded that a federal excise tax does not cease to be valid merely because it discourages or deters the activities taxed. Nor is the tax invalid because the revenue obtained is negligible. Appellee, however, argues that the sole purpose of the statute is to penalize only illegal gambling in the States through the guise of a tax measure. As with the above excise taxes which we have held to be valid, the instant tax has a regulatory effect. But regardless of its regulatory effect, the wagering tax produces

revenue. As such it surpasses both the narcotics and firearms taxes which we have found valid.

It is axiomatic that the power of Congress to tax is extensive and sometimes falls with crushing effect on businesses deemed unessential or inimical to the public welfare, or where, as in dealing with narcotics, the collection of the tax also is difficult. As is well known, the constitutional restraints on taxing are few. . . .

. . . Without any specific differentiation between the power to tax and other federal powers, the indirect results from the exercise of the power to tax have raised more doubts. . . . It is hard to understand why the power to tax should raise more doubts because of indirect effects than other federal powers.

Dissenting, Justice Frankfurter wrote: "[W]hen oblique use is made of the taxing power as to matters which substantively are not within the powers delegated to Congress, the Court cannot shut its eyes . . . merely because Congress wrapped the legislation in the verbal cellophane of a revenue measure."

Kahriger's attack upon the tax on persons engaged in the business of accepting wagers was based on two grounds. First, he asserted that Congress, under the pretense of a tax, had invaded the police power of the states. On this point, as we have seen, he lost. Second, he asserted that the registration provisions of the tax act violated the privilege against self-incrimination. On this point he also lost, but on it Justice Black filed a dissenting opinion, concurred in by Justice Douglas.

The scope of the protection of the self-incrimination clause was expanded in the 1960s, and in *Marchetti* v. *United States,* 390 US 37 (1968), Justice Harlan wrote that "nothing in the Court's opinion in *Kahriger* and *Lewis* now suffices to preclude petitioner's assertion of the constitutional privilege [against self-incrimination] as a defense to the indictments under which he was convicted. To this extent *Kahriger* and *Lewis* are overruled." This did not mean, of course, that the holding of *Kahriger* concerning the "tax penalty" doctrine was overruled. The language of *Kahriger* on that matter was repeated with approval by the Court in *Minor* v. *United States,* 396 US 87 (1969). *Marchetti* and related cases are discussed in chapter 12, section C, "Self-Incrimination."

Charles C. Steward Machine Co. v. Davis

301 US 548, 57 S Ct 883, 81 L Ed 1279 (1937)

The problem of unemployment is national as well as local, and Congress may use its fiscal powers to deal with the problem.

[The Social Security Act of 1935 levied a tax on employers of eight or more persons measured by a prescribed percentage of the wages paid. A credit of 90 percent of the tax was allowed for amounts paid into an approved state unemployment fund. Steward Machine Co. paid the tax under protest and sued to recover the payment made.]

MR. JUSTICE CARDOZO delivered the opinion of the Court.

The assailants of the statute say that its dominant end and aim is to drive the state legislatures under the whip of economic pressure into the enactment of unemployment compensation laws at the bidding of the central government. Supporters of the statute say that its operation is not constraint, but the creation of a larger freedom, the states and the nation joining in a cooperative endeavor to avert a common evil. Before Congress acted, unemployment compensation insurance was still, for the most part, a project and no more. Wisconsin was the pioneer. Her statute was adopted in 1931. At times bills for such insurance were introduced elsewhere, but they did not reach the stage of law. In 1935, four states (California, Massachusetts, New Hampshire and New York) passed unemployment laws on the eve of the adoption of the Social Security Act, and two others did likewise after the federal act and later in the year. The statutes differed to some extent in type, but were directed to a common end. In 1936, twenty-eight other states fell in line, and eight more the present year. But if states had been holding back before the passage of the federal law, inaction was not owing, for the most part, to the lack of sympathetic interest. Many held back through alarm lest, in laying such a toll upon their industries, they would place themselves in a position of economic disadvantage as compared with neighbors or competitors. . . . Two consequences ensued. One was that the freedom of a state to contribute its fair share to the solution of a national problem was paralyzed by fear. The other was that insofar as there was failure by the states to contribute relief according to the measure of their capacity, a disproportionate burden, and a mountainous one, was laid upon the resources of the Government of the nation.

The Social Security Act is an attempt to find a method by which all these public agencies may work together to a common end. Every dollar of the new taxes will continue in all likelihood to be used and needed by the nation as long as states are unwilling, whether through timidity or for other motives, to do what can be done at home. At least the inference is permissible that Congress so believed, though retaining undiminished freedom to spend the money as it pleased. On the other hand fulfilment of the home duty will be lightened and encouraged by crediting the taxpayer upon his account with the Treasury of the nation to the extent that his contributions under the laws of the locality have simplified or diminished the problem of relief and the probable demand upon the resources of the fisc. Duplicated taxes, or burdens that approach them, are recognized hardships that government, state or national, may properly avoid. . . . If Congress believed that the general welfare would better be promoted by relief through local units than by the system then in vogue, the cooperating localities ought not in all fairness to pay a second time.

Who then is coerced through the operation of this statute? Not the taxpayer. He pays in fulfilment of the mandate of the local legislature. Not the state. Even now she does not offer a suggestion that in passing the unemployment law she was affected by duress. . . . For all that appears she is satisfied with her choice, and would be sorely disappointed if it were now to be annulled. . . .

The judgment is

Affirmed.

[Dissenting opinions of JUSTICES MCREYNOLDS, SUTHERLAND, VAN DEVANTER, and BUTLER are omitted here.]

D. PROTECTION OF CIVIL RIGHTS

Katzenbach v. Morgan

384 US 641, 86 S Ct 1717, 16 L Ed2d 828 (1966)

Even though the judiciary has found that a state's use of an English language literacy test as a qualification for voting does not violate the Fourteenth Amendment, Congress may outlaw the use of such tests.

MR. JUSTICE BRENNAN delivered the opinion of the Court.

These cases concern the constitutionality of § 4(e) of the Voting Rights Act of 1965. That law, in the respects pertinent in these cases, provides that no person who has successfully completed the sixth primary grade in a public school in, or a private school accredited by, the Commonwealth of Puerto Rico in which the language of instruction was other than English shall be denied the right to vote in any election because of his inability to read or write English. Appellees, registered voters in New York City, brought this suit to challenge the constitutionality of § 4(e) insofar as it *pro tanto* prohibits the enforcement of the election laws of New York requiring an ability to read and write English as a condition of voting. Under these laws many of the several hundred thousand New York City residents who have migrated there from the Commonwealth of Puerto Rico had previously been denied the right to vote, and appellees attack § 4(e) insofar as it would enable many of these citizens to vote. Pursuant to § 14(b) of the Voting Rights Act of 1965, appellees commenced this proceeding in the District Court for the District of Columbia seeking a declaration that § 4(e) is invalid and an injunction prohibiting appellants, the Attorney General of the United States and the New York City Board of Elections, from either enforcing or complying with § 4(e). A three-judge district court was designated. . . . Upon cross motions for summary judgment, that court, one judge dissenting, granted the declaratory and injunctive relief appellees sought. The court held that in enacting § 4(e) Congress exceeded the powers granted to it by the Constitution and therefore usurped powers reserved to the States by the Tenth Amendment. . . . Appeals were taken directly to this Court, . . . and we noted probable jurisdiction. . . . We reverse. . . .

The Attorney General of the State of New York argues that . . . § 4(e) cannot be sustained as appropriate legislation to enforce the Equal Protection Clause unless the judiciary decides—even with the guidance of a congressional judgment—that the application of the English literacy requirement prohibited by § 4(e) is forbidden by the Equal Protection Clause itself. We disagree. . . .

Thus our task in this case is not to determine whether the New York English literacy requirement as applied to deny the right to vote to a person who successfully completed the sixth grade in a Puerto Rican school violates the Equal Protection Clause. Accordingly, our decision in *Lassiter* v. *Northampton Election Bd.*, 360 US 45, sustaining the North Carolina English literacy requirement as not in all circumstances prohibited by the first sections of the Fourteenth and Fifteenth Amendments, is inapposite. . . . *Lassiter* did not present the question before us here: Without regard to whether the judiciary would find that the Equal Protection Clause itself nullifies New York's English literacy requirement as so applied, could Congress prohibit the enforcement of the state law by legislating under § 5 of the Fourteenth Amendment? In answering this question, our task is limited to determining whether such legislation is, as required by § 5, appropriate legislation to enforce the Equal Protection Clause.

By including § 5 the draftsmen sought to grant to Congress, by a specific provision applicable to the Fourteenth Amendment, the same broad powers expressed in the Necessary and Proper Clause, Art. I, § 8, cl. 18. The classic formulation of the reach of those powers was established by Chief Justice Marshall in *McCulloch* v. *Maryland. . . .*

We therefore proceed to the consideration whether § 4(e) is "appropriate legislation" to enforce the Equal Protection Clause, that is, under the *McCulloch* v. *Maryland* standard, whether § 4(e) may be regarded as an enactment to enforce the Equal Protection Clause, whether it is "plainly adapted to that end" and whether it is not prohibited by but is consistent with "the letter and spirit of the constitution."[1]

There can be no doubt that § 4(e) may be regarded as an enactment to enforce the Equal Protection Clause. . . . More specifically, § 4(e) may be viewed as a measure to secure for the Puerto Rican community residing in New York nondiscriminatory treatment by government—both in the imposition of voting qualifications and the provision or administration of governmental services, such as public schools, public housing and law enforcement.

. . . It was for Congress, as the branch that made this judgment, to assess and weigh the various conflicting considerations—the risk or pervasiveness of the discrimination in governmental services, the effectiveness of eliminating the state restriction on the right to vote as a means of dealing with the evil, the adequacy or availability of alternative remedies, and the nature and significance of the state interests that would be affected by the nullification of the English literacy requirement as applied to residents who have successfully completed the sixth grade in a Puerto Rican school. It is not for us to review the congressional resolution of these factors. It is enough that we be able to perceive a basis upon which the Congress might resolve the conflict as it did. There plainly was such a basis to support § 4(e) in the application in question in this case. Any contrary conclusion would require us to be blind to the realities familiar to the legislators.

The result is no different if we confine our inquiry to the question whether § 4(e) was merely legislation aimed at the elimination of an invidious discrimination in establishing voter qualifications. . . .

We therefore conclude that § 4(e), in the application challenged in this case, is appropriate legislation to enforce the Equal Protection Clause and that the judgment of the District Court must be and hereby is

Reversed.

[JUSTICES HARLAN and STEWART dissented.]

---

1. Contrary to the suggestion of the dissent, *post*, p. 668, § 5 does not grant Congress power to exercise discretion in the other direction and to enact "statutes so as in effect to dilute equal protection and due process decisions of this Court." We emphasize that Congress' power under § 5 is limited to adopting measures to enforce the guarantees of the Amendment; § 5 grants Congress no power to restrict, abrogate, or dilute these guarantees. Thus, for example, an enactment authorizing the States to establish racially segregated systems of education would not be—as required by § 5—a measure "to enforce" the Equal Protection Clause since that clause of its own force prohibits such state laws. [Footnote by the Court.]

Oregon v. Mitchell

400 US 112, 91 S Ct 260, 27 L Ed2d 272 (1970)

Congress can lower the voting age to eighteen for national but not for state elections, and it can prescribe the residency requirement for voting in presidential elections.

Mr. Justice Black, announcing the judgments of the Court in an opinion expressing his own view of the cases.

In these suits, the States resist compliance with the voting Rights Act Amendments of 1970, Pub. L. 91-285, 84 Stat 314, because they believe that the Act takes away from them powers reserved to the States by the Constitution to control their own elections. By its terms the Act does three things. First: It lowers the minimum age of voters in both state and federal elections from 21 to 18. Second: Based upon a finding by Congress that literacy tests have been used to discriminate against voters on account of their color, the Act enforces the Fourteenth and Fifteenth Amendments by barring the use of such tests in all elections, state and national. Third: The Act forbids States from disqualifying voters in national elections for presidential and vice presidential electors because they have not met state residency requirements.

For the reasons set out in Part I of this opinion, I believe Congress can fix the age of voters in national elections, such as congressional, senatorial, Vice-Presidential and Presidential elections, but cannot set the voting age in state and local elections. . . .

For the reasons set out in Part II of this opinion, I believe that Congress in the exercise of its power to enforce the Fourteenth and Fifteenth Amendments, can prohibit the use of literacy tests or other devices used to discriminate against voters on account of their race in both state and federal elections. . . .

For the reasons set out in Part III of this opinion, I believe Congress can set residency requirements and provide for absentee balloting in elections for presidential and vice presidential electors. . . .

I

The Framers of our Constitution provided in Art. I, § 2, that members of the House of Representatives should be elected by the people and that the voters for Representatives should have "the Qualifications requisite for Electors of the most numerous Branch of the State Legislature." Senators were originally to be elected by the state legislatures, but under the Seventeeth Amendment Senators are also elected by the people, and voters for Senators have the same qualifications as voters for Representatives. In the very beginning the responsibility of the States for setting the qualifications of voters in congressional elections was made subject to the power of Congress to make or alter such regulations if it deemed advisable. This was done in Art. I, § 4, of the Constitution which provides:

"The Times, Places and Manner of holding Elections for Senators and Representatives, shall be prescribed in each state by the legislature thereof; *but the Congress may at any time by Law make or alter such Regulations,* except as to the Place of Choosing Senators." [Emphasis supplied.]

. . . I would hold, as have a long line of decisions in this Court, that Congress has ultimate supervisory power over congressional elections. Similarly, it is the prerogative of Congress to oversee the conduct of presidential and vice presidential elections and to set the qualifications for voters for electors for those offices. It cannot be seriously contended that Congress has less power over the conduct of presidential elections than it has over congressional elections.

On the other hand, the Constitution was also intended to preserve to the States the power that even the Colonies had to establish and maintain their own separate and independent governments, except insofar as the Constitution itself commands otherwise. My Brother HARLAN has persuasively demonstrated that the Framers of the Constitution intended the States to keep for themselves, as provided in the Tenth Amendment, the power to regulate elections. My major disagreement with my Brother HARLAN is that, while I agree as to the States' power to regulate the elections of their own officials, I believe, contrary to his view, that Congress has the final authority over federal elections. . . . [T]he Equal Protection Clause of the Fourteenth Amendment was never intended to destroy the States' power to govern themselves, making the Nineteenth and Twenty-Fourth Amendments superfluous. My Brother BRENNAN's opinion, if carried to its logical conclusion, would, under the guise of insuring equal protection, blot out all state power, leaving the 50 States little more than impotent figureheads. In interpreting what the Fourteenth Amendment means, the Equal Protection Clause should not be stretched to nullify the States' powers over elections which they had before the Constitution was adopted and which they have retained throughout our history.

Of course, the original design of the Founding Fathers was altered by the Civil War Amendments and various other amendments to the Constitution. The Thirteenth, Fourteenth, Fifteenth, and Nineteenth Amendments have expressly authorized Congress to "enforce" the limited prohibitions of those amendments by "appropriate legislation." The Solicitor General contends in these cases that Congress can set the age qualifications for voters in state elections under its power to enforce the Equal Protection Clause of the Fourteenth Amendment.

Above all else, the Framers of the Civil War Amendments intended to deny to the States the power to discriminate against persons on account of their race. . . .

To fulfill their goal of ending racial discrimination and to prevent direct or indirect state legislative encroachment on the rights guaranteed by the amendments, the Framers gave Congress power to enforce each of the Civil War Amendments. . . .

As broad as the congressional enforcement power is, it is not unlimited. . . .

In enacting the 18-year-old vote provisions of the Act now before the Court, Congress made no legislative findings that 21-year-old vote requirements were used by the States to disenfranchise voters on account of race. I seriously doubt that such a finding, if made, could be supported by substantial evidence. . . .

. . . In this case, it is the judgment of the Court that Title III, lowering the voting age to 18, is invalid as applied to voters in state and local elections. It is also the judgment of the Court that Title III is valid with respect to national elections. . . .

II

In Title II of the Amendments Congress prohibited the use of any test device resembling a literacy test in any national, state, or local election in any area of the

United States where such test is not already proscribed by the Voting Rights Act of 1965. The State of Arizona maintains that Title II cannot be enforced to the extent that it is inconsistent with Arizona's literacy test requirement. ... I would hold that the literacy test ban of the 1970 Amendments is constitutional under the Enforcement Clause of the Fifteenth Amendment and that it supersedes Arizona's conflicting statutes under the Supremacy Clause of the Federal Constitution.

In enacting the literacy test ban of Title II Congress had before it a long history of the discriminatory use of literacy tests to disfranchise voters on account of their race. ...

... Moreover, the history of this legislation suggests that concern with educational inequality was perhaps uppermost in the minds of the congressmen who sponsored the Act. The hearings are filled with references to educational inequality. Faced with this and other evidence that literacy tests reduce voter participation in a discriminatory manner not only in the South but throughout the Nation, Congress was supported by substantial evidence in concluding that a nationwide ban on literacy tests was appropriate to enforce the Civil War Amendments. ...

III

In Title II of the Voting Rights Act Amendments Congress also provided that in presidential and vice presidential elections, no voter could be denied his right to cast a ballot because he had not lived in the jurisdiction long enough to meet its residency requirements. Furthermore, Congress provided uniform national rules for absentee voting in presidential and vice presidential elections. In enacting these regulations for national elections Congress was attempting to insure a fully effective voice to all citizens in national elections. ...

[The concurring and dissenting opinions which cover 162 pages in the *United States Reports* are omitted here.]

Jones v. Alfred H. Mayer Co.

392 US 409, 88 S Ct 2186, 20 L Ed2d 1189 (1968)

The badges of slavery that the Thirteenth Amendment empowered Congress to eliminate include restraints upon the right to purchase property.

MR. JUSTICE STEWART delivered the opinion of the Court.

In this case we are called upon to determine the scope and the constitutionality of an Act of Congress, 42 USC § 1982, which provides that:

"All citizens of the United States shall have the same right, in every State and Territory, as is enjoyed by white citizens thereof to inherit, purchase, lease, sell, hold, and convey real and personal property."

On September 2, 1965, the petitioners filed a complaint in the District Court for the Eastern District of Missouri, alleging that the respondents had refused to sell them a home in the Paddock Woods community of St. Louis County for the sole reason that petitioner Joseph Lee Jones is a Negro. Relying in part upon § 1982, the petitioners sought injunctive and other relief. The District Court sustained the respondents' motion to dismiss the complaint, and the Court of Appeals for the Eighth Circuit affirmed, concluding that § 1982 applies only to state action and does not reach private refusals to sell. We granted *certiorari* to consider the questions thus presented. For the reasons that follow, we reverse the judgment of the Court of Appeals. We hold that § 1982 bars *all* racial discrimination, private as well as public, in the sale or rental of property, and that the statute, thus construed, is a valid exercise of the power of Congress to enforce the Thirteenth Amendment.

We begin with the language of the statute itself. In plain and unambiguous terms, § 1982 grants to all citizens, without regard to race or color, "the same right" to purchase and lease property "as is enjoyed by white citizens." As the Court of Appeals in this case evidently recognized, that right can be impaired as effectively by "those who place property on the market" as by the State itself. For, even if the State and its agents lend no support to those who wish to exclude persons from their communities on racial grounds, the fact remains that, whenever property "is placed on the market for whites only, whites have a right denied to Negroes." So long as a Negro citizen who wants to buy or rent a home can be turned away simply because he is not white, he cannot be said to enjoy "the *same* right . . . as is enjoyed by white citizens . . . to . . . purchase [and] lease . . . real and personal property." 42 USC § 1982. (Emphasis added.)

In its original form, 42 USC § 1982 was part of § 1 of the Civil Rights Act of 1866. . . . The crucial language for our purposes was that which guaranteed all citizens "the same right, in every State and Territory in the United States, . . . to inherit, purchase, lease, sell, hold, and convey real and personal property . . . as is enjoyed by white citizens. . . ." To the Congress that passed the Civil Rights Act of 1866, it was clear that the right to do these things might be infringed not only by "State or local law" but also by "custom, or prejudice." Thus, when Congress provided in § 1 of the Civil Rights Act that the right to purchase and lease property was to be enjoyed equally throughout the United States by Negro and white citizens alike, it plainly meant to secure that right against interference from any source whatever, whether governmental or private.

In light of the concerns that led Congress to adopt it and the contents of the debates that preceded its passage, it is clear that the Act was designed to do just what its terms suggest: to prohibit all racial discrimination, whether or not under color of law, with respect to the rights enumerated therein—including the right to purchase or lease property.

. . . The constitutional question in this case . . . comes to this: Does the authority of Congress to enforce the Thirteenth Amendment "by appropriate legislation" include the power to eliminate all racial barriers to the acquisition of real and personal property? We think the answer to that question is plainly yes.

"By its own unaided force and effect," the Thirteenth Amendment "abolished slavery, and established universal freedom." *Civil Rights Cases,* 109 US 3, 20. Whether or not the Amendment *itself* did any more than that—a question not involved in this case —it is at least clear that the Enabling Clause of that Amendment empowered Congress to do much more. For that clause clothed "Congress with power to pass *all laws necessary and proper for abolishing all badges and incidents of slavery in the United States.*" *Ibid.* (Emphasis added.)

Those who opposed passage of the Civil Rights Act of 1866 argued in effect that the Thirteenth Amendment merely authorized Congress to dissolve the legal bond by which the Negro slave was held to his master. Yet many had earlier opposed the Thirteenth Amendment on the very ground that it would give Congress virtually unlimited power to enact laws for the protection of Negroes in every State. . . .

Negro citizens, North and South, who saw in the Thirteenth Amendment a promise of freedom—freedom to "go and come at pleasure" and to "buy and sell when they please"—would be left with "a mere paper guarantee" if Congress were powerless to assure that a dollar in the hands of a Negro will purchase the same thing as a dollar in the hands of a white man. At the very least, the freedom that Congress is empowered to secure under the Thirteenth Amendment includes the freedom to buy whatever a white man can buy, the right to live wherever a white man can live. If Congress cannot say that being a free man means at least this much, then the Thirteenth Amendment made a promise the Nation cannot keep.

Representative Wilson of Iowa was the floor manager in the House for the Civil Rights Act of 1866. In urging that Congress had ample authority to pass the pending bill, he recalled the celebrated words of Chief Justice Marshall in *McCulloch* v. *Maryland,* 4 Wheaton 316, 421:

"Let the end be legitimate, let it be within the scope of the Constitution, and all means which are appropriate, which are plainly adapted to that end, which are not prohibited, but consist with the letter and spirit of the Constitution, are constitutional."

"The end is legitimate," the Congressman said, "because it is defined by the Constitution itself. The end is the maintenance of freedom. . . . A man who enjoys the civil rights mentioned in this bill cannot be reduced to slavery. . . . This settles the appropriateness of this measure, and that settles its constitutionality."

We agree. The judgment is

Reversed.

MR. JUSTICE DOUGLAS, concurring.

Enabling a negro to buy and sell real and personal property is a removal of one of many badges of slavery. . . .

MR. JUSTICE HARLAN, whom MR. JUSTICE WHITE joins, dissenting.

The decision in this case appears to me to be most ill-considered and ill-advised.

Like the Court, I begin analysis of § 1982 by examining its language. In its present form, the section provides:

"All citizens of the United States shall have the same right, in every State and Territory, as is enjoyed by white citizens thereof to inherit, purchase, lease, sell, hold, and convey real and personal property."

The Court finds it "plain and unambiguous," . . . that this language forbids purely private as well as state-authorized discrimination. With all respect, I do not find it so. For me, there is an inherent ambiguity in the term "right," as used in § 1982. The "right" referred to may either be a right to equal status under the law, in which case the statute operates only against state-sanctioned discrimination, or it may be an "absolute" right enforceable against private individuals. To me, the words of the statute, taken alone, suggest the former interpretation, not the latter.

The Court rests its opinion chiefly upon the legislative history of the Civil Rights Act of 1866. I shall endeavor to show that those debates do not, as the Court would have it, overwhelmingly support the result reached by the Court, and in fact that a contrary conclusion may equally well be drawn.

[The historical argument is omitted here for reason of space.]

Notes

1. *Griggs* v. *Duke Power Co.,* 401 US 424 (1971), involved the question "whether an employer is prohibited by the Civil Rights Act of 1964, Title VII, from requiring a high school education or passing of a standardized general intelligence test as a condition of employment in or transfer to jobs when (a) neither standard is shown to be significantly related to successful job performance, (b) both requirements operate to disqualify blacks at a substantially higher rate than white applicants, and (c) the jobs in question formerly had been filled only by white employees as part of a longstanding practice of giving preferences to whites." The Supreme Court gave an affirmative answer, despite the factural finding by the district court that there was "no showing of a discriminatory purpose in the adoption of the diploma and test requirements." "Congress directed the thrust of the Act to the *consequences* of employment practices, not simply to motivation. More than that, Congress has placed on the employer the burden of showing that any given requirement must have a manifest relationship to the employment in question" wrote Chief Justice Burger.

2. *Tillman* v. *Wheaton-Haven Recreation Association,* 410 US 431 (1973), held that the "private club" exemption under the Civil Rights Act of 1964 did not, under the circumstances of the case, remove a community swimming-pool from the ban against racial discrimination under the provisions of the Civil Rights Acts of 1866 and 1870.

Chapter 4

The States

A. INTRODUCTION

"The powers not delegated to the United States by the Constitution, nor prohibited by it to the States, are reserved to the States, respectively, or to the people," reads the Tenth Amendment. The extent of the powers of the national government, save in cases involving civil liberties, is today considered largely a legislative matter, and the Court is not inclined to declare acts of Congress void on the basis that they invade areas reserved to the states. But the extent of the powers of the states remains a live judicial issue.

The power vested by the Constitution in Congress to coin money and regulate the value thereof would appear by its very nature to be an exclusive power; and that it is an exclusive national power is made clear by the clause in the Constitution stating that no state shall coin money. But few of the powers of Congress are expressly made exclusive. Many powers of Congress, such as the power to tax, are obviously concurrent powers, to be exercised by both the national and the state governments. The most numerous and difficult cases have arisen in regard to the regulation and taxation of commerce. These constitute the subject matter of this chapter.

In the case of *Gibbons* v. *Ogden* (p. 93), Chief Justice Marshall flirted with the idea of holding the power to regulate interstate commerce to be an exclusive power of Congress, subject to no control by the states. He said "There is great force in this argument, and the Court is not satisfied that it has been refuted." Within a few years, however, he abandoned this idea, as shown in his opinion in *Willson* v. *Black Bird Creek Marsh Co.,* 2 Peters 245 (1829). A sloop owned by Willson "broke and injured" a dam on the Black Bird Creek, a tributary of the Delaware River, and the company owning the dam successfully sued for damages in the courts of Delaware. Contending that the state law authorizing the dam violated the commerce clause of the United States Constitution, Willson appealed the case to the United States Supreme Court. In affirming the state court's judgment, Marshall wrote: "The act of assembly by which the plaintiffs were authorized to construct their dam shows plainly that this is one of those many creeks passing through a deep level marsh adjoining the Delaware, up which the tide flows for some distance. The value of the property on its banks must be enhanced by excluding the water from the marsh, and the health of the inhabitants improved. Measures calculated to produce these objects, provided they do not come into collision with the powers of the general government, are undoubtedly within those which are reserved to the states." There being no act of Congress applicable to the case, Marshall found that the Delaware act was not repugnant to the congressional power in its "dormant state."

The power of the states to regulate interstate commerce was given broad application while Roger B. Taney was chief justice. The shift in the position of the Court is illustrated by the case of *New York* v. *Miln,* 11 Peters 102 (1837). The case involved the validity of a New York statute requiring the masters of vessels arriving in the port of New York to report detailed information concerning each immigrant brought in. It was first argued before the United States Supreme Court in 1834. The two Jackson appointees then on the Court (McLean and Baldwin) thought the New York law was constitutional, and Justice Thompson agreed with them; but Justices Story, Duvall, and Johnson, together with Chief Justice Marshall, thought it to be unconstitutional. Justices Duvall and Johnson, however, were absent at the time the case was argued before the Court. Instead of allowing the case to be decided by a three-to-two vote, Marshall announced a rule that, except in case of absolute necessity, in constitutional cases the Court would not deliver judgments unless four justices, constituting a majority of the whole Court, concurred in the opinion. He then postponed the *Miln* case for further arguments. The period was one of rapid change in the personnel of the Court, and when in 1837 the *Miln* case was taken up before Chief Justice Taney, only Story remained of the old Marshall Court. The vote was six to one to sustain the New York law. In dissenting, Justice Story wrote: "In this opinion I have the consolation to know that I had the entire concurrence, upon the same grounds, of that great consitutional jurist, the late Mr. Chief Justice Marshall." See Carl B. Swisher, *American Constitutional Development* (New York, 1954), p. 196.

The philosophy of the Taney Court is well represented in the decision in *Cooley* v. *Board of Wardens* (p. 125).

Munn v. *Illinois,* 94 US 113 (1877), sustained a state law fixing maximum charges for the storage of grain in warehouses. Most of the grain stored in the Chicago warehouses (elevators) was produced in the West and destined for shipment to markets outside Illinois. The principal argument in the Court was over the question of whether price-fixing by legislation was contrary to due process of law. In the closing paragraph of the Court's opinion, Chief Justice Waite wrote that the regulation of the warehouses "is a matter of domestic concern, and, certainly, until Congress acts in reference to their interstate relations, the State may exercise all the powers of government over them, even though in so doing it may indirectly operate upon commerce outside its immediate jurisdiction."

Wabash, St. Louis & Pacific Railway Co. v. *Illinois,* 118 US 557 (1886), held void a state statute prohibiting discriminatory freight rates as applied to interstate shipments. The Illinois statute prohibited any railroad from charging for the transportation of any passenger or freight within the state the same or a greater charge than charged for the transport in the same direction of any passenger or like quantity of freight of the same class over a greater distance of the same road. In the opinion of the Court, Justice Miller observed that in a general way the language of some of the earlier decisions of the Court could be construed as sanctioning state regulations of the type involved. But he concluded that even in the absence of congressional legislation, a state regulation of transportation rates was void when applied to interstate shipments, even though limited to the portion of the interstate shipment taking place within the state.

The following year Congress created the Interstate Commerce Commission. For a detailed analysis of the early history of this commission, see Isaiah L. Sharfman, *The Interstate Commerce Commission* (New York, 1947. 4 vols.). On the development of the commerce clause, see Felix Frankfurter, *The Commerce Clause under Marshall, Taney, and Waite* (Chapel Hill, 1937).

From 1890 to 1937 the Court adhered generally to a laissez-faire philosophy, and the commerce clause and due process clauses were used interchangeably to strike down state laws which the justices thought undesirable. In recent years, the Court has been more tolerant toward state regulations, albeit all judicial restraints have by no means been removed, as the cases in this chapter make clear.

Problems on state taxation of commerce run parallel to those of state regulation of commerce. A selection of the leading cases in the field, especially recent ones, is included in this chapter.

B. REGULATION OF COMMERCE

Cooley v. Board of Wardens of Port of Philadelphia

12 Howard 299, 13 L Ed 996 (1851)

Either absolutely to affirm or to deny that the power of Congress to regulate interstate and foreign commerce is exclusive is to lose sight of the diverse nature of the subjects of this power.

[A statute of Pennsylvania required that ships of designated classes and size employ a local pilot in entering and leaving Port of Philadelphia. There was a monetary penalty for failure to comply with the statute. Aaron B. Cooley, the consignee of two ships that sailed from Philadelphia without employing local pilots, was sued for the prescribed penalty. The Supreme Court of Pennsylvania sustained a judgment against Cooley. He brought the case to the United States Supreme Court by writ of error.]

CURTIS, J., delivered the opinion of the Court. . . .

[A] majority of the court are of opinion that a regulation of pilots is a regulation of commerce, within the grant to Congress of the commercial power, contained in the third clause of the eighth section of the first article of the Constitution. . . . Entertaining these views, we are brought directly and unavoidably to the consideration of the question, whether the grant of the commercial power to Congress, did *per se* deprive the States of all power to regulate pilots. . . .

The diversities of opinion . . . which have existed on this subject, have arisen from the different views taken of the nature of this power. But when the nature of a power like this is spoken of, when it is said that the nature of the power requires that it should be exercised exclusively by Congress, it must be intended to refer to the subjects of that power, and to say they are of such a nature as to require exclusive legislation by Congress. Now, the power to regulate commerce, embraces a vast field, containing not only many, but exceedingly various subjects, quite unlike in their nature; some imperatively demanding a single uniform rule, operating equally on the commerce of the United States in every port; and some, like the subject now in question, as imperatively demanding that diversity, which alone can meet the local necessities of navigation.

Either absolutely to affirm or deny that the nature of this power requires exclusive legislation by Congress, is to lose sight of the nature of the subjects of this power, and to assert concerning all of them, what is really applicable but to a part. Whatever subjects of this power are in their nature national, or admit only of one uniform system, or plan of regulation, may justly be said to be of such a nature as to require exclusive legislation by Congress. That this cannot be affirmed of laws for the regulation of pilots and pilotage, is plain. The Act of 1789 contains a clear and authoritative declaration by the first Congress that the nature of this subject is such that until Congress should find it necessary to exert its power, it should be left to the legislation of the States; that it is local and not national; that it is likely to be the best provided for, not by one system, or plan of regulations, but by as many as the legislative discretion of the several States should deem applicable to the local peculiarities of the ports within their limits. . . .

We have not adverted to the practical consequences of holding that the States possess no power to legislate for the regulation of pilots, though in our apprehension these would be of the most serious importance. For more than sixty years this subject has been acted on by the States, and the systems of some of them created and of others essentially modified during that period. To hold that pilotage fees and penalties demanded and received during that time have been illegally exacted, under color of void laws, would work an amount of mischief which a clear conviction of constitutional duty, if entertained, must force us to occasion, but which could be viewed by no just mind without deep regret. Nor would the mischief be limited to the past. If Congress were now to pass a law adopting the existing state laws, if enacted without authority, and in violation of the Constitution, it would seem to us to be a new and questionable mode of legislation. . . .

We are of opinion that this state law was enacted by the virtue of a power residing in the State to legislate, that it is not in conflict with any law of Congress; that it does not interfere with any system which Congress has established by making regulations, or by intentionally leaving individuals to their own unrestricted action; that this law is therefore valid, and the judgment of the Supreme Court of Pennsylvania in each case must be affirmed.

McLean, J., and Wayne, J., dissented; and Daniel, J., although he concurred in the judgment of the Court, yet dissented from its reasoning. . . .

Notes

1. *Transportation media.* *Hall* v. *DeCuir*, 95 US 485 (1878), held void as applied to interstate commerce a statute passed by the legislature of Louisiana in 1869 (during the Reconstruction Period) requiring those engaged in transportation to give all persons traveling in that state upon public conveyances equal rights and privileges in all parts of the conveyance, without discrimination on account of race. Hall operated a steamboat between New Orleans and Vicksburg. He was convicted of violating the statute by denying to DeCuir, a black, a cabin reserved for white persons. In reversing the conviction Chief Justice Waite wrote:

> But we think it may safely be said that state legislation which seeks to impose a direct burden upon interstate commerce, or to interfere directly with its freedom, does encroach upon the exclusive power of Congress. . . . While it [the statute] purports only to control the carrier when engaged within the state, it must necessarily influence his conduct in some extent in the management of his business throughout his entire voyage. . . . A passenger in the cabin set apart for the use of whites without the state must, when the boat comes within, share the accommodations of that cabin with such colored persons as may come on board afterwards, if the law is enforced. . . . The statute . . . to the extent that it requires those engaged in the transportation of passengers among the states to carry colored passengers in Louisiana in the same cabin with whites, is unconstitutional and void. If the public good requires such legislation, it must come from Congress.

Southern Pacific Co. v. *Arizona*, 325 US 761 (1945), held invalid an Arizona statute which made it unlawful to operate within the state a train of more than fourteen passenger cars or seventy freight cars. Dissenting, Justice Black wrote:

> The determination of whether it is in the interest of society for the length of trains to be governmentally regulated is a matter of public policy. . . . A century and a half of constitutional history and government admonishes this Court to leave that choice to the elected legislative representatives of the people themselves, where it properly belongs both on democratic principles and the requirements of efficient government.

Morgan v. *Virginia*, 328 US 373 (1946), held invalid a Virginia statute which required all motor-vehicle carriers to separate white and colored passengers so that contiguous seats would not be occupied by persons of different races. "The factual situation set out . . . emphasizes the soundness of this Court's early conclusion in *Hall* v. *DeCuir*," wrote Justice Reed.

Colorado Anti-Discrimination Commission v. *Continental Air Lines, Inc.*, 372 US 714 (1963), held that Colorado's fair employment law could be applied to airlines engaged in interstate commerce. Marlon D. Green, thirty-two, a black, had applied for a job with Continental Air Lines. The Colorado Anti-Discrimination Commission found that the only reason Continental refused to hire Green was his race. The Colorado Supreme Court held that to apply the state's anti-discrimination law to the employment of pilots for interstate commerce would violate the Commerce Clause. In reversing the state court, Justice Black disposed of opinions in earlier cases by stating that they were based on the assumption that one state might require segregation and another forbid it. But since all segregation laws are now considered void, conflict "simply cannot exist here."

2. *Natural resources.*   *Geer* v. *Connecticut,* 161 US 519 (1896), sustained state restrictions on the exportation of quail and other birds.

Hudson Water Co. v. *McCarter,* 209 US 349 (1908), held that a state "may protect the diversion of the waters of its important streams to points outside of its boundaries."

Sligh v. *Kirkwood,* 237 US 52 (1915), upheld the right of Florida to protect the reputation of its products by prohibiting the sale of immature citrus fruit.

Pennsylvania v. *West Virginia,* 262 US 553 (1923), held void a statute requiring that natural gas companies furnish, to the extent of their supply of gas produced within the state, the needs of domestic consumers before sending gas to customers in other states.

Panhandle Eastern Pipe Line Co. v. *Michigan Public Service Commission,* 341 US 329 (1951), upheld the power of Michigan to require a natural gas company seeking to sell gas in interstate commerce to the Ford Motor Company and other industrial consumers to obtain a certification of public convenience and necessity. The opinion stressed not only the inconvenience of using the streets for parallel pipe lines, but the overall cost of services by an existing company.

3. *People.*   *Edwards* v. *California,* 314 US 160 (1941), held invalid a California law making it a misdemeanor to bring or assist in bringing into the state any nonresident indigent person.

Leisy v. Hardin

135 US 100, 10 S Ct 681, 34 L Ed2d 128 (1890)

A state cannot prohibit the sale of intoxicating liquors by a person importing them into the state while the liquors remain in the sealed kegs and cans in which they were shipped.

[Iowa adapted a law prohibiting the sale or keeping for sale of intoxicating liquors. A. J. Hardin, a police officer, seized a quantity of beer from the premises of Leisy & Co. in the city of Keokuk. It had been shipped from Illinois and remained in its original sealed barrels and cases when seized. Leisy brought an action to recover the beer.]

MR. JUSTICE FULLER . . . delivered the opinion of the Court. . . .
. . . The power to regulate commerce among the States is a unit, but if particular subjects within its operation do not require the application of a general or uniform system, the States may legislate in regard to them with a view to local needs and circumstances, until Congress otherwise directs. . . .

Whenever, however, a particular power of the general government is one which must necessarily be exercised by it, and Congress remains silent, this it not only not a concession that the powers reserved by the States may be exerted as if the specific power had not been elsewhere reposed, but, on the contrary, the only legitimate conclusion is that the general government intended that power should not be affirmatively exercised, and the action of the States cannot be permitted to effect that which would be incompatible with such intention. Hence, inasmuch as interstate commerce, consisting in the transportation, purchase, sale and exchange of commodities, is national in its character, and must be governed by a uniform system, so long as Congress does not pass any law to regulate it, or allowing the States so to do, it thereby indicates its will that such commerce shall be free and untrammelled. . . .

That ardent spirits, distilled liquors, ale and beer are subjects of exchange, barter and traffic, like any other commodity in which a right of traffic exists, and are so recognized by the usages of the commercial world, the laws of Congress and the decisions of courts, is not denied. Being thus articles of commerce, can a State, in the absence of legislation on the part of Congress, prohibit their importation from abroad or from a sister State? or when imported prohibit their sale by the importer? If the importation cannot be prohibited without the consent of Congress, when does property imported from abroad, or from a sister State, so become part of the common mass of property within a State as to be subject to its unimpeded control?

In *Brown* v. *Maryland* [1827] the act of the state legislature drawn in question was held invalid as repugnant to the prohibition of the Constitution upon the States to lay any impost or duty upon imports or exports, and to the clause granting the power to regulate commerce; and it was laid down by the great magistrate who presided over this court for more than a third of a century, that the point of time when the prohibition ceases and the power of the State to tax commences, is not the instant when the article enters the country, but when the importer has so acted upon it that it has become incorporated and mixed up with the mass of property in the country, which happens when the original package is no longer such in his hands. . . .

The doctrine now firmly established is, as stated by Mr. Justice Field, in *Bowman* v. *Chicago &c. Railway Co.,* 125 US 507, "that where the subject upon which Congress can act under its commercial power is local in its nature or sphere of operation, such as harbor pilotage, the improvement of harbors, the establishment of beacons and buoys to guide vessels in and out of port, the construction of bridges over navigable rivers, the erection of wharves, piers and docks, and the like, which can be properly regulated only by special provisions adapted to their localities, the State can act until Congress interferes and supersedes its authority; but where the subject is national in its character, and admits and requires uniformity of regulation, affecting alike all the States, such as transportation between the States, including the importation of goods from one State into another, Congress can alone act upon it and provide the needed regulations. The absence of any law of Congress on the subject is equivalent to its declaration that commerce in that matter shall be free. . . . "

The conclusion follows that, as the grant of the power to regulate commerce among the States, so far as one system is required, is exclusive, the States cannot exercise that power without the assent of Congress, and, in the absence of legislation, it is left for the courts to determine when state action does or does not amount to such exercise, or, in other words, what is or is not a regulation of such commerce. When that is determined, controversy is at an end. Illustrations exemplifying the general rule are numerous. Thus we have held the following to be regulations of interstate commerce: A tax upon freight transported from State to State, *Case of the State Freight Tax,* 15

Wall 232; a statute imposing a burdensome condition on ship-masters as a prerequisite to the landing of passengers, *Henderson* v. *Mayor of New York,* 92 US 259; a statute prohibiting the driving or conveying of any Texas, Mexican or Indian cattle, whether sound or diseased, into the State between the first day of March and the first day of November in each year, *Railroad Co.* v. *Husen,* 95 US 465; a statute requiring every auctioneer to collect and pay into the state treasury a tax on his sales, when applied to imported goods in the original packages by him sold for the importer, *Cook* v. *Pennsylvania,* 97 US 566; a statute intended to regulate or tax, or to impose any other restriction upon, the transmission of persons or property, or telegraphic messages, from one State to another, *Wabash, St. Louis &c. Railway* v. *Illinois,* 118 US 557; a statute levying a tax upon nonresident drummers offering for sale or selling goods, wares or merchandise by sample, manufactured or belonging to citizens of other States, *Robbins* v. *Shelby Taxing District,* 126 US 489. . . .

The plaintiffs in error are citizens of Illinois, are not pharmacists, and have no permit, but import into Iowa beer, which they sell in original packages, as described. Under our decision in *Bowman* v. *Chicago &c. Railway Co., supra,* they had the right to sell it, by which act alone it would become mingled in the common mass of property within the State. Up to that point of time, we hold that in the absence of congressional permission to do so, the State had no power to interfere by seizure, or any other action, in prohibition of importation and sale by the foreign or non-resident importer. . . .

Reversed and the cause remanded for further proceedings not inconsistent with this opinion.

MR. JUSTICE GRAY, with whom concurred MR. JUSTICE HARLAN and MR. JUSTICE BREWER, dissenting. . . .

By the Tenth Amendment, "the powers not delegated to the United States by the Constitution, nor prohibited by it to the States, are reserved to the States respectively, or to the people."

Among the powers thus reserved to the several States is what is commonly called the police power—that inherent and necessary power, essential to the very existence of civil society, and the safeguard of the inhabitants of the State against disorder, disease, poverty and crime. . . .

The police power extends not only to things intrinsically dangerous to the public health, such as infected rags or diseased meat, but to things which, when used in a lawful manner, are subjects of property and of commerce, and yet may be used so as to be injurious or dangerous to the life, the health or the morals of the people. Gunpowder, for instance, is a subject of commerce and of lawful use, yet, because of its explosive and dangerous quality, all admit that the State may regulate its keeping and sale. And there is no article, the right of the State to control or to prohibit the sale or manufacture of which within its limits is better established, than intoxicating liquors. . . .

The statutes in question were enacted by the State of Iowa in the exercise of its undoubted power to protect its inhabitants against the evils, physical, moral and social, attending the free use of intoxicating liquors. They are not aimed at interstate commerce; they have no relation to the movement of goods from one State to another, but operate only on intoxicating liquors within the territorial limits of the State; they include all such liquors without discrimination, and do not even mention where they are made or whence they come. . . .

The decision in the *License Cases,* 5 Howard 504, by which the court ... unanimously adjudged that a general statute of a State, prohibiting the sale of intoxicating liquors without license from municipal authorities included liquors brought from another State and sold by the importer in the original barrel or package, should be upheld and followed. ...

The silence and inaction of Congress upon the subject, during the long period since the decision in the *License Cases,* appear to us to require the inference that Congress intended that the law should remain as thereby declared by this court; rather than to warrant the presumption that Congress intended that commerce among the States should be free from the indirect effect of such an exercise of the police power for the public safety, as had been adjudged by that decision to be within the constitutional authority of the States. ...

Note

Congressional power to divest interstate commerce for immunity from state control. The Court has not applied the rationale of the *Leisy* case with uniformity. For examples, it sustained against interstate commerce claims a Massachusetts prohibition on the sale of colored oleomargarine in *Plumley* v. *Massachusetts,* 155 US 461 (1894), and a New York requirement of certification against Bang's disease for cattle shipped into the state in *Mintz* v. *Baldwin,* 289 US 346 (1933). And when Congress has intervened to authorize state regulation of specific subjects of interstate commerce, the Court has always sustained the congressional acts. Acts subjecting intoxicating liquors to state control were sustained in *In re Rahrer,* 140 US 545 (1891), and *Clark Distilling Co.* v. *Western Maryland Ry. Co.,* 242 US 311 (1917). Compare *Prudential Insurance Co.* v. *Benjamin,* 328 US 408 (1946), dealing with a congressional act authorizing state regulation and taxation of the business of insurance.

Finch & Co. v. McKittrick

305 US 395, 59 S Ct 256, 83 L Ed 246 (1939)

Since the adoption of the Twenty-first Amendment, the right of a state to prohibit or regulate the importation of intoxicating liquor is not limited by the Commerce Clause.

MR. JUSTICE BRANDEIS delivered the opinion of the Court.

The State of Missouri approved April 8, 1937, an Act, sometimes called the Missouri Anti-Discrimination Act, sometimes the Missouri Retaliation Act. It provides in § 4:

"The transportation or importation into this state, or the purchase, sale, receipt or possession herein, by any licensee, of any alcoholic liquor manufactured in a 'state in which discrimination exists' is hereby prohibited, and it shall be unlawful for any licensee to transport or import into this state, or to purchase, receive, possess or sell in this state, any alcoholic liquor manufactured in any 'state in which discrimination exists' as herein defined."

The statute defines what exactions, prohibitions and restrictions imposed by laws of the several states shall be deemed "discriminations" imposed upon the importation into the several states of alcoholic liquor manufactured in Missouri; requires the Attorney General to determine whether there exists therein any such discrimination; and, if he find any such discriminatory law, to specify the same in a certificate to be filed with the Supervisor of Liquor Control. The Supervisor is directed to publish notice of the certificates and to advise all licensees that it will be unlawful to import into Missouri or to purchase, receive, sell or possess in Missouri any liquor manufactured in a discriminating state. Pursuant to these provisions, the Attorney General filed, in October, 1937, certificates with the Supervisor declaring that the States of Indiana, Pennsylvania, Michigan and Massachusetts are "states in which discriminations existed" as defined by the Missouri statute.

To enjoin enforcement of this provision of the Missouri statute, these five suits were brought, in the federal court for the western district of the state, against the Attorney General [Roy McKittrick] and the Supervisor of Liquor Control. . . .

The claim of unconstitutionality is rested, in this Court, substantially on the contention that the statute violates the commerce clause. It is urged that the Missouri law does not relate to protection of the health, safety and morality, or the promotion of their social welfare, but is merely an economic weapon of retaliation; and that, hence, the Twenty-first Amendment should not be interpreted as granting power to enact it. Since that amendment, the right of a State to prohibit or regulate the importation of intoxicating liquor is not limited by the commerce clause. As was said in *State Board of Equalization* v. *Young's Market Co.,* 299 US 59, 62, "The words used are apt to confer upon the State the power to forbid all importations which do not comply with the conditions which it prescribes." To limit the power of the states as urged "would involve not a construction of the Amendment, but a rewriting of it." . . .

Affirmed.

Notes

1. *Collins* v. *Yosemite Park Co.,* 304 US 518 (1938), held that California could not prevent the shipment into and through its territory of liquor destined for distribution and consumption in a national park. Compare *United States* v. *Mississippi Tax Comm'n,* 412 US 363 (1973).

2. *Hostetter* v. *Idlewild Liquor Corp.,* 377 US 324 (1964), sustained an injunction against the application of New York's Alcohol Control Law to a corporation making sales of alcohol at an international airport under an arrangement with its customers to put their purchases, under U.S. Customs Supervision, aboard planes so that deliveries would be made outside the United States.

3. *Dept. of Revenue* v. *Beam Distillers,* 377 US 341 (1964), held a Kentucky tax of ten cents per gallon on liquor imported into the state to be void as a violation of the Export-Import Clause of Article I, Sec. 10.

4. *Seagram & Sons* v. *Hostetter*, 384 US 35 (1966), sustained a New York statute which required that monthly price schedules for the sale of liquor, required to be filed with the State Liquor Authority, be accompanied by an affirmation that the prices were no higher than the lowest prices at which sales were made anywhere in the country in the preceding month by the brand owner or his agents.

5. *California* v. *LaRue*, 409 US 109 (1972), found support in the Twenty-first Amendment for a California regulation prohibiting explicitly live entertainment and films in establishments licensed to dispense liquor by the drink.

6. *Heublein* v. *S.C. Tax Comm'n*, 409 US 275 (1972), held that since South Carolina's Beverage Control Act requires that, as a condition of doing business, a manufacturer do more than solicit sales, Heublein, Inc., an out-of-state company, could not claim exemption under the federal ban (15 USC Sec 381) on states' imposition of income tax on corporations that do no more than solicit sales.

South Carolina State Highway Dept. v. Barnwell

303 US 177, 58 S Ct 510, 82 L Ed 734 (1938)

State restrictions on the size of trucks may be applied to trucks in interstate commerce.

MR. JUSTICE STONE delivered the opinion of the Court.

Act No. 259 of the General Assembly of South Carolina, of April 28, 1933 ... prohibits use on the state highways of motor trucks and "semi-trailer motor trucks" whose width exceeds 90 inches, and whose weight including load exceeds 20,000 pounds. ... The principal question for decision is whether these prohibitions impose an unconstitutional burden upon interstate commerce. ...

South Carolina has built its highways and owns and maintains them. It has received from the federal government, in aid of its highway improvements, money grants which have been expended upon the highways to which the injunction applies. But appellees do not challenge here the ruling of the district court that Congress has not undertaken to regulate the weight and size of motor vehicles in interstate motor traffic, and has left undisturbed whatever authority in that regard the states have retained under the Constitution.

While the constitutional grant to Congress of power to regulate interstate commerce has been held to operate of its own force to curtail state power in some measure, it did not forestall all state action affecting interstate commerce. Ever since *Willson* v. *Black Bird Creek Marsh Co.*, 2 Peters 245, and *Cooley* v. *Board of Wardens of Port of Philadelphia*, 12 Howard 299, it has been recognized that there are matters of local concern, the regulation of which unavoidably involves some regulation of interstate commerce but which, because of their local character and their number and diversity, may never be fully dealt with by Congress. Notwithstanding the commerce clause, such regulation in the absence of Congressional action has for the most part been left to the states by the decisions of this Court, subject to the other applicable constitutional restraints.

The commerce clause, by its own force, prohibits discrimination against interstate commerce, whatever its form or method, and the decisions of this Court have recognized that there is scope for its like operation when state legislation nominally of local concern is in point of fact aimed at interstate commerce, or by its necessary operation is a means of gaining a local benefit by throwing the attendant burdens on those without the state. . . .

But the present case affords no occasion for saying that the bare possession of power by Congress to regulate the interstate traffic forces the states to conform to standards which Congress might, but has not adopted, or curtails their power to take measures to insure the safety and conservation of their highways which may be applied to like traffic moving intrastate. Few subjects of state regulation are so peculiarly of local concern as is the use of state highways. . . . Unlike the railroads, local highways are built, owned and maintained by the state or its municipal subdivisions. The state has a primary and immediate concern in their safe and economical administration. The present regulations, or any others of like purpose, if they are to accomplish their end, must be applied alike to interstate and intrastate traffic both moving in large volume over the highways. The fact that they affect alike shippers in interstate and intrastate commerce in large number within as well as without the state is a safeguard against their abuse. . . .

Congress, in the exercise of its plenary power to regulate interstate commerce, may determine whether the burdens imposed on it by state regulation, otherwise permissible, are too great, and may, by legislation designed to secure uniformity or in other respects to protect the national interest in the commerce, curtail to some extent the state's regulatory power. But that is a legislative, not a judicial function, to be performed in the light of the Congressional judgment of what is appropriate regulation of interstate commerce, and the extent to which, in that field, state power and local interests should be required to yield to the national authority and interest. In the absence of such legislation the judicial function, under the commerce clause as well as the Fourteenth Amendment, stops with the inquiry whether the state legislature in adopting regulations such as the present has acted within its province, and whether the means of regulation chosen are reasonably adapted to the end sought. . . .

The fact that many states have adopted a different standard is not persuasive. The conditions under which highways must be built in the several states, their construction and the demands made upon them, are not uniform. The road building art, as the record shows, is far from having attained a scientific certainty and precision, and scientific precision is not the criterion for the exercise of the constitutional regulatory power of the states. . . . The legislature, being free to exercise its own judgment, is not bound by that of other legislatures. It would hardly be contended that if all the states had adopted a single standard none, in the light of its own experience and in the exercise of its judgment upon all the complex elements which enter into the problem, could change it. . . .

The regulatory measures taken by South Carolina are within its legislative power. They do not infringe the Fourteenth Amendment, and the resulting burden on interstate commerce is not forbidden.

Reversed.

Mr. Justice Cardozo and Mr. Justice Reed took no part in the consideration or decision of this case.

Notes

1.   *Bibb* v. *Navajo Freight Lines,* 359 US 520 (1959), held invalid as applied to interstate commerce an Illinois statute requiring trucks to use contour rear fender mudguards. "Such a new safety device—out of line with the requirements of other states—may be so compelling that the innovating state need not be the one to give way. But the present showing—balanced by the clear burden on commerce—is far too inconclusive to make this mudguard meet the test," wrote Justice Douglas.

2.   *Dean Milk Co.* v. *City of Madison,* 340 US 349 (1951), held void an ordinance of the city of Madison, Wisconsin, making it unlawful to sell any milk as pasteurized unless it had been pasteurized at a plant within a radius of five miles of the central square of Madison.

3.   *Huron Portland Cement Co.* v. *City of Detroit,* 362 US 400 (1960), sustained the application of the city's smoke-abatement code to the company's ships. "[W]hile the appellant argues that other local governments might impose differing requirements as to air pollution, it has pointed to none" wrote Justice Stewart. Contrast *Burbank* v. *Lockheed Air Terminal,* 411 US 624 (1973).

Hood & Sons v. Du Mond

336 US 525, 69 S Ct 657, 93 L Ed 865 (1949)

A state may not promote its own local economic advantage by curtailing the volume of interstate commerce.

MR. JUSTICE JACKSON delivered the opinion of the Court.

This case concerns the power of the State of New York to deny additional facilities to acquire and ship milk in interstate commerce where the grounds of denial are that such limitation upon interstate business will protect and advance local economic interests.

H. P. Hood & Sons, Inc., a Massachusetts corporation, has long distributed milk and its products to inhabitants of Boston. That city obtains about 90% of its fluid milk from states other than Massachusetts. Dairies located in New York State since about 1900 have been among the sources of Boston's supply, their contribution having varied but during the last ten years approximately 8%. The area in which Hood has been denied an additional license to make interstate purchases has been developed as a part of the Boston milkshed from which both the Hood Company and a competitor have shipped to Boston.

The state courts have held and it is conceded here that Hood's entire business in New York, present and proposed, is interstate commerce. This Hood has conducted for some time by means of three receiving depots, where it takes raw milk from farmers. The milk is not processed in New York but is weighed, tested and, if necessary, cooled and on the same day shipped as fluid milk to Boston. These existing plants have been operated under license from the State and are not in question here as the State has licensed Hood to continue them. The controversy concerns a proposed additional plant for the same kind of operation at Greenwich, New York.

Article 21 of the Agriculture and Markets Law of New York forbids a dealer to buy milk from producers unless licensed to do so by the Commissioner of Agriculture and Markets. For the license he must pay a substantial fee and furnish a bond to assure prompt payment to producers for milk. Under § 258, the Commissioner may not grant a license unless satisfied "that the applicant is qualified by character, experience, finanical responsibility and equipment to properly conduct the proposed business." The Hood Company concededly has met all the foregoing tests and license for an additional plant was not denied for any failure to comply with these requirements.

The Commissioner's denial was based on further provisions of this section which require him to be satisfied "that the issuance of the license will not tend to a destructive competition in a market already adequately served, and that the issuance of the license is in the public interest." . . .

In denying the application for expanded facilities, the Commissioner states his grounds as follows:

"If applicant is permitted to equip and operate another milk plant in this territory, and to take on producers now delivering to plants other than those which it operates, it will tend to reduce the volume of milk received at the plants which lose those producers, and will tend to increase the cost of handling milk in those plants. . . .

"The issuance of a license to applicant which would permit it to operate an additional plant, would tend to a destructive competition in a market already adequately served, and would not be in the public interest."

Denial of the license was sustained by the Court of Appeals over constitutional objections duly urged under the Commerce Clause and, because of the importance of the questions involved, we brought the case here by *certiorari.* . . .

Our decision in the milk litigation most relevant to the present controversy deals with the converse of the present situation. *Baldwin* v. *Seelig,* 294 US 511. In that case, New York placed conditions and limitations on the local sale of milk imported from Vermont designed in practical effect to exclude it, while here its order proposes to limit the local facilities for purchase of additional milk so as to withhold milk from export. . . .

"The Constitution," said Mr. Justice Cardozo [in *Baldwin* v. *Seelig*] for the unanimous Court, "was framed upon the theory that the peoples of the several states must sink or swim together, and that in the long run prosperity and salvation are in union and not division." He reiterated that the economic objective, as distinguished from any health, safety and fair-dealing purpose of the regulation, was the root of its invalidity. The action of the State would "neutralize the economic consequences of free trade among the states." "Such a power, if exerted, will set a barrier to traffic between one state and another as effective as if customs duties, equal to the price differential, had been laid upon the thing transported." "If New York, in order to promote the economic welfare of her farmers, may guard them against competition with the cheaper prices of Vermont, the door has been opened to rivalries and reprisals that were meant to be averted by subjecting commerce between the states to the power of the nation." . . .

This distinction between the power of the State to shelter its people from menaces to their health or safety and from fraud, even when those dangers emanate from interstate commerce, and its lack of power to retard, burden or constrict the flow of such commerce for their economic advantage, is one deeply rooted in both our history and our law. . . .

Since the statute as applied violates the Commerce Clause and is not authorized by federal legislation pursuant to that Clause, it cannot stand. The judgment is reversed and the cause remanded for proceedings not inconsistent with this opinion.

It is so ordered.

Mr. Justice Black, dissenting. . . .

The judicially directed march of the due process philosophy as an emancipator of business from regulation appeared arrested a few years ago. That appearance was illusory. That philosophy continues its march. The due process clause and commerce clause have been used like Siamese twins in a never-ending stream of challenges to government regulation. See for example, *Pacific Tel. Co.* v. *Tax Comm'n,* 297 US 403, 420. The reach of one twin may appear to be longer than that of the other, but either can easily be turned to remedy this apparent handicap. . . .

The basic question here is not the greatness of the commerce clause concept, but whether all local phases of interstate business are to be judicially immunized from state laws against destructive competitive business practices such as those prohibited by New York's law. Of course, there remains the bare possibility Congress might attempt to federalize all such local business activities in the forty-eight states. While I have doubt about the wisdom of this New York law, I do not conceive it to be the function of this Court to revise that state's economic judgments. Any doubt I may have concerning the wisdom of New York's law is far less, however, than is my skepticism concerning the ability of the Federal Government to reach out and effectively regulate all the local business activities in the forty-eight states. I would leave New York's law alone.

Mr. Justice Murphy joins in this opinion. . . .

[The dissenting opinion of Justice Frankfurter, concurred in by Justice Rutledge, is omitted.]

Note

Price fixing. The application of prices set by state public utilities commissions to gas and electricity sold in interstate commerce has been sustained where the local interest was deemed paramount and invalidated where the regulation was deemed to be discriminatory. The volume of the business being regulated which is interstate as compared to the volume of the local business is a factor in determining the validity of the state regulation. See *Public Utilities Commission of Rhode Island* v. *Attleboro Steam & Electric Co.,* 273 US 83 (1927).

Milk Control Board v. *Eisenberg Farm Products Co.,* 306 US 346 (1949), upheld a Pennsylvania minimum price law on the sale of milk when applied to milk purchased in Pennsylvania for shipment to New York.

Parker v. *Brown,* 317 US 341 (1943), upheld a state program requiring the cooperative marketing of raisins, under which more than half the crop was disposed of as by-products and withdrawn from the market.

Cities Service Co. v. *Peerless Co.,* 340 US 179 (1950), upheld the power of Oklahoma to fix a minimum wellhead price on all gas taken from wells in the state.

Polar Co. v. *Andrews,* 375 US 361 (1964), held invalid a Florida Milk Control Act which regulated prices and gave local producers a monopoly on the sale of Class I fluid milk.

Guss v. Utah Labor Board

353 US 1, 77 S Ct 598, 1 L Ed2d 601 (1957)

By vesting in the National Labor Relations Board jurisdiction over labor relations matters affecting interstate commerce, Congress has completely displaced state power to deal with such matters where the Board has declined to exercise its jurisdiction but has not ceded jurisdiction to a state agency pursuant to the proviso to § 10 (a) of the National Labor Relations Act.

MR. CHIEF JUSTICE WARREN delivered the opinion of the Court.

The question presented by this appeal ... is whether Congress, by vesting in the National Labor Relations Board jurisdiction over labor relations matters affecting interstate commerce, has completely displaced state power to deal with such matters where the Board has declined or obviously would decline to exercise its jurisdiction but has not ceded jurisdiction pursuant to the proviso to § 10 (a) of the National Labor Relations Act. ...

Some background is necessary for an understanding of this problem in federal-state relations and how it assumed its present importance. Since it was first enacted in 1935, the National Labor Relations Act has empowered the National Labor Relations Board "to prevent any person from engaging in any unfair labor practice ... [defined by the Act] affecting commerce." By this language and by the definition of "affecting commerce" elsewhere in the Act, Congress meant to reach to the full extent of its power under the Commerce Clause. ... The Board, however, has never exercised the full measure of its jurisdiction. For a number of years, the Board decided case-by-case whether to take jurisdiction. In 1950, concluding that "experience warrants the establishment and announcement of certain standards" to govern the exercise of its jurisdiction ... the Board published standards, largely in terms of yearly dollar amounts of interstate inflow and outflow. In 1954, a sharply divided Board ... revised the jurisdictional standards upward. This Court has never passed and we do not pass today upon the validity of any particular declination of jurisdiction by the Board or any set of jurisdictional standards.

How many labor disputes the Board's 1954 standards leave in the "twilight zone" between exercised federal jurisdiction and unquestioned state jurisdiction is not known. In any case, there has been recently a substantial volume of litigation raising the question stated at the beginning of this opinion, of which this case is an example.

Appellant [P. S. Guss], doing business in Salt Lake City, Utah, manufactures specialized photographic equipment for the Air Force on a contract basis. To fulfill his government contracts he purchased materials from outside Utah in an amount "a little less than $50,000." Finished products were shipped to Air Force bases, one within Utah and the others outside. In 1953 the United Steelworkers of America filed with the National Labor Relations Board a petition for certification of that union as the bargaining representative of appellant's employees. A consent election was agreed to, the agreement reciting that appellant was "engaged in commerce within the meaning of Section 2 (6), (7) of the National Labor Relations Act." The union won the election and was certified by the National Board as bargaining representative. Shortly thereafter the union filed with the National Board charges that appellant had engaged in unfair labor practices proscribed by . . . the Act. Meanwhile, on July 15, 1954, the Board promulgated its revised jurisdictional standards. The Board's Acting Regional Director declined to issue a complaint. He wrote on July 21:

"Further proceedings are not warranted, inasmuch as the operations of the Company involved are predominantly local in character, and it does not appear that it would effectuate the policies of the Act to exercise jurisdiction."

The union thereupon filed substantially the same charges with the Utah Labor Relations Board, pursuant to the Utah Labor Relations Act. Appellant urged that the State Board was without jurisdiction of a matter within the jurisdiction of the National Board. The State Board, however, found it had jurisdiction and concluded on the merits that appellant had engaged in unfair labor practices as defined by the Utah Act. It granted relief through a remedial order. On a Writ of Review, the Utah Supreme Court affirmed the decision and order of the state administrative agency. We noted probable jurisdiction. . . .

On these facts we start from the following uncontroverted premises:

(1) Appellant's business affects commerce within the meaning of the National Labor Relations Act and the National Labor Relations Board had jurisdiction. . . .

(2) The National Act expressly deals with the conduct charged to appellant which was the basis of the state tribunals' actions. Therefore, if the National Board had not declined jurisdiction, state action would have been precluded. . . .

(3) The National Board has not entered into any cession agreement with the Utah Board pursuant to § 10 (a) of the National Act.

Section 10(a) provides:

"The Board is empowered, as hereinafter provided, to prevent any person from engaging in any unfair labor practice (listed in section 8) affecting commerce. This power shall not be affected by any other means of adjustment or prevention that has been or may be established by agreement, law, or otherwise: *Provided, That the Board is empowered by agreement with any agency of any State or Territory to cede to such agency jurisdiction over any cases in any industry (other than mining, manufacturing, communications, and transportation except where predominantly local in character) even though such cases may involve labor disputes affecting commerce, unless the provision of the State or Territorial statute applicable to the determination of such cases by such agency is inconsistent with the corresponding provision of this Act or has received a construction inconsistent therewith.*" (Emphasis added.). . .

We hold that the proviso to § 10(a) is the exlusive means whereby States may be enabled to act concerning the matters which Congress has entrusted to the National Labor Relations Board. . . .

We are told by appellee that to deny the State jurisdiction here will create a vast no-man's-land, subject to regulation by no agency or court. We are told by appellant that to grant jurisdiction would produce confusion and conflicts with federal policy. Unfortunately, both may be right. We believe, however, that Congress has expressed its judgment in favor of uniformity. Since Congress' power in the area of commerce among the States is plenary, its judgment must be respected whatever policy objections there may be to creation of a no-man's-land.

Congress is free to change the situation at will. . . .

The judgment of the Supreme Court of Utah is

Reversed.

MR. JUSTICE WHITTAKER took no part in the consideration or decision of this case.

MR. JUSTICE CLARK, whom MR. JUSTICE BURTON joins, dissenting.

I believe the Court is mistaken in its interpretation of the proviso which Congress added to § 10(a) of the National Labor Relations Act in 1947. It is my view that the proviso was added merely to make it clear the the National Labor Relations Board had the power, by making specific agreements, to cede jurisdiction to state or territorial agencies over certain labor disputes. . . .

The Court's interpretation of the proviso is contrary to the established practice of the States and of the National Board, as well as to the considered position taken by the Board as *amicus curiae*. Congress has demonstrated a continuing and deep interest in providing governmental machinery for handling labor controversies. The creation by it of a large, unsupervised no man's land flies in the face of that policy. Due regard for our federal sytem suggests that all doubts on this score should be resolved in favor of a conclusion that would not leave the States powerless when the federal agency declines to exercise its jurisdiction. . . .

Notes

1. *Erie Railroad Co.* v. *New York,* 233 US 671 (1914), held void a state eight-hour work day law for railroad telegraph operators because of the existence of a five-hour law on the same subject by Congress.

2. *Napier* v. *Atlantic Coast Line Railroad Co.,* 272 US 605 (1926), held that the Federal Boiler Inspection Act of 1911, making it unlawful for a railroad to operate a locomotive not in safe operating condition, and providing for federal inspection, made invalid state laws requiring specific safety devices for locomotives.

3. *Campbell* v. *Hussey,* 368 US 297 (1961), held void a Georgia law requiring that tobacco grown in Georgia be identified as such when offered for sale at tobacco markets in Georgia. The Georgia law, designed to prevent large quantities of tobacco grown in other states and having a different flavor from being sold as Georgia-grown tobacco, was found to be in a field preempted by the Federal Tobacco Inspection Act.

4. *Brotherhood of Locomotive Engineers* v. *Chicago, R.I. & P. Rd. Co.,* 382 US 423 (1966), sustained an Arkansas statute which made it an offense for any railroad to operate in that state without specified numbers of crewmen, including a fireman and three brakemen. The Court held that the federal statute on which the railroad company relied as preempting the field was not intended to supersede state full-crew laws.

5. *Motor Coach Employees* v. *Lockridge,* 403 US 274 (1971), held that, Congress having placed exclusive jurisdiction over unfair labor practices in the NLRB, the courts of Idaho lacked power to decide a breach of contract suit brought by a former union member against the union. "Since pre-emption is designed to shield the [labor] system from conflicting regulation of conduct, the formal description of that conduct [as a breach of contract] is immaterial," held the majority. Four justices dissented.

6. *Burbank* v. *Lockheed Air Terminal,* 411 US 624 (1973), held that the Federal Aviation Act of 1958, as amended by the Noise Control Act of 1972, preempts a local ordinance prohibiting jet aircraft takeoffs during specified hours of the day. Four justices dissented.

7. *Kewanee Oil Co.* v. *Bicron Corp.,* 416 US 470 (1974), held Ohio's trade-secret law was not preempted by the federal patent law. "Just as the States may exercise regulatory power over writings [*Goldstein* v. *California,* 412 US 546 (1973)] so may the States regulate with respect to discoveries" so long as the state laws do not obstruct congressional policy.

8. *William E. Arnold Co.* v. *Carpenters District Council,* US (1974), held that a state court had jurisdiction to enforce a collective-bargaining agreement and to enjoin a strike in violation of a no-strike clause therein, even though the strike was arguably an unfair labor practice prohibited by federal law. The authority of the NLRB "is not exclusive and does not destroy the jurisdiction of the courts in suits under § 301."

C. TAXATION OF COMMERCE

Brown v. Maryland

12 Wheaton 419, 6 L Ed 678 (1827)

An article imported from abroad, remaining the property of the importer, and in the original package in which it was imported, is not subject to taxation by a state.

MARSHALL, C. J., delivered the opinion of the Court.

This is a writ of error to a judgment rendered in the court of appeals of Maryland, affirming a judgment of the city court of Baltimore, on an indictment found in that court against the plaintiffs in error, for violating an act of the legislature of Maryland. The indictment was founded on the 2d section of that act, which is in these words: "And be it enacted that all importers of foreign articles or commodities, of dry goods, wares, or merchandise, by bale or package, or of wine, rum, brandy, whiskey, and other distilled spirituous liquors, etc., and other persons selling the same by wholesale, bale or package, hogshead, barrel, or tierce, shall, before they are authorized to sell, take out a license . . . for which they shall pay fifty dollars; and in case of neglect or refusal to take out such license, shall be subject to the same penalties and forfeitures as are prescribed by the original act to which this is a supplement." The indictment charges the plaintiffs in error with having imported and sold one package of foreign dry goods without having license to do so. A judgment was rendered against them, on demurrer, for the penalty which the act prescribes for the offence; and that judgment is now before this court.

The cause depends entirely on the question whether the legislature of a state can constitutionally require the importer of foreign articles to take out a license from the State, before he shall be permitted to sell a bale or package so imported. . . .

The plaintiffs in error . . . insist that the act under consideration is repugnant to two provisions in the Constitution of the United States.

1. To that which declares that "no State shall, without the consent of Congress, lay any imposts or duties on imports or exports, except what may be absolutely necessary for executing its inspection laws."

2. To that which declares that Congress shall have power "to regulate commerce with foreign nations, and among the several States, and with the Indian tribes."

1. The first inquiry is into the extent of the prohibition upon States "to lay any imposts or duties on imports or exports." . . .

What . . . is the meaning of the words, "imposts or duties on imports or exports?"

An impost, or duty on imports, is a custom or a tax levied on articles brought into a country, and is most usually secured before the importer is allowed to exercise his rights of ownership over them, because evasions of the law can be prevented more certainly by executing it while the articles are in its custody. It would not, however, be less an impost or duty on the articles, if it were to be levied on them after they were landed. . . .

The counsel for the State of Maryland insist, with great reason, that if the words of the prohibition be taken in their utmost latitude, they will abridge the power of taxation, which all admit to be essential to the States, to an extent which has never yet been suspected, and will deprive them of resources which are necessary to supply revenue, and which they have heretofore been admitted to possess. These words must, therefore, be construed with some limitation; and, if this be admitted, they insist, that entering the country is the point of time when the prohibition ceases, and the power of the State to tax commences.

It may be conceded that the words of the prohibition ought not to be pressed to their utmost extent; that in our complex system, the object of the powers conferred on the Government of the Union, and the nature of the often conflicting powers which remain in the States, must always be taken into view, and may aid in expounding the words of any particular clause. But, while we admit that sound principles of construction ought to restrain all courts from carrying the words of the prohibition beyond the object the Constitution is intended to secure; that there must be a point of time when the prohibition ceases, and the power of the State to tax commences; we cannot admit that this point of time is the instant that the articles enter the country. It is, we think, obvious, that this construction would defeat the prohibition.

The constitutional prohibition on the States to lay a duty on imports, a prohibition which a vast majority of them must feel an interest in preserving, may certainly come in conflict with their acknowledged power to tax persons and property within their territory. The power, and the restriction on it, though quite distinguishable when they do not approach each other, may yet, like the intervening colors between white and black, approach so nearly as to perplex the understanding, as colors perplex the vision in marking the distinction between them. Yet the distinction exists, and must be marked as the cases arise. Till they do arise, it might be premature to state any rule as being universal in its application. It is sufficient for the present to say, generally, that when the importer has so acted upon the thing imported, that it has become incorporated and mixed up with the mass of property in the country, it has, perhaps, lost its distinctive character as an import, and has become subject to the taxing power of the State; but while remaining the property of the importer, in his warehouse, in the original form or package in which it was imported, a tax upon it is too plainly a duty on imports to escape the prohibition in the Constitution. . . .

But if it should be proved that duty on the article itself would be repugnant to the Constitution, it is still argued that this is not a tax upon the article, but on the person. The State, it is said, may tax occupations, and this is nothing more.

It is impossible to conceal from ourselves that this is varying the form without varying the substance. It is treating a prohibition which is general, as if it were confined to a particular mode of doing the forbidden thing. All must perceive that a tax on the sale of an article, imported only for sale, is a tax on the article itself. It is true the State may tax occupations generally, but this tax must be paid by those who employ the individual, or is a tax on his business. The lawyer, the physician, or the mechanic, must either charge more on the article in which he deals, or the thing itself is taxed through his person. This the State has a right to do, because no constitutional prohibition extends to it. So a tax on the occupation of an importer is, in like manner, a tax on importation. It must add to the price of the article, and be paid by the consumer, or by the importer himself, in like manner as a direct duty on the article itself would be made. This the State has not a right to do, because it is prohibited by the Constitution. . . .

2. Is it also repugnant to that clause in the Constitution which empowers "congress to regulate commerce with foreign nations, and among the several States, and with the Indian tribes?" . . .

What would be the language of a foreign government, which should be informed that its merchants, after importing according to law, were forbidden to sell the merchandise imported? What answer would the United States give to the complaints and just reproaches to which such an extraordinary circumstance would expose them? No apology could be received, or even offered. Such a state of things would break up commerce. . . .

We think there is error in the judgment of the court of appeals of the State of Maryland, in affirming the judgment of the Baltimore city court, because the act of the legislature of Maryland, imposing the penalty for which the said judgment is rendered, is repugnant to the constitution of the United States, and, consequently, void. The judgment is to be reversed, and the cause remanded to that court, with instructions to enter judgment in favor of the appellants.

[JUSTICE THOMPSON dissented.]

Notes

1. *The original package rule.*   The original package rule formulated in *Brown* v. *Maryland* appears to be still used in determining when foreign imports become subject to taxation. In 1945, the Court held that hemp imported and stored in original packages for three years was still exempt from taxation. *Hoover & Allison Co.* v. *Evatt,* 324 US 652. In *United States Plywood Corp.* v. *City of Algoma,* (decided together with *Youngstown Sheet & Tube Co.* v. *Bowers*), 358 US 534 (1958), the Court did relax the original package rule to the extent of permitting a city in Wisconsin to collect a property tax on imported lumber, some of it in "bundles" that had not been opened. The lumber was stored in the owner's plant and used as needed in the day-to-day operations of the plant, thus losing its character as an "import."

The dictum of Chief Justice Marshall in *Brown* v. *Maryland* that "we suppose the principles laid down in this case apply equally to importations from a sister state" has been rejected. In *Woodruff* v. *Parham,* 8 Wallace 123 (1869), the Court sustained a tax by the City of Mobile upon the sale of all merchandise when applied to the sale at auction in original packages of goods imported from other States. But it should be remembered that in *Brown* v. *Maryland,* Chief Justice Marshall held the state tax void both because it was a burden on foreign commerce and because it was a tax on an import. In *Woodruff* v. *Parham* the Court held that the words "imports and exports" used in Article I, Section 10, expressly forbidding any state to tax imports and exports, included "only merchandise brought in from, or transported to, foreign countries."

2. *The Passenger cases.*   In these cases, 7 Howard 283 (1849), the Court held void laws of New York and Massachusetts that placed a tax for each passenger on the master of each ship, the revenue from the tax to be used to defray the cost of examining the passengers for contagious diseases.

Kosydar v. National Cash Register Co.

416 US   , 94 S Ct 2108, 40 L Ed2d 660 (1974)

Machines built to foreign buyer's specifications and intended for exportation are subject to taxation until the process of exportation has begun.

MR. JUSTICE STEWART delivered the opinion of the Court.

The Import-Export Clause of the Constitution, Art. I, § 10, cl. 2, provides:

"No State shall, without the Consent of the Congress, lay any Imposts or Duties on Imports or Exports, except what may be absolutely necessary for executing its inspection Laws: and the net Produce of all Duties and Imports, laid by any State on Imports or Exports, shall be for the Use of the Treasury of the United States; and all such Laws shall be subject to the Revision and Control of the Congress."

The issue for decision in this case is whether the assessment of an *ad valorem* personal property tax by the petitioner Tax Commissioner of Ohio upon certain property of the respondent is in conflict with this Clause.

I

The respondent National Cash Register Company (NCR) has for many years engaged in the manufacture of cash registers, accounting machines, and electronic data processing systems, which it markets worldwide. Its home offices, main production plant, and warehouse are located in Dayton, Ohio. For marketing purposes, NCR is organized into two divisions, domestic and international, each wholly separated from the other. It is with the operations of the latter division that this case is concerned.

NCR maintains no inventory of machines which are available to meet incoming orders from foreign customers. Rather, when a salesman from the international division receives an order from a customer, an individual order form is completed. The machine is then built to specification, taking into account the commercial peculiarities of the country to which it is to be shipped and the buyer's individual needs.

After manufacture, the machine is inspected, packed, and crated for shipment abroad. The crated machine is then taken to an NCR warehouse in Dayton, to await foreign shipment. The machines relevant to this case were in storage in the Dayton warehouse, awaiting shipment, on December 31, 1967, when the petitioner Tax Commissioner assessed a personal property tax upon them.

NCR appealed the Commissioner's assessment to the Board of Tax Appeals of the Ohio Department of Taxation. Its basic claim was that the "international inventory" in the Dayton warehouse was made up of exports, and thus was immune from State taxation under the Import-Export Clause. In support of this contention, NCR offered evidence to show that, because of their unique construction and special adaptation for foreign use, the crated machines were not salable domestically. Further evidence was offered to show that no piece of equipment built for the international division has ever gone anywhere but into that division; that there is no recorded instance of a machine that was sold to a foreign purchaser being returned; and that no exported item has ever found its way back into the United States market.

The Board of Tax Appeals nonetheless upheld the Commissioner's assessment. It ruled that even if the crated machines were irrevocably committed to export, the immunity from State taxation conferred by Art. I, § 10, cl. 2, did not attach until the property actually started on its journey to a foreign destination. Since the machines here had not yet entered the export stream, the Board of Tax Appeals concluded that they were still subject to the personal property tax.

The Supreme Court of Ohio reversed this decision by a divided vote. . . . Relying on the evidence about the domestic nonsalability of the machines, the state court concluded that there was a "certainty of export" in this case. Given that "certainty," the court thought it irrelevant for Import-Export Clause purposes that the taxed machines had not, on the date of the assessment, been moved from the storage facility in Dayton. We granted *certiorari* . . . because the case seemed to present important questions touching the accommodation of state and federal interests under the Constitution.

II

By its own terms, the prohibition on taxation contained in the Import-Export Clause is absolute; no duties or imposts are allowed "except what may be absolutely necessary for executing [a State's] inspection Laws." Consequently the essential question in cases involving the Clause is a narrow one: is the property upon which a tax has been sought to be imposed an "export," and thus entitled to protection under the provisions' literal terms?

The seminal case on the subject is *Coe* v. *Errol*, 116 US 517. *Coe* involved a shipment of spruce logs that had been hewn at various locations in Maine and New Hampshire, and were to be floated down the Androgscoggin River for manufacture and sale in Lewiston, Maine. The logs were detained by low water in the town of Errol, New Hampshire, where the local selectmen assessed a number of taxes upon them. The owners of the logs contested the assessments, claiming that the property was immune from taxation under both the Commerce and Import-Export clauses, since the river served as a "public highway" for the interstate shipment of timber. The Supreme Court of New Hampshire sustained the tax, and this Court affirmed.

Writing for the Court, Mr. Justice Bradley viewed "the precise question for solution" as follows:

> "Do the owner's state of mind in relation to the goods, that is, his intent to export them, and his partial preparation to do so, exempt them from taxation?" 116 US, at 525.

That question was answered in the negative. Recognizing that its task was to set a "point in time when State jurisdiction over the commodities of commerce begins and ends," *id.*, at 526, the Court concluded that

> "[S]uch goods do not cease to be part of the general mass of property in the State, subject, as such, to its jurisdiction, and to taxation in the usual way, *until they have been shipped, or entered with a common carrier for transportation to another State, or have been started upon such transportation in a continuous route or journey.*" *Id.*, at 527 (emphasis added).

Since the logs in *Coe* had not begun a "final movement for transportation from the State of their origin to that of their destination," *id.*, at 525, the Court held that the Constitution provided no immunity from local taxation.

The basic principle of *Coe* v. *Errol* is a simple one—the exemption from taxation in the Import-Export Clause "attaches to the export and not to the article before its exportation." *Cornell* v. *Coyne*, 192 US 418, 427. This Court has adhered to that principle in the almost 90 years since *Coe* was decided, and the essential problem in cases involving the constitutional prohibition against taxation of exports has therefore been to decide whether a sufficient commencement of the process of exportation has occurred so as to immunize the article at issue from state taxation. Of necessity, the inquiry has usually been a factual one. For example, in *A. G. Spalding & Bros.* v. *Edwards*, 262 US 66, this Court decided that delivery of baseballs and bats to an export carrier for shipment to Venezuela constituted a significant "step in exportation," *id.*, at 68, and exempted the goods from a federal income tax. Similarly, in *Richfield Oil Corp.* v. *State Board of Equalization,* 329 US 69, it was held that the delivery of oil into the storage tanks of a New Zealand-bound steamer "marked the commencement of the movement of the oil abroad," *id.,* at 83, making the product immune from a California sales tax.

Yet, even if the inquiry in cases like *Spalding* and *Richfield Oil* was specifically directed at determining whether particular acts of movement toward a final destination constituted sufficient entrance into the export stream to invoke the protection of the Import-Export Clause, this Court has never lost sight of one basic principle—at least *some* such entrance is a prerequisite to the Clause's operation. That fact is well-illustrated by the opinion of the Court in *Empresa Siderurgica* v. *County of Merced,* 337 US 154. That case involved a California cement plant, which had been sold to a Colombian buyer. Title to the property has passed to the buyer, and a common carrier had begun to dismantle the plant and crate it for shipment to Colombia.

At a stage when 12% of the plant had been shipped out of the country, the county of Merced levied a personal property tax on the remaining 88%. This balance included about 10% of the original plant that had been dismantled and crated or prepared for shipment, but which had not yet begun its voyage to Colombia. This Court held that the tax on the 88%, including this crated portion, did not violate the Import-Export Clause. Adhering to the test of *Coe* v. *Errol,* the Court stated:

"Under that test it is not enough that there is an intent to export, or a plan which contemplates exportation, or an integrated series of events which will end in it. . . . It is the entrance of the articles into the export stream that marks the start of the process of exportation. Then there is certainty that the goods are headed for their foreign destination and will not be diverted to domestic use. Nothing less will suffice." *Id.,* at 156–157.

Since the 88% of the cement plant had not yet begun its out-of-state journey, the Court concluded that the California tax was not one upon "exports" within the meaning of the Clause.

We can find little in the case before us to take it outside the ambit of the *Empresa Siderurgica* holding. At the time that the respondent's machines were assessed for taxation, they were sitting in the Dayton warehouse awaiting shipment. Title and possession were in NCR, payment had not yet been made by the putative purchasers, no export license had issued, and the machines were in the complete control of the respondent. More important, there had simply been no movement of the goods—no shipment, and no commencement of the process of exportation. Given this factual setting, it would require a sharp departure from nearly a century of precedents under the Import-Export Clause for us to conclude that the machines were "exports" and exempt from state taxation.

In an effort to avoid the clear holdings of our prior cases, NCR emphasizes the peculiar nature of the taxed machines, and contends that their nonadaptability to domestic use brought about a "certainty of export." Because of this practical absence of "diversion potential," NCR argues that the ultimate placement of the machines into the stream of exportation is a mere formality, and that this Court should treat the crated property as already having become an export in the constitutional sense even as it sits in the Dayton warehouse.

As a practical matter, it might well be doubted that the "diversion potential" of the crated portions of the cement plant in *Empresa Siderurgica* was any greater than that present here. But, even assuming *arguendo* the validity of NCR's arguments about the practical certainty of export here, we think it plain that the warehoused machines are not entitled to the protection of the Import-Export Clause. Mr. Justice Frankfurter put the matter succinctly in *Joy Oil Co.* v. *State Tax Comm'n,* 337 US 286, 288:

> "The Export-Import Clause was meant to confer immunity from local taxation upon property being exported, not to relieve property eventually to be exported from its share of the cost of local services."

We may accept as fact the respondent's assurances that the prospect of eventual exportation here was virtually certain. "But that prospect, no matter how bright, does not start the process of exportation. On the tax date the movement to foreign shores had neither started nor been committed." *Empresa Siderurgica, supra,* at 157. Given the absence of an entrance of the respondent's machines into the export stream, the immunities of the Import-Export Clause are unavailable.

It may be said that insistence upon an actual movement into the stream of export in the case at hand represents an overly wooden or mechanistic application of the *Coe* doctrine. This is an instance, however, where we believe that simplicity has its virtues. The Court recognized long ago that even if it is not an easy matter to set down a rule determining the moment in time when articles obtain the protection of the Import-Export Clause, "it is highly important, both to the shipper and to the State, that it should be clearly defined so as to avoid all ambiguity or question." *Coe, supra,* at 526. As Mr. Justice Holmes put the matter in *A. G. Spalding, supra,* at 69:

> "[W]e have to fix a point at which, in view of the purpose of the Constitution, the export must be said to begin. As elsewhere in the law there will be other points very near to it on the other side, so that if the necessity of fixing one definitely is not remembered any determination may seem arbitrary."

Our prior cases have determined that the protections of the Import-Export Clause are not available until the article at issue begins its physical entry into the stream of exportation. We find no reason to depart from that settled doctrine.

For these reasons, the judgment of the Supreme Court of Ohio is

Reversed.

Best & Co. v. Maxwell

311 US 454, 61 S Ct 334, 85 L Ed 275 (1940)

A state tax which in practical operation works discrimination against interstate commerce is void.

MR. JUSTICE REED delivered the opinion of the Court.

Appellant, a New York retail merchandise establishment, rented a display room in a North Carolina hotel for several days during February, 1938, and took orders for goods corresponding to samples; it filled the orders by shipping direct to the customers from New York City. Before using the room appellant paid under protest the tax required by . . . the North Carolina Laws of 1937, which levies an annual privilege tax of $250 on every person or corporation, not a regular retail merchant in the state, who displays samples in any hotel room rented or occupied temporarily for the purpose of securing retail orders. Appellant not being a regular retail merchant of North Carolina admittedly comes within the statute. Asserting, however, that the tax was unconstitutional, especially in view of the commerce clause, it brought this suit for a refund and succeeded in the trial court. The Supreme Court of North Carolina reversed. . . .

The commerce clause forbids discrimination, whether forthright or ingenious. In each case it is our duty to determine whether the statute under attack, whatever its name may be, will in its practical operation work discrimination against interstate commerce. This standard we think condemns the tax at bar. Nominally the statute taxes all who are not regular retail merchants in North Carolina, regardless of whether they are residents or nonresidents. We must assume, however, on this record that those North Carolina residents competing with appellant for the sale of similar merchandise will normally be regular retail merchants. The retail stores of the state are the natural outlets for the merchandise, not those who sell only by sample. Some of these local shops may, like appellant, rent temporary display rooms in sections of North Carolina where they have no permanent store, but even these escape the tax at bar because the location of their central retail store somewhere within the state will qualify them as "regular retail merchants in the State of North Carolina." The only corresponding fixed-sum license tax to which appellant's real competitors are subject is a tax of $1 per annum for the privilege of doing business. Nonresidents wishing to display their wares must either establish themselves as regular North Carolina retail merchants at prohibitive expense, or else pay this $250 tax that bears no relation to actual or probable sales but must be paid in advance no matter how small the sales turn out to be. Interstate commerce can hardly survive in so hostile an atmosphere. A $250 investment in advance, required of out-of-state retailers but not of their real local competitors, can operate only to discourage and hinder the appearance of interstate commerce in the North Carolina retail market. Extrastate merchants would be compelled to turn over their North Carolina trade to regular local merchants selling by sample. North Carolina regular retail merchants would benefit, but to the same extent the commerce of the Nation would suffer discrimination.

The freedom of commerce which allows the merchants of each state a regional or national market for their goods is not to be fettered by legislation, the actual effect of which is to discriminate in favor of intrastate businesses, whatever may be the ostensible reach of the language.

Reversed.

Notes

1. *Drummers:* Robbins v. *Shelby County Taxing District,* 120 US 489 (1887), is the first in the long line of cases protecting "drummers" engaged in interstate commerce. Sabine Robbins was convicted and fined in Shelby County for displaying samples and soliciting orders for goods to be shipped in interstate

commerce without having paid a fee and obtained the license required of drummers by Tennessee law. In reversing the conviction, Justice Bradley wrote: "It is strongly urged . . . that no discrimination is made between domestic and foreign drummers—those of Tennessee and those of other States; that all are taxed alike. But that does not meet the difficulty. Interstate commerce cannot be taxed at all. . . ." Drummers, may, however, be regulated by a municipal ordinance forbidding as a nuisance the practice of going "in and upon private residences" for the purpose of soliciting orders when uninvited. *Breard* v. *Alexandria,* 341 US 622 (1951). Contrast, however, the decision in *Murdock* v. *Pennsylvania,* 319 US 105 (1943), where religious literature only was sold.

A review of the drummer cases is given in the opinions in *Eli Lilly & Co.* v. *Sav-on-Drugs,* 366 US 276 (1961). In that case the Court sustained a New Jersey statute requiring foreign corporations transacting business in the state to obtain a certificate of authority to do business there as a condition precedent to maintaining a suit in a state court. Lilly had nineteen salaried employees in New Jersey soliciting business, but contended that its business in the state was entirely in interstate commerce, and hence it could not be required to obtain a license as a condition to bringing suit in the New Jersey courts growing out of this business. The Court felt that the facts showed that Lilly was transacting intrastate as well as interstate business.

2. *Peddlers.*   While drummers taking orders for goods to be shipped into a state cannot be taxed for the privilege, hawkers and peddlers selling goods produced by out-of-state vendors are subject to taxation. *Wagner* v. *City of Covington,* 251 US 95 (1919). But a tax on peddlers of products produced outside the state, but not upon goods produced within the state, is discriminatory and void. *Walton* v. *Missouri,* 91 US 275 (1875).

Henneford v. Silas Mason Co.

300 US 577, 57 S Ct 524, 81 L Ed 814 (1937)

When goods imported in interstate commerce have become part of the common mass of property within the state of destination, that state may subject them to a property tax, or to a tax upon their use.

MR. JUSTICE CARDOZO delivered the opinion of the Court.

A statute of Washington taxing the use of chattels in that state is assailed in this suit as a violation of the commerce clause . . . insofar as the tax is applicable to chattels purchased in another state and used in Washington thereafter.

Plaintiffs [Silas Mason Co.] are engaged either as contractors or as subcontractors in the construction of the Grand Coulee Dam on the Columbia River. In the performance of that work they have brought into the state of Washington machinery, materials and supplies, such as locomotives, cars, conveyors, pumps, and trestle steel, which were bought at retail in other states. The cost of all the articles with transportation expenses added was $921,189.34. Defendants [Henneford *et al.*], the Tax Commission of Washington . . . gave notice that plaintiffs had become subject through the use of this property to a tax of $18,423.78, two per cent of the cost, and made demand for payment. A District Court of three judges . . . adjudged the statute void upon its face, and granted an interlocutory injunction. . . . The case is here upon appeal. . . .

Chapter 180 of the Laws of Washington for the year 1935 . . . lays a multitude of excise taxes on occupations and activities. Only two of these taxes are important for the purposes of the case at hand, the "tax on retail sales," imposed by Title III, and the "compensating tax," imposed by Title IV on the privilege of use. Title III provides that after May 1, 1935, every retail sale in Washington, with a few enumerated exceptions, shall be subject to a tax of 2% of the selling price. Title IV, with the heading "compensating tax," provides . . . that there shall be collected from every person in the state "a tax or excise for the privilege of using within this state any article of tangible personal property purchased subsequent to April 30, 1935," at the rate of 2% of the purchase price, including in such price the cost of transportation from the place where the article was purchased. If those provisions stood alone, they would mean that retail buyers within the state would have to pay a double tax, 2% upon the sale and 2% upon the use. Relief from such a burden is provided in another section which qualifies the use tax by allowing four exceptions. Only two of these exceptions (b and c) call for mention at this time. Subdivision (b) provides that the use tax shall not be laid unless the property has been bought at retail. Subdivision (c) provides that the tax shall not apply to the "use of any article of tangible personal property the sale or use of which has already been subjected to a tax equal to or in excess of that imposed by this title whether under the laws of this state or of some other state of the United States." If the rate of such tax is less than 2%, the exemption is not to be complete, but in such circumstances the rate is to be measured by the difference. . . .

The practical effect of a system thus conditioned is readily perceived. One of its effects must be that retail sellers in Washington will be helped to compete upon terms of equality with retail dealers in other states who are exempt from a sales tax or any corresponding burden. Another effect, or at least another tendency, must be to avoid the likelihood of a drain upon the revenues of the state, buyers being no longer tempted to place their orders in other states in the effort to escape payment of the tax on local sales. Do these consequences which must have been foreseen, necessitate a holding that the tax upon the use is either a tax upon the operations of interstate commerce or a discrimination against such commerce obstructing or burdening it unlawfully?

1. The tax is not upon the operations of interstate commerce, but upon the privilege of use after commerce is at an end.

Things acquired or transported in interstate commerce may be subjected to a property tax, non-discriminatory in its operation, when they have become part of the common mass of property within the state of destination. . . . A state is at liberty, if it pleases, to tax them all collectively, or to separate the faggots and lay the charge distributively. . . . Calling the tax an excise when it is laid solely upon the use . . . does not make the power to impose it less, for anything the commerce clause has to say of its validity, than calling it a property tax and laying it on ownership. "A nondiscriminatory tax upon local sales . . . has never been regarded as imposing a direct burden upon interstate commerce and has no greater or different effect upon that commerce than a general property tax to which all those enjoying the protection of the State may be subjected." . . . A tax upon the privilege of use or storage when the chattel used or stored has ceased to be in transit is now an import so common that its validity has been withdrawn from the arena of debate. . . .

2. The tax upon the use after the property is at rest is not so measured or conditioned as to hamper the transactions of interstate commerce or discriminate against them.

Equality is the theme that runs through all the sections of the statute. There shall be a tax upon the use, but subject to an offset if another use or sales tax has been paid for the same thing. This is true where the offsetting tax became payable to Washington by reason of purchase or use within the state. It is true in exactly the same measure where the offsetting tax has been paid to another state by reason of use or purchase there. . . .

[A] word of caution should be added here to avoid the chance of misconception. We have not meant to imply by anything said in this opinion that allowance of a credit for other taxes paid to Washington made it mandatory that there should be a like allowance for taxes paid to other states. A state, for many purposes, is to be reckoned as a self-contained unit, which may frame its own system of burdens and exemptions without heeding systems elsewhere. If there are limits to that power, there is no need to mark them now. It will be time enough to mark them when a taxpayer paying in the state of origin is compelled to pay again in the state of destination. This statute by its framework avoids that possibility. The offsetting allowance has been conceded, whether the concession was necessary or not, and thus the system has been divested of any semblance of inequality or prejudice. A taxing act is not invalid because its exemptions are more generous than the state would have been free to make them by exerting the full measure of her power. . . .

The interlocutory injunction was erroneously granted, and the decree must be

Reversed.

MR. JUSTICE McREYNOLDS and MR. JUSTICE BUTLER dissent.

Notes

1. *Sales taxes.*   *McGoldrick* v. *Burwind-White Coal Min. Co.,* 309 US 33 (1940), sustained the imposition of a New York City sales tax of 2 percent on the sale of coal to be shipped from Pennsylvania. Delivery of the coal was the taxable event and the sale was made in New York. Justice Stone emphasized that the sales tax was not aimed at and did not discriminate against interstate commerce.

McLeod v. *Dilworth Co.,* 322 US 327 (1944), modified the rule of the *McGoldrick* case by holding that a sales tax by the state of the buyer was invalid where the sale was made outside the state.

A sales tax on a sale in interstate commerce by the state of the seller was held void in *Freeman* v. *Hewit,* 329 US 249 (1946). In the majority opinion, Justice Frankfurter pointed out that a seller state had other means of extracting from interstate commerce a fair tithe for the local protection afforded it, for example, a tax on manufacturing, license taxes, and income taxes.

In a concurring opinion, Justice Rutledge made this statement: "The alternative methods available for avoiding the multiple state tax burden may now be stated. They are: (1) To apply the . . . ruling, stopping such taxes at the source, unless the tax is apportioned, thus eliminating the cumulative burdens; (2) to rule that either the state of origin or the state of market, but not both, can levy the exaction; (3) To determine factually in each case whether application of the tax can be made by one state without incurring actual danger of its being made in another or the risk of real uncertainty whether in fact it will be so made. . . . I think the solution most nearly in accord with the commerce clause . . . would be to vest the power to tax in the state of the market, subject to power in the forwarding state also to tax by allowing credit to the full amount of any tax paid or due at the destination. . . ."

2. *Use taxes.* Most states have adopted use taxes as a complement to their sales tax in order to avert evasion of their sales tax by purchasing outside the state. But how is a state to collect a use tax on goods purchased outside the state? The simplest solution is to make the vendor, wherever located, the state's tax collecting agency; but this cannot be done in all cases.

Nelson v. *Sears, Roebuck & Co.,* 312 US 359 (1941), held that Iowa could require a company maintaining a place of business in the state to collect a use tax on all goods sold for use within Iowa, including goods sold by mail order from out-of-state branches of the company.

General Trading Co. v. *Tax Commissioner,* 322 US 335 (1944), held that Iowa could require a company to collect its use tax even though it had no local office in Iowa when the company employed soliciting agents in Iowa. Compare the ruling in *Scripto* v. *Carson,* 362 US 207 (1960).

Miller Brothers Co. v. *Maryland,* 347 US 340 (1954), marked a limit to the power of a state to make vendors in other states collecting agents of use taxes. Miller Brothers operated a department store in Wilmington, Delaware. Maryland seized one of Miller Brothers' trucks while in Maryland delivering goods on the ground that Miller Brothers was indebted to Maryland for use taxes on goods sold to Maryland residents when the sale was accompanied by a request that the goods be delivered in Maryland. The Court held that this was insufficient jurisdictional basis for placing the burden of collecting the tax on Miller Brothers. Compare *National Bellas Hess* v. *Dept. of Revenue,* 386 US 753 (1967).

United Air Lines v. *Mahin,* 410 US 623 (1973), held that Illinois could collect a use tax on "all fuel stored in Illinois and loaded aboard United's aircraft for in-flight consumption." The taxable event was withdrawal from storage, not consumption.

Braniff Airways v. Nebraska

347 US 590, 74 S Ct 757, 98 L Ed 967 (1954)

A state tax on airplanes employed in interstate commerce, apportioned according to their use within the state, is valid.

MR. JUSTICE REED delivered the opinion of the Court.

The question presented by this appeal from the Supreme Court of Nebraska is whether the Constitution bars the State of Nebraska from levying an apportioned ad valorem tax on the flight equipment of appellant, an interstate air carrier. Appellant is not incorporated in Nebraska and does not have its principal place of business or home port registered under the Civil Aeronautics Act ... in that state. Such flight equipment is employed as a part of a system of interstate air commerce operating over fixed routes and landing on and departing from airports within Nebraska on regular schedules. Appellant does not challenge the reasonableness of the apportionment prescribed by the taxing statute or the application of such apportionment to its property. It contends only that its flight equipment used in interstate commerce is immune from taxation by Nebraska because without situs in that state and because of regulation of air navigation by the Federal Government precludes such state taxation ...

The home port registered with the Civil Aeronautics Authority and the overhaul base for the aircraft in question is the Minneapolis-St. Paul Airport, Minnesota. All of the aircraft not undergoing overhaul fly regular schedules upon a circuit ranging from Minot, North Dakota, to New Orleans, Louisiana, with stops in fourteen states including Minnesota, Nebraska and Oklahoma. ... The Nebraska stops are of short duration since utilized only for the discharge and loading of passengers, mail, express, and freight, and sometimes for refueling. Appellant neither owns nor maintains facilities for repairing, reconditioning, or storing its flight equipment in Nebraska, but rents depot space and hires other services as required. ...

It is stipulated that the tax in question is assessed only against regularly scheduled air carriers and is not applied to carriers who operate only intermittently in the state. The statute defines "flight equipment" as "aircraft fully equipped for flight," and provides that "any tax upon or measured by the value of flight equipment of air carriers incorporated or doing business in this state shall be assessed and collected by the Tax Commissioner." A formula is prescribed for arriving at the proportion of a carrier's flight equipment to be allocated to the state.[1]

Appellant relies upon cases involving ocean-going vessels to support its contention that its aircraft attained no tax situs in Nebraska. ...

[T]he situs issue devolves into the question of whether eighteen stops per day by appellant's aircraft is sufficient contact with Nebraska to sustain that state's power to levy an apportioned ad valorem tax on such aircraft. We think such regular contact is sufficient to establish Nebraska's power to tax even though the same aircraft do not land every day and even though none of the aircraft is continuously within the state. "The basis of the jurisdiction is the habitual employment of the property within the State." Appellant rents its ground facilities and pays for fuel it purchases in Nebraska. This leaves it in the position of other carriers such as rails, boats and motors that pay for the use of local facilities so as to have the opportunity to exploit the commerce, traffic, and trade that originates in or reaches Nebraska. Approximately one-tenth of appellant's revenue is produced by the pickup and discharge of Nebraska freight and

---

1. This section provides that "The proportion of flight equipment allocated to this state for purposes of taxation shall be the arithmetical average of the following three ratios: (1) The ratio which the aircraft arrivals and departures within this state scheduled by such air carrier during the preceding calendar year bears to the total aircraft arrivals and departures within and without this state scheduled by such carrier during the same period; *Provided,* that in the case of nonscheduled operations all arrivals and departures shall be substituted for scheduled arrivals and departures; (2) the ratio which the revenue tons handled by such air carrier at airports within this state during the preceding calendar year bears to the total revenue tons handled by such carrier at airports within and without this state during the same period; and (3) the ratio which such air carrier's originating revenue within this state for the preceding calendar year bears to the total originating revenue of such carrier within and without this state for the same period."

passengers. Nebraska certainly affords protection during such stops and these regular landings are clearly a benefit to appellant. . . .

Appellant urges that *Northwest Airlines* v. *Minnesota,* 322 US 292, precludes this tax unless that case is to be overruled. In that case Minnesota, as the domicile of the air carrier and its "home port," was permitted to tax the entire value of the fleet ad valorem although it ranged by fixed routes through eight states. While no one view mustered a majority of this Court, it seems fair to say that without the position stated in the Conclusion and Judgment which announced the decision of this Court, the result would have been the reverse. That position was that it was not shown "that a defined part of the domiciliary corpus has acquired a permanent location, i.e., a taxing situs, elsewhere." P 295. That opinion recognized the "doctrine of tax apportionment for instrumentalities engaged in interstate commerce," p 297, but held it inapplicable because no "property (or a portion of fungible units) is permanently situated in a State other than the domiciliary State." P 298. When *Standard Oil Co.* v. *Peck,* 342 US 384, was here, the Court interpreted the *Northwest Airlines* case to permit states other than those of the corporate domicile to tax boats in interstate commerce on the apportionment basis in accordance with their use in the taxing state. We adhere to that interpretation.

Affirmed.

[The concurring and dissenting opinions are omitted.]

Notes

1. *Airport service tax.* *Evansville-Vanderburgh Airport Authority* v. *Delta Airlines, Inc.,* 405 US 707 (1972), sustained a $1 service charge for each passenger emplaning on a commercial aircraft at Dress Memorial Airport, the fund to be used to improve the airport.

2. *Motor vehicles.* The Court has been inclined to sustain taxes upon trucks and busses engaged in interstate commerce under the theory that it is fair for these instrumentalities to bear a fair share of the cost of maintaining the highways. Registration fees and mileage taxes have been the most common type of taxes used. See *Capitol Greyhound Lines* v. *Brice,* 339 US 542 (1950).

Spector Motor Service v. *O'Connor,* 340 US 602 (1951), held void a Connecticut franchise tax as applied to a trucking firm doing only interstate business. The tax was held void as a direct tax upon the privilege of doing interstate business. If the state had denominated its tax as one in lieu of a property tax, or as a charge for the use of its roads, apparently the same fee could have been collected.

Chicago v. *Willett Co.,* 344 US 574 (1953), sustained, on a "home state" theory, a tax on the operation of trucks graduated by size when the trucks were used in a business inseparably commingling intrastate and interstate transportation.

Bode v. *Barrett,* 344 US 583 (1953), sustained an Illinois tax for the use of its highways measured by the weight of vehicles. Even though the tax ranged as high as $1,580 per truck, the Court disposed of the case by holding that all of the trucks involved were engaged in intrastate as well as interstate commerce without considering the merits of the argument that the tax was a burden on interstate commerce.

3. *Water vessels.* Seagoing vessels are taxable at the domicile of the owner. *Southern Pacific Co.* v. *Kentucky,* 222 US 63 (1911). *Ott* v. *Mississippi Barge Line Co.,* 336 US 169 (1949) held that vessels moving in interstate operations along the inland waters were taxable by a state other than the state of the owner's domicile when the tax was fairly apportioned to the commerce carried on within the taxing state.

4. *Rolling stock of railroads.* Where a just apportionment has been made, the Court has consistently sustained property taxes on the rolling stock of railroads. *Pullman's Palace Car Co.* v. *Pennsylvania,* 141 US 18 (1891), sustained a tax on the company's capital stock "taking as the basis of assessment such proportion of its capital stock as the number of miles of railroad over which cars were run by the defendant in Pennsylvania bore to the whole number of miles in this [Pennsylvania] and other states over which its cars were run."

5. *Other property taxes.* "Where property has come to rest within a state, being held there at the pleasure of the owner, for disposal or use, so that he may dispose of it either within the state or for shipment elsewhere" it is subject to taxation. Thus cattle delivered to a stockyard, and subject to disposal by their owner, are subject to taxation by the state in which the stockyard is located, even though the cattle remain in the state only a few days. *Minnesota* v. *Blasius,* 290 US 1 (1933).

In determining the value of the physical property of railroads and other public utilities for tax purposes, states consider the value of the property not in isolation but as a part of a going concern. In reality they use real property taxes to reach both tangible and intangible property values. So long as the apportionment formula used is not abusive, the taxes are sustained. Thus, in *Western Union Tel. Co.* v. *Massachusetts,* 125 US 530 (1888), the Court sustained a Massachusetts tax on the property of the telegraph company used by it in the state measured by such proportion of the value of its capital stock as the length of its lines in Massachusetts bore to the total mileage of the company's lines throughout the United States.

"Going business" is an intangible property value that may be assessed separately and added to the value of the physical property in assessing state taxes upon property of companies engaged in interstate commerce. *Railway Express Agency* v. *Virginia,* 358 US 434 (1959). But a gross discrepancy in the taxation of a railroad's property is void. *Norfolk & W. R. Co.* v. *Missouri State Tax Comm'n,* 390 US 317 (1968).

General Motors v. Washington

377 US 436, 84 S Ct 1564, 12 L Ed2d 430 (1964)

The validity of a state tax on interstate commerce rests upon whether the state is exacting a constitutionally fair demand for that aspect of interstate commerce to which it bears a special relation.

MR. JUSTICE CLARK delivered the opinion of the Court.

This appeal tests the constitutional validity, under the Commerce and Due Process Clauses, of Washington's tax imposed upon the privilege of engaging in business activities within the State. The tax is measured by the appellant's gross wholesale sales of motor vehicles, parts, and accessories delivered in the State. Appellant claims that the tax is levied on unapportioned gross receipts from such sales and is, therefore, a tax on the privilege of engaging in interstate commerce; is inherently discriminatory; results in the imposition of a multiple tax burden; and, is a deprivation of property without due process of law. The Washington Superior Court held that the presence of a branch office in Seattle rendered some of the Chevrolet transactions subject to tax, but, as to the remainder, held that the application of the statute would be repugnant to the Commerce and the Due Process Clauses of the United States Constitution. On appeal, the Supreme Court of Washington reversed the latter finding, holding that all of the appellant's transactions were subject to the tax on the ground that the tax bore a reasonable relation to the appellant's activities within the State. . . . We have concluded that the tax is levied on the incidents of a substantial local business in Washington and is constitutionally valid and, therefore, affirm the judgment.

We start with the proposition that "it was not the purpose of the commerce clause to relieve those engaged in interstate commerce from their just share of state tax burden even though it increases the cost of doing the business." *Western Live Stock* v. *Bureau of Revenue,* 303 US 250, 254 (1938). . . .

A careful analysis of the cases in this field teaches that the validity of the tax rests upon whether the State is exacting a constitutionally fair demand for that aspect of interstate commerce to which it bears a special relation. For our purposes the decisive issue turns on the operating incidence of the tax. In other words, the question is whether the State has exerted its power in proper proportion to appellant's activities within the State and to appellant's consequent enjoyment of the opportunities and protections which the State has afforded. Where, as in the instant case, the taxing State is not the domiciliary State, we look to the taxpayer's business activities within the State, i. e., the local incidents, to determine if the gross receipts from sales therein may be fairly related to those activities. As was said in *Wisconsin* v. *J. C. Penney Co.,* 311 US 435, 444 (1940), "the simple but controlling question is whether the state has given anything for which it can ask return."

Here it is admitted that General Motors has entered the State and engaged in activities therein. In fact, General Motors voluntarily pays considerable taxes on its Washington operations but contests the validity of the tax levy on four of its Divisions, Chevrolet, Pontiac, Oldsmobile and General Motors Parts. Under these circumstances appellant has the burden of showing that the operations of these Divisions in the State are "dissociated from the local business and interstate in nature. . . ."

With these principles in mind, we turn to the facts. . . .

General Motors is a Delaware corporation which was engaged in business in Washington during the period of time involved in this case, January 1, 1949, through June 30, 1953. Chevrolet, Pontiac, Oldsmobile and General Motors Parts are divisions of General Motors, but they operate substantially independently of each other. The corporation manufactures automobiles, trucks and other merchandise which are sold to dealers in Washington. However, all of these articles are manufactured in other States. In order to carry on the sale, in Washington, of the products of Chevrolet, Pontiac, Oldsmobile and General Motors Parts, the corporation maintains an organization of employees in each of these divisions on a national, regional and district level. During the taxing period in question, the State of Washington was located in the western region of the corporation's national organization and each division, except General Motors Parts, maintained a zone office at Portland, Oregon. These zone offices served General Motors' operations in Oregon, Washington, Idaho, portions of Montana and Wyoming and all of the then Territory of Alaska. Chevrolet Division also maintained a branch office at Seattle which was under the jurisdiction of the Portland zone office and which rendered special service to all except the nine southern counties of Washington, which were still serviced by the Portland office. The zone offices of each division were broken down into geographical district offices and it is in these districts that the dealers, to whom the corporation sold its products for resale, were selected and located. The orders for these products were sent by the dealers to the zone office located at Portland. They were accepted or rejected there or at the factory and the sales were completed by shipments f.o.b. the factories. . . .

In addition to the district manager, each of the Chevrolet, Pontiac and Oldsmobile Divisions also maintained service representatives who called on the dealers with regularity, assisting the service department in any troubles it experienced with General Motors products. . . .

"[I]t is beyond dispute," we said in *Northwestern States Portland Cement Co.* v. *Minnesota* [358 US 450], "that a State may not lay a tax on the 'privilege' of engaging in interstate commerce." But that is not this case. To so contend here is to overlook a long line of cases of this Court holding that an in-state activity may be a sufficient local incident upon which a tax may be based. As was said in *Spector Motor Service, Inc.* v. *O'Connor,* 340 US 602, 609 (1951), "the State is not precluded from imposing taxes upon other activities or aspects of this [interstate] business which, unlike the privilege of doing interstate business, are subject to the sovereign power of the State." This is exactly what Washington seeks to do here and we cannot say that appellant has shown that its activities within the State are not such incidents that the State can reach. . . . [T]he Pontiac and Oldsmobile Divisions had district managers, service representatives and other employees who were residents of the State and who performed substantial services in relation to General Motors' functions therein, particularly with relation to the establishment and maintenance of sales, upon which the tax was measured. We place little weight on the fact that these divisions had no formal offices in the State, since in actuality the homes of these officials were used as corporate offices. Despite their label as "homes" they served the corporation just as effectively as "offices." In addition, the corporation had a Chevrolet branch office and a General Motors Parts Division warehouse in Seattle.

Thus, in the bundle of corporate activity, which is the text here, we see General Motors activity so enmeshed in local connections that it voluntarily paid taxes on various of its operations but insists that it was not liable on others. Since General Motors elected to enter the State in this fashion, we cannot say that the Supreme Court of Washington erred in holding that these local incidents were sufficient to form the basis for the levy of a tax that would not run contrary to the Constitution. . . .

A more difficult question might arise from appellant's claim of multiple taxation. . . . The Court touched upon the problem of multiple taxation in *Northwest Airlines* v. *Minnesota, supra,* at 295, but laid it to one side as "not now before us." Thereafter, in *Northwestern States Portland Cement Co.* v. *Minnesota, supra,* at 463, we held that "in this type of case the taxpayers must show that the formula places a burden upon interstate commerce in a constitutional sense." Appellant has not done this. . . .

Affirmed.

Mr. Justice Goldberg, with whom Mr. Justice Stewart and Mr. Justice White join, dissenting. . . .

Although the opinion of the Court seems to imply that there still is some threshold requirement of in-state activity which must be found to exist before a "fairly apportioned" tax may be imposed on interstate sales, it is difficult to conceive of a state gross receipts tax on interstate commerce which could not be sustained under the rationale adopted today. Every interstate sale invariably involves some local incidents—some "in-state" activity. It is difficult, for example, to distinguish between the in-state activities of the representatives here involved and the in-state activities of solicitors or traveling salesmen—activities which this Court has held are insufficient to constitute a basis for imposing a tax on interstate sales. . . .

The opinion of the Court goes beyond a consideration of whether there has been in-state activity of appropriate character to satisfy a threshold requirement for imposing a tax on interstate sales. The Court asserts as a general principle that the validity of a tax on interstate commerce "rests upon whether the State is exacting a constitutionally fair demand for that aspect of interstate commerce to which it bears a special relation." . . . What is "fair"? How are we to determine whether a State has exerted its power in "proper proportion to appellant's activities within the state"?. . . . See Developments—Federal Limitations on State Taxation of Interstate Business, 75 Harv L Rev 953, 957 (1962). I submit, with due respect for the complexity of the problem, that the formulation suggested by the Court is unworkable. . . .

The dilemma inhering in the Court's formulation is revealed by its treatment of the "more difficult," but inextricably related, question arising from the alleged multiple taxation. . . . [I]f it is "fair" to subject the interstate sales to the Washington wholesale sales tax because of the activities of the sales representatives in Washington, then it would seem equally "fair" for Oregon, which is the site of the office directing and consummating these sales, to tax the same gross sales receipts. Moreover, it would seem "fairer" for California, Michigan or Missouri—states in which automobiles are manufactured, assembled or delivered—to impose a tax measured by, and effectively bearing upon, the same gross sales receipts. . . .

In my view the rules set forth in *Norton Co.* v. *Department of Revenue* [340 US 534] reflect an attempt to adhere to the basic purposes of the Commerce Clause. Therefore, in dealing with unapportioned taxes on interstate sales, I would adhere to the *Norton* rules instead of departing from them by adopting a standard of "fairness." I would hold that a manufacturer or wholesaler making interstate sales is not subject to a state gross receipts tax merely because those sales were solicited or processed by agents living or traveling in the taxing State. As *Norton* recognized, a different rule may be applied to the taxation of sales substantially connected with an office or warehouse making intrastate sales. The test adopted by the Court today, if followed logically in future cases, would seem to mean that States will be permitted to tax wholly interstate sales by any company selling through local agents or traveling salesmen. Such a rule may leave only mail-order houses free from state taxes on interstate sales. With full sympathy for the revenue needs of States, I believe there are other legitimate means of raising state revenues without undermining the common national market created by the Commerce Clause. I therefore respectfully dissent.

Mr. Justice Brennan, dissenting. . . .

In order to tax any transaction, the Due Process Clause requires that a State show a sufficient "nexus between such a tax and transactions within a state for which the tax is an exaction." . . . But the strictures of the Constitution on this power do not stop there. For in the case of a gross receipts tax imposed upon an interstate transaction, even though the taxing State can show "some minimum connection," . . . the Commerce Clause requires that "taxation measured by gross receipts from interstate commerce . . . [be] fairly apportioned to the commerce carried on within the taxing state."

. . . While the ratio of in-state to out-of-state sales is often taken into account as one factor among others in apportioning a firm's total net income, see e.g., the description of the "Massachusetts Formula" in Note, 75 Harv L Rev 953, 1011 (1962), it nevertheless remains true that if commercial activity in more than one State results in a sale in one of them, that State may not claim as all its own the gross receipts to which the activity within its borders has contributed only a part. Such a tax must be apportioned to reflect the business activity within the taxing State. . . . Since the Washington tax on wholesales is, by its very terms, applied to the "gross proceeds of sales" of those "engaging within this state in the business of making sales at wholesale," . . . it cannot be sustained under the standards required by the Commerce Clause.

Evco v. Jones

409 US 91, 93 S Ct 349, 34 L Ed2d 325 (1972)

A state cannot impose a gross receipts tax on the total proceeds received by a domestic corporation from contracts with out-of-state customers to develop instructional programs.

PER CURIAM.

The petitioner, Evco, is a New Mexico corporation that employs writers, artists, and draftsmen to create and design instructional programs. It develops an educational idea into a finished product, that generally consists of reproducible originals of books, films, and magnetic audio tapes. Typical of its contracts is Evco's agreement with the Department of Agriculture to develop camera-ready copies of programmed textbooks, notebooks, and manuals to be used in an orientation course for forest engineers. Evco's contracts are negotiated and entered into outside New Mexico; it creates the reproducible originals in New Mexico, and then delivers them to its out-of-state clients. The customers in turn use the originals to publish however many books and manuals are needed to implement the instructional program.

The Commissioner of Revenue for New Mexico levied the State's Emergency School Tax and its Gross Receipts Tax on the total proceeds Evco received from these contracts. The company appealed this assessment to the Court of Appeals of New Mexico, arguing that these taxes on out-of-state sales imposed an unconstitutional burden on interstate commerce in violation of Art. I, § 8, of the Constitution. That court found that though the taxes were imposed on the proceeds of out-of-state sales of tangible personal property, rather than on the receipts from sales of services, such taxes were not an unconstitutional burden on commerce. . . . The Supreme Court of New Mexico declined to review the judgment.

In his brief in opposition to the petition for *certiorari* which sought our review of that judgment, the Attorney General of New Mexico conceded that the State could not tax the receipts from sales of tangible personal property outside the State. We granted *certiorari,* vacated the judgment, and remanded the case to the Court of Appeals for reconsideration in light of the position taken by the Attorney General. . . .

On remand, the Court of Appeals adhered to its prior findings that these taxes were imposed on out-of-state sales of tangible property, not services, but it concluded that the constitutionality of the taxes should not depend on that distinction. It reinstated and reaffirmed its prior opinion finding the taxes constitutional. . . . The Supreme Court of New Mexico again declined to review the case, and we granted *certiorari* . . .

Our prior cases indicate that a State may tax the proceeds from services performed in the taxing State, even though they are sold to purchasers in another State. Hence, in *Department of Treasury* v. *Ingram-Richardson Mfg. Co.,* 313 US 252, the Court upheld a state gross income tax imposed on a taxpayer engaged in the process of enameling metal parts for its customers. We accepted the finding of the court below that this was a tax on income derived from services, not from the sales of finished products, and we found irrelevant the fact that the sales were made to out-of-state customers. The tax was validly imposed on the service performed in the taxing State. See also *Western Live Stock* v. *Bureau of Revenue,* 303 US 250.

But a tax levied on the gross receipts from the sales of tangible personal property in another State is an impermissible burden on commerce. In *J. D. Adams Mfg. Co.* v. *Storen,* 304 US 307, we rejected as unconstitutional a State's attempt to impose a gross receipts tax on a taxpayer's sales of road machinery to out-of-state customers.

> The vice of the statute as applied to receipts from interstate sales is that the tax includes in its measure, without apportionment, receipts derived from activities in interstate commerce; and that the exaction is of such a character that if lawful it may in substance be laid to the fullest extent by States in which the goods are sold as well as those in which they are manufactured. Interstate commerce would thus be subjected to the risk of a double tax burden to which intrastate commerce is not exposed, and which the commerce clause forbids. 304 US, at 311.

See also *Gwin, White & Prince, Inc.* v. *Henneford,* 305 US 434.

As on the previous petition for *certiorari,* both parties accept these propositions, and both agree that if the findings of the Court of Appeals are accepted, its judgment must be reversed.

The only real dispute between the parties centers on the factual question of the nature and effect of the taxes. The State contends that these taxes were actually imposed on the receipts from services performed in the State, not on the income from the sale of property outside the State. It argues that the out-of-state purchasers actually paid for the educational programs developed in New Mexico, not for the camera-ready copies that were only incidental to the services purchased. But the Court of Appeals rejected this interpretation of the facts. It found in effect that the reproducible originals were the *sine qua non* of the contract and that it was the sale of that tangible property in another State that New Mexico had taxed. "There are no exceptional circumstances of any kind that would justify us in rejecting the . . . Court's findings; they are not without factual foundation, and we accept them." *Lloyd A. Fry Roofing Co.* v. *Wood,*

344 US 157, 160. See also *Grayson* v. *Harris,* 267 US 352, 357–358; *Portland Ry. Light & Power Co.* v. *R.R. Commission,* 229 US 397, 411–412.

Accordingly, since the Court of Appeals approved the imposition of a tax on the proceeds of the out-of-state sales of tangible personal property, its judgment is

Reversed.

Note

Congressional action. The Constitution vests the power to regulate interstate commerce in Congress, and the need for comprehensive national legislation governing the taxation of interstate commerce is widely recognized. See Emanuel Celler, "The Development of a Congressional Program Dealing with State Taxation of Interstate Commerce," *Fordham Law Review* 36 (1967–68): 385–400. Noting the rapid trend toward a balkanization of the domestic economy, within a few months after the decision in *Northwestern States Portland Cement Co.* v. *Minnesota,* 358 US 450 (1959)—a case holding that, in the absence of federal legislation, a state could collect an income tax from a company engaged exclusively in interstate commerce—Congress passed a "stopgap" law (15 USC § 381) reading as follows:

(a) No State, or political subdivision thereof, shall have power to impose, for any taxable year ending after September 14, 1959, a net income tax on the income derived within such State by any person from interstate commerce if the only business activities within such State by or on behalf of such person during such taxable year are either, or both, of the following:

(1) the solicitation of orders by such person, or his representative, in such State for sales of tangible personal property, which orders are sent outside the State for approval or rejection, and, if approved, are filled by shipment or delivery from a point outside the State; and

(2) the solicitation of orders by such person, or his representative, in such State in the name of or for the benefit of a prospective customer of such person, if orders by such customer to such person to enable such customer to fill orders resulting from such solicitation are orders described in paragraph (1).

(b) The provisions of subsection (a) of this section shall not apply to the imposition of a new income tax by any State, or political subdivision thereof, with respect to—

(1) any corporation which is incorporated under the laws of such State; or

(2) any individual who, under the laws of such State, is domiciled in, or a resident of, such State.

(c) For purposes of subsection (a) of this section, a person shall not be considered to have engaged in business activities within a State during any taxable year merely by reason of sales in such State, or the solicitation of orders for sales in such State, of tangible personal property on behalf of such person by one or more independent contractors, or by reason of the maintenance of an office in such State by one or more independent contractors whose activities on behalf of such person in such State consist solely of making sales, or soliciting orders for sales, of tangible personal property.

For comment on the application of 15 USC § 381, see *Heublein* v. *South Carolina Tax Commission,* 309 US 275 (1972).

Chapter 5

Intergovernmental Relations

A. TAXATION

Introduction

Intergovernmental taxation is a perennial problem in our federal union. In declaring void a state tax upon the issuance of bank notes by the Bank of the United States, Chief Justice Marshall observed in *McCulloch* v. *Maryland* (1819) that "The power to tax involves the power to destroy. . . . If the States may tax one instrumentality, employed by the government in the execution of its powers, they may tax any and every other instrument. They may tax the mail; they may tax the mint; . . . they may tax all the means employed by the government to an excess which would defeat all the ends of government."

It was not until 1871 that the Supreme Court held void a federal tax upon a state "instrumentality." In an earlier case, *Dobbins* v. *Commissioners of Erie County,* 16 Peters 435 (1842), the Court had held that a state could not levy a tax upon the salary of an officer of the United States. By analogy, in *Collector* v. *Day* (1871) the Court held that the federal government could not impose a tax upon the salary of a judicial officer of a state.

Dissenting in *Collector* v. *Day,* Justice Bradley wrote:

> I dissent from the opinion . . . because it seems to me that the general government has the same power of taxing the income of officers of the State governments as it has of taxing that of its own officers. . . . No man ceases to be a citizen of the United States by being an officer under a State government. I cannot accede to the doctrine that the general government is to be regarded as in any sense foreign or antagonistic to the State governments, their officers, or people; nor can I agree that a presumption

can be admitted that the general government will act in a manner hostile to the existence or functions of the State governments, which are constituent parts of the system or body politic forming the basis on which the general government is founded. The taxation by the State governments of the instruments employed by the general government . . . is a very different thing. Such taxation involves an interference with the powers of a government in which other States and their citizens are equally interested with the State which imposes the taxation. In my judgment, the limitation of the power of taxation in the general government, which the present decision establishes, will be very difficult to control. Where are we to stop in enumerating the functions of the State governments which will be interfered with by Federal taxation?

Bradley's distinction between (a) taxation by the federal government upon state functions and (b) taxation by a state government upon a federal function had been expressed by Marshall as "The difference . . . between the action of the whole on a part, and the action of a part on the whole; between the laws of a government declared to be supreme, and those of a government which, when in opposition to those laws, is not supreme."

Bradley's prediction that the doctrine of immunity of state functions from federal taxation would be "very difficult to control" proved to be true. The constant expansion of state functions and the number of employees claiming exemptions from federal taxes because of their relation to state governments became an obstacle to the federal power to tax. Some relief came through application of the principle that only traditional state functions were immune. For example, in *South Carolina* v. *United States,* 199 US 437 (1905), the state itself was taxed for the privilege of carrying on the liquor business; but by the 1930s state immunity from federal taxation had become a major national problem.

Helvering v. *Gerhardt,* 304 US 405 (1938), sustained the application of the federal income tax to the salary of an employee of the Port of New York Authority, a state agency. In the opinion of the Court, Justice Stone explained that "where the tax laid upon individuals affects the state only as the burden is passed onto it by the taxpayer" sound policy "forbids recognition of the immunity when the burden on the state is so speculative and uncertain that if allowed it would restrict the federal taxing power without affording any corresponding tangible protection to the state government." The following year, in *Graves* v. *New York ex rel. O'Keefe,* 306 US 466 (1939), the Court sustained the application of a state income tax to the salary of an employee of a federal agency. No constitutional immunity from taxation appears to remain on the salaries of employees of either the state or federal governments or their instrumentalities. It is conceivable that Congress could grant a tax immunity to federal officers, but rather than granting immunity, the Public Salary Act of 1939 specifically approves taxation of the compensation of officers and employees of the United States by the duly constituted taxing authority having jurisdiction to tax such compensation "if such taxation does not discriminate against such officer or employee because of the sources of the compensation."

The immunity of national corporations and other agencies created by the national government from state taxation is a matter subject to the control of Congress. In the absence of a governing federal statute, the Court is inclined to sustain state taxes. Thus, in *Polar Co.* v. *Andrews,* 375 US 361 (1964), it sustained a Florida tax upon each gallon of milk distributed by a Florida distributor as applied to milk sold to the armed forces of the United States. The incidence of the tax was interpreted to be upon the processing or bottling of milk, activities occurring prior to the sale and delivery to the government.

The constitutional immunity of a state and its instrumentality from federal taxation is not clear. Emphasis in judicial decisions in recent years has been toward limiting such immunity, and it is debatable whether any such immunity remains. The opinion in *New York* v. *United States,* 326 US 572 (1946), sustaining a federal tax on the sale of mineral water by the state of New York, emphasized that the tax fell on all who earned by that business and did not discriminate against a state activity. This might be interpreted as implying that a discriminatory tax aimed at hampering a state activity would be void; but it is significant that no federal tax has in fact been declared void on this basis.

Cases Holding a Federal Tax Void

Cases in which the Supreme Court has held a federal tax to be void under the immunity doctrine are:

Collector v. *Day,* 11 Wallace 113 (1871), income tax applied to salary of state judge;

United States v. *Baltimore & Ohio R. Co.,* 17 Wallace 322 (1873), income of a municipality derived from ownership of railroad bonds;

Pollock v. *Farmers Loan & Trust Co.,* 157 US 429 (1895), income derived from the interest of bonds issued by a municipality;

Indian Motorcycle Co. v. *United States,* 383 US 570 (1931), sale of a motorcycle to a municipality;

Burnet v. *Colorado Oil & Gas Co.,* 285 US 393 (1932), income tax on private profits derived from state school lands held under lease;

Brush v. *Commissioner of Internal Revenue,* 300 US 352 (1937), income tax as applied to the salary of an engineer of the Bureau of Water Supply of the City of New York.

Cases Holding a State Tax Void

Leading cases in which a state tax has been held void under the immunity doctrine include:

McCulloch v. *Maryland,* 4 Wheaton 316 (1819), a Maryland tax on the Bank of the United States;

Osborn v. *Bank of the United States,* 9 Wheaton 738 (1824), an Ohio tax on banking as applied to the Bank of the United States;

Weston v. *Charleston,* 2 Peters 449 (1829), a tax on stock of the United States held by an individual;

Dobbins v. *Commissioners of Erie County,* 16 Peters 435 (1842), a tax on the salary of a federal employee;

Western Union Tel. Co. v. *Texas,* 105 US 460 (1882), a tax on telegraph messages as applied to messages on official government business;

Van Brocklin v. *Tennessee,* 117 US 151 (1886), a tax on land owned by the United States;

Choctaw O. & G. R. Co. v. *Harrison,* 235 US 292 (1914), a tax on the production of oil as applied to the lessee of restricted Indian lands (a long line of similar cases was overruled in *Oklahoma Tax Commission* v. *Texas Co.,* 336 US 342 (1949);

Gillespie v. *Oklahoma,* 257 US 501 (1922), an income tax on profits earned in private business on Indian lands leased from the United States;

Northwestern Mut. Life Ins. Co. v. *Wisconsin,* 275 US 136 (1927), a tax on income from United States securities;

Panhandle Oil Co. v. *Mississippi,* 277 US 218 (1928), a tax on the sale of gasoline to the Coast Guard;

Long v. *Rockwood,* 277 US 142 (1928), a tax on income derived from royalties for use of a patent issued by the United States—this decision was overruled in *Fox Film Corp.* v. *Doyal,* 286 US 123 (1932);

Mayo v. *United States,* 319 US 441 (1943), an inspection fee as applied to fertilizer owned and distributed by the United States under a Soil Conservation Act;

McClanahan v. *State Tax Comm'n of Arizona,* 411 US 164 (1973), a tax on the income of reservation Indians derived from reservation sources.

Sales Taxes

In many instances Congress has determined by statute the taxable status of designated federal agencies and activities associated therewith. Thus it has authorized the Atomic Energy Commission to make payments in lieu of taxes in states where it acquires property, 42 USC § 1809(b), and provided that independent contractors carrying on activities of the Atomic Energy Commission shall be subject to state sales taxes, 67 Stat 575. In the absence of a governing statute, in recent years the Court has tended to sustain state sales taxes. In *Alabama* v. *King & Boozer,* 314 US 1 (1941), it sustained a tax upon the sale of lumber to a contractor building army barracks under a cost-plus contract with the United States. The Court has, however, held void taxes based on sales directly to the United States. In *Standard Oil Co. of California* v. *Johnson,* 316 US 481 (1942), it held void a tax on the sale of gasoline to an army post exchange; and in *Kern-Limerick, Inc.* v. *Scurlock,* 347 US 110 (1954), it held void a tax on the sale of material to a contractor constructing a naval depot under a cost-plus contract with the navy when the contract provided that in procuring material for the work the contractor should act as purchasing agent for the government and that title thereto should pass directly from the vendor to the United States.

Corporate Income Derived from Government Contracts

James v. *Dravo Contracting Co.,* 302 US 134 (1937), sustained a state gross receipts tax applied to receipts of a contractor derived from the United States for the construction of locks in a navigable stream. An earlier case, *Metcalf* v. *Mitchell,* 269 US 514 (1926), had sustained a federal income tax as applied to a contractor performing work for a state government.

Taxes on Property

State taxes on land or other property of the United States have usually been declared void. *Van Brocklin* v. *Tennessee,* 117 US 151 (1886).

United States v. *Detroit,* 355 US 466 (1958), sustained a use tax on a corporation which leased an industrial plant owned by the United States, the amount of the use tax being measured by the value of the property leased. See also the related case, *Detroit* v. *Murray Corp.,* 355 US 489 (1958). But *Humble Pipe Line Co.* v. *Waggonner,* 376 US 369 (1964), held void a Louisiana ad valorem tax on pipeline and equipment located on land that constituted a part of a military base over which the United States had exclusive jurisdiction, even though a portion of the land constituting the military base was leased to the Humble Pipe Line Co.

The ability of states to tax property owned by federal agencies is governed extensively by statute. Thus Congress has authorized the states to tax real estate owned by National Banks and "real property" owned by the Reconstruction Finance Corporation, *R.F.C.* v. *Beaver County,* 328 US 204 (1946), but "property of any kind" owned by the United States Housing Authority is exempted from taxation, *Cleveland* v. *United States,* 322 US 329 (1945). In a number of instances, Congress has authorized federal agencies to make payments in lieu of taxes to local governments. See "Federal Contributions to State and Local Governmental Units with Respect to Federally Owned Real Estate," House Doc No. 216, 78th Congress, 1st sess.

Government Bonds

There are old decisions holding bonds of the United States and interest thereon to be immune from state taxation, and, by analogy, bonds of states and municipalities and interest thereon to be immune from federal taxation. (See the summary of cases in *Indian Motorcycle Co.* v. *United States,* 283 US 570 (1931).) Both types of bonds are currently exempted from intergovernmental taxation by statutory provisions. What ruling the present Court would make if presented with the question of the authority of one government to tax the bonds of another is debatable. Under present decisions, the following taxes are valid: a United States inheritance tax measured by net estate, including state bonds, *Greiner* v. *Lewellyn,* 258 US 384 (1922); a United States income tax on profit derived from the sale of state bonds, *Willcutts* v. *Bunn,* 282 US 216 (1931); a United States corporate franchise tax measured by income, including interest on state bonds, *Flint* v. *Stone Tracy Co.,* 220 US 107 (1911); and a state corporate franchise tax measured by the property of a corporation, including United States bonds, *Werner Mach. Co.* v. *Director of Taxation,* 350 US 492 (1956).

Congressional Control

The power of Congress to protect its agents and activities from state taxation is illustrated in the following cases.

Carson v. *Roane-Anderson Co.,* 342 US 232 (1951), held that Tennessee could not collect a sales or use tax from private contractors on activities growing out of contracts with the Atomic Energy Commission. The Atomic Energy Act of 1946 provided that "The Commission, and the property, activities, and income of the Commission, are hereby expressly exempt from taxation in any manner or form by any state. . . ." (Congress subsequently changed this statute. See *United States* v. *Boyd,* 378 US 39, 84 S Ct 1518, 12 L Ed2d 713 (1964).)

Damon v. *Brodhead,* 345 US 322 (1953), held that "When a serviceman domiciled in one state is assigned to military service in another state, the latter state is barred by . . . the Soldiers' and Sailors' Civil Relief Act of 1940 . . . from imposing a tax on his tangible personal property temporarily located within its borders—even when the state of his domicile has not taxed such property." Colorado had sought to collect from an Air Force officer a tax of $23.51 on his household goods located throughout the year in a privately rented apartment in Denver.

Offutt Housing Co. v. *Sarpy County,* 351 US 253 (1956), sustained a Nebraska tax on a housing corporation based on the value of buildings and improvements located on land which constituted a part of an Air Force base leased to the Housing Company. The company contended that it was merely a "managing agent" since the government prescribed the maximum rents, designated the occupants, and provided services. The Court held that "By the Military Leasing Act of 1947 . . . Congress consented to state taxation of petitioner's interest as lessee, though the area involved is subject to the federal power of 'exclusive legislation'."

Mescalero Apache Tribe v. *Jones,* 411 US 145 (1973), held that the Indian Reorganization Act of 1934 permits New Mexico to impose a nondiscriminatory gross receipts tax on a ski resort operated by the Apache Tribe on off-reservation land leased by the tribe from the United States; but the Act does not authorize a use tax on personalty installed by the tribe as a permanent improvement at the resort.

B. REGULATIONS

Introduction

National regulations of commerce may be applied to state agencies. For example, *United States* v. *California,* 297 US 175 (1936), sustained the application of a provision of the Federal Safety Appliance Act to a railroad owned and operated by California; *Case* v. *Bowles,* 327 US 92 (1946), sustained application of the Price Control Act to the sale of timber by a state; and *Maryland* v. *Wirtz,* 392 US 183 (1968), sustained the application of the Fair Labor Standards Act to employees of state-operated schools and hospitals. Writing for the Court, Justice Harlan rejected the argument that the Act interfered with "sovereign state functions" and held that in the exercise of its delegated power to regulate interstate commerce Congress "may override countervailing state interests whether these be described as 'governmental' or 'proprietary' in character." Dissenting, Justice Douglas argued that the principle of intergovernmental immunity developed in the field of taxation which (in his view) denied to Congress the power to tax state governmental functions should apply also to limit the power of Congress to regulate state governmental functions.

Johnson v. *Maryland,* 254 US 51 (1920), held that Maryland could not penalize an employee of the Post Office Department for driving without a state license while performing his official duties. *Miller* v. *Arkansas,* 352 US 187 (1956), held void an

Arkansas statute requiring contractors submitting bids and commencing work in the state to obtain a license from a state board, as applied to a contractor submitting a bid and commencing work on facilities at a United States Air Force Base. "Subjecting a federal contractor to the Arkansas contract license requirements would give the state's licensing board a virtual power of review over the federal determination of responsibility and would thus frustrate the express federal policy of selecting the lowest responsible bidder," stated the *per curiam* opinion.

Federal Enclaves

The United States owns a great deal of land located within the states of the Union. Its interest in this land varies all the way from that of a mere proprietor to that of the possessor of "exclusive legislation," as provided in Article I, Section 8 of the Constitution. Many problems have arisen in connection with federal enclaves. For one thing, there was sometimes no federal statute governing a particular crime committed on an enclave, and the applicability of state law was questionable. The Assimilative Crime Act of 1948 provides that anyone who within a federal enclave "is guilty of any act or omission which, although not made punishable by any enactment of Congress, would be punishable if committed or omitted within the jurisdiction of the state . . . in which such place is situated, by the laws thereof in force at the time of such act or omission, shall be guilty of a like offense and subject to a like punishment." 18 USC § 13.

Congress has authorized the states to apply their sales and use taxes to transactions occurring in federal areas. However, sales taxes, other than on gasoline, cannot be applied to sales by a government agency such as a post exchange. A statute also provides that no person shall be relieved from the payment of a state income tax by reason of his residing within a federal area. 4 USC § 106.

Evans v. *Cornman,* 398 US 419 (1970), held that residents of a federal enclave in Maryland were residents of that state for purposes of voting.

The most comprehensive treatment of legal problems involved in federal enclaves is entitled *Jurisdiction Over Federal Areas Within States,* a report by an Interdepartmental Committee for Study of Jurisdiction Over Federal Areas Within States (Washington, Part I, 1956; Part II, 1957).

C. STATE AND NATIONAL COURTS

Introduction

Throughout our history the national and state courts have used restraint to prevent interference with each other. However, with the courts of two governments operating over the same territory, some conflicts are inevitable.

Supremacy of National Law

The power of the Supreme Court of the United States to reverse the decision of a state court was established in *Martin* v. *Hunter's Lessee,* 1 Wheaton 304 (1816). This power is accepted by everyone today as a matter of course, but it was bitterly disputed at an early period. In his opinion in the *Martin* case, Justice Story pointed to the supremacy clause of Article VI of the Constitution and insisted that uniformity in interpretation required the review of decisions of state courts involving the Constitution by the Supreme Court. As he phrased it, "Judges of equal learning and integrity, in different states, might differently interpret a statute, or a treaty of the United States, or even the Constitution itself: if there were no revising authority to control these jarring and discordant judgments, and harmonize them into uniformity, the laws, the treaties, and the Constitution of the United States would be different in different states. . . ." From the Judiciary Act of 1789 onward, Congress has authorized the Supreme Court to review the final judgments rendered by the highest court of a state when designated questions are involved. For details, see pages 12–13 of this text.

Removal of Cases

For a discussion of the statutory provisions governing the right to remove a case from a state to a federal court, see page 8. An extensive discussion of these statutes is found in *Georgia* v. *Rachel,* 384 US 780 (1966). The case involved an application for the removal of a criminal prosecution of blacks for trespass under the state law, based on a sit-in in an Atlanta restaurant. The Civil Rights Act of 1964 provides that no person shall "punish or attempt to punish" any person for exercising rights secured by its public accommodations provisions. The Supreme Court held that the United States district court erred in remanding the case to the state court without giving the applicants an opportunity to show that they were ordered to leave the restaurant solely for racial reasons.

Abstention

Under a doctrine of abstention, a federal district court sometimes remits litigants to a state court for litigation of a state issue involved in a case. This is illustrated by *England* v. *Louisiana,* 375 US 411 (1964). England and other chiropractors sought to practice in Louisiana without complying with the Louisiana Medical Practice Act. They brought suit in a United States district court for a declaratory judgment that the Act was void under the Fourteenth Amendment. The district court remitted the parties to the state courts on the ground that a decision that the act did not apply to chiropractors would end the controversy. Compare *Lake Carrier's Ass'n* v. *MacMullan,* 406 US 498 (1972). In a case such as this, in submitting the state question to a state court, the party must inform that court of his federal claims so that the state statute may be construed in the light of these claims. If, without reservation, he submits both his state claims and his federal claims to the state court for decision, he thereby waives his right to return to the district court.

Federal Injunctions Against State Actions

That federal courts may be authorized to enjoin proceedings in a state court is not questioned, but as a matter of policy, Congress has restrained the exercise of such power. The present statute on the subject states: "A court of the United States may not grant an injunction to stay proceedings in a State court except as expressly authorized by Act of Congress, or where necessary in aid of its jurisdiction, or to protect or effectuate its judgments." 28 USC § 2283. In practice, the federal courts make many exceptions to this statutory rule by using equity power to prevent irreparable damage. They are, however, hesitant to enjoin criminal proceedings already instituted in a state court. A full discussion of this subject is given in *Younger* v. *Harris,* 401 US 37 (1971). See also *Mitchum* v. *Foster,* 407 US 225 (1972), and *Allee* v. *Medrano,* 416 US 802 (1974).

State Injunctions Against Federal Actions

Donovan v. *City of Dallas,* 377 US 408 (1964), dealt with the power of a state court to enjoin persons from prosecuting a case in the courts of the United States. Residents of Dallas had sought to restrain the city from issuing bonds to improve an airport. They lost their suit in the state courts. They then instituted proceedings for the same purpose in a United States district court. The Texas Court of Civil Appeals enjoined the plaintiffs from prosecuting their suit. The Supreme Court of the United States held this injunction to be void. "Whether or not a plea of *res judicata* in the second suit would be good is a question for the federal court to decide."

Habeas Corpus Proceedings

A state court cannot use the writ of habeas corpus as a means of discharging a person held under authority of the United States. This was established in *Ableman* v. *Booth,* 21 Howard 506 (1859). As Chief Justice Taney expressed it, "We do not question the authority of a state court, or judge, who is authorized by the laws of the state to issue the writ of habeas corpus, to issue it in any case where the party is imprisoned within its territorial limits, provided it does not appear, when the application is made, that the person imprisoned is in custody under the authority of the United States. . . . But, after the return is made, and the state judge or court judicially apprized that the party is in custody under the authority of the United States, they can proceed no further." A Wisconsin court had sought to release Booth, held by a United States marshal, pending trial for violating the Fugitive Slave Law.

The converse of *Ableman* v. *Booth* does not follow. A federal court can discharge a person held in custody by authority of a state. Under the governing statute, federal judges have broad power to extend a writ of habeas corpus to any prisoner "in custody in violation of the Constitution or laws or treaties of the United States." 28 USC § 2241.

A person convicted of crime in a state court and serving a sentence in a state prison can be released by a federal court upon habeas corpus proceedings. For many years the writ of habeas corpus was used in this respect as a means of checking upon the jurisdiction of the state court by which the convicted person was tried. However, beginning with *Moore* v. *Dempsey,* 261 US 86 (1923), habeas corpus proceedings have been used by judges of United States district courts to determine if the procedure used in criminal proceedings was in conformity with constitutional standards. The fact that an application to the Supreme Court for *certiorari* has been denied in the case does not bar an application to a district court for release from prison through habeas corpus proceedings. But a state prisoner is not required to seek *certiorari* in the Supreme Court before he applies to a district court for habeas corpus. He must, however, first exhaust his state remedies. *Fay* v. *Noia,* 372 US 391 (1963).

Traditionally the federal courts had used the writ of habeas corpus sparingly as a means of collateral attack upon judgments of state courts. Direct appeal to the highest state court and then to the United States Supreme Court was the normal procedure. However, under the guidelines set forth by Chief Justice Warren in *Townsend* v. *Sain,* 372 US 293 (1963), thousands of applications for the writ of habeas corpus began to be filed with the United States district courts annually, and the district courts were in fact rapidly being transformed into courts of appeals over state courts in criminal cases. To prevent this abuse and to "expedite the disposition of nonmeritorious and repetitious applications" for the writ, in 1966 Congress revised the governing statute (28 USC § 2254). The 1966 addition provides that in hearings in a federal court for a writ of habeas corpus by a person in custody pursuant to the judgment of a state court, the judgment of the state court shall "be presumed to be correct" unless specified defects appear, and "the burden shall rest upon the applicant to establish by convincing evidence that the factual determination by the State court was errone-ous."

The concurring opinion by Justice Powell in *Schneckloth* v. *Bustamonte,* 412 US 218 (1973), is an illuminating commentary on the excessive use of habeas corpus proceedings in cases involving searches and seizures.

D. RENDITION

Introduction

The Constitution provides that "A person charged in any state with treason, felony, or other crime, who shall flee from justice, and be found in another state, shall, on demand of the executive authority of the state from which he fled, be delivered up to be removed to the state having jurisdiction of the crime." Art. IV, Sec. 2, Par. 2. In *Kentucky* v. *Dennison,* 24 Howard 66 (1861), the Supreme Court held that both the Constitution and an act of Congress designed to implement it placed a moral duty upon the governor of a state to return a fugitive from justice, but that "there is no power delegated to the General Government, either through the Judicial Department or any other department, to use any coercive means to compel him." This decision has never been overruled, and there are occasional instances of a governor refusing to return a fugitive.

A Uniform Criminal Extradition Act written in 1936 had been adopted by most of the states. For its provisions, see *Uniform Laws Annotated,* vol. 9, pp. 263–355. There is also a Uniform Law to Secure the Attendance of Witnesses from Within and Without a State in Criminal Proceedings. Its constitutionality was sustained in *New York* v. *O'Neill,* 359 US 1 (1959). A federal statute (18 USC § 1073) makes it a crime to travel in interstate commerce to avoid prosecution for murder, robbery, and other specified crimes.

E. FULL FAITH AND CREDIT

Introduction

As a matter of comity, states often give recognition to the laws and judicial decisions of other states. A legal duty in this regard is imposed upon the states of the American Union in their dealings with each other by the opening sentence of Article IV of the Constitution which reads: "Full faith and credit shall be given in each State to the public acts, records, and judicial proceedings of every other State. And the Congress may by general laws prescribe the manner in which such acts, records, and proceedings shall be proved, and the effect thereof." Congress has provided the procedure for authenticating public records and judicial proceedings and enacted that they shall have the same effect "as they have by law or usage in the courts of the State from which they are taken." 28 USC § 687.

The greater number of cases arising under this clause relate to the effect to be given to the judgment of a court of one state in the courts of another state. Ordinarily such judgments are enforced, but occasionally they are successfully attacked on a collateral ground such as fraud in procurement or lack of jurisdiction. Thus in *Williams* v. *North Carolina,* 325 US 226 (1945), the courts of North Carolina refused to honor a divorce procured in Nevada. Williams, a resident of North Carolina, spent forty-two days in a Nevada tourist camp, obtained a divorce, returned to North Carolina, and married again. North Carolina prosecuted Williams for bigamy. A jury found that Williams did not go to Nevada with the intent of making it his home. Hence the North Carolina court ruled that Williams did not become a legal resident and that Nevada lacked jurisdiction to grant him a divorce. The United States Supreme Court refused to reverse the North Carolina decision. *Simons* v. *Miami Beach First National Bank,* 381 US 80 (1965), contains a summary of the federal cases on the effect of a divorce on property rights when obtained in an *ex parte* proceeding with one of the spouses outside the jurisdiction of the state.

The full faith and credit clause is closely associated with the broader problem of the conflict of laws. Assuming that full faith and credit is to be given, the law appropriate for application becomes a difficult problem in many cases. For example, in regard to a contract, the issue may be whether it is to be governed by the law of the state where the contract was made, by the law of the state where the contract is to be executed, by the law contemplated by the parties, or by a combination of factors. An introduction to the subject is presented in the following books: Brainerd Currie, *Selected Essays on the Conflict of Laws* (Durham, 1963); Albert A. Ehrenzweig, *Conflicts in a Nutshell* (St. Paul, 1970); Herbert F. Goodrich, *Handbook of the Conflict of Laws* (St. Paul, 1949); and George W. Stumberg, *Principles of Conflict of Laws* (Brooklyn, 1963).

F. INTERSTATE AGREEMENTS

Introduction

The Constitution prohibits a state from entering any "treaty, alliance, or confederation." These are terms signifying a political relationship. The states are also forbidden to enter "any agreement or compact with another State or with a foreign power" without the consent of Congress. Agreements among two or more states have been common on such matters as the construction of bridges, development of harbors, and promotion of education. See Council of State Governments, *The Book of the States, 1964–1965* (Chicago, 1964), pp. 269–77. The consent of Congress may be given specifically through resolution, or it may be implied. Thus *Virginia* v. *Tennessee,* 148 US 503 (1893), held that Congress had impliedly consented to the agreement concerning the boundary between these two states by its districting the two states for revenue and judicial purposes.

West Virginia v. *Sims,* 341 US 22 (1951), held that a state could not unilaterally nullify its obligations arising under an interstate conpact. West Virginia was one of eight states that entered an agreement to create a Sanitation Commission to control pollution of the Ohio River system. A question arose as to whether West Virginia could, under the terms of its Constitition, make the financial payment to the Sanitary Commission called for by the agreement. The Supreme Court of Appeals of West Virginia ruled that the state could not make the payments. All justices of the United States Supreme Court agreed that this decision should be reversed, but they had difficulty in expressing the reason on which to base their decision. Justice Jackson put it this way: "Whatever she [West Virginia] now says her Constitution means, she may not apply retroactively that interpretation to place an unforeseeable construction upon what the other States to this Compact were entitled to believe was a fully authorized act." On the general subject, see Richard H. Leach and Redding S. Sugg, Jr., *The Administration of Interstate Compacts* (Baton Rouge, 1959).

Part II

Civil

Rights

Chapter 6

The Original Constitution

A. INTRODUCTION

The Constitution of the United States as written by the Federal Convention of 1787 contained no distinct bill of rights. The theory that prevailed in the Convention was that the national government was to be limited to the powers given to it by the Constitution, and that no bill of rights was necessary. In *The Federalist,* No. 84, Alexander Hamilton wrote: "I go further, and affirm, that bills of rights . . . are not only unnecessary in the proposed constitution, but would even be dangerous. They would contain various exceptions not granted, and on this very account would afford a colourable pretext to claim more than was granted. For why declare that things shall not be done which there is no power to do?" But this line of argument did not prevail. In the arguments over ratification of the Constitution, the people preferred the view of George Mason and others who favored a bill of rights. Promises that clauses protecting fundamental freedoms would be written into the Constitution if it were adopted were fulfilled by the ratification of the first ten amendments in 1791.

While containing no separate bill of rights, the original Constitution did contain a number of significant safeguards of liberty and property. These are dealt with in this chapter.

B. WRIT OF HABEAS CORPUS

Introduction

The writ of habeas corpus is the great writ of the English law, used to afford protection against arbitrary arrest and imprisonment. A person sometimes has difficulty in securing relief through judicial action because he lacks standing to sue, but everyone has an interest in his own freedom and the freedom of everyone else; hence if a person is imprisoned, the writ of habeas corpus is available to test its legality. The writ takes its name from the first two words of the Latin sentence with which it customarily began, *Habeas corpus ad faciendum ad subjiciendum et recipiendum, etc.,* translated by Blackstone, "That you have or produce the body of the prisoner, with the day and cause of his caption and detention, to do, submit to, and receive whatsoever the judge or court awarding such writ shall consider in that behalf." T. M. Cooley, *Blackstone's Commentaries,* 4th ed. II (Chicago, 1899), p. 951. The writ is directed to a jailor or other person holding another in custody. He is supposed to produce the body of the prisoner and show cause why he should not be released. If sufficient cause is shown, the prisoner is returned to the jailor; if not, the prisoner is released, released on bail, or otherwise dealt with as appears appropriate. In practice, before issuing a writ of habeas corpus, judges often hold a hearing on the petition for the writ, to consider whether, upon the facts presented in the petition, the prisoner, if brought before the court, would be discharged.

Chapter 29 of the Magna Carta provided that "No freeman shall be taken and imprisoned . . . except by the lawful judgment of his peers or by the law of the land." Some seek to trace the writ of habeas corpus back to this famous document of 1215, but it is clearly of later origin. Writs of habeas corpus of a variety of forms were used by both the Court of Chancery and the common law courts. The writ of *habeas corpus ad subjiciendum,* the great writ of today, was largely a product of the seventeenth century.

History of Suspension of the Writ

The Consitution provides that "The privilege of the writ of habeas corpus shall not be suspended, unless when in cases of rebellion or invasion the public safety may require it."

To delineate with exactness the line of division between civilian and military authority is difficult; but the supremacy of civil authority over the military is considered fundamental in American government, and our tradition is against suspending the writ of habeas corpus.

There were no official suspensions of the writ prior to 1861. President Lincoln suspended the writ in specific areas early in the Civil War, and on September 24, 1862, he suspended it throughout the United States in respect to persons arrested or detained by the military. On March 3, 1863, Congress authorized the president to suspend the privilege of the writ of habeas corpus whenever, in his judgment, the public safety required it. The exact number of civilians arrested by the military during the Civil War is not known, but it certainly ran into the thousands. See Andrew C. McLaughlin, *A Constitutional History of the United States* (New York, 1935), p. 623.

When Judge Wylie issued a writ of habeas corpus for Mrs. Mary Eugenia Surratt the night before she was to be executed on conviction of participating in the plot to assassinate President Lincoln, President Johnson suspended the privilege of the writ and Mrs. Surratt was executed. The subsequent verdict of history has been that this execution was a ghastly miscarriage of justice. Guy W. Moore, *The Case of Mrs. Surratt* (Norman, Okla., 1954) p. 54.

Under the authority of the Ku Klux Klan Act, on October 17, 1871, President Grant suspended the writ in nine South Carolina counties. A state of rebellion was declared to exist there.

Despite the presence of a large and vociferous pro-German element in the United States, there was no instance during World War I when the writ was suspended. It was suspended in Hawaii during World War II, as explained in the *Duncan* case below.

Meaning of Suspension of the Writ

What does a suspension of the writ of habeas corpus mean? The Constitution uses the phrase "the privilege of the writ of habeas corpus," and in *Ex parte Milligan,* 4 Wallace 2 (1866), Justice Davis wrote: "The suspension of the privilege of the writ of habeas corpus does not suspend the writ itself. The writ issues as a matter of course; and on the return made to it the court decides whether the party applying is denied the right of proceeding any further with it." The theory here seems to be that, as long as the courts are open, the judges will issue writs of habeas corpus despite the fact that the privilege of the writ has been officially suspended. The jailer, military officer, or other person to whom a writ is directed will, in such cases, have to answer the writ. If he shows the official suspension of the writ, apparently the judge is to decide in each case whether the suspension is legal. If it is, the jailer will not have to justify further his detention of the prisoner. In the *Milligan* case, the Supreme Court held that the trial of a civilian (Lambdin P. Milligan) by a military tribunal at a time and place (Indiana in 1864) when the civil courts were open was illegal and that a writ of habeas corpus should issue to secure his release from military custody.

Duncan v. Kahanamoku

327 US 304, 66 S Ct 606, 90 L Ed 688 (1946)

When Congress passed the Hawaiian Organic Act and authorized the establishment of "martial law" it had in mind, and did not wish to exceed, the boundaries between military and civilian power, in which our people have always believed, which responsible military and executive officers had heeded, and which had become part of our philosophy and institutions.

[On December 7, 1941, after the Japanese attack upon Pearl Harbor, the governor of Hawaii by proclamation undertook to suspend the writ of habeas corpus and to place the territory under "martial law." The civilian courts were forbidden to try cases. Eight months later Harry E. White, a stockbroker in Honolulu, was convicted by a military tribunal of embezzling stock belonging to another civilian. Two years later, Lloyd C. Duncan, a civilian, was similarly convicted of an assault upon two military sentries. The Supreme Court considered petitions from White and Duncan in the same opinion. Kahanamoku was the sheriff of the city and county of Honolulu.

Under the Hawaiian Organic Act, the governor could, "in case of rebellion or invasion, or imminent danger thereof, when the public safety requires it, suspend the privilege of the writ of *habeas corpus,* or place the territory, or any part thereof, under martial law. . . ."]

MR. JUSTICE BLACK delivered the opinion of the Court. . . . Did the Organic Act during the period of martial law give the armed forces power to supplant all civilian laws and to substitute military for judicial trials under the conditions that existed in Hawaii at the time these petitioners were tried? . . .

We note first that at the time the alleged offenses were committed the dangers apprehended by the military were not sufficiently imminent to cause them to require civilians to evacuate the area or even to evacuate any of the buildings necessary to carry on the business of the courts. In fact, the buildings had long been open and actually in use for certain kinds of trials. . . .

If a power . . . to obliterate the judicial system of Hawaii can be found at all in the Organic Act, it must be inferred from § 67's provision for placing the Territory under "martial law." But the term "martial law" carries no precise meaning. The Constitution does not refer to "martial law" at all and no Act of Congress has defined the term. It has been employed in various ways by different people and at different times. By some it has been identified as "military law" limited to members of, and those connected with, the armed forces. Others have said that the term does not imply a system of established rules but denotes simply some kind of day to day expression of a general's will dictated by what he considers the imperious necessity of the moment. . . . In 1857 the confusion as to the meaning of the phrase was so great that the Attorney General in an official opinion had this to say about it: "The common law authorities and commentators afford no clue to what martial law, as understood in England, really is. . . . In this country it is still worse." 8 Op Atty Gen 365, 367, 368. What was true in 1857 remains true today. The language of § 67 thus fails to define adequately the scope of the power given to the military and to show whether the Organic Act provides that courts of law be supplanted by military tribunals. . . .

Since both the language of the Organic Act and its legislative history fail to indicate that the scope of "martial law" in Hawaii includes the supplanting of courts by military tribunals, we must look to other sources in order to interpret that term. We think the answer may be found in the birth, development and growth of our governmental institutions up to the time Congress passed the Organic Act. . . .

People of many ages and countries have feared and unflinchingly opposed the kind of subordination of executive, legislative and judicial authorities to complete military rule which, according to the Government, Congress has authorized here. In this country that fear has become part of our cultural and political institutions. The story of that development is well known and we see no need to retell it all. But we might mention a few pertinent incidents. As early as the 17th Century our British ancestors took political action against aggressive military rule. When James I and Charles I authorized martial law for purposes of speedily punishing all types of crimes committed by civilians the protest led to the historic Petition of Right which in uncompromising terms objected to this arbitrary procedure and prayed that it be stopped and never repeated. When later the American colonies declared their independence one of the grievances listed by Jefferson was that the King had endeavored to render the military superior to the civil power. The executive and military officials who later found it necessary to utilize the armed forces to keep order in a young and turbulent nation, did not lose sight of the philosophy embodied in the Petition of Right and the Declaration of Independence, that existing civilian government and especially the courts were not to be interfered with by the exercise of military power. In 1787, the year in which the Constitution was formulated, the Governor of Massachusetts Colony used the militia to cope with Shay's Rebellion. In his instructions to the Commander of the troops the Governor listed the "great objects" of the mission. The troops were to "protect the judicial courts . . .," "to assist the civil magistrates in executing the laws . . .," and to "aid them in apprehending the disturbers of the public peace. . . ." The Commander was to consider himself "constantly as under the direction of the civil officer, saving where any armed force shall appear and oppose . . . [his] marching to execute these orders." President Washington's instructions to the Commander of the troops sent into Pennsylvania to suppress the Whiskey Rebellion of 1794 were to the same effect. The troops were to see to it that the laws were enforced and were to deliver the leaders of armed insurgents to the regular courts for trial. The President admonished the Commanding General "that the judge cannot be controlled in his functions. . . ." In the many instances of the use of troops to control the activities of civilians that followed, the troops were generally again employed merely to aid and not to supplant the civilian authorities. . . .

We believe that when Congress passed the Hawaiian Organic Act and authorized the establishment of "martial law" it had in mind and did not wish to exceed the boundaries between military and civilian power, in which our people have always believed, which responsible military and executive officers had heeded, and which had become part of our political philosophy and institutions prior to the time Congress passed the Organic Act. The phrase "martial law" as employed in that Act, therefore, while intended to authorize the military to act vigorously for the maintenance of an orderly civil government and for the defense of the Islands against actual or threatened rebellion or invasion, was not intended to authorize the supplanting of courts by military tribunals. Yet the Government seeks to justify the punishment of both White and Duncan on the ground of such supposed congressional authorization. We hold that both petitioners are now entitled to be released from custody.

Reversed.

MR. CHIEF JUSTICE STONE, concurring. [Omitted here.]

MR. JUSTICE BURTON, with whom MR. JUSTICE FRANKFURTER concurs, dissenting. . . .

One way to test the soundness of a decision today that the trial of petitioner White on August 25, 1942, before a provost court on a charge of embezzlement and the trial of petitioner Duncan on March 2, 1944, before a similar court on a charge of maliciously assaulting marine sentries were unconstitutional procedures, is to ask ourselves whether or not on those dates, with the war against Japan in full swing, this Court would have, or should have, granted a writ of habeas corpus, an injunction or a writ of prohibition to release the petitioners or otherwise to oust the provost courts of their claimed jurisdiction. Such a test emphasizes the issue. I believe that this Court would not have been justified in granting the relief suggested at such times. Also I believe that this Court might well have found itself embarrassed had it ordered such relief and then had attempted to enforce its order in the theatre of military operations, at a time when the area was under martial law and the writ of habeas corpus was still suspended, all in accordance with the orders of the President of the United States and the Governor of Hawaii issued under their interpretation of the discretion and responsibility vested in them by the Constitution of the United States and by the Organic Act of Hawaii enacted by Congress.

C. BILL OF ATTAINDER

United States v. Lovett

328 US 303, 66 S Ct 1073, 90 L Ed 1252 (1946)

An act of Congress that cuts off the pay of named individuals found by Congress to be guilty of disloyalty is void as a bill of attainder.

[In a speech on the floor of the House of Representatives in 1943, Representative Martin Dies, chairman of the Committee on Un-American Activities, denounced thirty-nine named government employees as "irresponsible, unrepresentative, crackpot, radical bureaucrats" and affiliates of "Communist front organizations." The House attached an amendment to the Urgent Deficiencies Appropriation Act of 1943 providing that no federal funds should be used after November 15, 1943, "to pay any part of the salary . . . of Goodwin B. Watson, William E. Dodd, Junior, and Robert Morss Lovett. . . ." The imperative need for the funds involved led the president to sign the Act, but in doing so he noted that he thought the provision naming Watson, Dodd, and Lovett was unconstitutional. These men continued in their jobs, but their compensation was discontinued after November 15. To secure compensation for this post-November 15 work, they brought suit in the court of claims. The Supreme Court granted *certiorari.*]

MR. JUSTICE BLACK delivered the opinion of the Court.

We hold that § 304 falls precisely within the category of congressional actions which the Constitution barred by providing that "No Bill of Attainder or *ex post facto* Law shall be passed." In *Cummings* v. *Missouri,* 4 Wallace 277, 323, this Court said, "A bill of attainder is a legislative act which inflicts punishment without a judicial trial. If the punishment be less than death, the act is termed a bill of pains and penalties. Within the meaning of the Constitution, bills of attainder include bills of pains and penalties." The *Cummings* decision involved a provision of the Missouri Reconstruction Constitution which required persons to take an Oath of Loyalty as a prerequisite to practicing a profession. Cummings, a Catholic Priest, was convicted for teaching and preaching as a minister without taking the oath. The oath required an applicant to affirm that he had never given aid or comfort to persons engaged in hostility to the

United States and had never "been a member of, or connected with, any order, society, or organization, inimical to the government of the United States . . ." In an illuminating opinion which gave the historical background of the constitutional prohibition against bills of attainder, this Court invalidated the Missouri constitutional provision both because it constituted a bill of attainder and because it had an *ex post facto* operation. On the same day the *Cummings* case was decided, the Court, in *Ex parte Garland,* 4 Wallace 333, also held invalid on the same grounds an Act of Congress which required attorneys practicing before this Court to take a similar oath. Neither of these cases has ever been overruled. They stand for the proposition that legislative acts, no matter what their form, that apply either to named individuals or to easily ascertainable members of a group in such a way as to inflict punishment on them without a judicial trial are bills of attainder prohibited by the Constitution. Adherence to this principle requires invalidation of § 304. We do adhere to it. . . .

Section 304 . . . clearly accomplishes the punishment of named individuals without a judicial trial. The fact that the punishment is inflicted through the instrumentality of an Act specifically cutting off the pay of certain named individuals found guilty of disloyalty, makes it no less galling or effective than if it had been done by an Act which designated the conduct as criminal. No one would think that Congress could have passed a valid law, stating that after investigation it had found Lovett, Dodd, and Watson "guilty" of the crime of engaging in "subversive activities," defined that term for the first time, and sentenced them to perpetual exclusion from any government employment. Section 304, while it does not use that language, accomplishes that result. The effect was to inflict punishment without the safeguards of a judicial trial and "determined by no previous law or fixed rule." The Constitution declares that that cannot be done either by a State or by the United States.

When our Constitution and Bill of Rights were written, our ancestors had ample reason to know that legislative trials and punishments were too dangerous to liberty to exist in the nation of free men they envisioned. And so they proscribed bills of attainder. Section 304 is one. Much as we regret to declare that an Act of Congress violates the Constitution, we have no alternative here.

Section 304 therefore does not stand as an obstacle to payment of compensation to Lovett, Watson, and Dodd. The judgment in their favor is

Affirmed.

[Mr. Justice Frankfurter, whom Mr. Justice Reed joined, wrote a concurring opinion.]

Note

United States v. *Brown,* 381 US 437 (1965), held Sec 504 of the Labor-Management Reporting and Disclosure Act of 1959 void as a bill of attainder. The section makes it a crime for a member of the Communist Party to serve as an officer or (except in clerical or custodial positions) as an employee of a labor union. For the majority, Chief Justice Warren wrote:

[T]he Bill of Attainder Clause was intended ... as ... a general safeguard against legislative exercise of the judicial function, or more simply—trial by legislature. ... The statute does not set forth a generally applicable rule decreeing that any person who commits certain acts or possesses certain characteristics ... shall not hold union office, and leave to courts and juries the job of deciding what persons have committed the specified acts or possess the specified characteristics. Instead, it designates ... the persons ... —members of the Communist Party. ... The designation of Communists as those persons likely to cause political strikes ... rests ... upon an empirical investigation by Congress of the acts, characteristics and propensities of Communist Party members. ... Even assuming that Congress had reason to conclude that some Communists would use union positions to bring about political strikes, "it cannot automatically be inferred that all members share their evil purposes or participate in their illegal activities."

Dissenting, JUSTICE WHITE (joined by JUSTICES CLARK, HARLAN, and STEWART) held the basic flaw in the Court's reasoning to be

its too narrow view of the legislative process. ... [L]egislators seldom deal with abstractions, but with concrete situations and the regulation of specific abuses. Thus many regulatory measures are enacted after investigation into particular incidents or the practices of particular groups and after findings by the legislature that the practices disclosed are inimical to the public interest and should be prevented in the future. Not surprisingly, the resulting legislation may reflect in its specificity the specificity of the preceding legislative inquiry. ... But the fact that it does should not be taken, in itself, to be conclusive that the legislature's purpose is punitive.

D. EX POST FACTO LAWS

Calder v. Bull

3 Dallas 386, 1 L Ed 648 (1798)

A resolution, or law of the state of Connecticut, setting aside a decree of a court of probate, and granting a new hearing before the same court, with liberty of appeal, is not an *ex post facto* law within the meaning of the 10th section of the 1st Article of the Constitution of the United States.

[By a decree in March, 1793, the Court of Probate of Hartford disapproved and refused to record a will under which Caleb Bull claimed certain property. After eighteen months, all right of appeal was barred by Connecticut law. In May, 1795, the legislature of Connecticut passed a resolution which set aside the 1793 decree of the probate court and granted a new hearing by the same court. At this second hearing, the probate court approved the will in question and ordered it to be recorded. Bull claimed the property in dispute under this will. Calder, having another claim, sought to show that the resolution of the legislature granting the new hearing was an *ex post facto* law, and void.

Bull won in the Connecticut courts, and Calder took the case to the United States Supreme Court. . . . The justices delivered their opinions *seriatim.*]

CHASE, JUSTICE. ·. . . I shall endeavor to show what law is to be considered an *ex post facto* law, within the words and meaning of the prohibition in the federal constitution. The prohibition, "that no State shall pass any *ex post facto* law," necessarily requires some explanation; for naked and without explanation it is unintelligible, and means nothing. Literally it is only that a law shall not be passed concerning, and after the fact, or thing done, or action committed. I would ask, what fact; of what nature or kind; and by whom done? That Charles I, King of England, was beheaded; that Oliver Cromwell was protector of England, that Louis XVI, late King of France, was guillotined; are all facts that have happened, but it would be nonsense to suppose that the States were prohibited from making any law after either of these events, and with reference thereto. The prohibition in the letter is not to pass any law concerning and after the fact, but the plain and obvious meaning and intention of the prohibition is this, that the legislatures of the several States shall not pass laws after a fact done by a subject, or citizen, which shall have relation to such fact, and shall punish him for having done it. The prohibition, considered in this light, is an additional bulwark in favor of the personal security of the subject, to protect his person from punishment by legislative acts, having a retrospective operation. I do not think it was inserted to secure the citizen in his private rights of either property or contracts. The prohibitions not to make anything but gold and silver coin a tender in payment of debts, and not to pass any law impairing the obligation of contracts, were inserted to secure private rights; but the restriction not to pass any *ex post facto* law, was to secure the person of the subject from injury or punishment, in consequence of such law. If the prohibition against making *ex post facto* laws was intended to secure personal rights from being affected or injured by such laws, and the prohibition is sufficiently extensive for that object, the other restraints I have enumerated were unnecessary, and therefore improper, for both of them are retrospective.

I will state what laws I consider *ex post facto* laws, within the words and the intent of the prohibition. 1st. Every law that makes an action done before the passing of the law, and which was innocent when done, criminal; and punishes such action. 2d. Every law that aggravates a crime, or makes it greater than it was, when committed. 3d. Every law that changes the punishment, and inflicts a greater punishment than the law annexed to the crime, when committed. 4th. Every law that alters the legal rules of evidence, and receives less or different testimony than the law required at the time of the commission of the offence, in order to convict the offender. All these and similar laws are manifestly unjust and oppressive. . . .

[The opinions of JUSTICES IREDELL, PATERSON and CUSHING are omitted here.]

Judgment affirmed.

Notes

1. *Definition.* "It is sufficient now to say that a statute belongs to that class [of *ex post facto* laws], which by its necessary operation and in its relation to the

offense, or its consequences, alters the situation of the accused to his disadvantage." *Thompson* v. *Utah,* 170 US 343 (1898).

The retroactive application of a law providing for the deportation of aliens found practicing prostitution after entry into the United States was sustained. The court held that the determination of facts upon which to base deportation is not a conviction of crime and that deportation is not punishment. *Bugajewitz* v. *Adams,* 228 US 585 (1913).

Disqualifying anyone who had been convicted of crime from practicing medicine was held not to be a penal law. *Hawker* v. *New York,* 170 US 189 (1898). *Flemming* v. *Nestor,* 363 US 603 (1960), held that Sec 202(n) of the Social Security Act providing for the termination of benefit payments to an alien deported for Communist affiliation is neither a bill of attainder nor *ex post facto* law.

2. *Changes in procedure.*   Changes in procedure may be made, provided no substantial rights of the accused are impaired. Examples of procedural changes made by statutes which have been sustained include (1) shifting the place of trial from one county to another, *Gut* v. *Minnesota,* 9 Wallace 35 (1870); (2) changing the number of appellate judges, *Duncan* v. *Missouri,* 152 US 377 (1894); (3) granting a right of appeal to the state, *Mallett* v. *North Carolina,* 181 US 589 (1901); and (4) changing the method of selecting jurors, *Gibson* v. *Mississippi,* 162 US 565 (1896).

But *Thompson* v. *Utah,* 170 US 343 (1898), held that a law of the state of Utah providing for trial by a jury of eight persons was an *ex post facto* law when applied to Thompson. He had been convicted by a jury of twelve persons under the law of the territory before Utah became a state and granted a new trial.

In his *Treatise on Constitutional Limitations,* Ch. 9, Sec. 272, Thomas M. Cooley makes this statement:

> But so far as mere modes of procedure are concerned, a party has no more right, in a criminal than in a civil action, to insist that his case shall be disposed of under the law in force when the act to be investigated is charged to have taken place. Remedies must always be under the control of the legislature, and it would create endless confusion in legal proceedings if every case was to be conducted only in accordance with the rules of practice, and heard only by the courts in existence when its facts arose. The legislature may abolish courts and create new ones, and it may prescribe altogether different modes of procedure in its discretion, though it cannot lawfully, we think, in so doing, dispense with any of those substantial protections with which the existing law surrounds the persons accused of crime.

3. *Change in law by judiciary.*   The prohibition against *ex post facto* laws does not operate as a restraint upon changes in the law by the judiciary. *Ross* v. *Oregon,* 227 US 150 (1913).

E. THE CONTRACT CLAUSE

Protection of property, as well as life and liberty, has always been a basic tenet of American political thought. The Northwest Ordinance of 1787 provided that "in the just preservation of rights and property, it is understood and declared, that no law ought ever to be made or have force in the said territory, that shall, in any manner whatever, interfere with or affect private contracts, or engagements *bona fide,* and without fraud previously formed." In sending General Washington a copy of this Ordinance, Richard Henry Lee explained: "It seemed necessary, for the security of property among uninformed, and perhaps licentious people, as the greater part of those who go there are, that a strong toned government should exist, and the rights of property be clearly defined." B. F. Wright, *The Contract Clause of the Constitution* (Cambridge, Mass., 1938), p. 7.

During the critical period between the Revolution and the Federal Convention, property rights were jeopardized by laws staying or postponing payment of private debts, laws authorizing payments in installments rather than in lump sums, laws permitting payment in commodities rather than in cash, and laws providing for the issuance of paper money declared to be legal tender. It was against this background that the framers wrote into Article 1, Section 10 of the Constitution the provision that "No State shall . . . pass any . . . law impairing the obligation of contracts. . . ."

History of Clause

The clause was held to apply to contracts by the state governments as well as to private contracts and given a very broad application by Chief Justice Marshall. Protection of property rights was a characteristic feature of his decisions. These decisions were not overruled, but their application was diminished by the application of a doctrine of strict construction during the period that Taney was chief justice. The adoption of "reservation clauses" and an increased respect for the "police power" of the states further limited the application of the contract clause; yet it remained the most important clause for the protection of property rights throughout the nineteenth century. Excluding the commerce clause, the contract clause was the constitutional basis for more cases involving the validity of state laws than all the other clauses of the Constitution together.

The *Blaisdell* case of 1934 (p. 196) held that the contract clause was not to be applied with literal exactness. Thereafter, cases involving the clause were handled on what amounted to a due-process method of reasoning. Where legislation reflected a "studied indifference" to property rights growing out of a contract, the legislation was invalidated. See, for example, *W. B. Worthen Co.* v. *Kavanaugh,* 295 US 56 (1935). Where, on the other hand, the legislation reflected an honest effort to deal fairly with actual conditions, it was sustained. For example, *El Paso* v. *Simmons,* 379 US 497 (1965), sustained a Texas statute involving changes in the state's policy governing land claims when applied in such a way as to adversely affect rights acquired under previous statutes. According to the Court, "The measure taken to induce defaulting purchasers to comply with their contracts, requiring payment of interest in arrears within five years, was a mild one indeed, hardly burdensome to the purchaser who wanted to adhere to his contract of purchase, but nonetheless an important one to the State's interest. The Contract Clause does not forbid such a measure."

Judicial action

The contract clause is a restraint upon legislative action, not judicial. *Tidal Oil Co.* v. *Flanagan,* 263 US 444 (1924).

Eminent domain

The contract clause does not limit the power of eminent domain. This is illustrated by *West River Bridge Co.* v. *Dix,* 6 Howard 507 (1848). The state of Vermont had chartered a corporation and given it the exclusive right of operating a toll bridge over the West River. Later the state took the bridge by eminent domain and made it a free bridge. The corporation was unable to obtain judicial relief under the contract clause.

The Gold Clause Cases

In 1933 Congress devaluated the dollar, and a joint resolution of June 5, 1933, declared that every contract that provided for payment in gold, or in a particular kind of currency, was against public policy. A number of corporations had bonds outstanding payable by their express terms either in gold coin of a specified weight, or in an equivalent amount of currency. The Court held that Congress could impair such contracts. There is no "contract clause" limiting the power of Congress, and all contracts are made subject to the rightful authority of Congress to control the currency. *Norman* v. *Baltimore & Ohio R.R.,* 294 US 240 (1935).

The United States government had bonds outstanding "payable in United States gold coin of the present standard of value." Could the government repudiate this pledge? On this question the Court gave double-talk. It held that Congress had power to borrow "on the credit of the United States," a "plighted faith," not a vain promise. Yet the suit before the Court was for breach of contract, and, according to the majority, the plaintiff had not shown that he had suffered any loss. *Perry* v. *United States,* 294 US 330 (1935).

Fletcher v. Peck

6 Cranch 87, 3 L Ed 162 (1810)

If a legislature make a grant of lands in fee simple, a subsequent legislature cannot take away the title of a *bona fide* purchaser for a valuable consideration from the first grantee, upon the ground that the grant to the latter was fraudulent.

[Yielding to bribery, in 1795 the Legislature of Georgia voted to sell a vast area of the state's western land for approximately 1½ cents per acre. The next year the legislature repealed the Act authorizing the sale. Purchasers of the land refused to surrender their bargain. John Peck sold a tract of this land to Robert Fletcher. In the deed he included a covenant that the title to the land had not been legally impaired by the Repeal Act passed by the Legislature of Georgia in 1796. Fletcher brought suit against Peck upon this covenant in a United States circuit court. An appeal from its decision was taken to the Supreme Court.]

MARSHALL, C. J., delivered the opinion of the Court. . . .

Is the power of the legislature competent to the annihilation of such title, and to a resumption of the property thus held?

The principle asserted is, that one legislature is competent to repeal any act which a former legislature was competent to pass; and that one legislature cannot abridge the powers of a succeeding legislature.

The correctness of this principle, so far as respects general legislation, can never be controverted. But if an act be done under a law, a succeeding legislature cannot undo it. The past cannot be recalled by the most absolute power. Conveyances have been made, those conveyances have vested legal estates, and, if those estates may be seized by the sovereign authority, still, that they originally vested is a fact, and cannot cease to be a fact. . . .

The validity of this rescinding act, then, might well be doubted, were Georgia a single sovereign power. But Georgia cannot be viewed as a single, unconnected, sovereign power, on whose legislature no other restrictions are imposed than may be found in its own constitution. She is a part of a large empire; she is a member of the American Union; and that union has a constitution the supremacy of which all acknowledge, and which imposes limits to the legislatures of the several States, which none claim a right to pass. The Constitution of the United States declares that no State shall pass any bill of attainder, *ex post facto* law, or law impairing the obligation of contracts.

Does the case now under consideration come within the prohibitory section of the Constitution?

In considering this very interesting question, we immediately ask ourselves what is a contract? Is a grant a contract?

A contract is a compact between two or more parties, and is either executory or executed. An executory contract is one in which a party binds himself to do, or not to do, a particular thing; such was the law under which the conveyance was made by the governor. A contract executed is one in which the object of contract is performed; and this, says Blackstone, differs in nothing from a grant. The contract between Georgia and the purchasers was executed by the grant. A contract executed, as well as one which is executory, contains obligations binding on the parties. A grant, in its own nature, amounts to an extinguishment of the right of the grantor, and implies a contract not to reassert that right. A party is, therefore, always estopped by his own grant. . . .

If, under a fair construction of the Constitution, grants are comprehended under the term contracts, is a grant from the State excluded from the operation of the provision? Is the clause to be considered as inhibiting the State from impairing the obligation of contracts between two individuals, but as excluding from that inhibition contracts made with itself?

The words themselves contain no such distinction. They are general, and are applicable to contracts of every description. If contracts made with the State are to be exempted from their operation, the exception must arise from the character of the contracting party, not from the words which are employed. . . .

No State shall pass any bill of attainder, *ex post facto* law, or law impairing the obligation of contracts. . . .

In this form the power of the legislature over the lives and fortunes of individuals is expressly restrained. What motive, then, for implying, in words which import a general prohibition to impair the obligation of contracts, an exception in favor of the right to impair the obligation of those contracts into which the State may enter? . . .

It is . . . the unanimous opinion of the court, that, in this case, the estate having passed into the hands of a purchaser for a valuable consideration, without notice, the

State of Georgia was restrained, either by general principles which are common to our free institutions, or by the particular provisions of the Constitution of the United States, from passing a law whereby the estate of the plaintiff in the premises so purchased could be constitutionally and legally impaired and rendered null and void. . . .

Notes

1. *Fletcher* v. *Peck* was the first case in which the United States Supreme Court held a state statute unconstitutional.

2. In *Trustees of Dartmouth College* v. *Woodward,* 4 Wheaton 518, 4 L Ed 629 (1819), Marshall further expanded the protection of the contract clause by holding that "the circumstances of this case constitute a contract." The Trustees of Dartmouth College operated under a charter granted by the King of England before the American Revolution. The legislature of New Hampshire had passed an act increasing the membership of the trustees and, in effect, subjecting the college to political control. The Supreme Court held the act of the legislature to be void.

Charles River Bridge v. Warren Bridge

11 Peters 420, 9 L Ed 773 (1837)

A state law may be retrospective and divest vested rights, and yet not violate the Constitution of the United States.

[The Charles River Bridge Company obtained from the legislature of Massachusetts authority to build a toll bridge over the river between Boston and Cambridge. The legislature later authorized the construction of the Warren Bridge so near the Charles River Bridge as to diminish its toll revenue. The Charles River Bridge sought to enjoin operation of the Warren Bridge.]

MR. CHIEF JUSTICE TANEY delivered the opinion of the court. . . .
   Much has been said in the argument of the principles of construction by which this law is to be expounded, and what undertakings, on the part of the state, may be implied. The court thinks there can be no serious difficulty on that head. It is the grant of certain franchises by the public to a private corporation, and in a matter where the public interest is concerned. The rule of construction in such cases is well settled, both in England and by the decisions of our own tribunals. In 2 Barn. & Adol. 793, in the case of the Proprietors of the Stourbridge Canal v. Wheeley and others, the court say [sic], "The canal having been made under an act of parliament, the rights of the plaintiffs are derived entirely from that act. This, like many other cases, is a bargain between a company of adventurers and the public, the terms of which are expressed in the statute; and the rule of construction, in all such cases, is now fully established to be this; that any ambiguity in the terms of the contract must operate against the adventurers, and in favor of the public, and the plaintiffs can claim nothing that is not clearly given them by the act." . . .

Adopting the rule of construction above stated as the settled one, we proceed to apply it to the charter of 1785, to the proprietors of the Charles River Bridge. This act of incorporation is in the usual form, and the privileges such as are commonly given to corporations of that kind. It confers on them the ordinary faculties of a corporation, for the purpose of building the bridge; and establishes certain rates of toll, which the company are authorized to take: this is the whole grant. There is no exclusive privilege given to them over the waters of Charles River, above or below their bridge; no right to erect another bridge themselves, nor to prevent other persons from erecting one, no engagement from the state, that another shall not be erected; and no undertaking not to sanction competition, nor to make improvements that may diminish the amount of its income. Upon all these subjects, the charter is silent; and nothing is said in it about a line of travel, so much insisted on in the argument, in which they are to have exclusive privileges. No words are used from which an intention to grant any of these rights can be inferred; if the plaintiff is entitled to them, it must be implied, simply, from the nature of the grant; and cannot be inferred, from the words by which the grant is made.

The relative position of the Warren Bridge has already been described. It does not interrupt the passage over the Charles River Bridge, nor make the way to it, or from it, less convenient. None of the faculties or franchises granted to that corporation, have been revoked by the legislature; and its right to take the tolls granted by the charter remains unaltered. In short, all the franchises and rights of property, enumerated in the charter, and there mentioned to have been granted to it, remain unimpaired. But its income is destroyed by the Warren Bridge; which, being free, draws off the passengers and property which would have gone over it, and renders their franchise of no value. This is the gist of the complaint. For it is not pretended, that the erection of the Warren Bridge would have done them any injury, or in any degree affected their right of property, if it had not diminished the amount of their tolls. In order, then, to entitle themselves to relief, it is necessary to show, that the legislature contracted not to do the act of which they complain; and that they impaired, or in other words, violated, that contract by the erection of the Warren Bridge.

The inquiry, then, is, does the charter contain such a contract on the part of the state? Is there any such stipulation to be found in that instrument? It must be admitted on all hands, that there is none; no words that even relate to another bridge, or to the diminution of their tolls, or to the line of travel. If a contract on that subject can be gathered from the charter, it must be by implication; and cannot be found in the words used. Can such an agreement be implied? The rule of construction before stated is an answer to the question; in charters of their description, no rights are taken from the public, or given to the corporation, beyond those which the words of the charter, by their natural and proper construction, purport to convey. . . .

The judgment of the supreme judicial court of the commonwealth of Massachusetts, dismissing the plaintiffs' bill, must therefore, be affirmed, with costs. . . .

[MR. JUSTICE STORY dissented.]

Note

Atlantic Coast Line R. Co. v. *Phillips,* 332 US 168 (1947).   This is an example of a strict and narrow construction of a charter. To encourage investments in railroads, in 1833 the General Assembly of Georgia granted to the Georgia

Railroad Company a charter providing that "The stock of said company and its branches shall be exempt from taxation for and during the term of seventy years from and after the completion of said railroads or any one of them: and after that, shall be subject to a tax not exceeding one half per cent per annum on the net proceeds of their investments." The present case arose from an attempt by Phillips, the state revenue commissioner, to collect an income tax upon the lessee of the Georgia Railroad Company, computed at the rate of 5½ percent of its net income. In sustaining the tax, Justice Frankfurter wrote: "Not until the Civil War did Georgia, like the Federal Government, resort to what was indisputably an income tax. On the other hand, to read as the Georgia Supreme Court read the exemption provision of the Charter of 1833, as dealing with a tax on property, fairly reflects a practice, not unknown in the earlier days of assessing property for tax purposes not by its exchange value but by its earning power."

Stone v. Mississippi

101 US 814, 25 L Ed 1079 (1880)

In 1867, the legislature of Mississippi granted a charter to a lottery company for twenty-five years in consideration of a stipulated sum in cash, an annual payment of a further sum, and a percentage of receipts from the sale of tickets. A provision of the Constitution of Mississippi adopted in 1868 declares that "the legislature shall never authorize any lottery, nor shall the sale of lottery-tickets be allowed, nor shall any lottery heretofore authorized be permitted to be drawn, or tickets therein to be sold." The attorney general of Mississippi filed an information against John B. Stone and others, alleging that they were illegally operating a lottery. *Held,* a legislature cannot bargain away the police power.

Mr. Chief Justice Waite delivered the opinion of the court. . . .

It is now too late to contend that any contract which a State actually enters into when granting a charter to a private corporation is not within the protection of the clause in the Constitution of the United States that prohibits States from passing laws impairing the obligation of contracts. Art 1, sect 10. The doctrines of *Trustees of Dartmouth College* v. *Woodward* (4 Wheaton 518), announced by this court more than sixty years ago, have become so imbedded in the jurisprudence of the United States as to make them to all intents and purposes a part of the Constitution itself. In this connection, however, it is to be kept in mind that it is not the charter which is protected, but only any contract the charter may contain. If there is no contract, there is nothing in the grant on which the Constitution can act. Consequently, the first inquiry in this class of cases always is, whether a contract has in fact been entered into, and if so, what its obligations are.

In the present case the question is whether the State of Mississippi, in its sovereign capacity, did by the charter now under consideration bind itself irrevocably by a contract to permit "the Mississippi Agricultural, Educational, and Manufacturing Aid Society," for twenty-five years, "to receive subscriptions, and sell and dispose of certifications of subscription which shall entitle the holders thereof to . . . any property or thing that may be . . . awarded to them . . . by the casting of lots, or by lot, chance, or otherwise." There can be no dispute but that under this form of words the legislature of the State chartered a lottery company . . . for twenty-five years, and that in consideration thereof the company paid into the State treasury $5,000 for the use of a university, and agreed to pay . . . an annual tax of $1,000 and "one-half of one per cent on the amount of receipts derived from the sale of certificates or tickets." If the legislature that granted this charter had the power to bind the people of the State and all succeeding legislatures to allow the corporation to continue its corporate business during the whole term of its authorized existence, there is no doubt about the sufficiency of the language employed to effect that object. . . . Whether the alleged contract exists, therefore, or not, depends on the authority of the legislature to bind the State and the people of the State in that way.

All agree that the legislature cannot bargain away the police power of a State. "Irrevocable grants of property and franchises may be made if they do not impair the supreme authority to make laws for the right government of the State; but no legislature can curtail the power of its successors to make such laws as they may deem proper in matters of police." *Metropolitan Board of Excise* v. *Barrie,* 34 NY 657; . . . Many attempts have been made in this court and elsewhere to define the police power, but never with entire success. It is always easier to determine whether a particular case comes within the general scope of the power, than to give an abstract definition of the power itself which will be in all respects accurate. No one denies, however, that it extends to all matters affecting the public health or the public morals. . . . Neither can it be denied that lotteries are proper subjects for the exercise of this power. . . .

If lotteries are to be tolerated at all, it is no doubt better that they should be regulated by law, so that the people may be protected as far as possible against the inherent vices of the system; but that they are demoralizing in their effects, no matter how carefully regulated, cannot admit of a doubt. . . .

The question is therefore directly presented, whether, in view of these facts, the legislature of a State can, by the charter of a lottery company, defeat the will of the people, authoritatively expressed, in relation to the further continuance of such business in their midst. We think it cannot. No legislature can bargain away the public health or the public morals. The people themselves cannot do it, much less their servants. The supervision of both these subjects of governmental power is continuing in its nature, and they are to be dealt with as the special exigencies of the moment may require. Government is organized with a view to their preservation, and cannot divest itself of the power to provide for them. For this purpose the largest legislative discretion is allowed, and the discretion cannot be parted with any more than the power itself.

Judgment affirmed.

Note

Looker v. *Maynard,* 179 US 46, 45 L Ed 79, 21 S Ct 21 (1900), upheld the power of a state to reserve in its constitution a power in its legislature to alter, amend, or repeal future acts of incorporation.

Home Building and Loan Ass'n v. Blaisdell

290 US 398, 54 S Ct 231, 78 L Ed 413 (1934)

The contract clause is not to be applied with literal exactness but is one of the broad clauses of the Constitution which requires construction to fill out details.

MR. CHIEF JUSTICE HUGHES delivered the opinion of the Court.

Appellant [Bldg. & Loan Ass'n.] contests the validity of Chapter 339 of the Laws of Minnesota of 1933, p. 514, approved April 18, 1933, called the Minnesota Mortgage Moratorium Law, as being repugnant to the contract clause (Art 1, § 10) and the due process and equal protection clauses of the Fourteenth Amendment of the Federal Constitution. The statute was sustained by the Supreme Court of Minnesota, and the case comes here on appeal.

The Act provides that during the emergency declared to exist, relief may be had through authorized judicial proceedings with respect to foreclosures of mortgages, and execution sales, of real estate; that sales may be postponed and periods of redemption may be extended. ... The Act is to remain in effect "only during the continuance of the emergency and in no event beyond May 1, 1935." No extension of the period for redemption and no postponement of sale is to be allowed which would have the effect of extending the period of redemption beyond that date. ...

Invoking the relevant provision of the statute, appellees applied to the District Court of Hennepin County for an order extending the period of redemption from a foreclosure sale. Their petition stated that they owned a lot in Minneapolis which they had mortgaged to appellant; that the mortgage contained a valid power of sale by advertisement, and that by reason of their default the mortgage had been foreclosed and sold to appellant on May 2, 1932, for $3700.98; that appellant was the holder of the sheriff's certificate of sale; that, because of the economic depression, appellees had been unable to obtain a new loan or to redeem, and that, unless the period of redemption were extended, the property would be irretrievably lost; and that the reasonable value of the property greatly exceeded the amount due on the mortgage, including all liens, costs, and expenses.

On the hearing, appellant objected to the introduction of evidence upon the ground that the statute was invalid under the federal and state constitutions, and moved that the petition be dismissed. ...

The court entered its judgment extending the period of redemption to May 1, 1935, subject to the condition that the appellees should pay to the appellant $40 a month through the extended period from May 2, 1933, that is, that in each of the months of August, September, and October, 1933, the payments should be $80, in two installments, and thereafter $40 a month, all these amounts to go to the payment of taxes, insurance, interest, and mortgage indebtedness. It is this judgment, sustained by the Supreme Court of the State on the authority of its former opinion, which is here under review. ...

In determining whether the provisions for this temporary and conditional relief exceeds the power of the State by reason of the clause in the Federal Constitution prohibiting impairment of the obligations of contracts, we must consider the relation of emergency to constitutional power, the historical setting of the contract clause, the development of the jurisprudence of this Court in the construction of that clause, and the principles of construction which we may consider to be established.

Emergency does not create power. Emergency does not increase granted power or remove or diminish the restrictions imposed upon power granted or reserved. The Constitution was adopted in a period of grave emergency. Its grants of power to the Federal Government and its limitations of the power of the States were determined in the light of emergency, and they are not altered by emergency. What power was thus granted and what limitations were thus imposed are questions which have always been, and always will be, the subject of close examination under our constitutional system. . . .

The obligation of a contract is "the law which binds the parties to perform their agreement." . . . Chief Justice Marshall pointed out the distinction between obligation and remedy. *Sturges* v. *Crowninshield* [4 Wheaton 122], *supra*, p. 200. Said he: "The distinction between the obligation of a contract, and the remedy given by the legislature to enforce that obligation, has been taken at the bar, and exists in the nature of things. Without impairing the obligation of the contract, the remedy may certainly be modified as the wisdom of the nation shall direct." . . .

Not only is the constitutional provision qualified by the measure of control which the State retains over remedial processes, but the State also continues to possess authority to safeguard the vital interests of its people. It does not matter that legislation appropriate to that end "has the result of modifying or abrogating contracts already in effect." *Stephenson* v. *Binford,* 287 US 251, 276. Not only are existing laws read into contracts in order to fix obligations as between the parties, but the reservation of essential attributes of sovereign power is also read into contracts as a postulate of the legal order. The policy of protecting contracts against impairment presupposes the maintenance of a government by virtue of which contractual relations are worthwhile, —a government which retains adequate authority to secure the peace and good order of society. . . .

It is no answer to say that this public need was not apprehended a century ago, or to insist that what the provision of the Constitution meant to the vision of that day it must mean to the vision of our time. If by the statement that what the Constitution meant at the time of its adoption it means today, it is intended to say that the great clauses of the Constitution must be confined to the interpretation which the framers, with the conditions and outlook of their time, would have placed upon them, the statement carries its own refutation. It was to guard against such a narrow conception that Chief Justice Marshall uttered the memorable warning—"We must never forget, that it is *a constitution* we are expounding" (*McCulloch* v. *Maryland,* 4 Wheaton 316, 407)—"a constitution intended to endure for ages to come, and, consequently, to be adapted to the various crises of human affairs." Id., p. 415.

In the absence of legislation, courts of equity have exercised jurisdiction in suits for the foreclosure of mortgages to fix the time and terms of sale and to refuse to confirm sales upon equitable grounds where they were found to be unfair or inadequacy of price was so gross as to shock the conscience. The "equity of redemption" is the creature of equity. . . . Although the courts would have no authority to alter a statutory period of redemption, the legislation in question permits the courts to extend that period, within limits and upon equitable terms, thus providing a procedure and relief which are cognate to the historic exercise of the equitable jurisdiction. If it be determined, as it must be, that the contract clause is not an absolute and utterly unqualified restriction of the State's protective power, this legislation is clearly so reasonable as to be within the legislative competency. . . .

Judgment affirmed.

MR. JUSTICE SUTHERLAND, dissenting.

. . . A candid consideration of the history and circumstances which led up to and accompanied the framing and adoption of this clause will demonstrate conclusively that it was framed and adopted with the specific and studied purpose of preventing legislation designed to relieve debtors *especially* in time of financial distress. Indeed, it is not probable that any other purpose was definitely in the minds of those who composed the framers' convention or the ratifying state conventions which followed, although the restriction has been given a wider application upon principles clearly stated by Chief Justice Marshall in the *Dartmouth College* case, 4 Wheaton 518, 644–645. . . .

The defense of the Minnesota law is made upon grounds which were discountenanced by the makers of the Constitution and have many times been rejected by this court. That defense should not now succeed because it constitutes an effort to overthrow the constitutional provision by an appeal to facts and circumstances identical with those which brought it into existence . . .

The Minnesota statute either impairs the obligation of contracts or it does not. If it does not, the occasion to which it relates becomes immaterial, since then the passage of the statute is the exercise of a normal, unrestricted, state power and requires no special occasion to render it effective. If it does, the emergency no more furnishes a proper occasion for its exercise than if the emergency were nonexistent. . . .

A statute which materially delays enforcement of the mortgagee's contractual right of ownership and possession does not modify the remedy merely; it destroys, for the period of delay, *all* remedy so far as the enforcement of that right is concerned. The phrase "obligation of a contract" in the constitutional sense imports a legal duty to perform the specified obligation of *that* contract, not to substitute and perform, against the will of one of the parties, a different, albeit equally valuable, obligation. And a state, under the contract impairment clause, has no more power to accomplish such a substitution than has one of the parties to the contract against the will of the other. It cannot do so either by acting directly upon the contract or by bringing about the result under the guise of a statute in form acting only upon the remedy. . . .

I am authorized to say that MR. JUSTICE VAN DEVANTER, MR. JUSTICE McREYNOLDS, and MR. JUSTICE BUTLER concur in this opinion.

F. TRIAL BY JURY

Both the original Constitution and the Fifth Amendment provide for trial by jury. The subject is treated in chapter 12 of this text.

G. TREASON

The Constitution defines treason as follows: "Treason against the United States shall consist only in levying war against them, or in adhering to their enemies, giving them aid and comfort. No person shall be convicted of treason unless on testimony of two witnesses to the same overt act, or on confession in open court." James Madison commented on this clause in *The Federalist,* No. 43, as follows:

> As treason may be committed against the United States, the authority of the United States ought to be enabled to punish it. But as new-fangled and artificial treasons have been the great engines by which violent factions, the natural offspring of free governments, have usually wreaked their alternate malignity on each other, the convention have, with great judgment, opposed a barrier to this peculiar danger, by inserting a constitutional definition of the crime, fixing the proof necessary for conviction of it, and restraining the Congress, even in punishing it, from extending the consequence of guilt beyond the person of its author.

For the English background, see pages 253–54.

In the trial of Aaron Burr for his alleged conspiracy to establish an empire in the southwest, it was shown that he had laid plans of a treasonable nature; yet, he was acquitted because it was not proved that he had levied war against the United States or adhered to its enemies. A. J. Beveridge, *The Life of John Marshall,* vol. III (Boston, 1919), pp. 618–26. A plot to overthrow the government that has not progressed to an actual assembling of a body of men for the purpose is not treason. *Ex parte Bollman,* 4 Cranch 75 (1807). On the other hand, numerous acts constitute the offense of adhering to the enemies of the United States, giving them aid and comfort, such as, for example, communicating intelligence of military value to the enemy or furnishing him with materials. See Charles Warren, "What is Giving Aid and Comfort to the Enemy?" *Yale Law Journal* XXVII (January 1918): 331–49, and Willard Hurst, "Treason in the United States," *Harvard Law Review* XLVIII (1945–46): 226–72, 395–444, 806–57.

Attainder of Treason

The constitutional provision that "no attainder of treason shall work corruption of blood or forfeiture except during the life of the person attained" was meant, as explained by Madison in *The Federalist,* No. 42, to prevent the punishment for attainder—i.e., conviction—"from extending the consequences of guilt beyond the person of its author." Under early English practice, when a man was convicted of treason, both his own property and that of his descendants were forfeited to the Crown.

Lesser Offenses

It should be noted that the restricted definition of treason in the Constitution does not prevent Congress, in the exercise of its delegated powers, such as the war power, from providing punishment for a variety of disloyal acts essentially treasonable in character but not included in the constitutional definition of treason. The Espionage Act of 1917 is an example of such legislation.

World War II Cases

From the *Bollman* case of 1807 to 1945, no treason cases reached the Supreme Court. As an outgrowth of World War II, three such cases came before the Court, and in two of them convictions were sustained.

In *Cramer* v. *United States,* 325 US 1 (1945), the conviction of a person charged with harboring a saboteur sent to America on a German submarine was reversed in a five-to-four decision. Justice Jackson for the majority followed the view that the "overt act" had to be "openly manifest treason," and that under the two-witness principle, there could be no "imputation of incriminating acts to the accused by circumstantial evidence or by the testimony of a single witness."

In *Haupt* v. *United States,* 330 US 631 (1947), for the first time the Supreme Court sustained a conviction of treason. Haupt had aided his son, whom he knew to be an enemy agent who had entered this country for purposes of sabotage, to buy a car and secure employment in a plant manufacturing military equipment. The Court recognized that "the overt act and the intent with which it is done are separate and distinct elements of the crime. Intent need not be proved by two witnesses but may be inferred from all the circumstances surrounding the overt act."

Kawakita v. *United States,* 343 US 717 (1952), affirmed another conviction of treason. Kawakita, born in the United States, was in Japan during World War II and was employed as an interpreter for a mining company where American prisoners of war were worked. He kicked, beat, and otherwise brutally treated the prisoners. Upon returning to America in 1946, he was recognized by a former American prisoner of war, indicted, and tried for treason. In sustaining his conviction, Justice Douglas wrote:

> The jury found that each of the six overt acts of cruelty actually gave aid and comfort to the enemy. We agree. These were not acts innocent and commonplace in appearance and gaining treasonable significance only by reference to other evidence, as in *Cramer* v. *United States.* . . . These acts in their setting would help make all the prisoners fearful, docile, and subservient. . . . These acts would tend to give the enemy the "heart and courage to go on with the war." That was the test laid down by Lord Chief Justice Treby in *Trial of Captain Vaughan,* 13 Howard St Tr 485, 533. It is a sufficient measure of the overt act required by the Constitution.

H. RELIGIOUS TESTS

The last paragraph in Article VI reads: "The senators and representatives before mentioned, and the members of the several state legislatures, and all executive and judicial officers both of the United States and of the several states, shall be bound by oath or affirmation, to support this Constitution; but no religious test shall ever be required as a qualification to any office or public trust under the United States."

The clause prohibiting a religious test as a qualification for federal office has never been the subject of litigation. See, however, the decision in *Ex parte Garland* (p. 185). In *Torcaso* v. *Watkins,* 367 US 488 (1961), the Court held void a Maryland law requiring a declaration of belief in the existence of God as a qualification to hold office in that state.

Chapter 7

The Bill of Rights and the Fourteenth Amendment

A. INTRODUCTION

Freedom of religion, freedom of speech, and other provisions of the Bill of Rights are considered in detail in other chapters. Emphasis here is on the scope of application of the Bill of Rights and of the Fourteenth Amendment and on the relation between the two.

The few restrictions on the states in the Constitution prior to 1868 were examined in chapter 3. Section 1 of the Fourteenth Amendment, ratified in 1868, read as follows:

> All persons born or naturalized in the United States, and subject to the juridisction thereof, are citizens of the United States and of the State wherein they reside. No State shall make or enforce any law which shall abridge the privileges or immunities of citizens of the United States; nor shall any State deprive any person of life, liberty, or property, without due process of law; nor deny to any person within its juridiction the equal protection of the laws.

As any student of constitutional law knows, the decision of a case involving the application of a broad constitutional term like "due process of law" or "equal protection of the laws" depends more upon the philosophy espoused by the members of the Court at the time the case is heard than upon the words of the Constitution. Cases arising under the Fourteenth Amendment constitute no real exception to this general rule, but the wording of the amendment has been of sufficient importance to warrant committing it to memory.

Equal protection was the dominant note in American constitutional law during the 1950s and 1960s, but, during the century since the adoption of the Fourteenth

Amendment, considered as a whole, due process has been the dominant note. Separate chapters on each of these clauses appearing later in this text must be consulted for a detailed analysis of their scope of application. The next section of this chapter is designed to show that, while the Bill of Rights of 1791 does not per se apply as a limitation on the state governments, its provisions had long influenced the interpretation given to the Fourteenth Amendment, and by 1974 the Supreme Court had "incorporated" almost all of the guarantees of personal liberty in the Bill of Rights into its interpretation of the amendment's due-process clause. (For a list of the incorporated provisions, see p. 207.) However, to say that a certain provision is applicable to a case through incorporation is, as explained *Dutton* v. *Evans,* 400 US 74 (1970), "no more than the beginning of our inquiry." The Burger Court is inclined to give a generalized rather than a technical application to the specific provision of the Bill of Rights—e.g., trial by "jury" means trial by a group but not necessarily by a group of twelve.

The second sentence of the Fourteenth Amendment begins with the words, "No State Shall. . . ." In early cases involving application of this sentence, the Court held that it placed limitations on state action but not on private action. The section of this chapter entitled "The State Action Concept" grapples with the question, What is state action within the meaning of the Fourteenth Amendment?

In the present state of the law, no definitive answer can be given. But while the exact status of the law is not clear, recent cases make it apparent that only slight state involvement is needed to make the Fourteenth Amendment applicable. Moreover, the Court now recognizes congressional power under the Thirteenth Amendment to eradicate "badges of slavery" through legislation affecting private conduct unassociated with "state action."

While only a naive person would expect to find an exact analogy of what constitutes governmental action on the part of the state and national governments, the opinions in the 1973 case of *Columbia Broadcasting System* v. *Democratic National Committee* (p. 287) causes one to be skeptical of the contitutional basis of much that has been written about state action and to conclude that the justices tend to classify action as private or governmental according to the desired results.

B. SCOPE OF APPLICATION

Barron v. Baltimore

7 Peters 243, 9 L Ed 672 (1833)

The provision in the Fifth Amendment of the Constitution declaring that private property shall not be taken for public use without just compensation, is only a limitation of the power of the United States; it is not applicable to the legislation of the several states.

[In paving its streets, the city of Baltimore diverted certain streams from their natural course. This resulted in sand deposits that made the water shallow and prevented use of Barron's wharf. He sought to collect damages.]

MARSHALL, CH. J., delivered the opinion of the court. . . .

The judgment brought up by this writ of error having been rendered by the court of a state, this tribunal can exercise no jurisdiction over it, unless it be shown to come within the provisions of the 25th section of the judiciary act. The plaintiff in error contends, that it comes within that clause in the fifth amendment to the Constitution, which inhibits the taking of private property for public use, without just compensation. He insists, that this amendment being in favor of the liberty of the citizen, ought to be so construed as to restrain the legislative power of a state, as well as that of the United States. If this proposition be untrue, the court can take no jurisdiction of the cause.

The question thus presented is, we think of great importance, but not of much difficulty. The Constitution was ordained and established by the people of the United States for themselves, for their own government, and not for the government of the individual states. Each state established a constitution for itself, and in that constitution, provided such limitations and restrictions on the powers of its particular government, as its judgment dictated. The people of the United States framed such a government for the United States as they supposed best adapted to their situation and best calculated to promote their interests. The powers they conferred on this government were to be exercised by itself; and the limitations on power, if expressed in general terms, are naturally, and, we think, necessarily, applicable to the government created by the instrument. They are limitations of power granted in the instrument itself; not of distinct governments, framed by different persons and for different purposes.

If these propositions be correct, the fifth amendment must be understood as restraining the power of the general government, not as applicable to the states. In their several constitutions, they have imposed such restriction on their respective government, as their own wisdom suggested; such as they deemed most proper for themselves. It is a subject on which they judge exclusively, and with which others interfere no further than they are supposed to have a common interest. . . .

We are of opinion, that the provision in the fifth amendment to the Constitution, declaring that private property shall not be taken for public use, without just compensation, is intended solely as a limitation on the exercise of power by the government of the United States, and is not applicable to the legislation of the states. We are, therefore, of opinion, that there is no repugnancy between the several acts of the general assembly of Maryland, given in evidence by the defendants at the trial of this cause, in the court of that state, and the Constitution of the United States. This court, therefore, has no jurisdiction of the cause, and it is dismissed.

Adamson v. California

332 US 46, 67 S Ct 1672, 91 L Ed 1903 (1947)

The guaranty of the Fifth Amendment against self-incrimination is not made applicable by the Fourteenth Amendment to trials in state courts.

MR. JUSTICE REED delivered the opinion of the Court.

The appellant, Adamson, a citizen of the United States, was convicted, without recommendation for mercy, by a jury in a Superior Court of the State of California of murder in the first degree. After considering the same objections to the conviction that are pressed here, the sentence of death was affirmed by the Supreme Court of the State. . . . The provisions of California law which were challenged in the state proceedings as invalid under the Fourteenth Amendment . . . permit the failure of a defendant to explain or to deny evidence against him to be commented upon by court and by counsel and to be considered by court and jury. The defendant did not testify. As the trial court gave its instructions and the District Attorney argued the case in accordance with the constitutional and statutory provisions just referred to, we have for decision the question of their constitutionality. . . .

The appellant was charged in the information with former convictions for burglary, larceny and robbery and pursuant to § 1025, California Penal Code, answered that he had suffered the previous convictions. This answer barred allusion to these charges of convictions on the trial. Under California's . . . procedure, however, if the defendant, after answering affirmatively charges alleging prior convictions, takes the witness stand to deny or explain away other evidence that has been introduced "the commission of these crimes could have been revealed to the jury on cross-examination to impeach his testimony." . . . This forces an accused who is a repeated offender to choose between the risk of having his prior offenses disclosed to the jury or of having it draw harmful inferences from uncontradicted evidence that can only be denied or explained by the defendant.

In the first place, appellant urges that the provision of the Fifth Amendment that no person "shall be compelled in any criminal case to be a witness against himself" is a fundamental national privilege or immunity protected against state abridgment by the Fourteenth Amendment or a privilege or immunity secured, through the Fourteenth Amendment, against deprivation by state action because it is a personal right, enumerated in the federal Bill of Rights.

Secondly, appellant relies upon the due process of law clause of the Fourteenth Amendment to invalidate the provisions of the California law . . . as applied (a) because comment on failure to testify is permitted, (b) because appellant was forced to forego testimony in person because of danger of disclosure of his past convictions through cross-examination, and (c) because the presumption of innocence was infringed by the shifting of the burden of proof to appellant in permitting comment on his failure to testify.

We shall assume, but without any intention thereby of ruling upon the issue, that permission by law to the court, counsel and jury to comment upon and consider the failure of defendant "to explain or to deny by his testimony any evidence or facts in the case against him" would infringe defendant's privilege against self-incrimination under the Fifth Amendment if this were a trial in a court of the United States under a similar law. Such an assumption does not determine appellant's rights under the Fourteenth Amendment. . . .

. . . The due process clause of the Fourteenth Amendment . . . does not draw all the rights of the federal Bill of Rights under its protection. That contention was made and rejected in *Palko* v. *Connecticut* (1937) . . . *Palko* held that such provisions of the Bill of Rights as were "implicit in the concept of ordered liberty," . . . became secure from state interference by the clause. But it held nothing more.

Specifically, the due process clause does not protect, by virtue of its mere existence, the accused's freedom from giving testimony by compulsion in state trials that is secured to him against federal interference by the Fifth Amendment. . . . For a state to require testimony from an accused is not necessarily a breach of a state's obligation to give a fair trial. . . .

Generally, comment on the failure of an accused to testify is forbidden in American jurisdictions. This arises from state constitutional or statutory provisions. similar in character to the federal provisions. . . . California, however, is one of a few states that permit limited comment upon a defendant's failure to testify. . . . California has prescribed a method for advising the jury in the search for truth. However sound may be the legislative conclusion that an accused should not be compelled in any criminal case to be a witness against himself, we see no reason why comment should not be made upon his silence. It seems quite natural that when a defendant has opportunity to deny or explain facts and determines not to do so, the prosecution should bring out the strength of the evidence by commenting upon defendant's failure to explain or deny it. The prosecution evidence may be of facts that may be beyond the knowledge of the accused. If so, his failure to testify would have little if any weight. But the facts may be such as are necessarily in the knowledge of the accused. In that case a failure to explain would point to an inability to explain. . . .

Affirmed.

MR. JUSTICE FRANKFURTER, concurring. . . .

For historical reasons a limited immunity from the common duty to testify was written into the Federal Bill of Rights, and I am prepared to agree that, as part of that immunity, comment on the failure of an accused to take the witness stand is forbidden in federal prosecutions. It is so, of course, by explicit act of Congress. . . . But to suggest that such a limitation can be drawn out of "due process" in its protection of ultimate decency in a civilized society is to suggest that the Due Process Clause fastened fetters of unreason upon the States. . . .

The short answer to the suggestion that the provision of the Fourteenth Amendment, which ordains "nor shall any State deprive any person of life, liberty, or property, without due process of law," was a way of saying that every State must thereafter initiate prosecutions through indictment by a grand jury, must have a trial by a jury of twelve in criminal cases, and must have trial by such a jury in common law suits where the amount in controversy exceeds twenty dollars, is that it is a strange way of saying it. . . .

A construction which gives to due process no independent function but turns it into a summary of the specific provisions of the Bill of Rights would . . . tear up by the roots much of the fabric of law in the several States, and would deprive the States of opportunity for reforms in legal process designed for extending the area of freedom. It would assume that no other abuses would reveal themselves in the course of time than those which had become manifest in 1791. Such a view not only disregards the historic meaning of "due process." It leads inevitably to a warped construction of specific provisions of the Bill of Rights to bring within their scope conduct clearly condemned by due process but not easily fitting into the pigeon-holes of the specific provisions. It seems pretty late in the day to suggest that a phrase so laden with historic meaning should be given an improvised content consisting of some but not all of the provisions of the first eight Amendments, selected on an undefined basis, with improvisation of content for the provisions so selected.

And so, when as in a case like the present, a conviction in a State court is here for review under a claim that a right protected by the Due Process Clause of the Fourteenth Amendment has been denied, the issue is not whether an infraction of one of the specific provisions of the first eight Amendments is disclosed by the record. The relevant question is whether the criminal proceedings which resulted in conviction deprived the accused of the due process of law to which the United States Constitution entitled him. Judicial review of that guaranty of the Fourteenth Amendment inescapably imposes upon this Court an exercise of judgment upon the whole course of the proceedings in order to ascertain whether they offend those canons of decency and fairness which express the notions of justice of English-speaking peoples even toward those charged with the most heinous offenses. These standards of justice are not authoritatively formulated anywhere as though they were prescriptions in a pharmacopoeia. But neither does the application of the Due Process Clause imply that judges are wholly at large. The judicial judgment in applying the Due Process Clause must move within the limits of accepted notions of justice and is not to be based upon the idiosyncrasies of a merely personal judgment. The fact that judges among themselves may differ whether in a particular case a trial offends accepted notions of justice is not disproof that general rather than idiosyncratic standards are applied. An important safeguard against such merely individual judgment is an alert deference to the judgment of the State court under review.

MR. JUSTICE BLACK, dissenting. . . .

This decision reasserts a constitutional theory spelled out in *Twining* v. *New Jersey,* 211 US 78, that this Court is endowed by the Constitution with boundless power under "natural law" periodically to expand and contract constitutional standards to conform to the Court's conception of what at a particular time constitutes "civilized decency" and "fundamental liberty and justice." . . .

My study of the historical events that culminated in the Fourteenth Amendment, and the expressions of those who sponsored and favored, as well as those who opposed its submission and passage, persuades me that one of the chief objects that the provisions of the Amendment's first section, separately, and as a whole, were intended to accomplish was to make the Bill of Rights, applicable to the states. . . .

. . . I fear to see the consequences of the Court's practice of substituting its own concepts of decency and fundamental justice for the language of the Bill of Rights as its point of departure in interpreting and enforcing that Bill of Rights. If the choice must be between the selective process of the *Palko* decision applying some of the Bill of Rights to the States, or the *Twining* rule applying none of them, I would choose the *Palko* selective process. But rather than accept either of these choices, I would follow what I believe was the original purpose of the Fourteenth Amendment—to extend to all the people of the nation the complete protection of the Bill of Rights. To hold that this Court can determine what, if any, provisions of the Bill of Rights will be enforced, and if so to what degree, is to frustrate the great design of a written Constitution. . . .

Since *Marbury* v. *Madison* . . . was decided, the practice has been firmly established, for better or worse, that courts can strike down legislative enactments which violate the Constitution. This process, of course, involves interpretation, and since words can have many meanings, interpretation obviously may result in contraction or extension of the original purpose of a constitutional provision, thereby affecting policy. But to pass upon the constitutionality of statutes by looking to the particular standards enumerated in the Bill of Rights and other parts of the Constitution is one thing; to invalidate statutes because of application of "natural law" deemed to be above and undefined by the Constitution is another. "In the one instance, courts proceeding within clearly marked constitutional boundaries seek to excute policies written into the Constitution; in the other, they roam at will in the limitless area of their own beliefs as to reasonableness and actually select policies, a responsibility which the Constitution entrusts to the legislative representatives of the people." . . .

MR. JUSTICE DOUGLAS joins in this opinion.

MR. JUSTICE MURPHY, with whom MR. JUSTICE RUTLEDGE concurs, dissenting.

While in substantial agreement with the views of MR. JUSTICE BLACK, I have one reservation and one addition to make.

I agree that the specific guarantees of the Bill of Rights should be carried over intact into the first section of the Fourteenth Amendment. But I am not prepared to say that the latter is entirely and necessarily limited by the Bill of Rights. Occasions may arise where a proceeding falls so far short of conforming to fundamental standards of procedure as to warrant constitutional condemnation in terms of a lack of due process despite the absence of a specific provision in the Bill of Rights.

Note

Provisions incorporated. In *Duncan* v. *Louisiana,* 391 US 145 (1968), the Court gave the following summary statement, quoted here with the Court's footnotes placed in parentheses:

> The Fourteenth Amendment denies the States the power to "deprive any person of life, liberty, or property, without due process of law." In resolving conflicting claims concerning the meaning of this spacious language, the Court has looked increasingly to the Bill of Rights for guidance; many of the rights guaranteed by the first eight Amendments to the Constitution have been held to be protected against state action by the Due Process Clause of the Fourteenth Amendment. That clause now protects the right to compensation for property taken by the State (*Chicago, B. & Q. R. Co.* v. *Chicago,* 166 US 226 (1897)); the rights of speech, press, and religion covered by the First Amendment (see, *e.g., Fiske* v. *Kansas,* 274 US 380 (1927)); the Fourth Amendment rights to be free from unreasonable searches and seizures and to have excluded from criminal trials any evidence illegally seized; (See *Mapp* v. *Ohio,* 367 US 643 (1961); the right guaranteed by the Fifth Amendment to be free of compelled self-incrimination (*Malloy* v. *Hogan,* 378 US 643 (1961)); and the Sixth Amendment rights to counsel (*Gideon* v. *Wainwright,* 372 US 335 (1963)), to a speedy (*Klopfer* v. *North Carolina,* 386 US 213 (1967)) and public (*In re Oliver,* 333 US 257 (1948)) trial, to confrontation of opposing witnesses (*Pointer* v. *Texas,* 380 US 400 (1965)), and to compulsory process for obtaining witnesses (*Washington* v. *Texas,* 388 US 14 (1967)).

To this list the *Duncan* case added the "right of jury trial in all criminal cases which—were they to be tried in a federal court—would come within the Sixth Amendment's guarantee," and *Benton* v. *Maryland,* 395 US 784 (1969), added the double-jeopardy prohibition of the Fifth Amendment. The Eighth Amendment's prohibition against "cruel and unusual punishment" is also included. See *Robinson* v. *California,* 370 US 660 (1962), and *Furman* v. *Georgia,* 408 US 238 (1972).

C. THE "STATE ACTION" CONCEPT

Civil Rights Cases

109 US 3, 3 S Ct 18, 27 L Ed 835 (1883)

The Fourteenth Amendment is prohibitory upon the states only, and the legislation authorized to be adopted by Congress for enforcing it is not *direct* legislation on the matters respecting which the states are prohibited from making or enforcing certain laws, or doing certain acts, but is *corrective* legislation, such as may be necessary or proper for counteracting and redressing the effect of such laws or acts.

These cases were all founded on the first and second sections of the Act of Congress, known as the Civil Rights Act, passed March 1st, 1875, entitled "An Act to protect all citizens in their civil and legal rights." 18 Stat 335. Two of the cases, those against Stanley and Nichols, were indictments for denying to persons of color the accommodations and privileges of an inn or hotel; two of them, those against Ryan and Singleton, were . . . for denying to individuals the privileges and accommodations of a theatre, the information against Ryan being for refusing a colored person a seat in the dress circle of Maguire's theatre in San Francisco; and the indictment against Singleton was for denying to another person, whose color was not stated, the full enjoyment of the accommodations of the theatre known as the Grand Opera House in New York. . . . The case of Robinson and wife against the Memphis & Charleston R.R. Company was an action brought in the Circuit Court of the United States for the Western District of Tennessee, to recover the penalty of five hundred dollars given by the second section of the act; and the gravamen was the refusal by the conductor of the railroad company to allow the wife to ride in the ladies' car, for the reason, as stated in one of the counts, that she was a person of African descent. . . .

MR. JUSTICE BRADLEY delivered the opinion of the Court. After stating the facts in the above language he continued:

It is obvious that the primary and important question in all the cases is the constitutionality of the law: for if the law is unconstitutional none of the prosecutions can stand.

The sections of the law referred to provide as follows:

"Sec. 1. That all persons within the jurisdiction of the United States shall be entitled to the full and equal enjoyment of the accommocations, advantages, facilities, and privileges of inns, public conveyances on land or water, theatres, and other places of public amusement; subject only to the conditions and limitations established by law, and applicable alike to citizens of every race and color, regardless of any previous condition of servitude.

"Sec. 2. That any person who shall violate the foregoing section by denying to any citizen, except for reasons by law applicable to citizens of every race and color, and regardless of any previous condition of servitude, the full enjoyment of any of the accommodations, advantages, facilities, or privileges in said section enumerated, or by aiding or inciting such denial, shall for every such offence forfeit and pay the sum of five hundred dollars to the person aggrieved thereby, to be recovered in an action of debt, with full costs; and shall also for every such offence, be deemed guilty of a misdemeanor, and, upon conviction thereof, shall be fined not less than five hundred nor more than one thousand dollars, or shall be imprisoned not less than thirty days nor more than one year. . . ."

Has Congress constitutional power to make such a law? Of course, no one will contend that the power to pass it was contained in the Constitution before the adoption of the last three amendments. The power is sought, first, in the Fourteenth Amendment. . . .

The first section of the Fourteenth Amendment (which is the one relied on), after declaring who shall be citizens of the United States, and of the several States, is prohibitory in its character, and prohibitory upon the States. It declares that:

> "No State shall make or enforce any law which shall abridge the privileges or immunities of citizens of the United States; nor shall any State deprive any person of life, liberty, or property without due process of law; nor deny to any person within its jurisdiction the equal protection of the laws."

It is State action of a particular character that is prohibited. Individual invasion of individual rights is not the subject-matter of the amendment. It has a deeper and broader scope. It nullifies and makes void all State legislation, and State action of every kind, which impairs the privileges and immunities of citizens of the United States, or which injures them in life, liberty or property without due process of law, or which denies to any of them the equal protection of the laws. It not only does this, but, in order that the national will, thus declared, may not be a mere *brutum fulmen,* the last section of the amendment invests Congress with power to enforce it by appropriate legislation. To enforce what? To enforce the prohibition. To adopt appropriate legislation for correcting the effects of such prohibited State laws and State acts, and thus to render them effectually null, void, and innocuous. This is the legislative power conferred upon Congress and this is the whole of it. It does not invest Congress with power to legislate upon subjects which are within the domain of State legislation; but to provide modes of relief against State legislation, or State action, of the kind referred to.

An apt illustration of this distinction may be found in some of the provisions of the original Constitution. Take the subject of contracts, for example. The Constitution prohibited the States from passing any law impairing the obligation of contracts. This did not give to Congress power to provide laws for the general enforcement of contracts; nor power to invest the courts of the United States with jurisdiction over contracts, so as to enable parties to sue upon them in those courts. It did, however, give the power to provide remedies by which the impairment of contracts by State legislation might be counteracted and corrected: and this power was exercised. The remedy which Congress actually provided was that contained in the 25th section of the Judiciary Act of 1789, 1 Stat 85, giving to the Supreme Court of the United States jurisdiction by writ of error to review the final decisions of State courts whenever they should sustain the validity of a State statute or authority alleged to be repugnant to the Constitution or laws of the United States. By this means, if a State law was passed impairing the obligation of a contract, and the State tribunals sustained the validity of the law, the mischief could be corrected in this court. The legislation of Congress, and the proceedings provided for under it, were corrective in their character. No attempt was made to draw into the United States courts the litigation of contracts generally; and no such attempt would have been sustained. . . .

And so in the present case, until some State law has been passed, or some State action through its officers or agents has been taken, adverse to the rights of citizens sought to be protected by the Fourteenth Amendment, no legislation of the United States under said amendment, nor any proceeding under such legislation, can be called into activity: for the prohibitions of the amendment are against State laws and acts done under State authority. . . .

An inspection of the law shows that it makes no reference whatever to any supposed or apprehended violation of the Fourteenth Amendment on the part of the States. It is not predicated on any such view. It proceeds *ex directo* to declare that certain acts committed by individuals shall be deemed offences, and shall be prosecuted and punished by proceedings in the courts of the United States. . . .

If this legislation is appropriate for enforcing the prohibitions of the amendment, it is difficult to see where it is to stop. Why may not Congress with equal show of authority enact a code of laws for the enforcement and vindication of all rights of life, liberty and property? If it is supposable that the States may deprive persons of life, liberty, and property without due process of law (and the amendment itself does suppose this), why should not Congress proceed at once to prescribe due process of law for the protection of every one of these fundamental rights, in every possible case, as well as to prescribe equal privileges in inns, public conveyances, and theatres? The truth is, that the implication of a power to legislate in this manner is based upon the assumption that if the States are forbidden to legislate or act in a particular way on a particular subject, and power is conferred upon Congress to enforce the prohibition, this gives Congress power to legislate generally upon that subject, and not merely power to provide modes of redress against such State legislation or action. The assumption is certainly unsound. It is repugnant to the Tenth Amendment of the Constitution. . . .

On the whole we are of opinion, that no countenance of authority for the passage of the law in question can be found in either the Thirteenth or Fourteenth Amendment of the Constitution; and no other ground of authority for its passage being suggested, it must necessarily be declared void. . . .

And it is so ordered.

Mr. Justice Harlan dissenting.

The opinion in these cases proceeds, it seems to me, upon grounds entirely too narrow and artificial. I cannot resist the conclusion that the substance and spirit of the recent Amendments of the Constitution have been sacrificed by a subtle and ingenious verbal criticism. . . .

I do not contend that the 13th Amendment invests Congress with authority, by legislation, to define and regulate the entire body of the civil rights which citizens enjoy, or may enjoy, in the several States. But I hold that since slavery, as the court has repeatedly declared, *Slaughter-House Cases,* 16 Wall 36; *Strauder* v. *West Virginia,* 100 US 303, was the moving or principal cause of adoption of that Amendment, and since that institution rested wholly upon the inferiority, as a race, of those held in bondage, their freedom necessarily involved immunity from and protection against, all discrimination against them, because of their race, in respect of such civil rights as belong to freemen of other races. Congress, therefore, under its express power to enforce that Amendment, by appropriate legislation, may enact laws to protect that people against the deprivation, *because of their race,* of any civil rights granted to other freemen in the same State; and such legislation may be of a direct and primary character, operating upon States, their officers and agents and, also, upon, at least, such individuals and corporations as exercise public functions and wield power and authority under the State. . . .

Note

Contrast the decision in *Heart of Atlanta Motel, Inc.* v. *United States,* page 103 of this text.

Shelley v. Kraemer

334 US 1, 68 S Ct 836, 92 L Ed 1161 (1948)

Private agreements to exclude persons of designated race or color from the use or occupancy of real estate for residential purposes do not violate the Fourteenth Amendment; but it is violative of the equal protection clause of the Fourteenth Amendment for state courts to enforce them.

[Owners of property on a residential street in St. Louis signed an agreement restricting the occupancy of the property to persons of the Caucasian race. J. D. Shelley, a black, bought a home in the restricted area. Louis Kraemer, owner of other property on the street, bought suit in a Missouri court to restrain Shelley from occupying the property and to divest him of title. The trial court held the restrictive covenant ineffective because all property owners in the district concerned had not signed it. The Supreme Court of Missouri reversed and directed the trial court to grant the relief prayed. The United States Supreme Court granted *certiorari.*]

Mr. Chief Justice Vinson delivered the opinion of the Court.

Since the decision of this Court in the *Civil Rights Cases,* 109 US 3 (1883), the principle has become firmly embedded in our constitutional law that the action inhibited by the first section of the Fourteenth Amendment is only such action as may fairly be said to be that of the States. That Amendment erects no shield against merely private conduct, however discriminatory or wrongful.

We conclude, therefore, that the restrictive agreements standing alone cannot be regarded as violative of any rights guaranteed to petitioners by the Fourteenth Amendment. So long as the purposes of those agreements are effectuated by voluntary adherence to their terms, it would appear clear that there has been no action by the State and the provisions of the Amendment have not been violated. . . .

But here there was more. These are cases in which the purposes of the agreements were secured only by judicial enforcement by state courts of the restrictive terms of the agreements. . . .

That the action of state courts and judicial officers in their official capacities is to be regarded as action of the State within the meaning of the Fourteenth Amendment, is a proposition which has long been established by decisions of this Court. That principle was given expression in the earliest cases involving the construction of the terms of the Fourteenth Amendment. Thus, in *Virginia* v. *Rives,* 100 US 313, 318 (1880), this Court stated: "It is doubtless true that a State may act through different agencies,—either by its legislative, its executive, or its judicial authorities; and the prohibitions of the amendment extend to all action of the State denying equal protection of the laws, whether it be action by one of these agencies or by another." In *Ex parte Virginia,* 100 US 339, 347 (1880), the Court observed: "A State acts by its legislative, its executive, or its judicial authorities. It can act in no other way." In the *Civil Rights Cases,* 109 US 3, 11, 17 (1883), this Court pointed out that the Amendment makes void "State action of every kind" which is inconsistent with the guaranties therein contained, and extends to manifestation of "State authority in the shape of laws, customs, or judicial or executive proceedings." Language to like effect is employed no less than eighteen times during the course of that opinion. . . .

We have no doubt that there has been state action in these cases in the full and complete sense of the phrase. The undisputed facts disclose that petitioners were willing purchasers of properties upon which they desired to establish homes. The owners of the properties were willing sellers; and contracts of sale were accordingly consummated. It is clear that but for the active state power, petitioners would have been free to occupy the properties in question without restraint. . . .

Reversed.

[MR. JUSTICE REED, MR. JUSTICE JACKSON, and MR. JUSTICE RUTLEDGE took no part in the consideration or decision of these cases.]

Williams v. United States

341 US 97, 71 S Ct 576, 95 L Ed 774 (1951)

A special police officer who, in his official capacity, by use of force and violence, obtains a confession from a person suspected of crime may be prosecuted under what is now 18 USC § 242, which makes it an offense for any person, under color of law, willfully to subject any inhabitant of any state, territory, or district to the deprivation of any rights, privileges, or immunities secured or protected by the Constitution and laws of the United States.

MR. JUSTICE DOUGLAS delivered the opinion of the Court.

The question in this case is whether a special police officer who in his official capacity subjects a person suspected of crime to force and violence in order to obtain a confession may be prosecuted under § 20 of the Criminal Code, 18 USC (1946 ed) § 52, now 18 USC § 242.

Section 20 provides in pertinent part:

"Whoever, under color of any law, statute, ordinance, regulation, or custom, willfully subjects, or causes to be subjected, any inhabitant of any State, Territory, or District to the deprivation of any rights, privileges, or immunities secured or protected by the Constitution and laws of the United States . . . shall be fined not more than $1,000, or imprisoned not more than one year, or both."

The facts are these: The Lindsley Lumber Co. suffered numerous thefts and hired petitioner [Jay G. Williams], who operated a detective agency, to ascertain the identity of the thieves. Petitioner held a special police officer's card issued by the City of Miami, Florida, and had taken an oath and qualified as a special police officer. Petitioner and others over a period of three days took four men to a paint shack on the company's premises and used brutal methods to obtain a confession from each of them. A rubber hose, a pistol, a blunt instrument, a sash cord and other implements were used in the project. One man was forced to look at a bright light for fifteen minutes; when he was blinded, he was repeatedly hit with a rubber hose and a sash cord and finally knocked to the floor. Another was knocked from a chair and hit in the stomach again and again. He was put back in the chair and the procedure was repeated. One was backed against the wall and jammed in the chest with a club. Each was beaten, threatened, and unmercifully punished for several hours until he confessed. One Ford, a policeman, was sent by his superior to lend authority to the proceedings. And petitioner, who committed the assaults, went about flashing his badge.

The indictment charged among other things that petitioner acting under color of law used force to make each victim confess to his guilt and implicate others, and that the victims were denied the right to be tried by due process of law and if found guilty to be sentenced and punished in accordance with the laws of the state. Petitioner was found guilty by a jury under instructions which conformed with the rulings of the Court in *Screws* v. *United States,* 325 US 91. . . .

We think it clear that petitioner was acting "under color" of law within the meaning of § 20, or at least that the jury could properly so find. We interpreted this phrase of § 20 in *United States* v. *Classic,* 313 US 299, 326, "Misuse of power, possessed by virtue of state law and made possible only because the wrongdoer is clothed with the authority of state law, is action taken 'under color of' state law." . . .

The main contention is that the application of § 20 so as to sustain a conviction for obtaining a confession by use of force and violence is unconstitutional. The argument is the one that a clear majority of the Court rejected in *Screws* v. *United States,* and runs as follows:

Criminal statutes must have an ascertainable standard of guilt or they fall for vagueness. See *United States* v. *Cohen Grocery Co.,* 255 US 81; *Winters* v. *New York,* 333 US 507. Section 20, it is argued, lacks the necessary specificity when rights under the Due Process Clause of the Fourteenth Amendment are involved. We are pointed to the course of decisions by this Court under the Due Process Clause as proof of the vague and fluid standard for "rights, privileges, or immunities secured or protected by the Constitution" as used in § 20. We are referred to decisions where we have been closely divided on whether state action violated due process. More specifically we are cited many instances where the Court has been conspicuously in disagreement on the illegal character of confessions under the Due Process Clause. If the Court cannot agree as to what confessions violate the Fourteenth Amendment, how can one who risks criminal prosecutions for his acts be sure of the standard? Thus it is sought to show the police officers such as petitioner walk on ground far too treacherous for criminal responsibility.

Many criminal statues might be extended to circumstances so extreme as to make their application unconstitutional. Conversely, as we held in *Screws* v. *United States,* a close construction will often save an act from vagueness that is fatal. The present case is as good an illustration as any. It is as plain as a pikestaff that the present confessions would not be allowed in evidence whatever the school of thought concerning the scope and meaning of the Due Process Clause. This is the classic use of force to make a man testify against himself. The result is as plain as if the rack, the wheel, and the thumb-screw—the ancient methods of securing evidence by torture . . . were used to compel the confession. Some day the application of § 20 to less obvious methods of coercion may be presented and doubts as to the adequacy of the standard of guilt may be presented. There may be a similar doubt when an officer is tried under § 20 for beating a man to death. That was a doubt stirred in the *Screws* case; and it was the reason we held that the purpose must be plain, the deprivation of the constitutional right willful. But where police take matters in their own hands, seize victims, beat and pound them until they confess, there cannot be the slightest doubt that the police have deprived the victim of a right under the Constitution. It is the right of the accused to be tried by a legally constituted court, not by a kangaroo court. Hence when officers wring confessions from the accused by force and violence, they violate some of the most fundamental, basic, and well-established constitutional rights which every citizen enjoys. Petitioner and his associates acted willfully and purposely; their aim was precisely to deny the protection that the Constitution affords. It was an arrogant and brutal deprivation of rights which the Constitution specifically guarantees. Section 20 would be denied the high service for which it was designed if rights so palpably plain were denied its protection. Only casuistry could make vague and nebulous what our constitutional scheme makes so clear and specific. . . .

MR. JUSTICE BLACK dissents.

MR. JUSTICE FRANKFURTER, MR. JUSTICE JACKSON and MR. JUSTICE MINTON, dissenting.

Experience in the effort to apply the doctrine of *Screws* v. *United States,* 325 US 91, leads MR. JUSTICE FRANKFURTER, MR. JUSTICE JACKSON and MR. JUSTICE MINTON to dissent for the reasons set forth in the dissent in that case.

Notes

1. *Monroe* v. *Pape,* 365 US 167 (1961). Section 1 of the Ku Klux Act of 1871 now appears as 42 USC § 1983, reading as follows:

> Every person who, under color of any statute, ordinance, regulation, custom, or usage, of any State or Territory, subjects, or causes to be subjected, any citizen of the United States or other persons within the jurisdiction thereof to the deprivation of any rights, privileges, or immunities secured by the Constitution and laws, shall be liable to the party injured in an action at law, suit in equity, or other proper proceeding for redress.

In *Monroe* v. *Pape,* the Court gave the same construction to the phrase "under color of" state law as used in this section defining civil liability as it had given to the similar phrase in 18 USC § 242 defining criminal liability. It again rejected a contention that "under color of" state law included only action taken by officials pursuant to state law. It quoted with approval this statement from *United States* v. *Classic:* "Misuse of power, possessed by virtue of state law and made possible only because the wrong-doer is clothed with the authority of state law, is action taken 'under color of' state law." The case dealt with an alleged search without warrant and beating of Monroe by police officers of the city of Chicago. The facts alleged were held to constitute a cause of action against the policemen as individuals but not against the city of Chicago because "Congress did not intend to bring municipal corporations within the ambit of" the Ku Klux Act involved.

2. *Adickes* v. *Kress,* 398 US 144 (1970), involved Adickes, a white person from New York teaching blacks in a Mississippi "Freedom School," being refused service at Kress's lunch counter in Hattiesburg. She sued for damages under 42 USC § 1983. The opinions in the case contain an extensive study of the application of this code section.

3. *United States* v. *Guest,* 383 US 745 (1966), involved an indictment under a section of the Civil Rights Act of 1870, now appearing as 28 USC § 241, and reading as follows: "If two or more persons conspire to injure, oppress, or intimidate any citizen in the free exercise or enjoyment of any right or privilege secured to him by the Constitution or laws of the United States . . . they shall be fined not more than $5,000 or imprisoned not more than ten years, or both." The indictments alleged, among other things, that Guest and other named defendants conspired to deny to blacks the right "to travel freely to and from the State of Georgia" by "causing the arrest of Negroes by false reports that Negroes had committed criminal acts." The trial court dismissed the indictment on the ground that it alleged no state action. In reversing this decision, the Supreme Court held: "The allegation of the extent of official involvement in the present case is not clear. It may charge no more than co-operative private and state action similar to that involved in Bell [*Bell* v. *Maryland*], but it may go considerably further. For example, the allegation is broad enough to cover a charge of active connivance by agents of the State in the making of 'false reports,' or other conduct amounting to official discrimination clearly sufficient to constitute denial of rights protected by the Equal Protection Clause. Although it is possible that a bill of particulars, or the proof if the case goes to trial, would disclose no co-operative action of that kind by officials of the State, the allegation is enough to prevent dismissal of this branch of the indictment."

4. The Civil Rights Act of 1968 [82 Stat 73], passed a few weeks after the assassination of Dr. Martin Luther King, Jr., added a provision to the criminal code [18 USC § 245] reading in part as follows:

Whoever, whether or not acting under color of law, by force or threat of force willfully . . . interferes with (1) any person because he is or has been, or in order to intimidate such person . . . or any class of persons from (A) voting . . . ; (B) participating in or enjoying any benefit, service, privilege, program, facility or activity provided or administered by the United States; (C) applying for or enjoying employment . . . by any agency of the United States . . . or (2) any person because of his race, color, religion or national origin and because he is or has been (A) enrolling in or attending any public school or public college; (B) participating in . . . any . . .

activity provided or administered by any State or subdivision thereof; (C) applying for or enjoying employment ... by any private employer ... or joining or using the services or advantages of any labor organization ..., (F) enjoying the goods, services ... or accommodations of any inn, hotel, motel, or other establishment which provides lodging to transient guests ... or any ... place of exhibition or entertainment which serves the public and (i) which is located within the premises of any of the aforesaid establishments ... and (ii) which holds itself out as serving patrons of such establishments ... shall be fined not more than $1,000, or imprisoned not more than one year, or both. ...

5. *Griffin* v. *Breckenridge,* 403 US 88 (1971), makes it clear that the present Court, committed to the proposition that Congress is empowered to pass broad civil rights legislation under the terms of the Thirteenth Amendment, will give broader application to civil rights laws passed years ago.

In an earlier case, *Collins* v. *Handyman* (1951), the Court had interpreted Rev. Stat. Sec. 1980 as applicable only to conspiracies under color of state law. In *Griffin* v. *Breckenridge* Justice Stewart wrote:

> Whether or not *Collins* v. *Handyman* was correctly decided on its facts is a question with which we need not here be concerned. But it is clear, in the light of the evolution of decisional law in the years that have passed since that case was decided, that many of the constitutional problems there perceived simply do not exist. Little reason remains, therefore, not to accord to the words of the statute their apparent meaning. ... On their face, the words of the statute fully encompass the conduct of private persons. The provision speaks simply of "two or more persons" ... who "conspire to go in disguise on the highway or premises of another ... for the purpose of depriving ... any person or class of persons of the equal protection of the laws, or of equal privileges and immunities under the law."

Pennsylvania v. Board of Trusts

353 US 230 77 S Ct 806, 1 L Ed2d 792 (1957)

PER CURIAM.

The motion to dismiss the appeal for want of jurisdiction is granted. 28 USC § 1257 (2). Treating the papers whereon the appeal was taken as a petition for writ of *certiorari,* 28 USC § 2103, the petition is granted. 28 USC § 1257 (3).

Stephen Girard, by will probated in 1831, left a fund in trust for the erection, maintenance, and operation of a "college." The will provided that the college was to admit "as many poor white male orphans, between the ages of six and ten years, as the said income shall be adequate to maintain." The will named as trustee the City of Philadelphia. The provisions of the will were carried out by the State and City and the college was opened in 1848. Since 1869, by virtue of an act of the Pennsylvania Legislature, the trust has been administered and the college operated by the "Board of Directors of City Trusts of the City of Philadelphia." ...

In February 1954, the petitioners Foust and Felder applied for admission to the college. They met all qualifications except that they were Negroes. For this reason the

Board refused to admit them. They petitioned the Orphans' Court of Philadelphia County for an order directing the Board to admit them, alleging that their exclusion because of race violated the Fourteenth Amendment to the Constitution. The State of Pennsylvania and the City of Philadelphia joined in the suit also contending the Board's action violated the Fourteenth Amendment. The Orphans' Court rejected the constitutional contention and refused to order the applicants' admission. This was affirmed by the Pennsylvania Supreme Court. . . .

The Board which operates Girard College is an agency of the State of Pennsylvania. Therefore, even though the Board was acting as a trustee, its refusal to admit Foust and Felder to the college because they were Negroes was discrimination by the State. Such discrimination is forbidden by the Fourteenth Amendment. *Brown* v. *Board of Education,* 347 US 483. Accordingly, the judgment of the Supreme Court of Pennsylvania is reversed and the cause is remanded for further proceedings not inconsistent with this opinion.

It is so ordered.

Note

Subsequent development. Following the decision by the United States Supreme Court, the Pennsylvania courts substituted private trustees in order to carry out the dominant purpose of the Girard trust. The United States Supreme Court denied *certiorari.* 357 US 570 (1957). Ten years later, however, the Court of Appeals of the Third Circuit held the Pennsylvania court's substitution of private trustees to be unconstitutional state action. The Supreme Court again denied *certiorari,* 391 US 921 (1968), and blacks were admitted to the college in September, 1968.

Bell v. Maryland

378 US 226, 84 S Ct 1814, 12 L Ed2d 822 (1964)

Can a state enforce trespass laws when invoked on a racial basis?

MR. JUSTICE BRENNAN delivered the opinion of the Court.

Petitioners, 12 Negro students, were convicted in a Maryland state court as a result of their participation in a "sit-in" demonstration at Hooper's restaurant in the City of Baltimore in 1960. The convictions were based on a record showing in summary that a group of 15 to 20 Negro students, including petitioners, went to Hooper's restaurant to engage in what their counsel describes as a "sit-in protest" because the restaurant would not serve Negroes. The "hostess," on orders of Mr. Hooper, the president of the corporation owning the restaurant, told them, "solely on the basis of their color," that they would not be served. Petitioners did not leave when requested to by the hostess and the manager; instead they went to tables, took seats, and refused to leave, insisting that they be served. On orders of the owner the police were called, but they advised that a warrant would be necessary before they could arrest petitioners. The owner then went to the police station and swore out warrants, and petitioners were accordingly arrested.

The statute under which the convictions were obtained was the Maryland criminal trespass law . . . under which it is a misdemeanor to "enter upon or cross over the land, premises or private property of any person or persons in this State after having been duly notified by the owner or his agent not to do so." The convictions were affirmed by the Maryland Court of Appeals . . . and we granted *certiorari. . . .*

We do not reach the questions that have been argued under the Equal Protection and Due Process Clauses of the Fourteenth Amendment. It appears that a significant change has taken place in the applicable law of Maryland since these convictions were affirmed by the Court of Appeals. Under this Court's settled practice in such circumstances, the judgments must consequently be vacated and reversed and the case remanded so that the state court may consider the effect of the supervening change in state law.

Petitioners' convictions were affirmed by the Maryland Court of Appeals on January 9, 1962. Since that date, Maryland has enacted laws that abolish the crime of which petitioners were convicted. These laws accord petitioners a right to be served in Hooper's restaurant, and make unlawful conduct like that of Hooper's president and hostess in refusing them service becasue of their race. . . .

Accordingly, the judgment of the Maryland Court of Appeals should be vacated and the case remanded to that court, and to this end the judgment is

Reversed.

MR. JUSTICE DOUGLAS, with whom MR. JUSTICE GOLDBERG concurs as respects Parts II-V, reversing and directing dismissal of the indictment.

I reach the merits of this controversy. The issue is ripe for decision and petitioners, who have been convicted of asking for service in Hooper's restaurant, are entitled to an answer to their complaint here and now.

On this the last day of the Term, we studiously avoid decision of the basic issue of the right of public accommodation under the Fourteenth Amendment, remanding the case to the state court for reconsideration in light of an issue of state law. . . .

The issue in this case, according to those who would affirm, is whether a person's "personal prejudices" may dictate the way in which he uses his property and whether he can enlist the aid of the state to enforce those "personal prejudices." With all respect, that is not the real issue. The corporation that owns this restaurant did not refuse service to these Negroes because "it" did not like Negroes. The reason "it" refused service was because "it" thought "it" could make more money by running a segregated restaurant. . . .

I leave those questions to another part of this opinion and turn to an even more basic issue.

I now assume that the issue is the one stated by those who would affirm. The case in that posture deals with a relic of slavery—an institution that has cast a long shadow across the land, resulting today in a second-class citizenship in this area of public accommodations. . . .

When one citizen because of his race, creed, or color is denied the privilege of being treated as any other citizen in places of public accommodation, we have classes of citizenship, one being more degrading than the other. That is at war with the one class of citizenship created by the Thirteenth, Fourteenth, and Fifteenth Amendments. . . .

State judicial action is as clearly "state" action as state administrative action. Indeed, we held in *Shelly* v. *Kraemer,* 334 US 1, 20, that "State action, as that phrase is understood for the purposes of the Fourteenth Amendment, refers to exertions of state powers in all forms." . . .

Maryland's action against these Negroes was as authoritative as any case where the State in one way or another puts its full force behind a policy. The policy here was segregation in places of public accommodation; and Maryland enforced that policy with her police, her prosecutors, and her courts. . . .

MR. JUSTICE GOLDBERG [wrote a concurring opinion, joined by JUSTICE DOUGLAS and CHIEF JUSTICE WARREN].

MR. JUSTICE BLACK, with whom MR. JUSTICE HARLAN and MR. JUSTICE WHITE join, dissenting. . . .

Petitioners . . . contend that their conviction for trespass under the state statute was by itself the kind of discriminatory state action forbidden by the Fourteenth Amendment. This contention, on its face, has plausibility which considered along with general statements to the effect that under the Amendment forbidden "state action" may be that of the Judicial as well as of the Legislative or Executive Branches of Government. But a mechanical application of the Fourteenth Amendment to this case cannot survive analysis. The Amendment does not forbid a State to prosecute for crimes committed against a person or his property, however prejudiced or narrow the victim's views may be. Nor can whatever prejudice and bigotry the victim of a crime may have be automatically attributed to the State that prosecutes. Such a doctrine would not only be based on a fiction; it would also severely handicap a State's efforts to maintain a peaceful and orderly society. Our society has put its trust in a system of criminal laws to punish lawless conduct. To avert personal feuds and violent brawls it has led its people to believe and expect that wrongs against them will be vindicated in the courts. Instead of attempting to take the law into their own hands, people have been taught to call for police protection to protect their rights wherever possible. It would betray our whole plan for a tranquil and orderly society to say that a citizen, because of his personal prejudices, habits, attitudes, or beliefs, is cast outside the law's protection and cannot call for the aid of officers sworn to uphold the law and preserve the peace. The worst citizen no less than the best is entitled to equal protection of the laws of his State and of his Nation. . . .

In contending that the State's prosecution of petitioners for trespass is State action forbidden by the Fourteenth Amendment, petitioners rely chiefly on *Shelley* v. *Kraemer, supra.* That reliance is misplaced. . . .

It seems pretty clear that the reason judicial enforcement of the restrictive covenants in Shelley was deemed State action was, not merely the fact that a State court had acted, but rather that it had acted "to deny to petitioners, on the grounds of race or color, the enjoyment of property rights in premises which petitioners are willing and financially able to acquire and which the grantors are willing to sell." 344 US, at 19. In other words, this Court held that State enforcement of the covenants had the effect of denying to the parties their federally guaranteed right to own, occupy, enjoy, and use their property without regard to race or color. Thus, the line of cases from

Buchanan through *Shelley* establishes these propositions: (1) When an owner of property is willing to sell and a would-be purchaser is willing to buy, then the Civil Rights Act of 1866, which gives all persons the same right to "inherit, lease, sell, hold, and convey" property, prohibits a State, whether through its legislature, executive, or judiciary, from preventing the sale on the grounds of the race or color of one of the parties. . . . (2) Once a person has become a property owner, then he acquires all the rights that go with ownership: "the free use, enjoyment, and disposal of a person's acquisitions without control or diminution save by the law of the land." *Buchanan* v. *Warley, supra,* 245 US, at 74. This means that the property owner may, in the absence of a valid statute forbidding it, sell his property to whom he pleases and admit to that property whom he will; so long as *both* parties are willing parties, then the principles stated in *Buchanan* and *Shelley* protect this right. But equally, when one party is unwilling, as when the property owner chooses *not* to sell to a particular person or *not* to admit that person, then, as this Court emphasized in *Buchanan,* he is entitled to rely on the guarantee of due process of law, that is, "law of the land," to protect his free use and enjoyment of property and to know that only by valid legislation, passed pursuant to some constitutional grant of power, can anyone disturb this free use. But petitioners here would have us hold that, despite the absence of any valid statute restricting the use of his property, the owner of Hooper's restaurant in Baltimore must not be accorded the same federally guaranteed right to occupy, enjoy, and use property given to the parties in *Buchanan* and *Shelley;* instead, petitioners would have us say that Hooper's federal right must be cut down and he be compelled—though no statute said he must—to allow people to force their way into his restaurant and remain there over his protest. We cannot subscribe to such a mutilating, one-sided interpretation of federal guarantees the very heart of which is equal treatment under law to all. We must never forget that the Fourteenth Amendment protects "life, liberty, or property" of all people generally, not just some people's "life," some people's "liberty," and some kinds of "property." . . .

Notes

1. *The sit-in cases.* In more than a dozen cases decided in 1963 and 1964, the Court reversed decisions of state courts convicting blacks of refusing to leave restaurants when asked to leave by the manager. *Peterson* v. *Greenville,* 373 US 244, held that, when a local statute required racial segregation in restaurants, state action was involved and a black could not be convicted of trespass even if the restaurant manager would have sought to exclude the black in the absence of the ordinance. Compare *Lombard* v. *Louisiana,* 373 US 267 (1963), where the same result was reached in the absence of an ordinance, but where the mayor and superintendent of police had announced publicly that sit-in demonstrations would not be permitted.

    Hamm v. *City of Rock Hill,* 379 US 306 (1964), held that pending convictions for violating a state trespass law, based on conduct occurring prior to the passage of the Civil Rights Act of 1964, were abated by that law.

2. *Burton* v. *Wilmington Parking Authority,* 365 US 715 (1961). This case held that when a state leases public property, under the circumstances involved, to a private operator of a restaurant, the proscriptions of the Fourteenth Amendment must be applied.

Evans v. Abney

396 US 435, 90 S Ct 628, 24 L Ed2d 634 (1970)

Where a testator wills property to a city to be used as a park for white persons only, a state court can return the property to the heirs of the testator, even though it has been used as a public park for fifty years.

MR. JUSTICE BLACK delivered the opinion of the Court.

Once again this Court must consider the constitutional implications of the 1911 will of United States Senator A. O. Bacon of Georgia which conveyed property in trust to Senator Bacon's home city of Macon for the creation of a public park for the exclusive use of the white people of that city. As a result of our earlier decision in this case which held that the park, Baconsfield, could not continue to be operated on a racially discriminatory basis, *Evans* v. *Newton,* 382 US 296 (1966), the Supreme Court of Georgia ruled that Senator Bacon's intention to provide a park for whites only had become impossible to fulfill and that accordingly the trust had failed and the parkland and other trust property had reverted by operation of Georgia law to the heirs of the Senator. ... Petitioners, the same Negro citizens of Macon who have sought in the courts to integrate the park, contend that this termination of the trust violates their rights to equal protection and due process under the Fourteenth Amendment. We granted *certiorari* because of the importance of the questions involved. ... For the reasons to be stated, we are of the opinion that the judgment of the Supreme Court of Georgia should be, and it is, affirmed. ...

We are of the opinion that in ruling as they did the Georgia courts did no more than apply well-settled general principles of Georgia law to determine the meaning and effect of a Georgia will. ... The question ... properly before the Georgia Supreme Court was whether as a matter of state law the doctrine of *cy pres* should be applied to prevent the trust itself from failing. Petitioners urged that the *cy pres* doctrine allowed the Georgia courts to strike the racially restrictive clauses in Bacon's will so that the terms of the trust could be fulfilled without violating the Constitution. ...

In this case, Senator Bacon provided an unusual amount of information in his will from which the Georgia courts could determine the limits of his charitable purpose. ... Since racial separation was found to be an inseparable part of the testator's intent, the Georgia court held that the State's *cy pres* doctrine could not be used to alter the will to permit racial integration. ...

When a city park is destroyed because the Constitution required it to be integrated, there is reason for everyone to be disheartened. We agree with petitioners that in such a case it is not enough to find that the state court's result was reached through the application of established principles of state law. No state law or act can prevail in the face of contrary federal law, and the federal courts must search out the fact and truth of any proceeding or transaction to determine if the Constitution has been violated. ... Here, however, the action of the Georgia Supreme Court declaring the Baconsfield trust terminated presents no violation of constitutionally protected rights, and any harshness that may have resulted from the State court's decision can be attributed solely to its intention to effectuate as nearly as possible the explicit terms of Senator Bacon's will.

... [T]he situation presented in this case is ... easily distinguishable from that presented in *Shelley* v. *Kraemer,* 334 US 1 (1948), where we held unconstitutional state judicial action which had affirmatively enforced a private scheme of discrimination against Negroes. Here the effect of the Georgia decision eliminated all discrimination against Negroes in the park by eliminating the park itself, and the termination of the park was a loss shared equally by the white and Negro citizens of Macon since both races would have enjoyed a constitutional right of equal access to the park's facilities had it continued. ...

Petitioners also advance a number of considerations of public policy in opposition to the conclusion which we have reached. In particular, they regret, as we do, the loss of the Baconsfield trust to the City of Macon, and they are concerned lest we set a precedent under which other charitable trusts will be terminated. It bears repeating that our holding today reaffirms the traditional role of the States in determining whether or not to apply their *cy pres* doctrines to particular trusts. Nothing we have said here prevents a state court from applying its *cy pres* rule in a case where the Georgia court, for example, might not apply its rule. More fundamentally, however, the loss of charitable trusts such as Baconsfield is part of the price we pay for permitting deceased persons to exercise a continuing control over assets owned by them at death. This aspect of freedom of testation, like most things, has its advantages and disadvantages. The responsibility of this Court, however, is to construe and enforce the Constitution and laws of the land as they are and not to legislate social policy on the basis of our own personal inclinations. ...

The judgment is

Affirmed.

Mr. Justice Marshall took no part in the decision of this case.

Mr. Justice Douglas, dissenting. ...

The Georgia court held that the doctrine of *cy pres* "can not be applied to establish a trust for an entirely different purpose from that intended by the testator." ... That however does not state the issue realistically. No proposal to bar use of the park by whites has ever been made, except the reversion ordered to the heirs. Continuation of the use of the property as a municipal park or, for another municipal purpose carries out a larger share of Bacon's purpose than the complete destruction of such use by the decree we today affirm. ...

Moreover, putting the property in the hands of the heirs will not necessarily achieve the racial segregation which Bacon desired. We deal with city real estate. If a theatre is erected, Negroes cannot be excluded. If a restaurant is opened, Negroes must be served. If office or housing structures are erected, Negro tenants must be eligible. If a church is erected, mixed marriage ceremonies may be performed. If a court undertook to attach a racial use condition to the property once it became "private," that would be an unconstitutional convenant or condition.

Bacon's basic desire can be realized only by the repeal of the Fourteenth Amendment. So the fact is that in the vicissitudes of time there is no constitutional way to assure that this property will not serve the needs of Negroes.

The Georgia decision, which we today approve, can only be a gesture toward a state-sanctioned segregated way of life, now *passé*. It therefore should fail as the imposition of a penalty for obedience to a principle of national supremacy.

MR. JUSTICE BRENNAN, dissenting. . . .

. . . When it is as starkly clear as it is in this case that a public facility would remain open but for the constitutional command that it be operated on a non-segregated basis, the closing of that facility conveys an unambiguous message of community involvement in racial discrimination. . . .

This . . . is not a case of private discrimination. It is rather discrimination in which the State of Georgia is "significantly involved," and enforcement of the reverter is therefore unconstitutional. . . .

I would reverse the judgment of the Supreme Court of Georgia.

Notes

1. *Reitman* v. *Mulkey,* 387 US 369 (1967). The Mulkeys, husband and wife, sued Reitman for damages, alleging that he had refused to rent them an apartment solely on account of their race. The Unrah Act of 1959, under which the suit was filed, provided that "All persons within . . . this State are free and equal . . . and entitled to the full and equal accommodation . . . facilities . . . or services in all business establishments of every kind whatsoever. . . . Whosoever denies . . . or . . . makes any discrimination . . . on account of color . . . is liable . . . for actual damages, and two hundred fifty dollars ($250) in addition thereto. . . ." California also had the Rumford Fair Housing Act of 1963. In 1964, however, a popularly initiated Proposition 14 was placed on the statewide ballot and approved as an amendment to the California Constitution. It read: "Neither the State nor any subdivision or agency thereof shall deny, limit or abridge, directly or indirectly, the right of any person, who is willing or desires to sell, lease or rent any part or all of his real property, to decline to sell, lease or rent such property to such person or persons as he, in his absolute discretion, chooses." The California Supreme Court held that the 1964 constitutional amendment violated the equal protection clause of the Fourteenth Amendment because, by constitutionally prohibiting fair housing legislation, it encouraged segregation. By a five-to-four vote, the United States Supreme Court affirmed the judgment. Was it overruled *sub silentio* in the *Evans* case?

2. *Palmer* v. *Thompson,* 403 US 217 (1971), held that neither the Thirteenth nor the Fourteenth Amendment bars a city from closing public swimming pools.

3. *Moose Lodge No. 107* v. *Irvis,* 407 US 163 (1972), held that Pennsylvania's licensing of a private club to dispense liquor did not render the club's discriminatory policies "state action." Justices Brennan, Douglas, and Marshall dissented.

4. *Gilmore* v. *City of Montgomery,* 417 US 556 (1974), held that the city, having an affirmative duty to bring about a desegregated public school system under a district court order, could be enjoined from permitting private, racially segregated schools from using, however temporarily, public recreational facilities. For the Court, Justice Blackmun wrote:

> Although the Court of Appeals ruled out the *exclusive* use of city facilities by private schools, it went on to modify the District Court order "to make clear that the City of Montgomery is not prohibited from permiting nonexclusive access to public recreational facilities and general governmental services by private schools or school affiliated groups," 473 F. 2d, at 840, or from permitting access to these facilities by private organizations that have a racially discriminatory admissions policy. *Id.,* at 839. Upon this record, we are unable to draw a conclusion as to whether the use of zoos, museums, parks, and other recreational facilities by private school groups in common with others, and by private nonschool organizations, involves government so directly in the actions of those users as to warrant court intervention on constitutional grounds. . . .
>
> The difficulties that confront us on this record are readily apparent. Under appropriate circumstances, the District Court might conclude, as it did in the instance of exclusive use by private schools, that access in common to city facilities by private school groups would indeed contravene the school desegregation order. For example, all-white private school basketball teams might be invited to participate in a tournament conducted on public recreational facilities with desegregated private and public school teams. Because "discriminatory treatment exerts a pervasive influence on the entire educational process," *Norwood* v. *Harrison,* 413 US, at 469, citing *Brown* v. *Board of Education,* 347 US 483 (1954), such assistance, although proffered in common with fully desegragated groups, might so directly impede the progress of court-ordered school desegregation within the city that it would be appropriate to fashion equitable relief "adjusting and reconciling public and private needs." *Brown* v. *Board of Education,* 349 US 294, 300 (1955). The essential finding justifying further relief would be a showing of direct impairment of an outstanding school desegregation order. . . .
>
> "The Court has never held, of course, that discrimination by an otherwise private entity would be violative of the Equal Protection Clause if the private entity receives any sort of benefit or service at all from the State, or if it is subject to state regulation in any degree whatever." 407 US, at 173. Traditional state monopolies, such as electricity, water, and police and fire protection—all generalized governmental services —do not by their mere provision constitute a showing of state involvement in invidious discrimination. *Norwood* v. *Harrison,* 413 US, at 465; *Moose Lodge No. 107* v. *Irvis,* 407 US, at 173. The same is true of a broad spectrum of municipal recreational facilities: parks, playgrounds, athletic facilities, amphitheaters, museums, zoos, and the like. *Cf. Evans* v. *Newton,* 382 US, at 302. It follows, therefore, that the portion of the District Court's order prohibiting the mere use of such facilities by *any* segregated "private group, club or organization" is invalid because it was not predicated upon a proper finding of state action.
>
> If, however, the city or other governmental entity rations otherwise freely accessible recreational facilities, the case for state action will naturally be stronger than if the

facilities are simply available to all comers without condition or reservation. Here, for example, petitioners allege that the city engages in scheduling softball games for an all-white church league and provides balls, equipment, fields and lighting. The city's role in that situation would be dangerously close to what was found to exist in *Burton,* where the city had "elected to place its power, property and prestige behind the admitted discrimination." 365 US, at 725. We are reminded, however, that the Court has never attempted to formulate "an infallible test for determining whether the State . . . has become significantly involved in private discriminations" so as to constitute state action. *Reitman* v. *Mulkey,* 387 US, at 378. " 'Only by sifting facts and weighing circumstances' on a case-by-case basis can a 'nonobvious involvement of the State in private conduct be attributed its true significance'." *Id.,* quoting *Burton,* 365 US, at 722. This is the task for the District Court on remand.

We close with this word of caution. It should be obvious that the exclusion of any person or group—all-Negro, all-oriental, or all-white—from public facilities infringes upon the freedom of the individual to associate as he chooses. Mr. Justice Douglas emphasized this in his dissent, joined by Mr. Justice Marshall, in *Moose Lodge.* He observed, "The associational rights which our system honors permit all white, all black, all brown, and all yellow clubs to be formed. They also permit all Catholic, all Jewish, or all agnostic clubs to be established. Government may not tell a man or woman who his or her associates must be. The individual can be as selective as he desires," 407 US, at 179–180. The freedom to associate applies to the beliefs we share, and to those we consider reprehensible. It tends to produce the diversity of opinion that oils the machine of democratic government and insures peaceful, orderly change. Because its exercise is largely dependent on the right to own or use property, *Healy* v. *James,* 408 US 169, 181–183 (1972), any denial of access to public facilities must withstand close scrutiny and be carefully circumscribed. Certainly, a person's mere membership in an organization which possesses a discriminatory admissions policy would not alone be ground for his exclusion from public facilities. Having said this, however, we must also be aware that the very exercise of the freedom to associate by some may serve to infringe that freedom for others. Invidious discrimination takes its own toll on the freedom to associate, and it is not subject to affirmative constitutional protection when it involves state action. . . .

Chapter 8

Freedom of Religion

A. INTRODUCTION

The only provision in the original Constitution on freedom of religion is the clause in Article VI banning religious tests as a qualification for holding federal offices. In the Bill of Rights, however, religious freedom is given first place. The First Amendment reads: "Congress shall make no law respecting an establishment of religion, or prohibiting the free exercise thereof. . . ." *Cantwell* v. *Connecticut,* 310 US 296 (1940), expressly declared the "free exercise" provision of the First Amendment to be incorporated into the Fourteenth Amendment as a limitation on the states, and *Everson* v. *Board of Education,* 330 US 1 (1947), made a similar ruling on the "establishment of religion" clause.

As the case law has developed, there has emerged a conflict between the concepts of the "establishment of religion" and the "free exercise thereof." When a state enforces Sunday closing laws, is it establishing a religion or merely cooperating to facilitate the free exercise thereof? And which is involved when the United States defers conscientious objectors from combat duty? In these and many other situations, the concept of a neutral position is delusive. On this subject, contrast the views of Justices Harlan and White in *Welsh* v. *United States* (p. 231) and of Chief Justice Burger and Justice Powell in *Committee for Public Education* v. *Nyquist* (p. 248). In sustaining the right of members of the Amish religion not to send their children to a formal school after they had completed the eighth grade, Chief Justice Burger wrote: "The Court must not ignore the danger that an exception from a general obligation on religious grounds may run afoul of the Establishment Clause, but that danger cannot be allowed to prevent any exception no matter how vital it may be to the protection of values promoted by the right of free exercise." *Wisconsin* v. *Yoder,* page 238.

Free Exercise of Religion

The first case in which extensive consideration was given to religious freedom was *Reynolds* v. *United States* (p. 234) in 1878. However, it was not until after the incorporation of the "free exercise" clause into the due process requirement of the Fourteenth Amendment in 1940 that much litigation arose under it.

The *Cantwell* case of 1940 was brought to the Supreme Court by Jehovah's Witnesses. The Court reversed the decision of a Connecticut court holding Cantwell guilty of inciting to breach of the peace by accosting people on the street in a community dominantly Roman Catholic and playing records denouncing the Papacy. The next year, however, the Witnesses failed to secure a reversal of conviction of sixty-eight of their members for holding a parade in the streets of Manchester, New Hampshire, without securing a permit. *Cox* v. *New Hampshire,* 312 US 569 (1941). Two years later, in *West Virginia State Board of Education* v. *Barnette,* 319 US 624 (1943), the Court held that children of Jehovah's Witnesses attending a public school could not be required to salute the American flag, which the Witnesses regarded as a "graven image." The same year, in *Martin* v. *Struthers,* 319 US 141 (1943), the Court sustained the religious freedom of the Witnesses (each one regarding himself as a minister of the gospel) to go from house to house ringing doorbells for the purpose of religious propagandizing and, without paying any license fee, to solicit orders for their religious literature, *Murdock* v. *Pennsylvania,* 319 US 105 (1943). The next year, however, the Court refused to reverse the judgment holding Sarah Prince guilty of violating Massachusetts' child labor law by bringing her niece, Betty, a girl nine years of age, on the streets at night to sell the "Watchtower," the group's magazine. *Prince* v. *Massachusetts,* 421 US 158 (1944).

The most significant recent "free exercise" of religion cases other than those brought by Jehovah's Witnesses are *Sherbert* v. *Verner,* 374 US 398 (1963), and *Wisconsin* v. *Yoder,* 406 US 205 (1972). In *Sherbert* a member of the Seventh-Day Adventist Church was discharged by her South Carolina employer because she would not work on Saturday, the Sabbath Day of her faith. She was unable to obtain other employment because she would not work on Saturday, and she filed a claim for unemployment compensation benefits under the South Carolina Unemployment Compensation Act, which provides that a claimant is ineligible for benefits if he has failed, without good cause, to accept available, suitable work when offered him. The state employment commission denied appellant's application on the ground that she would not accept suitable work when offered, and its action was sustained by the state courts. The Supreme Court held that, as applied, the South Carolina statute abridged appellant's right to the free exercise of her religion.

Establishment of Religion

Problems of religious freedom have existed throughout recorded history, and religious intolerance ranks high among the causes of persecution and bloodshed. Europe was crippled by wars of religion in the sixteenth and seventeenth centuries. In the eighteenth century most of the European states had established churches, and dissenters from orthodoxy were persecuted. Many of the early settlers, notably the Puritans of New England, came to America to escape religious persecution, but intolerance soon arose in the colonies.

Virginia, like eight other of the thirteen colonies, had an established church. It continued to be supported financially by the state after the American Revolution. In 1786 Thomas Jefferson and James Madison led a movement to prevent the Virginia legislature from renewing the state's tax levy for support of the established church. They succeeded in having the assembly enact the famous "Virginia Bill for Religious Liberty." Its preamble proclaimed that "Almighty God hath created the mind free, that all attempts to influence it by temporal punishments or burthens, or by civil incapacitations, tend only to beget habits of hypocrisy and meanness . . . [and] that to compel a man to furnish contributions of money for the propagation of opinion which he disbelieves, is sinful and tyrannical. . . ." It was against this background that Madison introduced in Congress the resolution which became the First Amendment to the United States Constitution in 1791.

Attempts to have acts of Congress declared void as an establishment of religion have met with little success. *Bradford* v. *Roberts,* 175 US 291 (1899), held that money appropriated by Congress for the construction of two isolation buildings on the grounds of hospitals could be used by the commissioners of the District of Columbia to construct a building on the grounds of Providence Hospital, a hospital operated by a sisterhood under the auspices of the Roman Catholic Church. Under a contract between the hospital and the commissioners, the hospital was to provide care for indigent patients. The Court ruled that Providence Hospital was chartered as a private eleemosynary corporation, and "its powers, duties and character are to be solely measured by the charter under which it alone has any legal existence." The fact that it was conducted by a religious order was viewed to be immaterial.

Quick Bear v. *Leupp,* 210 US 50 (1907), sustained the use of funds derived from congressional appropriation for carrying out a contract between the Commissioner of Indian Affairs and the Catholic Indian mission for the education of Indians at St. Francis Mission Boarding School, a sectarian school.

As noted above, the *Everson* case of 1947 was the one in which the Court announced that the "establishment of religion" clause of the First Amendment would be considered as incorporated into the Fourteenth as a limitation on the states. It sustained a New Jersey practice of reimbursing to parents money spent for transporting their children by public transportation to either public schools or parochial schools. In substance, the majority opinion by Justice Black adopted the child-benefit theory. This theory had been advanced in *Cochran* v. *Board of Education,* 281 US 370 (1930), a case in which a Louisiana statute providing free textbooks for students attending both public and private schools was sustained against the charge that public funds were being used for private purposes.

Indirect Financial Aid to Religious Organizations

The *Everson* case discussed above might be placed under this heading. *Board of Education* v. *Allen,* 392 US 226 (1968), in which the Court sustained a New York practice of lending textbooks free of charge to students in grades seven to twelve, including those in private schools, was a similar case. *Walz* v. *New York,* 397 US 664 (1970), sustained the practice of granting tax exemptions to church property.

Lemon v. *Kurtzman,* 403 US 602 (1971), held that state support of the salaries of teachers in religious schools was unconstitutional. Chief Justice Burger wrote: "Every analysis in this area must begin with consideration of the cumulative criteria developed by the Court over many years. Three such tests may be gleaned from our cases. First, the statute must have a secular legislative purpose; second, its principal and primary effect must be one that neither advances nor inhibits religion . . .; finally, the statute must not foster 'an excessive entanglement with religion.' " The Court recognized that "a dedicated religious person, teaching in a school affiliated with his or her faith and operated to inculcate its tenets, will inevitably experience great difficulty in remaining religiously neutral. . . . Unlike a book, a teacher cannot be inspected once so as to determine the extent and intent of his or her personal beliefs and subjective acceptance of the limitations imposed by the First Amendment. These prophylactic contacts will involve excessive and enduring entanglement between state and church."

The Court has sought to distinguish between permissible state aid to church-related institutions for use for secular purposes, on the one hand, and, on the other, impermissible aid to any institution for use for religious purposes. Thus, *Tilton* v. *Richardson,* 403 US 672 (1971), sustained the Higher Education Facilities Act of 1963, except for one provision. The Act provided federal construction grants to colleges, including those affiliated with religious bodies, except for facilities "used or to be used for sectarian instruction or as a place of religious worship. . . ." The United States retained a twenty-year interest in any facility constructed with funds under the Act, during which time it could recover funds if the conditions under which they were granted were violated. This provision reflected the view of Congress that after twenty years "the public benefit accruing to the United States" from the use of the federally financed facility would "equal or exceed in value" the amount of the federal grant. The Court held this twenty-year provision to be void. It held that the restriction obligation could not expire while the building had "substantial value."

The Court has taken judicial notice that religious indoctrination is more pervasive in parochial schools than in church-related colleges. In *Hunt* v. *McNair,* 413 US 734 (1973), it held that the Baptist College of Charleston had no significant sectarian orientation and could participate in a state bonding program in order to construct facilities for secular purposes.

Religious Instruction

In *McCollum* v. *Board of Education,* 333 US 203 (1948), the Court sought to maintain a "wall of separation" between church and state by prohibiting public school authorities from permitting volunteer groups to give religious instruction at public schools in off-periods. However, in *Zorach* v. *Clauson* (p. 244) the Court held that released time in the public schools for religious instruction was permissible if the religious classes were not held in public school buildings.

Engel v. *Vitale* 370 US 421 (1962), and *Abington School District* v. *Schempp* (p. 247) banned the use of prayers or devotional reading of the Bible in public schools.

Epperson v. *Arkansas,* 393 US 97 (1968), held invalid as an establishment of religion an Arkansas law prohibiting teachers in public-supported schools from teaching "that mankind ascended or descended from a lower order of animals."

Sunday Closing Laws

In *McGowan* v. *Maryland,* 366 US 420 (1961), and three related cases the Court sustained state Sunday closing laws against charges that they violated freedom of religion and equal protection of law and also that they constituted an establishment of religion. The opinions in the four cases cover 222 pages. The Court concluded that "In the light of the evolution of our Sunday Closing Laws through the centuries, and of their more or less recent emphasis upon secular considerations, it is concluded that, as presently written and administered, most of them, at least, are of a secular rather than of religious character, and that presently they bear no relationship to establishment of religion, as those words are used in the Constitution of the United States. . . ."

Conscientious Objectors

In the *Selective Draft Law Cases,* 245 US 366 (1918), the Court sustained the statutory exemption for conscientious objectors to military service with this curt sentence by Chief Justice White: "And we pass without anything but statement the proposition that an establishment of religion . . . resulted from the exemption clause, because we think its unsoundness is too apparent to require us to do more."

In *Hamilton* v. *Regents of the University of California,* 293 US 245 (1934), the Court sustained a California statute requiring all male students at the state university to take a course in military science against an attack by a student whose religious beliefs forbade military training. It noted that attendance at the university was not compulsory and held that Hamilton had no right to attend without complying with the state's requirement.

United States v. *Seeger,* 380 US 163 (1965), dealt with the statutory provision exempting from military service those persons who by reason of religious training and belief are conscientiously opposed to participation in war. The term "religious training and belief" is defined in the statute as "an individual's belief in a relation to a Supreme Being. . . ." The Court held that the test under this statute "is whether a given belief that is sincere and meaningful occupies a place in the life of its possessor parallel to that filled by the orthodox belief in God. . . ."

In *Welsh* v. *United States,* 398 US 333 (1970), Mr. Justice Black for the Court held that for a registrant's conscientious objection to war to be "religious" within the meaning of the exemption statute, it was only necessary "that this opposition to war stem from the registrant's moral, ethical, or religious beliefs held with the strength of traditional religious conviction. . . . Because his beliefs function as a religion in his life, such an individual is as much entitled to a 'religious' conscientious objector exemption under § 6(j) as is someone who derives his conscientious opposition to war from traditional religious convictions."

Justice Harlan concurred in the judgment, not as a matter of statutory construction, but as a means "for salvaging a congressional policy of long standing that would otherwise have to be nullified." He wrote: "The constitutional question that must be faced in this case is whether a statute that defers to the individual's conscience only when his views emanate from adherence to theistic religious beliefs is within the power of Congress. Congress, of course, could, entirely consistently with the requirements of the Constitution, eliminate *all* exemptions for conscientious objectors. Such a course would be wholly 'neutral' and, in my view, would not offend the Free Exercise Clause. . . . However, having chosen to exempt, it cannot draw the line between theistic or non-theistic religious beliefs on the one hand and secular beliefs on the other. Any such distinctions are not, in my view, compatible with the Establishment Clause of the First Amendment. . . .

"The 'radius' of this legislation" continued Justice Harlan, "is the conscientiousness with which an individual opposes war in general, yet the statute, as I think it must be construed, excludes from its 'scope' individuals motivated by teachings of nontheistic religions, and individuals guided by an inner ethical voice that bespeaks secular and not 'religious' reflection. It not only accords a preference to the 'religious' but also disadvantages adherents of religions that do not worship a Supreme Being. The constitutional infirmity cannot be cured, moreover, even by an impermissible construction that eliminates the theistic requirement and simply draws the line between religious and nonreligious. This in my view offends the Establishment Clause and is that kind of classification that this court has condemned."

Joined by Chief Justice Burger and by Justice Stewart, in a dissenting opinion Justice White wrote:

> Congress may have granted this exemption because otherwise religious objectors would be forced into conduct that their religions forbid and because in the view of Congress to deny the exemption would violate the Free Exercise Clause or at least raise grave problems in this respect. . . .
>
> That judgment is entitled to respect. . . . [J]ust as in *Katzenbach* v. *Morgan,* 384 US 641 (1966), where we accepted the judgment of Congress as to what legislation was appropriate to enforce the Equal Protection Clause of the Fourteenth Amendment, here we should respect congressional judgment accommodating the Free Exercise Clause and the power to raise armies. . . .
>
> We have said that neither support nor hostility, but neutrality, is the goal of the religious clause of the First Amendment. "Neutrality," however, is not self-defining. If it is "favoritism" and not "neutrality" to exempt religious believers from the draft, is it "neutrality" and not "inhibition" of religion to compel religious believers to fight when they have special reasons for not doing so, reasons to which the Constitution gives particular recognition? . . . We should . . . not labor to find a violation of the Establishment Clause where free exercise values prompt Congress to relieve religious believers from the burdens of the law at least in those instances where the law is not merely prohibitory but commands the performance of military duties that are forbidden by a man's religion.

Church Property

Civil courts accept jurisdiction to settle disputes concerning the ownership or use of church property. In general, the courts apply to such controversies the ecclesiastical law of the particular church prior to the schism. *Kedroff* v. *St. Nicholas Cathedral of the Russian Orthodox Church in North America,* 344 US 94 (1952), involved a dispute over the use of a church in New York. The Court of Appeals of New York had decided in favor of an archbishop elected by a convention of American churches and against an archbishop appointed by the Patriarch of Moscow. Its decision was based on a New York statute making all incorporated Russian Orthodox churches in that state subject to the authority of the general convention of Russian Churches in America. In reversing the New York court, the United States Supreme Court held that "legislation which determines, in an hierarchial church, ecclesiastical administration or the appointment of the clergy, or transfers control of churches from one group to another, interferes with the free exercise of religion contrary to the Constitution."

Presbyterian Church in the United States v. *Hull Church,* 393 US 440 (1969), involved a dispute over property in Savannah, Georgia. By a resolution adopted on April 17, 1966, the congregation of the Hull Memorial Presbyterian Church voted to withdraw from the Presbyterian Church of the United States (the "general church") and to become autonomous. The resolution stated that the general church had departed from its original tenets of faith by "ordaining women as ministers and ruling elders, making pronouncements and recommendations concerning civil, economic, and political matters, . . . adopting certain Sunday School literature and teaching neo-orthodoxy alien to the Confession of Faith and Catechisms, as originally adopted by the general church, and causing all members to remain in the National Council of Churches of Christ and willingly accept its leadership which advocates named practices, such as the subverting of parental authority, civil disobedience and intermeddling in civil affairs." A similar secessionist resolution was passed by the Eastern Heights Presbyterian Church of Savannah on the same date. The general church appointed an administrative commission to look into the matter. Within a month this commission resolved that the two local ministers and all elders of both churches "except one not contacted and another who dissented, had removed themselves from office and membership in the general church"; hence the commission "will secure ministerial leadership and provide regular services of worship in the sanctuaries of [the two churches] for those members who wish to continue their membership in and communion with [the general church]. . . ."

Alleging that the Presbyterian Church of the United States had never contributed any financial support to the Savannah churches, that title to the property in dispute was vested in the local church trustees, and that they were threatened with trespass, the local churches sought injunctive relief in the state court. Georgia law implied a trust over the local church property for the benefit of the general church, on condition that the general church not substantially abandon the tenets of faith existing at the time of affiliation by the local churches. The case was tried by jury. After elaborate evidence and argument were introduced on both sides, the jury was instructed to determine whether the actions of the general church had amounted to a substantial abandonment of the original tenets "so that the new tenets and doctrines are utterly variant from the purposes for which the [general] church was founded." The jury found such an abandonment, and the trial court ruled in favor of the local churches. The Georgia Supreme Court affirmed the judgment. 224 Ga 61 (1968).

In reversing, the United States Supreme Court held that "Civil courts cannot . . . determine ecclesiastical questions in resolving property disputes; and since the departure-from-doctrine element in Georgia's implied trust theory requires civil courts to weigh the significance and meaning of religious doctrines, it can play *no* role in judicial proceedings." 393 US 440 (1969).

Upon demand, the Georgia Supreme Court held: "1. The Supreme Court of the United States having stricken a portion of Georgia's implied trust theory, the remainder falls also, and there is no implied trust on the local church property in favor of the general church. 2. Since legal title to the property is in the local churches, the judgments sustaining their claims to such property are affirmed." 225 Ga 259 (1969). The United States Supreme Court denied *certiorari.* Compare *Maryland and Virginia Eldership of the Churches of God* v. *Church of God at Sharpsburg, Inc.,* 396 US 1041 (1970).

B. FREE EXERCISE OF RELIGION

Reynolds v. United States

98 US 145, 25 L Ed 244 (1879)

A person's religious belief cannot be accepted as a justification for his committing an overt act, to wit, polygamy, made criminal by the law of the land.

MR. CHIEF JUSTICE WAITE delivered the opinion of the Court. . . .

On the trial, the plaintiff in error [George Reynolds] . . . proved that at the time of his alleged second marriage he was, and for many years before had been, a member of the Church of Jesus Christ of Latter-Day Saints, commonly called the Mormon Church, and a believer in its doctrines; that it was an accepted doctrine of that church "that it was the duty of male members of said church, circumstances permitting, to practice polygamy; . . . that this duty was enjoined by different books which the members of said church believed to be of divine origin, and among others the Holy Bible, and also that the members of the church believed that the practice of polygamy was directly enjoined upon the male members thereof by the Almighty God, in a revelation of Joseph Smith, the founder and prophet of said church; that the failing or refusing to practise polygamy by such male members of said church, when circumstances would admit, would be punished, and that the penalty for such failure and refusal would be damnation in the life to come." . . .

Upon this proof he asked the court to instruct the jury that if they found from the evidence that he "was married as charged—if he was married—in pursuance of and in conformity with what he believed at the time to be a religious duty, that the verdict must be 'not guilty'." This request was refused, and the court did charge "that there must have been a ciminal intent, but that if the defendant, under the influence of a religious belief that it was right,—under an inspiration, if you please, that it was right, —deliberately married a second time, having a first wife living, the want of consciousness of evil intent—the want of understanding on his part that he was committing a crime—did not excuse him; but the law inexorably in such case implies the criminal intent." . . .

The word "religion" is not defined in the Constitution. We must go elsewhere, therefore, to ascertain its meaning, and nowhere more appropriately, we think, than to the history of the times in the midst of which the provision was adopted. The precise point of the inquiry is, what is the religious freedom which has been guaranteed. . . .

[A]t the first session of the first Congress the amendment now under consideration was proposed with others by Mr. Madison. It met the views of the advocates of religious freedom, and was adopted. Mr. Jefferson afterwards, in reply to an address to him by a committee of the Danbury Baptist Association . . ., took occasion to say: "Believing with you that religion is a matter which lies solely between man and his God; that he owes account to none other for his faith or his worship; that the legislative powers of the government reach actions only, and not opinions,—I contemplate with sovereign reverence that act of the whole American people which declared that their legislature should 'make no law respecting an establishment of religion or prohibiting the free exercise thereof,' thus building a wall of separation between church and State. Adhering to this expression of the supreme will of the nation in behalf of the rights of conscience, I shall see with sincere satisfaction the progress of those sentiments which tend to restore man to all his natural rights, convinced he has no natural right in oposition to his social duties." Coming as this does from an acknowledged leader of the advocates of the measure, it may be accepted almost as an authoritative declaration of the scope and effect of the amendment thus secured. Congress was deprived of all legislative power over mere opinion, but was left free to reach actions which were in violation of social duties or subversive of good order.

Polygamy has always been odious among the northern and western nations of Europe, and, until the establishment of the Mormon Church, was almost exclusively a feature of the life of Asiatic and of African people. At common law, the second marriage was always void (2 Kent, Com 79), and from the earliest history of England polygamy has been treated as an offence against society. . . .

In our opinion, the statute immediately under consideration is within the legislative power of Congress. It is constitutional and valid as prescribing a rule of action for all those residing in the Territories, and in places over which the United States have exclusive control. This being so, the only question which remains is, whether those who make polygamy a part of their religion are excepted from the operation of the statute. If they are, then those who do not make polygamy a part of their religious belief may be found guilty and punished, while those who do, must be acquitted and go free. This would be introducing a new element into criminal law. Laws are made for the government of actions, and while they cannot interfere with mere religious belief and opinions, they may with practices. Suppose one believed that human sacrifices were a necessary part of religious worship, would it be seriously contended that the civil government under which he lived could not interfere to prevent a sacrifice? . . .

To permit this would be to make the professed doctrines of religious belief superior to the law of the land, and in effect to permit every citizen to become a law unto himself. Government could exist only in name under such circumstances. . . .

Judgment affirmed.

Pierce v. Society of Sisters

268 US 510, 45 S Ct 571, 69 L Ed 1070 (1925)

The fundamental theory of liberty upon which all governments of this union rest excludes any general power of the state to standardize its children by forcing them to accept instruction from public teachers only.

MR. JUSTICE MCREYNOLDS delivered the opinion of the Court.

These appeals are from decrees, based upon undenied allegations, which granted preliminary orders restraining appellants [Walter M. Pierce, Governor of Oregon, et al.] from threatening or attempting to enforce the Compulsory Education Act adopted November 7, 1922, under the initiative provision of her Constitution by the voters of Oregon. . . .

The challenged Act, effective September 1, 1926, requires every parent, guardian or other person having control or charge or custody of a child between eight and sixteen years to send him "to a public school for the period of time a public school shall be held during the current year" in the district where the child resides; and failure so to do is declared a misdemeanor. . . .

Appellee, the Society of Sisters, is an Oregon Corporation, organized in 1880, with power to care for orphans, educate and instruct the youth, establish and maintain academies or schools, and acquire necessary real and personal property. It has long devoted its property and effort to the secular and religious education and care of children, and has acquired the valuable good will of many parents and guardians. It conducts interdependent primary and high schools and junior colleges, and maintains orphanages for the custody and control of children between eight and sixteen. . . .

Under the doctrine of *Meyer* v. *Nebraska,* 262 US 390, we think it entirely plain that the Act of 1922 unreasonably interferes with the liberty of parents and guardians to direct the upbringing and education of children under their control. As often heretofore pointed out, rights guaranteed by the Constitution may not be abridged by legislation which has no reasonable relation to some purpose within the competency of the State. The fundamental theory of liberty upon which all governments in this Union repose excludes any general power of the State to standardize its children by forcing them to accept instruction from public teachers only. The child is not the mere creature of the State; those who nurture him and direct his destiny have the right, coupled with the high duty, to recognize and prepare him for additional obligations.

Appellees are corporations and therefore, it is said, they cannot claim for themselves the liberty which the Fourteenth Amendment guarantees. Accepted in the proper sense, this is true. . . . But they have business and property for which they claim protection. These are threatened with destruction through the unwarranted compulsion which appellants are exercising over present and prospective patrons of their schools. And this court has gone very far to protect against loss threatened by such action. . . .

Generally it is entirely true, as urged by counsel, that no person in any business has such an interest in possible customers as to enable him to restrain exercise of proper power of the State upon the ground that he will be deprived of patronage. But the injunctions here sought are not against the exercise of any *proper* power. Plaintiffs asked protection against arbitrary, unreasonable and unlawful interference with their business and property. . . .

The suits were not premature. The injury to appellees was present and very real, not a mere possibility in the remote future. If no relief had been possible prior to the effective date of the Act, the injury would have become irreparable. Prevention of impending injury by unlawful action is a well recognized function of courts of equity.

The decrees below are

Affirmed.

West Virginia Board of Education v. Barnette

319 US 624, 63 S Ct 1178, 87 L Ed 1628 (1943)

The action of a state in making it compulsory for children in the public schools to salute the flag and pledge allegiance violates the First and Fourteenth Amendments.

[In implementing a statute calling for courses of instruction designed to foster the ideals of Americanism, in 1941 the West Virginia Board of Education adopted a resolution making the salute of the flag and pledge of allegiance a regular part of a program of activities in the public schools. A similar resolution by a school board in Pennsylvania had been upheld in *Minersville School District* v. *Gobitis,* 310 US 586 (1940). Walter Barnette and others brought suit in a district court to enjoin enforcement of the West Virginia resolution against Jehovah's Witnesses. Their religious beliefs included a literal version of Exodus 20:4–5 which reads: "Thou shalt not make unto thee any graven image, or any likeness of anything that is in heaven above, or that is in the earth beneath, or that is in the water under the earth; thou shalt not bow down thyself to them nor serve them." They considered the flag to be an "image."]

MR. JUSTICE JACKSON delivered the opinion of the Court. . . .

This case calls upon us to reconsider a precedent decision, as the Court throughout its history often has been required to do. Before turning to the *Gobitis* case, however, it is desirable to notice certain characteristics by which this controversy is distinguished.

The freedom asserted by these appellees does not bring them into collision with rights asserted by any other individual. . . . Nor is there any question in this case that their behavior is peaceable and orderly. The sole conflict is between authority and rights of the individual. The State asserts power to condition access to public education on making a prescribed sign and profession and at the same time to coerce attendance by punishing both parent and child. The latter stand on a right of self-determination in matters that touch individual opinion and personal attitude.

As the present CHIEF JUSTICE [STONE] said in dissent in the *Gobitis* case, the State may "require teaching by instruction and study of all in our history and in the structure and organization of our government, including the guaranties of civil liberty, which tend to inspire patriotism and love of country." 310 US at 604. Here, however, we are dealing with a compulsion of students to declare a belief. They are not merely made acquainted with the flag salute so that they may be informed as to what it is or even what it means. The issue here is whether this slow and easily neglected route to aroused loyalties constitutionally may be shortcut by substituting a compulsory salute and slogan. This issue is not prejudiced by the Court's previous holding that where a State, without compelling attendance, extends college facilities to pupils who voluntarily enroll, it may prescribe military training as part of the course without offense to the Constitution. It was held that those who take advantage of its opportunities may not on ground of conscience refuse compliance with such conditions. *Hamilton* v. *Regents,* 293 US 245. In the present case attendance is not optional. That case is also to be distinguished from the present one because, independently of college privileges or requirements, the State has power to raise militia and impose the duties of service therein upon its citizens.

There is no doubt that, in connection with the pledges, the flag salute is a form of utterance. Symbolism is a primitive but effective way of communicating ideas. The use of an emblem or flag to symbolize some system, idea, institution, or personality, is a short cut from mind to mind. . . .

It is also to be noted that the compulsory flag salute and pledge requires affirmation of a belief and an attitude of mind. It is not clear whether the regulation contemplates that pupils forego any contrary convictions of their own and become unwilling converts to the prescribed ceremony or whether it will be acceptable if they simulate assent by words without belief and by a gesture barren of meaning. It is now a commonplace that censorship or suppression of expression of opinion is tolerated by our Constitution only when the expression presents a clear and present danger of action of a kind the State is empowered to prevent and punish. It would seem that involuntary affirmation could be commanded only on even more immediate and urgent grounds than silence. But here the power of compulsion is invoked without any allegation that remaining passive during a flag salute ritual creates a clear and present danger that would justify an effort even to muffle expression. To sustain the compulsory flag salute we are required to say that a Bill of Rights which guards the individual's right to speak his own mind, left it open to public authorities to compel him to utter what is not in his mind. . . .

If there is any fixed star in our constitutional constellation, it is that no official, high or petty, can prescribe what shall be orthodox in politics, nationalism, religion, or other matters of opinion or force citizens to confess by word or act their faith therein. If there are any circumstances which permit an exception, they do not now occur to us. . . .

The decision of this Court in *Minersville School District* v. *Gobitis* and the holdings of those few *per curiam* decisions which preceded and foreshadowed it are overruled, and the judgment enjoining enforcement of the West Virginia Regulation is

Affirmed.

[The concurring opinion of JUSTICES BLACK and DOUGLAS, and the dissenting opinions of JUSTICES ROBERTS, REED, and FRANKFURTER are omitted.]

Wisconsin v. Yoder

406 US 205, 92 S Ct 1526, 32 L Ed2d 15 (1972)

The importance of a simple way of life to their religion justifies the exemption of Amish children from compulsory high-school attendance.

MR. CHIEF JUSTICE BURGER delivered the opinion of the Court.

On petition of the State of Wisconsin, we granted the writ of *certiorari* in this case to review a decision of the Wisconsin Supreme Court holding that respondents' convictions of violating the State's compulsory school-attendance law were invalid under the Free Exercise Clause of the First Amendment to the United States Constitution made applicable to the States by the Fourteenth Amendment. For the reasons hereafter stated we affirm the judgment of the Supreme Court of Wisconsin.

Respondents Jonas Yoder and Wallace Miller are members of the Old Order Amish religion, and respondent Adin Yutzy is a member of the Conservative Amish Mennonite Church. They and their families are residents of Green County, Wisconsin. Wisconsin's compulsory school-attendance law required them to cause their children to attend public or private school until reaching age 16 but the respondents declined to send their children, ages 14 and 15, to public school after they completed the eighth grade. The children were not enrolled in any private school, or within any recognized exception to the compulsory-attendance law, and they are conceded to be subject to the Wisconsin statute.

On complaint of the school district administrator for the public schools, respondents were charged, tried, and convicted of violating the compulsory-attendance law in Green County Court and were fined the sum of $5 each. . . . The trial testimony showed that respondents believed, in accordance with the tenets of Old Order Amish communities generally, that their children's attendance at high school, public or private, was contrary to the Amish religion and way of life. They believed that by sending their children to high school, they would not only expose themselves to the danger of the censure of the church community, but, as found by the county court, also endanger their own salvation and that of their children. The State stipulated that respondents' religious beliefs were sincere.

In support of their position, respondents presented as expert witnesses scholars on religion and education whose testimony is uncontradicted. . . .

A . . . feature of Old Order Amish communities is their devotion to a life in harmony with nature and the soil, as exemplified by the simple life of the early Christian era that continued in America during much of our early national life. . . .

Amish objection to formal education beyond the eighth grade is firmly grounded in these central religious concepts. They object to the high school, and higher education generally, because the values they teach are in marked variance with Amish values and the Amish way of life; they view secondary school education as an impermissible exposure of their children to a "worldly" influence in conflict with their beliefs. . . .

Formal high school education beyond the eighth grade is contrary to Amish beliefs, not only because it places Amish children in an environment hostile to Amish beliefs with increasing emphasis on competition in class work and sports and with pressure to conform to the styles, manners, and ways of the peer group, but also because it takes them away from their community, physically and emotionally, during the crucial and formative adolescent period of life. During this period, the children must acquire Amish attitudes favoring manual work and self-reliance and the specific skills needed to perform the adult role of an Amish farmer or housewife. . . .

The Amish do not object to elementary education through the first eight grades as a general proposition because they agree that their children must have basic skills in the "three R's" in order to read the Bible, to be good farmers and citizens, and to be able to deal with non-Amish people when necessary in the course of daily affairs. . . .

There is no doubt as to the power of a State, having a high responsibility for education of its citizens, to impose reasonable regulations for the control and duration of basic education. See, *e.g., Pierce* v. *Society of Sisters,* 268 US 510, 534 (1925). Providing public schools ranks at the very apex of the function of a State. Yet even this paramount responsibility was, in *Pierce,* made to yield to the right of parents to provide an equivalent education in a privately operated system. There the Court held that Oregon's statute compelling attendance in a public school from age eight to age 16 unreasonably interfered with the interest of parents in directing the rearing of their offspring, including their education in church-operated schools. As that case suggests, the values of parental direction of the religious upbringing and education of their children in their early and formative years have a high place in our society. . . . Thus, a State's interest in universal education, however highly we rank it, is not totally free from a balancing process when it impinges on fundamental rights and interests, such as those specifically protected by the Free Exercise Clause of the First Amendment, and the traditional interest of parents with respect to the religious upbringing of their children so long as they, in the words of *Pierce,* "prepare [them] for additional obligations." 268 US, at 535.

It follows that in order for Wisconsin to compel school attendance beyond the eighth grade against a claim that such attendance interferes with the practice of a legitimate religious belief, it must appear either that the State does not deny the free exercise of religious belief by its requirement, or that there is a state interest of sufficient magnitude to override the interest claiming protection under the Free Exercise Clause. . . .

Giving no weight to such secular considerations. . . . we see that the record in this case abundantly supports the claim that the traditional way of life of the Amish is not merely a matter of personal preference, but one of deep religious conviction, shared by an organized group, and intimately related to daily living. . . .

. . . Their rejection of telephones, automobiles, radios, and television, their mode of dress, of speech, their habits of manual work do indeed set them apart from much of contemporary society; these customs are both symbolic and practical.

As the society around the Amish has become more populous, urban , industrialized, and complex, particularly in this century, government regulation of human affairs has correspondingly become more detailed and pervasive. The Amish mode of life has thus come into conflict increasingly with requirements of contemporary society exerting a hydraulic insistence on conformity to majoritarian standards. So long as compulsory education laws were confined to eight grades of elementary basic education imparted in a nearby rural schoolhouse, with a large proportion of students of the Amish faith, the Old Order Amish had little basis to fear that school attendance would expose their children to the worldly influence they reject. But modern compulsory secondary education in rural areas is now largely carried on in a consolidated school, often remote from the student's home and alien to his daily home life. As the record so strongly shows, the values and programs of the modern secondary school are in sharp conflict with the fundamental mode of life mandated by the Amish religion; modern laws requiring compulsory secondary education have accordingly engendered great concern and conflict. The conclusion is inescapable that secondary schooling . . . contravenes the basic religious tenets and practice of the Amish faith, both as to the parent and the child.

The impact of the compulsory-attendance law on respondents' practice of the Amish religion is not only severe, but inescapable, for the Wisconsin law affirmatively compels them, under threat of criminal sanction, to perform acts undeniably at odds with fundamental tenets of their religious beliefs. . . . It carries with it precisely the kind of objective danger to the free exercise of religion that the First Amendment was designed to prevent. As the record shows, compulsory school attendance to age 16 for Amish children carries with it a very real threat of undermining the Amish community and religious practice as they exist today; they must either abandon belief and be assimilated into society at large, or be forced to migrate to some other and more tolerant region. . . .

Wisconsin concedes that under the Religion Clauses religious beliefs are absolutely free from the State's control, but it argues that "actions," even though religiously grounded, are outside the protection of the First Amendment. But our decisions have rejected the idea that religiously grounded conduct is always outside the protection of the Free Exercise Clause. It is true that activities of individuals, even when religiously based, are often subject to regulation by the States in the exercise of their undoubted power to promote the health, safety, and general welfare, or the Federal Government in the exercise of its delegated powers. See, *e.g., Gillette* v. *United States,* 401 US 437 (1971); *Braunfeld* v. *Brown,* 366 US 599 (1961); *Prince* v. *Massachusetts,* 321 US 158 (1944); *Reynolds* v. *United States,* 98 US 145 (1879). But to agree that religiously grounded conduct must often be subject to the broad police power of the State is not to deny that there are areas of conduct protected by the Free Exercise Clause of the First Amendment and thus beyond the power of the State to control, even under regulations of general applicability. *E.g., Sherbert* v. *Verner,* 374 US 398 (1963); *Murdock* v. *Pennsylvania,* 319 US 105 (1943); *Cantwell* v. *Connecticut,* 310 US 296, 303–304 (1940). This case, therefore, does not become easier because respondents were convicted for their "actions" in refusing to send their children to the public high school; in this context belief and action cannot be neatly confined in logic-tight compartments. . . .

The State attacks respondents' position as one fostering "ignorance" from which the child must be protected by the State. No one can question the State's duty to protect children from ignorance but this argument does not square with the facts disclosed in the record. Whatever their idiosyncrasies as seen by the majority, this record strongly shows that the Amish community has been a highly successful social unit within our society, even if apart from the conventional "mainstream." . . .

It is neither fair nor correct to suggest that the Amish are opposed to education beyond the eighth grade level. What this record shows is that they are opposed to conventional formal education of the type provided by a certified high school because it comes at the child's crucial adolescent period of religious development. . . .

There is nothing in this record to suggest that the Amish qualities of reliability, self-reliance, and dedication to work would fail to find ready markets in today's society. Absent some contrary evidence supporting the State's position, we are unwilling to assume that persons possessing such valuable vocational skills and habits are doomed to become burdens on society should they determine to leave the Amish faith, nor is there any basis in the record to warrant a finding that an additional one or two years of formal school education beyond the eighth grade would serve to eliminate any such problem that might exist. . . .

For the reasons stated we hold, with the Supreme Court of Wisconsin, that the First and Fourteenth Amendments prevent the State from compelling respondents to cause their children to attend formal high school to age 16. . . . It cannot be overemphasized that we are not dealing with a way of life and mode of education by a group claiming to have recently discovered some "progressive" or more enlightened process for rearing children for modern life. . . .

Affirmed.

[The concurring opinions of JUSTICES STEWART and WHITE and the opinion of JUSTICE DOUGLAS, dissenting in part, are omitted here.]

C. ESTABLISHMENT OF RELIGION

Everson v. Board of Education

330 US 1, 67 S Ct 504, 91 L Ed 711 (1947)

Pursuant to a New Jersey statute authorizing district boards of education to make rules and contracts for the transportation of children to and from schools other than private schools operated for profit, a board of education by resolution authorized the reimbursement of parents for fares paid for the transportation by public carrier of children attending public and Catholic schools. *Held:* The expenditure of tax-raised funds thus authorized was for a public purpose and did not violate the due process clause of the Fourteenth Amendment. . . .

MR. JUSTICE BLACK delivered the opinion of the Court.

A New Jersey statute authorizes its local school districts to make rules and contracts for the transportation of children to and from schools. The appellee, a township board of education, acting pursuant to this statute, authorized reimbursement to parents of money expended by them for the bus transportation of their children on regular busses operated by the public transportation system. Part of this money was for the payment of transportation of some children in the community to Catholic parochial schools. These church schools give their students, in addition to secular education, regular religious instruction conforming to the religious tenets and modes of worship of the Catholic Faith. The superintendent of these schools is a Catholic priest.

The appellant [Arch R. Everson], in his capacity as a district taxpayer, filed suit in a state court challenging the right of the Board to reimburse parents of parochial school students. He contended that the statute and the resolution passed pursuant to it violated both the State and the Federal Constitutions. . . . The case is here on appeal. . . .

The New Jersey statute is challenged as a "law respecting an establishment of religion." The First Amendment, as made applicable to the states by the Fourteenth, commands that a state "shall make no law respecting an establishment of religion, or prohibiting the free exercise thereof. . . ."

The "establishment of religion" clause of the First Amendment means at least this: Neither a state nor the Federal Government can set up a church. Neither can pass laws which aid one religion, aid all religions, or prefer one religion over another. Neither can force nor influence a person to go to or to remain away from church against his will or force him to profess a belief or disbelief in any religion. No person can be punished for entertaining or professing religious beliefs or disbeliefs, for church attendance or non-attendance. No tax in any amount, large or small, can be levied to support any religious activities or institutions, whatever they may be called, or whatever form they may adopt to teach or practice religion. Neither a state nor the Federal Government can, openly or secretly, participate in the affairs of any religious organizations or groups and *vice versa*. In the words of Jefferson, the clause against establishment of religion by law was intended to erect "a wall of separation between church and State." . . .

We must consider the New Jersey statute in accordance with the foregoing limitations imposed by the First Amendment. But we must not strike that state statute down if it is within the States's constitutional power even though it approaches the verge of that power. . . . New Jersey cannot hamper its citizens in the free exercise of their own religion. Consequently, it cannot exclude individual Catholics, Lutherans, Mohammedans, Baptists, Jews, Methodists, Non-believers, Presbyterians, or the members of any other faith, *because of their faith, or lack of it,* from receiving the benefits of public welfare legislation. While we do not mean to intimate that a state could not provide transportation only to children attending public schools, we must be careful, in protecting the citizens of New Jersey against state-established churches, to be sure that we do not inadvertently prohibit New Jersey from extending its general state law benefits to all its citizens without regard to their religious belief.

Measured by these standards, we cannot say that the First Amendment prohibits New Jersey from spending tax-raised funds to pay the bus fares of parochial school pupils as a part of a general program under which it pays the fares of pupils attending public and other schools. . . .

Affirmed.

MR. JUSTICE JACKSON, dissenting.

I find myself, contrary to first impressions, unable to join in this decision. I have a sympathy, though it is not ideological, with Catholic citizens who are compelled by law to pay taxes for public schools, and also feel constrained by conscience and discipline to support other schools for their own children. Such relief to them as this case involves is not in itself a serious burden to taxpayers and I had assumed it to be as little serious in principle. Study of this case convinces me otherwise. The Court's opinion marshals every argument in favor of state aid and puts the case in its most favorable light, but much of its reasoning confirms my conclusions that there are no good grounds upon which to support the present legislation. In fact, the undertones of the opinion, advocating complete and uncompromising separation of Church from State, seem utterly discordant with its conclusion yielding support to their commingling in educational matters. The case which irresistibly comes to mind as the most fitting precedent is that of Julia who, according to Byron's reports, "whispering 'I will ne'er consent,'—consented." . . .

Whether the taxpayer constitutionally can be made to contribute aid to parents of students because of their attendance at parochial schools depends upon the nature of those schools and their relation to the Church. . . .

The function of the Church school is a subject on which this record is meager. It shows only that the schools are under superintendence of a priest and that "religion is taught as part of the curriculum." But we know that such schools are parochial only in name—they, in fact, represent a world-wide and age-old policy of the Roman Catholic Church. Under the rubric "Catholic Schools," the Canon Law of the Church, by which all Catholics are bound, provides:

"1215. Catholic children are to be educated in schools where not only nothing contrary to Catholic faith and morals is taught, but rather in schools where religious and moral training occupy first place. . . ."

[W]e cannot have it both ways. Religious teaching cannot be a private affair when the state seeks to impose regulations which infringe on it indirectly, and a public affair when it comes to taxing citizens of one faith to aid another, or those of no faith to aid all. If these principles seem harsh in prohibiting aid to Catholic education, it must not be forgotten that it is the same Constitution that alone assures Catholics the right to maintain these schools at all when predominant local sentiment would forbid them. . . . Nor should I think that those who have done so well without this aid would want to see this separation between Church and State broken down. If the state may aid these religious schools, it may therefore regulate them. Many groups have sought aid from tax funds only to find that it carried political controls with it. Indeed this Court has declared that "It is hardly lack of due process for the Government to regulate that which it subsidizes." *Wickard* v. *Filburn,* 317 US 111, 131. . . .

MR. JUSTICE FRANKFURTER joins in this opinion.

[A dissenting opinion by JUSTICE RUTLEDGE, joined by JUSTICES FRANKFURTER, JACKSON, and BURTON, is omitted.]

Zorach v. Clauson

343 US 306, 72 S Ct 679, 96 L Ed 954 (1952)

New York City permits its public schools to release students during school hours, on written requests of their parents, so that they may leave the school buildings and grounds and go to religious centers for religious instruction or devotional exercises. By this system, New York has neither prohibited the "free exercise" of religion nor made a law "respecting an establishment of religion" within the meaning of the First Amendment.

MR. JUSTICE DOUGLAS delivered the opinion of the Court.

New York City has a program which permits its public schools to release students during the school day so that they may leave the school buildings and school grounds and go to religious centers for religious instruction or devotional exercises. A student is released on written request of his parents. Those not released stay in the classrooms. The churches make weekly reports to the schools, sending a list of children who have been released from public school but who have not reported for religious instruction.

This "released time" program involves neither religious instruction in public school classrooms nor the expenditure of public funds. All costs, including the application blanks, are paid by the religious organizations. The case is therefore unlike *McCollum* v. *Board of Education,* 333 US 203, which involved a "released time" program from Illinois. In that case the classrooms were turned over to religious instructors. We accordingly held that the program violated the First Amendment which (by reason of the Fourteenth Amendment) prohibits the states from establishing religion or prohibiting its free exercise.

Appellants [Tessim Zorach *et al.*], who are taxpayers and residents of New York City and whose children attend its public schools, challenge the present law, contending it is in essence not different from the one involved in the *McCollum* case. Their argument, stated elaborately in various ways, reduces itself to this: the weight and influence of the school is put behind a program for religious instruction; public school teachers police it, keeping tab on students who are released; the classroom activities come to a halt while the students who are released for religious instruction are on leave; the school is a crutch on which the churches are leaning for support in their religious training; without the cooperation of the schools this "released time" program, like the one in the McCollum case, would be futile and ineffective. . . .

There is a suggestion that the system involves the use of coercion to get public school students into religious classrooms. There is no evidence in the record before us that supports that conclusion. The present record indeed tells us that the school authorities [Andrew O. Clauson *et al.*] are neutral in this regard and do no more than release students whose parents so request. If in fact coercion were used, if it were established that any one or more teachers were using their office to persuade or force students to take the religious instruction, a wholly different case would be presented. Hence we put aside that claim of coercion both as respects the "free exercise" of religion and "an establishment of religion" within the meaning of the First Amendment. . . .

The First Amendment . . . does not say that in every and all respects there shall be a separation of Church and State. Rather, it studiously defines the manner, the specific ways, in which there shall be no concert or union or dependency one on the other. That is the common sense of the matter. Otherwise the state and religion would be aliens to each other—hostile, suspicious, and even unfriendly. Churches could not be required to pay even property taxes. Municipalities would not be permitted to render police or fire protection to religious groups. Policemen who helped parishioners into their places of worship would violate the Constitution. Prayers in our legislative halls; the appeals to the Almighty in the messages of the Chief Executive; the proclamations making Thanksgiving Day a holiday; "so help me God" in our courtroom oaths—these and all other references to the Almighty that run through our laws, our public rituals, our ceremonies would be flouting the First Amendment. A fastidious atheist or agnostic could even object to the supplication with which the Court opens each session: "God save the United States and this Honorable Court."

We would have to press the concept of separation of Church and State to these extremes to condemn the present law on constitutional grounds. The nullification of this law would have wide and profound effects. A Catholic student applies to his teacher for permission to leave the school during hours on a Holy Day of Obligation to attend a mass. A Jewish student asks his teacher for permission to be excused for Yom Kippur. A Protestant wants the afternoon off for a family baptismal ceremony. In each case the teacher requires parental consent in writing. In each case the teacher, in order to make sure the student is not a truant, goes further and requires a report from the priest, the rabbi, or the minister. The teacher in other words cooperates in a religious program to the extent of making it possible for her students to participate in it. Whether she does it occasionally for a few students, regularly for one, or pursuant to a systematized program designed to further the religious needs of all the students does not alter the character of the act.

We are a religious people whose institutions presuppose a Supreme Being. We guarantee the freedom to worship as one chooses. We make room for as wide a variety of beliefs and creeds as the spiritual needs of man deem necessary. We sponsor an atitude on the part of government that shows no partiality to any one group and that lets each flourish according to the zeal of its adherents and the appeal of its dogma. When the state encourages religious instruction or cooperates with religious authorities by adjusting the schedule of public events to sectarian needs, it follows the best of our traditions. For it then respects the religious nature of our people and accommodates the public service to their spiritual needs. To hold that it may not would be to find in the Constitution a requirement that the government show a callous indifference to religious groups. That would be preferring those who believe in no religion over those who do believe. Government may not finance religious groups nor undertake religious instruction nor blend secular and sectarian education nor use secular institutions to force one or some religion on any person. But we find no constitutional requirement which makes it necessary for government to be hostile to religion and to throw its weight against efforts to widen the effective scope of religious influence. . . .

Affirmed.

MR. JUSTICE BLACK, dissenting.

Illinois ex rel. McCollum v. *Board of Education,* 333 US 203, held invalid as an "establishment of religion" an Illinois system under which school children, compelled by law to go to public schools, were freed from some hours of required school work on condition that they attend special religious classes held in the school buildings. Although the classes were taught by sectarian teachers neither employed nor paid by the state, the state did use its power to further the program by releasing some of the children from regular class work, insisting that those released attend the religious classes, and requiring that those who remained behind do some kind of academic work while the others received their religious training. We said this about the Illinois system:

> "Pupils compelled by law to go to school for secular education are released in part from their legal duty upon the condition that they attend the religious classes. This is beyond all question a utilization of the tax-established and tax-supported public school system to aid religious groups to spread their faith. And it falls squarely under the ban of the First Amendment. . . ." *McCollum* v. *Board of Education, supra,* at pp. 209–210.

I see no significant difference between the invalid Illinois system and that of New York here sustained. Except for the use of the school buildings in Illinois, there is no difference between the systems which I consider even worthy of mention. . . .

State help to religion injects political and party prejudices into a holy field. It too often substitutes force for prayer, hate for love, and persecution for persuasion. Government should not be allowed, under cover of the soft euphemism of "co-operation," to steal into the sacred area of religious choice.

[Dissenting opinions by JUSTICES FRANKFURTER and JACKSON are omitted.]

School District of Abington v. Schempp

374 US 203, 83 S Ct 1560, 10 L Ed 844 (1963)

No state law or school board may require that passages from the Bible be read or that the Lord's Prayer be recited in the public schools.

MR. JUSTICE CLARK delivered the opinion of the Court. . . .

These companion cases present the issue [of the constitutionality] of state action requiring that schools begin each day with readings from the Bible. . . .

The facts in . . . No. 142. The Commonwealth of Pennsylvania by law . . . requires that "At least ten verses from the Holy Bible shall be read without comment, at the opening of each public school on each school day. Any child shall be excused from such Bible reading, or attending such Bible reading, upon the written request of his parent or guardian." The Schempp family, husband and wife and two of their three children, brought suit to enjoin enforcement of the statute, contending that their rights under the Fourteenth Amendment to the Constitution of the United States are, have been, and will continue to be violated unless this statute be declared unconstitutional. . . . A three-judge District Court . . . held that the statute is violative of the Establishment Clause. . . . On appeal by the [School] District. . . . we noted probable jurisdiction.

No. 119. In 1905 the Board of School Commissioners of Baltimore City adopted a rule pursuant to Art 77, § 202 of the Annotated Code of Maryland. The rule provided for the holding of opening exercises in the schools of the city, consisting primarily of the "reading, without comment, of a chapter in the Holy Bible and/or the use of the Lord's Prayer." The petitioners, Mrs. Madalyn Murray and her son, William J. Murray III, are both professed atheists. Following unsuccessful attempts to have the respondent school board rescind the rule, this suit was filed for *mandamus* to compel its rescission and cancellation. . . .

As we have indicated, the Establishment Clause has been directly considered by this Court eight times in the past score of years and, with only one Justice dissenting on the point, it has consistently held that the clause withdrew all legislative power respecting religious belief or the expression thereof. The test may be stated as follows: what are the purpose and the primary effect of the enactment? If either is the advancement or inhibition of religion then the enactment exceeds the scope of legislative power as circumscribed by the Constitution. That is to say that to withstand the strictures of the Establishment Clause there must be a secular legislative purpose and a primary effect that neither advances nor inhibits religion. . . .

The conclusion follows that in both cases the laws require religious exercises and such exercises are being conducted in direct violation of the rights of the appellees and petitioners. Nor are these required exercises mitigated by the fact that individual students may absent themselves upon parental request, for that fact furnishes no defense to a claim of unconstitutionality under the Establishment Clause. See *Engel* v. *Vitale* . . . [370 US 421] at 430. . . .

It is insisted that unless these religious exercises are permitted a "religion of secularism" is established in the schools. We agree of course that the State may not establish a "religion of secularism" in the sense of affirmatively opposing or showing hostility to religion, thus "preferring those who believe in no religion over those who do believe." *Zorach* v. *Clauson, supra,* at 314. We do not agree, however, that this decision in any sense has that effect. In addition, it might well be said that one's education is not complete without a study of comparative religion or the history of religion and its relationship to the advancement of civilization. It certainly may be said that the Bible is worthy of study for its literary and historic qualities. Nothing we have said here indicates that such study of the Bible or of religion, when presented objectively as part of a secular program of education, may not be effected consistently with the First Amendment. But the exercises here do not fall into those categories. They are religious exercises, required by the States in violation of the command of the First Amendment that the Government maintain strict neutrality, neither aiding nor opposing religion.

Finally, we cannot accept that the concept of neutrality, which does not permit a State to require a religious exercise even with the consent of the majority of those affected, collides with the majority's right to free exercise of religion. While the Free Exercise Clause clearly prohibits the use of state action to deny the rights of free exercise to *anyone,* it has never meant that a majority could use the machinery of the State to practice its beliefs. . . .

The place of religion in our society is an exalted one, achieved through a long tradition of reliance on the home, the church and the inviolable citadel of the individual heart and mind. We have come to recognize through bitter experience that it is not within the power of government to invade that citadel, whether its purpose or effect be to aid or oppose, to advance or retard. In the relationship between man and religion, the State is firmly committed to a position of neutrality. Though the application of that rule requires interpretation of a delicate sort, the rule itself is clearly and concisely stated in the words of the First Amendment. Applying that rule to the facts of these cases, we affirm the judgment in No. 142. In No. 119, the judgment is reversed and the cause remanded to the Maryland Court of Appeals for further proceedings consistent with this opinion.

It is so ordered.

[Concurring opinions by Justices Douglas and Brennan and a dissenting opinion by Justice Stewart are omitted.]

Committee for Public Education v. Nyquist

413 US 756, 93 S Ct 2955, L Ed2d (1973)

A law that has a primary effect that advances religion is void.

Mr. Justice Powell delivered the opinion of the Court. . . .

In May 1972, the Governor of New York signed into law several amendments to the State's Education and Tax Laws. The first five sections of these amendments established three distinct financial aid programs for nonpublic elementary and secondary schools.

Almost immediately after the signing of these measures a complaint was filed in the United States District Court for the Southern District of New York challenging each of the three forms of aid as violative of the Establishment Clause. The plaintiffs were an unincorporated association known as the Committee for Public Education and Religious Liberty (PEARL), and several individuals who were residents and taxpayers in New York, some of whom had children attending public schools. Named as defendants were the State Commissioner of Education [Ewald B. Nyquist], the Comptroller, and the Commissioner of Taxation and Finance. . . .

The first section of the challenged enactment, entitled "Health and Safety Grants for Nonpublic School Children," provides for direct money grants from the State to "qualifying" nonpublic schools to be used for the "maintenance and repair of . . . school facilities and equipment to ensure the health, welfare and safety of enrolled pupils." A "qualifying" school is any nonpublic, nonprofit elementary or secondary school which "has been designated during the [immediately preceding] year as serving a high concentration of pupils from low-income families for purposes of Title IV of the Federal Higher Education Act of 1965. . . ." Such schools are entitled to receive a grant of $30 per pupil per year, or $40 per pupil per year if the facilities are more than 25 years old. Each school is required to submit to the Commissioner of Education an audited statement of its expenditures for maintenance and repair during the preceding year, and its grant may not exceed the total of such expenses. The Commissioner is also required to ascertain the average per-pupil cost for equivalent maintenance and repair services in the public schools, and in no event may the grant to nonpublic qualifying schools exceed 50% of that figure. . . .

The remainder of the challenged legislation—§§ 2 through 5—is a single package captioned the "Elementary and Secondary Education Opportunity Program." It is composed, essentially, of two parts, a tuition grant program and a tax benefit program. Section 2 establishes a limited plan providing tuition reimbursements to parents of children attending elementary or secondary nonpublic schools. To qualify under this section the parent must have an annual taxable income of less than $5,000. The amount of reimbursement is limited to $50 for each grade school child and $100 for each high school child. Each parent is required, however, to submit to the Commissioner of Education a verified statement containing a receipted tuition bill, and the amount of state reimbursement may not exceed 50% of that figure. No restrictions are imposed on the use of the funds by the reimbursed parents.

This section, like § 1, is prefaced by a series of legislative findings designed to explain the impetus for the State's action. Expressing a dedication to the "vitality of our pluralistic society," the findings state that a "healthy competitive and diverse alternative to public education is not only desirable but indeed vital to a state and nation that have continually reaffirmed the value of individual differences." The findings further emphasize that the right to select among alternative educational systems "is diminished or even denied to children of lower-income families, whose parents, of all groups, have the least options in determining where their children are to be educated." Turning to the public schools, the findings state that any "precipitous decline in the number of nonpublic school pupils would cause a massive increase in public school enrollment and costs," an increase that would "aggravate an already serious fiscal crisis in public education" and would "seriously jeapardize the quality education for all children. . . ."

The remainder of the "Elementary and Secondary Education Opportunity Program," contained in §§ 3, 4, and 5 of the challenged law, is designed to provide a form of tax relief to those who fail to qualify for tuition reimbursement. . . .

The history of the Establishment Clause has been recounted frequently and need not be repeated here. . . . What our cases require is careful examination of any law challenged on establishment grounds with a view to ascertaining whether it furthers any of the evils against which that Clause protects. Primary among those evils have been "sponsorship, financial support, and active involvement of the sovereign in religious activity. . . ."

The "maintenance and repair" provisions of § 1 authorize direct payments to nonpublic schools, virtually all of which are Roman Catholic schools in low income areas. The grants, totaling $30 or $40 per pupil depending on the age of the institution, are given largely without restriction on usage. So long as expenditures do not exceed 50% of comparable expenses in the public school system, it is possible for a sectarian elementary or secondary school to finance its entire "maintenance and repair" budget from state tax-raised funds. No attempt is made to restrict payments to those expenditures related to the upkeep of facilities used exclusively for secular purposes, nor do we think it possible within the context of these religion-oriented institutions to impose such restrictions. . . .

The state officials nevertheless argue that these expenditures for "maintenance and repair" are similar to other financial expenditures approved by this Court. Primarily they rely on *Everson* v. *Board of Education, supra; Board of Education* v. *Allen, supra;* and *Tilton* v. *Richardson, supra.* . . .

These cases simply recognize that sectarian schools perform secular, educative functions as well as religious functions, and that some forms of aid may be channelled to the secular without providing direct aid to the sectarian. . . .

What we have said demonstrates that New York's maintenance and repair provisions violate the Establishment Clause because their effect, inevitably, is to subsidize and advance the religious mission of sectarian schools. . . .

New York's tuition reimbursement program also fails the "effect" test, for much the same reasons that govern its maintenance and repair grants. The state program is designed to allow direct, unrestricted grants of $50 to $100 per child (but no more than 50% of tuition actually paid) as reimbursement to parents in low-income brackets who send their children to nonpublic schools. To qualify, a parent must have earned less than $5,000 in taxable income and must present a receipted tuition bill from a nonpublic school, the bulk of which are concededly sectarian in orientation.

There can be no question that these grants could not, consistently with the Establishment Clause, be given directly to sectarian schools, since they would suffer from the same deficiency that renders invalid the grants for maintenance and repair. . . . The controlling question here, then, is whether the fact that the grants are delivered to parents rather than schools is of such significance as to compel a contrary result. The State and intervenor-appellees rely on *Everson* and *Allen* for their claim that grants to parents, unlike grants to institutions, respect the "wall of separation" required by the Constitution. . . .

In *Everson,* the Court found the bus fare program analogous to the provision of services such as police and fire protection, sewage disposal, highways, and sidewalks for parochial schools. . . . Such services, provided in common to all citizens, are "so separate and so indisputably marked off from the religious function," *id.,* at 18, that they may fairly be viewed as reflections of a neutral posture toward religious institutions. *Allen* is founded upon a similar principle. The Court there repeatedly emphasized that upon the record in that case there was no indication that textbooks would be provided for anything other than purely secular courses. "Of course books are different from buses. Most bus rides have no inherent religious significance, while religious books are common. However, the language of [the law under consideration] does not authorize the loan of religious books, and the State claims no right to distribute religious literature. . . . Absent evidence, we cannot assume that school authorities . . . are unable to distinguish between secular and religious books or that they will not honestly discharge their duties under the law." . . .

The tuition grants here are subject to no such restrictions. There has been no endeavor "to guarantee the separation between secular and religious educational functions and to ensure that State financial aid supports only the former." *Lemon* v. *Kurtzman, supra,* at 613. Indeed, it is precisely the function of New York's law to provide assistance to private schools, the great majority of which are sectarian. By reimbursing parents for a portion of their tuition bill, the State seeks to relieve their financial burdens sufficiently to assure that they continue to have the option to send their children to religion-oriented schools. And while the other purposes for that aid— to perpetuate a pluralistic educational environment and to protect the fiscal integrity of overburdened public schools—are certainly unexceptionable, the effect of the aid is unmistakably to provide desired financial support for nonpublic, sectarian institutions. . . .

Finally, the State argues that its program of tuition grants should survive scrutiny because it is designed to promote the free exercise of religion. The State notes that only "low-income parents" are aided by this law, and without state assistance their right to have their children educated in a religious environment "is diminished or even denied." It is true, of course, that this Court has long recognized and maintained the right to choose nonpublic over public education. *Pierce* v. *Society of Sisters,* 268 US 510 (1925). It is also true that a state law interfering with a parent's right to have his child educated in a sectarian school would run afoul of the Free Exercise Clause. But this Court repeatedly has recognized that tension inevitably exists between the Free Exercise and the Establishment Clauses, . . . and that it may often not be possible to promote the former without offending the latter. As a result of this tension, our cases require the State to maintain an attitude of "neutrality," neither "advancing" nor "inhibiting" religion. In its attempt to enhance the opportunities of the poor to choose between public and nonpublic education, the State has taken a step which can only be regarded as one "advancing" religion. However great our sympathy, *Everson* v. *Board of Education, supra,* at 18 (Jackson, J., dissenting), for the burdens experienced by those who must pay public school taxes at the same time that they support other schools because of the constraints of "conscience and discipline," *ibid.,* and notwithstanding the "high social importance" of the State's purposes, *Wisconsin* v. *Yoder,* 406 US 205, 214 (1972), neither may justify an eroding of the limitations of the Establishment Clause now firmly emplanted.

Sections, 3, 4, and 5 . . . allow parents of children attending nonpublic elementary and secondary schools to subtract from adjusted gross income a specified amount if they do not receive a tuition reimbursement under § 2, and if they have an adjusted gross income of less than $25,000. . . .

In . . . light of the practical similarity between . . . [the] tax and tuition reimbursement programs, we hold that neither form of aid is sufficiently restricted to assure that
it will not have the impermissible effect of advancing the sectarian activities of religious
schools.

Because we have found that the challenged sections have the impermissible effect of
advancing religion, we need not consider whether such aid would result in entanglement of the State with religion in the sense of "[a] comprehensive, discriminating, and
continuing state surveillance." *Lemon* v. *Kurtzman,* 403 US, at 619. But the importance of the competing societal interests implicated in this case prompts us to make the
further observation that, apart from any specific entanglement of the State in particular
religious programs, assistance of the sort here involved carries grave potential for entanglement in the broader sense of continuing political strife over aid to religion. . . .

MR. CHIEF JUSTICE BURGER, joined in part by MR. JUSTICE WHITE, and joined by
MR. JUSTICE REHNQUIST, concurring in part and dissenting in part.

I join in that part of the Court's opinion which hold the New York "maintenance
and repair" provision unconstitutional under the Establishment Clause because it is a
direct aid to religion. I disagree, however, with the Court's decisions in *Nyquist* and
in *Sloan* v. *Lemon, post,* to strike down the New York and Pennsylvania tuition grant
programs and the New York tax relief provisions. . . .

While there is no straight line running through our decisions interpreting the Establishment and Free Exercise clauses of the First Amendment, our cases do, it seems to
me, lay down one solid, basic principle: that the Establishment Clause does not forbid
governments, state or federal, from enacting a program of general welfare under which
benefits are distributed to private individuals, even though many of those individuals
may elect to use those benefits in ways that "aid" religious instruction or worship. . . .

The essence of all these decisions, I suggest, is that government aid to individuals generally stands on an entirely different footing from direct aid to religious institutions. . . .

This fundamental principle which I see running through our prior decisions in this
difficult and sensitive field of law, and which I believe governs the present cases, is
premised more on experience and history than on logic. It is admittedly difficult to
articulate the reasons why a State should be permitted to reimburse parents of private-
school children—partially at least—to take into account the State's enormous savings
in not having to provide schools for those children, when a State is not allowed to pay
the same benefit directly to sectarian schools on a per-pupil basis. In either case, the
private individual makes the ultimate decision that may indirectly benefit church
sponsored schools; to that extent the state involvement with religion is substantially
attenuated. The answer, I believe, lies in the experienced judgment of various members
of this Court over the years that the balance between the policies of free exercise and
establishment of religion tips in favor of the former when the legislation moves away
from direct aid to religious institutions and takes on the character of general aid to
individual families. This judgment reflects the caution with which we scrutinize any
effort to give official support to religion and the tolerance with which we treat general
welfare legislation. But, whatever its basis, that principle is established in our cases,
from the early case of *Quick Bear* to the more recent holdings in *Everson* and *Allen,*
and it ought to be followed here.

The tuition grant and tax relief programs now before us are, in my view, indistinguishable in principle, purpose and effect from the statutes in *Everson* and *Allen.* . . .

Chapter 9

Freedom of Speech and Association

The First Amendment provides that "Congress shall make no law . . . abridging freedom of speech or of the press," and the due process clause of the Fourteenth Amendment is interpreted as including a like prohibition on the state governments. In a footnote to his opinion in *United States* v. *Carolene Products Co.,* 304 US 144 (1938), Justice Stone suggested that the freedoms protected by the First Amendment enjoy a "preferred position" in our constitutional law. This freedom is essential to a free people, but it is not absolute. As Mr. Justice Holmes stated, no one would hold that a man has the right to shout "Fire!" in a crowded theatre. Because of the complexity of the subject, a topical approach is used in this chapter.

Section 1. Seditious Speech

INTRODUCTION

English Background

Statements showing disloyalty to the King, for example, calling him a fool or a whoremonger, were frequently punished by death in England under the ancient common law as treason. The undefined scope of this offense was restricted by the Statute of Treasons enacted in 1351 which included as treason, among other things, a manifest intent to kill the King, Queen, or Prince, levying war against the King, adhering to his enemies, and giving them aid and comfort. Acts and utterances which tended to disturb the public tranquility, and which at an earlier period would have been punished as treason, began to be punished as sedition. The crimes of "seditious speech," "seditious libel" (for printed matter), and "seditious conspiracy" were not clearly defined but involved the concept of intent to defame a member of the royal family or the government, or to incite the subjects to attempt to change the government "otherwise than by lawful means."

The definition of sedition that finally came to prevail in England is found in the charge to the jury by Judge Cave in 1886 in the trial of John Burns, accused of uttering seditious words at a meeting of unemployed in Trafalgar Square, followed by a riot. Judge Cave defined seditious intention as "an intention to bring into hatred or contempt, or to excite disaffection against the person of Her Majesty, her heirs or successors, or the Government and Constitution of the United Kingdom, as by law established, or either House of Parliament, or the administration of justice, or to excite Her Majesty's subjects to attempt, otherwise than by lawful means, the alteration of any matter in church or state by law established, or to raise discontent or disaffection amongst Her Majesty's subjects, or to promote feelings of ill-will and hostility between different classes of such subjects." But he added this qualifying sentence: "An intention to show that Her Majesty has been misled or mistaken in her measures, or to point out errors or defects in the government or constitution as by law established, with a view to their reformation, or to excite Her Majesty's subjects to attempt by lawful means the alteration of any matter in church or state by law established, or to point out, in order to their removal, matters which are producing or have a tendency to produce, feelings of hatred and ill-will between classes of Her Majesty's subjects, is not a seditious intention."[1]

Conviction of sedition was aided by the judicial procedure that limited the jury to special verdicts in prosecutions for this crime. As a general rule, the judge has the function of determining the law applicable in a case, and the jury has the function of determining the facts. But who is to determine the application of the law to the facts? In some types of cases, this can be done best by the jury; in others, by the judge. Until near the end of the eighteenth century, the judges insisted that it was their function to apply the law to the facts in sedition cases. The jury was not given a statement of the law and asked to bring in a general verdict of guilty or not guilty. Instead, they were limited to bringing in a special verdict of whether or not the accused uttered or wrote the statement which he was accused of having made. If they found that the accused made the statement, the judge applied the law to this fact and determined whether or not the accused was guilty of sedition.

The same rule applied in the colonies. However, in 1735 in his defense of John Peter Zenger, publisher of the New York *Weekly Journal,* Andrew Hamilton of Philadelphia insisted that the jury should pass not only upon the question of whether Zenger published the allegedly seditious articles, but whether they were in fact seditious. The jury returned a verdict of "not guilty." The phrase "Philadelphia lawyer" was coined as a result of Hamilton's performance in this case.

The limited-verdict rule was under frequent attack throughout the eighteenth century. Finally, in 1792, Parliament passed James Fox's Libel Act which allowed the jury

---

1. *Regina* v. *Burns* (1866), 2 TLR 510; 16 Cox, CC 355.

to give a general verdict in prosecutions for seditious libel. This act was quickly copied throughout the United States.[2]

Another common law rule that aided conviction in sedition prosecutions was the doctrine that true criticism was punishable as well as false criticism. "The greater the truth, the greater the libel" was an oft-quoted maxim. Although the judge charged the jury otherwise, in the *Zenger* case Andrew Hamilton argued that truth of the statements made was a valid defense in libel suits. Hamilton's position was later enacted into law in many American states.

American Experience to 1940

Aside from the Alien and Sedition Acts of 1798, which expired after two years, sedition played little part in American law prior to the twentieth century. The common law crime of seditious libel had no place in the national law, for there are no common law crimes against the United States. The only mention of sedition in the federal law was in the conspiracy section of the Criminal Code, and this section required proof of an overt act for conviction. And there was little or no state legislation on sedition during the nineteenth century. The century affords examples of mob violence and rough action by police officers, but little legislation on sedition. Laissez-faire in economy was accompanied by laissez-faire in speech.

The assassination of President McKinley was followed by the enactment by New York of a Criminal Anarchy Act in 1902 and a federal statute excluding anarchists in 1903. A number of other states soon adopted statutes against criminal anarchism and syndicalism.

World War I led to the passage of the Espionage Act of 1917 and the Sedition Act of 1918 by Congress and numerous related statutes by state legislatures. Thousands of prosecutions were made under these statutes, and the appellate courts, both federal and state, were inclined to sustain convictions found in the trial courts. *Schenck* v. *United States* (1919) was the first case in which the Supreme Court considered the federal espionage act. The conviction of Schenck was sustained, but in the opinion of the Court Justice Holmes announced a test which, if adhered to, would protect legitimate expression. "The question in every case," wrote Holmes, "is whether the words used are used in such circumstances and are of such a nature as to create a clear and present danger that they will bring about the substantive evils that Congress has a right to prevent." Holmes and Brandeis clarified this test in dissenting opinions in a number of subsequent cases when the Court departed from it. *Gitlow* v. *New York* (1925) is typical of cases of the period in which convictions of violating state criminal-anarchy statutes were sustained. The Court applied a "bad-tendency" test under which a revolutionary spark could be quenched before it kindled a fire that might eventually burst into a destructive conflagration.

World War II and Afterwards

The Second World War and its aftermath produced the Smith Act of 1940, the Subversive Activities Control Act of 1950, and the Communist Control Act of 1954.

---

2. Zechariah Chafee, Jr., *Free Speech in the United States* (Cambridge, 1946), p. 504.

Of these, the Smith Act has been the subject of most litigation. The act makes it unlawful for any person "to knowingly or willfully advocate, abet, advise, or teach the duty, necessity, desirability, or propriety of overthrowing or destroying any government in the United States by force or violence, . . . to help organize any group that advocates such action, or to be a member of such a group, knowing the purposes thereof."

The Supreme Court has sustained very few convictions under these statutes. It has not declared the statutes void, but it has required such rigorous standards of proof and been so inclined to reverse convictions on technical grounds as to frustrate any serious effort to enforce the federal anti-Communist legislation. At the same time, the Court has prevented the enforcement of state laws banning the advocacy of overthrow of the United States government by force and violence. In *Pennsylvania* v. *Nelson,* 350 US 497 (1956), the Court held that the federal Smith Act of 1940 superseded state laws on subversion against the United States.

In the period from 1940 to the present considered as a whole, the phrase "clear and present danger" was used most frequently by the Supreme Court to label its conclusions in reversing the judgments of trial courts in cases where persons had been found guilty under antisubversion statutes. A notable instance of departure from the use of this standard and the sustaining of convictions under the Smith Act was *Dennis* v. *United States,* 341 US 494 (1950). For the majority, Chief Justice Vinson wrote:

> . . . In this case we are squarely presented with the application of the "clear and present danger" test, and must decide what that phrase imports. . . . Obviously, the words cannot mean that before the Government may act, it must wait until the *putsch* is about to be executed, the plans have been laid and the signal is awaited. . . . The situation with which Justices Holmes and Brandeis were concerned in *Gitlow* was a comparatively isolated event, bearing little relation in their minds to any substantial threat to the safety of the community. . . . Chief Judge Learned Hand, writing for the majority below, interpreted the phrase as follows: "In each case [courts] must ask whether the gravity of the "evil," discounted by its improbability, justifies such invasion of free speech as is necessary to avoid the danger." . . . We adopt this statement of the rule. [Paragraphs not indicated.]

Encouraged by the decision in the *Dennis* case of 1950, the Department of Justice moved against other Communist leaders in the United States. Within six years eighty-nine convictions of violation of the Smith Act were obtained in the district courts. Then came the 1957 decisions in *Yates* v. *United States* in which the convictions of fourteen leaders of the Communist party in California were all reversed and the "balancing of interests" of the *Dennis* case pushed aside in favor of a return to something akin to the clear and present danger test.

Brandenburg v. *Ohio,* 395 US 444 (1969), held that recent decisions "have fashioned the principle that the constitutional guarantees of free speech and free press do not permit a State to forbid or proscribe advocacy of the use of force or violation of law except where such advocacy is directed to inciting or producing imminent lawless action and is likely to incite or produce such action." As a practical matter, from 1940 to 1974 the Court prevented either the national government or the states from punishing anyone on the sole ground that the content of something he had said or written was subversive.

Schenck v. United States

249 US 47, 39 S Ct 247, 63 L Ed 470 (1919)

A conspiracy to circulate among men called and accepted for military service a circular tending to influence them to obstruct the draft, with the intent to effect that result, and followed by the sending of such circulars, presents a clear and present danger, within the power of Congress to punish.

MR. JUSTICE HOLMES delivered the opinion of the Court.

This is an indictment in three counts. The first charges a conspiracy to violate the Espionage Act of June 15, 1917 . . . by causing or attempting to cause insubordination, etc., in the military and naval forces of the United States, and to obstruct the recruiting and enlistment service of the United States, when the United States was at war with the German Empire, to-wit, that the defendants [Charles T. Schenck et al.] wilfully conspired to have printed and circulated to men who had been called and accepted for military service under the Act of May 18, 1917, a document set forth and alleged to be calculated to cause such insubordination and obstruction. The count alleges overt acts in pursuance of the conspiracy, ending in the distribution of the document set forth. The second count alleges a conspiracy to commit an offence against the United States, to-wit, to use the mails for the transmission of matter declared to be non-mailable by Title XII, § 2 of the Act of June 15, 1917, to-wit, the above mentioned document, with an averment of the same overt acts. The third count charges an unlawful use of the mails for the transmission of the same matter and otherwise as above. The defendants were found guilty on all the counts. They set up the First Amendment to the Constitution forbidding Congress to make any law abridging the freedom of speech, or of the press, and bringing the case here on that ground have argued some other points also of which we must dispose. . . . The document in question upon its first printed side recited the first section of the Thirteenth Amendment, said that the idea embodied in it was violated by the Conscription Act and that a conscript is little better than a convict. In impassioned language it intimated that conscription was despotism in its worst form and a monstrous wrong against humanity in the interest of Wall Street's chosen few. It said "Do not submit to intimidation," but in form at least confined itself to peaceful measures such as petition for the repeal of the act. The other and later printed side of the sheet was headed "Assert Your Rights." It stated reasons for alleging that any one violated the Constitution when he refused to recognize "your right to assert your opposition to the draft," and went on "If you do not assert and support your rights, you are helping to deny or disparage rights which it is the solemn duty of all citizens and residents of the United States to retain." It described the arguments on the other side as coming from cunning politicians and a mercenary capitalist press, and even silent consent to the conscription law as helping to support an infamous conspiracy. It denied the power to send our citizens away to foreign shores to shoot up the people of other lands, and added that words could not express the condemnation such cold-blooded ruthlessness deserves, etc., etc., winding up "You must do your share to maintain, support and uphold the rights of the people of this country." Of course the document would not have been sent unless it had been intended to have some effect, and we do not see what effect it could be expected to have upon persons subject to the draft except to influence them to obstruct the carrying it out. The defendants do not deny that the jury might find against them on this point.

But it is said, suppose that that was the tendency of this circular, it is protected by the First Amendment to the Constitution. Two of the strongest expressions are said to be quoted respectively from well-known public men. It well may be that the prohibition of laws abridging the freedom of speech is not confined to previous restraints, although to prevent them may have been the main purpose, as intimated in *Patterson* v. *Colorado,* 205 US 454, 462. We admit that in many places and in ordinary times the defendants in saying all that was said in the circular would have been within their constitutional rights. But the character of every act depends upon the circumstances in which it is done. . . . The most stringent protection of free speech would not protect a man in falsely shouting fire in a theatre and causing a panic. It does not even protect a man from an injunction against uttering words that may have all the effect of force. . . . The question in every case is whether the words used are used in such circumstances and are of such a nature as to create a clear and present danger that they will bring about the substantive evils that Congress has a right to prevent. It is a question of proximity and degree. When a nation is a war many things that might be said in time of peace are such a hindrance to its effort that their utterance will not be endured so long as men fight and that no Court could regard them as protected by any constitutional right. It seems to be admitted that if an actual obstruction of the recruiting service were proved, liability for words that produced that effect might be enforced. The statute of 1917 in § 4 punishes conspiracies to obstruct as well as actual obstruction. If the act (speaking, or circulating a paper), its tendency and the intent with which it is done are the same, we perceive no ground for saying that success alone warrants making the act a crime. . . .

Judgments affirmed.

Gitlow v. New York

268 US 652, 45 S Ct 625, 69 L Ed 1138 (1925)

A state in the exercise of its police power may punish those who abuse freedom of speech by utterances inimical to the public welfare, tending to corrupt public morals, incite to crime, or disturb the public peace.

[Benjamin Gitlow was convicted in the courts of New York of violating a statute against advocating criminal anarchy. He was a member of the Left Wing Section of the Socialist party and took a prominent part in publishing a Manifesto that condemned moderate socialism and advocated "revolutionary mass action." Gitlow's counsel had requested that the jury be charged that to constitute criminal anarchy within the meaning of the statute, it was necessary that the language used should advocate "some definite, or immediate act or acts" of violence or unlawfulness directed toward overthrow of the government. This request had been refused. An appeal was taken to the United States Supreme Court.]

MR. JUSTICE SANFORD delivered the opinion of the Court.

For present purposes we may and do assume that freedom of speech and of the press —which are protected by the First Amendment from abridgment by Congress—are among the fundamental personal rights and "liberties" protected by the due process clause of the Fourteenth Amendment from impairment by the States. . . .

It is a fundamental principle, long established, that the freedom of speech and of the press which is secured by the Constitution, does not confer an absolute right to speak or publish, without responsibility, whatever one may choose, or an unrestricted and unbridled license that gives immunity for every possible use of language and prevents the punishment of those who abuse this freedom. . . .

That a State in the exercise of its police power may punish those who abuse this freedom by utterances inimical to the public welfare, tending to corrupt public morals, incite to crime, or disturb the public peace, is not open to question. . . .

And, for yet more imperative reasons, a State may punish utterances endangering the foundations of organized government and threatening its overthrow by unlawful means. These imperil its own existence as a constitutional State. . . .

By enacting the present statute the State has determined, through its legislative body, that utterances advocating the overthrow of organized government by force, violence and unlawful means, are so inimical to the general welfare and involve such danger of substantive evil that they may be penalized in the exercise of its police power. That determination must be given great weight. Every presumption is to be indulged in favor of the validity of the statute. . . . That utterances inciting to the overthrow of organized government by unlawful means, present a sufficient danger of substantive evil to bring their punishment within the range of legislative discretion, is clear. Such utterances, by their very nature, involve danger to the public peace and to the security of the State. They threaten breaches of the peace and ultimate revolution. And the immediate danger is none the less real and substantial, because the effect of a given utterance cannot be accurately foreseen. The State cannot reasonably be required to measure the danger from every such utterance in the nice balance of a jeweler's scale. A single revolutionary spark may kindle a fire that, smouldering for a time, may burst into a sweeping and destructive conflagration. It cannot be said that the State is acting arbitrarily or unreasonably when in the exercise of its judgment as to the measures necessary to protect the public peace and safety, it seeks to extinguish the spark without waiting until it has enkindled the flame or blazed into the conflagration. . . .

We cannot hold that the present statute is an arbitrary or unreasonable exercise of the police power of the State unwarrantably infringing the freedom of speech or press; and we must and do sustain its constitutionality.

Affirmed.

MR. JUSTICE HOLMES, dissenting.

MR. JUSTICE BRANDEIS and I are of opinion that this judgment should be reversed. The general principle of free speech, it seems to me, must be taken to be included in the Fourteenth Amendment, in view of the scope that has been given to the word "liberty" as there used, although perhaps it may be accepted with a somewhat larger latitude of interpretation than is allowed to Congress by the sweeping language that governs or ought to govern the laws of the United States. If I am right, then I think that the criterion sanctioned by the full Court in *Schenck* v. *United States,* 249 US 47, 52, applies. "The question in every case is whether the words used are used in such circumstances and are of such a nature as to create a clear and present danger that they will bring about the substantive evils that [the State] has a right to prevent." It is true that in my opinion this criterion was departed from in *Abrams* v. *United States,* 250 US 616, but the convictions that I expressed in that case are too deep for it to be possible for me as yet to believe that it and *Schaefer* v. *United States,* 251 US 466, have settled the law. If what I think the correct test is applied, it is manifest that there was no present danger of an attempt to overthrow the government by force on the part of the admittedly small minority who shared the defendant's views. It is said that this manifesto was more than a theory, that it was an incitement. Every idea is an incitement. It offers itself for belief and if believed it is acted on unless some other belief outweighs it or some failure of energy stifles the movement at its birth. The only difference between the expression of an opinion and an incitement in the narrower sense is the speaker's enthusiasm for the result. Eloquence may set fire to reason. But whatever may be thought of the redundant discourse before us it had no chance of starting a present conflagration. If in the long run the beliefs expressed in proletarian dictatorship are destined to be accepted by the dominant forces of the community, the only meaning of free speech is that they should be given their chance and have their way. . . .

Yates v. United States

354 US 298, 77 S Ct 1064, 1 L Ed2d 1356 (1957)

> The Smith Act does not prohibit advocacy and teaching of forcible overthrow of the government as an abstract principle, divorced from any effort to instigate action to that end; the trial court's charge to the jury furnished wholly inadequate guidance on this central point in the case; and the conviction cannot be allowed to stand.

MR. JUSTICE HARLAN delivered the opinion of the Court. . . .

These 14 petitioners [Oleta Yates and others] stand convicted, after a jury trial in the United States District Court for the Southern District of California, upon a single count indictment charging them with conspiring (1) to advocate and teach the duty and necessity of overthrowing the Government of the United States by force and violence, and (2) to organize, as the Communist Party of the United States, a society of persons who so advocate and teach, all with the intent of causing the overthrow of the Government by force and violence as speedily as circumstances would permit. . . . The conspiracy is alleged to have originated in 1940 and continued down to the date of the indictment in 1951. The indictment charged that in carrying out the conspiracy the defendants and their co-conspirators would (a) become members and officers of the Communist Party, with knowledge of its unlawful purposes, and assume leadership in carrying out its policies and activities; (b) cause to be organized units of the Party in California and elsewhere; (c) write and publish, in the "Daily Worker" and other Party organs, articles on the proscribed advocacy and teaching; (d) conduct schools for the indoctrination of Party members in such advocacy and teaching; and (4) recruit new Party members, particularly from among persons employed in the key industries of the nation. Twenty-three overt acts in furtherance of the conspiracy were alleged.

Upon conviction each of the petitioners was sentenced to five years' imprisonment and a fine of $10,000. The Court of Appeals affirmed. 225 F2d 146. We granted *certiorari.* . . .

For reasons given hereafter, we conclude that these convictions must be reversed and the case remanded to the District Court with instructions to enter judgments of acquittal as to certain of the petitioners, and to grant a new trial as to the rest.

. . . After telling the jury that it could not convict the defendants for holding or expressing merely opinions, beliefs, or predictions relating to violent overthrow, the trial court defined the content of the proscribed advocacy or teaching in the following terms, which are crucial here:

"Any advocacy or teaching which does not include the urging of force and violence as the means of overthrowing and destroying the Government of the United States is not within the issue of the indictment here and can constitute no basis for any finding against the defendants.

"The kind of advocacy and teaching which is charged and upon which your verdict must be reached is not merely a desirability but a necessity that the Government of the United States be overthrown and destroyed by force and violence and not merely a propriety but a duty to overthrow and destroy the Government of the United States by force and violence. . . ."

We are thus faced with the question whether the Smith Act prohibits advocacy and teaching of forcible overthrow as an abstract principle, divorced from any effort to instigate action to that end, so long as such advocacy or teaching is engaged in with evil intent. We hold that it does not.

The distinction between advocacy of abstract doctrine and advocacy directed at promoting unlawful action is one that has been consistently recognized in the opinions of this Court. . . .

What we find lacking in the instructions here is illustrated by contrasting them with the instructions given to the Dennis jury, upon which this Court's sustaining of the conviction in that case was bottomed. There the trial court charged:

"In further construction and interpretation of the statute [the Smith Act] I charge you that it is *not the abstract doctrine* of overthrowing or destroying organized government by unlawful means which is denounced by this law, but the teaching and advocacy of *action* for the accomplishment of that purpose, *by language reasonably and ordinarily calculated to incite persons to such action.* Accordingly, you cannot find the defendants or any of them guilty of the crime charged unless you are satisfied beyond a reasonable doubt that they conspired . . . to advocate and teach the duty and necessity of overthrowing or destroying the Government of the United States by force and violence, with the intent that such teaching and advocacy *be of a rule or principle of action* and *by language reasonably and ordinarily calculated to incite persons to such action,* all with the intent to cause the overthrow . . . as speedily as circumstances would permit." (Emphasis added.) 9 FRD 367, 391; and see 341 US, at 511–512.

We recognize that distinctions between advocacy or teaching of abstract doctrines, with evil intent, and that which is directed to stirring people to action, are often subtle and difficult to grasp, for in a broad sense, as Mr. Justice Holmes said in his dissenting opinion in *Gitlow, supra,* 268 US, at 673: "Every idea is an incitement." But the very subtlety of these distinctions required the most clear and explicit instructions with reference to them, for they concerned an issue which went to the very heart of the charges against these petitioners. . . . We cannot allow a conviction to stand on such "an equivocal direction to the jury on a basic issue."

. . . The judgment of the Court of Appeals is reversed, and the case remanded to the District Court for further proceedings consistent with this opinion.

It is so ordered.

[Concurring and dissenting opinions are omitted here.]

Lamont v. Postmaster General

381 US 301, 85 S Ct 1493, 14 L Ed2d 398 (1965)

The congressional act restricting the use of postal service for Communist political propaganda is, as applied, void.

MR. JUSTICE DOUGLAS delivered the opinion of the Court.

These appeals present the same question: is § 305(a) of the Postal Service and Federal Employees Salary Act of 1962, 76 Stat 840, constitutional as construed and applied? The statute provides in part:

"Mail matter, except sealed letters, which originates or which is printed or otherwise prepared in a foreign country and which is determined by the Secretary of the Treasury pursuant to rules and regulations to be promulgated by him to be 'communist political propaganda,' shall be detained by the Postmaster General upon its arrival for delivery in the United States, or upon its subsequent deposit in the United States domestic mails, and the addressee shall be notified that such matter has been received and will be delivered only upon the addressee's request, except that such detention shall not be required in the case of any matter which is furnished pursuant to subscription or which is otherwise ascertained by the Postmaster General to be desired by the addressee." 39 USC 4008 (a). . . .

To implement the statute the Post Office maintains 10 or 11 screening points through which is routed all unsealed mail from the designated foreign countries. At these points the nonexempt mail is examined by Customs authorities. When it is determined that a piece of mail is "communist political propaganda," the addressee is mailed a notice identifying the mail being detained and advising that it will be destroyed unless the addressee requests delivery by returning an attached reply card within 20 days. . . .

No. 491 arose out of the Post Office's detention in 1963 of a copy of the Peking Review #12 addressed to appellant, Dr. Corliss Lamont, who is engaged in the publishing and distributing of pamphlets. . . .

Like Lamont, appellee Heilberg in No. 848, when his mail was detained, refused to return the reply card and instead filed a complaint in the District Court for an injunction against enforcement of the statute. . . .

We conclude that the Act as construed and applied is unconstitutional because it requires an official act (*viz.* returning the reply card) as a limitation on the unfettered exercise of the addressee's First Amendment rights. As stated by Mr. Justice Holmes in *Milwaukee Pub. Co.* v. *Burleson,* 255 US 407, 437 (dissenting): "The United States may give up the Post Office when it sees fit, but while it carries it on, the use of the mails is almost as much a part of free speech as the right to use our tongues. . . ."

. . . The Act sets administrative officials astride the flow of mail to inspect it, appraise it, write the addressee about it, and await a response before dispatching the mail. Just as the licensing or taxing authorities in the *Lovell, Thomas,* and *Murdock* cases sought to control the flow of ideas to the public so here federal agencies regulate the flow of mail. We do not have here, any more than we had in *Hannegan* v. *Esquire, Inc.,* 327 US 146, any question concerning the extent to which Congress may classify the mail and fix the charges for its carriage. Nor do we reach the question whether the standard here applied could pass constitutional muster. Nor do we deal with the right of customs to inspect material from abroad for contraband. We rest on the narrow ground that the addressee in order to receive his mail must request in writing that it be delivered. This amounts in our judgment to an unconstitutional abridgment of the addressee's First Amendment rights. The addressee carries an affirmative obligation which we do not think the Government may impose on him. This requirement is almost certain to have a deterrent effect, especially as respects those who have sensitive positions. Their livelihood may be dependent on a security clearance. Public officials, like schoolteachers who have no tenure, might think they would invite disaster if they read what the Federal Government says contains the seeds of treason. Apart from them, any addressee is likely to feel some inhibition in sending for literature which federal officials have condemned as "communist political propaganda." The regime of this Act is at war with the "uninhibited, robust, and wide-open" debate and discussion that are contemplated by the First Amendment. *New York Times Co.* v. *Sullivan,* 376 US 254, 270.

We reverse the judgment in No. 491 and affirm that in No. 848.

It is so ordered.

[The concurring opinions are omitted.]

Section 2. Special Problems Relating to Speech

A. OBSCENITY

Introduction

Prior to the Warren Court, obscenity had been considered outside the area of First Amendment freedoms, and there were no major opinions by the Supreme Court on the subject. The 1957 case of *Roth* v. *United States* was the first in which a major opinion on the subject was written. That opinion did not abolish the traditional rule placing obscenity outside the reach of constitutional protection, but it introduced a new definition of obscenity. Thereafter, the question of what materials could be banned as obscene became almost as debatable as what could be banned as a clear and present danger.

In *Memoirs* v. *Massachusetts* (1966) the opinion of the Court by Justice Brennan held that for material to be obscene, "three elements must coalesce: it must be established that (a) the dominant theme of the material taken as a whole appeals to a prurient interest in sex; (b) the material is patently offensive because it affronts contemporary community standards relating to the description or representation of sexual matters; and (c) the matter is utterly without redeeming social value."

Dissenting, Justice White wrote: "If 'social importance' is to be used as the prevailing opinion uses it today, obscene material, however far beyond customary limits of candor, is immune if it has any literary style, if it contains any historical references or language characteristic of a bygone day, or even if it is printed or bound in an interesting way. Well written, especially effective obscenity is protected; the poorly written is vulnerable."

Many state-court decisions holding publications or films to be obscene were reversed by the Warren Court in *per curiam* decisions. There were, however, plenty of cases with lengthy opinions. In *Ginsberg* v. *New York* (1968), Justice Harlan pointed out that "In the 13 obscenity cases since Roth in which a signed opinion was written for the Court, there have been a total of 55 separate opinions among the Justices . . . ," and concluded that the upshot of all this divergence was "utter bewilderment." For his own part, Harlan thought that "no improvement in this chaotic state of affairs is likely to come until it is recognized that this whole problem is primarily one of state concern. . . ."

In February, 1971, the Supreme Court reversed decisions by three district courts in each of which injunctions had been issued halting pending prosecutions in state courts under obscenity statutes. These cases gave no added information on the definition of obscenity, but they reflected a growing disposition to curtail the use of injunctions by the federal courts, thus giving an advantage in time to the states. See the dissenting opinion by Justice Brennan in *Byrne* v. *Karalexis,* 401 US 216 (1971). In *Miller* v. *California* (p. 000), the Court relaxed the restraints it had imposed on the enforcement of state laws regulating obscenity.

Roth v. United States

354 US 476, 77 S Ct 1304, 1 L Ed2d 1498 (1957)

Obscenity is not within the area of constitutionally protected freedom of speech or press —either (1) under the First Amendment, as to the federal government, or (2) under the Due Process Clause of the Fourteenth Amendment, as to the states.

MR. JUSTICE BRENNAN delivered the opinion of the Court. . . .

[Samuel] Roth conducted a business in New York in the publication and sale of books, photographs and magazines. He used circulars and advertising matter to solicit sales. He was convicted by a jury in the District Court for the Southern District of New York upon 4 counts of a 26-count indictment charging him with mailing obscene circulars and advertising, and an obscene book, in violation of the federal obscenity statute. His conviction was affirmed by the Court of Appeals for the Second Circuit. We granted *certiorari*. . . .

The dispositive question is whether obscenity is utterance within the area of protected speech and press. Although this is the first time the question has been squarely presented to this Court, either under the First Amendment or under the Fourteenth Amendment, expressions found in numerous opinions indicate that this Court has always assumed that obscenity is not protected by the freedoms of speech and press. . . .

The guaranties of freedom of expression in effect in 10 of the 14 States which by 1792 had ratified the Constitution, gave no absolute protection for every utterance. Thirteen of the 14 States provided for the prosecution *of libel, and all of those States made either blasphemy or profanity, or both, statutory crimes. As early as 1712, Massachusetts made it criminal to publish "any filthy, obscene, or profane song, pamphlet, libel or mock sermon" in imitation or mimicking of religious services. . . .

In light of this history, it is apparent that the unconditional phrasing of the First Amendment was not intended to protect every utterance. . . .

The protection given speech and press was fashioned to assure unfettered interchange of ideas for the bringing about of political and social changes desired by the people. . . .

All ideas having even the slightest redeeming social importance—unorthodox ideas, controversial ideas, even ideas hateful to the prevailing climate of opinion—have the full protection of the guaranties, unless excludable because they encroach upon the limited area of more important interests. But implicit in the history of the First Amendment is the rejection of obscenity as utterly without redeeming social importance. This rejection for that reason is mirrored in the universal judgment that obscenity should be restrained, reflected in the international agreement of over 50 nations, in the obscenity laws of all of the 48 States, and in the 20 obscenity laws enacted by the Congress from 1842 to 1956. . . .

It is strenuously urged that these obscenity statutes offend the constitutional guaranties because they punish incitation to impure sexual *thoughts,* not shown to be related to any overt antisocial conduct which is or may be incited in the persons stimulated to such *thoughts.* In Roth, the trial judge instructed the jury: "The words 'obscene, lewd and lascivious' as used in the law, signify that form of immorality which has related to sexual impurity and has a tendency to excite lustful *thoughts.*" . . . It is insisted that the constitutional guaranties are violated because convictions may be had without proof either that obscene material will perceptibly create a clear and present danger of antisocial conduct, or will probably induce its recipients to such conduct. But, in light of our holding that obscenity is not protected speech, the complete answer to this argument is the holding of this Court in *Beauharnais* v. *Illinois, infra,* at page 301:

"Libelous utterances not being within the area of constitutionally protected speech, it is unnecessary, either for us or for the State courts, to consider the issues behind the phrase 'clear and present danger.' Certainly no one would contend that obscene speech, for example, may be punished only upon a showing of such circumstances. Libel, as we have seen, is in the same class."

However, sex and obscenity are not synonymous. . . .

. . . It is therefore vital that the standards for judging obscenity safeguard the protection of freedom of speech and press for material which does not treat sex in a manner appealing to prurient interest.

The early leading standard of obscenity allowed material to be judged merely by the effect of an isolated excerpt upon particularly susceptible persons. *Regina* v. *Hicklin*, [1868] LR 3 QB 360. Some American courts adopted this standard but later decisions have rejected it and substituted this test: whether to the average person, applying contemporary community standards, the dominant theme of the material taken as a whole appeals to prurient interest. The *Hicklin* test, judging obscenity by the effect of isolated passages upon the most susceptible persons, might well encompass material legitimately treating with sex, and so it must be rejected as unconstitutionally restrictive of the freedoms of speech and press. On the other hand, the substituted standard provides safeguards adequate to withstand the charge of constitutional infirmity.

Affirmed.

[The concurring opinion of CHIEF JUSTICE WARREN and the dissenting opinion of JUSTICE HARLAN are omitted.]

MR. JUSTICE DOUGLAS, with whom MR. JUSTICE BLACK concurs, dissenting.

When we sustain these convictions, we make the legality of a publication turn on the purity of thought which a book or tract instills in the mind of the reader. I do not think we can approve that standard and be faithful to the command of the First Amendment. . . .

The tests by which these convictions were obtained require only the arousing of sexual thoughts. Yet the arousing of sexual thoughts and desires happens every day in normal life in dozens of ways. . . .

The absence of dependable information on the effect of obscene literature on human conduct should make us wary. It should put us on the side of protecting society's interest in literature, except and unless it can be said that the particular publication has an impact on action that the government can control. . . .

Any test that turns on what is offensive to the community's standards is too loose, too capricious, too destructive of freedom of expression to be squared with the First Amendment. Under that test, juries can censor, suppress, and punish what they don't like, provided the matter relates to "sexual impurity" or has a tendency "to excite lustful thoughts." This is community censorship in one of its worst forms. . . .

I do not think that the problem can be resolved by the Court's statement that "obscenity is not expression protected by the First Amendment." . . .

I would give the broad sweep of the First Amendment full support. I have the same confidence in the ability of our people to reject noxious literature as I have in their capacity to sort out the true from the false in theology, economics, politics, or any other field.

Notes

1. *Smith* v. *California,* 361 US 147 (1959), held that strict liability could not be applied to a bookseller for having obscene materials in his place of business. He could be held criminally liable only if he knew that the materials were obscene. However, in *Hamling* v. *United States,* 418 US 87 (1974), the Court applied an older, relaxed standard of scienter, holding that "only those who are in some manner aware of the character of the material they attempt to distribute should be punished. To require proof of the defendant's knowledge of the legal status of the materials would permit the defendant to avoid prosecution by simply claiming that he had not brushed up on the law."

2. *Ginzburg* v. *United States,* 383 US 463 (1966), introduced the concept of giving consideration in obscenity cases to the context of publication—that is, whether the materials were sold "as stock in trade of the business of pandering, *i.e.,* the purveying of publications openly advertised to appeal to customers' erotic interest."

3. *Mishkin* v. *New York,* 383 US 502 (1966), held that "Where the material is designed for and primarily disseminated to a clearly defined deviant sexual group, rather than to the public at large, the prurient-appeal requirement of the *Roth* test is satisfied if the dominant theme of the material taken as a whole appeals to the prurient interest in sex of the members of that group."

4. *Ginsberg* v. *New York,* 390 US 629 (1968), sustained a conviction for violating a statute making it illegal knowingly to sell to a minor under seventeen "any picture which depicts nudity . . . and is harmful to minors" or any magazine containing such pictures. The Court ruled that "The State has power to adjust the definition of obscenity as applied to minors. . . ."

5. *Stanley* v. *Georgia,* 394 US 557 (1969), held that a statute imposing criminal sanctions upon the mere knowing possession of obscene matter in the privacy of the home was void. The Court rejected the argument that prohibition of possession of obscene material is a necessary incident to statutory schemes prohibiting distribution.

6. *Rowan* v. *United States Post Office Department,* 397 US 728 (1970), sustained the constitutionality of a statute of 1967 (81 Stat 645) entitled "Prohibition of pandering advertisements in the mail." The statute provides a procedure whereby any householder may insulate himself from advertisements that offer for sale "matter which the addressee in his sole discretion believes to be erotically arousing or sexually provocative." He has only to request the Postmaster to issue an order directing the sender of such advertisements to delete his name from the sender's mailing lists. The Court found that, in the issue at hand, the right of every person "to be let alone" weighed more heavily than the right of others to communicate.

7. *United States* v. *Thirty-Seven Photographs,* 402 US 363 (1971), held that "obscene materials may be removed from the channels of commerce when discovered in the luggage of a returning foreign traveler even though intended solely for his private use. . . . [A] port of entry is not a traveler's home."

Miller v. California

413 US 15, 93 S Ct 2607, 36 L Ed2d 410 (1973)

A state may use contemporary community standards in defining obscenity and ban the sale or exposure of hard core pornography.

MR. CHIEF JUSTICE BURGER delivered the opinion of the Court.

This is one of a group of "obscenity-pornography" cases being reviewed by the Court in a re-examination of standards enunciated in earlier cases involving what Mr. Justice Harlan called "the intractable obscenity problem." ...

Appellant conducted a mass mailing campaign to advertise the sale of illustrated books, euphemistically called "adult" material. After a jury trial, he was convicted of violating [the] California Penal Code ... by knowingly distributing obscene matter. ... Appellant's conviction was specifically based on his conduct in causing five unsolicited advertising brochures to be sent through the mail in an envelope addressed to a restaurant in Newport Beach, California. The envelope was opened by the manager of the restaurant and his mother. They had not requested the brochures; they complained to the police.

The brochures advertise four books entitled "Intercourse," "Man-Woman," "Sex Orgies Illustrated," and "An Illustrated History of Pornography," and a film entitled "Marital Intercourse." While the brochures contain some descriptive printed material, primarily they consist of pictures and drawings very explicitly depicting men and women in groups of two or more engaging in a variety of sexual activities, with genitals often prominently displayed.

I

This case involves the application of a State's criminal obscenity statute to a situation in which sexually explicit materials have been thrust by aggressive sales action upon unwilling recipients who had in no way indicated any desire to receive such materials. This Court has recognized that the States have a legitimate interest in prohibiting dissemination or exhibition of obscene material when the mode of dissemination carries with it a significant danger of offending the sensibilities of unwilling recipients or of exposure to juveniles. ... It is in this context that we are called on to define the standards which must be used to identify obscene material that a State may regulate without infringing the First Amendment as applicable to the States through the Fourteenth Amendment. ...

In *Roth* v. *United States,* 354 US 476 (1957), the Court sustained a conviction under a federal statute punishing the mailing of "obscene, lewd, lascivious or filthy ..." materials. The key to that holding was the Court's rejection of the claim that obscene materials were protected by the First Amendment. ...

Nine years later in *Memoirs* v. *Massachusetts,* 383 US 413 (1966), the Court veered sharply away from the *Roth* concept. ...

While *Roth* presumed "obscenity" to be "utterly without redeeming social value," *Memoirs* required that to prove obscenity it must be affirmatively established that the material is *"utterly* without redeeming social value." Thus, even as they repeated the words of *Roth,* the *Memoirs* plurality produced a drastically altered test that called on the prosecution to prove a negative, *i.e.,* that the material was *"utterly* without redeeming social value"—a burden virtually impossible to discharge under our criminal standards of proof. . . .

. . . [T]he *Memoirs* test has been abandoned as unworkable by its author and no member of the Court today supports the *Memoirs* formulation.

II

. . . We acknowledge . . . the inherent dangers of undertaking to regulate any form of expression. State statutes designed to regulate obscene materials must be carefully limited. . . .

The basic guidelines for the trier of fact must be: (a) whether "the average person, applying contemporary community standards" would find that the work, taken as a whole, appeals to the prurient interest, . . . (b) whether the work depicts or describes, in a patently offensive way, sexual conduct specifically defined by the applicable state law, and (c) whether the work, taken as a whole, lacks serious literary, artistic, political, or scientific value. We do not adopt as a constitutional standard the *"utterly* without redeeming social value" test of *Memoirs* v. *Massachusetts.* . . . If a state law that regulates obscene material is thus limited, as written or construed, the First Amendment values applicable to the States through the Fourteenth Amendment are adequately protected by the utilimate power of appellate courts to conduct an independent review of constitutional claims when necessary. . . .

We emphasize that it is not our function to propose regulatory schemes for the States. That must await their concrete legislative efforts. It is possible, however, to give a few plain examples of what a state statute could define for regulation under the second part (b) of the standard announced in this opinion, *supra:*

(a) Patently offensive representations or descriptions of ultimate sexual acts, normal or perverted, actual or simulated.

(b) Patently offensive representations or descriptions of masturbation, excretory functions, and lewd exhibition of the genitals.

Sex and nudity may not be exploited without limit by films or pictures exhibited or sold in places of public accommodation any more than live sex and nudity can be exhibited or sold without limit in such public places. . . .

Under the holdings announced today, no one will be subject to prosecution for the sale or exposure of obscene materials unless these materials depict or describe patently offensive "hard core" sexual conduct specifically defined by the regulating state law, as written or construed. We are satisfied that these specific prerequisites will provide fair notice to a dealer in such materials that his public and commercial activities may bring prosecution. . . .

III

. . . When triers-of-fact are asked to decide whether "the average person, applying contemporary community standards" would consider certain materials "prurient," it would be unrealistic to require that the answer be based on some abstract formulation. The adversary system, with lay jurors as the usual ultimate factfinders in criminal prosecutions, has historically permitted triers-of-fact to draw on the standards of their community, guided always by limiting instructions on the law. To require a State to structure obscenity proceedings around evidence of a *national* "community standard" would be an exercise in futility.

IV

... The First Amendment protects works which, taken as a whole, have serious literary, artistic, political or scientific value, regardless of whether the government or a majority of the people approve of the ideas these works represent. "The protection given speech and press was fashioned to assure unfettered interchange of *ideas* for the bringing about of political and social changes desired by the people," *Roth* v. *United States, supra,* 354 US, at 484 (1957) (emphasis added). ... But the public portrayal of hard core sexual conduct for its own sake, and for the ensuing commerical gain, is a different matter. ...

[JUSTICES DOUGLAS, BRENNAN, STEWART, and MARSHALL dissented.]

Notes

1. *Paris Adult Theatre I* v. *Slayton,* 413 US 49 (1973), categorically disapproved the theory "that obscene, pornographic films acquire constitutional immunity from state regulation simply because they are exhibited for consenting adults only." Justices Douglas, Brennan, Stewart, and Marshall dissented. Justice Brennan wrote that "after 15 years of experimentation and debate, I am reluctantly forced to conclude that none of the available formulas [for defining obscenity] can reduce the vagueness to a tolerable level. ..." He therefore proposed that the court abandon attempts to define a class of sexually oriented expression that may be suppressed. Instead, the Court should approach the problem of suppressing expression in terms of the state's interest in suppression. "The opinions in *Redrup* and *Stanley* v. *Georgia* reflected our emerging view that the state interests in protecting children and in protecting unconsenting adults may stand on a different footing from the other asserted state interests. It may well be, as one commentator has argued, that 'exposure to [erotic material] is for some persons an intense emotional experience. A communication of this nature, imposed upon a person contrary to his wishes, has all the characteristics of a physical assault. ...' "

2. *Jenkins* v. *Georgia,* 418 US 153 (1974), held that juries could properly be instructed to apply "community standards" without further specification. However, the Court reversed the finding that the film "Carnal Knowledge" was obscene. Justice Rehnquist wrote: "Even though questions of appeal to the 'prurient interest' or of patent offensiveness are 'essentially questions of fact,' it would be a serious misreading of *Miller* to conclude that juries have unbridled discretion in determining what is 'patently offensive.' ... Our own view of the film satisfies us that 'Carnal Knowledge' could not be found under the *Miller* standards to depict sexual conduct in a patently offensive way. ... While the subject matter of the picture is, in a broader sense, sex, and there are scenes in which sexual conduct including 'ultimate sexual acts' is to be understood to be taking place, the camera does not focus on the bodies of the actors at such times. There is no exhibition

whatever of the actors' genitals, lewd or otherwise, during these scenes. There are occasional scenes of nudity, but nudity alone is not enough to make material legally obscene under the *Miller* standards."

B. LIBEL

Introduction

At common law it was libelous per se to publish a defamatory statement, for example, a statement that a man was a bootlegger, or that a woman was unchaste. The burden of proof was on the person who published the libelous statement. Each of the American states developed its own libel laws. In some states proof that a defamatory statement was true was a complete defense; in others it was necessary to prove both that the statement was true and that it was made for a good motive and justifiable end.

In *New York Times Co.* v. *Sullivan* (1964), the Supreme Court adopted a policy of subjecting judgments in libel suits to judicially created tests designed to promote freedom of expression. Justice Brennan wrote: "The constitutional guarantee requires, we think, a federal rule that prohibits a public official from recovering damages for a defamatory falsehood relating to his official conduct unless he proves that the statement was made with 'actual malice'—that is, with knowledge that it was false or with reckless disregard of whether it was false or not."

The actual-malice rule of the *Times* case was designed to limit public officers in collecting damages for libel. It was first extended to "public figures" and next to anyone associated with an event of legitimate public interest. In *Rosenbloom* v. *Metromedia,* 403 US 29 (1971), Justice White summarized the spectrum of views of justices then on the Court and concluded that "it would seem that at least five members of the Court would support each of the following rules:

"For public officers and public figures to recover for damages to their reputations for libelous falsehoods, they must prove either knowing or reckless disregard of the truth. All other plaintiffs must prove at least negligent falsehood, but if the publication about them was in an area of legitimate public interest, then they too must prove deliberate or reckless error. In all actions for libel or slander, actual damages must be proved, and awards of punitive damages will be strictly limited."

In Gertz v. Welch, Inc., 418 US 323 (1974), the Court retracted the *Rosenbloom* expansion. It held that a publisher of defamatory statements about an individual who is neither a public officer nor a public figure is liable for resulting injury, even though the defamatory statements concern matters of public interest. The liability is confined to actual damages, however, unless "actual malice" is proved.

For the Court, Justice Powell wrote:

> We would not lightly assume that a citizen's participation in community and professional affairs rendered him a public figure for all purposes. Absent clear evidence of general fame or notoriety in the community, and pervasive involvement in the affairs of society, an individual should not be deemed a public personality for all aspects of his life. It is preferable to reduce the public figure question to a more meaningful context by looking to the nature and extent of an individual's participation in the particular controversy giving rise to the defamation.
>
> In this context it is plain that petitioner was not a public figure. He played a minimal role at the coroner's inquest, and his participation related solely to his representation

of a private client. He took no part in the criminal prosecution of officer Nuccio. Moreover, he never discussed either the criminal or civil litigation with the press and was never quoted as having done so. He plainly did not trust himself into the vortex of this public issue, nor did he engage the public's attention in an attempt to influence its outcome. We are persuaded that the trial court did not err in refusing to characterize petitioner as a public figure for the purpose of this litigation.

We therefore conclude that the *New York Times* standard is inapplicable to this case and that the trial court erred in entering judgment for respondent. Because the jury was allowed to impose liability without fault and was permitted to presume damages without proof of injury, a new trial is necessary. We reverse and remand for further proceedings in accord with this opinion.

In a concurring opinion, Justice Blackmun wrote:

> The Court . . . seeks today to strike a balance between competing values where necessarily uncertain assumptions about human behavior color the result. Although the Court's opinion in the present case departs from the rationale of the *Rosenbloom* plurality, in that the Court now conditions a libel action by a private person upon a showing of negligence, as contrasted with a showing of willful or reckless disregard, I am willing to join, and do join, the Court's opinion and its judgment for two reasons:
>
> 1. By removing the spectres of presumed and punitive damages in the absence of *New York Times* malice, the Court eliminates significant and powerful motives for self-censorship that otherwise are present in the traditional libel action. By so doing, the Court leaves what should prove to be sufficient and adequate breathing space for a vigorous press. What the Court has done, I believe, will have little, if any, practical effect on the functioning of responsible journalism.
>
> 2. The Court was sadly fractionated in *Rosenbloom.* A result of that kind inevitably leads to uncertainty. I feel that it is of profound importance for the Court to come to rest in the defamation area and to have a clearly defined majority position that eliminates the unsureness engendered by *Rosenbloom's* diversity. If my vote were not needed to create a majority, I would adhere to my prior view. A definitive ruling, however, is paramount. . . .

Dissenting opinions were written by Chief Justice Burger and by Justices Douglas, Brennan, and White.

New York Times Co. v. Sullivan

376 US 254, 84 S Ct 710, 11 L Ed2d 686 (1964)

A state cannot award damages to a public official for defamatory falsehood relating to his official conduct unless he proves "actual malice."

MR. JUSTICE BRENNAN delivered the opinion of the Court.

We are required for the first time in this case to determine the extent to which the constitutional protections for speech and press limit a State's power to award damages in a libel action brought by a public official against critics of his official conduct. . . .

Respondent's complaint alleged that he had been libeled by statements in a full-page advertisement that was carried in the *New York Times* on March 29, 1960. Entitled "Heed Their Rising Voices," the advertisement began by stating that "As the whole world knows by now, thousands of Southern Negro students are engaged in widespread non-violent demonstrations in positive affirmation of the right to live in human dignity as guaranteed by the U.S. Constitution and the Bill of Rights." It went on to charge that "in their efforts to uphold these guarantees, they are being met by an unprecedented wave of terror by those who would deny and negate that document which the whole world looks upon as setting the pattern for modern freedom. . . . "

Of the 10 paragraphs of text in the advertisement, the third and a portion of the sixth were the basis of respondent's claim of libel. They read as follows:

Third paragraph:

"In Montogomery, Alabama, after students sang "My Country 'Tis of Thee" on the State Capitol steps, their leaders were expelled from school, and truckloads of police armed with shotguns and tear-gas ringed the Alabama State College Campus. When the entire student body protested to state authorities by refusing to re-register, their dining hall was padlocked in an attempt to starve them into submission." . . .

Respondent relies heavily, as did the Alabama courts, on statements of this Court to the effect that the Constitution does not protect libelous publications. . . . Like "insurrection," contempt, advocacy of unlawful acts, breach of the peace, obscenity, solicitation of legal business, and the various other formulae for the repression of expression that have been challenged in this Court, libel can claim no talismanic immunity from constitutional limitations. It must be measured by standards that satisfy the First Amendment. . . .

[W]e consider this case against the background of a profound national commitment to the principle that debate on public issues should be uninhibited, robust, and wide-open, and that it may well include vehement, caustic, and sometimes unpleasantly sharp attacks on government and public officials. . . .

[E]rroneous statement is inevitable in free debate, and . . . it must be protected if the freedoms of expression are to have the "breathing space" that they "need . . . to survive." *NAACP* v. *Button,* 371, US 415. . . .

A rule compelling the critic of official conduct to guarantee the truth of all his factual assertions—and to do so on pain of libel judgments virtually unlimited in amount—leads to a comparable "self-censorship." Allowance of the defense of truth, with the burden of proving it on the defendant, does not mean that only false speech will be deterred. Even courts accepting this defense as an adequate safeguard have recognized the difficulties of adducing legal proofs that the alleged libel was true in all its factual particulars. . . .

The constitutional guarantees require, we think, a federal rule that prohibits a public official from recovering damages for a defamatory falsehood relating to his official conduct unless he proves that the statement was made with "actual malice"—that is, with knowledge that it was false or with reckless disregard of whether it was false or not. . . .

This Court's duty is not limited to the elaboration of constitutional principles; we must also in proper cases review the evidence to make certain that those principles have been constitutionally applied. This is such a case, particularly since the question is one of alleged trespass across "the line between the speech unconditionally guaranteed and speech which may legitimately be regulated." . . . We must "make an independent examination of the whole record," . . . so as to assure ourselves that the judgment does not constitute a forbidden intrusion on the field of free expression. . . .

. . . We think the evidence against the *Times* supports at most a finding of negligence in failing to discover the misstatements, and is constitutionally insufficient to show the recklessness that is required for a finding of actual malice. . . .

Reversed and remanded.

[The concurring opinions are omitted here.]

C. FIGHTING WORDS

Chaplinsky v. New Hampshire

315 US 568, 62 S Ct 766, 86 L Ed 1031 (1942)

The Court notices judicially that the appellations "damned racketeer" and "damned Fascist" are epithets likely to provoke the average person to retaliation, and thereby cause a breach of the peace.

MR. JUSTICE MURPHY delivered the opinion of the Court.

Appellant [Walter Chaplinsky] a member of the sect known as Jehovah's Witnesses, was convicted in the municipal court of Rochester, New Hampshire, for violation of Chapter 378, § 2, of the Public Laws of New Hampshire:

"No person shall address any offensive, derisive or annoying word to any other person who is lawfully in any street or other public place, nor call him by any offensive or derisive name, nor make any noise or exclamation in his presence and hearing with intent to deride, offend or annoy him, or to prevent him from pursuing his lawful business or occupation."

The complaint charged that appellant, "with force and arms, in a certain public place in said city of Rochester, to wit, on the public sidewalk on the easterly side of Wakefield Street, near unto the entrance of the City Hall, did unlawfully repeat, the words following, addressed to the complainant, that is to say, 'You are a God damned racketeer' and a 'damned Fascist and the whole government of Rochester are Fascists or agents of Fascists,' the same being offensive, derisive and annoying words and names." . . .

By motions and exceptions, appellant raised the questions that the statute was invalid under the Fourteenth Amendment of the Constitution of the United States, in that it placed an unreasonable restraint on freedom of speech, freedom of the press, and freedom of worship, and because it was vague and indefinite. These contentions were overruled and the case comes here on appeal. . . .

Allowing the broadest scope to the language and purpose of the Fourteenth Amendment, it is well understood that the right of free speech is not absolute at all times and under all circumstances. There are certain well-defined and narrowly limited classes of speech, the prevention and punishment of which have never been thought to raise any Constitutional problem. These include the lewd and obscene, the profane, the libelous, and the insulting or "fighting" words—those which by their very utterance inflict injury or tend to incite an immediate breach of the peace. It has been well observed that such utterances are no essential part of any exposition of ideas, and are of such slight social value as a step to truth that any benefit that may be derived from them is clearly outweighed by the social interest in order and morality. . . .

The state statute here challenged comes to us authoritatively construed by the highest court of New Hampshire. . . .

On the authority of its earlier decisions, the state court declared that the statute's purpose was to preserve the public peace, no words being "forbidden except such as have a direct tendency to cause acts of violence by the persons to whom, individually, the remark is addressed." . . .

We are unable to say that the limited scope of the statute as thus construed contravenes the Constitutional right of free expression. . . .

Affirmed.

Notes

1. *Cohen* v. *California,* 403 US 15 (1971), reversed a conviction under California law which prohibits "maliciously and willfully disturb[ing] the peace or quiet of any neighborhood or person . . . by . . . offensive conduct. . . . " Cohen had worn a jacket bearing the words "Fuck the Draft" while in the corridor of the Los Angeles Municipal Court. For the majority of the Supreme Court, Justice Harlan wrote: "While the four-letter word displayed by Cohen in relation to the draft is not uncommonly employed in a personally provocative fashion, in this instance it was clearly not 'directed to the person of the hearer.' . . . No individual actually or likely to be present could reasonably have regarded the words on the appellant's jacket as a direct personal insult. Nor do we have here an instance of the exercise of the State's police power to prevent a speaker from intentionally provoking a given group to hostile reaction. . . . There is, as noted above, no showing that anyone who saw Cohen was in fact violently aroused or that appellant intended such a result." Four justices dissented.

2. *Gooding* v. *Wilson,* 405 US 518 (1972), held void on its face for vagueness and overbreadth a Georgia statute providing that "[a]ny person who shall, without provocation, use to or of another, and in his presence . . . opprobrious words or abusive language, tending to cause a breach of the peace . . . shall be guilty of a misdemeanor. . . . " For the majority, Justice Brennan concluded that "the Georgia appellate decisions have not construed § 26-6303 to be limited in application, as in *Champlinsky,* to words that 'have a direct tendency to cause acts of violence by the person to whom, individually, the remark is addressed'."

Dissenting, Justice Blackmun wrote: "It seems strange indeed that in this day a man may say to a police officer, who is attempting to restore access to a public building, 'White son of a bitch, I'll kill you' and 'You son of a bitch, I'll choke you to death,' and say to an accompanying officer, 'You son of a bitch, if you ever put your hands on me again, I'll cut you to pieces.' and yet constitutionally cannot be prosecuted and convicted under a statute which makes it a misdemeanor to 'use to or of another, and in his presence, opprobrious words or abusive language, tending to cause a breach of the peace. . . . ' This, however, is precisely what the Court pronounces as the law today."

3. *Lewis* v. *City of New Orleans,* 415 US 130 (1974), held void as overbroad an ordinance making it unlawful "for any person wantonly to curse or revile or to use obscene or opprobrious language toward or with reference to any member of the city police while in the actual performance of his duties." For the majority, Justice Brennan wrote: "At the least, the proscription of the use of 'opprobrious language,' embraces words that do not 'by their very utterance inflict injury or tend to excite an immediate breach of the peace.' " Justice Powell filed a concurring opinion. Justice Blackmun filed a dissenting opinion in which the chief justice and Justice Rehnquist joined.

D. CONTEMPT OF COURT

Introduction

The British courts have effectively used their power to punish for contempt as a means of preventing news media from unduly influencing pending litigation. A summary of the British practice is given in Mr. Justice Frankfurter's opinion in *Maryland* v. *Baltimore Radio Show,* 338 US 912 (1949).

The use by a judge of a state court of the power of contempt to punish the publisher of an out-of-court statement was first questioned by the United States Supreme Court in 1941. Since then, it has been the subject of litigation in four Supreme Court cases: *Bridges* v. *California,* 314 US 252 (1941); *Pennekamp* v. *Florida,* 328 US 331 (1946); *Craig* v. *Harney,* 331 US 367 (1947); and *Wood* v. *Georgia,* 370 US 375 (1962). In all four cases, the Court used the "clear and present danger" test in reversing the convictions. The *Craig* case is presented below.

By sharp contrast, in numerous cases decided by the Court in which the validity of a verdict in a criminal case was contested on the ground of prejudice to the accused by news media, the verdicts of guilty have been reversed. Some of the recent cases are presented in chapter 12.

Craig v. Harney

331 US 367, 67 S Ct 1249, 91 L Ed 1546 (1947)

The publication in a newspaper of news articles, which unfairly reported events in a case pending in a state court, and an editorial, which vehemently attacked the trial judge (a layman elected for a short term) while a motion for a new trial was pending, did not, in the circumstances of this case, constitute a clear and present danger to the administration of justice; and the conviction of the newspapermen for contempt violated the freedom of the press guaranteed by the First and Fourteenth Amendments.

Opinion of the Court by MR. JUSTICE DOUGLAS, announced by MR. JUSTICE REED.

Petitioners [Conway C. Craig and others] are a publisher, an editorial writer, and a news reporter of newspapers published in Corpus Christi, Texas. The County Court had before it a forcible detainer case, *Jackson* v. *Mayes,* whereby Jackson sought to regain possession from Mayes of a business building in Corpus Christi which Mayes (who was at the time in the armed services and whose affairs were being handled by an agent, one Burchard) claimed under a lease. That case turned on whether Mayes' lease was forfeited because of non-payment of rent. At the close of the testimony each side moved for an instructed verdict. The judge instructed the jury to return a verdict for Jackson. That was on May 26, 1945. The jury returned with a verdict for Mayes. The judge refused to accept it and again instructed the jury to return a verdict for Jackson. The jury returned a second time with a verdict for Mayes. Once more the judge refused to accept it and repeated his prior instruction. It being the evening of May 26th and the jury not having complied, the judge recessed the court until the morning of May 27th. Again the jury balked at returning the instructed verdict. But finally it complied, stating that it acted under coercion of the court and against its conscience.

On May 29th Mayes moved for a new trial. That motion was denied on June 6th. On June 4th an officer of the County Court filed with that court a complaint charging petitioners with contempt by publication. The publications referred to were an editorial and news stories published on May 26, 27, 28, 30, and 31 in the newspapers with which petitioners are connected. . . . [In these publications] Browning, the judge, who is a layman and who holds an elective office, was criticised for taking the case from the jury. That ruling was called "arbitrary action" and a "travesty on justice." It was deplored that a layman, rather than a lawyer, sat as judge. Groups of local citizens were reported as petitioning the judge to grant Mayes a new trial and it was said that one group had labeled the judge's ruling as a "gross miscarriage of justice." It was also said that the judge's behavior had properly brought down "the wrath of public opinion upon his head," that the people were aroused because a service man "seems to be getting a raw deal," and that there was "no way of knowing whether justice was done, because the first rule of justice, giving both sides an opportunity to be heard, was repudiated." And the fact that there could be no appeal from the judge's ruling to a court "familiar with proper procedure and able to interpret and weigh motions and arguments by opposing counsel" was deplored.

The trial judge concluded that the reports and editorial were designed falsely to represent to the public the nature of the proceedings and to prejudice and influence the court in its ruling on the motion for a new trial then pending. Petitioners contended at the hearing that all that was reported did no more than to create the same impression that would have been created upon the mind of an average intelligent layman who sat through the trial. They disclaimed any purpose to impute unworthy motives to the judge or to advise him how the case should be decided or to bring the court into disrepute. The purpose was to "quicken the conscience of the judge" and to "make him more careful in discharging his duty." . . .

... The history of the power to punish for contempt ... and the unequivocal command of the First Amendment serve as constant reminders that freedom of speech and of the press should not be impaired through the exercise of that power, unless there is no doubt that the utterances in question are a serious and imminent threat to the administration of justice.

In a case where it is asserted that a person has been deprived by a state court of a fundamental right secured by the Constitution, an independent examination of the facts by this Court is often required to be made. ...

We start with the news articles. ...

The articles of May 26, 27, and 28 were partial reports of what transpired at the trial. They did not reflect good reporting, for they failed to reveal the precise issue before the judge. They said that Mayes, the tenant, had tendered a rental check. They did not disclose that the rental check was post-dated and hence, in the opinion of the judge, not a valid tender. In that sense the news articles were by any standard an unfair report of what transpired. But inaccuracies in reporting are commonplace. Certainly a reporter could not be laid by the heels for contempt because he missed the essential point in a trial or failed to summarize the issues to accord with the views of the judge who sat on the case. Conceivably, a plan of reporting on a case could be so designed and executed as to poison the public mind, to cause a march on the court house, or otherwise so disturb the delicate balance in a highly wrought situation as to imperil the fair and orderly functioning of the judicial process. But it takes more imagination than we possess to find in this rather sketchy and one-sided report of a case any imminent or serious threat to a judge of reasonable fortitude. See *Pennekamp* v. *Florida, supra* [328 US 331].

The accounts of May 30 and 31 dealt with the news of what certain groups of citizens proposed to do about the judge's ruling in the case. So far as we are advised, it was a fact they planned to take the proposed action. ...

The only substantial question raised pertains to the editorial. ... It deplored the fact that the judge was a "layman" and not a "competent attorney." It concluded that the "first rule of justice" was to give both sides an opportunity to be heard and when that rule was "repudiated," there was "no way of knowing whether justice was done."

This was strong language, intemperate language, and, we assume, an unfair criticism. But a judge may not hold in contempt one "who ventures to publish anything that tends to make him unpopular or to belittle him. ... " See *Craig* v. *Hecht,* 263 US 255, 281, Mr. Justice Holmes dissenting. The vehemence of the language used is not alone the measure of the power to punish for contempt. The fires which it kindles must constitute an imminent, not merely a likely, threat to the administration of justice. The danger must not be remote or even probable; it must immediately imperil. ...

"Legal trials are not like elections, to be won through the use of the meeting-hall, the radio, and the newspaper." *Bridges* v. *California, supra,* p. 271. But there was here no threat or menace to the integrity of the trial. ...

Reversed.

Mr. Justice Murphy, concurring. ...

In my view, the Constitution forbids a judge from summarily punishing a newspaper editor for printing an unjust attack upon him or his method of dispensing justice. The only possible exception is in the rare instance where the attack might reasonably cause a real impediment to the administration of justice. Unscrupulous and vindictive criticism of the judiciary is regrettable. But judges must not retaliate by a summary suppression of such criticism for they are bound by the command of the First Amendment. . . .

MR. JUSTICE FRANKFURTER, with whom THE CHIEF JUSTICE [VINSON] concurs, dissenting.

Today's decision, in effect though not in terms, holds unconstitutional a power the possession of which by the States this Court has heretofore deemed axiomatic.

It cannot be repeated too often that the freedom of the press so indispensable to our democratic society presupposes an independent judiciary which will, when occasion demands, protect that freedom. . . .

We are not dealing here with criticisms, whether temperate or unbridled, of action in a case after a judge is through with it, or of his judicial qualifications, or of his conduct in general. . . .

The publications now in question did not constitute merely a narrative of a judge's conduct in a particular case nor a general commentary upon his competence or his philosophy. Nor were they a plea for reform of the Texas legal system to the end that county court judges should be learned in the law and that a judgment in a suit of forcible detainer may be appealable. The thrust of the articles was directed to what the judge should do on a matter immediately before him, namely to grant a motion for a new trial. . . .

Corpus Christi, the locale of the drama, had a population of less than 60,000 at the last census, and Neuces County about 92,000. The three papers which published the articles complained of are under common control and are the only papers of general circulation in the area. It can hardly be a compelling presumption that such papers so controlled had no influence, at a time when patriotic fervor was running high, in stirring up sentiment of powerful groups in a small community in favor of a veteran to whom, it was charged, a great wrong had been done. It would seem a natural inference, as the court below in effect found, that these newspapers whipped up public opinion against the judge to secure reversal of his action and then professed merely to report public opinion. We cannot say that the Texas Court could not properly find that these newspapers asked of the judge, and instigated powerful sections of the community to ask of the judge, that which no one has any business to ask of a judge, except the parties and their counsel in open court, namely, that he should decide one way rather than another. . . . Because it is a question of degree, the field in which a court, like a jury, may "exercise its judgment is, necessarily, a wide one." Mr. Justice Brandeis in *Schaefer v. United States,* 251 US 466, 483. Of course, the findings by a State court of what are usually deemed facts cannot foreclose our scrutiny of them if a constitutional right depends on a fair appraisal of those facts. But it would be novel doctrine indeed to say that we may consider the record as it comes before us from a State court as though it were our duty or right to ascertain the facts in the first instance. A State cannot by torturing facts preclude us from considering whether it has thereby denied a constitutional right. Neither can this Court find a violation of a constitutional right by denying to a State its right to a fair appraisal of facts and circumstances peculiarly its concern. . . .

We think the judgment should be affirmed.

MR. JUSTICE JACKSON, dissenting. . . . [Omitted.]

Note

Gelbard v. *United States,* 408 US 41 (1972), held that a grand jury witness charged with contempt for refusing "without just cause" to testify could invoke as a defense the ban imposed by 18 USC 2515 on use of warrantless wiretapped evidence. The four Nixon appointees dissented. See also *Branzburg* v. *Hayes,* page 301.

E. PREVIOUS RESTRAINT

Previous restraint is censorship. From an early period the Crown exercised an effective restraint upon publications by requiring advance approval. John Milton's *Areopagitica* (1644) leveled a telling blow at censorship, but it was not until 1695 that the practice was abolished in England. William Blackstone, whose *Commentaries on the Laws of England* was published in 1765, considered the absence of censorship to be the real meaning of freedom of the press.

That the freedom of speech guaranteed by the Constitution means more than the prevention of censorship is recognized by all. Blackstone's concept of free speech leaves the individual to the discretion of legislatures and juries. Our Constitution, as interpreted by the Supreme Court, permits the justices to interpose a veto upon legislation which they consider to violate the right of freedom of speech. But while not the whole of it, protection from censorship or previous restraint is nonetheless an important part of the American concept of freedom of speech.

Near v. Minnesota

283 US 697, 51 S Ct 625, 75 L Ed 1357 (1931)

> The fact that the liberty of the press may be abused by miscreant purveyors of scandal does not make any the less necessary the immunity from previous restraint in dealing with official misconduct.

[A Minnesota statute authorized injunctions against the publication of a "malicious, scandalous and defamatory newspaper." J. M. Near was publisher of the *Saturday Press.* It published articles which charged that "a Jewish gangster was in control of gambling, bootlegging and racketeering in Minneapolis, and that law enforcing officers and agencies were not energetically performing their duties." Alleging that nine consecutive issues of the paper had been largely devoted to malicious, scandalous and defamatory articles, a county attorney sought an injunction. The trial court found the *Saturday Press* to be a public nuisance. Its judgment perpetually enjoined Near from publishing a malicious, scandalous or defamatory newspaper and "from further conducting said nuisance under the name and title of said, 'The Saturday Press' or any other name or title." From a judgment of the Supreme Court of Minnesota affirming the judgment of the trial court, Near appealed to the United States Supreme Court.]

Mr. Chief Justice Hughes delivered the opinion of the Court. . . .

This statute, for the suppression as a public nuisance of a newspaper or periodical, is unusual, if not unique, and raises questions of grave importance transcending the local interests involved in the particular action. . . .

If we cut through mere details of procedure, the operation and effect of the statute in substance is that public authorities may bring the owner or publisher of a newspaper or periodical before a judge upon a charge of conducting a business of publishing scandalous and defamatory matter—in particular that the matter consists of charges against public officers of official dereliction—and unless the owner or publisher is able and disposed to bring competent evidence to satisfy the judge that the charges are true and are published with good motives and for justifiable ends, his newspaper or periodical is suppressed and further publication is made punishable as a contempt. This is of the essence of censorship. . . .

The struggle in England, directed against the legislative power of the licenser, resulted in renunciation of the censorship of the press. The liberty deemed to be established was thus described by Blackstone: "The liberty of the press is indeed essential to the nature of a free state; but this consists in laying no *previous* restraints upon publications, and not in freedom from censure for criminal matter when published. Every freeman has an undoubted right to lay what sentiments he pleases before the public; to forbid this, is to destroy the freedom of the press; but if he publishes what is improper, mischievous or illegal, he must take the consequence of his own temerity." 41 Bl Com 151, 152. . . .

The criticism upon Blackstone's statement has not been because immunity from previous restraint upon publication has not been regarded as deserving of special emphasis, but chiefly because that immunity cannot be deemed to exhaust the conception of the liberty guaranteed by state and federal constitutions. . . .

The objection has also been made that the principle as to immunity from previous restraint is stated too broadly, if every such restraint is deemed to be prohibited. That is undoubtedly true; the protection even as to previous restraint is not absolutely unlimited. But the limitation has been recognized only in exceptional cases: "When a nation is at war many things that might be said in time of peace are such a hindrance to its effort that their utterance will not be endured so long as men fight and that no Court could regard them as protected by any constitutional right." *Schenck* v. *United States,* 249 US 47, 52. No one would question but that a government might prevent actual obstruction to its recruiting service or the publication of the sailing dates of transports or the number and location of troops. On similar grounds, the primary requirements of decency may be enforced against obscene publications. The security of the community life may be protected against incitements to acts of violence and the overthrow by force of orderly government. The constitutional guaranty of free speech does not "protect a man from an injunction against uttering words that may have all the effect of force. *Gompers* v. *Buck Stove and Range Co.,* 221 US 418, 439." *Schenck* v. *United States, supra.* These limitations are not applicable here. Nor are we now concerned with questions as to the extent of authority to prevent publication in order to protect private rights according to the principles governing the exercise of the jurisdiction of courts of equity. . . .

The fact that the liberty of the press may be abused by miscreant purveyors of scandal does not make any the less necessary the immunity of the press from previous restraint in dealing with official misconduct. Subsequent punishment for such abuses as may exist is the appropriate remedy, consistent with constitutional privilege. . . .

The statute in question cannot be justified by reason of the fact that the publisher is permitted to show, before injunction issues, that the matter published is true and is published with good motives and for justifiable ends. . . .

Equally unavailing is the insistence that the statute is designed to prevent the circulation of scandal which tends to disturb the public peace and to provoke assaults and the commission of crime. Charges of reprehensible conduct, and in particular of official malfeasance, unquestionably create a public scandal, but the theory of the constitutional guaranty is that even a more serious public evil would be caused by authority to prevent publication. . . .

Judgment reversed.

MR. JUSTICE BUTLER, dissenting.

The publications themselves disclose the need and propriety of the legislation. They show:

In 1913 one Guilford, orginally a defendant in this suit, commenced the publication of a scandal sheet called the *Twin City Reporter;* in 1916 Near joined him in the enterprise, later bought him out and engaged the services of one Bevans. In 1919 Bevans acquired Near's interest, and has since, alone or with others, continued the publication. Defendants admit that they published some reprehensible articles in the *Twin City Reporter,* deny that they personally used it for blackmailing purposes, admit that by reason of their connection with the paper their reputation did become tainted and state that Bevans, while so associated with Near, did use the paper for blackmailing purposes. And Near says it was for that reason he sold his interest to Bevans.

In a number of the editions defendants charge that, ever since Near sold his interest to Bevans in 1919, the *Twin City Reporter* has been used for blackmail, to dominate public gambling and other criminal activities and as well to exert a kind of control over public officers and the government of the city.

The articles in question also state that, when defendants announced their intention to publish the *Saturday Press,* they were threatened, and that soon after the first publication Guilford was waylaid and shot down before he could use the firearm which he had at hand for the purpose of defending himself against anticipated assaults. It also appeares that Near apprehended violence and was not unprepared to repel it. There is much more of like significance.

The long criminal career of the *Twin City Reporter*—if it is in fact as described by defendants—and the arming and shooting arising out of the publication of the *Saturday Press,* serve to illustrate the kind of conditions, in respect of the business of publishing malicious, scandalous and defamatory periodicals, by which the state legislature presumably was moved to enact the law in question. It must be deemed appropriate to deal with conditions existing in Minnesota.

It is of the greatest importance that the States shall be untrammeled and free to employ all just and appropriate measures to prevent abuses of the liberty of the press. . . .

The Court quotes Blackstone in support of its condemnation of the statute as imposing a previous restraint upon publication. But the *previous restraints* referred to by him subjected the press to the arbitrary will of an administrative officer. . . .

The Minnesota statute does not operate as a *previous* restraint on publication within the proper meaning of that phrase. It does not authorize administrative control in advance such as was formerly exercised by the licensers and censors but prescribes a remedy to be enforced by a suit in equity. In this case there was previous publication made in the course of the business of regularly producing malicious, scandalous and defamatory periodicals. . . . There is no question of the power of the State to denounce such transgressions. The restraint authorized is only in respect of continuing to do what has been duly adjudged to constitute a nuisance. The controlling words are "All persons guilty of such nuisance may be enjoined, as hereinafter provided. . . . Whenever any such nuisance is committed . . . an action in the name of the State" may be brought "to perpetually enjoin the person or persons committing, conducting or maintaining any such nuisance, *from further committing, conducting or maintaining any such nuisance. . . .*"

The judgment should be affirmed.

Mr. Justice Van Devanter, Mr. Justice McReynolds and Mr. Justice Sutherland concur in this opinion.

Notes

1. *Obscene matter.* A New York statute authorizing the courts to enjoin the sale or distribution of obscene prints and articles under specified conditions was sustained in *Kingsley Books, Inc.* v. *Brown,* 354 US 436 (1957). The statute authorized the chief executive of a municipality in which any person had in his possession any writing or picture of an indecent character with intent to distribute the same to bring an action for an injunction to prevent sale or distribution of the obscene matter. The person or firm sought to be enjoined was entitled to a trial of the issue within one day after joinder of issue, and, under the statute, "a decision shall be rendered by the court within two days of the conclusion of the trial."

Speedy judicial determination of the issue was the redeeming feature of the statutory scheme involved in the *Kingsley Books* case. Contrast the decision in *Blount* v. *Rizzi,* 400 US 410 (1971), and *United States* v. *Thirty-Seven Photographs,* 402 US 363 (1971).

2. *Motion pictures.* In *Joseph Burstyn, Inc.* v. *Wilson,* 343 US 495 (1952), the Court held that motion pictures are included within the free speech and free press guaranty of the First and Fourteenth Amendments, but that motion pictures were not "necessarily subject to the precise rules governing any other particular method of expression. Each method tends to present its own peculiar problems." In *Time Film Corp.* v. *Chicago,* 365 US 43 (1961), the Supreme Court sustained the judgment of a district court refusing to issue an injunction requiring the commissioner of police to issue a permit for the showing of the film "Don Juan." Time Film Corp. had refused to submit the film for censorship, contending that the ordinance requiring the submission of films to censorship was void on its face. The majority of the Court failed to see in the Constitution any "complete and absolute freedom to exhibit, at least once, any and every kind of motion picture." The application of these early cases was limited by the decision in *Freedman* v.

Maryland, 380 US 51 (1965). This case held that, to be constitutional, any censorship system must place the burden of proof that a film is obscene on the censor and must require him to go to court in order to enforce his determination. Moreover, any judicially imposed restraint on exhibition prior to final determination on the merits must be for the shortest period compatible with sound judicial action.

Recent cases dealing with procedure in the seizure of obscene films include *Paris Adult Theatre I* v. *Slayton,* 413 US 49 (1973), *Heller* v. *New York,* 413 US 483 (1973), and *Roaden* v. *Kentucky,* 413 US 496 (1973).

Lovell v. City of Griffin

303 US 444, 58 S Ct 666, 82 L Ed 949 (1938)

A city ordinance forbidding as a nuisance the distribution, by hand or otherwise, of literature of any kind without first obtaining written permission from the city manager strikes at the very foundation of the freedom of the press by subjecting it to license and censorship.

MR. CHIEF JUSTICE HUGHES delivered the opinion of the Court.

Appellant, Alma Lovell, was convicted in the Recorder's Court of the City of Griffin, Georgia, of the violation of a city ordinance.

The ordinance in question is as follows:

"Section 1. That the practice of distributing either by hand or otherwise, circulars, handbooks, advertising, or literature of any kind, whether said articles are being delivered free, or whether same are being sold, within the limits of the City of Griffin, without first obtaining written permission from the City Manager of the City of Griffin, ... shall be deemed a nuisance, and punishable as an offense against the City of Griffin. ..."

The violation, which is not denied, consisted of the distribution without the required permission of a pamphlet and magazine in the nature of the religious tracts, setting forth the gospel of the "Kingdom of Jehovah." Appellant did not apply for a permit, as she regarded herself as sent "by Jehovah to do His work" and that such an application would have been "an act of disobedience to His commandment." ...

We think that the ordinance is invalid on its face. Whatever the motive which induced its adoption, its character is such that it strikes at the very foundation of the freedom of the press by subjecting it to license and censorship. ...

The liberty of the press is not confined to newspapers and periodicals. It necessarily embraces pamphlets and leaflets. These indeed have been historic weapons in the defense of liberty, as the pamphlets of Thomas Paine and others in our own history abundantly attest. The press in its historic connotation comprehends every sort of publication which affords a vehicle of information and opinion. ...

The ordinance cannot be saved because it relates to distribution and not to publication. "Liberty of circulating is as essential to that freedom as liberty of publishing;

indeed, without the circulation, the publication would be of little value." *Ex parte Jackson,* 96 US 727, 733 . . .

Reversed.

Notes

1. *Taxation and license fees.* In *Murdock* v. *Pennsylvania,* 319 US 105 (1943), a municipal ordinance imposing a license tax on peddlers was held to be invalid when applied to Jehovah's Witnesses who went from door to door selling religious pamphlets. "A State may not impose a charge for the enjoyment of a right granted by the Federal Constitution," stated Justice Douglas in the opinion of the Court. Four justices dissented, among them Justice Frankfurter. In his view, "A legislature undoubtedly can tax all those who engage in an activity upon an equal basis. . . . [A tax cannot] be invalidated because the exercise of a constitutional privilege is conditioned upon its payment. It depends upon the nature of the condition that is imposed, its justification, and the extent to which it hinders or restricts the exercise of the privilege."

2. *Requirement of identification card.* In *Thomas* v. *Collins,* 323 US 516 (1945), by a five-to-four vote, the Court held void a Texas statute that required every labor union organizer to obtain an identification card from the secretary of state before soliciting members for his organization.

New York Times Co. v. United States

403 US 713, 91 S Ct 2140, 29 L Ed2d 822 (1971)

The heavy presumption against the validity of any injunction restraining publication was not overcome by the government in this case.

PER CURIAM.

We granted *certiorari* in these cases in which the United States seeks to enjoin the *New York Times* and the *Washington Post* from publishing the contents of a classified study entitled "History of U.S. Decision-Making Process on Viet Nam Policy."

"Any system of prior restraints of expression comes to this Court bearing a heavy presumption against its constitutional validity." *Bantam Books, Inc.* v. *Sullivan,* 372 US 58, 70 (1963); see also *Near* v. *Minnesota,* 283 US 697 (1931). The Government "thus carries a heavy burden of showing justification for the enforcement of such a restraint." *Organization for a Better Austin* v. *Keefe,* 402 US 415 (1971). The District Court for the Southern District of New York in the *New York Times* case and the District Court for the District of Columbia and the Court of Appeals for the District of Columbia Circuit in the *Washington Post* case held that the Government had not met that burden. We agree.

The judgment of the Court of Appeals for the District of Columbia Circuit is therefore affirmed. The order of the Court of Appeals for the Second Circuit is reversed and the case is remanded with directions to enter a judgment affirming the judgment of the District Court for the Southern District of New York. The stays entered June 25, 1971, by the Court are vacated. The mandates shall issue forthwith.

So ordered.

MR. JUSTICE BLACK, with whom MR. JUSTICE DOUGLAS joins, concurring.

I adhere to the view that the Government's case against the *Washington Post* should have been dismissed and that the injunction against the *New York Times* should have been vacated without oral argument when the cases were first presented to this Court. I believe that every moment's continuance of the injunctions against these newspapers amounts to a flagrant, indefensible, and continuing violation of the First Amendment. . . .

In the First Amendment the Founding Fathers gave the free press the protection it must have to fulfill its essential role in our democracy. The press was to serve the governed, not the governors. The Government's power to censor the press was abolished so that the press would remain forever free to censure the Government. The press was protected so that it could bare the secrets of government and inform the people. Only a free and unrestrained press can effectively expose deception in government. And paramount among the responsiblities of a free press is the duty to prevent any part of the government from deceiving the people and sending them off to distant lands to die of foreign fevers and foreign shot and shell. In my view, far from deserving condemnation for their courageous reporting, the *New York Times,* the *Washington Post,* and other newspapers should be commended for serving the purpose that the Founding Fathers saw so clearly. In revealing the workings of government that led to the Viet Nam war, the newspapers nobly did precisely that which the Founders hoped and trusted they would do. . . .

. . . And the Government argues in its brief that in spite of the First Amendment, "[t]he authority of the Executive Department to protect the nation against publication of information whose disclosure would endanger the national security stems from two interrelated sources: the constitutional power of the President over the conduct of foreign affairs and his authority as Commander-in-Chief." . . .

The word "security" is a broad, vague generality whose contours should not be invoked to abrogate the fundamental law embodied in the First Amendment. The guarding of military and diplomatic secrets at the expense of informed representative government provides no real security for our Republic. The Framers of the First Amendment, fully aware of both the need to defend a new nation and the abuses of the English and Colonial governments, sought to give this new society strength and security by providing that freedom of speech, press, religion, and assembly should not be abridged. . . .

[Concurring opinions by JUSTICES DOUGLAS, BRENNAN, STEWART, and WHITE are omitted.]

MR. CHIEF JUSTICE BURGER, dissenting.

. . . In this case, the imperative of a free and unfettered press comes into collision with another imperative, the effective functioning of a complex modern government and specifically the effective exercise of certain constitutional powers of the Executive. Only those who view the First Amendment as an absolute in all circumstances—a view I respect, but reject—can find such a case as this to be simple or easy. . . .

It is not disputed that the *Times* has had unauthorized possession of the documents for three to four months, during which it has had its expert analysts studying them, presumably digesting them and preparing the material for publication. During all of this time, the *Times,* presumably in its capacity as trustee of the public's "right to know," has held up publication for purposes it considered proper and thus public knowledge was delayed. No doubt this was for a good reason; the analysis of 7,000 pages of complex material drawn from a vastly greater volume of material would inevitably take time and the writing of good news stories takes time. But why should the United States Government, from whom this information was illegally acquired by someone, along with all the counsel, trial judges, and appellate judges be placed under needless pressure? After these months of deferral, the alleged right-to-know has somehow and suddenly become a right that must be vindicated instanter. . . .

. . . The course followed by the *Times,* whether so calculated or not, removed any possibility of orderly litigation of the issues. If the action of the judges up to now has been correct, that result is sheer happenstance.

Our grant of the writ before final judgment in the *Times* case aborted the trial in the District Court before it had made a complete record pursuant to the mandate of the Court of Appeals, Second Circuit.

The consequence of all this melancholy series of events is that we literally do not know what we are acting on. . . .

I would affirm the Court of Appeals for the Second Circuit and allow the District Court to complete the trial aborted by our grant of *certiorari* meanwhile preserving the *status quo* in the *Post* case. I would direct that the District Court on remand give priority to the *Times* case to the exclusion of all other business of that court but I would not set arbitrary deadlines. . . .

[Dissenting opinions by JUSTICES HARLAN and BLACKMUN are omitted.]

F. REGULATION OF MEDIA

Columbia Broadcasting System v. Democratic National Committee

412 US 94, 93 S Ct 2080, 36 L Ed2d 772 (1973)

Neither the Communications Act nor the First Amendment requires broadcasters to accept paid editorial advertisements.

MR. CHIEF JUSTICE BURGER delivered the opinion of the Court. . . .

In two orders announced the same day, the Federal Communications Commission ruled that a broadcaster who meets his public obligation to provide full and fair coverage of public issues is not required to accept editorial advertisements. . . .

The complainants in these actions are the Democratic National Committee (DNC) and the Business Executives' Move for Vietnam Peace (BEM), a national organization of businessmen opposed to United States involvement in the Vietnam conflict. . . .

A majority of the Court of Appeals reversed the Commission, holding that "a flat ban on paid public issue announcements is in violation of the First Amendment, at least when other sorts of paid announcements are accepted." 450 F.2d, at 646. Recognizing that the broadcast frequencies are a scarce resource inherently unavailable to all, the court nevertheless concluded that the First Amendment mandated an "abridgeable" right to present editorial advertisements. The court reasoned that a broadcaster's policy of airing commercial advertisements but not editorial advertisements constitutes unconstitutional discrimination. . . .

MR. JUSTICE WHITE's opinion for the Court in *Red Lion Broadcasting Co.* v. *FCC,* 395 US 367 (1969), makes clear that the broadcast media pose unique and special problems not present in the traditional free speech case. Unlike other media, broadcasting is subject to an inherent physical limitation. Broadcast frequencies are a scarce resource; they must be portioned out among applicants. All who possess the financial resources and the desire to communicate by television or radio cannot be satisfactorily accommodated. . . .

. . . Congress and its chosen administrative agency have established a delicately balanced system of regulation intended to serve the interests of all concerned. . . .

. . . The judgment of the legislative branch cannot be ignored or undervalued simply because one segment of the broadcast constituency casts its claims under the umbrella of the First Amendment. . . . Thus before confronting the specific legal issues in these cases, we turn to an examination of the legislative and administrative development of our broadcast system over the last half century. . . . [Omitted here.]

That "Congress shall make no law . . . abridging the freedom of speech, or of the press" is a restraint on government action, not that of private persons. *Public Utility Commission* v. *Pollak,* 343 US 451, 461 (1952). The Court has not previously considered whether the action of a broadcast licensee such as that challenged here is "governmental action" for purposes of the First Amendment. . . .

[W]ith the advent of radio a half century ago Congress was faced with a fundamental choice between total government ownership and control of the new medium—the choice of most other countries—or some other alternative. Long before the impact and potential of the medium was realized, Congress opted for a system of private broadcasters licensed and regulated by Government. The legislative history suggests that this choice was influenced not only by traditional attitudes toward private enterprise, but by a desire to maintain for licensees, so far as consistent with necessary regulation, a traditional journalistic role. . . .

[T]he Commission has not fostered the licensee policy challenged here; it has simply declined to command particular action because it fell within the area of journalistic discretion. The Commission explicitly emphasized that "there is of course no Commission policy thwarting the sale of time to comment on public issues." . . . The Commission's reasoning, consistent with nearly 40 years of precedent, is that so long as a licensee meets its "public trustee" obligation to provide balanced coverage of issues and events, it has broad discretion to decide how that obligation will be met. . . .

Thus, it cannot be said that the government is a "partner" to the action of broadcast licensee complained of here, nor is it engaged in a "symbiotic relationship" with the licensee, profiting from the invidious discrimination of its proxy. . . . The First Amendment does not reach acts of private parties in every instance where the Congress or the Commission has merely permitted or failed to prohibit such acts. . . .

Were we to read the First Amendment to spell out governmental action in the circumstances presented here, few licensee decisions on the content of broadcasts or the processes of editorial evaluation would escape constitutional scrutiny. In this sensitive area so sweeping a concept of governmental action would go far in practical effect to undermine nearly a half century of unmistakable congressional purpose to maintain—no matter how difficult the task—essentially private broadcast journalism held only broadly accountable to public interest standards. . . .

. . . We therefore conclude that the policies complained of do not constitute governmental action violative of the First Amendment. . . .

There remains for consideration the question whether the "public interest" standard of the Communications Act requires broadcasters to accept editorial advertisements or, whether, assuming governmental action, broadcasters are required to do so by reason of the First Amendment. In resolving those issues, we are guided by the "venerable principle that the construction of a statute by those charged with its execution should be followed unless there are compelling indications that it is wrong. . . ."

[N]othing in the language of the Communications Act or its legislative history compels a conclusion different from that reached by the Commission. . . .

Conceivably at some future date Congress or the Commission—or the broadcasters —may devise some kind of limited right of access that is both practicable and desirable. . . .

[T]he history of the Communications Act and the activities of the Commission over a period of 40 years reflect a continuing search for means to achieve reasonable regulation compatible with the First Amendment rights of the public and the licensees. The Commission's pending hearings are but one step in this continuing process. At the very least, courts should not freeze this necessarily dynamic process into a constitutional holding. . . .

The judgment of the Court of Appeals is

Reversed.

Mr. Justice Douglas.

While I join the Court in reversing the judgment below, I do so for quite different reasons.

My conclusion is that the TV and radio stand in the same protected position under the First Amendment as do newspapers and magazines. The philosophy of the First Amendment requires that result, for the fear that Madison and Jefferson had of government intrusion is perhaps even more relevant to TV and radio than it is to newspapers and other like publications. . . .

Mr. Justice Stewart, concurring. . . .

The First Amendment prohibits the Government from imposing controls upon the press. Private broadcasters are surely part of the press. *United States* v. *Paramount Pictures, Inc.,* 334 US 131, 166. Yet here the Court of Appeals held, and the dissenters today agree, that the First Amendment *requires* the Government to impose controls upon private broadcasters—in order to preserve First Amendment "values." The appellate court accomplished this strange convolution by the simple device of holding that private broadcasters *are* Government. This is a step along a path that could eventually lead to the proposition that private *newspapers* "are" Government. Freedom of the press would then be gone. In its place we would have such governmental controls upon the press as a majority of this Court at any particular moment might consider First Amendment "values" to require. It is a frightening specter. . . .

MR. JUSTICE WHITE, concurring. . . .

I do not suggest that the conduct of broadcasters must always, or even often, be considered that of a government for the purposes of the First Amendment. But it is at least arguable, and strongly so, that the Communications Act and the policies of the Commission, including the Fairness Doctrine, are here sufficiently implicated to require review of the Commission's orders under the First Amendment. . . .

[A]ssuming *arguendo,* as the Court does in Part IV of its opinion, that Congress or the Commission is sufficiently involved in the denial of access to the broadcasting media to require review under the First Amendment, I would reverse the judgment of the Court of Appeals. Given the constitutionality of the Fairness Doctrine, and accepting Part IV of the Court's opinion, I have little difficulty in concluding that statutory and regulatory recognition of broadcaster freedom and discretion to make up their own programs and to choose their method of compliance with the Fairness Doctrine is consistent with the First Amendment.

MR. JUSTICE BLACKMUN, with whom MR. JUSTICE POWELL joins, concurring.

In Part IV the Court determines "whether assuming governmental action, broadcasters are required" to accept editorial advertisements "by reason of the First Amendment." The Court concludes that the Court of Appeals erred when it froze the "continuing search for means to achieve reasonable regulation compatible with the First Amendment rights of the public and the licensees" into "a constitutional holding." . . . The Court's conclusion that the First Amendment does not compel the result reached by the Court of Appeals demonstrates that the governmental action issue does not affect the outcome of this case. I therefore refrain from deciding it.

MR. JUSTICE BRENNAN, with whom MR. JUSTICE MARSHALL concurs, dissenting.

These cases require us to consider whether radio and television broadcast licensees may, with the approval of the Federal Communications Commission, refuse *absolutely* to sell any part of their advertising time to groups or individuals wishing to speak out on controversial issues of public importance. In practical effect, the broadcaster policy here under attack permits airing of only those paid presentations which advertise products or deal with "noncontroversial" matters, while relegating the discussion of controversial public issues to formats such as documentaries, the news, or panel shows, which are tightly controlled and edited by the broadcaster. The Court holds today that this policy . . . is consistent with the "public interest" requirements of the Communications Act of 1934. . . . The Court also holds that the challenged policy does not violate the First Amendment. It is noteworthy that, in reaching this result, the Court does *not* hold that there is insufficient "governmental involvement" in the promulgation and enforcement of the challenged ban to activate the commands of the First Amendment. On the contrary, only THE CHIEF JUSTICE, and my Brothers STEWART and REHNQUIST express the view that the First Amendment is inapplicable to this case. My Brothers WHITE, BLACKMUN, and POWELL quite properly do not decide that question, for they find that the broadcaster policy here under attack does not violate the "substance" of the First Amendment. Similarly, there is no Court for the *holding* that the challenged ban does not violate the "substance" of the First Amendment. For although THE CHIEF JUSTICE, and my Brother REHNQUIST purport to "decide" that question, their disposition of the "governmental involvement" issue necessarily renders their subsequent discussion of the "substantive" question mere *dictum.*

In my view, the principle at stake here is one of fundamental importance, for it concerns the people's right to engage in and to hear vigorous public debate on the broadcast media. And balancing what I perceive to be the competing interests of broadcasters, the listening and viewing public, and individuals seeking to express their views over the electronic media, I can only conclude that the exclusionary policy upheld today can serve only to inhibit, rather than to further our "profound national commitment to the principle that debate on public issues should be uninhibited, robust, and wide-open." *New York Times Co.* v. *Sullivan,* 376 US 254, 270 (1964). I would therefore affirm the determination of the Court of Appeals that the challenged broadcaster policy is violative of the First Amendment.

Notes

1. *Pittsburgh Press Co.* v. *Human Relations Comm'n,* 413 US 376 (1973), held that an ordinance forbidding newspapers to carry "help-wanted" advertisements in six designated columns did not violate freedom of the press. Chief Justice Burger and Justices Blackmun, Douglas, and Stewart dissented.

2. *Miami Herald Publishing Co.* v. *Tornillo,* 418 US 241 (1974), held void a Florida "right to reply" statute. The statute read as follows:

If any newspaper in its columns assails the personal character of any candidate for nomination or for election in any election, or charges said candidate with malfeasance or misfeasance in office, or otherwise attacks his official record, or gives to another free space for such purpose, such newspaper shall upon request of such candidate immediately publish free of cost any reply he may make thereto in as conspicuous a place and in the same kind of type as the matter that calls for such reply, provided such reply does not take up more space than the matter replied to. Any person or firm failing to comply with the provisions of this section shall be guilty of a misdemeanor of the first degree. . . .

For a unanimous Court, Chief Justice Burger wrote:

Even if a newspaper would face no additional costs to comply with a compulsory access law and would not be forced to forego publication of news or opinion by the inclusion of a reply, the Florida statute fails to clear the barriers of the First Amendment because of its intrusion into the function of editors. A newspaper is more than a passive receptacle or conduit for news, comment, and advertising. The choice of material to go into a newspaper, and the decisions made as to limitations on the size of the paper, and content, and treatment of public issues and public officials—whether fair or unfair—constitutes the exercise of editorial control and judgment. It has yet to be demonstrated how governmental regulation of this crucial process can be exercised consistent with First Amendment guarantees of a free press as they have evolved to this time. . . .

Mr. Justice Brennan, joined by Justice Rehnquest, wrote, concurring:

> I join the Court's opinion which, as I understand it, addresses only "right of reply" statutes and implies no view upon the constitutionality of "retraction" statutes affording plaintiffs able to prove defamatory falsehoods a statutory action to require publication of a retraction. See generally Note, Vindication of the Reputation of a Public Official, 80 Harv L Rev 1730, 1739–1747 (1967).

Section 3.　Special Problems Relating to Speech and Association

A.　FORCED DISCLOSURE

NAACP v. Alabama

357 US 449, 78 S Ct 1163, 2 L Ed2d 1488 (1958)

> The state has failed to show a controlling justification for the deterrent effect on the free enjoyment of the right to associate which disclosure of petitioner's membership lists is likely to have. Accordingly, the judgment of civil contempt and the fine which resulted from petitoner's refusal to produce its membership lists must fall.

MR. JUSTICE HARLAN delivered the opinion of the Court.

We review from the standpoint of its validity under the Federal Constitution a judgment of civil contempt entered against petitioner, the National Association for the Advancement of Colored People, in the courts of Alabama. ...

Alabama has a statute similar to those of many other States which requires a foreign corporation, except as exempted, to qualify before doing business by filing its corporate charter with the Secretary of State and designating a place of business and an agent to receive service of process. The statute imposes a fine on a corporation transacting intrastate business before qualifying and provides for criminal prosecution of officers of such a corporation. ... The National Association for the Advancement of Colored People is a nonprofit membership corporation organized under the laws of New York. Its purposes, fostered on a nationwide basis, are those indicated by its name, and it operates through chartered affiliates which are independent unincorporated associations, with membership therein equivalent to membership in petitioner. The first Alabama affiliates were chartered in 1918. Since that time the aims of the Association have been advanced through activities of its affiliates, and in 1951 the Association itself opened a regional office in Alabama, at which it employed two supervisory persons and one clerical worker. The Association has never complied with the qualification statute, from which it considered itself exempt.

In 1956, the Attorney General of Alabama brought an equity suit in the State Circuit Court, Montgomery County, to enjoin the Association from conducting further activities within, and to oust it from, the State. Among other things the bill in equity alleged that the Association had opened a regional office and had organized various affiliates in Alabama; had recruited members and solicited contributions within the State; had given financial support and furnished legal assistance to Negro students seeking admission to the state university; and had supported a Negro boycott of the bus lines in Montgomery to compel the seating of passengers without regard to race. The bill recited that the Association, by continuing to do business in Alabama without complying with the qualification statute, was ". . . causing irreparable injury to the property and civil rights of the residents and citizens of the State of Alabama for which criminal prosecution and civil actions at law afford no adequate relief. . . ." On the day the complaint was filed, the Circuit Court issued *ex parte* an order restraining the Association, *pendente lite,* from engaging in further activities within the State and forbidding it to take any steps to qualify itself to do business therein.

Petitioner demurred to the allegations of the bill and moved to dissolve the restraining order. It contended that its activities did not subject it to the qualification requirements of the statute and that in any event what the State sought to accomplish by its suit would violate rights to freedom of speech and assembly guaranteed under the Fourteenth Amendment to the Constitution of the United States. Before the date set for a hearing on this motion, the State moved for the production of a large number of the Association's records and papers, including bank statements, leases, deeds, and records containing the names and addresses of all Alabama "members" and "agents" of the Association. It alleged that all such documents were necessary for adequate preparation for the hearing, in view of petitioner's denial of the conduct of intrastate business within the meaning of the qualification statute. Over petitioner's objections, the court ordered the production of a substantial part of the requested records, including the membership lists, and postponed the hearing on the restraining order to a date later than the time ordered for production.

Thereafter petitioner filed its answer to the bill in equity. It admitted its Alabama activities substantially as alleged in the complaint and that it had not qualified to do business in the State. Although still disclaiming the statute's application to it, petitioner offered to qualify if the bar from qualification made part of the restraining order were lifted, and it submitted with the answer an executed set of the forms required by the statute. However petitioner did not comply with the production order, and for this failure was adjudged in civil contempt and fined $10,000. The contempt judgment provided that the fine would be subject to reduction or remission if compliance were forthcoming within five days but otherwise would be increased to $100,000.

At the end of the five-day period petitioner produced substantially all the data called for by the production order except its membership lists, as to which it contended that Alabama could not constitutionally compel disclosure, and moved to modify or vacate the contempt judgment, or stay its execution pending appellate review. This motion was denied. While a similar stay application, which was later denied, was pending before the Supreme Court of Alabama, the Circuit Court made a further order adjudging petitioner in continuing contempt and increasing the fine already imposed to $100,000. Under Alabama law, . . . the effect of the contempt adjudication was to foreclose petitioner from obtaining a hearing on the merits of the underlying ouster action, or from taking any steps to dissolve the temporary restraining order which had been issued *ex parte,* until it purged itself of contempt. . . .

The State Supreme Court thereafter twice dismissed petitions for *certiorari* to review this final contempt judgment, the first time, . . . for insufficiency of the petition's allegations and the second time on procedural grounds. . . . We granted *certiorari* because of the importance of the constitutional questions presented. . . .

We hold that this Court has jurisdiction to entertain petitioner's federal claims. . . .

. . . [W]e reject respondent's argument that the Association lacks standing to assert here constitutional rights pertaining to the members, who are not of course parties to the litigation. . . .

We thus reach petitioner's claim that the production order in the state litigation trespasses upon fundamental freedoms protected by the Due Process Clause of the Fourteenth Amendment. . . .

. . . It is beyond debate that freedom to engage in association for the advancement of beliefs and ideas is an inseparable aspect of the "liberty" assured by the Due Process Clause of the Fourteenth Amendment, which embraces freedom of speech. . . .

. . . This Court has recognized the vital relationship between freedom to associate and privacy in one's associations. When referring to the varied forms of governmental action which might interfere with freedom of assembly, it said in *American Communications Assn.* v. *Douds, supra* [339 US 382], at 402: "A requirement that adherents of particular religious faiths or political parties wear identifying arm-bands, for example, is obviously of this nature." Compelled disclosure of membership in an organization engaged in advocacy of particular beliefs is of the same order. Inviolability of privacy in group association may in many circumstances be indispensable to preservation of freedom of association, particularly where a group espouses dissident beliefs. . . .

We think that the production order, in the respects here drawn in question, must be regarded as entailing the likelihood of a substantial restraint upon the exercise by petitioner's members of their right to freedom of association. Petitioner has made an uncontroverted showing that on past occasions revelation of the identity of its rank-and-file members has exposed these members to economic reprisal, loss of employment, threat of physical coercion, and other manifestations of public hostility. Under these circumstances, we think it apparent that compelled disclosure of petitioner's Alabama membership is likely to affect adversely the ability of petitioner and its members to pursue their collective effort to foster beliefs which they admittedly have the right to advocate, in that it may induce members to withdraw from the Association and dissuade others from joining it because of fear of exposure of their beliefs shown through their associations and of the consequences of this exposure. . . .

We turn to the final question whether Alabama has demonstrated an interest in obtaining the disclosures it seeks from petitioner which is sufficient to justify the deterrent effect which we have concluded these disclosures may well have on the free exercise by petitioner's members of their constitutionally protected right of association. . . . Such a ". . . subordinating interest of the State must be compelling," *Sweezy* v. *New Hampshire,* 354 US 234, 265 (concurring opinion). . . .

Whether there was "justification" in this instance turns solely on the substantiality of Alabama's interest in obtaining the membership lists. During the course of a hearing before the Alabama Circuit Court on a motion of petitioner to set aside the production order, the State's Attorney General presented at length, under examination by petitioner, the State's reason for requesting the membership lists. The exclusive purpose was to determine whether petitioner was conducting intrastate business in violation of the Alabama foreign corporation registration statute, and the membership lists were expected to help resolve this question. The issues in the litigation commenced by Alabama by its bill in equity were whether the character of petitioner and its activities in Alabama had been such as to make petitioner subject to the registration statute, and whether the extent of petitioner's activities without qualifying suggested its permanent ouster from the State. Without intimating the slightest view upon the merits of these issues, we are unable to perceive that the disclosure of the names of petitioner's rank-and-file members has a substantial bearing on either of them. As matters stand in the state court, petitioner (1) has admitted its presence and conduct of activities in Alabama since 1918; (2) has offered to comply in all respects with the state qualification statute, although preserving its contention that the statute does not apply to it; and (3) has apparently complied satisfactorily with the production order, except for the membership lists, by furnishing the Attorney General with varied business records, its charter and statement of purposes, the names of all of its directors and officers, and with the total number of its Alabama members and the amount of their dues. These last items would not on this record appear subject to constitutional challenge and have been furnished, but whatever interest the State may have in obtaining names of ordinary members has not been shown to be sufficient to overcome petitioner's constitutional objections to the production order.

From what has already been said, we think it apparent that *Bryant* v. *Zimmerman,* 278 US 63, cannot be relied on in support of the State's position, for that case involved markedly different considerations in terms of the interest of the State in obtaining disclosure. There, this Court upheld, as applied to a member of a local chapter of the Ku Klux Klan, a New York statute requiring any unincorporated association which demanded an oath as a condition to membership to file with state officials copies of its ". . . constitution, by-laws, rules, regulations and oath of membership, together with a roster of its membership and a list of its officers for the current year." NY Laws 1923, c 664, §§ 53, 56. In its opinion, the Court took care to emphasize the nature of the Klan's activities, involving acts of unlawful intimidation and violence, which the Court assumed was before the state legislature when it enacted the statute, and of which the Court itself took judicial notice. Furthermore, the situation before us is significantly different from that in Bryant, because the organization there had made no effort to comply with any of the requirements of New York's statute but rather had refused to furnish the State with *any* information as to its local activities.

. . . [W]e conclude that Alabama has fallen short of showing a controlling justification for the deterrent effect on the free enjoyment of the right to associate which disclosure of membership lists is likely to have. Accordingly, the judgment of civil contempt and the $100,000 fine which resulted from petitioner's refusal to comply with the production order in this respect must fall. . . .

Reversed.

Note

Communist Party v. *Control Board,* 367 US 1 (1961), sustained the provisions of the Subversive Activities Control Act of 1950 which required "Communist-action" organizations to register and file a membership list. In the lengthy opinion of the Court (115 pages) Justice Frankfurter wrote:

> The Communist Party would have us hold that the First Amendment prohibits Congress from requiring the registration and filing of information, including membership lists, by organizations substantially dominated or controlled by the foreign powers controlling the world Communist movement and which operate primarily to advance the objectives of that movement: the overthrow of existing government by any means necessary and the establishment in its place of a Communist totalitarian dictatorship. . . . We cannot find such a prohibition in the First Amendment and the great ends for the well-being of our democracy that it serves.
>
> No doubt, a governmental regulation which requires a registration as a condition upon the exercise of speech may in some circumstances affront the constitutional guarantee of free expression. *Thomas* v. *Collins,* 323 US 516. . . .
>
> Similarly, we agree that compulsory disclosure of the names of an organization's members may in certain instances infringe constitutionally protected rights of association. *NAACP* v. *Alabama,* 357 US 449; *Bates* v. *Little Rock,* 361 US 516; *Shelton* v. *Tucker,* 364 US 479. But to say this much is only to recognize one of the points of reference from which analysis must begin. To state that individual liberties may be affected is to establish the condition for, not to arrive at the conclusion of, constitutional decision. Against the impediments which particular governmental regulation causes to entire freedom of individual action, there must be weighed the value to the public of the ends which the regulation may achieve. . . .
>
> The present case differs from *Thomas* v. *Collins* and from *NAACP, Bates,* and *Shelton* in the magnitude of the public interests which the registration and disclosure provisions are designed to protect and in the pertinence which registration and disclosure bear to the protection of those interests. Congress itself has expressed in § 2 of the Act both what those interests are and what, in its view, threatens them. . . .
>
> It is not for the courts to re-examine the validity of these legislative findings and reject them. . . .
>
> We certainly cannot dismiss them as unfounded or irrational imaginings. . . .

Chief Justice Warren and Justices Black, Douglas, and Brennan dissented at length (eighty-seven pages).

The registration order was never complied with. After four more years of litigation (the issue had been in the federal courts since 1953), in 1965 the Supreme Court held that it would violate the constitutional provision against self-incrimination to require members of the Communist party to register. *Albertson* v. *SACB,* 382 US 71 (1965).

Barenblatt v. United States

360 US 109, 79 S Ct 1081, 3 L Ed2d 1115 (1959)

Where First Amendment rights are asserted to bar governmental interrogation, resolution of the issue always involves a balancing by the courts of the competing private and public interests at stake in the particular circumstances shown.

MR. JUSTICE HARLAN delivered the opinion of the Court. . . .

Pursuant to a subpoena, and accompanied by counsel, petitioner [Lloyd Barenblatt] on June 28, 1954, appeared as a witness before this congressional Subcommittee [of the House Committee on Un-American Activities]. After answering a few preliminary questions and testifying that he had been a graduate student and teaching fellow at the University of Michigan from 1947 to 1950 and an instructor in psychology at Vassar College from 1950 to shortly before his appearance before the Subcommittee, petitioner objected generally to the right of the Subcommittee to inquire into his "political" and "religious" beliefs or any "other personal and private affairs" or "associational activities," upon grounds set forth in a previously prepared memorandum which he was allowed to file with the Subcommittee. Thereafter petitioner specifically declined to answer each of the following five questions:

"Are you now a member of the Communist Party? [Count One.]
"Have you ever been a member of the Communist Party? [Count Two.]
"Now, you have stated that you knew Francis Crowley. Did you know Francis Crowley as a member of the Communist Party? [Count Three.]
"Were you ever a member of the Haldane Club of the Communist Party while at the University of Michigan? [Count Four.]
"Were you a member while a student of the University of Michigan Council of Arts, Sciences, and Professions?" [Count Five.]

In each instance the grounds of refusal were those set forth in the prepared statement. Petitioner expressly disclaimed reliance upon "the Fifth Amendment."

Following receipt of the Subcommittee's report of these occurrences the House duly certified the matter to the District of Columbia United States Attorney for contempt proceedings. An indictment in five Counts, each embracing one of petitioner's several refusals to answer, ensued. With the consent of both sides the case was tried to the court without a jury, and upon conviction under all Counts a general sentence of six months' imprisonment and a fine of $250 was imposed. . . .

Since this sentence was less than the maximum punishment authorized by the statute for conviction under any one Count, the judgment below must be upheld if the conviction upon any of the Counts is sustainable. . . . As we conceive the ultimate issue in this case to be whether petitioner could properly be convicted of contempt for refusing to answer questions relating to his participation in or knowledge of alleged Communist Party activities at educational institutions in this country, we find it unnecessary to consider the validity of his conviction under the Third and Fifth Counts, the only ones involving questions which on their face do not directly relate to such participation or knowledge.

Petitioner's various contentions resolve themselves into three propositions: First, the compelling of testimony by the Subcommittee was neither legislatively authorized nor constitutionally permissible because of the vagueness of Rule XI of the House of Representatives, Eighty-third Congress, the charter of authority of the parent Committee. Second, petitioner was not adequately apprised of the pertinency of the Subcommittee's questions to the subject matter of the inquiry. Third, the questions petitioner refused to answer infringed rights protected by the First Amendment. . . .

At the outset it should be noted that Rule XI authorized this Subcommittee to compel testimony within the framework of the investigative authority conferred on the

Un-American Activities Committee.[1] Petitioner contends that *Watkins* v. *United States, supra* [354 US 178], nevertheless held the grant of this power in all circumstances ineffective because of the vagueness of Rule XI in delineating the Committee jurisdiction to which its exercise was to be appurtenant. . . .

The *Watkins* case cannot properly be read as standing for such a proposition. . . .

[W]hile Watkins was critical of Rule XI, it did not involve the broad and inflexible holding petitioner now attributes to it.

Petitioner also contends, independently of *Watkins,* that the vagueness of Rule XI deprived the Subcommittee of the right to compel testimony in this investigation into Communist activity. We cannot agree with this contention, which in its furthest reach would mean that the House Un-American Activities Committee under its existing authority has no right to compel testimony in any circumstances. Granting the vagueness of the rule, we may not read it in isolation from its long history in the House of Representatives. Just as legislation is often given meaning by the gloss of legislative reports, administrative interpretation, and long usage, so the proper meaning of an authorization to a congressional committee is not to be derived alone from its abstract terms unrelated to the definite content furnished them by the course of congressional actions. The Rule comes to us with a "persuasive gloss of legislative hsitory." *United States* v. *Witkovich,* 353 US 194, 199, which shows beyond doubt that in pursuance of its legislative concerns in the domain of "national security" the House has clothed the Un-American Activities Committee with pervasive authority to investigate Communist activities in this country. . . .

We are urged, however, to construe Rule XI so as at least to exclude the field of education from the Committee's compulsory authority. . . .

To the contrary, the legislative gloss on Rule XI is again compelling. Not only is there no indication that the House ever viewed the field of education as being outside the Committee's authority under Rule XI, but the legislative history affirmatively evinces House approval of this phase of the Committee's work. . . .

Undeniably a conviction for contempt under 2 USC § 192 cannot stand unless the questions asked are pertinent to the subject matter of the investigation. *Watkins* v. *United States, supra,* at 214–215. But the factors which led us to rest decision on this ground in *Watkins* were very different from those involved here. . . .

First of all, it goes without saying that the scope of the Committee's authority was for the House, not a witness, to determine, subject to the ultimate reviewing responsibility of this Court. What we deal with here is whether petitioner was sufficiently apprised of "the topic under inquiry" thus authorized "and the connective reasoning whereby the precise questions asked relate[d] to it." *Id.,* at 215. In light of his prepared memorandum of constitutional objections there can be no doubt that this petitioner was well aware of the Subcommittee's authority and purpose to question him as it did. . . .

The first question is whether this investigation was related to a valid legislative purpose, for Congress may not constitutionally require an individual to disclose his

---

[1] "The Committee on Un-American Activities, as a whole or by subcommittee, is authorized to make from time to time investigations of (1) the extent, character, and objects of un-American propaganda activities in the United States, (2) the diffusion within the United States of subversive and un-American propaganda that is instigated from foreign countries or of a domestic origin and attacks the principle of the form of government as guaranteed by our Constitution, and (3) all other questions in relation thereto that would aid Congress in any necessary remedial legislation." H Res 5, 83d Cong, 1st Sess, 99 Cong Rec 15, 18, 24. The Rule remains current in the same form. H Res 7, 86th Cong, 1st Sess, Cong Rec, Jan 7, 1959, p 13. [Footnote by the Court.]

political relationships or other private affairs except in relation to such a purpose. See *Watkins* v. *United States, supra,* at 198.

That Congress has wide power to legislate in the field of Communist activity in this Country, and to conduct appropriate investigations in aid thereof, is hardly debatable. . . .

We think that investigatory power in this domain is not to be denied Congress solely because the field of education is involved. Nothing in the prevailing opinions in *Sweezy* v. *New Hampshire, supra* [354 US 234], stands for a contrary view. The vice existing there was that the questioning of Sweezy, who had not been shown ever to have been connected with the Communist Party, as to the contents of a lecture he had given at the University of New Hampshire, and as to his connections with the Progressive Party, then on the ballot as a normal political party in some 26 States, was too far removed from the premises on which the constitutionality of the State's investigation had to depend to withstand attack under the Fourteenth Amendment. See the concurring opinion in *Sweezy, supra,* at 261, 265, 266, n 3. This is a very different thing from inquiring into the extent to which the Communist Party has succeeded in infiltrating into our universities, or elsewhere, persons and groups committed to furthering the objective of overthrow. . . .

We conclude that the balance between the individual and the governmental interests here at stake must be struck in favor of the latter, and that therefore the provisions of the First Amendment have not been offended.

We hold that petitioner's conviction for contempt of Congress discloses no infirmity, and that the judgment of the Court of Appeals must be

Affirmed.

MR. JUSTICE BLACK, with whom THE CHIEF JUSTICE and MR. JUSTICE DOUGLAS concur, dissenting. . . .

It goes without saying that a law to be valid must be clear enough to make its commands understandable. For obvious reasons, the standard of certainty required in criminal statutes is more exacting than in noncriminal statutes. This is simply because it would be unthinkable to convict a man for violating a law he could not understand. This Court has recognized that the stricter standard is as much required in criminal contempt cases as in all other criminal cases, and has emphasized that the "vice of vagueness" is especially pernicious where legislative power over an area involving speech, press, petition and assembly is involved. . . .

Measured by the foregoing standards, Rule XI cannot support any conviction for refusal to testify. In substance it authorizes the Committee to compel witnesses to give evidence about all "un-American propaganda," whether instigated in this country or abroad. The word "propaganda" seems to mean anything that people say, write, think or associate together about. The term "un-American" is equally vague. As was said in *Watkins* v. *United States,* 354 US 178, 202, "Who can define [its] meaning . . .? What is that single, solitary 'principle of the form of government as guaranteed by our Constitution'?" I think it clear that the boundaries of the Committee are, to say the least, "nebulous." Indeed, "It would be difficult to imagine a less explicit authorizing resolution." *Ibid.* . . .

The First Amendment says in no equivocal language that Congress shall pass no law abridging freedom of speech, press, assembly or petition. The activities of this Committee, authorized by Congress, do precisely that, through exposure, obloquy and public scorn. . . .

I do not agree that laws directly abridging First Amendment freedoms can be justified by a congressional or judicial balancing process. There are, of course, cases suggesting that a law which primarily regulates conduct but which might also indirectly affect speech can be upheld if the effect on speech is minor in relation to the need for control of the conduct. With these cases I agree. Typical of them are *Cantwell* v. *Connecticut,* 310 US 296, and *Schneider* v. *Irvington,* 308 US 147. Both of these involved the right of a city to control its streets. . . . Neither these cases, nor any others, can be read as allowing legislative bodies to pass laws abridging freedom of speech, press and association merely because of hostility to views peacefully expressed in a place where the speaker had a right to be. Rule XI, on its face and as here applied, since it attempts inquiry into beliefs, not action—ideas and association, not conduct—does just that. . . .

The fact is that once we allow any group which has some political aims or ideas to be driven from the ballot and from the battle for men's minds because some of its members are bad and some of its tenets are illegal, no group is safe. Today we deal with Communists or suspected Communists. In 1920, instead, the New York Assembly suspended duly elected legislators on the ground that, being Socialists, they were disloyal to the country's principles. In the 1830's the Masons were hunted as outlaws and subversives, and abolitionists were considered revolutionaries of the most dangerous kind in both North and South. Earlier still, at the time of the universally unlamented alien and sedition laws, Thomas Jefferson's party was attacked and its members were derisively called "Jacobins." Fisher Ames described the party as a "French faction" guilty of "subversion" and "officered, regimented and formed to subordination." Its members, he claimed, intended to "take arms against the laws as soon as they dare." History should teach us then, that in times of high emotional excitement minority parties and groups which advocate extremely unpopular social or governmental innovations will always be typed as criminal gangs and attempts will always be made to drive them out. It was knowledge of this fact, and of its great dangers, that caused the Founders of our land to enact the First Amendment as a guarantee that neither Congress nor the people would do anything to hinder or destroy the capacity of individuals and groups to seek converts and votes for any cause, however radical or unpalatable their principles might seem under the accepted notions of the time. . . .

Finally, I think Barenblatt's conviction violates the Constitution because the chief aim, purpose and practice of the House Un-American Activities Committee, as disclosed by its many reports, is to try witnesses and punish them because they are or have been Communists or because they refuse to admit or deny Communist affiliations. The punishment imposed is generally punishment by humiliation and public shame. There is nothing strange or novel about this kind of punishment. It is in fact one of the oldest forms of governmental punishment known to mankind; branding, the pillory, ostracism and subjection to public hatred being but a few examples of it. Nor is there anything strange about a court's reviewing the power of a congressional committee to inflict punishment. In 1880 this Court nullified the action of the House of Representatives in sentencing a witness to jail for failing to answer questions of a congressional committee. *Kilbourn* v. *Thompson,* 103 US 168. The Court held that the Committee in its investigation of the Jay Cooke bankruptcy was seeking to exercise judicial power, and this, it emphatically said, no committee could do. It seems to me that the proof that the Un-American Activities Committee is here undertaking a purely judicial function is overwhelming, far stronger, in fact, than it was in the Jay Cooke investigation which, moreover, concerned only business transactions, no freedom of association. . . .

I would reverse this conviction.

Mr. Justice Brennan, dissenting. [Omitted.]

Notes

1. *Watkins* v. *United States,* 354 US 178 (1957), was the first case in which the Supreme Court clearly recognized the right of a witness to rely upon freedom of speech and association as a basis for refusing to testify before a legislative committee. The opinion of the Court contains a list of former cases in which witnesses had relied upon the self-incrimination clause of the Fifth Amendment. Dissenting, Justice Clark wrote: "While there may be no restraint by the Government of one's beliefs, the right of free belief has never been extended to include the withholding of knowledge of past events or transactions. There is no general privilege of silence."

2. *Gibson* v. *Florida Legislative Committee,* 372 US 539 (1963), marked the greatest extreme to which the Warren Court pushed the concept of associational freedom. The Committee was investigating the infiltration of Communists into various local organizations. In the course of its proceedings, it developed information indicating that, of fifty-two residents of Dade County implicated as Communist, fourteen were also members of the local branch of the National Association for the Advancement of Colored People. The Committee then summoned Gibson, a black clergyman who was and had for five years been president and custodian of the records of the local NAACP chapter. He was asked to consult his records and inform the Committee which, if any, of the fifty-two named persons were or had been members of the NAACP Miami Branch. The Court held that the evidence was "not sufficient to show a substantial connection between the Miami Branch of the Association and Communist activities [as distinguished from *associations*], or to demonstrate a compelling and subordinating state interest necessary to sustain the State's right to inquire into the membership lists of the Association." Justices Harlan, Clark, Stewart, and White dissented. Compare the division on the Court in *Jenkins* v. *McKeithen,* 395 US 411 (1969).

Branzburg v. Hayes

408 US 665, 92 S Ct 2645, 33 L Ed2d 626 (1972)

Newsmen have no First Amendment privilege to refuse to appear or to refuse to answer relevant questions asked during a good faith investigation by a grand jury.

Opinion of the Court by Mr. Justice White. . . .

The issue in these cases is whether requiring newsmen to appear and testify before State or federal grand juries abridges the freedom of speech and press guaranteed by the First Amendment. We hold that it does not.

The writ of *certiorari* in No. 70–85 . . . brings before us two judgments of the Kentucky Court of Appeals, both involving petitioner Branzberg, a staff reporter for the *Courier-Journal,* a daily newspaper published in Louisville, Jefferson County, Kentucky.

On November 15, 1969, the *Courier-Journal* carried a story under petitioner's by-line describing in detail his observations of two young residents of Jefferson County synthesizing hashish from marihuana, an activity which, they asserted, earned them about $5,000 in three weeks. The article included a photograph of a pair of hands working above a laboratory table on which was a substance identified by the caption as hashish. The article stated that petitioner had promised not to reveal the identity of the two hashish makers. Petitioner was shortly subpoenaed by the Jefferson County grand jury; he appeared, but refused to identify the individuals he had seen possessing marihuana or the persons he had seen making hashish from marihuana. A state trial court judge ordered petitioner to answer these questions. . . .

In the Matter of Paul Pappas, No. 70–94, originated when petitioner Pappas, a television newsman-photographer working out of the Providence, Rhode Island, office of a New Bedford, Massachusetts, television station, was called to New Bedford on July 30, 1970, to report on civil disorders there which involved fires and other turmoil. He intended to cover a Black Panther news conference at that group's headquarters in a boarded-up store. Petitioner found the streets around the store barricaded, but he ultimately gained entrance to the area and recorded and photographed a prepared statement read by one of the Black Panther leaders at about 3:00 P.M. He then asked for and received permission to re-enter the area. Returning at about 9:00 P.M. that evening, he was allowed to enter and remain inside Panther headquarters. As a condition of entry, Pappas agreed not to disclose anything he saw or heard inside the store except an anticipated police raid which Pappas, "on his own," was free to photograph and report as he wished. Pappas stayed inside the headquarters for about three hours, but there was no police raid, and petitioner wrote no story and did not otherwise reveal what had transpired in the store while he was there. Two months later, petitioner was summoned before the Bristol County Grand Jury and appeared, answered questions as to his name, address, employment, and what he had seen and heard outside Panther headquarters, but refused to answer any questions about what had taken place inside headquarters while he was there, claiming that the First Amendment afforded him a privilege to protect confidential informants and their information. . . .

United States v. *Caldwell,* No. 70–57, arose from subpoenas issued by a federal grand jury in the Northern District of California to respondent Earl Caldwell, a reporter for the *New York Times* assigned to cover the Black Panther Party and other black militant groups. . . .

. . . Respondent refused to appear before the grand jury, and the court issued an order to show cause why he should not be held in contempt. . . .

Respondent Caldwell appealed the contempt order, and the Court of Appeals reversed. . . .

Petitioners Branzberg and Pappas and respondent Caldwell press First Amendment claims that may be simply put: that to gather news it is often necessary to agree either not to identify the source of information published or to publish only part of the facts revealed, or both; that if the reporter is nevertheless forced to reveal these confidences to a grand jury, the source so identified and other confidential sources of other reporters will be measurably deterred from furnishing publishable information, all to the detriment of the free flow of information protected by the First Amendment. . . . The heart of the claim is that the burden on news gathering resulting from compelling reporters to disclose confidential information outweighs any public interest in obtaining the information. . . .

The sole issue before us is the obligation of reporters to respond to grand jury subpoenas as other citizens do and to answer questions relevant to an investigation into the commission of crime. Citizens generally are not constitutionally immune from grand jury subpoenas; and neither the First Amendment nor other constitutional provision protects the average citizen from disclosing to a grand jury information that he has received in confidence. The claim is, however, that reporters are exempt from these obligations because if forced to respond to subpoenas and identify their sources or disclose other confidences, their informants will refuse or be reluctant to furnish newsworthy information in the future. This asserted burden on news gathering is said to make compelled testimony from newsmen constitutionally suspect and to require a privileged position for them. . . .

A number of States have provided newsmen a statutory privilege of varying breadth, but the majority have not done so, and none has been provided by federal statute. Until now the only testimonial privilege for unofficial witnesses that is rooted in the Federal Constitution is the Fifth Amendment privilege against compelled self-incrimination. We are asked to create another by interpreting the First Amendment to grant newsmen a testimonial privilege that other citizens do not enjoy. This we decline to do. Fair and effective law enforcement aimed at providing security for the person and property of the individual is a fundamental function of government, and the grand jury plays an important, constitutionally mandated role in this process. On the records now before us, we perceive no basis for holding that the public interest in law enforcement and in ensuring effective grand jury proceedings is insufficient to override the consequential, but uncertain, burden on news gathering which is said to result from insisting that reporters, like other citizens, respond to relevant questions put to them in the course of a valid grand jury investigation or criminal trial.

This conclusion itself involves no restraint on what newspapers may publish or on the type or quality of information reporters may seek to acquire, nor does it threaten the vast bulk of confidential relationships between reporters and their sources. Grand juries address themselves to the issues of whether crimes have been committed and who committed them. Only where news sources themselves are implicated in crime or possess information relevant to the grand jury's task need they or the reporter be concerned about grand jury subpoenas. Nothing before us indicates that a large number or percentage of *all* confidential news sources fall into either category and would in any way be deterred by our holding that the Constitution does not, as it never has, exempt the newsman from performing the citizen's normal duty of appearing and furnishing information relevant to the grand jury's task. . . .

Accepting the fact . . . that an undetermined number of informants not themselves implicated in crime will nevertheless, for whatever reason, refuse to talk to newsmen if they fear identification by a reporter in an official investigation, we cannot accept the argument that the public interest in possible future news about crime from undisclosed, unverified sources must take precedence over the public interest in pursuing and prosecuting those crimes reported to the press by informants and in thus deterring the commission of such crimes in the future. . . .

The administration of a constitutional newsman's privilege would present practical and conceptual difficulties of a high order. Sooner or later, it would be necessary to define those categories of newsmen who qualified for the privilege, a questionable procedure in light of the traditional doctrine that liberty of the press is the right of the lonely pamphleteer who uses carbon paper or a mimeograph just as much as of the large metropolitan publisher who utilizes the latest photocomposition methods. . . . The informative function asserted by representatives of the organized press in the present cases is also performed by lecturers, political pollsters, novelists, academic researchers, and dramatists. Almost any author may quite accurately assert that he is contributing to the flow of information to the public, that he relies on confidential sources of information, and that these sources will be silenced if he is forced to make disclosures before a grand jury. . . .

Finally, as we have earlier indicated, news gathering is not without its First Amendment protections, and grand jury investigations if instituted or conducted other than in good faith, would pose wholly different issues for resolution under the First Amendment. Official harassment of the press undertaken not for purposes of law enforcement but to disrupt a reporter's relationship with his news sources would have no justification. Grand juries are subject to judicial control and subpoenas to motions to quash. We do not expect courts will forget that grand juries must operate within the limits of the First Amendment as well as the Fifth.

We turn, therefore, to the disposition of the cases before us. From what we have said, it necessarily follows that the decision in *United States* v. *Caldwell,* No. 70–57, must be reversed. If there is no First Amendment privilege to refuse to answer the relevant and material questions asked during a good-faith grand jury investigation, then it is *a fortiori* true that there is no privilege to refuse to appear before such a grand jury until the Government demonstrates some "compelling need" for a newsman's testimony. . . .

The decisions in No. 70–85, *Branzburg* v. *Hayes* and *Branzburg* v. *Meigs* must be affirmed. Here, petitioner refused to answer questions that directly related to criminal conduct which he had observed and written about. . . . In both cases, if what petitioner wrote was true, he had direct information to provide the grand jury concerning the commission of serious crimes.

The only question presented at the present time in *In the Matter of Paul Pappas,* No. 70–94, is whether petitioner Pappas must appear before the grand jury to testify pursuant to subpoena. The Massachusetts Supreme Judicial Court characterized the record in this case as "meager," and it is not clear what petitioner will be asked by the grand jury. It is not even clear that he will be asked to divulge information received in confidence. We affirm the decision of the Massachusetts Supreme Judicial Court and hold that petitioner must appear before the grand jury to answer the questions put to him, subject, of course, to the supervision of the presiding judge as to "the propriety, purposes, and scope of the grand jury inquiry and the pertinence of the probable testimony."

So ordered.

MR. JUSTICE POWELL, concurring in the opinion of the Court. . . .

As indicated in the concluding portion of the opinion, the Court states that no harassment of newsmen will be tolerated. If a newsman believes that the grand jury investigation is not being conducted in good faith he is not without remedy. Indeed, if the newsman is called upon to give information bearing only a remote and tenuous relationship to the subject of the investigation, or if he has some other reason to believe that his testimony implicates confidential source relationships without a legitimate need of law enforcement, he will have access to the Court on a motion to quash and an appropriate protective order may be entered. The asserted claim to privilege should be judged on its facts by the striking of a proper balance between freedom of the press and the obligation of all citizens to give relevant testimony with respect to criminal conduct. The balance of these vital constitutional and societal interests on a case-by-case basis accords with the tried and traditional way of adjudicating such questions. . . .

MR. JUSTICE DOUGLAS, dissenting. . . .

Caldwell, a Black, is a reporter for the *New York Times* and was assigned to San Francisco with the hope that he could report on the activities and attitudes of the Black Panther Party. Caldwell in time gained the complete confidence of its members and wrote in-depth articles about them. . . .

It is my view that there is no "compelling need" that can be shown which qualifies the reporter's immunity from appearing or testifying before a grand jury, unless the reporter himself is implicated in a crime. His immunity in my view is therefore quite complete, for absent his involvement in a crime, the First Amendment protects him against an appearance before a grand jury and if he is involved in a crime, the Fifth Amendment stands as a barrier. Since in my view there is no area of inquiry not protected by a privilege, the reporter need not appear for the futile purpose of invoking one to each question. And, since in my view a newsman has an absolute right not to appear before a grand jury it follows for me that a journalist who voluntarily appears before that body may invoke his First Amendment privilege to specific questions. . . .

MR. JUSTICE STEWART, with whom MR. JUSTICE BRENNAN and MR. JUSTICE MARSHALL join, dissenting. . . .

The crux of the Court's rejection of any newsman's privilege is its observation that only "where news sources themselves are implicated in crime or possess information *relevant* to the grand jury's task need they or the reporter be concerned about grand jury subpoenas.". . . But this is a most misleading construct. For it is obviously not true that the only persons about whom reporters will be forced to testify will be those "confidential informants involved in actual criminal conduct" and those having "information suggesting illegal conduct by others.". . . As noted above, given the grand jury's extraordinarily broad investigative powers and the weak standards of relevance and materiality that apply during such inquiries, reporters, if they have no testimonial privilege, will be called to give information about informants who have neither committed crimes nor have information about crime. It is to avoid deterrence of such sources and thus to prevent needless injury to First Amendment values that I think the government must be required to show probable cause that the newsman has information which is clearly relevant to a specific probable violation of criminal law.

Similarly, a reporter may have information from a confidential source which is "related" to the commission of crime, but the government may be able to obtain an indictment or otherwise achieve its purposes by subpoenaing persons other than the reporter. It is an obvious but important truism that when government aims have been fully served, there can be no legitimate reason to disrupt a confidential relationship between a reporter and his source. To do so would not aid the administration of justice and would only impair the flow of information to the public. Thus, it is to avoid deterrence of such sources that I think the government must show that there are no alternative means for the grand jury to obtain the information sought.

Both the "probable cause" and "alternative means" requirements would thus serve the vital function of mediating between the public interest in the administration of justice and the constitutional protection of the full flow of information. . . .

B. LOYALTY AND SECURITY

Loyalty Oaths

Article VI of the Constitution provides that "The senators and representatives before mentioned, and the members of the several state legislatures, and all executive and judicial officers, both of the United States and of the several states, shall be bound by oath or affirmation to support this Constitution. . . ." A positive oath of this character has never been questioned, but objection has been raised against negative oaths, requiring public officials to swear that they do not believe in the overthrow of the government by violence and that they are not members of any organization advocating violent revolution.

In *American Communications Ass'n.* v. *Douds,* 339 US 382 (1950), the Supreme Court sustained a non-Communist oath prescribed by the National Labor Relations Act. The section of the Act in question provided that services of the National Labor Relations Board should not be available to a labor union unless the union had on file with the Board an affidavit, executed by each of its officers, "that he is not a member of the Communist Party or affiliated with such party, and that he does not believe in, and is not a member of or supports any organization that believes in or teaches, the overthrow of the United States Government by force. . . ." The Court held that "Congress might reasonably find that Communists, unlike members of other political parties, and persons who believe in the overthrow of the Government by force, unlike persons of other beliefs, represent a continuing danger of disruptive political strikes when they hold positions of union leadership."

In *Gerende* v. *Election Board,* 341 US 56 (1951), the Court sustained a Maryland law requiring that each candidate for public office take an oath that he is not engaged "in one way or another in the attempt to overthrow the government by force or violence" and that he is not knowingly a member of an organization engaged in such an attempt. Knowledge of the subversive character of an organization which one joined was the crucial test of a loyalty oath in the pre-Warren Court. See *Wieman* v. *Updegraff,* 344 US 183 (1952).

Under Chief Justice Warren, the Supreme Court moved progressively in the direction of holding all loyalty oaths to be invalid. *Speiser* v. *Randall,* 357 US 513 (1958), held void a loyalty oath required by California as a prerequisite to certain tax exemptions. The Court interpreted the oath, in the context in which it was administered, as placing upon the taxpayer the burden of proof that he did not advocate the violent overthrow of government. *Shelton* v. *Tucker,* 364 US 479 (1960), held void an Arkansas statute which required each teacher in state-supported schools to file an annual affidavit listing every organization to which he had belonged within the last five years. According to the majority opinion, "The unlimited and indiscriminate sweep of the statute . . . brings it within the ban of our prior cases." *Baggett* v. *Bullitt,* 377 US 360 (1964), held void the loyalty oaths required of state employees in Washington on the ground that they were "unduly vague, uncertain and broad." The Court was critical of the statutory definition of "subversive organization" employed by Washington, and the use of such phrases as "undivided allegiance to the government of the United States."

Elfbrandt v. *Russell,* 384 US 11 (1966), held void an Arizona oath because it did not distinguish between knowledge of the subversive purposes of an organization and specific intent on the part of one of its members to further these unlawful purposes. Under the theory of the Court, while the primary purpose of the Communist party might be to overthrow the government of the United States, the party could have other purposes, and a person might join it for one of these other purposes, for example, entertainment. "Laws such as this which are not restricted in scope to those who join with the 'specific intent' to further illegal actions impose, in effect, a conclusive presumption that the member shares the unlawful aims of the organization."

Keyishian v. *Board of Regents,* 385 US 589 (1967), held void a New York statute which made knowing membership in the Communist party even *prima facie* evidence of disqualification for employment as a teacher in the public schools. Dissenting, Justice Clark wrote: "The majority says the Feinberg Law is bad because it has an 'overbroad sweep.' I regret to say that the majority has by its broadside swept away one of our most precious rights, namely, the right of self-preservation."

In 1971 the Court divided five to four in several loyalty oath cases, with Justice Stewart's vote being decisive. In general, since Warren E. Burger became chief justice the Court has relaxed moderately its tendency to invalidate loyalty oaths.

Law Students Civil Rights Research Council, Inc. v. *Wadmond,* 401 US 154 (1971), sustained the procedure used by New York for admission to the bar. An applicant was required to affirm that he "believes in the form of the government of the United States and is loyal to such government." This was interpreted by New York as requiring only an oath to support the Constitution of the United States as well as that of the State of New York. The majority of the Supreme Court found no objection in requiring a bar applicant to take this oath "in good faith."

In re Stolar, 401 US 23 (1971), held that Ohio could not deny admission to its bar on the ground that the applicant refused to answer the question: "State whether you have been, or presently are . . . a member of any organization which advocates the overthrow of the government of the United States by force. . . ." A similar result was reached in *Baird* v. *State Bar of Arizona,* 401 US 1 (1971).

Connell v. *Higginbotham,* 403 US 1 (1971), dealt with a loyalty oath required by Florida of school teachers reading as follows: "I do hereby solemnly swear or affirm (1) that I will support the Constitution of the United States and of the State of Florida; and (2) that I do not believe in the overthrow of the government of the United States or of the State of Florida by force or violence." The Court upheld the first section of the oath but held the second section to be void.

In *Cole* v. *Richardson,* 405 US 672 (1972), the Court sustained an oath required of all public employees in Massachusetts which read as follows: "I do solemnly swear (or affirm) that I will uphold and defend the Constitution of the United States of America and the Constitution of the Commonwealth of Massachusetts and that I will oppose the overthrow of the government of the United States of America or of this Commonwealth by force, violence, or by any illegal or unconstitutional method." The opinion of the Court, written by the Chief Justice, summarizes the history of litigation on loyalty oaths. Justices Brennan, Douglas, and Marshall dissented.

In *Communist Party of Indiana* v. *Whitcomb,* 414 US 441 (1974), the Court held void a state requirement that "[n]o existing or newly-organized political party or organization shall be permitted on or to have the name of its candidates printed on the ballot at any election unless it has filed an affidavit . . . that it does not advocate the overthrow of local, state or national government by force or violence. . . . " For the Court, Justice Brennan wrote:

> We most recently summarized the constitutional principles that have evolved in this area in *Brandenburg* v. *Ohio*, 395 US 444 (1969). We expressly overruled the earlier holding of *Whitney* v. *California,* 274 US 357 (1927), that without more, "advocating" violent means to effect political and economic change involves such danger to the security of the State that the State may outlaw it. . . .
>
> This principle that "the constitutional guarantees of free speech and free press do not permit a state to forbid or proscribe advocacy of the use of force or of law violation except where such advocacy is directed to inciting or producing imminent lawless action and is likely to incite or produce such action" has been applied not only to statutes that directly forbid or proscribe advocacy, see *Scales* v. *United States,* 367 US 203 (1961); *Noto* v. *United States,* 367 US 290 (1961); *Yates* v. *United States,* 354 US 298 (1957), but also to regulatory schemes that determine eligibility for public employment, *Keyishian* v. *Board of Regents,* 385 US 589 (1967); *Elfbrandt* v. *Russell,* 384 US 11 (1966); *Cramp* v. *Board of Public Instruction,* 368 US 278 (1961); see also *United States* v. *Robel,* 389 US 258 (1967), tax exemptions, *Speiser* v. *Randall,* 357 US 513 (1958), and moral fitness justifying disbarment, *Schware* v. *Board of Bar Examiners,* 353 US 232 (1957).
>
> Appellees argue that the principle should nevertheless not obtain in cases of state regulation of access to the ballot. We perceive no reason to make an exception, and appellees suggest none.

The four Nixon appointees concurred in the judgment. For them, Justice Powell wrote:

> I concur in the result. In my view it was quite unnecessary to reach the issue addressed by the Court.
>
> It was established at trial that appellants had certified the Democratic and Republican parties despite the failure of party officials to submit the prescribed affidavits under Ind Stat § 29–3812. In *Williams* v. *Rhodes,* 393 US 23, 31 (1968), this Court held that a discriminatory preference for established parties under a State's electoral system can be justified only by a "compelling state interest." In the present case, no colorable justification has been offered for placing on appellants burdens not imposed on the two established parties. It follows that the appellees' discriminatory application of the Indiana statute denied appellants equal protection under the Fourteenth Amendment.

Security Programs

Section 1 of this chapter dealt with cases involving subversive speech arising under the Smith Act of 1940 and the Subversive Activities Control Act of 1950. In addition to proscribing certain types of subversive speech, the 1950 Act also proscribed certain action on the part of members of Communist-action organizations. Section 6 provided that:

> (a)When a Communist organization . . . is registered, or there is in effect a final order of the Board requiring such organization to register, it shall be unlawful for any member of such organization, with knowledge or notice that such organization is so registered or that such order has become final—
> (1) to make application for a passport, or the renewal of a passport, to be issued or renewed by or under the authority of the United States; or
> (2) to use or attempt to use any such passport.

In *Aptheker* v. *Secretary of State,* 378 US 500 (1964), the Court held that "freedom of travel is a constitutional liberty closely related to rights of free speech and association" and that the statute under review was void on its face because it "sweeps too widely and too indiscriminately." The "appellants in this case [the chairman of the Communist party of the United States and the editor of the party's "theoretical organ," *Political Affairs*] should not be required to assume the burden of demonstrating that Congress could not have written a statute constitutionally prohibiting their travel."

Kleindienst v. *Mandel,* 408 US 753 (1972), sustained the right of the attorney general to deny a temporary immigration visa to a Belgian journalist and Marxian theoretician whom American plaintiffs had invited to participate in conferences in this country. For the majority Justice Blackmun wrote: "When, as in this case, the Attorney General decides for a legitimate and bona fide reason not to waive the statutory exclusion of an alien, courts will not look behind his decision or weigh it against the First Amendment interests of those who would personally communicate with the alien."

A section of the Subversive Activities Control Act of 1950 provides that when any Communist-action organization is under a final order to register, it shall be unlawful for any member of the organization "to engage in any employment in any defense facility." This provision came before the Court for invalidation in *United States* v. *Robel,* 389 US 258 (1967). Chief Justice Warren wrote: "It is precisely because that statute sweeps indiscriminately across all types of association with Communist-action groups, with regard to the quality and degree of membership, that it runs afoul of the First Amendment." Dissenting, Justice White wrote: "The Court's motives are worthy. It seeks the widest bounds for the exercise of individual liberty consistent with the security of the country. In so doing it arrogates to itself an independent judgment of the requirements of national security."

Presidential program. In addition to the congressional security program, the president of the United States administered a presidential "loyalty" program in the period following World War II. By executive order, in 1947 President Truman required that all federal employees pass tests to determine their loyalty to the United States. Millions of dollars were spent on the program, but its effectiveness remains a subject of speculation. In its annual report of 1953 the Civil Service Commission stated that a total of 560 persons were dismissed or denied employment under President Truman's loyalty order during the five years it was in effect. President Eisenhower abolished the controversial Loyalty Review Board of the Truman administration and made each department head responsible for insuring that employment practices within his department were "clearly consistent with the interest of national security." Subsequent presidents have continued this policy.

The Supreme Court never passed directly upon the constitutionality of any presidential loyalty program. The longest opinions are in *Joint Anti-Fascist Refugee Committee* v. *McGrath,* 344 US 123 (1951), but that case was disposed of on a technical ground.

On the question of whether an employee could be dismissed for disloyalty on the basis of confidential information without being given an opportunity to confront those who informed against him, the Court divided four to four in two cases in 1951 (*Bailey* v. *Richardson,* 341 US 918, and *Washington* v. *McGrath,* 341 US 923). In both cases, the lower courts had sustained the removals, and these decisions were permitted to stand. In subsequent years the Court never met this question squarely, but it frequently ruled in favor of the employee on statutory or technical grounds. *Peters* v. *Hobby,* 349 US 331 (1955), held that the old Loyalty Review Board exceeded the authority given it by the president; *Cole* v. *Young,* 350 US 900 (1955), held that the president exceeded his authority in classifying a position in the Department of Health, Education, and Welfare as "sensitive"; *Service* v. *Dulles,* 354 US 363 (1957), held that the secretary of state had failed to observe one of his own procedural rules in dismissing on security grounds a member of the foreign service; *Greene* v. *McElroy,* 360 US 474 (1959), held that the secretary of defense could not, in the absence of explicit authorization, revoke the security clearance of an aeronautical engineer on the basis of confidential information; and *Vitarelli* v. *Seaton*, 359 US 535 (1959), held that a department must adhere to its own rules in dismissing a person on loyalty grounds. However, *Cafeteria Workers* v. *McElroy,* 367 US 203 (1961), held that a cook employed by a restaurant concessionaire at a naval gun factory could be denied admission to the factory because of the withdrawal of her security badge without a hearing. According to the majority opinion, "The Fifth Amendment does not require a trial-type hearing in every conceivable case of government impairment of private interests. . . . Where it has been possible to characterize the private interest as a mere privilege subject to the Executive's plenary power, it has traditionally been held that notice and hearing are not constitutionally required." Compare *Arnett* v. *Kennedy,* page 344.

C. STUDENTS AND GOVERNMENT EMPLOYEES

Healy v. James

408 US 169, 92 S Ct 2338, 33 L Ed2d 266 (1972)

A state college may not deny associational rights to students because of their beliefs or because of assumed relationships with the SDS; it may, however, refuse to recognize a student organization that refuses to abide by reasonable campus regulations.

MR. JUSTICE POWELL delivered the opinion of the Court. . . .

Petitioners are students attending Central Connecticut State College (CCSC), a state-supported institution of higher learning. In September 1969 they undertook to organize what they then referred to as a "local chapter" of Students for a Democratic Society (SDS). Pursuant to procedures established by the College, petitioners filed a request for official recognition as a campus organization with the Student Affairs Committee, a committee composed of four students, three faculty members and the Dean of Student Affairs. The request specified three purposes for the proposed organization's existence. It would provide "a forum of discussion and self-education for students developing an analysis of American society"; it would serve as "an agency for integrating thought with action so as to bring about constructive changes"; and it would endeavor to provide "a coordinating body for relating the problems of leftist students" with other interested groups on campus and in the community. The Committee, while satisfied that the statement of purposes was clear and unobjectionable on its face, exhibited concern over the relationship between the proposed local group and the National SDS organization. In response to inquiries, representatives of the proposed organization stated that they would not affiliate with any national organization and that their group would remain "completely independent." . . .

By a vote of six to two the Committee ultimately approved the application and recommended to the President of the College, Dr. James, that the organization be accorded official recognition. In approving the application, the majority indicated that its decision was premised on the belief that varying viewpoints should be represented on campus and that since the Young Americans for Freedom, the Young Democrats, the Young Republicans, and the Liberal Party all enjoyed recognized status, a group should be available with which "left wing" students might identify. The majority also noted and relied on the organization's claim of independence. Finally, it admonished the organization that immediate suspension would be considered if the group's activities proved incompatible with the school's policies against interference with the privacy of other students or destruction of property. The two dissenting members based their reservation primarily on the lack of clarity regarding the organization's independence.

Several days later, the President rejected the Committee's recommendation, and issued a statement indicating that petitioners' organization was not to be accorded the benefits of official campus recognition. . . .

Their efforts to gain recognition having proved ultimately unsuccessful, and having been made to feel the burden of nonrecognition, petitioners resorted to the courts. . . .

At the outset we note that state colleges and universities are not enclaves immune from the sweep of the First Amendment. "It can hardly be argued that either students or teachers shed their constitutional rights to freedom of speech or expression at the schoolhouse gate." *Tinker* v. *Des Moines Independent Community School District*, 393 US 503, 506 (1969). Of course, as Mr. Justice Fortas made clear in *Tinker*, First Amendment rights must always be applied "in light of the special characteristics of the . . . environment" in the particular case. *Ibid.* And, where state-operated educational institutions are involved, this Court has long recognized "the need for affirming the comprehensive authority of the States and of school officials, consistent with fundamental constitutional safeguards, to prescribe and control conduct in the schools." *Id.*, at 507. Yet, the precedents of this Court leave no room for the view that, because of the acknowledged need for order, First Amendment protections should apply with less force on college campuses than in the community at large. Quite to the contrary, "[t]he vigilant protection of constitutional freedoms is nowhere more vital than in the community of American schools." *Shelton* v. *Tucker,* 364 US 479, 487 (1960). The college classroom with its surrounding environs is peculiarly the "market place of ideas" and we break no new constitutional ground in reaffirming this Nation's dedication to safeguarding academic freedom. . . .

Among the rights protected by the First Amendment is the right of individuals to associate to further their personal beliefs. While the freedom of association is not explicitly set out in the Amendment, it has long been held to be implicit in the freedoms of speech, assembly and petition. . . . There can be no doubt that denial of official recognition, without justification, to college organizations burdens or abridges that associational right. The primary impediment to free association flowing from nonrecognition is the denial of use of campus facilities for meetings and other appropriate purposes. The practical effect of nonrecognition was demonstrated in this case when, several days after the President's decision was announced, petitioners were not allowed to hold a meeting in the campus coffee shop because they were not an approved group.

Petitioners' associational interests also were circumscribed by the denial of the use of campus bulletin boards and the school newspaper. If an organization is to remain a viable entity in a campus community in which new students enter on a regular basis, it must possess the means of communicating with these students. Moreover, the organization's ability to participate in the intellectual give and take of campus debate, and to pursue its stated purposes, is limited by denial of access to the customary media for communicating with the administration, faculty members, and other students. Such impediments cannot be viewed as insubstantial. . . .

The opinions below assumed that petitioners had the burden of showing entitlement to recognition by the College. While petitioners have not challenged the procedural requirement that they file an application in conformity with the rules of the College, they do question the view of the courts below that final rejection could rest on their failure to convince the administration that their organization was unaffiliated with the National SDS. For reasons to be stated later in this opinion, we do not consider the issue of affiliation to be a controlling one. But apart from any particular issue, once petitioners had filed an application in conformity with the requirements, the burden was upon the College administration to justify its decision of rejection. . . . It is to be remembered that the effect of the College's denial of recognition was a form of prior restraint, denying to petitioners' organization the range of associational activities described above. While a college has a legitimate interest in preventing disruption on the campus, which under circumstances requiring the safeguarding of that interest may justify such restraint, a "heavy burden" rests on the college to demonstrate the appropriateness of that action. . . .

These fundamental errors—discounting the existence of a cognizable First Amendment interest and misplacing the burden of proof—require that the judgments below be reversed. But we are unable to conclude that no basis exists upon which nonrecognition might be appropriate. Indeed, based on a reasonable reading of the ambiguous facts of this case, there appears to be at least one potentially acceptable ground for a denial of recognition. Because of this ambiguous state of the record we conclude that the case should be remanded, and, in an effort to provide guidance to the lower courts upon reconsideration, it is appropriate to discuss the several bases of President James' decision. Four possible justifications for nonrecognition, all closely related, might be derived from the record and his statements. Three of those grounds are inadequate to substantiate his decision: a fourth, however, has merit. . . . [The] references in the record to the group's equivocation regarding how it might respond to "issues of violence" and whether it could ever "envision . . . interrupting a class," suggest a fourth possible reason why recognition might have been denied to these petitioners. These remarks might well have been read as announcing petitioners' unwillingness to be bound by reasonable school rules governing conduct. The College's Statement of Rights, Freedoms and Responsibilities of Students, contains, as we have seen, an explicit statement with respect to campus disruption. The regulation, carefully differentiating between advocacy and action, is a reasonable one, and petitioners have not questioned it directly. Yet their statements raise considerable question whether they intend to abide by the prohibitions contained therein.

As we have already stated, the critical line for First Amendment purposes must be drawn between advocacy, which is entitled to full protection, and action, which is not. Petitioners may, if they so choose, preach the propriety of amending or even doing away with any or all campus regulations. They may not, however, undertake to flout these rules. MR. JUSTICE BLACKMUN, at the time he was a circuit judge on the Eighth Circuit, stated:

> "We . . . hold that a college has the inherent power to promulgate rules and regulations; that it has the inherent power properly to discipline; that it has power appropriately to protect itself and its property; that it may expect that its students adhere to generally accepted standards of conduct. *Esteban* v. *Central Missouri State College,* 415 F. 2d 1077, 1089 (CA8 1969), cert. denied, 398 U.S. 965 (1970)."

Just as in the community at large, reasonable regulations with respect to the time, the place, and the manner in which student groups conduct their speech-related activities must be respected. A college administration may impose a requirement, such as may have been imposed in this case, that a group seeking official recognition affirm in advance its willingness to adhere to reasonable campus law. . . .

. . . Since we do not have the terms of a specific prior affirmation rule before us, we are not called on to decide whether any particular formulation would or would not prove constitutionally acceptable. Assuming the existence of a valid rule, however, we do conclude that the benefits of participation in the internal life of the college community may be denied to any group that reserves the right to violate any valid campus rules with which they disagree. . . .

Reversed and remanded.

[The concurring opinions of CHIEF JUSTICE BURGER and JUSTICE REHNQUIST and the dissenting opinion of JUSTICE DOUGLAS are omitted here.]

U.S. Civil Service Comm'n v. Letter Carriers

413 US 548, 93 S Ct 2880, 37 L Ed2d 796 (1973)

The provisions of the Hatch Act barring federal employees from taking "an active part in political management or in political campaigns" are valid.

MR. JUSTICE WHITE delivered the opinion of the Court.

On December 11, 1972, we noted probable jurisdiction of this appeal, 409 US 1058, based on a jurisdictional statement presenting the single question whether the prohibition in § 9(a) of the Hatch Act, now codified in 5 USC § 7324(a) (2), against federal employees taking "an active part in political management or in political campaigns," is constitutional on its face. Section 7324(a) provides:

"An employee in an Executive agency or an individual employed by the government of the District of Columbia may not—

"(1) use his official authority or influence for the purpose of interfering with or affecting the result of an election; or

"(2) take an active part in political management or in political campaigns.

"For the purpose of this subsection, the phrase 'an active part in political management or in political campaigns' means those acts of political management or political campaigning which were prohibited on the part of employees in the competitive service before July 19, 1940, by determinations of the Civil Service Commission under the rules prescribed by the President"

A divided three-judge court sitting in the District of Columbia had held the section unconstitutional. 346 F. Supp. 578 (1972). We reverse the judgment of the District Court. . . .

As the District Court recognized, the constitutionality of the Hatch Act's ban on taking an active part in political management or political campaigns has been here before. This very prohibition was attacked in the *Mitchell* case [page 25] by a labor union and various federal employees as being violative of the First, Ninth, and Tenth Amendments and as contrary to the Fifth Amendment as being vague and indefinite, arbitrarily discriminatory, and a deprivation of liberty. The Court there first determined that with respect to all but one of the plaintiffs there was no case or controversy present within the meaning of Art. III because the Court could only speculate as to the type of political activity the appellants there desired to engage in or as to the contents of their proposed public statements or the circumstances of their publication. As to the plaintiff Poole, however, the court noted that "he was a ward executive committeeman of a political party and was politically active on election day as a worker at the polls and a paymaster for the services of other party workers." 330 US, at 94. Plainly, the Court thought, these activities fell within the prohibition of § 9 of the Hatch Act against taking an active part in political management or political campaigning; and "[t]hey [were] also covered by the prior determinations of the [Civil Service] Commission." . . .

We unhesitatingly reaffirm the *Mitchell* holding that Congress had, and has, the power to prevent Mr. Poole and others like him from holding a party office, working at the polls and acting as party paymaster for other party workers. An Act of Congress going no farther would in our view unquestionably be valid. So would it be if, in plain and understandable language, the statute forbade activities such as organizing a political party or club; actively participating in fund-raising activities for a partisan candidate or politicial party; becoming a partisan candidate for, or campaigning for, an elective public office; actively managing the campaign of a partisan candidate for public office; initiating or circulating a partisan nominating petition or soliciting votes for a partisan candidate for public office; or serving as a delegate, alternate or proxy to a political party convention. Our judgment is that neither the First Amendment nor any other provision of the Constitution invalidates a law barring this kind of partisan political conduct by federal employees. . . .

[T]he government has an interest in regulating the conduct and "the speech of its employees that differ[s] significantly from those it possesses in connection with regulation of the speech of the citizenry in general. The problem in any case is to arrive at a balance between the interest of the [employee], as a citizen, in commenting upon matters of public concern and the interest of the [government], as an employer, in promoting the efficiency of the public services it performs through its employees." Although Congress is free to strike a different balance than it has, if it so chooses, we think the balance it has so far struck is sustainable by the obviously important interests sought to be served by the limitations on partisan political activities now contained in the Hatch Act.

It seems fundamental in the first place that employees in the Executive Branch of the Government, or those working for any of its agencies, should administer the law in accordance with the will of Congress, rather than in accordance with their own or the will of a political party. They are expected to enforce the law and execute the programs of the Government without bias or favoritism for or against any political party or group or the members thereof. A major thesis of the Hatch Act is that to serve this great end of Government—the impartial execution of the laws—it is essential that federal employees not, for example, take formal positions in political parties, not undertake to play substantial roles in partisan political campaigns and not run for office on partisan political tickets. Forbidding activities like these will reduce the hazards to fair and effective government. . . .

For the foregoing reasons, the judgment of the District Court is reversed.

So ordered.

MR. JUSTICE DOUGLAS, with whom MR. JUSTICE BRENNAN and MR. JUSTICE MARSHALL concur, dissenting. . . .

The chilling effect of these vague and generalized prohibitions is so obvious as not to need elaboration. That effect would not be material to the issue of constitutionality if only the normal contours of the police power were involved. On the run of social and economic matters the "rational basis" standard . . . would suffice. But . . . [w]e deal here with a First Amendment right to speak, to propose, to publish, to petition Government, to assemble. Time and place are obvious limitations. Thus no one could object if employees were barred from using office time to engage in outside activities whether political or otherwise. But it is of no concern of Government what an employee does in his or her spare time, whether religion, recreation, social work, or politics is his hobby—unless what he or she does impairs efficiency or other facets of the merits of his job. . . .

D. SOLDIERS

Parker v. Levy

417 US 733, 94 S Ct 2547, 41 L Ed 439 (1974)

While military personnel are not excluded from First Amendment protection, the necessity for discipline and obedience renders permissible within the military that which would be constitutionally impermissible outside it.

[Howard Levy, a physician, was a captain in the army stationed at Fort Jackson, South Carolina. He was convicted by court-martial of violating the following articles of the Uniform Code of Military Justice: Art. 90—"Any person subject to this chapter who . . . willfully disobeys a lawful command of his superior commanding officer . . ."; Art. 133—"Any commissioned officer . . . who is convicted of conduct unbecoming an officer and a gentleman . . ."; Art. 134—"Though not specifically mentioned in this chapter, all disorders and neglects to the prejudice of good order and discipline in the armed forces . . . shall be taken cognizance of by . . . court-martial . . . and shall be punished at the discretion of that court."

The following statement was described as representative of several public statements made by Levy to enlisted men at the post:

"The United States is wrong in being involved in the Viet Nam War. I would refuse to go to Viet Nam if ordered to do so. I don't see why any colored soldier would go to Viet Nam: They should refuse to go to Viet Nam and if sent should refuse to fight because they are discriminated against and denied their freedom in the United States, and they are sacrificed and discriminated against in Viet Nam by being given all the hazardous duty and they are suffering the majority of casualties. If I were a colored soldier I would refuse to go to Viet Nam and if I were a colored soldier and were sent I would refuse to fight. Special Forces personnel are liars and thieves and killers of peasants and murders of women and children."

Levy's appeal within the military was unsuccessful. He then sought habeas corpus relief. A decision by a district court denying relief was reversed by a court of appeals which in turn was reversed by the Supreme Court.]

MR. JUSTICE REHNQUIST delivered the opinion of the Court. . . .

This Court has long recognized that the military is, by necessity, a specialized society separate from civilian society. We have also recognized that the military has, again by necessity, developed laws and traditions of its own during its long history. The differences between the military and civilian communities result from the fact that "it is the primary business of armies and navies to fight or be ready to fight wars should the occasion arise." *Toth* v. *Quarles,* 350 US 11, 17 (1955). In *In re Grimley,* 137 US 147, 153 (1890), the Court observed: "An army is not a deliberative body. It is an executive arm. Its law is that of obedience. No question can be left open as to the right to command in the officer, or the duty of obedience in the solider." . . .

Just as military society has been a society apart from civilian society, so "[m]ilitary law . . . is a jurispurdence which exists separate and apart from the law which governs in our federal judicial establishment." *Burns* v. *Wilson, supra,* 346 US, at 140. And to maintain the discipline essential to perform its mission effectively, the military has developed what "may not unfitly be called the customary military law" or "general usage of the military service." *Martin* v. *Mott,* 12 Wheaton 19, 35 (1827). As the opinion in *Martin* v. *Mott* demonstrates, the Court has approved the enforcement of those military customs and usages by courts-martial from the early days of this Nation. . . .

The differences noted by this settled line of authority, first between the military community and the civilian community, and second between military law and civilian law, continue in the present day under the Uniform Code of Military Justice. . . .

Appellee urges that both Arts. 133 and 134 ("the General Article") are "void for vagueness" under the Due Process Clause of the Fifth Amendment and overbroad in violation of the First Amendment. . . . Each of these Articles has been construed by the United States Court of Military Appeals or by other military authorities in such a manner as to at least partially narrow its otherwise broad scope. . . .

Because of the factors differentiating military society from civilian society, we hold that the proper standard of review for a vagueness challenge to the Articles of the U.C.M.J. is the standard which applies to criminal statutes regulating economic affairs. Clearly, that standard is met here. . . .

Since appellee could have had no reasonable doubt that his published statements urging Negro enlisted men not to go to Vietnam if ordered to do so was both "unbecoming an officer and a gentleman," and "to the prejudice of good order and discipline in the armed forces," in violation of the provisions of Art. 133 and Art. 134, respectively, his challenge to them as unconstitutionally vague under the Due Process Clause of the Fifth Amendment must fail.

We likewise reject appellee's contention that Arts. 133 and 134 are facially invalid because of their "overbreadth." . . .

While the members of the military are not excluded from the protection granted by the First Amendment, the different character of the military community and of the military mission requires a different application of those protections. The fundamental necessity for obedience, and the consequent necessity for imposition of discipline, may render permissible within the military that which would be constitutionally impermissible outside it. . . .

Reversed.

MR. JUSTICE MARSHALL took no part in the consideration or decision of this case.

MR. JUSTICE BLACKMUN, with whom THE CHIEF JUSTICE joins. [This concurring opinion is omitted here.]

MR. JUSTICE DOUGLAS, dissenting. . . . This is the first case that presents to us a question of what protection, if any, the First Amendment gives people in the Armed Services:

"Congress shall make no law . . . abridging the freedom of speech, or of the press."

On its face there are no exceptions—no preferred classes for whose benefits the First Amendment extends, no exempt classes. . . .

The power to draft an army includes of course the power to curtail considerably the "liberty" of the people who make it up. But Congress in these Articles has not undertaken to cross the forbidden First Amendment line. Making a speech or comment on one of the most important and controversial public issues of the past two decades cannot by any stretch of dictionary meaning be included in "disorders and neglects to the prejudice of good order and discipline in the armed forces." Nor can what Capt. Levy said possibly be "conduct of a nature to bring discredit upon the armed forces." He was uttering his own belief—an article of faith that he sincerely held. This was no mere ploy to perform a "subversive" act. Many others who loved their country shared his views. They were not saboteurs. Uttering one's beliefs is sacrosanct under the First Amendment. Punishing the utterances is an "abridgement" of speech in the constitutional sense.

MR. JUSTICE STEWART, with whom MR. JUSTICE DOUGLAS and MR. JUSTICE BRENNAN join, dissenting.

Article 133 of the Uniform Code of Military Justice, 10 USC § 933 (1970), makes it a criminal offense to engage in "conduct unbecoming an officer and a gentleman." Article 134, 10 USC § 934 (1970), makes criminal "all disorders and neglects to the prejudice of good order and discipline in the armed forces" and "all conduct of a nature to bring discredit upon the armed forces." The Court today, reversing a unanimous judgment of the Court of Appeals, upholds the constitutionality of these statutes. I find it hard to imagine criminal statutes more patently unconstitutional than these vague and uncertain General Articles, and I would, accordingly, affirm the judgment before us.

Note

Compare *Secretary of the Navy* v. *Avrech,*   US   (1974).

E. PRISONERS

Procunier v. Martinez

416 US 396, 94 S Ct 1800, 40 L Ed2d 224 (1974)

Censorship of the correspondence of prisoners must be no greater than is necessary to serve the legitimate governmental interests involved, and it must be accompanied by procedural safeguards against abuse.

MR. JUSTICE POWELL delivered the opinion of the Court.

This case concerns the constitutionality of certain regulations promulgated by appellant Procunier in his capacity as Director of the California Department of Corrections. Appellees [Martinez et al.] brought a class action on behalf of themselves and all other inmates of penal institutions under the Department's jurisdiction to challenge the rules relating to censorship of prisoner mail and the ban against the use of law students and legal paraprofessionals to conduct attorney-client interviews with inmates. ... [A] three-judge United States District Court was convened to hear appellees' request for declaratory and injunctive relief. That court entered summary judgment enjoining continued enforcement of the rules in question and ordering appellants to submit new regulations for the court's approval. ... While the first proposed revisions of the Department's regulations were pending before the District Court, appellants brought this appeal to contest that court's decision holding the original regulations unconstitutional. ...

We begin our analysis of the proper standard of review for constitutional challenges to censorship of prisoner mail with a somewhat different premise than that taken by the other federal courts that have considered the question. For the most part, these courts have dealt with challenges to censorship of prisoner mail as involving broad questions of "prisoners' rights." ... In our view this inquiry is unnecessary. In determining the proper standard of review of prison restrictions on inmate correspondence, we have no occasion to consider the extent to which an individual's right to free speech survives incarceration, for a narrower basis of decision is at hand. In the case of direct personal correspondence between inmates and those who have a particularized interest in communicating with them, mail censorship implicates more than the right of prisoners.

Communication by letter is not accomplished by the act of writing words on paper. Rather, it is effected only when the letter is read by the addressee. Both parties to the correspondence have an interest in securing that result, and censorship of the communication between them necessarily impinges on the interest of each. Whatever the status of a prisoner's claim to uncensored correspondence with an outsider, it is plain that the latter's interest is grounded in the First Amendment's guarantee of freedom of speech. And this does not depend on whether the nonprisoner correspondent is the author or intended recipient of a particular letter, for the addressee as well as the sender of direct personal correspondence derives from the First and Fourteenth Amendments a protection against unjustified governmental interference with the intended communication. ... We do not deal here with difficult questions of the so-called "right to hear" and third-party standing but with a particular means of communication in which the interests of both parties are inextricably meshed. The wife of a prison inmate who is not permitted to read all that her husband wanted to say to her has suffered an abridgement of her interest in communicating with him as plain as that which results from censorship of her letter to him. In either event, censorship of prisoner mail works a consequential restriction on the First and Fourteenth Amendments rights of those who are not prisoners.

Accordingly, we reject any attempt to justify censorship of inmate correspondence merely by reference to certain assumptions about the legal status of prisoners. ... We ... turn for guidance not to cases involving questions of "prisoners' rights" but to decisions of this Court dealing with the general problem of incidental restrictions on First Amendment liberties imposed in furtherance of legitimate governmental activities.

As the Court noted in *Tinker* v. *Des Moines School District,* 393 US 503, 506 (1969), First Amendment guarantees must be "applied in light of the special characteristics of the ... environment." *Tinker* concerned the interplay between the right to freedom of speech of public high school students and "the need for affirming the comprehensive authority of the States and of school officials, consistent with fundamental constitutional safeguards, to prescribe and control the conduct in schools." *Id.,* at 507. In overruling a school regulation prohibiting the wearing of anti-war armbands, the Court undertook a careful analysis of the legitimate requirements of orderly school administration in order to ensure that the students were afforded maximum freedom of speech consistent with those requirements. The same approach was followed in *Healy* v. *James,* 408 US 169 (1972). ...

Applying the teachings of our prior decisions to the instant context, we hold that censorship of prisoner mail is justified if the following criteria are met. First, the regulation or practice in question must further an important or substantial governmental interest unrelated to the suppression of expression. Prison officials may not censor inmate correspondence simply to eliminate unflattering or unwelcome opinions or factually inaccurate statements. Rather, they must show that a regulation authorizing mail censorship furthers one or more of the substantial governmental interests of security, order, and rehabilitation. Second, the limitation of First Amendment freedoms must be no greater than is necessary or essential to the protection of the particular governmental interest involved. Thus a restriction on inmate correspondence that furthers an important or substantial interest of penal administration will nevertheless be invalid if its sweep is unnecessarily broad. This does not mean, of course, that prison administrators may be required to show with certainty that adverse consequences would flow from the failure to censor a particular letter. Some latitude in anticipating the probable consequences of allowing certain speech in a prison environment is essential to the proper discharge of an administrator's duty. But any regulation or practice that restricts inmate correspondence must be generally necessary to protect one or more of the legitimate governmental interests identified above.

On the basis of this standard, we affirm the judgment of the District Court. The regulations invalidated by that court authorized ... censorship of prisoner mail far broader than any legitimate interest of penal administration demands and were properly found invalid by the District Court.

We also agree with the District Court that the decision to censor or withhold delivery of a particular letter must be accompanied by minimum procedural safeguards. The interests of prisoners and their correspondents in uncensored communication by letter, grounded as it is in the First Amendment, is plainly a "liberty" interest within the meaning of the Fourteenth Amendment even though qualified of necessity by the circumstance of imprisonment. As such, it is protected from arbitrary governmental invasion. ... This District Court required that an inmate be notified of the rejection of a letter written by or addressed to him, that the author of that letter be given a reasonable opportunity to protest that decision, and that complaints be referred to a prison official other than the person who originally disapproved the correspondence. These requirements do not appear to be unduly burdensome, nor do appellants so contend. Accordingly, we affirm the judgment of the District Court with respect to the Department's regulations relating to prisoner mail.

The District Court also enjoined continued enforcement of Administrative Rule MV-IV-02, which provides in pertinent part:

"Investigators for an attorney-of-record will be confined to not more than two. Such investigators must be licensed by the State or must be members of the State Bar. Designation must be made in writing by the Attorney." By restricting access to prisoners to members of the bar and licensed private investigators, this regulation imposed an absolute ban on the use by attorneys of law students and legal paraprofessionals to interview inmate clients. In fact attorneys could not even delegate to such persons the task of obtaining prisoners' signatures on legal documents. The District Court reasoned that this rule constituted an unjustifiable restriction on the right of access to the courts. We agree. . . .

The judgment is

Affirmed.

MR. JUSTICE DOUGLAS, with whom MR. JUSTICE BRENNAN and MR. JUSTICE MARSHALL join, concurring.

I have joined Part II of MR. JUSTICE MARSHALL's opinion because I think it makes abundantly clear that foremost among the Bill of Rights of prisoners in this country, whether under state or federal dention, is the First Amendment. Prisoners are still "persons" entitled to all constitutional rights except and unless their liberty has been constitutionally curtailed in the procedures that satisfy all of the requirements of due process. . . .

MR. JUSTICE MARSHALL, with whom MR. JUSTICE BRENNAN joins, concurring.

I concur in the opinion and judgment of the Court. I write separately only to emphasize my view that prison authorities do not have a general right to open and read all incoming and outgoing prison mail. Although the issue of the First Amendment rights of inmates is explicitly reserved by the Court, I would reach that issue and hold that prison authorities may not read inmate mail as a matter of course.

As Mr. Justice Holmes observed over a half century ago, ". . . the use of the mails is almost as much a part of free speech as the right to use our tongues. . . ." . . . A prisoner does not shed such basic First Amendment rights at the prison gate. Rather, he " . . . retains all the rights of an ordinary citizen except those expressly, or by necessary implication, taken from him by law." *Coffin* v. *Reichard,* 143 F.2d 443, 445 (CA6 1944). Accordingly, prisoners are, in my view, entitled to use the mails as a medium of free expression not as a privilege, but rather as a constitutionally guaranteed right. . . .

Note

Pell v. *Procunier,*   US   (1974), sustained prison regulations which prohibited interviews between prison inmates and representatives of the news media. *Wolff* v. *McDonnell,*   US   (1974), contains a review of judicial holdings relating to the rights of prisoners.

Section 4.   Time, Place, and Manner of Expression

A.   SYMBOLIC SPEECH

Smith v. Goguen

415 US 566, 94 S Ct 1242, 39 L Ed2d 605 (1974)

A conviction cannot rest upon a charge of publicly treating contemptuously the flag of the United States.

MR. JUSTICE POWELL delivered the opinion of the Court.

The Sheriff of Worcester County, Massachusetts [Joseph Smith], appeals from a judgment of the United States Court of Appeals for the First Circuit holding the contempt provision of the Massachusetts flag misuse statute unconstitutionally vague and overbroad. . . . We affirm on the vagueness ground. We do not reach the correctness of the holding below on overbreadth or other First Amendment grounds.

The slender record in this case reveals little more than that Goguen wore a small cloth version of the United States flag sewn to the seat of his trousers. The flag was approximately four by six inches and was displayed to the left rear of Goguen's blue jeans. On January 30, 1970, two police officers in Leominster, Massachusetts saw Goguen bedecked in that fashion. The first officer encountered Goguen standing and talking with a group of persons on a public street. The group apparently was not engaged in any demonstration or other protest associated with Goguen's apparel. No disruption of traffic or breach of the peace occurred. When this officer approached Goguen to question him about the flag, the other persons present laughed. Some time later, the second officer observed Goguen in the same attire walking in the downtown business district of Leominister.

The following day the first officer swore out a complaint against Goguen under the contempt provision of the Massachusetts flag misuse statute. The relevant part of the statute then read:

> "Whoever publicly mutilates, tramples upon, defaces or treates contemptuously the flag of the United States . . ., whether such flag is public or private property . . ., shall be punished by a fine of not less than ten nor more than one hundred dollars or by imprisonment for not more than one year, or both. . . ."

Despite the first six words of the statute, Goguen was not charged with any action of physical desecration. As permitted by the disjunctive structure of the desecration and contempt portion of the statute, the officer charged specifically and only that Goguen "did publicly treat contemptuously the flag of the United States. . . . "

After jury trial in the Worcester County Superior Court, Goguen was found guilty. The court imposed a sentence of six months in the Massachusetts House of Corrections. Goguen appealed to the Massachusetts Supreme Judicial Court, which affirmed. . . .

After Goguen began serving his sentence, he was granted bail and then ordered released on a writ of habeas corpus by the United States District Court for the District of Massachusetts. . . . The District Court found the flag contempt portion of the Massachusetts statute impermissibly vague under the Due Process Clause of the Fourteenth Amendment as well as overbroad under the First Amendment. . . .

The Court of Appeals, with one judge concurring, affirmed the District Court on both First Amendment and vagueness grounds. . . .

We agree with the holdings of the District Court and the Court of Appeals on the due process doctrine of vagueness. . . .

Flag contempt statutes have been characterized as void for lack of notice on the theory that "[w]hat is contemptuous to one man may be a work of art to another." Goguen's behavior can hardly be described as art. Immaturity or "silly conduct" probably comes closer to the mark. But we see the force of the District Court's observation that the flag has become "an object of youth fashion and high camp. . . ."

In its terms, the language at issue is sufficiently unbounded to prohibit, as the District Court noted, "any public deviation from formal flag etiquette. . . ." Statutory language of such a standardless sweep allows policemen, prosecutors, and juries to pursue their personal predilections. Legislatures may not so abdicate their responsibilities for setting the standards of the criminal law. . . .

There are areas of human conduct where, by the nature of the problems presented, legislatures simply cannot establish standards with great precision. Control of the broad range of disorderly conduct that may inhibit a policeman in the performance of his official duties may be one such area, requiring as it does an on-the-spot assessment of the need to keep order. . . . But there is no comparable reason for committing broad discretion to law enforcement officials in the area of flag contempt. Indeed, because display of the flag is so common and takes so many forms, changing from one generation to another and often difficult to distinguish in principle, a legislature should define with some care the flag behavior it intends to outlaw. Certainly nothing prevents a legislature from defining with substantial specificity what constitutes forbidden treatment of United States flags. The statutory language at issue here fails to approach that goal and is void for vagueness. The judgment is affirmed.

It is so ordered.

MR. JUSTICE WHITE, concurring in the judgment.

. . . Although I concur in the judgment of affirmance . . . I cannot agree with [the] rationale.

I am . . . confident that the statute was not vague with respect to the conduct for which Goguen was arrested and convicted. It should not be beyond the reasonable comprehension of anyone who would conform his conduct to the law to realize that sewing a flag on the seat of his pants is contemptuous of the flag. The Supreme Judicial Court of Massachusetts, in affirming the conviction, stated that the "jury could infer that the violation was intentional. . . . " If he thus intended the very act which the statute forbids, Goguen can hardly complain that he did not realize his acts were in violation of the statute. . . .

The unavoidable inquiry, therefore, becomes whether the "treats contemptuously" provision of the statute, as applied in this case, is unconstitutional under the First Amendment. . . .

I would affirm Goguen's conviction, therefore, had he been convicted for mutilating, trampling upon or defacing the flag, or for using the flag as a billboard for commercial advertisements or other displays. The Massachusetts statute, however, does not stop with proscriptions against defacement or attaching foreign objects to the flag. It also makes it a crime if one "treats contemptuously" the flag of the United States, and Goguen was convicted under this part of the statute. To violate the statute in this respect, it is not enough that one "treat" the flag; he must also treat it "contemptuously," which, in ordinary understanding, is the expression of contempt for the flag. In the case before us, as has been noted, the jury must have found that Goguen not only wore the flag on the seat of his pants but also that the act—and hence Goguen himself—was contemptuous of the flag. To convict on this basis is to convict not to protect the physical integrity or to protect against acts interfering with the proper use of the flag, but to punish for communicating ideas about the flag unacceptable to the ontrolling majority in the legislature.

. . . In *O'Brien,* the Court sustained a conviction for draft card burning, although admittedly the burning was itself expressive. There, destruction of draft cards, whether communicative or not, was found to be inimical to important governmental considerations. But the Court made clear that if the concern of the law was with the expression associated with the act, the result would be otherwise:

> "The case at bar is therefore unlike one where the alleged governmental interest in regulating conduct arises in some measure because the communication allegedly integral to the conduct is itself thought to be harmful. In *Stromberg v. California,* 283 US 359 (1931), for example, this Court struck down a statutory phrase which punished people who expressed their "opposition to organized government" by displaying "any flag, badge, banner, or device." Since the statute there was aimed at suppressing communication it could not be sustained as a regulation of noncommunicative conduct." 391 US 367, 382 (1968).

It would be difficult, therefore, to believe that the conviction in *O'Brien* would have been sustained had the statute proscribed only contemptuous burning of draft cards.

Any conviction under the "treats contemptuously" provision of the Massachusetts statute would suffer from the same infirmity. This is true of Goguen's conviction. And if it be said that the conviction does not violate the First and Fourteenth Amendments because Goguen communicated nothing at all by his conduct and did not intend to do so, there would then be no evidentiary basis whatsoever for convicting him of being "contemptuous" of the flag. I concur in the Court's judgment.

MR. JUSTICE BLACKMUN, with whom THE CHIEF JUSTICE joins, dissenting. . . .

I agree with MR. JUSTICE REHNQUIST when he concludes that the First Amendment affords no shield to Goguen's conduct. . . . [T]he Massachusetts court, in upholding the conviction, . . . limited the scope of the statute to protecting the physical integrity of the flag. . . . I accept the Massachusetts court's opinion at what I regard to be its face value.

MR. JUSTICE REHNQUIST, with whom THE CHIEF JUSTICE joins, dissenting. . . .

. . . Goguen was convicted of treating the flag contemptuously by the act of wearing it where he did, and I have difficulty seeing how Goguen could be found by a jury to have treated the flag contemptuously by his act and still not to have expressed any idea at all. There are, therefore, in my opinion, at least marginal elements of "symbolic speech" in Goguen's conduct as reflected by this record.

Many cases which could be said to involve conduct no less expressive than Goguen's, however, have never been thought to require analysis in First Amendment terms because of the presence of other factors. One who burns down the factory of a company whose products he dislikes can expect his First Amendment defense to a consequent arson prosecution to be given short shrift by the courts. The arson statute safeguards the government's substantial interest in preventing the destruction of property by means dangerous to human life, and an arsonist's motive is quite irrelevant. . . . Yet Goguen . . . has so far as this record shows infringed on the ordinary property rights of no one.

That Goguen owned the flag with which he adorned himself, however, is not dispositive of the First Amendment issue. . . . [T]here are so many well-established exceptions to the proposition that one may do what he likes with his own property that it cannot be said to have even the status of a general rule.

. . . Land use regulations in a residential zoning district typically do not merely exclude malodorous and unsightly rendering plants; they often also prohibit erection of buildings or monuments, including ones open to the public, which might itself in an aesthetic sense involve substantial elements of "expressive conduct." . . .

As may land, so may other kinds of property be subjected to close regulation and control. A person with an ownership interest in controlled drugs, or in firearms, cannot use them, sell them, and transfer them in whatever manner he pleases. . . .

Even . . . laws regulating use of the flag are by no means unique. A number of examples can be found of statutes enacted by Congress which protect only a peculiarly governmental interest in property otherwise privately owned. 18 USC § 504 prohibits the printing or publishing in actual size or in actual color of any United States postage or revenue stamp, or of any obligation or security of the United States. It likewise prohibits the importation of any plates for the purpose of such imprinting. 18 USC § 331 prohibits the alteration of any Federal Reserve note or national bank note, and 18 USC § 333 prohibits the disfiguring or defacing of any national bank note or coin. . . .

My Brother WHITE says, however, that whatever may be said of neutral statutes simply designed to protect a governmental interest in private property, which in the case of the flag may be characterized as an interest in preserving its physical integrity, the Massachusetts statute here is not neutral. It punishes only those who treat the flag contemptuously, imposing no penalty on those who "treat" it otherwise, that is, those who impair its physical integrity in some other way. . . .

But Massachusetts metes out punishment to anyone who publicly mutilates, tramples, or defaces the flag, regardless of his motive or purpose. It also punishes the display of any "words, figures, advertisements or designs" on the flag, or the use of a flag in a parade as a receptacle for depositing or collecting money. Likewise prohibited is the offering or selling of any article on which is engraved a representation of the United States flag. . . .

In *United States* v. *O'Brien,* 391 US 367 (1968), the Court observed:

> "We cannot accept the view that an apparently limitless variety of conduct can be labeled 'speech' whenever the person engaging in the conduct intends thereby to express an idea."
> 391 US, at 376.

Then, proceeding "on the assumption that the alleged communicative element in O'Brien's conduct was sufficient to bring into play the First Amendment," the Court held that a regulation of conduct was sufficiently justified

> "if it is within the constitutional power of the Government; if it furthers an important or substantial governmental interest; if the governmental interest is unrelated to the suppression of free expression; and if the incidental restriction on alleged First Amendment freedoms is no greater than is essential to the furtherance of that interest." 391 US, at 377.

While I have some doubt that the first enunciation of a group of tests such as those established in *O'Brien* sets them in concrete for all time, it does seem to me that the Massachusetts statute substantially complies with those tests. . . .

. . . [The flag] is the one visible embodiment of the authority of the National Government, through which the laws of the Nation and the guarantees of the Constitution are enforced.

The permissible scope of government regulation of this unique physical object cannot be adequately dealt with in terms of the law of private property or by a highly abstract, scholastic interpretation of the First Amendment. Massachusetts has not prohibited Goguen from wearing a sign sewn to the seat of his pants expressing in words his low opinion of the flag, of the country, or anything else. It has prohibited him from wearing there a particular symbol of extraordinary significance and content, for which significance and content Goguen is in no wise responsible. The flag of the United States is not just another "thing," and it is not just another "idea"; it is not primarily an idea at all.

Here Goguen was, so far as this record appears, quite free to express verbally whatever views it was he was seeking to express by wearing a flag sewn to his pants, on the streets of Leominster or in any of its parks or commons where free speech and assembly was customarily permitted. . . . He was simply prohibited from impairing the physical integrity of a unique national symbol which has been given content by generations of his and our forebears, a symbol of which he had purchased a copy. I believe Massachusetts had a right to enact this prohibition.

Note

Spence v. *Washington,* 418 US 405 (1974), reversed the conviction of a student for displaying a privately owned United States flag upside down with a large peace symbol affixed thereto from his apartment window in violation of a statute forbidding the exhibition of a United States flag to which is superimposed symbols or other extraneous material.

B. PICKETS AND HANDBILLS

Pickets

In *Thornhill* v. *Alabama,* 310 US 88 (1940), the Court made sweeping statements about the right to picket. In subsequent cases, however, the Court recognized that picketing was something more than free speech and that a state could prohibit picketing in a context of violence or as a means toward obtaining an illegal objective. A concise history of the cases dealing with picketing is given in *International Brotherhood of Teamsters* v. *Vogt,* 354 US 284 (1957).

Amalgamated Food Employees v. *Logan Valley Plaza,* 391 US 308 (1967), reversed an injunction of a Pennsylvania court restraining union members from "Picketing and trespassing upon the private property of the plaintiff, Weis Markets, Inc., Store No. 40, located at Logan Valley Mall, Altoona, Pennsylvania, including as such private property the storeroom, porch and parcel pick-up area." The opinion of the Court by Justice Marshall relied heavily upon the concept of some privately owned private property being dedicated to public use, citing *Marsh* v. *Alabama,* 326 US 501 (1946), a case sustaining the right of Jehovah's Witnesses to distribute literature on the streets of a company-owned town. Justice Black, who wrote the opinion in the *Marsh* case, dissented, saying: "It seems clear to me, in light of the customary way that supermarkets now must operate, that pickup zones are as much a part of these stores as the inside counters. . . . I cannot conceive how such a pickup zone, even by the wildest stretching of *Marsh* . . . could ever be considered dedicated to the public or to pickets."

Handbills

Talley v. *California,* 362 US 60 (1960), held void on its face a Los Angeles ordinance prohibiting the distribution of any handbill which did not have printed on it the name and address of (a) "The person who printed, wrote, compiled or manufactured the same" and (b) "The person [or organization] who caused the same to be distributed. . . ." For the Court, Justice Black wrote: "[A]s in *Griffin,* the ordinance here is not limited to handbills whose content is 'obscene or offensive to public morals or that advocates unlawful conduct.' Counsel has urged that this ordinance is aimed at providing a way to identify those responsible for fraud, false advertising and libel. Yet the ordinance is in no manner so limited, nor have we been referred to any legislative history indicating such a purpose. Therefore we do not pass on the validity of an ordinance limited to prevent these or any other supposed evils." Justices Clark, Frankfurther, and Whittaker dissented.

Lloyd Corporation v. *Tanner,* 407 US 551 (1972), narrowly restricted earlier cases and ruled against any general right to distribute handbills on private property merely because it is open to the public. Lloyd Center is a large retail shopping center in Portland, Oregon, sprawling over fifty acres, with a perimeter of almost one and one-half miles. Five public streets traverse the center and several others run partly into or around it. These streets and the adjacent sidewalks are the only parts of the center not owned by the Lloyd Corporation, Ltd., which enforces a policy against the distribution of handbills within the building complex and its malls. In a quiet and orderly manner, five young people began to distribute handbills protesting the Vietnam War on a mall walkway. Security guards warned that they would be arrested unless they stopped distributing the handbills on the Corporation's property. They brought suit seeking injunctive relief. The district court found the center to be the "functional equivalent of a public business district" and ruled that its ban on handbills violated First Amendment rights.

The Supreme Court reversed this decision. For the majority, Justice Powell wrote:

> The basic issue in this case is whether respondents, in the exercise of asserted First Amendment rights, may distribute handbills on Lloyd's private property contrary to its wishes and contrary to a policy enforced against *all* handbilling. In addressing this issue, it must be remembered that the First and Fourteenth Amendments safeguard the rights of free speech and assembly by limitations on *state* action, not on action by the owner of private property used nondiscriminatorily for private purposes only. The Due Process Clauses of the Fifth and Fourteenth Amendments are also relevant to this case. They provide that "no person shall . . . be deprived of life, liberty or property, without due process of law." There is the further proscription in the Fifth Amendment against the taking of "private property . . . for public use, without just compensation."
>
> Although accommodations between the values protected by these three Amendments are sometimes necessary, and the courts properly have shown a special solicitude for the guarantees of the First Amendment, this Court has never held that a trespasser or an uninvited guest may exercise general rights of free speech on property privately owned and used nondiscriminatorily for private purposes only. . . .
>
> Nor does property lose its private character merely because the public is generally invited to use it for designated purposes.

Organization for a Better Austin v. *Keefe,* 402 US 415 (1971), held void an injunction issued by an Illinois court banning a community organization from distributing leaflets charging a real estate broker with the use of "blockbusting" and "panic peddling" tactics. The state court had issued the injunction on the theory that the leaflets were coercive and intimidating rather than informative, and hence an invasion of privacy. This argument was unappealing to the Supreme Court.

C. UNWILLING AUDIENCE

Terminiello v. Chicago

337 US 1, 69 S Ct 894, 93 L Ed2d 1131 (1949)

An ordinance which permits punishment of a person for speech stirring people to anger, inviting public dispute, or bringing about a condition of unrest is void.

MR. JUSTICE DOUGLAS delivered the opinion of the Court.

Petitioner [Arthur Terminiello] after jury trial was found guilty of disorderly conduct in violation of a city ordinance of Chicago and fined. The case grew out of an address he delivered in an auditorium in Chicago under the auspices of the Christian Veterans of America. The meeting commanded considerable public attention. The auditorium was filled to capacity with over eight hundred persons present. Others were turned away. Outside of the auditorium a crowd of about one thousand persons gathered to protest against the meeting. A cordon of policemen was assigned to the meeting to maintain order; but they were not able to prevent several disturbances. The crowd outside was angry and turbulent.

Petitioner in his speech condemned the conduct of the crowd outside and vigorously, if not viciously, criticized various political and racial groups whose activities he denounced as inimical to the nation's welfare.

The trial court charged that "breach of the peace" consists of any "misbehavior which violates the public peace and decorum"; and that the "misbehavior may constitute a breach of the peace if it stirs the public to anger, invites dispute, brings about a condition of unrest, or creates a disturbance, or if it molests the inhabitants in the enjoyment of peace and quiet by arousing alarm." Petitioner did not take exception to that instruction. But he maintained at all times that the ordinance as applied to his conduct violated his right of free speech under the Federal Constitution. The judgment of conviction was affirmed by the Illinois Appellate Court and by the Illinois Supreme Court. The case is here on a petition for *certiorari* which we granted because of the importance of the question presented. . . .

As we have noted, the statutory words "breach of the peace" were defined in instructions to the jury to include speech which "stirs the public to anger, invites dispute, brings about a condition of unrest, or creates a disturbance. . . ." That construction of the ordinance is a ruling on a question of state law that is as binding on us as though the precise words had been written into the ordinance. . . .

The vitality of civil and political institutions in our society depends on free discussion. . . .

Accordingly a function of free speech under our system of government is to invite dispute. It may indeed best serve its high purpose when it induces a condition of unrest, creates dissatisfaction with conditions as they are, or even stirs people to anger. Speech is often provocative and challenging. It may strike at prejudices and preconceptions and have profound unsettling effects as it presses for acceptance of an idea. That is why freedom of speech, though not absolute, . . . is nevertheless protected against censorship or punishment, unless shown likely to produce a clear and present danger of a serious substantive evil that rises far above public inconvenience, annoyance, or unrest. . . . There is no room under our Constitution for a more restrictive view. For the alternative would lead to standardization of ideas either by legislatures, courts or dominant political or community groups.

The ordinance as construed by the trial court seriously invaded this province. It permitted conviction of petitioner if his speech stirred people to anger, invited public dispute, or brought about a condition of unrest. A conviction resting on any of those grounds may not stand. . . .

Reversed.

Mr. Justice Jackson, dissenting.

The Court reverses this conviction by reiterating generalized approbations of freedom of speech with which, in the abstract, no one will disagree. Doubts as to their applicability are lulled by avoidance of more than passing reference to the circumstances of Terminiello's speech and judging it as if he had spoken to persons as dispassionate as empty benches, or like a modern Demosthenes practicing his Philippics on a lonely seashore.

But the local court that tried Terminiello was not indulging in theory. It was dealing with a riot and with a speech that provoked a hostile mob and incited a friendly one, and threatened violence between the two. When the trial judge instructed the jury that it might find Terminiello guilty of inducing a breach of peace if his behavior stirred the public to anger, invited dispute, brought about unrest, created a disturbance or molested peace and quiet by arousing alarm, he was not speaking of these as harmless or abstract conditions. He was addressing his words to the concrete behavior and specific consequences disclosed by the evidence. He was saying to the jury, in effect, that if this particular speech added fuel to the situation already so inflamed as to threaten to get beyond police control, it could be punished as inducing a breach of peace. . . .

Terminiello, advertised as a Catholic Priest, but revealed at the trial to be under suspension by his Bishop, was brought to Chicago from Birmingham, Alabama, to address a gathering that assembled in response to a call signed by Gerald L. K. Smith, which, among other things, said:

> " . . . The same people who hate Father Coughlin hate Father Terminiello. They have persecuted him, hounded him, threatened him, but he has remained unaffected by their anti-Christian campaign against him. You will hear all sorts of reports concerning Father Terminiello. But remember that he is a Priest in good standing and a fearless lover of Christ and America."

The jury may have considered that this call attempted to capitalize the hatreds this man had stirred and foreshadowed, if it did not intend to invite, the kind of demonstration that followed.

Terminiello's own testimony shows the conditions under which he spoke. So far as material it follows:

> " . . . We got there (the meeting place) approximately fifteen or twenty minutes past eight. The car stopped at the front entrance. There was a crowd of three or four hundred congregated there shouting and cursing and picketing. . . .
>
> "When we got there the pickets were not marching; they were body to body and covered the sidewalk completely, some on the steps so that we had to form a flying wedge to get through. Police escorted us to the building, and I noticed four or five others there.
>
> "They called us 'God damned Fascists, Nazis, ought to hang the so and sos.' When I entered the building I heard the howls of the people outside. . . . There were four or five plain clothes officers standing at the entrance to the stage and three or four at the entrance to the back door.
>
> "The officers threatened that if they broke the door again they would arrest them and every time they opened the door a little to look out something was thrown at the officers, including ice-picks and rocks. . . ."

The court below, in addition to this recital, heard other evidence, that the crowd reached an estimated number of 1,500. Picket lines obstructed and interfered with access to the building. The crowd constituted "a surging, howling mob hurling epithets" at those who would enter and "tried to tear their clothes off." One young woman's coat was torn off and she had to be assisted into the meeting by policemen. Those inside the hall could hear loud noises and hear those on the outside yell, "Fascists," "Hitlers" and curse words like "damn Fascists." Bricks were thrown through windowpanes before and during the speaking. About 28 windows were broken. The street was black with people on both sides for at least a block either way; bottles, stink bombs and brickbats were thrown. Police were unable to control the mob, which kept breaking the windows at the meeting hall, drowning out the speaker's voice at times and breaking in through the back door of the auditorium. About 17 of the group outside were arrested by the police.

Knowing of this environment, Terminiello made a long speech, from the stenographic record of which I omit relatively innocuous passages and add emphasis to what seems especially provocative:

> "Father Terminiello: Now I am going to whisper my greetings to you, Fellow Christians. I will interpret it. I said, *'Fellow Christians,'* and I suppose there are *some of the scum got in by mistake,* so I want to tell a story about the *scum:*
>
> " . . . And nothing I could say tonight could begin to express the contempt I have for the slimy scum that got in by mistake.
>
> " . . . The subject I want to talk to you tonight about is the attempt *that is going on right outside this hall tonight,* the attempt that is going on to *destroy America by revolution.* . . .
>
> "My friends, it is no longer true that it can't happen here. It is happening here, and it only depends upon you, good people, who are here tonight, depends upon all of us together, as Mr. Smith said. The tide is changing, and if you and I turn and run from that tide, we will all be drowned in this tidal wave of Communism which is going over the world. . . ."

Such was the speech. Evidence showed that it stirred the audience not only to cheer and applaud but to expressions of immediate anger, unrest and alarm. One called the speaker a "God damned liar" and was taken out by the police. Another said that "Jews, niggers and Catholics would have to be gotten rid of. . . ."

Many speeches, such as that of Terminiello, may be legally permissible but may nevertheless in some surroundings be a menace to peace and order. When conditions show the speaker that this is the case, as it did here, there certainly comes a point beyond which he cannot indulge in provocations to violence without being answerable to society.

This Court has gone far toward accepting the doctrine that civil liberty means the removal of all restraints from these crowds and that all local attempts to maintain order are impairments of the liberty of the citizen. The choice is not between order and liberty. It is between liberty with order and anarchy without either. There is danger that, if the Court does not temper its doctrinaire logic with a little practical wisdom, it will convert the constitutional Bill of Rights into a suicide pact.

I would affirm the conviction.

[CHIEF JUSTICE VINSON, JUSTICE FRANKFURTER, and JUSTICE BURTON also dissented.]

Notes

1. *Ringing doorbells.* In *Martin* v. *Struthers,* 319 US 141 (1943), a member of Jehovah's Witnesses was convicted of going to the homes of strangers, knocking on doors, and ringing doorbells in order to distribute leaflets advertising a religious meeting. The municipal ordinance which Martin violated read: "It is unlawful for any person distributing handbills, circulars or other advertisements to ring the door

bell, sound the door knocker, or otherwise summon the . . . inmates of any residence to the door for the purpose of receiving such handbills, circulars or other advertisements. . . ." In declaring the ordinance void, Mr. Justice Black wrote: "For centuries it has been a common practice in this and other countries for persons not specifically invited to go from home to home and knock on doors or ring doorbells to communicate ideas to the occupants or to invite them to political, religious, or other kinds of public meetings. Whether such visiting shall be permitted has in general been deemed to depend upon the will of the individual master of each household, and not upon the determination of the community."

The *Struthers* ruling may be limited to religious literature. In *Breard* v. *Alexandria,* 341 US 622 (1950), the Court sustained an ordinance prohibiting "going in and upon private residences for the purpose of soliciting orders" for commercial publications.

2. *Accosting on streets.* In *Cantwell* v. *Connecticut,* 310 US 296 (1940), defendant

> while on the public street endeavoring to interest passersby in the purchase of publications, or in making contributions, in the interest of what he believed to be true religion, induced individuals to listen to the playing of a phonograph record describing the publications. The record contained a verbal attack upon the religious denomination of which the listeners were members, provoking their indignation and a desire on their part to strike the defendant who thereupon picked up his books and phonograph and went on his way. There was no showing that defendant's deportment was noisy, truculent, overbearing or offensive; nor was it claimed that he intended to insult or affront the listeners by playing the record; nor was it shown that the sound of the phonograph disturbed persons living nearby, drew a crowd, or impeded traffic. *Held,* that defendant's conviction of the common law offense of breach of the peace was violative of constitutional guarantees of religious liberty and freedom of speech.

3. *Sound amplifiers.* In *Saia* v. *New York,* 334 US 558 (1948), the Court struck down as void on its face a municipal ordinance which prohibited the use on the streets of sound trucks without the permission of the chief of police. A year later, in *Kovacs* v. *Cooper,* 336 US 77 (1949), the Court sustained an ordinance of Trenton, New Jersey, which prohibited the use of sound trucks that emit "loud and raucous noises."

In *Public Utilities Commission* v. *Pollack,* 343 US 451 (1952), the Court found no constitutional objection to "music as you ride" provided by a street railway company in the District of Columbia. Justice Douglas, dissenting, referred to the streetcar audience as a "captive audience."

4. *Transit-car advertisements. Lehman* v. *City of Shaker Heights,* 418 US 298(1974), sustained the right of a city which operates a public transit system and sells advertising space for car cards on its vehicles to refuse to accept paid political advertisements from a candidate for public office.

D. PARADES AND DEMONSTRATIONS

Introduction

The communication of subversive ideas is no constitutional problem in America today. The country is wide open for that. But a serious problem facing the nation is how to deal with freedom of expression carried out in the form of mass demonstrations, many of which have resulted in deaths, looting, and the burning of whole city blocks.

In 170 cases sustaining the right of mass racial demonstrations in the early 1960s, the Court relied on freedom of association as well as freedom of speech as a basis for its decisions. *NAACP* v. *Alabama* (1958) formed an important background to the mass demonstration cases.

In *Garner* v. *Louisiana,* 368 US 157 (1961), an early sit-in case, the Court reversed the conviction of three groups of blacks convicted under Louisiana law of commission of an act "in such a manner as to unreasonably disturb or alarm the public." In the opinion of the Court, Chief Justice Warren ruled out any consideration of the fact that these sit-ins were a part of a widespread program designed to create racial tension and concluded that there was no evidence to support the convictions. This judicial fiction was of only passing interest. The doctrine on which mass demonstrations would thrive was enunciated in a concurring opinion by Justice Harlan:

> . . . There was more to the conduct of those petitioners than a bare desire to remain at the "white" lunch counter and their refusal of a police request to move from the counter. We would surely have to be blind not to recognize that petitioners were sitting at these counters, where they knew they would not be served, in order to demonstrate that their race was being segregated in dining facilities in this part of the country.
>
> Such a demonstration, in the circumstances of these two cases, is as much a part of the "free trade in ideas" as is verbal expression, more commonly thought of as "speech." It, like speech, appeals to good sense and to "the power of reason as applied through public discussion" . . . just as much as, if not more than, a public oration delivered from a soapbox at a street corner. This Court has never limited the right to speak, a protected "liberty" under the Fourteenth Amendment . . . to mere verbal expression. . . . If the act of displaying a red flag as a symbol of opposition to organized government is a liberty encompassed within free speech as protected by the Fourteenth Amendment . . . , the act of sitting at a privately owned lunch counter with the consent of the owner, as a demonstration of opposition to enforced segregation, is surely within the same range of protection. . . .
>
> . . . when a State seeks to subject to criminal sanctions conduct which, except for a demonstrated paramount state interest, would be within the range of freedom of expression as assured by the Fourteenth Amendment, it cannot do so by means of a general and all-inclusive breach of the peace prohibition. It must bring the activity sought to be proscribed within the ambit of a statute or clause "narrowly drawn to define and punish specific conduct as constituting a clear and present danger to a substantial interest of the State." . . . And of course that interest must be a legitimate one. A State may not "suppress free communication of views, religious or other, under the guise of conserving desirable conditions." . . .

Two years later, in *Edwards* v. *South Carolina,* 372 US 229 (1963), the free-speech tag for racial demonstrations moved up to first place in the Court's opinion. South Carolina had arrested 187 blacks for staging a demonstration and refusing to obey orders by the police to disperse. For the majority, Justice Stewart wrote: "And it is clear to us that in arresting the petitioners . . . South Carolina infringed the petitioner's constitutionally protected rights of free speech, free assembly, and freedom to petition for redress of their grievances. . . . The circumstances in this case reflect an exercise of these basic constitutional rights in their most pristine and classic form."

Justice Clark, dissenting, held that the manner in which the blacks exercised these rights "was by no means the passive demonstration which this Court relates; rather, as the City Manager of Columbia testified, 'a dangerous situation was really building up' which South Carolina courts expressly found had created 'an actual interference with traffic and an imminently threatened, disturbance of the peace of the community'."

In more than a dozen cases decided in 1963 and 1964, the Court reversed decisions of state courts convicting blacks of trespass and breach of the peace. The decisions were written in terms of "state action." The black demonstrations of this period throughout the South were encouraged not only by the federal courts but also by white liberals in the North and by the national news media. Congress responded by passing the Civil Rights Act of 1964 banning segregation in public accommodations.

The next year in *Cox* v. *Louisiana,* 379 US 536 (1965), the Court reversed the conviction of Cox, the leader of a demonstration by 2,000 blacks near the courthouse in Baton Rouge. While the conviction of Cox was reversed, the number of dissents on the Court showed an increase, and Justice Goldberg, for the majority, stated: "We emphatically reject the notion urged by appellant that the First and Fourteenth Amendments afford the same kind of freedom to those who would communicate ideas by conduct such as patrolling, marching, and picketing on streets and highways, as those amendments afford to those who communicate ideas by pure speech."

The tide in judicial opinion was turning, but symbolic speech in the form of mass racial demonstrations in defiance of local law was to spread from the South to the nation as a whole before losing its shield of protection by the Supreme Court.

The first conviction of racial demonstrators was sustained in *Adderly* v. *Florida,* 385 US 39 (1967). The case involved a conviction of "malicious trespass" for participation in a demonstration on the premises of a county jail by some 200 blacks and their refusal to leave upon the request of the Sheriff. Justice Black, now speaking for the majority of the Court, wrote:

> ... The State, no less than a private owner of property, has power to preserve the property under its control for the use to which it is lawfully dedicated. For this reason there is no merit to the petitioners' argument that they had a constitutional right to stay on the property, over the jail custodian's objections, because this "area chosen for the peaceful civil rights demonstration was not only 'reasonable' but also particularly appropriate. . . ." Such an argument has as its major unarticulated premise the assumption that people who want to propagandize protests or views have a constitutional right to do so whenever and however and wherever they please. That concept of constitutional law was vigorously and forthrightly rejected in two of the cases petitioners rely on, *Cox* v. *Louisiana, supra,* at 554–555 and 563–564. We reject it again. The United States Constitution does not forbid a State to control the use of its own property for its own lawful nondiscriminatory purpose.
>
> These judgments are
>
> *Affirmed.*

Joined by Justices Brennan and Fortas in a dissenting opinion, Mr. Justice Douglas wrote:

> The jailhouse, like an executive mansion, a legislative chamber, a courthouse, or the statehouse itself (*Edwards* v. *South Carolina, supra*) is one of the seats of government,

whether it be the Tower of London, the Bastille, or a small county jail. And when it houses political prisoners or those who many think are unjustly held, it is an obvious center for protest. . . .

Today a trespass law is used to penalize people for exercising a constitutional right. Tomorrow a disorderly conduct statute, a breach-of-the-peace statute, a vagrancy statute will be put to the same end. . . . [B]y allowing these orderly and civilized protests against injustice to be suppressed, we only increase the forces of frustration which the conditions of second-class citizenship are generating amongst us.

Colten v. Kentucky

407 US 104, 92 S Ct 1953, 32 L Ed2d 584 (1972)

The state has a legitimate interest in enforcing its traffic laws and may punish bystanders who refuse to obey appropriate police orders to move on.

MR. JUSTICE WHITE delivered the opinion of the Court. . . .

Appellant Colten and 15 to 20 other college students gathered at the Blue Grass Airport outside Lexington, Kentucky, to show their support for a state gubernatorial candidate and to demonstrate their lack of regard for Mrs. Richard Nixon, then about to leave Lexington from the airport after a public appearance in the city. When the demonstration had ended, the students got into their automobiles and formed a procession of six to 10 cars proceeding along the airport access road to the main highway. A state policeman, observing that one of the first cars in the entourage carried an expired Louisiana license plate, directed the driver, one Mendez, to pull off the road. He complied. Appellant Colten, followed by other motorists in the procession, also pulled off the highway, and Colton approached the officer to find out what was the matter. The policeman explained that the Mendez car bore an expired plate and that a traffic summons would be issued. Colton made some effort to enter into a conversation about the summons. His theory was that Mendez may have received an extension of time in which to obtain new plates. In order to avoid Colten and to complete the issuance of the summons, the policeman took Mendez to the patrol car. Meanwhile, other students had left their cars and additional policemen, having completed their duties at the airport and having noticed the roadside scene, stopped their cars in the traffic lane abreast of the students' vehicles. At least one officer took responsibility for directing traffic, although testimony differed as to the need for doing so. Testimony also differed as to the number of policemen and students present, how many students left their cars and how many were at one time or another standing in the roadway. A state police captain asked on four or five occasions that the group disperse. At least five times police asked Colten to leave. A state trooper made two requests, remarking at least once: "Now, this is none of your affair, get back in your car and move on and clear the road." In response to at least one of these requests Colten replied that he wished to make a transportation arrangement for his friend Mendez and the occupants of the Mendez car, which he understood was to be towed away. Another officer asked three times that Colten depart and when Colten failed to move away he was arrested for violating Kentucky's disorderly conduct statute. . . . The arresting officer testified that

Colten's response to the order had been to say that he intended to stay and see what might happen. Colten disputed this. He testified that he expressed a willingness to leave but wanted first to make a transportation arrangement. At trial he added that he feared violence on the part of the police. . . .

I

Colten was convicted of violating Ky Rev Stat § 437.016(1) (f) (Cum. Supp. 1968), which states:

> "(1) A person is guilty of disorderly conduct if, with intent to cause public inconvenience, annoyance or alarm, or recklessly creating a risk thereof, he: . . .
> "(f) Congregates with other persons in a public place and refuses to comply with a lawful order of the police to disperse. . . ."

The Kentucky Court of Appeals interpreted the statute in the following way:

> "As reasonably construed, the statute does not prohibit the lawful exercise of any constitutional right. We think that the plain meaning of the statute, in requiring that the proscribed conduct be done 'with intent to cause public inconvenience, annoyance or alarm, or recklessly creating a risk thereof,' is that the specified intent must be the *dominant* intent. Predominance can be determined either (1) from the fact that no bona fide intent to exercise a constitutional right appears to have existed or (2) from the fact that the interest to be advanced by the particular exercise of the constitutional right is insignificant in comparison with the inconvenience, annoyance or alarm caused by the exercise." 467 S.W.2d, at 377.

The evidence warranted a finding, the Kentucky court concluded, that at the time of his arrest, "Colten was not undertaking to exercise any constitutionally protected freedom." Rather, he "appears to have had no purpose other than to cause inconvenience and annoyance. So the statute as applied here did not chill or stifle the exercise of any constitutional right." *Id.,* at 378.

Based on our own examination of the record, we perceive no justification for setting aside the conclusion of the state court that when arrested appellant was not engaged in activity protected by the First Amendment. Colten insists that in seeking to arrange transportation for Mendez and in observing the issuance of a traffic citation he was disseminating and receiving information. But this is a strained, near-frivolous contention and we have little doubt that Colten's conduct in refusing to move on after being directed to do so was not, without more, protected by the First Amendment. Nor can we believe that Colten, although he was not trespassing or disobeying any traffic regulation himself, could not be required to move on. He had no constitutional right to observe the issuance of a traffic ticket or to engage the issuing officer in conversation at that time. The State has a legitimate interest in enforcing its traffic laws and its officers were entitled to enforce them free from possible interference or interruption from bystanders, even those claiming a third-party interest in the transaction. Here the police had cause for apprehension that a roadside strip, crowded with persons and automobiles, might expose the entourage, passing motorists and police to the risk of accident. We cannot disagree with the finding below that the order to disperse was suited to the occasion. We thus see nothing unconstitutional in the manner in which the statute was applied.

II

Neither are we convinced that the statute is either impermissibly vague or broad. We perceive no violation of "[t]he underlying principle . . . that no man shall be held criminally responsible for conduct which he could not reasonably understand to be proscribed." . . .

Colten also argues that the Kentucky statute is overbroad. He relies on *Cox* v. *Louisiana,* 379 US 536 (1965), where the Court held unconstitutional a breach of peace statute construed to forbid causing agitation or disquiet coupled with refusing to move on when ordered to do so. The Court invalidated the statute on the ground that it permitted conviction where the mere expression of unpopular views prompted the order which is disobeyed. Colten argues that the Kentucky statute must be stricken down for the same reason.

As the Kentucky statute was construed by the state court, however, a crime is committed only where there is no bona fide intention to exercise a constitutional right —in which event, by definition, the statute infringes no protected speech or conduct —or where the interest so clearly outweighs the collective interest sought to be asserted that the latter must be deemed insubstantial. The court hypothesized, for example, that one could be convicted for disorderly conduct if at a symphony concert he arose and began lecturing to the audience on leghorn chickens. 467 S.W.2d, at 377. In so confining the reach of its statute, the Kentucky court avoided the shortcomings of the statute invalidated in the *Cox* case. Individuals may not be convicted under the Kentucky statute merely for expressing unpopular or annoying ideas. The statute comes into operation only when the individual's interest in expression, judged in the light of all relevant factors, is "miniscule" compared to a particular public interest in preventing that expression or conduct at that time and place. As we understand this case, petitioner's own conduct was not immune under the First Amendment and neither is his conviction vulnerable on the ground that the statute threatens constitutionally protected conduct of others. . . .

The judgment of the Kentucky Court of Appeals is

Affirmed.

Mr. Justice Douglas, dissenting. . . .

The Court of Appeals sustained the statute as applied because the inconvenience and annoyance to the police far outweighed petitioner's speech which fell "far below the level of minimum social value." . . . That court, citing our obscenity cases, said if "the lack of redeeming social value is a basis upon which the right of freedom of speech may be required to yield to the protection of contemporary standards of morality . . . it would seem that the public's interest in being protected from inconvenience, annoyance or alarm should prevail over any claimed right to utter speech that has no social value."

But the speech involved here was nonerotic, having no suggestion or flavor of the pornographic.

The speech here was quiet, not boisterous and it was devoid of "fighting words."

Moreover, this was not a case where speech had moved into action, involving overt acts. There were no fisticuffs, no disorderly conduct in the normal meaning of the words.

The Court of Appeals said "Colten was not seeking to express a thought to any listener or to disseminate any idea." ... Nor was he, it said, "exercising the right of peaceable assembly."

He was, however, speaking to a representative of government, the police. And it is to government that one goes "for a redress of grievances," to use an almost forgotten phrase of the First Amendment. But it is said that the purpose was "to cause inconvenience and annoyance." Since when have we Americans been expected to bow submissively to authority and speak with awe and reverence to those who represent us? The constitutional theory is that we the people are the sovereigns, the state and federal officials only our agents. We who have the final word can speak softly or angrily. We can seek to challenge and annoy, as we need not stay docile and quiet. The situation might have indicated that Colten's techniques were ill-suited to the mission he was on, that diplomacy would have been more effective. But at the constitutional level speech need not be a sedative; it can be disruptive. As we said in *Terminello* v. *Chicago,* 337 US 1,4:

> " ... a function of free speech under our system of government is to invite dispute. It may indeed best serve its high purpose when it induces a condition of unrest, creates dissatisfaction with conditions as they are, or even stirs people to anger. Speech is often provocative and challenging. It may strike at prejudices and preconceptions and have profound unsettling effects as it presses for acceptance of an idea.

Under that test this conviction should be set aside.

MR. JUSTICE MARSHALL, dissenting. [Omitted here.]

Note

Grayned v. *City of Rockford,* 408 US 104 (1973), sustained a conviction for participation in a "Black cause" demonstration in front of a high school.

Chapter 10

Due Process of Law

The Fifth Amendment prohibits the national government from depriving any person of "life, liberty, or property without due process of law," and the Fourteenth Amendment places the same limitation on the state governments. The phrase "due process of law" is associated with the phrase "law of the land" used in Magna Carta in 1215. It connotes an idea of fairness and has often been associated with the concept of natural law.

A. PROCEDURE

Introduction

Fair trial.   A man prosecuted for crime has the right to a fair trial, as required by due process of law. Thus it is contrary to due process to try an accused before a judge who has a pecuniary interest in the outcome of the case. *Tumey* v. *Ohio,* 273 US 510 (1927). As was pointed out in chapter 7, due process also includes protection against unreasonable searches and seizures, protection against self-incrimination, the right to counsel, the right to a speedy and public trial by jury, the right to protection against double jeopardy and against cruel and unusual punishment, and the right to be confronted with opposing witnesses and to compulsory process for obtaining favorable witnesses. These subjects are treated in chapter 12.

Notice and hearing.   Another basic element of due process is the right of a person to notice and hearing on matters vitally affecting his life, liberty, or property. Thus a statutory procedure whereby a creditor can garnishee a debtor's wages before he was informed in the matter is void. *Sniadach* v. *Family Finance Corporation,* 395 US 337 (1969).

The courts use the due process clause as a basis for reviewing the action of administrative agencies, both national and state, to see that fair play is observed. The voluminous litigation in this area is covered adequately only in courses in administrative law. See Reginald Parker, *Administrative Law* (Boston, 1968). In *Citizens to Preserve Overton Park* v. *Volpe,* 401 US 402 (1971), the opinion by Justice Marshall summarizes much of the law governing judicial review of administrative agencies.

Clear and reasonable.   A criminal statute is void for vagueness if it "either forbids or requires the doing of an act in terms so vague that men of common intelligence must necessarily guess at its meaning and differ as to its application. . . ." *Connally* v. *General Construction Co.,* 269 US 385 (1932). Application of this principle is found in numerous cases in the previous chapter.

A criminal statute must also be reasonable. Thus, the Supreme Court held void a federal statute which provided that when firearms were found in the possession of a convict or a fugitive from justice the law would presume that the weapons had been shipped in interstate commerce in violation of the Federal Firearms Act. "Under our decisions a statutory presumption cannot be sustained if there be no rational connection between the fact proved and the ultimate fact presumed, if the inference of the one from proof of the other is arbitrary because of lack of connection between the two in common experience." *Tot* v. *United States,* 319 US 463 (1943). A "conclusive presumption," that is, one which the law will not permit to be rebutted by facts to the contrary, is frequently found to violate due process. The doctrine of unreasonable presumptions is of great current interest.

Likewise, a statute may violate due process by "overbreadth," that is, by violating the principle that "a governmental purpose to control or prevent activities constitutionally subject to state regulation may not be achieved by means which sweep unnecessarily broadly and thereby invade the area of protected freedoms." *NAACP* v. *Alabama,* 377 US 288 (1964). This doctrine was applied extensively by the Warren Court and numerous illustrations are found in chapter 9. See also the lucid explanation by Justice Brennan in *Zwickler* v. *Koota,* 389 US 241 (1967).

The principle of overbreadth can be labeled as "procedure" or as "substance," depending on one's point of view. Procedure consistent with due process must be observed in the application of any law affecting "Individual Rights," the subject of the whole of Part II of this text. Cases presented elsewhere are not repeated here, but two recent cases are presented because of their current interest.

Cleveland Board of Education v. LaFleur

414 US 632, 94 S Ct 791, 39 L Ed2d 52 (1974)

A rule creating a conclusive presumption that a teacher four or five months pregnant is physically incapable of continuing her duties is arbitrary and void.

MR. JUSTICE STEWART delivered the opinion of the Court.

The respondents in No. 72–777 [Jo Carol LaFleur and Ann Elizabeth Nelson] and the petitioner in No. 72–1129 are female public school teachers. During the 1970–1971 school year, each informed her local school board that she was pregnant; each was compelled by a mandatory maternity leave rule to quit her job without pay several months before the expected birth of her child. These cases call upon us to decide the constitutionality of the school board's rules. . . .

The petitioner in No. 72–1129, Susan Cohen, was employed by the School Board of Chesterfield County, Virginia. That school board's maternity leave regulation requires that a pregnant teacher leave work at least four months prior to the expected birth of her child. . . .

We granted *certiorari* in both cases . . . in order to resolve the conflict between the Courts of Appeals regarding the constitutionality of such mandatory maternity leave rules for public school teachers.

This Court has long recognized that freedom of personal choice in matters of marriage and family life is one of the liberties protected by the Due Process Clause of the Fourteenth Amendment. . . .

. . . Because public school maternity leave rules directly affect "one of the basic civil rights of man," *Skinner* v. *Oklahoma, supra,* at 541, the Due Process Clause of the Fourteenth Amendment requires that such rules must not needlessly, arbitrarily, or capriciously impinge upon this vital area of a teacher's constitutional liberty. The question before us in these cases is whether the interests advanced in support of the rules of the Cleveland and Chesterfield County School Boards can justify the particular procedures they have adopted.

The school boards in these cases have offered two essentially overlapping explanations for their mandatory maternity leave rules. First, they contend that the firm cut-off dates are necessary to maintain continuity of classroom instruction, since advance knowledge of when a pregnant teacher must leave facilitates the finding and hiring of a qualified substitute. Secondly, the school boards seek to justify their maternity rules by arguing that at least some teachers become physically incapable of adequately performing certain of their duties during the latter part of pregnancy.

We . . . conclude that the arbitrary cut-off dates embodied in the mandatory leave rules before us have no rational relationship to the valid state interest of preserving continuity of instruction. As long as the teacher is required to give substantial advance notice of her condition, the choice of firm dates later in pregnancy would serve the boards' objectives just as well, while imposing a far lesser burden on the women's exercise of constitutionally protected freedom.

The question remains as to whether the fifth and sixth month cut-off dates can be justified on the other ground advanced by the school boards—the necessity of keeping physically unfit teachers out of the classroom. There can be no doubt that such an objective is perfectly legitimate, both on educational and safety grounds. And, despite the plethora of conflicting medical testimony in these cases, we can assume *arguendo* that at least some teachers become physically disabled from effectively performing their duties during the latter stages of pregnancy.

The mandatory termination provisions of the Cleveland and Chesterfield County rules surely operate to insulate the classroom from the presence of potentially incapacitated pregnant teachers. But the question is whether the rules sweep too broadly. See *Shelton* v. *Tucker,* 364 US 479. That question must be answered in the affirmative, for the provisions amount to a conclusive presumption that every pregnant teacher who reaches the fifth and sixth month of pregnancy is physically incapable of continuing. There is no individualized determination by the teacher's doctor—or the school board's—as to any particular teacher's ability to continue at her job. The rules contain an irrebuttable presumption of physical incompetency, and that presumption applies even when the medical evidence as to an individual woman's physical status might be wholly to the contrary.

As the Court noted last Term in *Vlandis* v. *Kline,* 412 US 441, 446, "permanent irrebuttable presumptions have long been disfavored under the Due Process Clauses of the Fifth and Fourteenth Amendments." In *Vlandis,* the Court declared unconstitutional, under the Due Process Clause, a Connecticut statute mandating an irrebuttable presumption of nonresidency for the purposes of qualifying for reduced tuition rates at a state university. We said in that case, 412 US, at 452:

> "[I]t is forbidden by the Due Process Clause to deny an individual the resident rates on the basis of a permanent and irrebuttable presumption of nonresidence, when that presumption is not necessarily or universally true in fact, and when the state has reasonable alternative means of making the crucial determination."

Similarly, in *Stanley* v. *Illinois,* 405 US 645, the Court held that an Illinois statute containing an irrebuttable presumption that unmarried fathers are incompetent to raise their children violated the Due Process Clause. Because of the statutory presumption, the State took custody of all illegitimate children upon the death of the mother, without allowing the father to attempt to prove his parental fitness. As the Court put the matter:

> "It may be, as the State insists, that most unmarried fathers are unsuitable and neglectful parents. It may also be that Stanley is such a parent and that his children should be placed in other hands. But all unmarried fathers are not in this category; some are wholly suited to have custody of their children." *Id.,* at 654 (footnotes omitted).

Hence, we held that the State could not conclusively presume that any particular unmarried father was unfit to raise his child; the Due Process Clause required a more individualized determination. See also *United States Dept. of Agriculture* v. *Murry,* 413 US 588; *id.,* at 514–517 (concurring opinion); *Bell* v. *Burson,* 402 US 535; *Carrington* v. *Rash,* 380 US 89.

These principles control our decision in the cases before us. While the medical experts in these cases differed on many points, they unanimously agreed on one—the ability of any particular pregnant woman to continue at work past any fixed time in her pregnancy is very much an individual matter. Even assuming *arguendo* that there are some women who would be physically unable to work past the particular cut-off dates embodied in the challenged rules, it is evident that there are large numbers of teachers who are fully capable of continuing work for longer than the Cleveland and Chesterfield County regulations will allow. Thus, the conclusive presumption embodied in these rules, like that in *Vlandis,* is neither "necessarily nor universally true," and is violative of the Due Process Clause. . . .

Accordingly, the judgment in No. 72–777 is affirmed; the judgment in No. 72–1129 is reversed, and the case is remanded to the Court of Appeals for the Fourth Circuit for further proceedings consistent with this opinion.

It is so ordered.

Mr. Justice Douglas concurs in the result. [Omitted.]

Mr. Justice Rehnquist, with whom The Chief Justice joins, dissenting.

The Court rests its invalidation of the school regulations involved in these cases on the Due Process Clause of the Fourteenth Amendment, rather than on any claim of sexual discrimination under the Equal Protection Clause of that Amendment. My Brother STEWART thereby enlists the Court in another quixotic engagement in his apparently unending war on irrebuttable presumptions. In this case we are told that although a regulation "requiring a termination of employment at some firm date during the last few weeks of pregnancy" (n. 13, opinion of the Court), might pass muster, the regulations here challenged requiring termination at the end of the fourth or fifth month of pregnancy violate due process of law.

As THE CHIEF JUSTICE pointed out in his dissent last year in *Vlandis* v. *Kline,* 412 US 441, "literally thousands of state statutes create classifications permanent in duration, which are less than perfect, as all legislative classifications are, and might be improved on by individualized determinations. . . ." *Id.,* at 462. Hundreds of years ago in England, before Parliament came to be thought of as a body having general lawmaking power, controversies were determined on an individualized basis without benefit of any general law. Most students of government consider the shift from this sort of determination, made on an *ad hoc* basis by the king's representative, to a relatively uniform body of rules enacted by a body exercising legislative authority, to have been a significant step forward in the achievement of a civilized political society. It seems to me a little late in the day for this Court to weigh in against such an established consensus.

Countless state and federal statutes draw lines such as those drawn by the regulations here which, under the Court's analysis, might well prove to be arbitrary in individual cases. The District of Columbia Code, for example, draws lines with respect to age for several purposes. The Code requires that a person to be eligible to vote be 18 years of age, that a male by 18 and a female be 16 before a valid marriage may be contracted, that alcoholic beverages not be sold to a person under age 21 years, or beer or light wines to any person under the age of 18 years. A resident of the District of Columbia must be 16 years of age to obtain a permit to operate motor vehicle, and the District of Columbia delegate to the United States Congress must be 25 years old. Nothing in the Court's opinion clearly demonstrates why its logic would not equally well sustain a challenge to these laws from a 17-year-old who insists that he is just as well informed for voting purposes as an 18-year-old, from a 20-year-old who insists that he is just as able to carry his liquor as a 21-year-old, or from the numerous other persons who fall on the outside of lines drawn by these and similar statutes.

More closely in point is the jeopardy in which the Court's opinions places longstanding statutes providing for mandatory retirement of government employees. . . .

. . . If legislative bodies are to be permitted to draw a general line anywhere short of the delivery room, I can find no judicial standard of measurement which says the ones drawn here were invalid. I therefore dissent.

Note

Geduldig v. *Aiello,*   US   (1974), held that California's exclusion of disability due to normal pregnancy from its disability program for employees did not violate equal protection.

Arnett v. Kennedy

US   , 94 S Ct 1633, 40 L Ed2d 15 (1974)

The statutory provision that an individual in the competitive service may be removed or suspended "only for such causes as will promote the efficiency of the service" is not void for vagueness, and a post-removal evidentiary trial-type hearing satisfies due process requirements in this setting.

Mr. Justice Rehnquist announced the judgment of the Court in an opinion in which The Chief Justice and Mr. Justice Stewart join.

Prior to the events leading to his discharge, appellee Wayne Kennedy was a nonprobationary federal employee in the competitive Civil Service. He was a field representative in the Chicago Regional Office of the Office of Economic Opportunity (OEO). In March 1972, he was removed from the federal service pursuant to the provisions of the Lloyd-LaFollette Act, 5 USC § 7501, after Wendell Verduin, the Regional Director of the OEO, upheld written administrative charges made in the form of a "notification of proposed adverse action" against appellee. The charges listed five events occurring in November and December 1971; the most serious of the charges was that appellee "without any proof whatsoever and in reckless disregard of the actual facts" known to him or reasonably discoverable by him had publicly stated that Verduin and his administrative assistant had attempted to bribe a representative of a community action organization with whom the OEO had dealings. The alleged bribe consisted of an offer of a $100,000 grant of OEO funds if the representative would sign a statement against appellee and another OEO employee.

Appellee was advised of his right under regulations promulgated by the Civil Service Commission and the OEO to reply to the charges orally and in writing, and to submit affidavits to Verduin. He was also advised that the material on which the notice was based was available for his inspection in the Regional Office, and that a copy of the material was attached to the notice of proposed adverse action.

Appellee did not respond to the substance of the charges against him, but instead asserted that the charges were unlawful because he had a right to a trial-type hearing before an impartial hearing officer before he could be removed from his employment, and because statements made by him were protected by the First Amendment to the United States Constitution. On March 20, 1972, Verduin notified appellee in writing that he would be removed from his position at the close of business on March 27, 1972. Appellee was also notified of his right to appeal Verduin's decision either to the Office of Economic Opportunity or to the Civil Service Commission.

Appellee then instituted this suit in the United States District Court for the Northern District of Illinois on behalf of himself and others similarly situated, seeking both injunctive and declaratory relief. In his amended complaint, appellee contended that the standards and procedures established by and under the Lloyd-LaFollette Act for the removal of nonprobationary employees from the federal service unwarrantedly interfere with those employees' freedom of expression and deny them procedural due process of law. The three-judge District Court ... granted summary judgment for appellee. The court held that the discharge procedures authorized by the Act and attendant Civil Service Commission and OEO regulations denied appellee due process of law because they failed to provide for a trial-type hearing before an impartial agency official prior to removal; the court also held the Act and implementing regulations unconstitutionally vague because they failed to furnish sufficiently precise guidelines as to what kind of speech may be made the basis of a removal action. . . .

The numerous affidavits submitted to the District Court by both parties not unexpectedly portray two widely differing versions of the facts which gave rise to this lawsuit. Since the District Court granted summary judgment to appellee, it was required to resolve all genuine disputes as to any material facts in favor of appellant, and we therefore take as true for purposes of this opinion the material particulars of appellee's conduct which were set forth in the notification of proposed adverse action dated February 18, 1972. . . .

The statutory provisions which the District Court held invalid are found in 5 USC § 7501. Subsection (a) of that section provides that "[a]n individual in the competitive service may be removed or suspended without pay only for such cause as will promote the efficiency of the service."

Subsection (b) establishes the administrative procedures by which an employee's rights under subsection (a) are to be determined, providing:

"(b) An individual in the competitive service whose removal or suspension without pay is sought is entitled to reasons in writing and to—
"(1) notice of the action sought and of any charges preferred against him;
"(2) a copy of the charges;
"(3) a reasonable time for filing a written answer to the charges, with affidavits; and
"(4) a written decision on the answer at the earliest practicable date.
"Examination of witnesses, trial, or hearing is not required but may be provided in the discretion of the individual directing the removal or suspension without pay. . . ."

Both the Commission and OEO also follow regulations enlarging the procedural protections accorded by the Act itself. The Commission's regulations provide, *inter alia,* that the employing agency must give 30 days' advance written notice to the employee prior to removal, and make available to him the material on which the notice is based. They also provide that the employee shall have an opportunity to appear before the official vested with authority to make the removal decision in order to answer the charges against him, that the employee must receive notice of an adverse decision on or before its effective date, and that the employee may appeal from an adverse decision. This appeal may be either to a reviewing authority within the employing agency, or directly to the Commission, and the employee is entitled to an evidentiary trial-type hearing at the appeal stage of the proceeding. The only trial-type hearing available within the OEO is, by virtue of its regulations and practice, typically held after actual removal; but if the employee is reinstated on appeal, he receives full back pay. . . .

Appellee recognizes that our recent decisions in *Board of Regents of State Colleges* v. *Roth,* 408 US 564 (1972), and *Perry* v. *Sinderman,* 408 US 503 (1972), are those most closely in point with respect to the procedural rights constitutionally guaranteed public employees in connection with their dismissal from employment. Appellee contends that he had a property interest or an expectancy of employment which could not be divested without first affording him a full adversary hearing.

In *Board of Regents* v. *Roth, supra,* we said:

> "Property interests, of course, are not created by the Constitution. Rather, they are created and their dimensions are defined by existing rules or understandings that stem from an independent source such as state law—rules or understandings that secure certain benefits and that support claims of entitlement to those benefits." 408 US, at 577.

Here appellee did have a statutory expectancy that he not be removed other than for "such cause as will promote the efficiency of the service." But the very section of the statute which granted him that right, a right which had previously existed only by virtue of administrative regulation, expressly provided also for the procedure by which "cause" was to be determined, and expressly omitted the procedural guarantees which appellee insists are mandated by the Constitution. Only by bifurcating the very sentence of the Act of Congress which conferred upon appellee the right not to be removed save for cause could it be said that he had an expectancy of that substantive right without the procedural limitations which Congress attached to it. In the area of federal regulation of government employees, where in the absence of statutory limitation the governmental employer has had virtually uncontrolled latitude in decisions as to hiring and firing, *Cafeteria Workers* v. *McElroy,* 367 US 886, 896–897, we do not believe that a statutory enactment such as the Lloyd-LaFollette Act may be passed as discretely as appellee urges. Congress was obviously intent on according a measure of statutory job security to governmental employees which they had not previously enjoyed, but was likewise intent on excluding more elaborate procedural requirements which it felt would make the operation of the new scheme unnecessarily burdensome in practice. Where the focus of legislation was this strongly on the procedural mechanism for enforcing the substantive right which was simultaneously conferred, we decline to conclude that the substantive right may be viewed wholly apart from the procedure provided for its enforcement. The employee's statutorily defined right is not a guarantee against removal without cause in the abstract, but such a guarantee as enforced by the procedures which Congress has designated for the determination of cause.

Appellees urge that the judgment of the District Court must be sustained on the authority of cases such as *Goldberg* v. *Kelly,* 397 US 254, *Fuentes* v. *Shevin,* 407 US 67, *Bell* v. *Burson,* 402 US 535, and *Sniadach* v. *Family Finance Corp.,* 395 US 337. *Goldberg* held that welfare recipients are entitled under the Due Process Clause of the Fifth and Fourteenth Amendments to an adversay hearing before their benefits are terminated. *Fuentes* v. *Shevin* held that a hearing was generally required before one could have his property seized under a writ of replevin. In *Bell* v. *Burson* the Court held that due process required a procedure for determining whether there was a reasonable possibility of a judgment against a driver as a result of an accident before his license and vehicle registration could be suspended for failure to post security under Georgia's uninsured motorist statute. And in *Sniadach* v. *Family Finance Corp.* a Wisconsin statute providing for prejudgment garnishment without notice to the debtor or prior hearing was struck down as violative of the principles of due process. These cases deal with areas of the law dissimilar to one another and dissimilar to the area of governmental employer-employee relationships with which we deal here. The types of "liberty" and "property" protected by the Due Process Clause vary widely, and what may be required under that clause in dealing with one set of interests which it protects may not be required in dealing with another set of interests.

"The very nature of due process negates any concept of inflexible procedures universally applicable to every imaginable situation." *Cafeteria Workers* v. *McElroy,* 367 US 886, 895.

Here the property interest which appellee had in his employment was itself conditioned by the procedural limitations which had accompanied the grant of that interest. The Government might, then, under our holdings dealing with government employees in *Roth, supra,* and *Perry, supra,* constitutionally deal with appellee's claims as it proposed to do here. . . .

Appellee urges that the delays in processing agency and Civil Service Commission appeals, amounting to more than three months in over 50% of agency appeals, mean that the available administrative appeals do not suffice to protect his liberty interest recognized in *Roth.* During the pendency of his administrative appeals, appellee asserts, a discharged employee suffers from both the stigma and the consequent disadvantage in obtaining a comparable job that result from dismissal for cause from government employment. We assume that some delay attends vindication of an employee's reputation throughout the hearing procedures provided on appeal, and conclude that at least the delays cited here do not entail any separate deprivation of a liberty interest recognized in *Roth.*

Appellee also contends that the provisions of 5 USC § 7501(a), authorizing removal or suspension without pay "for such cause as will promote the efficiency of the service," are vague and overbroad. . . .

A certain anomaly attends appellee's substantive constitutional attack on the Lloyd-LaFollette Act just as it does his attack on its procedural provisions. Prior to the enactment of this language in 1912, there was no such statutory inhibition on the authority of the Government to discharge a federal employee, and an employee could be discharged with or without cause for conduct which was not protected under the First Amendment. Yet under the District Court's holding, a federal employee after the enactment of the Lloyd-LaFollette Act may not even be discharged for conduct which constitutes "cause" for discharge and which is not protected by the First Amendment, because the guarantee of job security which Congress chose to accord employees is "vague" and "overbroad."

We hold the standard of "cause" set forth in the Lloyd-LaFollette Act as a limitation on the Government's authority to discharge federal employees is constitutionally sufficient against the charges both of overbreadth and of vagueness. . . .

Congress sought to lay down an admittedly general standard, not for the purpose of defining criminal conduct, but in order to give myriad different federal employees performing widely disparate tasks a common standard of job protection. We do not believe that Congress was confined to the choice of enacting a detailed code of employee conduct, or else granting no job protection at all. . . .

Because of the infinite variety of factual situations in which public statements by government employees might reasonably justify dismissal for "cause," we conclude that the Act describes, as explicitly as is required, the employee conduct which is grounds for removal. . . .

We have no hesitation in saying, as did the District Court, that on the facts alleged in the administrative charges against appellee, the appropriate tribunal would infringe no constitutional right of appellee in concluding that there was "cause" for his discharge. *Pickering* v. *Board of Education,* 391 US 563, 569. Nor have we any doubt that satisfactory proof of these allegations could constitute "such cause as will promote the efficiency of the service" within the terms of 5 USC § 7501(a). Appellee's contention then boils down to the assertion that although no constitutionally protected conduct of his own was the basis for his discharge on the Government's version of the facts, the statutory language in question must be declared inoperative, and a set of more particularized regulations substituted for it, because the generality of its language might result in marginal situations in which other persons seeking to engage in constitutionally protected conduct would be deterred from doing so. But we have held that Congress in establishing a standard of "cause" for discharge did not intend to include within that term any constitutionally protected conduct. . . .

In sum, we hold that the Lloyd-LaFollette Act, in at once conferring upon nonprobationary federal employees the right not to be discharged except for "cause" and prescribing the procedural means by which that right was to be protected, did not create an expectancy of job retention in those employees requiring procedural protection under the Due Process Clause beyond that afforded here by the statute and related agency regulations. We also conclude that the post termination hearing procedures provided by the Civil Service Commission and OEO adequately protect those federal employees' liberty interest, recognized in *Roth, supra,* in not being wrongfully stigmatized by untrue and unsupported administrative charges. Finally, we hold that the standard of employment protection imposed by Congress in the Lloyd-LaFollette Act, is not impermissibly vague or overbroad in its regulation of the speech of federal employees and therefore unconstitutional on its face. Accordingly, we reverse the decision of the District Court on both grounds on which it granted summary judgment and remand for further proceedings not inconsistent with this opinion.

Reversed.

MR. JUSTICE POWELL, with whom MR. JUSTICE BLACKMUN joins, concurring in part and concurring in the result in part.

For the reasons stated by MR. JUSTICE REHNQUIST, I agree that the provisions of 5 USC § 7501(a) are neither unconstitutionally vague nor overbroad. I also agree that appellee's discharge did not contravene the Fifth Amendment guarantee of procedural due process. Because I reach that conclusion on the basis of different reasoning, I state my views separately. . . .

The plurality opinion evidently reasons that the nature of appellee's interest in continued federal employment is necessarily defined and limited by the statutory procedures for discharge and that the constitutional guarantee of procedural due process accords to appellee no procedural protections against arbitrary or erroneous discharge other than those expressly provided in the statute. The plurality would thus conclude that the statute governing federal employment determines not only the nature of appellee's property interest, but also the extent of the procedural protections to which he may lay claim. It seems to me that this approach is incompatible with the principles laid down in *Roth* and *Sindermann.* Indeed, it would lead directly to the conclusion that whatever the nature of an individual's statutorily-created property interest, deprivation of that interest could be accomplished without notice or a hearing at any time. This view misconceives the origin of the right to procedural due process. That right is conferred not by legislative grace but by constitutional guarantee. While the legislature may elect not to confer a property interest in federal employment, it may not constitutionally authorize the deprivation of such an interest, once conferred, without appropriate procedural safeguards. As our cases have consistently recognized, the adequacy of statutory procedures for deprivation of a statutorily created property interest must be analyzed in constitutional terms. . . .

Having determined that the constitutional guarantee of procedural due process applies to appellee's discharge from public employment, the question arises whether an evidentiary hearing, including the right to present favorable witnesses and to confront and examine adverse witnesses, must be accorded *before* removal. The resolution of this issue depends on a balancing process in which the Government's interest in expeditious removal of an unsatisfactory employee is weighed against the interest of the affected employee in continued public employment. . . .

In the present case, the Government's interest, and hence the public's interest, is the maintenance of employee efficiency and discipline. Such factors are essential if the Government is to perform its responsibilities effectively and economically. To this end, the Government, as an employer, must have wide discretion and control over the management of its personnel and internal affairs. This includes the prerogative to remove employees whose conduct hinders efficient operation and to do so with dispatch. . . .

On balance, I would conclude that a prior evidentiary hearing is not required and that the present statute and regulations comport with due process by providing a reasonable accommodation of the competing interests.

MR. JUSTICE WHITE, concurring in part and dissenting in part. . . .

In my view, three issues must be addressed in this case. First, does the Due Process Clause require that there be a full trial-type hearing *at some time* when a Federal Government employee in the competitive service is terminated? Secondly, if such be the case, must this hearing be held *prior* to the discharge of the employee, and, if so, was the process afforded in this case adequate? Third, and as an entirely separate matter, are the Lloyd-LaFollette Act and its attendant regulations void for vagueness or overbreadth? I join in the Court's opinion as to the third issue.

I differ basically with the Court's view that "where the grant of a substantive right is inextricably intertwined with the limitations on the procedures which are to be employed in determining that right, a litigant in the position of appellee must take the bitter with the sweet," and that "the property interest which appellee had in his employment was itself conditioned by the procedural limitations which had accompanied the grant of that interest." . . .

. . . A fundamental requirement of due process is "the opportunity to be heard." *Grannis* v. *Ordean,* 234 US 385 (1914). "It is an opportunity which must be granted at a meaningful time and in a meaningful manner." *Armstrong* v. *Manzo,* 380 US 545, 552 (1965). Where the Court has rejected the need for a hearing prior to the initial "taking," a principal rationale has been that a hearing would be provided before the taking became final. . . .

I conclude, therefore, that as a matter of due process, a hearing must be held at some time before a competitive civil service employee may be finally terminated for misconduct. . . .

In passing upon claims to a hearing before the preliminary but nonfinal deprivations, the usual rule of this Court has been that a full hearing at some time suffices. "We have repeatedly held that no hearing at the preliminary stage is required by due process so long as the requisite hearing is held before the final administrative order becomes effective. It is sufficient, where only property rights are concerned, that there is at some stage an opportunity for a hearing and a judicial determination." . . .

In recent years, however, in a limited number of cases, the Court has held that a hearing must be furnished at the first stage of taking, even where a later hearing was provided. This has been true in the revocation of a state-granted license, *Bell* v. *Burson,* 402 US 535 (1971), and in suits between private parties, where summary replevin procedures, *Fuentes* v. *Shevin,* 407 US 67 (1972), or garnishment procedures, were attacked, *Sniadach* v. *Family Finance Corp.,* 395 US 337 (1969), and when the State has sought to terminate welfare benefits. *Goldberg* v. *Kelley,* 397 US 254 (1970).

These conflicting lines of cases demonstrate, as the Court stated in *Cafeteria & Restaurant Workers Union* v. *McElroy, supra,* 367 US, at 895, that "consideration of what procedures due process may require under any given set of circumstances must begin with a determination of the precise nature of the government function involved as well as of the private interest that has been affected by governmental action." . . .

[T]he debate on the Lloyd-LaFollette Act indicates that constitutional considerations were present in the minds of congressmen speaking in favor of the legislation. In any event, I conclude that the statute's provisions to the extent they require 30 days advance notice and a right to make a written presentation satisfy minimum constitutional requirements.

Appellee in this case not only asserts that he is entitled to . . . an impartial hearing examiner, an opportunity to present witnesses, and the right to engage in cross-examination. In other words, his claim is not only to a pretermination hearing, but one in which full trial-type procedures are available.

The facts in this case show that the Regional Director Verduin, who charged appellee Kennedy with making slanderous statements about him as to an alleged bribe offer, also ruled in the preliminary hearing that Kennedy should be terminated. . . .

In considering appellee's claim to have an impartial hearing examiner, we might start with a first principle: "No man shall be a judge in his own cause." *Bonham's Case,* 8 Co. 114a, 118a (1610). Verduin's reputation was certainly at stake in the charges brought against Kennedy. Indeed, the heart of the charge was that Kennedy had spoken of Verduin in reckless disregard of the truth. . . .

We have also stressed the need for impartiality in administrative proceedings. . . .

My view is a narrower one, however. Fairness and accuracy are not always threatened simply because the hearing examiner is the supervisor of an employee, or, as in this case, the Regional Director over many employees, including appellee. But here the hearing official was the object of slander that was the basis for the employee's proposed discharge. . . . We need not hold that the Lloyd-LaFollette Act is unconstitutional for its lack of provision of an impartial hearing examiner. Congress is silent on the matter.

We would rather assume that because of the constitutional problems in not so providing that, if faced with the question, at least on the facts of this case, Congress would have so provided. . . .

Appellee also claims a right to a full trial-type hearing at the pretermination stage, particularly asserting that he is denied due process, if not given the opportunity to present and cross-examine witnesses. . . .

. . . We think the clear implication of *Bell* to be that "full adjudication," including presentation of witnesses and cross-examination, need not be provided in every case where a pretermination hearing of some kind is required by due process or provided by the statute.

In *Goldberg* v. *Kelly,* the Court struck a different note on procedures. Although stating that the only function of the pretermination hearing was "to produce an initial determination of the welfare department's grounds for discontinuance of payments," and seemingly adopting a probable cause standard, the Court required cross-examination of witnesses relied upon by the Department. The Court was careful to observe, however, that these procedural rules were "tailored to the capacities and circumstances of those who are to be heard." 397 US, at 267, 269. The decision to cut off AFDC welfare payments leaves the recipient literally without any means to survive or support a family. While this level of deprivation may not be insisted upon as a necessary condition for requiring some kind of pretermination hearing, it may well be decisive in requiring the Government to provide specific procedures at the predetermination stage. . . .

In this case, the employee is not totally without prospect for some form of support during the period between the pretermination and final hearing on appeal, though it may not be equivalent in earnings or tenure to his prior competitive service position. . . . Necessarily, to some extent, the Court must share with Congress, in an area where one is called upon to judge the efficacy of particular procedures, a role in defining constitutional requirements, and Congress explicitly left it to the discretion of the agency as to whether such procedures were required. I would not upset that judgment in this case.

In accord with these views, I would affirm the judgment of the three-judge court, ordering reinstatement and backpay, due to the failure to provide an impartial hearing officer at the pretermination hearing. I would reverse that part of the court's order enjoining the application of the statute on First Amendment vagueness and overbreadth grounds.

MR. JUSTICE DOUGLAS, dissenting.

The federal bureaucracy controls a vast conglomerate of people who walk more and more submissively to the dictates of their superiors. Our federal employees have lost many important political rights. *CSC* v. *Letter Carriers,* 413 US 548, held that they could be barred from taking "an active part in political management or in political campaigns," a restriction that some of us thought to be unconstitutional, *id.,* 595 *et seq.* Today's decision deprives them of other important First Amendment rights. . . .

. . . Appellee is in my view being penalized by the Federal Government for exercising his right to speak out. The excuse or pretense is an Act of Congress and an agency's regulations promulgated under it in the teeth of the First Amendment; "Congress shall make no law . . . abridging the freedom of speech or of the press. . . ." Losing one's job with the Federal Government because of one's discussion of an issue in the public domain is certainly an abridgement of speech.

MR. JUSTICE MARSHALL, with whom MR. JUSTICE DOUGLAS and MR. JUSTICE BRENNAN concur, dissenting.

I would affirm the judgment of the District Court, both in its holding that a tenured government employee must be afforded an evidentiary hearing prior to a dismissal for cause and in its decision that 5 USC § 7501 is unconstitutionally vague and overbroad as a regulation of employees' speech.

The first issue in this case is a relatively narrow one—whether a federal employee in the competitive service, entitled, by statute, to serve in his job without fear of dismissal except for cause, must be given an evidentiary hearing before he is discharged. We are hardly writing on a clean slate in this area. In just the last five years, the Court has held that such a hearing must be afforded before wages can be garnished, *Sniadach* v. *Family Finance Corp.,* 395 US 337 (1969); welfare benefits terminated, *Goldberg* v. *Kelly,* 397 US 254 (1970); a driver's license revoked, *Bell* v. *Burson,* 402 US 535 (1971); consumer goods repossessed, *Fuentes* v. *Shevin,* 407 US 67 (1972); parole revoked, *Morrissey* v. *Brewer,* 408 US 471 (1972); or a tenured college professor fired by a public educational institution, *Board of Regents* v. *Roth,* 408 US 564 (1972); *Perry* v. *Sindermann,* 408 US 593 (1972). . . .

The court below also held that the provision of the Lloyd-LaFollette Act which authorizes dismissal of tenured Government employees for "such cause as will promote the efficiency of the service" is unconstitutionally vague and overbroad.

There is no dispute but that the phrase " 'such cause as will promote the efficiency of the service' as a standard of employee job protection is intended to authorize dismissal for speech. . . .

The majority purports to solve this potential overbreadth problem merely by announcing that the standard in the Act "excludes protected speech." Nonetheless, it leaves the statutory standard intact and offers no guidance other than general observation as to what conduct is or is not punishable. . . .

The District Court found that "[b]ecause employees faced with the standard of 'such cause as will promote the efficiency of the service' can only guess as to what utterances may cost them their jobs, there can be little question that they will be deterred from exercising their First Amendment rights to the fullest extent." I agree with that characterization of the effect of the standard and would, therefore, uphold the conclusion of the District Court that the statute is unconstitutionally vague and overbroad.

I respectfully dissent.

Notes

1. *Mitchell* v. *W. T. Grant Co.,*   US   (1974), sustained a Louisiana statute which made available to a lien holder a writ of sequestration to forestall waste or alienation of encumbered property. The writ could be issued only upon a judge's authorization after the creditor filed a sworn affidavit and posted sufficient bond, and provision was made whereby the debtor could seek immediate dissolution of the writ. *Fuentes* v. *Shevin,* 407 US 67 (1972), was distinguished. Justice Stewart

filed a dissenting opinion in which Justices Douglas and Marshall joined, and in which Justice Brennan joined in part.

2. *Astol Calero-Toledo* v. *Pearson Yacht Leasing Co.,* 416 US 663 (1974), sustained the seizure without notice or prior hearing of a yacht found with marihuana aboard. The case presented an "extraordinary" situation in which postponement of notice and hearing did not violate due process. The Puerto Rican statute involved served the purpose of permitting the government to assert *in rem* jurisdiction over the yacht in forfeiture proceedings, thus preventing it from either fleeing the jurisdiction or being used further for illicit purposes. *Fuentes* v. *Shevin,* 407 US 67, was distinguished.

B. SUBSTANCE

Introduction

In 1927 Justice Brandeis wrote: "Despite arguments to the contrary which had seemed to me persuasive, it is settled that the due process clause of the Fourteenth Amendment applies to matters of substantive law as well as to matters of procedure." *Whitney* v. *California,* 274 US 357. It is not surprising that a judiciary exercising final authority over the constitutionality of laws should have discovered in the vague contours of "due process" authority to pass upon both procedure and substance.

In the period before the adoption of the Fourteenth Amendment, the Court found authority to invalidate state laws most frequently in the commerce and in the contract clauses of Article I. After the Fourteenth Amendment was added to the Constitution of 1868, for a quarter of a century its due process clause was interpreted primarily as a limitation on procedure and not on the substance of legislation. Thus *Munn* v. *Illinois,* 94 US 113 (1877), sustained a statute regulating the rates to be charged for the storage of grain on the theory that this was a matter of legislative prerogative. But near the close of the nineteenth century the Court began to apply due process as a limitation on substance. For example, *Smyth* v. *Ames,* 169 US 466 (1898), held void a railroad rate established by a state legislature on the theory that the rate did not allow the railroad a fair return on its investment. The year before in *Allgeyer* v. *Louisiana,* 165 US 578 (1897), the Court had read into the liberty phase of "life, liberty, and property" the concept of "liberty of contract." In the years ahead the Court frequently substituted its judgment for that of the legislature, both national and state, on economic matters. In 1944 Justice Frankfurter observed that "it was decided more than fifty years ago that the final say [on economic regulations] under the Constitution lies with the judiciary and not with the legislature." *Federal Power Commission* v. *Hope Natural Gas Co.,* 320 US 529. In the decades ahead, however, the Court abandoned this philosophy and left to the legislatures, both state and national, the power to regulate economic matters. In 1974 in sustaining a municipal tax of 20 percent on the gross receipts obtained from transactions involving the parking of motor vehicles, Justice White wrote for a unanimous Court:

> The claim that a particular tax is so unreasonably high and unduly burdensome as to deny due process is both familiar and recurring, but the Court has consistently

refused either to undertake the task of passing on the "reasonableness" of a tax that otherwise is within the power of Congress or of state legislative authorities, or to hold that a tax is unconstitutional because it renders a business unprofitable. . . .

Nor are we convinced that the ordinance loses character as a tax and may be stricken down as too burdensome under the Due Process Clause if the taxing authority, directly or through an instrumentality enjoying the various forms of tax exemption, competes with the taxpayer in a manner thought to be unfair by the judiciary. This approach would demand not only that the judiciary undertake to separate those taxes that are too burdensome from those that are not, but also would require judicial oversight of the terms and circumstances under which the Government or its tax-exempt instrumentalities may undertake to compete with the private sector. The teaching of prior cases is that this is not a task that the Due Process Clause of the Federal Constitution demands of or permits to the judiciary. *City of Pittsburgh* v. *Alco Parking Corp.,* 417 US 369.

After 1936 when the Court showed more interest in other types of civil rights, it found authority for many of its new policies in the equal protection clause of the Fourteenth Amendment; but since there was no equal protection clause governing the federal government, the same results could be obtained under the due process clause of the Fifth Amendment. As we have seen, it was the due process clause of the Fourteenth Amendment that served as the basis for incorporating almost all of the Bill of Rights as limitations on the states. The difficulty which the justices themselves have had in recent years in deciding whether to write their opinions in terms of due process or in terms of equal protection can be observed by comparing the cases in the first section of this chapter with the cases in section 3 of chapter 11.

Lochner v. New York

198 US 45, 25 S Ct 539, 49 L Ed 937 (1905)

There is no reasonable ground, on the score of health, for interfering with the liberty of the person or the right of free contract, by determining the hours of labor, in the occupation of a baker. Nor can a law limiting such hours be justified as a health law to safeguard the public health, or the health of the individuals following that occupation.

MR. JUSTICE PECKHAM . . . delivered the opinion of the Court.

The indictment, it will be seen, charges that the plaintiff in error [Joseph Lochner] violated the one hundred and tenth section of article 8, chapter 415, of the Laws of 1897, known as the labor law of the State of New York, in that he wrongfully and unlawfully required and permitted an employe working for him to work more than sixty hours in one week. . . .

The statute necessarily interferes with the right of contract between the employer and employes, concerning the number of hours in which the latter may labor in the bakery of the employer. The general right to make a contract in relation to his business is part of the liberty of the individual protected by the Fourteenth Amendment of the Federal Constitution. *Allgeyer* v. *Louisiana,* 165 US 578. . . .

... Therefore, when the State, by its legislature in the assumed exercise of its police powers, has passed an act which seriously limits the right to labor or the right of contract in regard to their means of livelihood between persons who are *sui juris* (both employer and employe), it becomes of great importance to determine which shall prevail—the right of the individual to labor for such time as he may choose, or the right of the State to prevent the individual from laboring or from entering into any contract to labor, beyond a certain time prescribed by the State. ...

It must, of course, be conceded that there is a limit to the valid exercise of the police power by the State. There is no dispute concerning this general proposition. Otherwise the Fourteenth Amendment would have no efficacy and the legislatures of the States would have unbounded power, and it would be enough to say that any piece of legislation was enacted to conserve the morals, the health or the safety of the people; such legislation would be valid, no matter how absolutely without foundation the claim might be. ...

This is not a question of substituting the judgment of the court for that of the legislature. If the act be within the power of the State it is valid, although the judgment of the court might be totally opposed to the enactment of such a law. But the question would still remain: Is it within the police power of the State? and that question must be answered by the court. ...

We think the limit of the police power has been reached and passed in this case. There is, in our judgment, no reasonable foundation for holding this to be necessary or appropriate as a health law to safeguard the public health or the health of the individuals who are following the trade of a baker. ...

The judgment of the Court of Appeals of New York as well as that of the Supreme Court and of the County Court of Oneida County must be reversed and the case remanded to the County Court for further proceedings not inconsistent with this opinion.

Reversed.

Mr. Justice Harlan, with whom Mr. Justice White and Mr. Justice Day concurred, dissenting. [Omitted]. ...

Mr. Justice holmes dissenting.

I regret sincerely that I am unable to agree with the judgment in this case, and that I think it my duty to express my dissent.

This case is decided upon an economic theory which a large part of the country does not entertain. If it were a question whether I agreed with that theory, I should desire to study it further and long before making up my mind. But I do not conceive that to be my duty, because I strongly believe that my agreement or disagreement has nothing to do with the right of a majority to embody their opinions in law. ... Some of these laws embody convictions or prejudices which judges are likely to share. Some may not. But a constitution is not intended to embody a particular economic theory, whether of paternalism and the organic relation of the citizen to the State or of laissez faire. It is made for people of fundamentally differing views, and the accident of our finding certain opinions natural and familiar or novel and even shocking ought not to conclude our judgment upon the question whether statutes embodying them conflict with the Constitution of the United States.

General propositions do not decide concrete cases. The decision will depend on a judgment or intuition more subtle than any articulate major premise. But I think that the proposition just stated, if it is accepted, will carry us far toward the end. Every opinion tends to become a law. I think that the word liberty in the Fourteenth Amendment is perverted when it is held to prevent the natural outcome of a dominant opinion, unless it can be said that a rational and fair man necessarily would admit that the statute proposed would infringe fundamental principles as they have been understood by the traditions of our people and our law. It does not need research to show that no such sweeping condemnation can be passed upon the statute before us. A reasonable man might think it a proper measure on the score of health. Men whom I certainly could not pronounce unreasonable would uphold it as a first instalment of a general regulation of the hours of work. Whether in the latter aspect it would be open to the charge of inequality I think it unnecessary to discuss.

Coppage v. Kansas

236 US 1, 35 S Ct 240, 59 L Ed 441 (1915)

The Kansas statute declaring it a misdemeanor punishable by fine or imprisonment for an employer to require an employe to agree not to become or remain a member of any labor organization during the time of the employment . . . *held*, repugnant to the "due process" clause of the Fourteenth Amendment.

MR. JUSTICE PITNEY delivered the opinion of the Court.

In a local court in one of the counties of Kansas, plaintiff in error was found guilty . . . upon an information charging him with a violation of an act of the legislature of that State, approved March 13, 1903. . . . The act reads as follows:

"AN ACT to provide a penalty for coercing or influencing or making demands upon or requirements of employes, servants, laborers, and persons seeking employment.

"*Be it Enacted, etc.:*

"Section 1. That it shall be unlawful for any individual or member of any firm, or any agent, officer or employe of any company or corporation, to coerce, require, demand or influence any person or persons to enter into any agreement, either written or verbal, not to join or become or remain a member of any labor organization or association, as a condition of such person or persons securing employment, or continuing in the employment of such individual, firm, or corporation. . . ."

The facts, as recited in the opinion of the Supreme Court, are as follows: About July 1, 1911, one Hedges was employed as a switchman by the St. Louis & San Francisco Railway Company, and was a member of a labor organization called the Switchmen's Union of North America. Plaintiff in error [T. B. Coppage] was employed by the railway company as superintendent, and as such he requested Hedges to sign an agreement, which he presented to him in writing, at the same time informing him that if he did not sign it he could not remain in the employ of the company. The following is a copy of the paper thus presented:

Fort Scott, Kansas, _____ __, 1911.

Mr. T. B. Coppage, Superintendent Frisco Lines, Fort Scott:

We, the undersigned, have agreed to abide by your request, that is, to withdraw from the Switchmen's Union, while in the service of the Frisco Company.

(Signed) _____

Hedges refused to sign this, and refused to withdraw from the labor organization. Thereupon plaintiff in error, as such superintendent, discharged him from the service of the company. . . .

In *Adair* v. *United States,* 208 US 161, this court had to deal with a question not distinguishable in principle from the one now presented. . . .

Unless it is to be overruled, this decision is controlling upon the present controversy; for if Congress is prevented from arbitrary interference with the liberty of contract because of the "due process" provision of the Fifth Amendment, it is too clear for argument that the States are prevented from the like interference by virtue of the corresponding clause of the Fourteenth Amendment. . . .

An interference with this liberty so serious as that now under consideration, and so disturbing of equality of right, must be deemed to be arbitrary, unless it be supportable as a reasonable exercise of the police power of the State. But, notwithstanding the strong general presumption in favor of the validity of state laws, we do not think the statute in question, as construed and applied in this case, can be sustained as a legitimate exercise of that power. . . .

As to the interest of the employed, it is said by the Kansas Supreme Court (87 Kansas, p. 759) to be a matter of common knowledge that "employes, as a rule, are not financially able to be as independent in making contracts for the sale of their labor as are employers in making contracts of purchase thereof." No doubt, wherever the right of private property exists, there must and will be inequalities of fortune; and thus it naturally happens that parties negotiating about a contract are not equally unhampered by circumstances. This applies to all contracts, and not merely to that between employer and employe. Indeed a little reflection will show that wherever the right of private property and the right of contract co-exist, each party when contracting is inevitably more or less influenced by the question whether he has much property, or little, or none; for the contract is made to the very end that each may gain something that he needs or desires more urgently than that which he proposes to give in exchange. And, since it is self-evident that, unless all things are held in common, some persons must have more property than others, it is from the nature of things impossible to uphold freedom of contract and the right of private property without at the same time recognizing as legitimate those inequalities of fortune that are the necessary result of the exercise of those rights. But the Fourteenth Amendment, in declaring that a State shall not "deprive any person of life, liberty or property without due process of law," gives to each of these an equal sanction; it recognizes "liberty" and "property" as co-existent human rights, and debars the States from any unwarranted interference with either. . . .

To ask a man to agree, in advance, to refrain from affiliation with the union while retaining a certain position of employment, is not to ask him to give up any part of his constitutional freedom. He is free to decline the employment on those terms, just as the employer may decline to offer employment to any other; for "It takes two to make a bargain." . . .

Upon both principle and authority, therefore, we are constrained to hold that the Kansas act of March 13, 1903, as construed and applied so as to punish with fine or imprisonment an employer or his agent for merely prescribing, as a condition upon which one may secure employment under or remain in the service of such employer, that the employe shall enter into an agreement not to become or remain a member of any labor organization while so employed, is repugnant to the "due process" clause of the Fourteenth Amendment, and therefore void.

Judgment reversed, and the cause remanded for further proceedings not inconsistent with this opinion.

MR. JUSTICE HOLMES [dissented]. . . .

MR. JUSTICE DAY with whom MR. JUSTICE HUGHES concurs [dissented]. . . .

West Coast Hotel Co. v. Parrish

300 US 379, 57 S Ct 578, 81 L Ed 703 (1937)

Deprivation of liberty to contract is forbidden by the Constitution if without due process of law; but restraint or regulation of this liberty, if reasonable in relation to its subject and if adopted for the protection of the community against evils menacing the health, safety, morals and welfare of the people, is due process.

MR. CHIEF JUSTICE HUGHES delivered the opinion of the Court. . . .

The appellant conducts a hotel. The appellee Elsie Parrish was employed as a chambermaid and (with her husband) brought this suit to recover the difference between the wages paid her and the minimum wage fixed pursuant to the state law. The minimum wage was $14.50 per week of 48 hours. The appellant challenged the act as repugnant to the due process clause of the Fourteenth Amendment of the Constitution of the United States. . . .

The appellant relies upon the decision of this Court in *Adkins* v. *Children's Hospital,* 261 US 525, which held invalid the District of Columbia Minimum Wage Act, which was attacked under the due process clause of the Fifth Amendment. . . .

The principle which must control our decision is not in doubt. The constitutional provision invoked is the due process clause of the Fourteenth Amendment governing the States, as the due process clause involved in the *Adkins* case governed Congress. In each case the violation alleged by those attacking minimum wage regulation for women is deprivation of freedom of contract. What is this freedom? The Constitution does not speak of freedom of contract. It speaks of liberty and prohibits the deprivation of liberty without due process of law. In prohibiting that deprivation the Constitution does not recognize an absolute and uncontrollable liberty. Liberty in each of its phases has its history and connotation. But the liberty safeguarded is liberty in a social organization which requires the protection of law against the evils which menace the health, safety, morals and welfare of the people. Liberty under the Constitution is thus necessarily subject to the restraints of due process, and regulation which is reasonable in relation to its subject and is adopted in the interests of the community is due process. . . .

The minimum wage to be paid under the Washington statute is fixed after full consideration by representatives of employers, employees and the public. It may be assumed that the minimum wage is fixed in consideration of the services that are performed in the particular occupations under normal conditions. Provision is made for special licenses at less wages in the case of men who are incapable of full service. The statement of Mr. Justice Holmes in the *Adkins* case is pertinent: "This statute does not compel anybody to pay anything. It simply forbids employment at rates below those fixed as the minimum requirement of health and right living. It is safe to assume that women will not be employed at even the lowest wages allowed unless they earn them, or unless the employer's business can sustain the burden. In short, the law in its character and operation is like hundreds of so-called police laws that have been upheld." . . .

We think that the views thus expressed are sound and that the decision in the *Adkins* case was a departure from the true application of the principles governing the regulation by the State of the relation of employer and employed. . . .

There is an additional and compelling consideration which recent economic experience has brought into a strong light. The exploitation of a class of workers who are in an unequal position with respect to bargaining power and are thus relatively defenceless against the denial of a living wage is not only detrimental to their health and well being but casts a direct burden for their support upon the community. What these workers lose in wages the taxpayers are called upon to pay. The bare cost of living must be met. We may take judicial notice of the unparalleled demands for relief which arose during the recent period of depression and still continue to an alarming extent despite the degree of economic recovery which has been achieved. . . . Our conclusion is that the case of *Adkins* v. *Children's Hospital, supra,* should be, and it is, overruled. The judgment of the Supreme Court of the State of Washington is

Affirmed.

Mr. Justice Sutherland, dissenting:
Mr. Justice Van Devanter, Mr. Justice McReynolds, Mr. Justice Butler and I think the judgment of the court below should be reversed. [Opinion omitted here.]

Notes

1. *Pennsylvania Coal Co.* v. *Mahon,* 260 US 393 (1922), held void a mining statute as applied in the case. Mahon had acquired surface rights to designated property sold by the Coal Company under a contract containing a reservation of the right to remove coal under the land sold. A subsequent statute prohibited mining under a structure used as a human habitation. For the majority, Justice Holmes wrote that

"while property may be regulated to a certain extent, if regulation goes too far it will be recognized as a taking." Compare *United States* v. *Causby,* 328 US 256 (1946), which held that frequent low-altitude flights by military planes over a poultry farm was a partial taking of the property requiring compensation. Contrast *Miller* v. *Schoene,* 276 US 272 (1928), sustaining a Virginia statute which required owners of ornamental red cedar trees (host plants for cedar rust) located near an apple orchard to cut the trees. See also *Berman* v. *Parker,* 348 US 26 (1954), sustaining the District of Columbia Redevelopment Act.

2. *Nebbia* v. *New York,* 291 US 502 (1934), sustained a statute giving a milk control board power to fix prices for the sale of milk. The Court recognized price fixing, like other economic regulations, to be primarily a matter of legislative discretion. Prior to 1934 the Court had permitted the states to regulate prices only in businesses said to be "affected with a public interest"—i.e., public utilities.

3. *State Tax Commission* v. *Aldrich,* 316 US 174 (1942), held that "there is no constitutional rule or immunity from taxation of intangibles by more than one State"; *First National Bank* v. *Maine,* 284 US 312 (1932), was overruled.

4. *Lincoln Federal Labor Union* v. *Northwestern Iron & Metal Co.,* 335 US 525 (1949), sustained the validity of "right to work" laws of Nebraska and North Carolina. The statutes provided that no person should be denied the opportunity to obtain or retain employment because he is or is not a member of a labor organization. For the Court, Justice Black wrote: "Appellants now ask us to return, at least in part, to the due process philosophy that has been deliberately discarded. Claiming that the Federal Constitution itself affords protection for union members against discrimination, they nevertheless assert that the same Constitution forbids a state from providing the same protection for non-union members. Just as we have held that the due process clause erects no obstacle to block legislative protection of union members, we now hold that legislative protection can be afforded non-union workers."

5. *Williamson* v. *Lee Optical Co.,* 348 US 483 (1955), sustained an Oklahoma statute which made it unlawful for any person other than licensed optometrists and ophthalmologists to fit or duplicate lenses. Justice Douglas wrote: "The day is gone when this Court uses the Due Process Clause . . . to strike down state laws, regulatory of business and industrial conditions, because they may be unwise, improvident, or out of harmony with a particular school of thought. . . . We emphasize again what Chief Justice Wait said in *Munn* v. *Illinois,* 94 US 113, 134, 'For protection against abuses by legislatures the people must resort to the polls, not to the courts.' "

6. *Ferguson* v. *Scrupa,* 372 US 726 (1962), sustained a Kansas statute making it a misdemeanor for persons other than lawyers to engage "in the business of debt adjusting." Justice Black wrote: "The doctrine that prevailed in *Lochner, Coppage, Adkins, Burns,* and like cases—that due process authorizes courts to hold laws unconstitutional when they believe the legislature has acted unwisely—has long since been discarded."

7. *North Dakota State Bd. of Pharmacy* v. *Snyders Drug Stores, Inc.,* 414 US 156 (1974), sustained a statute limiting the operation of a pharmacy to a registered

pharamcist or "a corporation or association, the majority stock in which is owned by registered pharamacists. . . ."

Griswold et al. v. Connecticut

381 US 479, 85 S Ct 1678, 14 L Ed2d 510 (1965)

A state statute prohibiting the use of contraceptives or the giving of counsel on their use is unconstitutional.

MR. JUSTICE DOUGLAS delivered the opinion of the Court.

Appellant Griswold is Executive Director of the Planned Parenthood League of Connecticut. Appellant Buxton is a licensed physician and a professor at the Yale Medical School who served as Medical Director for the League at its Center in New Haven—a center open and operating from November 1 to November 10, 1961, when appellants were arrested.

They gave information, instruction, and medical advice to *married persons* as to the means of preventing conception. They examined the wife and prescribed the best contraceptive device or material for her use. Fees were usually charged, although some couples were serviced free.

The statutes whose constitutionality is involved in this appeal are §§ 53–32 and 54–196 of the General Statutes of Connecticut (1958 rev.). The former provides:

"Any person who uses any drug, medicinal article or instrument for the purpose of preventing conception shall be fined not less than fifty dollars or imprisoned not less than sixty days nor more than one year or be both fined and imprisoned."

Section 54–196 provides:

"Any person who assists, abets, counsels, causes, hires or commands another to commit any offense may be prosecuted and punished as if he were the principal offender."

The appellants were found guilty as accessories and fined $100 each, against the claim that the accessory statute as so applied violated the Fourteenth Amendment. The Appellate Division of the Circuit Court affirmed. The Supreme Court of Errors affirmed that judgment. We noted probable jurisdiction. . . .

Coming to the merits, we are met with a wide range of questions that implicate the Due Process Clause of the Fourteenth Amendment. . . . We do not sit as a super-legislature to determine the wisdom, need, and propriety of laws that touch economic problems, business affairs, or social conditions. This law, however, operates directly on an intimate relation of husband and wife and their physician's role in one aspect of that relation.

The association of people is not mentioned in the Constitution nor in the Bill of Rights. The right to educate a child in a school of the parents' choice—whether public or private or parochial—is also not mentioned. Nor is the right to study any particular subject or any foreign language. Yet the First Amendment has been construed to include certain of those rights. . . .

The . . . cases suggest that specific guarantees in the Bill of Rights have penumbras, formed by emanations from those guarantees that help give them life and substance. . . .

The present case, then, concerns a relationship lying within the zone of privacy created by several fundamental constitutional guarantees. And it concerns a law which, in forbidding the *use* of contraceptives rather than regulating their manufacture or sale, seeks to achieve its goals by means having a maximum destructive impact upon that relationship. Such a law cannot stand in light of the familiar principle, so often applied by this Court, that a "governmental purpose to control or prevent activities constitutionally subject to state regulation may not be achieved by means which sweep unnecessarily broadly and thereby invade the area of protected freedoms." *NAACP* v. *Alabama,* 377 US 288, 307. Would we allow the police to search the sacred precincts of marital bedrooms for telltale signs of the use of contraceptives? The very idea is repulsive to the notions of privacy surrounding the marriage relationship.

We deal with a right of privacy older than the Bill of Rights—older than our political parties, older than our school system. Marriage is a coming together for better or for worse, hopefully enduring, and intimate to the degree of being sacred. It is an association that promotes a way of life, not causes; a harmony in living, not political faiths; a bilateral loyalty, not commercial or social projects. Yet it is an association for as noble a purpose as any involved in our prior decisions.

Reversed.

Mr. Justice Goldberg, whom The Chief Justice and Mr. Justice Brennan join, concurring.

I agree with the Court that Connecticut's birth-control law unconstitutionally intrudes upon the right of marital privacy, and I join in its opinion and judgment. Although I have not accepted the view that "due process" as used in the Fourteenth Amendment incorporates all of the first eight Amendments . . . I do agree that the concept of liberty protects those personal rights that are fundamental, and is not confined to the specific terms of the Bill of Rights. . . .

Mr. Justice Harlan, concurring in the judgment.

I fully agree with the judgment of reversal, but find myself unable to join the Court's opinion. The reason is that it seems to me to evince an approach to this case very much like that taken by my Brothers Black and Stewart in dissent, namely: the Due Process Clause of the Fourteenth Amendment does not touch this Connecticut statute unless the enactment is found to violate some right assured by the letter or penumbra of the Bill of Rights.

In other words, what I find implicit in the Court's opinion is that the "incorporation" doctrine may be used to *restrict* the reach of Fourteenth Amendment Due Process. For me this is just as unacceptable constitutional doctrine as is the use of the "incorporation" approach to *impose* upon the States all the requirements of the Bill of Rights as found in the provisions of the first eight amendments and in the decisions of this Court interpreting them. . . .

In my view, the proper constitutional inquiry in this case is whether this Connecticut statute infringes the Due Process Clause of the Fourteenth Amendment because the enactment violates basic values "implicit in the concept of ordered liberty." *Palko* v. *Connecticut,* 302 US 319, 325. For reasons stated at length in my dissenting opinion in *Poe* v. *Ullman, supra,* I believe that it does. While the relevant inquiry may be aided by resort to one or more of the provisions of the Bill of Rights, it is not dependent on them or any of their radiations. The Due Process Clause of the Fourteenth Amendment stands, in my opinion, on its own bottom. . . .

MR. JUSTICE WHITE, concurring in the judgment.

In my view this Connecticut law as applied to married couples deprives them of "liberty" without due process of law, as that concept is used in the Fourteenth Amendment. I therefore concur in the judgment of the Court reversing these convictions under Connecticut's aiding and abetting statute. . . .

The nature of the right invaded is pertinent . . . for statutes regulating sensitive areas of liberty do, under the cases of this Court, require "strict scrutiny," . . . .

MR. JUSTICE BLACK, with whom MR. JUSTICE STEWART joins, dissenting. . . .

The Court talks about a constitutional "right of privacy" as though there is some constitutional provision of provisions forbidding any law ever to be passed which might abridge the "privacy" of individuals. But there is not. There are, of course, guarantees in certain specific constitutional provisions which are designed in part to protect privacy at certain times and places with respect to certain activities. Such, for example, is the Fourth Amendment's gurantee against "unreasonable searches and seizures." To treat it that way is to give it a niggardly interpretation, not the kind of liberal reading I think any Bill of Rights provision should be given. The average man would very likely not have his feelings soothed any more by having his property seized openly than by having it seized privately and by stealth. He simply wants his property left alone. And a person can be just as much, if not more irritated, annoyed and injured by an unceremonious public arrest by a policeman as he is by a seizure in the privacy of his office or home.

One of the most effective ways of diluting or expanding a constitutionally gauranteed right is to substitute for the crucial word or words of a constitutional guarantee another word or words, more or less flexible and more or less restricted in meaning. This fact is well illustrated by the use of the term "right of privacy" as a comprehensive substitute for the Fourth Amendment's guarantee against "unreasonable searches and seizures." "Privacy" is a broad, abstract and ambiguous concept which can easily be shrunken in meaning but which can also, on the other hand, easily be interpreted as a constitutional ban against many things other than searches and seizures. . . .

I realize that many good and able men have eloquently spoken and written, sometimes in rhapsodical strains, about the duty of the Court to keep the Constitution in tune with the times. The idea is that the Constitution must be changed from time to time and that this Court is charged with a duty to make those changes. For myself, I must with all deference reject that philosophy. The Constitution makers knew the need for change and provided for it. Amendments suggested by the people's elected representatives can be submitted to the people or their selected agents for ratification. That method of change was good for our Fathers, and being somewhat old-fashioned I must add it is good enough for me. . . . The late Judge Learned Hand, after emphasizing his view that judges should not use the due process formula suggested in the concurring opinions today or any other formula like it to invalidate legislation offensive to their "personal preferences," made the statement, with which I fully agree, that:

"For myself it would be most irksome to be ruled by a bevy of Platonic Guardians, even if I knew how to choose them, which I assuredly do not."

So far as I am concerned, Connecticut's law as applied here is not forbidden by any provision of the Federal Constitution as that Constitution was written, and I would therefore affirm.

MR. JUSTICE STEWART, whom MR. JUSTICE BLACK joins, dissenting.

. . . In the course of its opinion the Court refers to no less than six Amendments to the Constitution: the First, the Third, the Fourth, the Fifth, the Ninth, and the Fourteenth. But the Court does not say which of these Amendments, if any, it thinks is infringed by this Connecticut law. . . .

The Court also quotes the Ninth Amendment, and my Brother GOLDBERG's concurring opinion relies heavily upon it. But to say that the Ninth Amendment has anything to do with this case is to turn somersaults with history. . . .

At the oral argument in this case we were told that the Connecticut law does not "conform to current community standards." But it is not the function of this Court to decide cases on the basis of community standards. We are here to decide cases "agreeably to the Constitution and laws of the United States." It is the essence of judicial duty to subordinate our own personal views, our own ideas of what legislation is wise and what is not. If, as I should surely hope, the law before us does not reflect the standards of the people of Connecticut, the people of Connecticut can freely exercise their true Ninth and Tenth Amendment rights to persuade their elected representatives to repeal it. That is the constitutional way to take this law off the books.

Notes

1. *Roe* v. *Wade,* 410 US 113 (1973), held void a Texas statute banning all abortions not necessary to save the mother's life as a violation of the fundamental right to privacy. According to the Court, the state's interest in the protection of potential life does not become sufficiently "compelling" to justify a ban on abortion prior to the time the fetus becomes "viable."

2. *Village of Belle Terre* v. *Boraas,*   US   (1974), sustained a zoning ordinance restricting land use to one-family dwellings, defining the word "family" as "one or more persons related by blood, adoption, or marriage, living and cooking together as a single household unit, exclusive of household servants. A number of persons but not exceeding two (2) living and cooking together as a single housekeeping unit though not related by blood, adoption, or marriage shall be deemed to constitute a family."

Chapter 11

Equal Protection

INTRODUCTION

The Fourteenth Amendment provides that no State shall "deny to any person within its jurisdiction the equal protection of the laws." Like due process, equal protection is a clause to which meaning must be assigned. In the first case in which the Supreme Court construed the clause (the *Slaughterhouse Cases* of 1873), Justice Miller wrote that in the light of the history of the Fourteenth Amendment and of the evil sought to be remedied by the clause, "we doubt very much whether any action of a State not directed by way of discrimination against the Negroes as a class, or on account of their race, will ever be held to come within the purview of this provision." Thirteen years later, however, the Court accepted the theory that the word "person" in the Fourteenth Amendment included corporations as well as natural persons, *Santa Clara County* v. *Southern Pacific Rr.,* 118 US 394 (1886), and, as illustrated in the last chapter, for the next half century the Court's dominant interest was in the protection of property rights.

Prior to 1950, due process was a broader and more frequently applied concept than equal protection. Justice Holmes referred to equal protection as "the usual last resort of constitutional argument." Under the Warren Court, however, equal protection became the dominant concept.

Under the old concept of equal protection, the Court presumed all statutes, state and national, to be valid, and was hesitant to substitute its own judgment for that of legislatures on matters of public policy. Adjectives used to describe statutes which the Court did invalidate were "unreasonable," "irrational," "irrelevant," "arbitrary," or "invidious."

Under the new concept of equal protection, the Court played a more active part in formulating public policy. Classification based on race, alienage, sex, illegitimacy, and indigency were subjected to close scrutiny. All classifications based on race, and occasionally others, were branded as "suspect." The burden of proof to justify a classification thus labeled was placed on the state, and nothing short of a "compelling state interest" would suffice.

This same difficult standard was applied to laws making classifications which the Court viewed as impinging upon fundamental rights conferred by the Constitution, for example, the right to vote and the right to travel. The "heavy burden of proof" placed on the state demanded a showing that its statute was precisely worded to encompass only its legitimate objective by the least drastic means imaginable. In short, "compelling state interest" was the language used to explain the use of a judicial veto on legislation.

Some have traced the origin of the compelling state interest concept to the opinion by Justice Douglas in *Skinner* v. *Oklahoma,* 315 US 535 (1942), which struck down a statute authorizing sterilization of persons convicted more than twice of designated felonies. Pointing to the fact that the statute covered larceny but not embezzlement, Douglas held that it ran afoul of the equal protection clause. He wrote: "We are dealing here with legislation which involves one of the basic civil rights of man. Marriage and procreation are fundamental to the very existence and survival of the race. . . . We mention these matters . . . in emphasis of our view that strict scrutiny . . . is essential. . . .''

Justice Frankfurter was, we believe, the first to use the adjective "compelling" in describing a state's interest. In *Sweezy* v. *New Hampshire,* 354 US 234 (1957), a case dealing with the right of association, he wrote: "For a citizen to be made to forego even a part of so basic a liberty as his political autonomy, the subordinating interest of the State must be compelling." Justice Harlan quoted this language with approval in his opinion in *NAACP* v. *Alabama,* 357 US 449 (1958), but he rejected the "compelling State interest" doctrine as it developed in the late 1960s and early 1970s. (See his opinion in *Shapiro* v. *Thompson,* p. 419.)

Decisions showing freer use of judicial review were by no means all written in terms of "compelling State interests." The doctrine of overbreadth, that is, statutes with "too broad a sweep," first developed in cases dealing with freedom of speech and association, was readily transplanted to the equal protection field.

It is difficult today to present a neat classification of the cases decided in terms of equal protection. Dissenting in *San Antonio Independent School District* v. *Rodriguez,* 411 US 1 (1973), Justice Marshall, who advocated a "variable standard of review," wrote:

> The Court apparently seeks to establish today that equal protection cases fall into one of two neat categories which dictate the appropriate standard of review—strict scrutiny or mere rationality. But this Court's decisions in the field of equal protection defy such easy categorization. A principled reading of what this Court has done reveals that it has applied a spectrum of standards in reviewing discriminations allegedly violative of the Equal Protection Clause. This spectrum clearly comprehends variations in the degree of care with which the Court will scrutinize particular classifications, depending, I believe, on the constitutional and societal importance of the interest adversely affected and the recognized invidiousness of the basis upon which the particular classification is drawn.

The equal protection clause confers no substantive rights. It is used to test the constitutionality of classifications made by legislatures. And, "Though the test has been variously stated, the end result is whether the line drawn is a rational one." Douglas, J., in *Levy* v. *Louisiana,* 391 US 68 (1968).

Section 1.   Traditional Analysis

A.   BACKGROUND

Lindsley v. Natural Carbonic Gas Co.

220 US 61, 31 S Ct 337, 55 L Ed 369 (1911)

A person challenging the validity of a statute on equal protection grounds must carry the burden of proving that the statute does not rest upon a reasonable basis.

[Lindsley, a stockholder of the Natural Carbonic Gas Company, sought to enjoin the company from obeying a New York statute entitled "An act for the protection of the natural mineral springs of the State and to prevent waste and impairment of its natural mineral waters." From an adverse decision in the circuit court, an appeal was taken to the Supreme Court.]

MR. JUSTICE VAN DEVANTER . . . delivered the opinion of the court. . . .

[W]e overlook the allegation in the bill that the gas company's pumps do not exert any force upon waters in or under adjoining lands, but lift to the surface only such waters "as flow by reason of the laws of nature into the wells"; but we regard it as of little importance, because if the wells reach a common source of supply excessive or wasteful pumping from them may affect injuriously the rights of other surface owners, although the force exerted by the pumps does not reach their lands.

Because the statute is directed against pumping from wells bored or drilled into the rock, but not against pumping from wells not penetrating the rock, and because it is directed against pumping for the purpose of collecting the gas and vending it apart from the waters, but not against pumping for other purposes, the contention is made that it is arbitrary in its classification, and consequently denies the equal portion of the laws to those whom it affects.

The rules by which this contention must be tested, as is shown by repeated decisions of this court, are these: 1. The equal protection clause of the Fourteenth Amendment does not take from the State the power to classify in the adoption of police laws, but admits of the exercise of a wide scope of discretion in that regard, and avoids what is done only when it is without any reasonable basis and therefore is purely arbitrary. 2. A classification having some reasonable basis does not offend against that clause merely because it is not made with mathematical nicety or because in practice it results in some inequality. 3. When the classification in such a law is called in question, if any state of facts reasonably can be conceived that would sustain it, the existence of that state of facts at the time the law was enacted must be assumed. 4. One who assails the classification in such a law must carry the burden of showing that it does not rest upon any reasonable basis, but is essentially arbitrary. . . .

Unfortunately the allegations of the bill shed but little light upon the classification in question. They do not indicate that pumping from wells not penetrating the rock appreciably affects the common supply therein, or is calculated to result in injury to the rights of others, and neither do they indicate that such pumping as is done for purposes other than collecting and vending the gas apart from the waters is excessive or wasteful, or otherwise operates to impair the rights of others. In other words, for aught that appears in the bill, the classification may rest upon some substantial difference between pumping from wells penetrating the rock and pumping from those not penetrating it, and between pumping for the purpose of collecting and vending the gas apart from the waters and pumping for other purposes, and this difference may afford a reasonable basis for the classification. . . .

From statements made in the briefs of counsel and in oral argument we infer that wells not penetrating the rock reach such waters only as escape naturally therefrom through breaks or fissures, and if this be so, it well may be doubted that pumping from such wells has anything like the same effect—if, indeed, it has any—upon the common supply or upon the rights of others, as does pumping from wells which take the waters from within the rock where they exist under great hydrostatic pressure. . . .

For these reasons none of the objections urged against the statute can be sustained, and so the decree dismissing the bill is

Affirmed.

Notes

1. *Santa Clara County* v. *Southern Pacific R. Co.,* 118 US 394 (1886), held that the word "person" in the Fourteenth Amendment includes corporations. The Court declined to hear arguments on the question because, Chief Justice Waite explained, "We are all of the opinion that it does." In a dissenting opinion in *Connecticut General Life Ins. Co.* v. *Johnson,* 303 US 77 (1938), Justice Black challenged this holding.

2. *Sioux City Bridge Co.* v. *Dakota County,* 260 US 441 (1928), held that intentional assessment of the property of one owner at its true value while other like property is systematically assessed much lower is a violation of equal protection and that the aggrieved owner has a right to have his assessment reduced to the common level.

3. *The Great A. & P. Tea Co.* v. *Grosjean,* 301 US 412 (1937), sustained a tax graduated according to the number of stores in a chain. Earlier cases had held similar taxes void.

4. *Goesaert* v. *Cleary,* 335 US 464 (1948), sustained a Michigan statute denying a bartender's license to a female other than "the wife or daughter of the male owner" of the bar.

5. *Railway Express Agency* v. *New York,* 336 US 106 (1949), sustained a New York statute which prohibited business advertisements on a truck, other than advertisements of products sold by the owner of the truck. Justice Douglas wrote: "It is by . . . practical considerations based on experience rather than by theoretical inconsistencies that the question of equal protection is to be answered."

6. *Morey* v. *Doud,* 354 US 457 (1957), held void the Illinois Commodity Exchange Act of 1955 which placed stringent requirements upon currency exchanges that issue money orders but exempted the American Express Co. Justices Black, Frankfurter, and Harlan dissented. Justice Frankfurter thought the majority of the Court emphasized abstractions instead of actualities.

7. *Lynch* v. *Household Finance Corp.,* 405 US 538 (1972) held that the district court erred in dismissing a suit for relief against enforcement of an allegedly unconstitutional garnishment law. The district court dismissed the complaint on the ground that it lacked jurisdiction because 28 USC § 1343 (3) applied only if "personal" rights, as opposed to "property" rights, were impaired. In reversing, the Supreme Court held that "the dichotomy between personal liberties and property rights is a false one. Property does not have rights. People have rights. The right to enjoy property without unlawful deprivation, no less than the right to speak or the right to travel, is, in truth a 'personal' right. . . . ."

B.   RECENT CASES

Lehnhausen v. Lake Shore Auto Parts Co.

410 US 356, 93 S Ct 1001, 35 L Ed2d 351 (1973)

A state may levy ad valorem taxes on personalty owned by corporations while exempting individuals from such taxes.

MR. JUSTICE DOUGLAS delivered the opinion of the Court.

In 1970 the people of Illinois amended her constitution adding Art. IX-A to become effective January 1, 1971, and reading:

"Not withstanding any other provision of this Constitution, the taxation of personal property by valuation is prohibited as to individuals." . . .

Respondent Lake Shore Auto Parts Co., a corporation, brought an action against Illinois officials on its behalf and on behalf of all other corporations and "non-individuals" subject to the personal property tax, claiming it violated the Equal Protection

Clause of the Fourteenth Amendment since it exempts from personal property taxes all personal property owned by individuals but retains such taxes as to personal property owned by corporations and other "non-individuals." The Circuit Court held Art. IX-A unconstitutional as respects corporations by reason of the Equal Protection Clause of the Fourteenth Amendment. . . . The cases are here on petitions for writs of *certiorari* which we granted. . . .

The Equal Protection Clause does not mean that a State may not draw lines that treat one class of individuals or entities different from the others. The test is whether the difference in treatment is an invidious discrimination. . . . Where taxation is concerned and no specific federal right, apart from equal protection, is imperilled, the States have large leeway in making classifications and drawing lines which in their judgment produce reasonable systems of taxation. . . .

It is true that in *Quaker City Cab Co.* v. *Pennsylvania,* 277 US 389, the Court held that a gross receipts tax levied on corporations doing a taxi business violated the Equal Protection Clause of the Fourteenth Amendment, when no such tax was levied on individuals and partnerships operating taxicabs in competition with the corporate taxpayers. Justice Holmes, Justice Brandeis, and Justice Stone dissented. . . .

[C]ases following *Quaker City Cab* have somewhat undermined it. *White River Co.* v. *Arkansas,* 279 US 692, sustained a state statute for collection of back taxes on lands owned by corporations but not individuals. The Court sustained the tax. Justice Butler, Chief Justice Taft, and Justice Van Devanter dissented, asserting that *Quaker City Cab* was not distinguishable. The majority made no effort to distinguish *Quaker City Cab* beyond saying that it did not involve, as did *White River,* a tax on back taxes. . . .

In *Madden* v. *Kentucky,* 309 US 83, a State laid an ad valorem tax of 50¢ per $100 on deposits in banks outside the State and only 10¢ for $1,000 in deposits within the State. The classification was sustained against the charge of invidious discrimination, the Court noting that "in taxation, even more than in other fields, legislatures possess the greatest freedom in classification." *Id.,* at 88. There is a presumption of constitutionality which can be overcome "only by the most explicit demonstration that a classification is a hostile and oppressive discrimination against particular persons and classes." *Ibid.* That idea has been elaborated. Thus in *Carmichael* v. *Southern Coal Co.,* 301 US 495, the Court in sustaining an unemployment tax on employers said:

> "A state legislature, in the enactment of laws, has the widest possible latitude within the limits of the Constitution. In the nature of the case it cannot record a complete catalogue of the considerations which move its members to enact laws. In the absence of such a record courts cannot assume that its action is capricious, or that, with its informed acquaintance with local conditions to which the legislation is to be applied, it was not aware of facts which afford reasonable basis for its action. Only by faithful adherence to this guiding principle of judicial review of legislation is it possible to preserve to the legislative branch its rightful independence and its ability to function." *Id.,* at 510. . . .

We could strike down this tax as discriminatory only if we substituted our judgment on facts of which we can be only dimly aware for a legislative judgment that reflects a vivid reaction to pressing fiscal problems. *Quaker City Cab Co.* v. *Pennsylvania* is only a relic of a bygone era. We cannot follow it and stay within the narrow confines of judicial review, which is an important part of our constitutional tradition.

Reversed.

San Antonio Independent School District v. Rodriguez

411 US 1, 93 S Ct 1278, 36 L Ed2d 16 (1973)

The Constitution contains no guarantee of education as a "fundamental" right; hence a challenge to a state's educational policy alleging discrimination against the "poor" but showing no such definable class will be judged by traditional equal protection standards, not by the stringent "compelling state interest" test.

MR. JUSTICE POWELL delivered the opinion of the Court.

This suit attacking the Texas system of financing public education was initiated by Mexican-American parents whose children attend the elementary and secondary schools in the Edgewood Independent School District, an urban school district in San Antonio, Texas. They brought a class action on behalf of school children throughout the State who are members of minority groups or who are poor and reside in school districts having a low property tax base. Named as defendants were the State Board of Education, the Commissioner of Education, the State Attorney General, and the Texas County (San Antonio) Board of Trustees. The complaint was filed in the summer of 1968 and a three-judge court was impaneled in January 1969. In December 1971 the panel rendered its judgment in a *per curiam* opinion holding the Texas school finance system unconstitutional under the Equal Protection Clause of the Fourteenth Amendment. The State appealed, and we noted probable jurisdiction to consider the far-reaching constitutional questions presented. . . . For the reasons stated in this opinion we reverse the decision of the District Court. . . .

Recognizing the need for increased state funding to help offset disparities in local spending and to meet Texas' changing educational requirements, the state legislature in the late 1940's undertook a thorough evaluation of public education with an eye toward major reform. . . . [T]he passage of the Gilmer-Aiken bills . . . established the Texas Minimum Foundation School Program. Today this Program accounts for approximately half of the total educational expenditures in Texas.

The Program calls for state and local contributions to a fund earmarked specifically for teacher salaries, operating expenses, and transportation costs. The State, supplying funds from its general revenues, finances approximately 80% of the Program, and the school districts are responsible—as a unit—for providing the remaining 20%. The districts' share, known as the Local Fund Assignment, is apportioned among the school districts under a formula designed to reflect each district's relative taxpaying ability. . . .

In the years since this program went into operation in 1949, expenditures for education—from State as well as local sources—have increased steadily. . . .

Despite these recent increases, substantial interdistrict disparities in school expenditures found by the District Court to prevail in San Antonio and in varying degrees throughout the State still exist. And it was these disparities, largely attributable to differences in the amounts of money collected through local property taxation, that led the District Court to conclude that Texas' dual system of public school finance violated the Equal Protection Clause. The District Court held that the Texas system discriminates on the basis of wealth in the manner in which education is provided for its people. . . . Finding that wealth is a "suspect" classification and that education is a "fundamental" interest, the District Court held that the Texas system could be sustained only if the State could show that it was premised upon some compelling state interest. . . .

Texas virtually concedes that its historically rooted dual system of financing education could not withstand the strict judicial scrutiny that this Court has found appropriate in reviewing legislative judgments that interfere with fundamental constitutional rights or that involve suspect classifications. If, as previous decisions have indicated, strict scrutiny means that the State's system is not entitled to the usual presumption of validity, that the State rather than the complainants must carry a "heavy burden of justification," that the State must demonstrate that its educational system has been structured with "precision" and is "tailored" narrowly to serve legitimate objectives and that it has selected the "least drastic means" for "effectuating its objectives," the Texas financing system and its counterpart in virtually every other State will not pass muster. The State candidly admits that "[n]o one familiar with the Texas system would contend that it has yet achieved perfection." Apart from its concession that educational finance in Texas has "defects" and "imperfections," the State defends the system's rationality with vigor and disputes the District Court's finding that it lacks a "reasonable basis."

This, then, establishes the framework for our analysis. We must decide, first, whether the Texas system of financing public education operates to the disadvantage of some suspect class or impinges upon a fundamental right explicitly or implicitly protected by the Constitution, thereby requiring strict judicial scrutiny. If so, the judgment of the District Court should be affirmed. If not, the Texas scheme must still be examined to determine whether it rationally furthers some legitimate, articulated state purpose and therefore does not constitute an invidious discrimination in violation of the Equal Protection Clause of the Fourteenth Amendment.

The District Court's opinion does not reflect the novelty and complexity of the constitutional questions posed by appellees' challenge to Texas' system of school finance. In concluding that strict judicial scrutiny was required, that court relied on decisions dealing with the rights of indigents to equal treatment in the criminal trial and appellate processes, and on cases disapproving wealth restrictions on the right to vote. Those cases, the District Court concluded, established wealth as a suspect classification. Finding that the local property tax system discriminated on the basis of wealth, it regarded those precedents as controlling. It then reasoned, based on decisions of this Court affirming the undeniable importance of education, that there is a fundamental right to education and that, absent some compelling state justification, the Texas system could not stand.

We are unable to agree that this case, which in significant aspects is *sui generis,* may be so neatly fitted into the conventional mosaic of constitutional analysis under the Equal Protection Clause. Indeed, for the several reasons that follow, we find neither the suspect classification nor the fundamental interest analysis persuasive. . . .

The case comes to us with no definitive description of the classifying facts or delineation of the disfavored class. Examination of the District Court's opinion and of appellees' complaint, briefs, and contentions at oral argument suggests, however, at least three ways in which the discrimination claimed here might be described. The Texas system of school finance might be regarded as discriminating (1) against "poor" persons whose incomes fall below some identifiable level of poverty or who might be characterized as functionally "indigent," or (2) against those who are relatively poorer than others, or (3) against all those who, irrespective of their personal incomes, happen to reside in relatively poorer school districts. Our task must be to ascertain whether, in fact, the Texas system has been shown to discriminate on any of these possible bases and, if so, whether the resulting classification may be regarded as suspect. . . .

However described, it is clear that appellees' suit asks this Court to extend its most exacting scrutiny to review a system that allegedly discriminates against a large, diverse, and amorphous class, unified only by the common factor of residence in districts that happen to have less taxable wealth than other districts. The system of alleged discrimination and the class it defines have none of the traditional indicia of suspectness: the class is not saddled with such disabilities, or subjected to such a history of purposeful unequal treatment, or relegated to such a position of political powerlessness as to command extraordinary protection from the majoritarian political process.

We thus conclude that the Texas system does not operate to the peculiar disadvantage of any suspect class. But in recognition of the fact that this Court has never heretofore held that wealth discrimination alone provides an adequate basis for invoking strict scrutiny, appellees have not relied solely on this contention. They also assert that the State's system impermissibly interferes with the exercise of a "fundamental" right and that accordingly the prior decisions of this Court require the application of the strict standard of judicial review. . . . It is this question—whether education is a fundamental right, in the sense that it is among the rights and liberties protected by the Constitution—which has so consumed the attention of courts and commentators in recent years. . . .

[T]he importance of a service performed by the State does not determine whether it must be regarded as fundamental for purposes of examination under the Equal Protection Clause. Mr. Justice Harlan, dissenting from the Court's application of strict scrutiny to a law impinging upon the right of interstate travel, admonished that "[v]irtually every state statute affects important rights." *Shapiro* v. *Thompson,* 394 US 618, 655, 661 (1969). In his view, if the degree of judicial scrutiny of state legislation fluctuated depending on a majority's view of the importance of the interest affected, we would have gone "far toward making this Court a 'super-legislature.' " *Ibid.* We would indeed then be assuming a legislative role and one for which the Court lacks both authority and competence. But Mr. Justice Stewart's response in *Shapiro* to Mr. Justice Harlan's concern correctly articulates the limits of the fundamental rights rationale employed in the Court's equal protection decisions:

> "The Court today does *not* 'pick out particular human activities, characterize them as "fundamental," and give them added protection. . . .' To the contrary, the Court simply recognizes, as it must, an established constitutional right, and gives to that right no less protection than the Constitution itself demands." 304 US, at 642. (Emphasis from original.)

Mr. Justice Stewart's statement serves to underline what the opinion of the Court in *Shapiro* makes clear. In subjecting to strict judicial scrutiny state welfare eligibility statutes that imposed a one-year durational residency requirement as a precondition to receiving AFDC benefits, the Court explained:

> "in moving from State to State . . . appellees were exercising a constitutional right, and any classification which serves to penalize the exercise of that right, unless shown to be

necessary to promote a *compelling* governmental interest, is unconstitutional." *Id.,* at 634. (Emphasis from original.)

The right to interstate travel had long been recognized as a right of constitutional significance, and the Court's decision therefore did not require an *ad hoc* determination as to the social or economic importance of that right." ...

[By contrast] ... in *Dandridge* v. *Williams,* 397 US 471 (1970), the Court's explicit recognition of the fact that the "administration of public welfare assistance ... involves the most basic economic needs of impoverished human beings," *id.,* at 485, provided no basis for departing from the settled mode of constitutional analysis of legislative classifications involving questions of economic and social policy. As in the case of housing, the central importance of welfare benefits to the poor was not an adequate foundation for requiring the State to justify its law by showing some compelling state interest. See also *Jefferson* v. *Hackney,* 406 US 535 (1972); *Richardson* v. *Belcher,* 404 US 78 (1971).

The lesson of these cases in addressing the question now before the Court is plain. It is not the province of this Court to create substantive constitutional rights in the name of guaranteeing equal protection of the laws. Thus the key to discovering whether education is "fundamental" is not to be found in comparisons of the relative societal significance of education as opposed to subsistence or housing. Nor is it to be found by weighing whether education is as important as the right to travel. Rather, the answer lies in assessing whether there is a right to education explicitly or implicitly guaranteed by the Constitution. ...

Even if it were conceded that some identifiable quantum of education is a constitutionally protected prerequisite to the meaningful exercise of either right, we have no indication that the present levels of educational expenditure in Texas provide an education that falls short. ...

... Every step leading to the establishment of the system Texas utilizes today—including the decisions permitting localities to tax and expend locally, and creating and continuously expanding state aid—was implemented in an effort to *extend* public education and to improve its quality. Of course, every reform that benefits some more than others may be criticized for what it fails to accomplish. But we think it plain that, in substance, the thrust of the Texas system is affirmative and reformatory and, therefore, should be scrutinized under judicial principles sensitive to the nature of the State's efforts and to the rights reserved to the States under the Constitution.

It should be clear, for the reasons stated above and in accord with the prior decisions of this Court, that this is not a case in which the challenged state action must be subjected to the searching judicial scrutiny reserved for laws that create suspect classifications or impinge upon constitutionally protected rights.

We need not rest our decision, however, solely on the inappropriateness of the strict scrutiny test. A century of Supreme Court adjudication under the Equal Protection Clause affirmatively supports the application of the traditional standard of review, which requires only that the State's system be shown to bear some rational relationship to legitimate state purposes. ...

In addition to matters of fiscal policy, this case also involves the most persistent and difficult questions of educational policy, another area in which this Court's lack of specialized knowledge and experience counsels against premature interference with the informed judgments made at the state and local levels. ...

It must be remembered also that every claim arising under the Equal Protection Clause has implications for the relationship between national and state power under our federal system. Questions of federalism are always inherent in the process of determining whether a State's laws are to be accorded the traditional presumption of constitutionality, or are to be subjected instead to rigorous judicial scrutiny. . . .

The foregoing considerations buttress our conclusion that Texas' system of public school finance is an inappropriate candidate for strict judicial scrutiny. These same considerations are relevant to the determination whether that system, with its conceded imperfections, nevertheless bears some rational relationship to a legitimate state purpose. It is to this question that we next turn our attention. . . .

Appellees do not question the propriety of Texas' dedication to local control of education. To the contrary, they attack the school finance system precisely because, in their view, it does not provide the same level of local control and fiscal flexibility in all districts. Appellees suggest that local control could be preserved and promoted under other financing systems that resulted in more equality in educational expenditures. While it is no doubt true that reliance on local property taxation for school revenues provides less freedom of choice with respect to expenditures for some districts than for others, the existence of "some inequality" in the manner in which the State's rationale is achieved is not alone a sufficient basis for striking down the entire system. . . . It may not be condemned simply because it imperfectly effectuates the State's goals. . . . Nor must the financing system fail because, as appellees suggest, other methods of satisfying the State's interest, which occasion "less drastic" disparities in expenditures, might be conceived. Only where state action impinges on the exercise of fundamental constitutional rights or liberties must it be found to have chosen the least restrictive alternative. . . . The people of Texas may be justified in believing that other systems of school finance, which place more of the financial responsibility in the hands of the State, will result in a comparable lessening of desired local autonomy. That is, they may believe that along with increased control of the purse strings at the state level will go increased control over local policies. . . .

. . . The consideration and initiation of fundamental reforms with respect to state taxation and education are matters reserved for the legislative processes of the various States, and we do no violence to the values of federalism and separation of powers by staying our hand. . . . [T]he ultimate solutions must come from the lawmakers and from the democratic pressures of those who elect them.

Reversed.

MR. JUSTICE STEWART, concurring.

The method of financing public schools in Texas, as in almost every other State, has resulted in a system of public education that can fairly be described as chaotic and unjust. It does not follow, however, and I cannot find, that this system violates the Constitution of the United States. I join the opinion and judgment of the Court because I am convinced that any other course would mark an extraordinary departure from principled adjudication under the Equal Protection Clause of the Fourteenth Amendment. The uncharted directions of such a departure are suggested, I think, by the imaginative dissenting opinion my Brother MARSHALL has filed today.

Unlike other provisions of the Constitution, the Equal Protection Clause confers no substantive rights and creates no substantive liberties. The function of the Equal Protection Clause, rather, is simply to measure the validity of *classifications* created by state laws.

There is hardly a law on the books that does not affect some people differently from others. But the basic concern of the Equal Protection Clause is with state legislation whose purpose or effect is to create discrete and objectively identifiable classes. And with respect to such legislation, it has long been settled that the Equal Protection Clause is offended only by laws that are invidiously discriminatory—only by classifications that are wholly arbitrary or capricious. . . .

MR. JUSTICE BRENNAN, dissenting.

Although I agree with my Brother WHITE that the Texas statutory scheme is devoid of any rational basis, and for that reason is violative of the Equal Protection Clause, I also record my disagreement with the Court's rather distressing assertion that a right may be deemed "fundamental" for the purposes of equal protection analysis only if it is "explicitly or implicitly guaranteed by the Constitution." . . . As my Brother MARSHALL convincingly demonstrates, our prior cases stand for the proposition that "fundamentality" is, in large measure, a function of the right's importance in terms of the effectuation of those rights which are in fact constitutionally guaranteed. Thus, "[a]s the nexus between the specific constitutional guarantee and the nonconstitutional interest draws closer, the nonconstitutional interest becomes more fundamental and the degree of judicial scrutiny applied when the interest is infringed on a discriminatory basis must be adjusted accordingly." . . .

Here, there can be no doubt that education is inextricably linked to the right to participate in the electoral process and to the rights of free speech and association guaranteed by the First Amendment. . . . This being so, any classification affecting education must be subjected to strict judicial scrutiny, and since even the State concedes that the statutory scheme now before us cannot pass constitutional muster under this stricter standard of review, I can only conclude that the Texas school financing scheme is constitutionally invalid.

MR. JUSTICE WHITE, with whom MR. JUSTICE DOUGLAS and MR. JUSTICE BRENNAN join, dissenting.

The Texas public schools are financed through a combination of state fundings, local property tax revenue, and some federal funds. Concededly, the system yields wide disparity in per-pupil revenue among the various districts. In a typical year, for example, the Alamo Heights district had total revenues of $504 per pupil, while the Edgewood district had only $356 per student. . . .

The difficulty with the Texas system . . . is that it provides a meaningful option to Alamo Heights and like school districts but almost none to Edgewood and those other districts with a low per-pupil real estate tax base. In these latter districts, no matter how desirous parents are of supporting their schools with greater revenues, it is impossible to do so through the use of the real estate property tax. . . .

The Equal Protection Clause permits discriminations between classes but requires that the classification bear some rational relationship to a permissible object sought to be attained by the statute. It is not enough that the Texas system before us seeks to achieve the valid, rational purpose of maximizing local initiative; the means chosen by the State must also be rationally related to the end sought to be achieved. . . .

Neither Texas nor the majority heeds this rule. If the State aims at maximizing local initiative and local choice, by permitting school districts to resort to the real property tax if they choose to do so, it utterly fails in achieving its purpose in districts with property tax bases so low that there is little if any opportunity for interested parents, rich or poor, to augment school district revenues. Requiring the State to establish only that unequal treatment is in furtherance of a permissible goal, without also requiring the State to show that the means chosen to effectuate that goal are rationally related to its achievement, makes equal protection analysis no more than an empty gesture. In my view, the parents and children in Edgewood, and in like districts, suffer from an invidious discrimination violative of the Equal Protection Clause. . . .

MR. JUSTICE MARSHALL, with whom MR. JUSTICE DOUGLAS concurs, dissenting.

The Court today decides, in effect, that a State may constitutionally vary the quality of education which it offers its children in accordance with the amount of taxable wealth located in the school districts within which they reside. The majority's decision represents an abrupt departure from the mainstream of recent state and federal court decisions concerning the unconstitutionality of state educational financing schemes dependent upon taxable local wealth. More unfortunately, though, the majority's holding can only be seen as a retreat from our historic commitment to equality of educational opportunity and as unsupportable acquiescence in a system which deprives children in their earliest years of the chance to reach their full potential as citizens. The Court does this despite the absence of any substantial justification for a scheme which arbitrarily channels educational resources in accordance with the fortuity of the amount of taxable wealth within each district.

In my judgment, the right of every American to an equal start in life, so far as the provision of a state service as important as education is concerned, is far too vital to permit state discrimination on grounds as tenuous as those presented by this record. Nor can I accept the notion that it is sufficient to remit these appellees to the vagaries of the political process which, contrary to the majority's suggestion, has proven singularly unsuited to the task of providing a remedy for this discrimination. . . .

Section 2. Suspect Classifications

A. RACE

Schools

Plessy v. Ferguson

163 US 597, 16 S Ct 1138, 41 L Ed 256 (1896)

The statute of Louisiana requiring railway companies carrying passengers in their coaches in that state to provide equal, but separate, accommodations for the white and colored races . . . [is] not in conflict with the provisions either of the Thirteenth Amendment or of the Fourteenth Amendment to the Constitution of the United States.

[Homer A. Plessy, seven-eighths Caucasian and one-eighth African, insisted upon going into a railroad coach reserved for white passengers. Upon arrest and prosecution, he filed a petition for a writ of prohibition, challenging the constitutionality of the statute under which he was being prosecuted.]

MR. JUSTICE BROWN ... delivered the opinion of the Court.

This case turns upon the constitutionality of an act of the General Assembly of the State of Louisiana, passed in 1890, providing for separate railway carriages for the white and colored races. . . .

That it does not conflict with the Thirteenth Amendment, which abolished slavery and involuntary servitude, except as a punishment for crime, is too clear for argument. . . .

The object of the [Fourteenth] amendment was undoubtedly to enforce the absolute equality of the two races before the law, but in the nature of things it could not have been intended to abolish distinctions based upon color, or to enforce social, as distinguished from political equality, or a comingling of the two races upon terms unsatisfactory to either. Laws permitting, and even requiring, their separation in places where they are liable to be brought into contact do not necessarily imply the inferiority of either race to the other, and have been generally, if not universally, recognized as within the competency of the state legislatures in the exercise of their police power. The most common instance of this is connected with the establishment of separate schools for white and colored children, which has been held to be a valid exercise of the legislative power even by courts of States where the political rights of the colored race have been longest and most earnestly enforced.

One of the earliest of these cases is that of *Roberts* v. *City of Boston,* 5 Cush 198, in which the Supreme Judicial Court of Massachusetts held that the general school committee of Boston had power to make provision for the instruction of colored children in separate schools established exclusively for them, and to prohibit their attendance upon other schools. . . .

Laws forbidding the intermarriage of the two races may be said in a technical sense to interfere with the freedom of contract, and yet have been universally recognized as within the police power of the State. *State* v. *Gibson,* 36 Indiana, 389. . . .

So far, then, as a conflict with the Fourteenth Amendment is concerned, the case reduces itself to the question whether the statute of Louisiana is a reasonable regulation, and with respect to this there must necessarily be a large discretion on the part of the legislature. In determining the question of reasonableness it is at liberty to act with reference to the established usages, customs and traditions of the people, and with a view to the promotion of their comfort, and the preservation of the public peace and good order. Gauged by this standard, we cannot say that a law which authorizes or even requires the separation of the two races in public conveyances is unreasonable, or more obnoxious to the Fourteenth Amendment than the acts of Congress requiring separate schools for colored children in the District of Columbia, the constitutionality of which does not seem to have been questioned, or the corresponding acts of state legislatures.

We consider the underlying fallacy of the plaintiff's argument to consist in the assumption that the enforced separation of the two races stamps the colored race with a badge of inferiority. If this be so, it is not by reason of anything found in the act, but solely because the colored race chooses to put that construction upon it. . . . The argument also assumes that social prejudices may be overcome by legislation, and that equal rights cannot be secured to the negro except by an enforced commingling of the two races. We cannot accept this proposition. If the two races are to meet upon terms of social equality, it must be the result of natural affinities, a mutual appreciation of each other's merits and a voluntary consent of individuals. . . .

The judgment of the court below is, therefore,

Affirmed.

MR. JUSTICE HARLAN dissenting. . . .

The white race deems itself to be the dominant race in this country. And so it is, in prestige, in achievement, in education, in wealth and in power. So, I doubt not, it will continue to be for all time, if it remains true to its great heritage and holds fast to the principles of constitutional liberty. But in view of the Constitution, in the eye of the law, there is in this country no superior, dominant, ruling class of citizens. There is no caste here. Our Constitution is color-blind, and neither knows nor tolerates classes among citizens. In respect of civil rights, all citizens are equal before the law. The humblest is the peer of the most powerful. The law regards man as man, and takes no account of his surroundings or of his color when his civil rights as guaranteed by the supreme law of the land are involved. It is, therefore, to be regretted that this high tribunal, the final expositor of the fundamental law of the land, has reached the conclusion that it is competent for a State to regulate the enjoyment by citizens of their civil rights solely upon the basis of race. . . .

Brown v. Board of Education

347 US 483, 74 S Ct 686, 98 L Ed 873 (1954)

Segregation of white and black children in the public schools of a state solely on the basis of race, pursuant to state laws permitting or requiring such segregation, denies to black children the equal protection of the laws guaranteed by the Fourteenth Amendment—even though the physical facilities and other "tangible" factors of white and black schools may be equal.

MR. CHIEF JUSTICE WARREN delivered the opinion of the Court.

These cases come to us from the States of Kansas, South Carolina, Virginia, and Delaware. They are premised on different facts and different local conditions, but a common legal question justifies their consideration together in this consolidated opinion.

In each of the cases, minors of the Negro race, through their legal representatives, seek the aid of the courts in obtaining admission to the public schools of their community on a nonsegregated basis. In each instance, they had been denied admission to schools attended by white children under laws requiring or permitting segregation according to race. . . .

The plaintiffs contend that segregated public schools are not "equal" and cannot be made "equal," and that hence they are deprived of the equal protection of the laws. Because of the obvious importance of the question presented, the Court took jurisdiction. Argument was heard in the 1952 Term, and reargument was heard this Term on certain questions propounded by the Court.

Reargument was largely devoted to the circumstances surrounding the adoption of the Fourteenth Amendment in 1868. It covered exhaustively consideration of the Amendment in Congress, ratification by the states, then existing practices in racial segregation, and the views of proponents and opponents of the Amendment. This discussion and our own investigation convince us that, although these sources cast some light, it is not enough to resolve the problem with which we are faced. At best, they are inconclusive. . . .

An additional reason for the inconclusive nature of the Amendment's history, with respect to segregated schools, is the status of public education at that time. In the South, the movement toward free common schools, supported by general taxation, had not yet taken hold. . . . Even in the North, the conditions of public education did not approximate those existing today. The curriculum was usually rudimentary; ungraded schools were common in rural areas; the school term was but three months a year in many states; and compulsory school attendance was virtually unknown. As a consequence, it is not surprising that there should be so little in the history of the Fourteenth Amendment relating to its intended effect on public education. . . .

Today, education is perhaps the most important function of state and local governments. Compulsory school attendance laws and the great expenditures for education both demonstrate our recognition of the importance of education to our democratic society. . . .

We come then to the question presented: Does segregation of children in public schools solely on the basis of race, even though the physical facilities and other "tangible" factors may be equal, deprive the children of the minority group of equal educational opportunities? We believe that it does. . . .

In *McLaurin* v. *Oklahoma State Regents, supra,* the Court, in requiring that a Negro admitted to a white graduate school be treated like all other students, again resorted to intangible considerations: ". . . his ability to study, to engage in discussions and exchange views with other students, and, in general, to learn his profession." Such considerations apply with added force to children in grade and high schools. To separate them from others of similar age and qualifications solely because of their race generates a feeling of inferiority as to their status in the community that may affect their hearts and minds in a way unlikely ever to be undone. . . . Whatever may have been the extent of psychological knowledge at the time of *Plessy* v. *Ferguson,* this finding is amply supported by modern authority. Any language in *Plessy* v. *Ferguson* contrary to this finding is rejected.

We conclude that in the field of public education the doctrine of "separate but equal" has no place. Separate educational facilities are inherently unequal. Therefore, we hold that the plaintiffs and others similarly situated for whom the actions have been brought are, by reason of the segregation complained of, deprived of the equal protection of the laws guaranteed by the Fourteenth Amendment. . . .

Because these are class actions, because of the wide applicability of this decision, and because of the great variety of local conditions, the formulation of decrees in these cases presents problems of considerable complexity. . . . In order that we may have the full assistance of the parties in formulating decrees, the cases will be restored to the docket, and the parties are requested to present further argument. . . . The Attorney General of the United States is again invited to participate. The Attorneys General of the states requiring or permitting segregation in public education will also be permitted to appear as *amici curiae* upon request to do so by September 15, 1954, and submission of briefs by October 1, 1954.

It is so ordered.

Notes

1. *Brown II.* In the second opinion in the *Brown* case, 349 US 294 (1955), the Supreme Court sent the segregation cases back to the courts in which they had originated. In doing so the Court explained:

Full implementation of these constitutional principles may require solution of varied local school problems. School authorities have the primary responsibility for elucidating, assessing, and solving these problems; courts will have to consider whether the action of school authorities constitutes good faith implementation of the governing constitutional principles. Because of their proximity to local conditions and the possible need for further hearings, the courts which originally heard these cases can best perform this judicial appraisal. Accordingly, we believe it appropriate to remand the cases to those courts.

In fashioning and effectuating the decrees, the courts will be guided by equitable principles. Traditionally, equity has been characterized by a practical flexibility in shaping its remedies and by a facility for adjusting and reconciling public and private needs. . . .

While giving weight to these public and private considerations, the courts will require that the defendants make a prompt and reasonable start toward full compliance with our May 17, 1954, ruling. Once such a start has been made, the courts may find that additional time is necessary to carry out the ruling in an effective manner. The burden rests upon the defendants to establish that such time is necessary in the public interest and is consistent with good faith compliance at the earliest practicable date. To that end, the courts may consider problems related to administration, arising from the physical condition of the school plant, the school transportation system, personnel, revision of school districts and attendance areas into compact units to achieve a system of determining admission to the public schools on a nonracial basis, and revision of local laws and regulations which may be necessary in solving the foregoing problems. They will also consider the adequacy of any plans the defendants may propose to meet these problems and to effectuate a transition to a racially nondiscriminatory school system. During this period of transition, the courts will retain jurisdiction of these cases.

2. *District of Columbia.* In *Bolling* v. *Sharpe,* 347 US 497 (1954), Chief Justice Warren wrote: "The Fifth Amendment, which is applicable to the District of Columbia, does not contain an equal protection clause as does the Fourteenth Amendment which applies to the states. . . . We hold that racial segregation in the

public schools of the District of Columbia is a denial of the due process of law guaranteed by the Fifth Amendment to the Constitution."

3. *Higher education.*   The rationale of a "separate but equal" doctrine was first undermined in cases dealing with higher education. *Missouri ex rel. Gaines* v. *Canada,* 305 US 337 (1938), held that a state must provide equal protection within its own borders, and that it could not refuse to admit a black to the law school of the state university solely because of his race even though the state offered to pay tuition for the black to attend a law school in a neighboring state.

Attempts on the part of southern states to preserve segregation by providing equal physical facilities for blacks proved futile. A new law school for blacks was established in Texas with high quality facilities. The Court found that the new black law school was not equal to the University of Texas Law School in qualities incapable of objective measurement, including reputation of the faculty, position and influence of alumni, and traditions. *Sweatt* v. *Painter,* 339 US 629 (1950).

4. *Early pupil assignment laws.*   Following the *Brown* case, several states passed statutes giving local boards of education broad power in the assignment of pupils to schools. An Alabama statute authorizing local boards to consider a variety of factors, including home environment and psychological relationships, in assigning pupils to schools was held not to be void on its face in *Shuttlesworth* v. *Birmingham Board of Education,* 358 US 101 (1958).

Goss v. *Board of Education of Knoxville,* 373 US 683 (1963), held void a provision in a school integration plan that permitted a student, upon request, to transfer from the school to which he was assigned by virtue of rezoning, and in which he would be in the racial minority, back to his former school where his race would be in the majority.

5. *Prince Edward County.*   This Virginia county discontinued its public schools in 1959. In 1960 both Virginia and Prince Edward County adopted tuition grant programs for children attending private schools. In *Griffin* v. *Prince Edward County,* 377 US 218 (1964), the Supreme Court held:

> A State, of course, has a wide discretion in deciding whether laws shall operate statewide or shall operate only in certain counties, the legislature 'having in mind the needs and desires of each.' *Salsburg* v. *Maryland, supra,* 346 US, at 552. A State may wish to suggest, as Maryland did in Salsburg, that there are reasons why one county ought not to be treated like another. 346 US, at 553–554. But the record in the present case could not be clearer that Prince Edward's public schools were closed and private schools operated in their place with state and county assistance, for one reason, and one reason only: to ensure, through measures taken by the county and the State, that white and colored children in Prince Edward County would not, under any circumstances, go to the same school. Whatever nonracial grounds might support a State's allowing a county to abandon public schools, the object must be a constitutional one, and grounds of race and opposition to desegregation do not qualify as constitutional. . . .
>
> The District Court enjoined the county officials from paying county tuition grants or giving tax exemptions and from processing applications for state tuition grants so long as the county's public schools remained closed. We have no doubt of the power of the court to give this relief to enforce the discontinuance of the county's racially discriminatory practices. . . . For the same reasons the District Court may, if necessary

to prevent further racial discrimination, require the Supervisors to exercise the power that is theirs to levy taxes to raise funds adequate to reopen, operate, and maintain without racial discrimination a public school system in Prince Edward County like that operated in other counties in Virginia. . . .

6. *Freedom of choice plans.* *Green* v. *County School Board,* 391 US 430 (1968), considered the constitutionality of a plan under which a pupil was permitted to choose the public school which he would attend. The Court placed emphasis upon the duty of the local school board to adopt a plan involving the affirmative steps necessary to eradicate the segregated pattern long imposed by state law and "to convert to a unitary system in which racial discrimination would be eliminated root and branch." This, the Court found, the school board in New Kent County, Virginia, had failed to do. However, the Court added:

> We do not hold that "freedom of choice" can have no place in such a plan. We do not hold that a "freedom of choice" plan might of itself be unconstitutional, although that argument has been urged upon us. Rather, all we decide today is that in desegregating a dual system a plan utilizing "freedom of choice" is not an end in itself. . . . [I]f there are reasonably available other ways, such for illustration as zoning, promising speedier and more effective conversion to a unitary, nonracial school system, "freedom of choice" must be held unacceptable.

7. *Faculty and staff.* *United States* v. *Montgomery County Board of Education,* 395 US 225 (1969), sustained a district judge's order that the school board must move toward a goal whereby "in each school the ratio of white to Negro faculty members is substantially the same as it is throughout the system."

8. *Timing.* *Alexander* v. *Holmes County Board of Education* 396 US 19 (1969), held, *per curiam,* that in considering a case from Mississippi "the Court of Appeals should have denied all motions for additional time because continued operation of segregated schools under a standard of allowing 'all deliberate speed' for desegregation is no longer constitutionally possible. Under explicit holdings of this Court the obligation of every school district is to terminate dual school systems at once and to operate hereafter only unitary schools."

9. *Busing.* The concept of a "segregated" school was never clearly defined, and as integration was carried out in the South the federal courts gradually changed their definitions. They moved from a doctrine of state neutrality ("the law is color blind") to a doctrine of affirmative state action involving busing and other devices to achieve racial balance.

In the Civil Rights Act of 1964, Congress defined desegregation as "the assignment of students to public schools and within such schools without regard to their race, color, religion, or national origin, but 'desegregation' shall not mean the assignment of students to public schools in order to overcome racial imbalance." Moreover, the Act specifically provided that "nothing herein shall empower any official or court of the United States to issue an order seeking to achieve a racial balance in any school by requiring the transportation of pupils or students from one school to another or one school district to another in order to achieve such racial balance. . . ." Despite this act, the federal district courts ordered the use of busing, pairing, and other devices to achieve rigid racial quotas in southern schools. In *Swann* v. *Charlotte-Mecklenburg Board of Education,* 402 US 1 (1971), the Supreme Court sustained this practice, holding that the courts were exercising inherent powers not dependent upon any act of Congress.

In *Milliken* v. *Bradley,*   US   (1974), however, the Supreme Court reversed lower court orders under which busing would have been required to achieve racial balance in Detroit and fifty-three outlying school districts. The lower federal courts had held that a "Detroit only" integration plan "would make the Detroit system more identifiably black ... thereby increasing flights of whites from the City and the system." For the Supreme Court, Chief Justice Burger wrote:

> Viewing the record as a whole it seems clear that the District Court and the Court of Appeals shifted the primary focus from a Detroit remedy to the metropolitan area only because of their conclusion that total desegration of Detroit would not produce the racial balance which they perceived as desirable. Both courts proceeded on an assumption that Detroit schools could not be truly desegregated—in their view of what constituted desegregation—unless the racial composition of the student body of each school substantially reflected the racial composition of the population of the metropolitan area as a whole. The metropolitan area was then defined as Detroit plus 53 of the outlying school districts. ...
>
> The controlling principle consistently expounded in our holdings is that the scope of the remedy is determined by the nature and extent of the constitutional violation. *Swann, supra,* at 16. Before the boundaries of separate and autonomous school districts may be set aside by consolidating the separate units for remedial purposes or by imposing a cross-district remedy, it must first be shown that there has been a constitutional violation within one district that produces a significant segregative effect in another district. Specifically it must be shown that racially discriminatory acts of the state and local school districts or of a single school district have been a substantial cause of inter-district segregation. Thus an inter-district remedy might be in order where the racially discriminatory acts of one or more school districts caused racial segregation in an adjacent district, or where district lines have been deliberately drawn on the basis of race. In such circumstances an inter-district remedy would be appropriate to eliminate the inter-district segregation directly caused by the constitutional violation. Conversely, without an inter-district violation and inter-district effect, there is no constitutional wrong calling for an inter-district remedy. ...
>
> The constitutional right of the Negro respondents residing in Detroit is to attend a unitary school system in that district. Unless petitioners drew the district lines in a discriminatory fashion, or arranged for the white students residing in the Detroit district to attend schools in Oakland and Macomb counties, they were under no constitutional duty to make provision for Negro students to do so. ...

Justice Marshall, with whom Justices Douglas, Brennan, and White joined, wrote in dissent:

> Today's holding, I fear, is more a reflection of a perceived public mood that we have gone far enough in enforcing the Constitution's guarantee of equal justice than it is the product of neutral principles of law. In the short run, it may seem to be the easiest course to allow our great metropolitan areas to be divided up each into two cities—one white, the other black—but it is a course, I predict, our people will ultimately regret. I dissent.

10. *De facto* v. *de jure segregation.*   Once viewed as a southern problem only, racial segregation became an American national problem with the rapid migration of blacks to the cities of the North and West after World War II. The 1968 *Report*

of the National Advisory Commission on Civil Disorders included the following statement:

> In 1950, at least one of every ten Americans was Negro; in 1966, one of nine. If this trend continues, one of every eight Americans will be Negro by 1972. . . .
>
> Almost all Negro population growth is occurring within metropolitan areas, primarily within central cities. . . .
>
> The 12 largest central cities—New York, Chicago, Los Angeles, Philadelphia, Detroit, Baltimore, Houston, Cleveland, Washington, D.C., St. Louis, Milwaukee, and San Francisco—now contain over two-thirds of the Negro population outside the South, and almost one-third of the total in the United States. . . .
>
> The bleak record of public education for ghetto children is growing worse. In the critical skills—verbal and reading ability—Negro students fall further behind whites with each year of school completed. For example, in the metropolitan Northeast Negro students on the average begin the first grade with somewhat lower scores than whites on standard achievement tests, are about 1.6 grades behind by the sixth grade and have fallen 3.3 grades behind white students by the twelfth grade. The failure of the public schools to equip these students with basic verbal skills is reflected in their performance on the Selective Service Mental Test. During the period June 1964—December 1965, 67 percent of Negro candidates failed the examination. The failure rate for whites was 19 percent. . . .
>
> The vast majority of inner-city schools are rigidly segregated. In 75 major central cities surveyed by the U.S. Commission on Civil Rights in its study, "Racial Isolation in the Public Schools," 75 percent of all Negro students in elementary grades attended schools with enrollments that were 90 percent or more Negro. Almost 90 percent of all Negro students attended schools which had a majority of Negro students. In the same cities, 83 percent of all white students in those grades attended schools with 90 to 100 percent white enrollments. . . .
>
> Urban schools are becoming more segregated. . . . By 1975, it is estimated that, if current policies and trends persist, 80 percent of all Negro pupils in the twenty largest cities, comprising nearly one-half of the nation's Negro population, will be attending 90 to 100 percent Negro schools. . . .

In *Keyes* v. *Denver,* 413 US 921 (1973), the Supreme Court gave its first opinion in a school desegregation case involving a city outside the South—Denver, Colorado. That city's school system had never been operated under statutory provisions for racial segregation. But the charge in the case was that the School Board alone, "by use of various techniques such as the manipulation of student attendance zones, school site selection and neighborhood school policy, created or maintained racially . . . segregated schools throughout the school district. . . ." The district court had found evidence of intentional segregation in only one area of the Denver school district and had ordered busing and other positive action to achieve integration only in that area. The Supreme Court, however, ruled that proof of intentional segregation in one area of a school district was prima facie evidence of a dual school system for the district as a whole. The burden of proof to disprove intentional segregation then shifted to the School Board, and failure in this proof would place upon it the same affirmative duty of achieving racial integration that school districts in the South had borne.

In a concurring opinion Justice Powell called for an abandonment of the *de jure/de facto* distinction and the application of the same constitutional principles throughout the nation. "The focus of the school desegregation problem has now shifted from the South to the country as a whole. Unwilling and footdragging as the process was in most places, substantial progress toward achieving integration has been made in southern States.[1] No comparable progress has been made in many nonsouthern cities with large minority populations primarily because of the *de facto/de jure* distinction nurtured by the courts and accepted complacently by many of the same voices which denounced the evils of segregated schools in the South. But if our national concern is for those who attend such schools rather than for perpetuating a legalism rooted in history rather than present reality, we must recognize that the evil of operating separate schools is not less in Denver than in Atlanta."

Voting

Black suffrage was introduced in the South by the Reconstruction Acts of 1867. During the Reconstruction period, and increasingly so after the withdrawal of federal troops, southern whites used violence and intimidation to discourage blacks from voting. Tiring of these illegal means, southern leaders sought to circumvent the Fourteenth and Fifteenth Amendments by literacy tests, grandfather clauses, and poll taxes. The Supreme Court found no objection to a literacy clause which, theoretically, applied to whites as well as to blacks. *Williams* v. *Mississippi,* 170 US 213 (1898). The grandfather clauses set up lineal descent from a person qualified to vote in 1867 as an alternative to property ownership and literacy tests as qualifications for voting. Most of the grandfather clauses were temporary measures, never tested in the courts. In *Guinn* v. *United States,* 238 US 348 (1915), an Oklahoma grandfather clause reached the Supreme Court and was held void as a violation of the Fifteenth Amendment.

The most effective device used by the southern states to disfranchise the black during the first half of the Twentieth century was the Democratic white primary. Only white persons were permitted to vote in Democratic primaries, and under the one-party system, nomination in the primary was tantamount to election. *Nixon* v. *Herndon,* 272 US 536 (1927), held void a Texas statute providing that "in no event shall a Negro be eligible to participate in a Democratic primary election." The Democratic party of Texas responded by adopting a party rule excluding blacks. In *Grovey* v. *Townsend,* 295 US 45 (1935), the Supreme Court denied relief to a black excluded by the party rule, finding no "State action" involved. However, this position was short lived. *Smith* v. *Allwright,* 321 US 649 (1944), held that "When primaries become a part of the machinery for choosing officials, state and national, as they have here, the same tests to determine the character of discrimination . . . should be applied to the primary as are applied to the general election." Sporadic attempts after 1944 to exclude blacks from primaries were held void under the doctrine that the purpose and effect was to violate the Constitution. See *Terry* v. *Adams,* 345 US 461 (1953).

---

1. "According to the 1971 HEW estimate, 43.9 percent of Negro pupils attended majority white schools in the South as opposed to only 27.8 percent who attended such schools in the North and West. Fifty-seven percent of all Negro pupils in the North and West attend schools with over 80 percent minority population as opposed to 32.6 percent who do so in the South. 118 Cong. Rec. S145." [Footnote by Justice Powell.]

It will be observed that many of these cases were decided in terms of "State action." There is a close relation between cases decided in terms of State action, equal protection of law, and the power of Congress to enforce the Fourteenth Amendment.

Anderson v. *Martin,* 375 US 399 (1964), held a Louisiana statue requiring that the race of candidates for office be placed on all election ballots to be void as a violation of the equal protection clause. *Louisiana* v. *United States,* 380 US 145 (1965), held that the provisions of the Louisiana Constitution which required voters to satisfy registrars of their ability to understand and give a reasonable interpretation of the Constitution violated the Fourteenth and Fifteenth Amendments as well as acts of Congress designed to enforce these amendments.

Cohabitation

Loving v. Virginia

388 US 1, 87 S Ct 1817, 18 L Ed2d 1010 (1967)

A state cannot prevent marriage between black and white persons.

MR. CHIEF JUSTICE WARREN delivered the opinion of the Court.

This case presents a constitutional question never addressed by this Court: whether a statutory scheme adopted by the State of Virginia to prevent marriages between persons solely on the basis of racial classifications violates the Equal Protection and Due Process Clauses of the Fourteenth Amendment. For reasons which seem to us to reflect the central meaning of those constitutional commands, we conclude that these statutes cannot stand consistently with the Fourteenth Amendment.

In June 1958, two residents of Virginia, Mildred Jeter, a Negro woman, and Richard Loving, a white man, were married in the District of Columbia pursuant to its laws. Shortly after their marriage, the Lovings returned to Virginia and established their marital abode in Caroline County. At the October Term, 1958, of the Circuit Court of Caroline County, a grand jury issued an indictment charging the Lovings with violating Virginia's ban on interracial marriages. On January 6, 1959, the Lovings pleaded guilty to the charge and were sentenced to one year in jail; however, the trial judge suspended the sentence for a period of 25 years on the condition that the Lovings leave the State and not return to Virginia together for 25 years. . . .

Virginia is now one of 16 States which prohibit and punish marriages on the basis of racial classifications. Penalties for miscegenation arose as an incident to slavery and have been common in Virginia since the colonial period. . . .

In upholding the constitutionality of these provisions in the decision below, the Supreme Court of Appeals of Virginia referred to its 1955 decision in *Naim* v. *Naim* . . . as stating the reasons supporting the validity of these laws. In *Naim,* the state court concluded that the State's legitimate purposes were "to preserve the racial integrity of its citizens" and to prevent "the corruption of blood," "a mongrel breed of citizens," and "the obliteration of racial pride," obviously an endorsement of the doctrine of White Supremacy. . . . The court also reasoned that marriage has traditionally been subject to state regulation without federal intervention, and, consequently, the regulation of marriage should be left to exclusive state control by the Tenth Amendment. . . .

The State argues that statements in the Thirty-ninth Congress about the time of the passage of the Fourteenth Amendment indicate that the Framers did not intend the Amendment to make unconstitutional state miscegenation laws. Many of the statements alluded to by the State concern the debates over the Freedmen's Bureau Bill, which President Johnson vetoed, and the Civil Rights Act of 1866, 14 Stat 27, enacted over his veto. While these statements have some relevance to the intention of Congress in submitting the Fourteenth Amendment, it must be understood that they pertained to the passage of specific statutes and not to the broader, organic purpose of a constitutional amendment. As for the various statements directly concerning the Fourteenth Amendment, we have said in connection with a related problem, that although these historical sources "cast some light" they are . . . "inconclusive." . . .

There can be no question but that Virginia's miscegenation statutes rest solely upon distinctions drawn according to race. . . .

. . . We have consistently denied the constitutionality of measures which restrict the rights of citizens on account of race. There can be no doubt that restricting the freedom to marry solely because of racial classifications violates the central meaning of the Equal Protection Clause. . . .

These convictions must be reversed.

It is so ordered.

MR. JUSTICE STEWART, concurring.

I have previously expressed the belief that "it is simply not possible for a state law to be valid under our Constitution which makes the criminality of an act depend upon the race of the actor." *McLaughlin* v. *Florida,* 379 US 184, 198 (concurring opinion). Because I adhere to that belief, I concur in the judgment of the Court.

Juries

As early as 1880 the Supreme Court reversed the conviction of a black by an all-white jury in a state limiting jury service to white men. *Strauder* v. *West Virginia,* 100 US 303. Uncontradicted testimony that no black had even been known to serve on the jury in the county concerned was taken as evidence of the exclusion of blacks in *Norris* v. *Alabama,* 294 US 587 (1935). However, the Court has rejected the notion that the Constitution requires proportional representation of races on juries. The leading cases are summarized in *Alexander* v. *Louisiana,* 405 US 625 (1972). *Peters* v. *Kiff,* 407 US 493 (1972), held that a white man indicted and convicted by juries from which blacks were excluded was denied equal protection and due process.

Miscellaneous

Statutes or ordinances providing for racial segregation have been held to be invalid in cases dealing with public bathing beaches, *Mayor of Baltimore* v. *Dawson,* 350

US 877 (1955); municipal golf courses, *Holmes* v. *City of Atlanta,* 350 US 879 (1955); parks, *New Orleans City Parks Improvement Ass'n* v. *Detiege,* 358 US 5 (1958); athletic contests, *State Athletic Commission* v. *Dorsey,* 359 US 533 (1959); court rooms, *Johnson* v. *Virginia,* 373 US 61 (1963); municipal auditoriums, *Schiro* v. *Bynum,* 375 US 395 (1964); voting records, *Virginia State Board of Elections* v. *Hamm,* 379 US 19 (1964); and prison facilities, except under special circumstances, *Lee* v. *Washington,* 390 US 333 (1968). The leading cases dealing with discrimination against blacks in transportation have been decided under the commerce clause. See *Morgan* v. *Virginia,* 328 US 373 (1946), and *Boynton* v. *Virginia,* 364 US 454 (1960). The cases on open housing are given in chapter 3, page 119. *Griggs* v. *Duke Power Co.,* 401 US 424 (1971), held that the company violated the Civil Rights Act of 1964 by requiring high school graduation and using general aptitude tests in its employment practice.

B. ALIENAGE

Takahashi v. Fish And Game Commission

334 US 410, 68 S Ct 1138, 92 L Ed 1478 (1948)

A California statue barring issuance of commercial fishing licenses to persons "ineligible to citizenship," which classification included resident alien Japanese and precluded such a one from earning his living as a commercial fishermen in the ocean waters off the coast of the state, *held* invalid.

MR. JUSTICE BLACK delivered the opinion of the Court.

The respondent, Torao Takahashi, born in Japan, came to this country and became a resident of California in 1907. Federal laws, based on distinctions of "color and race," *Toyota* v. *United States,* 268 US 402, 411–412, have permitted Japanese and certain other non-white racial groups to enter and reside in the country, but have made them ineligible for United States citizenship. The question presented is whether California can, consistently with the Federal Constitution and laws passed pursuant to it, use this federally created racial ineligibility for citizenship as a basis for barring Takahashi from earning his living as a commercial fisherman in the ocean waters off the coast of California. . . .

Takahashi brought this action for *mandamus* in the Superior Court of Los Angeles County, California, to compel the Commission to issue a license to him. That court granted the petition for *mandamus.* . . .

We may well begin our consideration of the principles to be applied in this case by a summary of this Court's holding in *Truax* v. *Raich,* 239 US 33, not deemed controlling by the majority of the California Supreme Court, but regarded by the dissenters as requiring the invalidation of the California law. That case involved an attack upon an Arizona law which required all Arizona employers of more than five workers to hire not less than eighty (80) per cent qualified electors or native-born citizens of the United States. Raich, an alien who worked as a cook in a restaurant which had more than five employees, was about to lose his job solely because of the state law's coercive effect on the restaurant owner. This Court, in upholding Raich's contention that the Arizona law was invalid, declared that Raich, having been lawfully admitted into the country under federal law, had a federal privilege to enter and abide in "any State in the Union" and thereafter under the Fourteenth Amendment to enjoy the equal protection of the laws of the state in which he abided: that this privilege to enter in and abide in any state carried with it the "right to work for a living in the common occupations of the community," a denial of which right would make of the Amendment "a barren form of words." ...

The *Truax* opinion pointed out that the Arizona law, aimed as it was against employment of aliens in *all* vocations, failed to show a "special public interest with respect to any particular business ... that could possibly be deemed to support the enactment." The Court noted that it had previously upheld various state laws which restricted the privilege of planting oysters in the tidewater rivers of a state to citizens of that state, and which denied to aliens within a state the privilege of possessing a rifle and of shooting game within that state; it also referred to decisions recognizing a state's broad powers, in the absence of overriding treaties, to restrict the devolution of real property to non-aliens.

California now urges, and the State Supreme Court held, that the California fishing provision here challenged falls within the rationale of the "special public interest" cases distinguished in the *Truax* opinion, and thus that the state's ban upon commercial fishing by aliens ineligible to citizenship is valid. ...

We are unable to find that the "special public interest" on which California relies provides support for this state ban on Takahashi's commercial fishing. ...

To whatever extent the fish in the three-mile belt off California may be "capable of ownership" by California, we think that "ownership" is inadequate to justify California in excluding any or all aliens who are lawful residents of the State from making a living by fishing in the ocean off its shores while permitting all others to do so. ...

The judgment is reversed and remanded for proceedings not inconsistent with this opinion

Reversed.

MR. JUSTICE MURPHY, with whom MR. JUSTICE RUTLEDGE agrees, concurring. [Omitted.]

MR. JUSTICE REED, dissenting.

The reasons which lead me to conclude that the judgment of the Supreme Court of California should be affirmed may be briefly stated. As fishing rights have been treated traditionally as a natural resource, in the absence of federal regulation, California as a sovereign state has power to regulate the taking and handling of fish in the waters bordering its shores. It is, I think, one of the natural resources of the state that may be preserved from exploitation by aliens. The ground for this power in the absence of any exercise of federal authority is California's authority over its fisheries. ...

MR. JUSTICE JACKSON joins in this dissent.

Notes

1. *Fujii* v. *California,* 242 P2d 617 (1952), held void California's law prohibiting aliens from owning land.

2. *Graham* v. *Richardson,* 403 US 365 (1971), voided state laws which denied welfare benefits to resident aliens.

3. *Sugarman* v. *Dougall,* 413 US 634 (1973), voided a New York Statute which provided that only United States citizens could hold positions in the competitive class of the state civil service. The Court recognized the power of a state to add citizenship "not only to the qualifications of voters, but also to persons holding state elective or important nonelective executive, legislative, and judicial positions," but declared New York's statute to be too broad.

4. *In Re Griffiths,* 413 US 717 (1973), voided Connecticut's requirement of citizenship to practice law.

C. ILLEGITIMACY

Weber v. Aetna Casualty & Surety Co.

406 US 164, 92 S Ct 1400, 31 L Ed2d 768 (1972)

A state workmen's compensation law that relegates dependent unacknowledged illegitimate children to an inferior classification is void.

MR. JUSTICE POWELL delivered the opinion of the Court.

The question before us, on writ of *certiorari* to the Supreme Court of Louisiana, concerns the right of dependent unacknowledged, illegitimate children to recover under Louisiana workmen's compensation laws benefits for the death of their natural father on an equal footing with his dependent legitimate children. We hold that Louisiana's denial of equal recovery rights to dependent unacknowledged illegitimates violates the Equal Protection Clause of the Fourteenth Amendment. . . .

On June 22, 1967, Henry Clyde Stokes died in Louisiana of injuries received during the course of his employment the previous day. At the time of his death Stokes resided and maintained a household with one Willie Mae Weber, to whom he was not married. Living in the household were four legitimate minor children, born of the marriage between Stokes and Adlay Jones Stokes who was at the time committed to a mental hospital. Also living in the home was one unacknowledged illegitimate child born of the relationship between Stokes and Willie Mae Weber. A second illegitimate child of Stokes and Weber was born posthumously.

On June 29, 1967, Stokes' four legitimate children, through their maternal grandmother as guardian, filed a claim for their father's death under Louisiana's workmen's compensation law. The defendant employer and its insurer, impleaded Willie Mae Weber who appeared and claimed compensation benefits for the two illegitimate children.

Meanwhile, the four legitimate children had brought another suit for their father's death against a third-party tort feasor which was settled for an amount in excess of the maximum benefits allowable under workmen's compensation. The illegitimate children did not share in this settlement. Subsequently, the employer in the initial action requested the extinguishment of all parties' workmen's compensation claims by reason of the tort settlement.

The trial judge awarded the four legitimate children the maximum allowable amount of compensation and declared their entitlement had been satisfied from the tort suit settlement. Consequently, the four legitimate children dismissed their workmen's compensation claim. Judgment was also awarded to Stokes' two illegitimate offspring to the extent that maximum compensation benefits were not exhausted by the four legitimate children. Since such benefits had been entirely exhausted by the amount of the tort settlement, in which only the four dependent legitimate offspring participated, the two dependent illegitimate children received nothing.

I

For purposes of recovery under workmen's compensation, Louisiana law defines children to include "only legitimate children, stepchildren, posthumous children, and illegitimate children acknowledged under the provisions of the Civil Code. . . ." Thus legitimate children and acknowledged illegitimates may recover on an equal basis. Unacknowledged illegitimate children, however, are relegated to the lesser status of "other dependents" . . . and may recover *only* if there are not enough surviving dependents in the preceding classifications to exhaust the maximum allowable benefits. Both the Louisiana Court of Appeal and a divided Louisiana Supreme Court sustained these statutes over appellants' constitutional objections, holding that our decision in *Levy* [v. *Louisiana*, 391 US 68] was not controlling.

We disagree. In *Levy*, the Court held invalid as denying equal protection of law, a Louisiana statue which barred an illegitimate child from recovering for the wrongful death of its mother when such recoveries by legitimate children were authorized. The Court there decided that the fact of a child's birth out of wedlock bore no reasonable relation to the purpose of wrongful death statutes which compensate children for the death of a mother. . . .

Respondent contends that our recent ruling in *Labine* v. *Vincent*, 401 US 532 (1971), controls this case. In *Labine*, the Court upheld, against constitutional objections, Louisiana intestacy laws which had barred an acknowledged illegitimate child from sharing equally with legitimate children in her father's estate. The decision reflected, in major part, the traditional deference to a State's prerogative to regulate the disposition at death of property within its borders. . . . The Court has long afforded broad scope to state discretion in this area. Yet the substantial state interest in providing for "the stability of . . . land titles and the prompt and definitive determination of the valid ownership of property left by decedents," . . . is absent in the case at hand.

Both the statute in *Levy* and the statute in the present case involve state-created compensation schemes, designed to provide close relatives and dependents of a deceased a means of recovery for his often abrupt and accidental death. Both wrongful death statutes and workmen's compensation codes represent outgrowths and modifications of our basic tort law. The former alleviated the harsh common-law rule under which "no person could inherit the personal right of another for tortious injuries to his body"; the latter removed difficult obstacles to recovery in work-related injuries by offering a more certain, though generally less remunerative compensation. In the instant case, the recovery sought under the workmen's compensation statute was in lieu of an action under the identical death statute which was at issue in *Levy.* Given the similarities in the origins and purposes of these two statutes, and the similarity of Louisiana's pattern of discrimination in recovery rights, it would require a disregard of precedent and the principles of *stare decisis* to hold that *Levy* did not control the facts of the case before us. It makes no difference that illegitimates are not so absolutely or broadly barred here as in *Levy;* the discrimination remains apparent.

II

Having determined that *Levy* is the applicable precedent, we briefly reaffirm here the reasoning which produced that result. The tests to determine the validity of state statutes under the Equal Protection Clause have been variously expressed, but this Court requires, at a minimum, that a statutory classification bear some rational relationship to a legitimate state purpose. . . . Though the latitude given state economic and social regulation is necessarily broad, when state statutory classifications approach sensitive and fundamental personal rights, this Court exercises a stricter scrutiny. . . . The essential inquiry in all the foregoing cases is, however, inevitably a dual one: What legitimate state interest does the classification promote? What fundamental personal rights might the classification endanger?

The Louisiana Supreme Court emphasized strongly the State's interest in protecting "legitimate family relationships," . . . and the regulation and protection of the family unit has indeed been a venerable state concern. We do not question the importance of that interest; what we do question is how the challenged statute will promote it. . . . Nor can it be thought here that persons will shun illicit relations because the offspring may not one day reap the benefits of workmen's compensation. . . .

The status of illegitimacy has expressed through the ages society's condemnation of irresponsible liaisons beyond the bonds of marriage. But visiting this condemnation on the head of an infant is illogical and unjust. Moreover, imposing disabilities on the illegitimate child is contrary to the basic concept of our system that legal burdens should bear some relationship to individual responsibility or wrongdoing. Obviously, no child is responsible for his birth and penalizing the illegitimate child is an ineffectual —as well as an unjust—way of deterring the parent. Courts are powerless to prevent the social opprobrium suffered by these hapless children, but the Equal Protection Clause does enable us to strike down discriminatory laws relating to status of birth where—as in this case—the classification is justified by no legitimate state interest, compelling or otherwise.

Reversed and remanded.

Mr. Justice Rehnquist, dissenting. . . .

As noted in *Levy,* in the field of economic and social legislation, the Court has given great latitude to the legislatures in making classification. . . . The test has been whether there is "any rational basis" for the legislative classification. . . . Under this test, so long as the "discrimination is founded upon a reasonable distinction, or difference in state policy," . . . the Court will not attempt to weigh its social value or determine whether the classification might have been more finely drawn. . . . However, this salutary principle has been departed from by the Court in recent years, as pointed out in its opinion here, where the Court has felt that the classification has affected what it conceives to be "fundamental personal rights."

The difficulty with this approach, devoid as it is of any historical or textual support in the language of the Equal Protection Clause, is that it leaves apparently to the Justices of this Court the determination of what are, and what are not, "fundamental personal rights." . . .

Although the majority argues that "the state interest in minimizing problems of proof is not *significantly* disturbed by our decision," . . . it clearly recognizes, as it must, that under its decision additional and sometimes more difficult problems of proof of paternity and dependency may be raised. This is particularly true with respect to petitioner's posthumous child, who was not born until after the death of his father. I believe that a State's desire to lessen these problems under its statutory scheme is a rational basis for difference in treatment of the two classes.

Finally, the majority apparently draws some comfort from the fact that the illegitimate children here could not have been acknowledged, since the decedent remained married to another woman while he raised these children. However, I do not believe that it follows from this fact that the statutory classification is irrational. On the contrary, this element of the statutory scheme points up another possible legislative purpose which I do not believe this Court should so freely dismiss. Louisiana, like many other States, has a wide variety of laws designed to encourage legally recognized and responsible family relationships. I believe this particular statutory provision, forbidding acknowledgment of illegitimate children when the parents were not free to marry (in this case because the father was already married to another women), might be considered part of that statutory pattern designed to discourage formation of illicit family relationships. Whether this is a wise state policy, or whether this particular statute will be particularly effective in advancing it, are not matters for this Court's determination. . . .

D.   SEX (?)

Frontiero v. Richardson

411 US 213, 93 S Ct 1764, 36 L Ed2d 583 (1973)

A classification based on sex is void unless it advances a legitimate purpose.

MR. JUSTICE BRENNAN announced the judgment of the Court and an opinion in which MR. JUSTICE DOUGLAS, MR. JUSTICE WHITE, and MR. JUSTICE MARSHALL join.

The question before us concerns the right of a female member of the uniformed services to claim her spouse as a "dependent" for the purposes of obtaining increased quarters allowances and medical and dental benefits under 37 USC §§ 401, 403, and 10 USC §§ 1072, 1076, on an equal footing with male members. Under these statutes, a serviceman may claim his wife as a "dependent" without regard to whether she is in fact dependent upon him for any part of her support. . . . A servicewoman, on the other hand, may not claim her husband as a "dependent" under these programs unless he is in fact dependent upon her for over one-half of his support. . . .

Appellant Sharron Frontiero, a lieutenant in the United States Air Force, sought increased quarters allowances, and housing and medical benefits for her husband, appellant Joseph Frontiero, on the ground that he was her "dependent." Although such benefits would automatically have been granted with respect to the wife of a male member of the uniformed services, appellant's application was denied because she failed to demonstrate that her husband was dependent on her for more than one-half of his support. Appellants then commenced this suit, contending that, by making this distinction, the statutes unreasonably discriminate on the basis of sex in violation of the Due Process Clause of the Fifth Amendment. In essence, appellants asserted that the discriminatory impact of the statutes is two-fold: first, as a procedural matter, a female member is required to demonstrate her spouse's dependency, while no such burden is imposed upon male members; and second, as a substantive matter, a male member who does not provide more than one-half of his wife's support receives benefits, while a similarly situated female member is denied such benefits. Appellants therefore sought a permanent injunction against the continued enforcement of these statutes and an order directing the appellees to provide Lieutenant Frontiero with the same housing and medical benefits that a similarly situated male member would receive.

At the outset, appellants contend that classifications based upon sex, like classifications based upon race, alienage, and national origin, are inherently suspect and must therefore be subjected to close judicial scrutiny. We agree and, indeed, find at least implicit support for such an approach in our unanimous decision only last Term in *Reed* v. *Reed,* 404 US 71 (1971).

In *Reed,* the Court considered the constitutionality of an Idaho statute providing that, when two individuals are otherwise equally entitled to appointment as administrator of an estate, the male applicant must be preferred to the female. Appellant, the mother of the deceased, and appellee, the father, filed competing petitions for appointment as administrator of their son's estate. Since the parties, as parents of the deceased, were members of the same entitlement class, the statutory perference was invoked and the father's petition was therefore granted. Appellant claimed that this statute, by giving a mandatory preference to males over females without regard to their individual qualifications, violated the Equal Protection Clause of the Fourteenth Amendment.

The Court noted that the Idaho statute "provides that different treatment be accorded to the applicants on the basis of their sex; it thus establishes a classification subject to scrutiny under the Equal Protection Clause." 404 US, at 75. Under "traditional" equal protection analysis, a legislative classification must be sustained unless it is "patently arbitrary" and bears no rational relationship to a legitimate governmental interest. . . .

There can be no doubt that our Nation has had a long and unfortunate history of sex discrimination. Traditionally, such discrimination was rationalized by an attitude of "romantic paternalism" which, in practical effect, put women not on a pedestal, but in a cage. . . .

As a result . . . our statute books gradually became laden with gross, sterotypical distinctions between the sexes and, indeed, throughout much of the 19th century the position of women in our society was, in many respects, comparable to that of blacks under the pre-Civil War slave codes. Neither slaves nor women could hold office, serve on juries, or bring suit in their own names, and married women traditionally were denied the legal capacity to hold or convey property or to serve as legal guardians of their own children. See generally, L. Kantowitz, Women and the Law: The Unfinished Revolution 5–6 (1969); G. Mydral, An American Dilemma 1073 (2d ed. 1962). And although blacks were guaranteed the right to vote in 1870, women were denied even that right—which is itself "preservative of other basic civil and political rights"—until adoption of the Nineteenth Amendment half a century later.

It is true, of course, that the position of women in America has improved markedly in recent decades. Nevertheless, it can hardly be doubted that, in part because of the high visibility of the sex characteristic, women still face pervasive, although at times more subtle, discrimination in our educational institutions, on the job market and, perhaps most conspicuously, in the political arena. See generally, K. Amundsen, The Silenced Majority: Women and American Democracy (1971); The President's Task Force on Women's Rights and Responsibilities, A Matter of Simple Justice (1970).

Moreover, since sex, like race and national origin, is an immutable characteristic determined solely by the accident of birth, the imposition of special disabilities upon the members of a particular sex because of their sex would seem to violate "the basic concept of our system that legal burdens should bear some relationship to individual responsibility. . . ." And what differentiates sex from such nonsuspect statutes as intelligence or physical disability, and aligns it with the recognized suspect criteria, is that the sex characteristic frequently bears no relation to ability to perform or contribute to society. As a result, statutory distinctions between the sexes often have the effect of invidiously relegating the entire class of females to inferior legal status without regard to the actual capabilities of its individual members.

We might also note that, over the past decade, Congress has itself manifested an increasing sensitivity to sex-based classifications. In Tit. VII of the Civil Rights Act of 1964, for example, Congress expressly declared that no employer, labor union, or other organization subject to the provisions of the Act shall discriminate against any individual on the basis of "race, color, religion, *sex,* or national origin." Similarly, the Equal Pay Act of 1963 provides that no employer covered by the Act "shall discriminate . . . between employees on the basis of *sex.*" And § 1 of the Equal Rights Amendment, passed by Congress on March 22, 1972, and submitted to the legislatures of the States for ratification, declares that "[e]quality of rights under the law shall not be denied or abridged by the United States or by any State on account of sex." Thus, Congress has itself concluded that classifications based upon sex are inherently invidious, and this conclusion of a coequal branch of Government is not without significance to the question presently under consideration. . . .

. . . We therefore conclude that, by according differential treatment to male and female members of the uniformed services for the sole purpose of achieving administrative convenience, the challenged statutes violate the Due Process Clause of the Fifth

Amendment insofar as they require a female member to prove the dependency of her husband.

Reversed.

MR. JUSTICE STEWART concurs in the judgment, agreeing that the statutes before us work an invidious discrimination in violation of the Constitution. . . .

MR. JUSTICE REHNQUIST dissents for the reasons stated by Judge Rives in his opinion for the District Court, *Frontiero* v. *Laird,* 341 F. Supp. 201 (1972).

MR. JUSTICE POWELL, with whom THE CHIEF JUSTICE and MR. JUSTICE BLACK-MUN join, concurring in the judgment.

I agree that the challenged statutes consitute an unconstitutional discrimination against service women in violation of the Due Process Clause of the Fifth Amendment, but I cannot join the opinion of MR. JUSTICE BRENNAN, which would hold that all classifications based upon sex, "like classifications based upon race, alienage, and national origin," are "inherently suspect and must therefore be subjected to close judicial scrutiny." . . . It is unnecessary for the Court in this case to characterize sex as a suspect classification, with all of the far-reaching implications of such a holding. . . .

. . . The Equal Rights Amendment, which if adopted will resolve the substance of this precise question, has been approved by the Congress and submitted for ratification by the States. If this Amendment is duly adopted, it will represent the will of the people accomplished in the manner prescribed by the Constitution. By acting prematurely and unnecessarily, as I view it, the Court has assumed a decisional responsibility at the very time when state legislatures, functioning within the traditional democratic process, are debating the proposed Amendment. It seems to me that this reaching out to pre-empt by judicial action a major political decision which is currently in process of resolution does not reflect appropriate respect for duly prescribed legislative processes.

Notes

1. *Corning Glass Works* v. *Brennan,*   US   (1974), gave broad application to the Equal Pay Act of 1963.

2. *Kahn* v. *Shevin,*   US   (1974), sustained a Florida statute granting a $500 property tax exemption to widows, but not to widowers. For the Court, Justice Douglas wrote:

> There can be no dispute that the financial difficulties confronting the lone woman . . . exceeded those facing the man. Whether from overt discrimination or from the socialization process of a male dominated culture, the job market is inhospitable to the woman seeking any but the lowest paid jobs. There are of course efforts underway to remedy this situation. . . . But firmly entrenched practices are resistant to such pressures. . . . We deal here with a state tax law reasonably designed to further the state policy of cushioning the financial impact of spousal loss upon the sex for whom that loss imposes a disproportionately heavy burden.

Justices White, Brennan, and Marshall dissented.

Section 3.   Classifications Affecting Fundamental Rights

A.   VOTING RIGHTS

Apportionment

Reynolds v. Sims

377 US 533, 84 S Ct 1362, 12 L Ed2d 506 (1964)

Election districts for both houses of a state legislature must be as nearly of equal population as is practicable.

Mr. Justice Warren delivered the opinion of the Court. . . .

Plaintiffs below alleged that the last apportionment of the Alabama Legislature was based on the 1900 federal census, despite the requirement of the State Constitution that the legislature be reapportioned decennially. They asserted that, since the population growth in the State from 1900 to 1960 had been uneven, Jefferson and other counties were now victims of serious discrimination with respect to the allocation of legislative representation. As a result of the failure of the legislature to reapportion itself, plaintiffs asserted, they were denied "equal suffrage in free and equal elections . . . and the equal protection of the laws" in violation of the Alabama Constitution and the Fourteenth Amendment to the Federal Constitution. The complaint asserted that plaintiffs had no other adequate remedy, and that they had exhausted all forms of relief other than that available through the federal courts. . . .

A three-judge District Court was convened. . . .

On July 21, 1962, the District Court held that the inequality of the existing representation in the Alabama Legislature violated the Equal Protection Clause of the Fourteenth Amendment. . . .

The District Court then directed its concern to the providing of an effective remedy. It indicated that it was adopting and ordering into effect for the November 1962 election a provisional and temporary reapportionment plan. . . .

Notices of appeal to this Court from the District Court's decision were timely filed by defendants below . . . and by two groups of intervenor-plaintiffs. . . .

Undeniably the Constitution of the United States protects the right of all qualified citizens to vote, in state as well as in federal elections. . . . And history has seen a continuing expansion of the scope of the right of suffrage in this country. The right to vote freely for the candidate of one's choice is of the essence of a democratic society, and any restrictions on that right strike at the heart of representative government. And the right of suffrage can be denied by a debasement or dilution of the weight of a citizen's vote just as effectively as by wholly prohibiting the free exercise of the franchise. . . .

A predominant consideration in determining whether a State's legislative apportionment scheme constitutes an invidious discrimination violative of rights asserted under the Equal Protection Clause is that the rights allegedly impaired are individual and personal in nature. . . .

Legislators represent people, not trees or acres. Legislators are elected by voters, not farms or cities or economic interests. As long as ours is a representative form of government, and our legislatures are those instruments of government elected directly by and directly representative of the people, the right to elect legislators in a free and unimpaired fashion is a bedrock of our political system. . . .

We hold that, as a basic constitutional standard, the Equal Protection Clause requires that the seats in both houses of a bicameral state legislature must be apportioned on a population basis. Simply stated, an individual's right to vote for state legislators is unconstitutionally impaired when its weight is in a substantial fashion diluted when compared with votes of citizens living in other parts of the State. . . .

Much has been written since our decision in *Baker* v. *Carr* about the applicability of the so-called federal analogy to state legislative apportionment arrangements. After considering the matter, the court below concluded that no conceivable analogy could be drawn between the federal scheme and the apportionment of seats in the Alabama Legislature under the proposed constitutional amendment. We agree with the District Court, and find the federal analogy inapposite and irrelevant to state legislative districting schemes. Attempted reliance on the federal analogy appears often to be little more than an after-the-fact rationalization offered in defense of maladjusted state apportionment arrangements. . . .

By holding that as a federal constitutional requisite both houses of a state legislature must be apportioned on a population basis, we mean that the Equal Protection Clause requires that a State make an honest and good faith effort to construct districts, in both houses of its legislature, as nearly of equal population as is practicable. We realize that it is a practical impossibility to arrange legislative districts so that each one has an identical number of residents, or citizens, or voters. Mathematical exactness or precision is hardly a workable constitutional requirement. . . .

A State may legitimately desire to maintain the integrity of various political subdivisions, insofar as possible, and provide for compact districts of contiguous territory in designing a legislative apportionment scheme. Valid considerations may underlie such aims. Indiscriminate districting, without any regard for political subdivision or natural or historical boundary lines, may be little more than an open invitation to partisan gerrymandering. Single-member districts may be the rule in one State, while another State might desire to achieve some flexibility by creating multimember or floterial districts. Whatever the means of accomplishment, the overriding objective must be substantial equality of population among the various districts, so that the vote of any citizen is approximately equal in weight to that of any other citizen in the State. . . .

History indicates, however, that many States have deviated, to a greater or lesser degree, from the equal-population principle in the apportionment of seats in at least one house of their legislatures. . . .

A consideration that appears to be of . . . substance in justifying some deviations from population-based representation in state legislatures is that of insuring some voice to political subdivisions, as political subdivisions. Several factors make more than insubstantial claims that a State can rationally consider according political subdivisions some independent representation in at least one body of the state legislature, as long as the basic standard of equality of population among districts is maintained. Local governmental entities are frequently charged with various responsibilities incident to the operation of state government. In many States much of the legislature's activity involves the enactment of so-called local legislation, directed only to the concerns of particular political subdivisions. And a State may legitimately desire to construct districts along political subdivision lines to deter the possibilities of gerrymandering. However, permitting deviations from population-based representation does not mean that each local governmental unit or political subdivision can be given separate representation, regardless of population. Carried too far, a political subdivision (for example, to each county) could easily result, in many States, in a total subversion of the equal-population principle in that legislative body. . . .

We find, therefore, that the action taken by the District Court in this case . . . was an appropriate and well-considered exercise of judicial power. . . . In retaining jurisdiction while deferring a hearing on the issuance of a final injunction in order to give the provisionally reapportioned legislature an opportunity to act effectively, the court below proceeded in a proper fashion. . . . [W]e affirm the judgment below and remand the cases for further proceedings consistent with the views stated in this opinion.

It is so ordered.

MR. JUSTICE CLARK, concurring in the affirmance.

The Court goes much beyond the necessities of this case in laying down a new "equal population" principle for state legislative apportionment. . . .

I . . . do not reach the question of the so-called "federal analogy." But in my view, if one house of the State Legislature meets the population standard, representation in the other house might include some departure from it so as to take into account, on a rational basis, the various elements of the State. See my dissenting opinion in *Lucas* v. *Forty-Fourth General Assembly of Colorado, post,* p. 741, decided this date.

MR. JUSTICE STEWART.

All of the parties have agreed with the District Court's finding that legislative inaction for some 60 years in the face of growth and shifts in population has converted Alabama's legislative apportionment plan enacted in 1901 into one completely lacking in rationality. Accordingly, for the reasons stated in my dissenting opinion in *Lucas* v. *Forty-Fourth General Assembly of Colorado, post,* p. 744, I would affirm the judgment of the District Court holding that this apportionment violated the Equal Protection Clause. . . .

MR. JUSTICE HARLAN, dissenting. . . .

. . . Whatever may be thought of this holding as a piece of political ideology—and even on that score the political history and practices of this country from its earliest beginnings leave wide room for debate (see the dissenting opinion of Frankfurter, J., in *Baker* v. *Carr,* 369 US 186, 266, 301–323)—I think it demonstrable that the Fourteenth Amendment does not impose this political tenet on the States or authorize this Court to do so. . . .

The Court says . . . that "legislators represent people, not trees or acres," *ante,* p. 562; that "citizens, not history or economic interests, cast votes," *ante,* p. 580; that "people, not land or trees or pastures, vote," *ibid.* All this may be conceded. But it is surely equally obvious, and, in the context of elections, more meaningful to note that people are not ciphers and that legislators can represent their electors only by speaking for their interests—economic, social, political—many of which do reflect the place where the electors live. The Court does not establish, or indeed even attempt to make a case for the proposition that conflicting interests within a State can only be adjusted by disregarding them when voters are grouped for purposes of representation.

Notes

1. *Lucas* v. *Forty-Fourth General Assembly of Colorado,* 377 US 713 (1964), was one of the reapportionment cases decided on June 15, 1964. Chief Justice Warren wrote in the opinion of the Court:

We hold that the fact that a challenged legislative apportionment plan was approved by the electorate is without federal constitutional significance, if the scheme adopted fails to satisfy the basic requirements of the Equal Protection Clause, as delineated in our opinion in *Reynolds* v. *Sims.* And we conclude that the fact that a practicably available political remedy, such as initiative referendum, exists under state law provides justification only for a court of equity to stay its hand temporarily while recourse to such a remedial device is attempted or while proposed initiated measures relating to legislative apportionment are pending and will be submitted to the State's voters at the next election.

Justice Stewart, dissenting in the *Colorado* case, wrote:

What the Court has done is to convert a particular political philosophy into a constitutional rule, binding upon each of the 50 States, from Maine to Hawaii, from Alaska to Texas, without regard and without respect for the many individualized and differentiated characteristics of each state, characteristics stemming from each State's distinct history, distinct geography, distinct distribution of population, and distinct political heritage. My own understanding of the various theories of representative government is that no one theory has ever commanded unanimous assent among political scientists, historians, or others who have considered the problem. . . .
　　The fact is, of course, that population factors must often to some degree be subordinated in devising a legislative apportionment plan which is to achieve the important goal of ensuring a fair, effective, and balanced representation of the regional, social, and economic interests within a State. And the further fact is that throughout our history the apportionments of State Legislatures have reflected the strongly felt American tradition that the public interest is composed of many diverse interests, and that in the long run it can better be expressed by a medley of component voices than by the majority's monolithic command. What constitutes a rational plan reasonably designed to achieve this objective will vary from State to State, since each State is unique, in terms of topography, geography, demography, history, heterogeneity and concentration of population, variety of social and economic interests, and in the operation and inter-relation of its political institutions. But so long as a State's

apportionment plan reasonably achieves, in the light of the State's own characteristics, effective and balanced representation of all substantial interests, without sacrificing the principle of effective majority rule, that plan cannot be considered irrational.

2. *American Federation of Musicians* v. *Wittstein,* 379 US 171 (1964), held that a provision of the Labor Act of 1959 requiring that an increase in dues be approved "by majority vote of the delegates voting at a regular convention" did not prohibit the weighing of the votes of convention delegates according to the number of members in the local which they represented.

3. *Fortson* v. *Dorsey,* 379 US 433 (1965), held that equal protection did not necessarily require formation of all districts in a state's legislative apportionment scheme on a "single-member" basis. Compare *Whitcomb* v. *Chavis,* 403 US 124 (1971).

4. *Avery* v. *Midland County,* 390 US 474 (1968), held that the "one man, one vote" rule applied to the election of members of the governing body of a political subdivision within a state—in this case, a county.

5. *Hadley* v. *Junior College District,* 397 US 50 (1970), held that the "one man, one rule" applied to elections for the election of trustees of a metropolitan junior college. For the majority, Justice Black wrote:

> When a court is asked to decide whether a State is required by the Constitution to give each qualified voter the same power in an election open to all, there is no discernible, valid reason why constitutional distinctions should be drawn on the basis of the purpose of the election. If one person's vote is given less weight through unequal apportionment, his right to equal voting participation is impaired just as much when he votes for a school board member as when he votes for a state legislator. While there are differences in the powers of different officials, the crucial consideration is the right of each qualified voter to participate on an equal footing in the election process. It should be remembered that in cases like this one we are asked by voters to insure that they are given equal treatment, and from their perspective the harm from unequal treatment is the same in any election, regardless of the officials selected. . . .
>
> In holding that the guarantee of equal voting strength for each voter applies in all elections of governmental officials, we do not feel that the States will be inhibited in finding ways to insure that legitimate political goals of representation are achieved. We have previously upheld against constitutional challenge an election scheme that required that candidates be residents of certain districts that did not contain equal numbers of people. . . . Since all the officials in that case were elected at large, the right of each voter was given equal treatment. We have also held that where a State chooses to select members of an official body by appointment rather than election, and that choice does not itself offend the Constitution, the fact that each official does not "represent" the same number of people does not deny those people equal protection of the laws. . . . And a State may, in certain cases, limit the right to vote to a particular group or class of people. As we said before, "[v]iable local governments may need many innovations, numerous combinations of old and new devices, great flexibility in municipal arrangements to meet changing urban conditions. We see nothing in the Constitution to prevent experimentation." . . . But once a State has decided to use the

process of popular election and "once the class of voters is chosen and their qualifications specified, we see no constitutional way by which equality of voting power may be evaded."

Chief Justice Burger and Justices Harlan and Stewart dissented.

6. *Abate* v. *Mundt,* 403 US 182 (1971), sustained a plan for electing members of the county board for Rockland County, New York, from districts corresponding to the five towns that made up the county, even though the plan produced a 11.9 percent total deviation from population equality. The opinion of the Court, by Justice Marshall, emphasized "the long history of, and perceived need for, close cooperation between the county and its constituent towns." The plan approved, "by preserving an exact correspondence between each town and one of the county legislative districts, continues to encourage that town supervisors also serve on the county board."

7. *Wells* v. *Edwards,* 409 US 1095 (1973), affirmed a holding that the "one man, one vote" principle did not apply to districts for electing judges. Justices White, Douglas, and Marshall dissented.

8. *Mahan* v. *Howell,* 410 US 315 (1973), sustained a Virginia legislative apportionment statute containing a 16 percent population variation between districts. The opinion explained that the "absolute equality" test announced in *Kirkpatrick* v. *Preisler* (394 US 526) for congressional districts was not applicable to state legislative districts.

9. *Salyer Land Co.* v. *Tulane Basin Water Storage District,* 410 US 719 (1973), sustained a California provision for election of the board of directors of a water storage district by district landowners only, whether or not they were residents, apportioning votes according to assessed land values.

Poll Tax

Harper v. Virginia Board of Elections

383 US 663, 86 S Ct 1079, 16 L Ed2d 169 (1966)

Payment of a poll tax cannot be required as a condition for voting.

Mr. Justice Douglas delivered the opinion of the Court.

These are suits by Virginia residents to have declared unconstitutional Virginia's poll tax. The three-judge District Court, feeling bound by our decision in *Breedlove* v. *Suttles,* 302 US 277, ... dismissed the complaint. ...

While the right to vote in federal elections is conferred by Art. I. § 2, of the Constitution . . . the right to vote in state elections is nowhere expressly mentioned. It is argued that the right to vote in state elections is implicit, particularly by reason of the First Amendment and that it may not constitutionally be conditioned upon the payment of a tax or fee. . . . We do not stop to canvass the relation between voting and political expression. For it is enough to say that once the franchise is granted to the electorate, lines may not be drawn which are inconsistent with the Equal Protection Clause. . . .

We conclude that a State violates the Equal Protection Clause of the Fourteenth Amendment whenever it makes the affluence of the voter or payment of any fee an electoral standard. Voter qualifications have no relation to wealth nor to paying or not paying this or any other tax. Our cases demonstrate that the Equal Protection Clause of the Fourteenth Amendment restrains the States from fixing voter qualifications which invidiously discriminate. . . .

Long ago in *Yick Wo* v. *Hopkins,* the Court referred to "the political franchise of voting" as a "fundamental political right." . . .

It is argued that a State may exact fees from citizens for many different kinds of licenses; that if it can demand from all an equal fee for a driver's license, it can demand from all an equal poll tax for voting. But we must remember that the interest of the State, when it comes to voting, is limited to the power to fix qualifications. Wealth, like race, creed, or color, is not germane to one's ability to participate intelligently in the electoral process. Lines drawn on the basis of wealth or property, like those of race . . . are traditionally disfavored. . . .

MR. JUSTICE BLACK, dissenting.

[The Court] overrules *Breedlove* in part, but its opinion reveals that it does so not by using its limited power to interpret the original meaning of the Equal Protection Clause, but by giving that clause a new meaning which it believes represents a better governmental policy. From this action I dissent. . . .

. . . The equal protection cases carefully analyzed boil down to the principle that distinctions drawn and even discriminations imposed by state laws do not violate the Equal Protection Clause so long as these distinctions and discriminations imposed by state laws are not "irrational," "irrelevant," "unreasonable," "arbitrary," or "invidious." These vague and indefinite terms do not, of course, provide a precise formula or an automatic mechanism for deciding cases arising under the Equal Protection Clause. The restrictive connotations of these terms, however . . . are a plain recognition of the fact that under a proper interpretation of the Equal Protection Clause States are to have the broadest kind of leeway in areas where they have a general constitutional competence to act. . . . State poll tax legislation can "reasonably," "rationally" and without an "invidious" or evil purpose to injure anyone be found to rest on a number of state policies including (1) the State's desire to collect its revenue, and (2) its belief that voters who pay a poll tax will be interested in furthering the State's welfare when they vote. Certainly it is rational to believe that people may be more likely to pay taxes if payment is a prerequisite to voting. And if history can be a factor in determining the "rationality" of discrimination in a state law (which we held it could in *Kotch* v. *River Port Pilots Comms.* [330 US 552]), then whatever may be our personal opinion, history is on the side of "rationality" of the State's poll tax policy. Property qualifications existed in the Colonies and were continued by many States after the Constitution was adopted. . . .

MR. JUSTICE HARLAN, whom MR. JUSTICE STEWART joins, dissenting. [Omitted.]

Name on Ballot

Lubin v. Panish

415 US 709, 94 S Ct 1315, 39 L Ed2d 702 (1974)

In the absence of reasonable alternative means of ballot access, a state may not require from an indigent candidate filing fees he cannot pay.

MR. CHIEF JUSTICE BURGER delivered the opinion of the Court.

We granted *certiorari* to consider petitioner's claim that the California statute requiring payment of a filing fee of $701.60 in order to be placed on the ballot in the primary election for nomination to the position of County Supervisor, while providing no alternative means of access to the ballot, deprived him, as an indigent person unable to pay the fee, and others similarly situated, of the equal protection guaranteed by the Fourteenth Amendment and rights of expression and association guaranteed by the First Amendment.

The California Election Code provides that forms required for nomination and election to congressional, state, and county offices are to be issued to candidates only upon prepayment of a nonrefundable filing fee. . . . Generally, the required fees are fixed at a percentage of the salary for the office sought. The fee for candidates for United States Senator, Governor, and other state offices and some county offices, is 2% of the annual salary. Candidates for Representative to Congress, State Senator or Assemblyman, or for judicial office or district attorney, must pay 1%. . . .

Petitioner with others commenced this class action on February 17, 1972, by petitioning the Los Angeles Superior Court for a writ of mandate against the Secretary of State and the Los Angeles County Registrar-Recorder. The suit was filed on behalf of petitioner and all those similarly situated persons who were unable to pay the filing fees and who desired to be nominated for public office. . . .

The Los Angeles Superior Court denied the requested writ of mandate on March 6, 1972. Petitioner alleged that he was a serious candidate, that he was indigent and that he was unable to pay the $701.60 filing fee; no evidence was taken during the hearing. The superior court found the fees to be "reasonable, as a matter of law." . . .

That "laundry list" ballots discourage voter participation and confuse and frustrate those who do participate is too obvious to call for extended discussion. The means of testing the seriousness of a given candidacy may be open to debate; the fundamental importance of ballots of reasonable size limited to serious candidates with some prospects of public support is not. Rational results within the framework of our system are not likely to be reached if the ballot for a single office must list a dozen or more aspirants who are relatively unknown or have no prospects of success.

This legitimate state interest, however, must be achieved by a means that does not unfairly or unnecessarily burden either a minority party's or an individual candidate's equally important interest in the continued availability of political opportunity. The interests involved are not merely those of parties or individual candidates; the voters can assert their preferences only through candidates or parties or both and it is this broad interest that must be weighed in the balance. The right of a party or an individual to a place on a ballot is entitled to protection and is intertwined with the rights of voters.

> "The right to vote is heavily burdened if that vote may be cast only for one of two parties at a time when other parties are clamoring for a place on the ballot." *Williams* v. *Rhodes,* 393 US 23, 30 (1968). . . .

In *Bullock* [v. *Carter,* 405 US 134] we expressly rejected the validity of filing fees as the sole means of determining a candidate's "seriousness". . . .

The absence of any alternate means of gaining access to the ballot inevitably renders the California system exclusionary as to some aspirants. As we have noted, the payment of a fee is an absolute not an alternative condition, and failure to meet it is a disqualification from running for office. Thus, California has chosen to achieve the important and legitimate interest of maintaining the integrity of elections by means which can operate to exclude some potentially serious candidates from the ballot without providing them with any alternative means of coming before the voters. Selection of candidates solely on the basis of ability to pay a fixed fee without providing any alternative means is not reasonably necessary to the accomplishment of the State's legitimate election interests. Accordingly, we hold that in the absence of reasonable alternative means of ballot access, a State may not, consistent with constitutional standards, require from an indigent candidate filing fees he cannot pay.

In so holding, we note that there are obvious and well known means of testing the "seriousness" of a candidacy which do not measure the probability of attracting significant voter support solely by the neutral fact of payment of a filing fee. States may, for example, impose on minor political parties the precondition of demonstrating the existence some reasonable quantum of voter support by requiring such parties to file petitions for a place on the ballot signed by a percentage of those who voted in a prior election. See *American Party of Texas* v. *White,* No. 72-887 (decided March, 1974). Similarly, a candidate who establishes that he cannot pay the filing fee required for a place on the primary ballot may be required to demonstrate the "seriousness" of his candidacy by persuading a substantial number of voters to sign a petition in his behalf. The point, of course, is that ballot access must be genuinely open to all subject to reasonable requirements. *Jenness* v. *Fortson,* 402 US 431, 439 (1971). California's present system has not met this standard.

Reversed and remanded for further consideration not inconsistent with this opinion.

Note

Storer v. *Brown,* 415 US 724 (1974), held that, in the interest of political stability, a state could deny a ballot position as an independent to a candidate who had registered affiliation with a political party within the past year.

Residence and Time of Registration

Dunn v. Blumstein

405 US 330, 92 S Ct 995, 31 L Ed2d 274 (1972)

A state requirement that bona fide residents have a "durational residence" of one year in the state and three months in the county as a qualification to register to vote is void.

Mr. Justice Marshall delivered the opinion of the Court.

Various Tennessee public officials (hereinafter "Tennessee") appeal from a decision by a three-judge federal court holding that Tennessee's durational residence requirements for voting violate the Equal Protection Clause of the United States Constitution. The issue arises in a class action for declaratory and injunctive relief brought by appellee James Blumstein. Blumstein moved to Tennessee on June 12, 1970, to begin employment as an assistant professor of law at Vanderbilt University in Nashville. With an eye towards voting in the upcoming August and November elections, he attempted to register to vote on July 1, 1970. The county registrar refused to register him, on the ground that Tennessee law authorizes the registration of only those persons who, at the time of the next election, will have been residents of the State for a year and residents of the county for three months.

After exhausting state administrative remedies, Blumstein brought this action challenging these residence requirements on federal constitutional grounds. A three-judge court . . . concluded that Tennessee's durational residence requirements were unconstitutional (1) because they impermissibly interfered with the right to vote and (2) because they created a "suspect" classification penalizing some Tennessee residents because of recent interstate movement. . . . For the reasons which follow, we affirm the decision below.

I

The subject of this lawsuit is the durational residence requirement. Appellee does not challenge Tennessee's power to restrict the vote to bona fide Tennessee residents. Nor has Tennessee ever disputed that appellee was a bona fide resident of the State and county when he attempted to register. But Tennessee insists that, in addition to *being* a resident, a would-be voter must *have been* a resident for a year in the State and three months in the county. It is this additional *durational* residence requirement which appellee challenges.

Durational residence laws penalize those persons who have traveled from one place to another to establish a new residence during the qualifying period. Such laws divide residents into two classes, old residents and new residents, and discriminate against the latter to the extent of totally denying them the opportunity to vote. The constitutional question presented is whether the Equal Protection Clause of the Fourteenth Amendment permits a State to discriminate in this way among its citizens.

To decide whether a law violates the Equal Protection Clause, we look, in essence, to three things: the character of the classification in question; the individual interests affected by the classification; and the governmental interests asserted in support of the classifiation. . . . In considering laws challenged under the Equal Protection Clause, this Court has evolved more than one test, depending upon the interests affected and the classification involved. First, then, we must determine what standard of review is appropriate. In the present case, whether we look to the benefit withheld by the classification (the opportunity to vote) or the basis for the classifications (recent interstate travel) we conclude that the State must show a substantial and compelling reason for imposing durational residence requirements.

A

Durational residence requirements completely bar from voting all residents not meeting the fixed durational standards. By denying some citizens the right to vote, such laws deprive them of "a fundamental political right, . . . preservative of all rights." . . .

B

This exacting test is appropriate for another reason, never considered in *Drueding* [v. *Devlin,* 380 US 125]: Tennessee's durational residence laws classify bona fide residents on the basis of recent travel, penalizing those persons, and only those persons, who have gone from one jurisdiction to another during the qualifying period. Thus, the durational residence requirement directly impinges on the exercise of a second fundamental personal right, the right to travel. . . .

C

In sum, durational residence laws must be measured by a strict equal protection test: they are unconstitutional unless the State can demonstrate that such laws are *"necessary* to promote a *compelling* governmental interest." . . . Thus phrased, the constitutional question may sound like a mathematical formula. But legal "tests" do not have the precision of mathematical formulas. The key words emphasize a matter of degree: that a heavy burden of justification is on the State, and that the statute will be closely scrutinized in light of its asserted purposes. . . .

II

We turn, then, to the question of whether the State has shown that durational residence requirements are needed to further a sufficiently substantial state interest. We emphasize again the difference between bona fide residence requirements and durational residence requirements. We have in the past noted approvingly that the States have the power to require that voters be bona fide residents of the relevant political subdivision. . . . An appropriately defined and uniformly applied requirement of bona fide residence may be necessary to preserve the basic conception of a political community, and therefore could withstand close constitutional scrutiny. But *durational* residence requirements, representing a separate voting qualification imposed on bona fide residents, must be separately tested by the stringent standard. . . .

It is worth noting at the outset that Congress has, in a somewhat different context, addressed the question whether durational residence laws further compelling state interests. In § 202 of the 1970 Federal Voting Rights Act, Congress outlawed state durational residence requirements for presidential and vice presidential elections, and prohibited the States from closing registration more than 30 days before such elections. . . .

Tennessee tenders "two basic purposes" served by it durational residence requirements:

> "(1) INSURE PURITY OF BALLOT BOX—Protection against fraud through colonization and inability to identify persons offering to vote, and
> "(2) KNOWLEDGEABLE VOTER—Afford some surety that the voter has, in fact, become a member of the community and that as such, he has a common interest in all matters pertaining to its government and is, therefore, more likely to exercise his right more intelligently." Appellants' Brief, p. 15, citing 18 Am. Jur., Elections, p. 217.

We consider each in turn.

A

Preservation of the "purity of the ballot box" is a formidable sounding state interest. The impurities feared, variously called "dual voting" and "colonization," all involve voting by nonresidents, either singly or in groups. The main concern is that nonresidents will temporarily invade the State or county, falsely swear that they are residents to become eligible to vote, and, by voting, allow a candidate to win by fraud. Surely the prevention of such fraud is a legitimate and compelling government goal. But it is impossible to view durational residence requirements as necessary to achieve that state interest. . . .

Durational residence laws may once have been necessary to prevent a fraudulent evasion of state voter standards, but today in Tennessee, as in most other States, this purpose is served by a system of voter registration. . . . Given this system, the record is totally devoid of any evidence that durational residence requirements are in fact necessary to identify bona fide residents. The qualifications of the would-be voter in Tennessee are determined when he registers to vote, which he may do until 30 days before the election. . . . His qualifications—including bona fide residence—are established then by oath. . . . There is no indication in the record that Tennessee routinely goes behind the would-be voter's oath to determine his qualifications. Since false swearing is no obstacle to one intent on fraud, the existence of burdensome voting qualifications like durational residence requirements cannot prevent corrupt nonresidents from fraudulent registering and voting. As long as the State relies on the oath-swearing system to establish qualifications, a durational residence requirement adds nothing to a simple residence requirement in the effort to stop fraud. The nonresident intent on committing election fraud will as quickly and effectively swear that he has been a resident for the requisite period of time as he would swear that he was simply a resident. Indeed, the durational residence requirement becomes an effective voting obstacle only to residents who tell the truth and have no fraudulent purposes. . . .

. . . To prevent dual voting, state voting officials simply have to cross-check lists of new registrants with their former jurisdictions. . . . Objective information tendered as relevant to the question of bona fide residence under Tennessee law—places of dwelling, occupation, car registration, driver's license, property owned, etc.—is easy to double check, especially in light of modern communications. Tennessee itself concedes that "[i]t might well be that these purposes can be achieved under requirements of shorter duration than that imposed by the State of Tennessee. . . . " Appellants' Brief, p. 10. Fixing a constitutionally acceptable period is surely a matter of degree. It is sufficient to note here that 30 days appears to be an ample period of time for the State to complete whatever administrative tasks are necessary to prevent fraud—and a year, or three months, too much. . . .

Our conclusion that the waiting period is not the least restrictive means necessary for preventing fraud is bolstered by the recognition that Tennessee has at its disposal a variety of criminal laws which are more than adequate to detect and deter whatever fraud may be feared. At least six separate sections of the Tennessee Code define offenses to deal with voter fraud. For example, Tenn. Code Ann. § 2-324 makes it a crime "for any person to register or to have his name registered as a qualified voter . . . when he is not entitled to be so registered . . . or to induce or procure any other person to register or be registered when such person is not legally qualified to be registered as such. . . ." In addition to the various criminal penalties, Tennessee permits the bona fides of a voter to be challenged on election day. . . .

B

The argument that durational residence requirements further the goal of having "knowledgeable voters" appears to involve three separate claims. The first is that such requirements "afford some surety that the voter has, in fact, become a member of the community." But here the State appears to confuse a bona fide residence requirement with a durational residence requirement. As already noted, a State does have an interest in limiting the franchise to bona fide members of the community. But this does not justify or explain the exclusion from the franchise of persons, not because their bona fide residence is questioned, but because they are recent rather than long-time residents.

The second branch of the "knowledgeable voters" justification is that durational residence requirements assure that the voter "has a common interest in all matters pertaining to [the community's] government. . . . " By this, presumably, the State means that it may require a period of residence sufficiently lengthy to impress upon its voters the local viewpoint. This is precisely the sort of argument this Court has repeatedly rejected. . . .

III

Concluding that Tennessee has not offered an adequate justification for its durational residence laws, we affirm the judgment of the court below.

Mr. Justice Powell and Mr. Justice Rehnquist took no part in the consideration or decision of this case.

Mr. Justice Blackmun, concurring in the result. . . .
The Tennessee plan, based both in statute and in the State's constitution, is not ideal. I am content that the one-year and three-month requirements be struck down for want of something more closely related to the State's interest. It is, of course, a matter of line-drawing, as the Court concedes. . . . But if 30 days pass constitutional muster, what of 35 or 45 or 75? The resolution of these longer measures, less than those today struck down, the Court leaves, I suspect, to the future.

MR. CHIEF JUSTICE BURGER, dissenting.

The holding of the Court in *Pope* v. *Williams, supra,* is as valid today as it was at the turn of the century. It is no more a denial of Equal Protection for a State to require newcomers to be exposed to state and local problems for a reasonable period such as one year before voting, than it is to require children to wait 18 years before voting. ... In both cases some informed and responsible persons are denied the vote, while others less informed and less responsible are permitted to vote. Some lines must be drawn. To challenge such lines by the "compelling state interest" standard is to condemn them all. So far as I am aware, no state law has ever satisfied this seemingly insurmountable standard, and I doubt one ever will, for it demands nothing less than perfection.

The existence of a constitutional "right to travel" does not persuade me to the contrary. If the imposition of a durational residency requirement for voting abridges the right to travel, surely the imposition of an age qualification penalizes the young for being young, a status I assume the Constitution also protects.

Notes

1. *Evans* v. *Cornman,* 398 US 419 (1970), held that residents on the grounds of the National Institutes of Health are treated by Maryland, in which the federal enclave is located, as state residents to such an extent that it violated equal protection to deny them the right to vote in that state.

2. *Marston* v. *Lewis,* 410 US 679 (1973), sustained Arizona's fifty-day durational residency requirement for registration.

Kusper v. Pontikes

414 US 51, 94 S Ct 303, 38 L Ed2d 260 (1974)

While a state has a legitimate interest in preventing party "raiding," it cannot lock the voter in his pre-existing party affiliation for the substantial period of twenty-three months.

MR. JUSTICE STEWART delivered the opinion of the Court.

Under § 7–43 (d) of the Illinois Election Code, a person is prohibited from voting in the primary election of a political party if he has voted in the primary of any other party within the preceding 23 months. Appellee Harriet G. Pontikes is a qualified Chicago voter who voted in a Republican primary in February of 1971; she wanted to vote in a March 1972 Democratic primary, but was barred from doing so by this "twenty-three months rule." She filed a complaint for declaratory and injunctive relief in the United States District Court for the Northern District of Illinois, alleging that § 7–43 (d) unconstitutionally abridged her freedom to associate with the political party of her choice by depriving her of the opportunity to vote in the Democratic primary. A statutory three-judge court was convened, and held, one judge dissenting, that the

23-months rule is unconstitutional. . . . We noted probable jurisdiction of this appeal from that judgment. . . .

To be sure, administration of the electoral process is a matter that the Constitution largely entrusts to the States. But, in exercising their powers of supervision over elections and in setting qualifications for voters, the States may not infringe upon basic constitutional protections. . . .

. . . While the Illinois statute did not absolutely preclude Mrs. Pontikes from associating with the Democratic party, it did absolutely preclude her from voting in that party's 1972 primary election. Under our political system, a basic function of a political party is to select the candidates for public office to be offered to the voters at general elections. A prime objective of most voters in associating themselves with a particular party must surely be to gain a voice in that selection process. By preventing the appellee from participating at all in Democratic primary elections during the statutory period, the Illinois statute deprived her of any voice in choosing the party's candidates, and thus substantially abridged her ability to associate effectively with the party of her choice. . . .

As our past decisions have made clear, a significant encroachment upon associational freedom cannot be justified upon a mere showing of a legitimate state interest. . . . For even when pursuing a legitimate interest, a State may not choose means that unnecessarily restrict constitutionally protected liberty. . . . If the State has open to it a less drastic way of satisfying its legitimate interests, it may not choose a legislative scheme that broadly stifles the exercise of fundamental personal liberties. . . .

The appellants here urge that the 23-months rule serves the purpose of preventing "raiding"—the practice whereby voters in sympathy with one party vote in another's primary in order to distort that primary's results. It is said that our decision in *Rosario* v. *Rockefeller,* 410 US 752, recognized the state interest in inhibiting "raiding," and upheld the constitutional validity of legislation restricting a voter's freedom to change parties, enacted as a means of serving that interest.

It is true, of course, that the Court found no constitutional infirmity in the New York delayed-enrollment statute under review in *Rosario.* That law required a voter to enroll in the party of his choice at least 30 days before a general election in order to be eligible to vote in the next party primary, and thus prevented a change in party affiliation during the approximately 11 months between the deadline and the primary election. It is also true that the Court recognized in *Rosario* that a State may have a legitimate interest in seeking to curtail "raiding," since that practice may affect the integrity of the electoral process. 410 US, at 761. But it does not follow from *Rosario* that the Illinois statutory procedures also pass muster under the Fourteenth Amendment, for the Illinois Election Code differs from the New York delayed-enrollment law in a number of important respects.

The New York statute at issue in *Rosario* did not prevent voters from participating in the party primary of their choice; it merely imposed a time limit on enrollment. Under the New York law, a person who wanted to vote in a different party primary every year was not precluded from doing so; he had only to meet the requirement of declaring his party allegiance 30 days before the preceding general election. The New York law did not have the consequence of "locking" a voter into an unwanted party affiliation from one election to the next; any such confinement was merely the result of the elector's voluntary failure to take timely measures to enroll. *Id.,* at 757–759. The Court therefore concluded that the New York delayed-enrollment law did not prevent voters "from associating with the political party of their choice." *Id.,* at 762. And see *id.,* at 758 and n. 8.

The basic difference in the Illinois law is obvious. Since the appellee here voted in the 1971 Republican primary, the state law absolutely precluded her from participating in the 1972 Democratic primary. Unlike the petitioners in *Rosario,* whose disenfranchisement was caused by their own failure to take timely measures to enroll, there was no action that Mrs. Pontikes could have taken to make herself eligible to vote in the 1972 Democratic primary. The Illinois law, unlike that of New York, thus "locks" voters into a preexisting party affiliation from one primary to the next, and the only way to break the "lock" is to forego voting in *any* primary for a period of almost two years.

In other words, while the Court held in *Rosario* that the New York delayed-enrollment scheme did not prevent voters from exercising their constitutional freedom to associate with the political party of their choice, the Illinois 23-months rule clearly does just that. It follows that the legitimate interest of Illinois in preventing "raiding" cannot justify the device it has chosen to effect its goal. For that device conspicuously infringes upon basic constitutional liberty. Far from supporting the validity of the Illinois legislation, the Court's decision in *Rosario* suggests that the asserted state interest can be attained by "less drastic means," which do not unnecessarily burden the exercise of constitutionally protected activity.

We conclude, therefore, that § 7–43 (d) of the Illinois Election Code unconstitutionally infringes upon the right of free political association protected by the First and Fourteenth Amendments. The judgment of the District Court is accordingly

Affirmed.

THE CHIEF JUSTICE concurs in the result.

MR. JUSTICE BLACKMUN, dissenting.

The deprivation Mrs. Pontikes claims to have suffered, and which the Court today enshrouds with the mantle of unconstitutionality, is that she has been restrained by the Illinois statute from voting in *one* primary election of *one* party in the relatively minor context of a personal desire to undo an established party affiliation. Apart from this meager restraint, appellee Pontikes is fully free to associate with the party of her varying choice. She is, and has been, completely free to vote as she chooses in any general election. And she was free to vote in the primary of the party with which she had affiliated and voted in the preceding primary.

It is important, I think—and deserving of repeated emphasis—to note that this very limited statutory restriction on the appellee's exercise of her franchise is triggered solely by her personal and voluntary decision. This being so, the Court's conclusion seems to me to dilute an important First Amendment concept the vitality of which, in the long run, necessarily will suffer from strained and artificial applications of this kind. The mere fact that a state statute lightly brushes upon the right to vote and the right of association, important as these are, should not automatically result in invalidation. Prior case law does not require a conclusion of invalidity where, as here, the intrusion is so minor. . . .

MR. JUSTICE REHNQUIST, with whom MR. JUSTICE BLACKMUN joins, dissenting.

The Court decides that the Illinois rule disqualifying a person from voting in the primary of one political party if he has voted in the primary of another political party during the preceding 23 months imposes an impermissible burden on Illinois voters' exercise of their right of free political association. In so doing it distinguishes *Rosario v. Rockefeller* . . . decided last Term. I find *Rosario* more difficult to distinguish than does the Court. . . .

Both the Illinois rule struck down today and the New York rule upheld in *Rosario* restrict voters' freedom to associate with the political party of their choice. In both instances the State has sought to justify the restrictions as promoting the State's legitimate interest in preventing "raiding." While neither rule is perfectly fashioned to accomplish that and no other result, I cannot conclude that the Illinois rule imposes a significantly greater burden on the exercise of associational freedom than does the New York rule we upheld last Term in *Rosario.*

Notes

1. *Phoenix* v. *Kolodziejski,* 399 US 204 (1970), held that "the Equal Protection Clause does not permit a State to restrict the franchise to real property taxpayers in elections to approve the issuance of general obligation bonds."

2. *Gordon* v. *Lance,* 403 US 1 (1971), sustained West Virginia's requirement that political subdivisions secure the approval of 60% of the voters in a referendum election in order to incur bonded indebtedness. The Court did not find the requirement to discriminate against any identifiable class.

3. *Richardson* v. *Ramirez,* 418 US 24 (1974), sustained California's continued disfranchisement of convicted felons who have completed their sentences.

Limited Purpose Elections

Kramer v. Union Free School District

395 US 621, 89 S Ct 1886, 23 L Ed2d 583 (1969)

A statute aimed at restricting the franchise in school district elections to those "primarily interested in school affairs" must be drawn with precision to withstand strict judicial scrutiny.

MR. CHIEF JUSTICE WARREN delivered the opinion of the Court.

In this case we are called on to determine whether § 2012 of the New York Education Law is constitutional. The legislation provides that in certain New York school districts [where the school board is elected at an annual meeting of qualified school district voters] residents who are otherwise eligible to vote in state and federal elections may vote in the school district election only if they (1) own (or lease) taxable real property within the district, or (2) are parents (or have custody of) children enrolled in the local public schools. Appellant, a bachelor who neither owns nor leases taxable real property, filed suit in federal court claiming that § 2012 denied him equal protection of the laws in violation of the Fourteenth Amendment. With one judge dissenting, a three-judge District Court dismissed appellant's complaint. Finding that § 2012 does violate the Equal Protection Clause of the Fourteenth Amendment, we reverse. . . .

Appellant asserts that excluding him from participation in the district elections denies him equal protection of the laws. He contends that he and others of his class are substantially interested in and significantly affected by the school meeting decisions. All members of the community have an interest in the quality and structure of public education, appellant says, and he urges that "the decisions taken by local boards . . . may have grave consequences to the entire population." Appellant also argues that the level of property taxation affects him, even though he does not own property, as property tax levels affect the price of goods and services in the community.

We turn therefore to question whether the exclusion is necessary to promote a compelling state interest. First, appellees argue that the State has a legitimate interest in limiting the franchise in school district elections to "members of the community of interest"—those "primarily interested in such elections." Second, appellees urge that the State may reasonably and permissibly conclude that "property taxpayers" (including lessees of taxable property who share the tax burden through rent payments) and parents of the children enrolled in the district's schools are those "primarily interested" in school affairs. . . .

[A]ssuming, *arguendo,* that New York legitimately might limit the franchise in these school district elections to those "primarily interested in school affairs," close scrutiny of the § 2012 classifications demonstrates that they do not accomplish this purpose with sufficient precision to justify denying appellant the franchise.

Whether classifications allegedly limiting the franchise to those resident citizens "primarily interested" deny those excluded equal protection of the laws depends, *inter alia,* on whether all those excluded are in fact substantially less interested or affected than those the statute includes. In other words, the classifications must be tailored so that the exclusion of appellant and members of his class is necessary to achieve the articulated state goal. Section 2012 does not meet the exacting standard of precision we require of statutes which selectively distribute the franchise. The classifications in § 2012 permit inclusion of many persons who have, at best, a remote and indirect interest in school affairs and, on the other hand, exclude others who have a distinct and direct interest in the school meeting decisions. . . .

The judgment of the United States District Court for the Eastern District of New York is therefore reversed. The case is remanded for further proceedings consistent with this opinion.

It is so ordered.

MR. JUSTICE STEWART, with whom MR. JUSTICE BLACK and MR. JUSTICE HARLAN join, dissenting.

In *Lassiter* v. *Northampton Election Bd.,* 360 US 45, this Court upheld against constitutional attack a literacy requirement, applicable to voters in all state and federal elections, imposed by the State of North Carolina. Writing for a unanimous Court, Mr. Justice Douglas said:

> "The States have long been held to have broad powers to determine the conditions under which the right of suffrage may be exercised, *Pope* v. *Williams,* 193 US 621, 633; *Mason* v. *Missouri,* 179 US 328, 335, absent of course the discrimination which the Constitution condemns." 360 US, at 50–51.

Believing that the appellant in this case is not the victim of any "discrimination which the Constitution condemns," I would affirm the judgment of the District Court. . . .

. . . This case does not involve racial classifications, which in light of the genesis of the Fourteenth Amendment have traditionally been viewed as inherently "suspect." And this statute is not one that impinges upon a constitutionally protected right, and that consequently can be justified only by a "compelling" state interest. For "the Constitution of the United States does not confer the right of suffrage upon any one. . . ." *Minor* v. *Happersett,* 21 Wallace 162, 178.

In any event, it seems to me that under *any* equal protection standard, short of a doctrinaire insistent that universal suffrage is somehow mandated by the Constitution, the appellant's claim must be rejected. . . .

B.   ACCESS TO COURTS

Griffin v. Illinois

351 US 12, 76 S Ct 585, 100 L Ed 891 (1956)

Appellate review cannot be conditioned upon ability to pay costs.

Mr. Justice Black announced the judgment of the Court and an opinion in which The Chief Justice, Mr. Justice Douglas, and Mr. Justice Clark join.

Illinois law provides that "Writs of error in all criminal cases are writs of right and shall be issued of course." The question presented here is whether Illinois may, consistent with the Due Process and Equal Protection Clauses of the Fourteenth Amendment, administer this statute so as to deny adequate appellate review to the poor while granting such review to all others.

The petitioners Griffin and Crenshaw were tried together and convicted of armed robbery in the Criminal Court of Cook County, Illinois. Immediately after their conviction they filed a motion in the trial court asking that a certified copy of the entire record, including a stenographic transcript of the proceedings, be furnished them without cost. They alleged that they were "poor persons with no means of paying the necessary fees to acquire the Transcript and Court Records needed to prosecute an appeal. . . ." These allegations were not denied. Under Illinois law in order to get full direct appellate review of alleged errors by a writ of error it is necessary for the defendant to furnish the appellate court with a bill of exceptions or report of proceedings at the trial certified by the trial judge. As Illinois concedes, it is sometimes impossible to prepare such bills of exceptions or reports without a stenographic transcript of the trial proceedings. Indigent defendants sentenced to death are provided with a free transcript at the expense of the county where convicted. In all other criminal cases defendants needing a transcript, whether indigent or not, must themselves buy it. The petitioners contended in their motion before the trial court that failure to provide them with the needed transcript would violate the Due Process and Equal Protection Clauses of the Fourteenth Amendment. The trial court denied the motion without a hearing.

. . . The Illinois Supreme Court affirmed the dismissal . . . on the ground that the charges raised no substantial state or federal constitutional questions. . . . We granted *certiorari.* . . .

. . . Both equal protection and due process emphasize the central aim of our entire judicial system—all people charged with crime must, so far as the law is concerned, "stand on an equality before the bar of justice in every American court." . . .

Surely no one would contend that either a State or the Federal Government could constitutionally provide that defendants unable to pay court costs in advance should be denied the right to plead not guilty or to defend themselves in court. Such a law would make the constitutional promise of a fair trial a worthless thing. Notice, the right to be heard, and the right to counsel would under such circumstances be meaningless promises to the poor. In criminal trials a State can no more discriminate on account of poverty than on account of religion, race, or color. Plainly the ability to pay costs in advance bears no rational relationship to a defendant's guilt or innocence and could not be used as an excuse to deprive a defendant of a fair trial. . . .

There is no meaningful distinction between a rule which would deny the poor the right to defend themselves in a trial court and one which effectively denies the poor an adequate appellate review accorded to all who have money enough to pay the costs in advance. It is true that a State is not required by the Federal Constitution to provide appellate courts or a right to appellate review at all. . . . But that is not to say that a State that does grant appellate review can do so in a way that discriminates against some convicted defendants on account of their poverty. Appellate review has now become an integral part of the Illinois trial system for finally adjudicating the guilt or innocence of a defendant. Consequently at all stages of the proceedings the Due Process and Equal Protection Clauses protect persons like petitioners from invidious discriminations. . . .

The Illinois Supreme Court denied these petitioners relief under the Post-Conviction Act because of its holding that no constitutional rights were violated. In view of our holding to the contrary the State Supreme Court may decide that petitioners are now entitled to a transcript, as the State's brief suggests. . . . We do not hold, however, that Illinois must purchase a stenographer's transcript in every case where a defendant cannot buy it. The Supreme Court may find other means of affording adequate and effective appellate review to indigent defendants. For example, it may be that bystanders' bills of exceptions or other methods of reporting trial proceedings could be used in some cases. The Illinois Supreme Court appears to have broad power to promulgate rules of procedure and appellate practice. We are confident that the State will provide corrective rules to meet the problem which this case lays bare.

The judgment of the Supreme Court of Illinois is vacated and the cause is remanded to that court for further action not inconsistent with the foregoing paragraph. MR. JUSTICE FRANKFURTER joins in this disposition of the case.

Vacated and remanded.

MR. JUSTICE BURTON and MR. JUSTICE MINTON, whom MR. JUSTICE REED and MR. JUSTICE HARLAN join, dissenting. [Omitted.]

MR. JUSTICE HARLAN, dissenting.
Much as I would prefer to see free transcripts furnished to indigent defendants in all felony cases, I find myself unable to join in the Court's holding that the Fourteenth Amendment requires a State to do so or to furnish indigents with equivalent means of exercising a right to appeal. . . .
. . . It is said that a State cannot discriminate between the "rich" and the "poor" in its system of criminal appeals. That statement of course commands support, but it hardly sheds light on the true character of the problem confronting us here. Illinois has not imposed any arbitrary conditions upon the exercise of the right of appeal nor any requirements unnecessary to the effective working of its appellate system. Trial errors cannot be reviewed without an appropriate record of the proceedings below; if a transcript is used, it is surely not unreasonable to require the appellant to bear its cost; and Illinois has not foreclosed any other feasible means of preparing such a record. Nor is this a case where the State's own action has prevented a defendant from appealing. . . . All that Illinois has done is to fail to alleviate the consequences of differences in economic circumstances that exist wholly apart from any state action.
The Court thus holds that, at least in this area of criminal appeals, the Equal Protection Clause imposes on the States an affirmative duty to lift the handicaps flowing from differences in economic circumstances. That holding produces the anomalous result that a constitutional admonition to the States to treat all persons equally means in this instance that Illinois must give to some what it requires others to pay for. Granting that such a classification would be reasonable, it does not follow that a State's failure to make it can be regarded as discrimination. It may as accurately be said that the real issue in this case is not whether Illinois *has* discriminated but whether it has a duty to discriminate. . . .
I do not understand the Court to dispute either the necessity for a bill of exceptions or the reasonableness of the general requirement that the trial transcript, if used in its preparation, be paid for by the appealing party. The Court finds in the operation of these requirements, however, an invidious classification between the "rich" and the "poor." But no economic burden attendant upon the exercise of a privilege bears equally upon all, and in other circumstances the resulting differentiation is not treated as an invidious classification by the State, even though discrimination against "indigents" by name would be unconstitutional. Thus, while the exclusion of "indigents" from a free state university would deny them equal protection, requiring the payment of tuition fees surely would not, despite the resulting exclusion of those who could not afford to pay the fees. And if imposing a condition of payment is not the equivalent of a classification by the State in one case, I fail to see why it should be so regarded in another. . . .

Notes

1. *Mayer* v. *Chicago,* 404 US 189 (1972), held that even in misdemeanor cases the state must supply an indigent with a "record of sufficient completeness to permit proper consideration" of his claims on appeal.

2. *Douglas* v. *California,* 372 US 353 (1963), held that where a state grants, as a matter of right to rich and poor alike, the right to appeal criminal convictions to an appellate court, failure to provide counsel to indigents in their first appeal is a denial of equal protection. In *Ross* v. *Moffitt,*   US   (1974), the Court refused to extend the *Douglas* rule so as "to require counsel for discretionary state appeals and for applications for review to this Court."

3. *Tate* v. *Short,* 401 US 395 (1971), held that "It is a denial of equal protection to limit punishment to payment of a fine for those who are able to pay it but to convert the fine to imprisonment for those who are unable to pay it."

4. *Schilb* v. *Kuebel,* 404 US 357 (1971), sustained, by a four-to-three vote, the provisions of Illinois' bail system permitting release without charge (a) on personal recognizance or (b) on bond secured by full cash deposit, but (c) retaining 1 percent of the deposit when release was secured by bond accompanied with a 10 percent deposit.

5. *Lindsey* v. *Normet,* 405 US 56 (1972), dealt with Oregon's "forceful entry and wrongful detainer statute." The statute (1) required trial within six days after service of a complaint unless security for accruing rent was provided, (2) limited the triable issue to the tenant's default, defenses based on the landlord's breach of duty to maintain the premises being precluded, and (3) required the posting of bond in twice the amount of rent expected to accrue as a condition of appeal. The Supreme Court sustained the first two provisions but invalidated the third. It held that the "double-bond prerequisite for appealing . . . does violate the Equal Protection Clause as it arbitrarily discriminates against tenants wishing to appeal from adverse FED decisions."

C. TRAVEL

Shapiro v. Thompson

394 US 618, 89 S Ct 1322, 22 L Ed2d 600 (1969)

> Regulations limiting welfare benefits to indigents who have been residents for a year violate equal protection of law.

MR. JUSTICE BRENNAN delivered the opinion of the Court.

These three appeals were restored to the calendar for reargument. . . . Each is an appeal from a decision of a three-judge District Court holding unconstitutional a State or District of Columbia statutory provision which denies welfare assistance to residents of the State or District who have not resided within their jurisdictions for at least one year immediately preceding their applications for such assistance. We affirm the judgments of the District Courts in the three cases. . . .

There is no dispute that the effect of the waiting-period requirement in each case is to create two classes of needy resident families indistinguishable from each other except that one is composed of residents who have resided a year or more, and the second of residents who have resided less than a year, in the jurisdiction. On the basis of this sole difference the first class is granted and the second class is denied welfare aid upon which may depend the ability of the families to obtain the very means to subsist—food, shelter, and other necessities of life. In each case, the District Court found that appellees met the test for residence in their jurisdictions, as well as all other eligibility requirements except the requirements of residence for a full year prior to their applications. On reargument, appellees' central contention is that the statutory prohibition of benefits to residents of less than a year creates a classification which constitutes an invidious discrimination denying them equal protection of the laws. We agree. The interests which appellants assert are promoted by the classification either may not constitutionally be promoted by government or are not compelling governmental interests.

Primarily, appellants justify the waiting period requirement as a protective device to preserve the fiscal integrity of state public assistance programs. It is asserted that people who require welfare assistance during their first year of residence in a State are likely to become continuing burdens on state welfare programs. Therefore, the argument runs, if such people can be deterred from entering the jurisdiction by denying them welfare benefits during the first year, state programs to assist long-time residents will not be impaired by a substantial influx of indigent newcomers. . . .

We do not doubt that the one-year waiting-period device is well suited to discourage the influx of poor families in need of assistance. An indigent who desires to migrate, resettle, find a new job, and start a new life will doubtless hesitate if he knows that he must risk making the move without the possibility of falling back on state welfare assistance during his first year of residence, when his need may be most acute. But the purpose of inhibiting migration by needy persons into the State is constitutionally impermissible.

This Court long ago recognized that the nature of our Federal Union and our constitutional concepts of personal liberty unite to require that all citizens be free to travel throughout the length and breadth of our land unihibited by statutes, rules, or regulations which unreasonably burden or restrict this movement. That proposition was early stated by Chief Justice Taney in the *Passenger Cases,* 7 Howard 283, 492 (1849). . . .

We have no occasion to ascribe the source of this right to travel interstate to a particular constitutional provision. It suffices that, as Mr. Justice Stewart said for the Court in *United States* v. *Guest,* 383 US 745, 757–758 (1966):

"The constitutional right to travel from one State to another . . . occupies a position fundamental to the concept of our Federal Union. It is a right that has been firmly established and repeatedly recognized. . . ."

Alternatively, appellants argue that even if it is impermissible for a State to attempt to deter the entry of all indigents, the challenged classification may be justified as a permissible state attempt to discourage those indigents who would enter the State solely to obtain larger benefits. We observe first that none of the statutes before us is tailored to serve that objective. Rather, the class of barred newcomers is all-inclusive, lumping the great majority who come to the State for other purposes with those who come for the sole purpose of collecting higher benefits. In actual operation, therefore, the three statutes enact what in effect are nonrebuttable presumptions that every applicant for assistance in his first year of residence came to the jurisdiction solely to obtain higher benefits. Nothing whatever in any of these records supplies any basis in fact for such a presumption. . . .

Appellants argue further that the challenged classification may be sustained as an attempt to distinguish between new and old residents on the basis of the contribution they have made to the community through the payment of taxes. We have difficulty seeing how long-term residents who qualify for welfare are making a greater present contribution to the State in taxes than indigent residents who have recently arrived. . . .

Appellants next advance as justification certain administrative and related governmental objectives allegedly served by the waiting-period requirement. They argue that the requirement (1) facilitates the planning of the welfare budget; (2) provides an objective test of residency; (3) minimizes the opportunity for recipients fraudulently to receive payments from more than one jurisdiction; and (4) encourages early entry of new residents into the labor force.

At the outset, we reject appellants' argument that a mere showing of a rational relationship between the waiting period and these four admittedly permissible state objectives will suffice to justify the classification. . . . The waiting-period provision denies welfare benefits to otherwise eligible applicants solely because they have recently moved into the jurisdiction. But in moving from State to State or to the District of Columbia appellees were exercising a constitutional right, and any classification which serves to penalize the exercise of that right, unless shown to be necessary to promote a *compelling* governmental interest, is unconstitutional. . . .

The argument that the waiting-period requirement facilitates budget predictability is wholly unfounded. . . .

The argument that the waiting period serves as an administratively efficient rule of thumb for determining residency similarly will not withstand scrutiny. . . . * Similarly, there is no need for a State to use the one-year waiting period as a safeguard against fraudulent receipt of benefits; for less drastic means are available. . . .

We conclude therefore that appellants in these cases do not use and have no need to use the one-year requirement for the governmental purposes suggested. Thus, even under traditional equal protection tests a classification of welfare applicants according to whether they have lived in the State for one year would seem irrational and unconstitutional. But, of course, the traditional criteria do not apply in these cases. Since the classification here touches on the fundamental right of interstate movement, its constitutionality must be judged by the stricter standard of whether it promotes a *compelling* state interest. Under this standard, the waiting-period requirement clearly violates the Equal Protection Clause. . . .

The waiting-period requirement in the District of Columbia Code involved in No. 33 is also unconstitutional even though it was adopted by Congress as an exercise of federal power. In terms of federal power, the discrimination created by the one-year requirement violates the Due Process Clause of the Fifth Amendment. . . .

Accordingly, the judgments in Nos. 9, 33, and 34 are

Affirmed.

Mr. Justice Stewart, concurring. [Omitted.]

Mr. Chief Justice Warren, with whom Mr. Justice Black joins, dissenting. . . .

The Court insists that § 402 (b) of the Social Security Act "does not approve, much less prescribe, a one-year requirement." . . . From its reading of the legislative history it concludes that Congress did not intend to authorize the States to impose residence requirements. An examination of the relevant legislative materials compels, in my view, the opposite conclusion, *i.e.,* Congress intended to authorize state residence requirements of up to one year. . . .

Appellees suggest, however, that Congress was not motivated by rational considerations. Residence requirements are imposed, they insist, for the illegitimate purpose of keeping poor people from migrating. Not only does the legislative history point to an opposite conclusion, but it also must be noted that "[i]nto the motives which induced members of Congress to [act] . . . this Court may not enquire." . . .

The Court's decision reveals only the top of the iceberg. Lurking beneath are the multitude of situations in which States have imposed residence requirements including eligibility to vote, to engage in certain professions or occupations or to attend a state-supported university. Although the Court takes pains to avoid acknowledging the ramifications of its decision, its implications cannot be ignored. I dissent.

Mr. Justice Harlan, dissenting.

The Court today holds unconstitutional Connecticut, Pennsylvania, and District of Columbia statutes which restrict certain kinds of welfare benefits to persons who have lived within the jurisdiction for at least one year immediately preceding their applications. The Court has accomplished this result by an expansion of the comparatively new constitutional doctrine that some state statutes will be deemed to deny equal protection of the laws unless justified by a "compelling" governmental interest, and by holding that the Fifth Amendment's Due Process Clause imposes a similar limitation on federal enactments. Having decided that the "compelling interest" principle is applicable, the Court then finds that the governmental interests here asserted are either wholly impermissible or are not "compelling." For reasons which follow, I disagree both with the Court's result and with its reasoning. . . .

I conclude with the following observations. Today's decision, it seems to me, reflects to an unusual degree the current notion that this Court possesses a peculiar wisdom all its own whose capacity to lead this Nation out of its present troubles is contained only by the limits of judicial ingenuity in contriving new constitutional principles to meet each problem as it arises. For anyone who, like myself, believes that it is an essential function of this Court to maintain the constitutional divisions between state and federal authority and among the three branches of the Federal Government, today's decision is a step in the wrong direction. This resurgence of the expansive view of "equal protection" carries the seeds of more judicial interference with the state and federal legislative process, much more indeed than does the judicial application of "due process" according to traditional concepts, . . . about which some members of this Court have expressed fears as to its potentialities for setting us judges "at large." I consider it particularly unfortunate that this judicial roadblock to the powers of Congress in this field should occur at the very threshold of the current discussions regarding the "federalizing" of these aspects of welfare relief.

Note

Memorial Hospital v. *Maricopa*, 415 US 250 (1974), held void an Arizona statute requiring a year's residence as a condition to an indigent's receiving hospital or medical care at the county's expense.

D. PRIVACY

The opinion of the Court in *Roe* v. *Wade*, 410 US 113 (1973), holding void the abortion law of Texas, read in part as follows:

> The Constitution does not explicitly mention any right of privacy. In a line of decisions, however, going back perhaps as far as *Union Pacific R. Co.* v. *Botsford,* 141 US 250, 251 (1891), the Court has recognized that a right of personal privacy, or a guarantee of certain areas or zones of privacy, does exist under the Constitution. In varying contexts the Court or individual Justices have indeed found at least the roots of that right in the First Amendment, *Stanley* v. *Georgia,* 394 US 557, 564 (1969); in the Fourth and Fifth Amendments, *Terry* v. *Ohio,* 392 US 1, 8–9 (1968), *Katz* v. *United States,* 389 US 347, 350 (1967), *Boyd* v. *United States,* 116 US 616 (1886), see *Olmstead* v. *United States,* 277 US 438, 478 (1928) (BRANDEIS, J. dissenting); in the penumbras of the Bill of Rights, *Griswold* v. *Connecticut,* 381 US 479, 484–485 (1965); in the Ninth Amendment, *id.,* at 486 (GOLDBERG, J., concurring); or in the concept of liberty guaranteed by the first section of the Fourteenth Amendment, see *Meyer* v. *Nebraska,* 262 US 390, 399 (1923). These decisions make it clear that only personal rights that can be deemed "fundamental" or "implicit in the concept of ordered liberty," *Palko* v. *Connecticut,* 302 US 319, 325 (1937), are included in this guarantee of personal privacy. They also make it clear that the right has some extension to activities relating to marriage, *Loving* v. *Virginia,* 388 US 1, 12 (1967), procreation, *Skinner* v. *Oklahoma,* 316 US 535, 541–542 (1942), contraception, *Eisenstadt* v. *Baird,* 405 US 438, 453–454 (1972); *id.,* at 460, 463–465 (WHITE, J., concurring), family relationships, *Prince* v. *Massachusetts,* 321 US 158, 166 (1944), and child rearing and education, *Pierce* v. *Society of Sisters,* 268 US 510, 535 (1925), *Meyer* v. *Nebraska, supra.*
>
> This right of privacy, whether it be founded in the Fourteenth Amendment's concept of personal liberty and restrictions upon state action, as we feel it is, or, as the District Court determined, in the Ninth Amendment's reservation of rights to the people, is broad enough to encompass a woman's decision whether or not to terminate her pregnancy. . . .

Justice Blackmun delivered this opinion of the Court in which Chief Justice Burger and Justices Douglas, Brennan, Stewart, Marshall, and Powell joined. The decision and opinion of the Court, buttressed by three concurring opinions, clearly established the right to privacy as a constitutionally protected right. The opinion, however, was written in terms of due process instead of equal protection. I know of no case in which a majority of the justices have singled out privacy as a "fundamental" right entitled to the protection of strict scrutiny by the courts under the Equal Protection Clause. *Eisenstadt* v. *Baird,* 405 US 438 (1972), was a close contender for that distinction.

Chapter 12

Criminal Procedure

The provisions of the original Constitution dealing with criminal procedure were discussed in chapter 6. To these the Bill of Rights adds many other safeguards, almost all of which have been incorporated into the Fourteenth Amendment as limitations on the states. A half-dozen of these provisions are singled out here for emphasis.

A. SEARCHES AND SEIZURES

Introduction

"The right of the people to be secure in their persons, houses, papers, and effects, against unreasonable searches and seizures, shall not be violated, and no warrants shall issue but upon probable cause, supported by oath or affirmation, and particularly describing the place to be searched, and the persons or things to be seized," reads the Fourth Amendment. Invasion of the privacy of colonial homes by the issuance of "writs of assistance," or blanket search warrants, authorizing British customs officers to search any house for smuggled goods had been roundly denounced by James Otis in the decade preceding the American Revolution.

As a means of making the prohibition against unreasonable searches meaningful, in *Weeks* v. *United States,* 232 US 383 (1914), the Supreme Court enunciated a rule that evidence seized through an unlawful search by federal officers could not be used as evidence in the federal courts. This was a departure from the English common law which judged the admissibility of evidence by pertinency and relevance. There was much debate over whether the rule of the *Weeks* case was derived from the Constitution or was merely a rule imposed over the lower federal courts by the Supreme Court in its supervisory power. Prior to *Mapp* v. *Ohio,* 367 US 643 (1961), the exclusionary rule did not apply to trials in state courts. That case held the exclusionary rule to be a constitutional rule, applicable in both federal and state courts. Debate over the matter continues, however. See the opinion by Chief Justice Burger in *Bivens* v. *Six Unknown Named Agents,* page 437.

Issuance of Warrant

The question of what constitutes "probable cause" for the issuance of a search warrant has been the subject of considerable attention. *Aguilar* v. *Texas,* 378 US 108 (1964), held that, to authorize the issuance of a search warrant, the affidavit made to a magistrate must contain not mere conclusions, but facts or an account of circumstances from which the magistrate may judge probable cause. Compare *Spinelli* v. *United States,* 393 US 410 (1969), and *Whiteley* v. *Warden,* 401 US 560 (1971). A city may authorize the issuance of arrest warrants by a court clerk who is disengaged from law enforcement. *Shadwick* v. *City of Tampa,* 407 US 345 (1972).

Exceptions to Requirement of Warrant

1. *Consent.* *Schneckloth* v. *Bustamonte,* 412 US 218 (1973), reaffirmed the principles that a valid search of property can be made without a warrant if proper consent is voluntarily given. It held that "voluntariness" was to be determined from the totality of the surrounding circumstances, and that the state was not required to prove that the person giving the consent knew that he had a right to withhold his consent.

   United States v. *Matlock,* 415 US 164 (1974), held that the state is not limited to proof that consent to search was given by the defendant but may show that permission was obtained from a third party possessing common authority over the premises searched.

2. *Circumstances Where Warrant Is Impractical.* *Carroll* v. *United States,* 267 US 132 (1925), sustained the right of the government, upon probable cause, to search an automobile without a warrant under circumstances making it "impracticable to secure a warrant because the vehicle can be quickly moved out of the locality or jurisdiction in which the warrant must be sought." But Chief Justice Taft emphasized that it would be "intolerable and unreasonable" for police to stop and search cars indiscriminately. "[Those] entitled to use the public highways have a right to free passage without interruption or search unless there is known to a competent official authorized to search, probable cause for believing that their vehicles are carrying contraband or illegal merchandise."

   The absence of this element of probable cause led the Court in *Almeida-Sanchez* v. *United States,* 413 US 266 (1973), to hold illegal a warrantless search of an automobile by the Border Patrol twenty-five miles north of the Mexican border. In dissent, Justice White wrote: "The judgment of Congress obviously was that there are circumstances in which it is reasonably necessary, in the enforcement of the immigration laws, to search vehicles and other private property for aliens, without warrant or probable cause, and at locations other than at the border. To disagree with the legislative judgment is to invalidate § 1357 in the face of the contrary opinion of

Congress that its legislation comported with the standard of reasonableness of the Fourth Amendment."

Cardwell v. *Lewis,*   US   (1974), expanded the "automobile exception" to the requirement of a warrant. Lewis, suspected of murder, was arrested under a warrant. Later, his automobile, found on a commercial parking lot, was towed to a police impoundment. The next day a warrantless examination of the outside of the car revealed that one of its tires matched the cast of a tire impression made at the crime scene and that paint samples taken from the car matched the paint on the fender of the victim's car. In a five- to-four decision, the Court sustained use of this evidence in the trial of Lewis. Justice Blackmun wrote: "A car has little capacity for escaping public scrutiny. It travels public thoroughfares where both its occupants and its contents are in plain view. 'What a person knowingly exposes to the public, even in his own home or office, is not a subject of Fourth Amendment protection.' . . . This is not to say that no part of the interior of an automobile has Fourth Amendment protection; the exercise of a desire to be mobile does not, of course, waive one's right to be free of unreasonable government intrusion. But insofar as Fourth Amendment protection extends to a motor vehicle, it is the right of privacy that is the touchstone of our inquiry. . . . With the 'search' limited to the examination of the tire on the wheel and the taking of paint scrapings from the exterior of the vehicle left in the public parking lot, we fail to comprehend what expectation of privacy was infringed."

Terry v. *Ohio,* 392 US 1 (1968), sustained the right of a police officer, upon observing "unusual conduct which leads him reasonably to conclude in light of his experience that criminal activity may be afoot," to stop and frisk a suspect and to seize any assault weapon discovered. The Court held, however, that if a policeman's action in thrusting his hand into a suspect's pocket is neither motivated by nor limited to the objective of protection but is a search to find narcotics, it is reversible error. *Sibron* v. *New York,* 392 US 40 (1968).

3. *Incident to Lawful Arrest.*   A search may be made incident to a lawful arrest, and a warrant is not always needed for an arrest. It is undebatable that a police officer may seize the culprit if he sees a crime being committed, and the general rule is that an arrest without a warrant is also valid if at the time the officers made the arrest "the facts and circumstances within their knowledge and of which they had reasonably trustworthy information were sufficient to warrant a prudent man in believing that the petitioner had committed or was committing an offense." *Beck* v. *Ohio,* 379 US 89 (1964), quoted approvingly in *McCray* v. *Illinois,* 386 US 300 (1967). It is debatable whether the "reasonable grounds" necessary for an arrest without a warrant are any weightier than the "probable cause" necessary for the issuance of a search warrant.

Cady v. *Dombrowski,* 413 US 433 (1973), sustained the use of evidence secured by a warrantless search of a wrecked automobile the day after the accident when the automobile was in a garage to which the police had towed it and the drunken driver was in jail. Justices Brennan, Douglas, Stewart, and Marshall dissented.

United States v. *Edwards,* 415 US 800 (1974), sustained the use of evidence obtained from a warrantless seizure of a prisoner's clothes the day after he was arrested. Edwards was arrested shortly after 11 P.M. and taken to jail. The next morning when substitute clothing became available, the police took Edwards' clothing for laboratory analysis. A majority of the justices held this to be reasonable. Four justices dissented, holding that the Fourth Amendment's requirement of a warrant had been ignored.

4. *Administrative Inspection.* "In *Camara* v. *Municipal Court* [387 US 523 (1967)] an inspection of every structure in an entire area to enforce the building codes was deemed reasonable under the Fourth Amendment without probable cause, or suspicion that any particular house or structure was in violation of law, although a warrant, issuable without probable cause, or reasonable suspicion of a violation, was required with respect to nonconsenting property owners. Also, in *Collonade Catering Corp.* v. *United States,* 397 US 72 (1970), MR. JUSTICE DOUGLAS, writing for the Court and recognizing that the Fourth Amendment bars only unreasonable searches and seizures, ruled that the historic power of the Government to control the liquor traffic authorized warrantless inspection of licensed premises without probable cause, or reasonable suspicion, not to check on liquor quality or conditions under which it was sold, but solely to enforce the collection of the federal excise tax. *United States* v. *Biswell,* 406 US 311 (1972), involved the Gun Control Act of 1968 and its authorization to federal officers to inspect firearms dealers. That public need to enforce an important regulatory program was held to justify random inspection of licensed establishments without warrant and probable cause." White, J., in *Almeida-Sanchez* v. *United States,* 413 US 266 (1973).

Wyman v. *James,* 400 US 307 (1971), rejected the thesis, as applied in the context, "that home visitation is a search and, when not consented to, or when not supported by a warrant based on probable cause, violates the beneficiary's Fourth and Fourteenth Amendment rights." The chief facts involved were as follows: Barbara James of New York City applied for AFDC assistance shortly before childbirth. A caseworker visited her apartment, and assistance was authorized. Two years later a caseworker wrote Mrs. James that she would visit her home on May 14. "Mrs. James telephoned the worker that, although she was willing to supply information 'reasonable and relevant' to her need for public assistance, any discussion was not to take place at her home. The worker told Mrs. James that she was required by law to visit in her home, and that refusal to permit the visit would result in the termination of assistance. Permission was still denied."

The Court held that a caseworker's home visit was not "unreasonable," even though it be assumed that it be a "search." In dispensing charitable funds, the state has a right to know how the funds are being used, explained Justice Blackmun. "Mrs. James has the 'right' to refuse the home visit, but a consequence in the form of cessation of aid . . . flows from that refusal. The choice is entirely hers, and nothing of constitutional magnitude is involved."

Air Pollution Variance Board v. *Western Alfalfa Corp.,*   US   (1974), sustained the right of a health inspector to conduct air quality tests on a company's outdoor premises without a warrant or consent. The Court branded the alleged invasion of privacy as "abstract and theoretical."

5. *Postal Inspection.* *United States* v. *Van Leeuwen,* 397 US 249 (1970), reaffirmed the established principle that first-class mail "can only be opened and examined under like warrant . . . as is required when papers are subjected to search in one's own household." In the *Van Leeuwen* case, however, a conviction of illegally importing gold coins based upon evidence secured through postal opening of first-class mail was sustained. Van Leeuwen mailed two twelve-pound packages at a small

post office in Washington, near the Canadian border. "When the postal clerk told a policeman who happened to be present that he was suspicious of the packages, the policeman at once noticed that the return address on the packages was a vacant housing area . . . and that the license plates of respondent's car were British Columbia." The postman retained the two packages for twenty-nine hours, during which time the police found out that both addressees (one in California and the other in Tennessee) were under investigation for trafficking in illegal coins, and they obtained a search warrant. They then opened, inspected, resealed, and sent the packages on their way. The Court held that the action in this case could not be said to be "unreasonable."

Conclusion. The Court is frequently closely divided on cases involving searches and seizures without a warrant. Justices voting to sustain exceptions to the warrant place emphasis upon the first half of the Searches and Seizure Clause which reads: "The right of the people to be secure . . . against unreasonable searches and seizures shall not be violated. . . ." They concern themselves with whether the search was reasonable. Whereas justices voting against exceptions to requirement of a warrant emphasize the second half, ". . . and no warrant shall issue but upon probable cause, supported by oath or affirmation, and particularly describing the places to be searched, and the persons or things to be seized."

Extent of Search

A warrant must describe "particularly . . . the place to be searched, and the person or things to be seized"; but how far may police go in searching incident to a lawful arrest with or without an arrest warrant?

Dicta in the 1968 frisking cases raised doubt as to the extent to which a police officer may go in searching the person of a suspect placed under lawful arrest. *United States* v. *Robinson,* 42 LW 4055 (1973), held that "in the case of a lawful custodial arrest a full search of the person is not only an exception to the warrant requirement of the Fourth Amendment, but is also a 'reasonable' search under that Amendment." The case sustained the use in evidence of heroin seized from the pocket of a person arrested for driving without a license.

Earlier cases had given state police much leeway in determining the extent to which the premises where an arrest was made should be searched. *Chimel* v. *California,* 395 US 752 (1969), however, sharply limited the area of the search. The majority opinion stated: "There is ample justification . . . for a search of the arrestee's person and the area 'within his immediate control'—construing that phrase to mean the area from within which he might gain possession of a weapon or destructible evidence. There is no comparable justification, however, for routinely searching any room other than that in which an arrest occurs—or, for that matter, for searching through all the desk drawers or other closed or concealed areas in that room itself. Such searches, in the absence of well-recognized exceptions, may be made only under the authority of a search warrant." *Williams* v. *United States,* 401 US 646 (1971), held that the limitations imposed by the *Chimel* case would not be applied retroactively. *Coolidge* v. *New Hampshire,* 403 US 443 (1971), revealed a wide diversity of views by the justices. Mr. Justice Harlan remarked that "it is apparent that the law of search and seizure is due for an overhauling."

Wiretapping and Electronic Surveillance

Olmstead v. *United States,* 277 US 438 (1928), held that wiretapping by police was not an unreasonable search and seizure within the meaning of the Fourth Amendment because no physical intrusion into the home (or trespass) was involved. The effect of this ruling was diminished by the holding in *Nardone* v. *United States,* 302 US 379 (1937), that the Communications Act of 1934 made wiretapping illegal. In *Katz* v. *United States,* 389 US 347 (1967), the trespass doctrine of the *Olmstead* case was greatly modified.

Katz was convicted under an indictment charging him with transmitting wagering information by telephone across state lines in violation of federal law. The prosecution used evidence of Katz's end of conversations, overheard by FBI agents who had attached an electronic listening and recording device to the outside of the telephone booth from which the calls were made. In reversing the conviction, the majority of the Court adopted the theory that the electronic surveillance used was a "search and seizure" and "that searches conducted outside the judicial process, without prior approval by judge or magistrate, are *per se* unreasonable under the Fourth Amendment—subject only to a few specifically established and well-delineated exceptions."

Alderman v. *United States,* 394 US 165 (1969), held that "Suppression of the product of a Fourth Amendment violation can be successfully urged only by those whose rights were violated by the search itself, and not those who are aggrieved solely by the introduction of damaging evidence. Thus, codefendants and coconspirators have no special standing and cannot prevent the admission against them of information which has been obtained through electronic surveillance which is illegal against another."

United States v. *White,* 401 US 745 (1971), sustained a conviction of narcotics violations where evidence was admitted which had been obtained by a government agent who carried a concealed electronic transmitter without a warrant. In announcing the judgment of the Court, Justice White wrote:

> The Court of Appeals understood *Katz* to render inadmissible against White the agent's testimony concerning conversations which Jackson broadcast to them. We cannot agree. *Katz* involved no revelation to the Government by a party to conversations with the defendant nor did the Court indicate in any way that a defendant has a justifiable and constitutionally protected expectation that a person with whom he is conversing will not then or later reveal the conversation to the police.

> *Hoffa* v. *United States,* 385 US 293 (1966), which was left undisturbed by *Katz,* held that however strongly a defendant may trust an apparent colleague, his expectations in this respect are not protected by the Fourth Amendment when it turns out that the colleague is a government agent regularly communicating with the authorities. In these circumstances, "no interest legitimately protected by the Fourth Amendment is involved," for that amendment affords no protection to "a wrongdoer's misplaced belief that a person to whom he voluntarily confides his wrongdoing will not reveal it." *Hoffa* v. *United States,* at 302. No warrant to "search and seize" is required in such circumstances, nor is it when the Government sends to defendant's home a secret agent who conceals his identity and makes a purchase of narcotics from the accused, *Lewis* v. *United States,* 385 US 206 (1966), or when the same agent,

unbeknown to the defendant, carries electronic equipment to record the defendant's words and the evidence so gathered is later offered in evidence. *Lopez* v. *United States,* 373 US 427 (1963). . . .

Concededly a police agent who conceals his police connections may write down for official use his conversations with a defendant and testify concerning them, without a warrant authorizing his encounters with the defendant and without otherwise violating the latter's Fourth Amendment rights. . . . For constitutional purposes, no different result is required if the agent instead of immediately reporting and transcribing his conversations with defendant, either (1) simultaneously records them with electronic equipment which he is carrying on his person, *Lopez* v. *United States, supra;* (2) or carries radio equipment which simultaneously transmits the conversations either to recording equipment located elsewhere or to other agents monitoring the transmitting frequency. On *Lee* v. *United States, supra.* If the conduct and revelations of an agent operating without electronic equipment do not invade the defendant's constitutionally justifiable expectations of privacy, neither does a simultaneous recording of the same conversations made by the agent, or by others from transmissions received from the agent to whom the defendant is talking and whose trustworthiness the defendant necessarily risks.

Omnibus Crime Control and Safe Streets Act of 1968. Title III of this act (82 Stat 197) prohibits the interception of any wire or oral communication by use of any mechanical device, except as specified, and it prohibits the use of evidence secured in violation of its terms against any "aggrieved person" in any legal proceeding, national, state, or local. It permits national, state, and local police officers to secure judicial warrants authorizing wiretapping and electronic surveillance under conditions similar to those governing the granting of search warrants. One section of the act (18 USC § 2511(3)) states that "Nothing contained in this chapter . . . shall limit the constitutional power of the President to take such measures as he deems necessary to protect . . . the security of the United States. . . ."

United States v. *United States District Court,* 407 US 297 (1972), held that this section conferred no authority but was merely a recognition that the President had a responsibility under the Constitution to protect the national security, subject to the limitations of the Fourth Amendment. "[T]hose charged with investigative and prosecutorial duty should not be the sole judges of when to utilize constitutionally sensitive means in pursuing their tasks. The historical judgment which the Fourth Amendment accepts, is that unreviewed executive discretion may yield too readily to pressure to obtain incriminating evidence and overlook potential invasion of privacy and protected speech." The case dealt with evidence gained by wiretap against domestic organizations engaged in subversion. "We have not addressed, and express no opinion as to, the issues which may be involved with respect to activities of foreign powers or their agents," stated the Court.

United States v. *Kahn,* 415 US 143 (1974), sustained a broad application of the wiretap provision of the 1968 act. Upon probable cause, the Department of Justice secured a court order authorizing the interception of wire communication of Irving Kahn and "others as yet unknown" over two named telephone lines in order to obtain information concerning gambling offenses. Government agents intercepted incriminating calls made between Kahn and his wife and also between Mrs. Kahn and "a known gambling figure." The lower federal courts sustained a motion to suppress use of the conversations between Mrs. Kahn and the known gambling figure. The Supreme Court reversed, holding the conversations to be admissible evidence. Justices Douglas, Brennan, and Marshall dissented. Condemning general warrants, Douglas wrote: "Under today's decision a wiretap warrant apparently need specify but one name and a national dragnet becomes effective. Members of the family of the suspect, visitors in his home, doctors, ministers, merchants, teachers, attorneys, and everyone having any possible connection with the Kahn household are caught up in this web."

United States v. *Giordano,* 416 US 505 (1974), held inadmissible evidence obtained against narcotics offense suspects through wiretaps authorized by the chief judge of the District Court of the District of Columbia upon an application made by the attorney general's executive assistant. The decision was based on statutory rather than constitutional grounds.

The Omnibus Crime Control of 1968 provides in 18 USC § 2516 (1) that "the Attorney General, or any Assistant Attorney General specially designated by the Attorney General, may authorize an application to a Federal judge of competent jurisdiction for, and such judge may grant in conformity with section 2518 of this chapter an order authorizing or approving the interception of wire or oral communications. . . ." For a unanimous Court, Justice White wrote:

> The Act is not as clear in some respects as it might be, but it is at once apparent that it not only limits the crimes for which intercept authority may be obtained but also imposes important preconditions to obtaining any intercept authority at all. Congress legislated in considerable detail in providing for applications and orders authorizing wiretapping and evinced the clear intent to make doubly sure that the statutory authority be used with restraint and only where the circumstances warrant the surreptitious interception of wire and oral communications. These procedures were not to be routinely employed as the initial step in criminal investigation. Rather, the applicant must state and the court must find that normal investigative procedures have been tried and failed or reasonably appear to be unlikely to succeed if tried or to be too dangerous. §§ 2518 (1) (c) and (3) (c). The Act plainly calls for the prior, informed judgment of enforcement officers desiring court approval for intercept authority, and investigative personnel may not themselves ask a judge for authority to wiretap or eavesdrop. The mature judgment of a particular, responsible Department of Justice official is interposed as a critical precondition to any judicial order.

The Court held inadmissible not only the evidence obtained illegally under the original court order granted upon application of the attorney general's executive assistant, but also all evidence secured by an extension of the original court order granted upon application of the attorney general himself. For the majority, Justice White wrote: "In our view, the results of the conversations overheard under the initial order were essential, both in fact and in law, to any extension of the intercept authority. Accordingly, communications intercepted under the extension order are derivative evidence and must be suppressed." On this point, Chief Justice Burger and Justices Blackmun, Powell, and Rehnquist dissented. Justice Powell wrote:

> . . . the derivative taint of illegal activity does not extend to the ends of the earth but only until it is dissipated by an intervening event. Of course, the presence of an independent source would always suffice.

The independent source rule has as much validity in the context of a search warrant as in any other. . . . The ultimate inquiry on a motion to suppress evidence seized pursuant to a warrant is not whether the underlying affidavit contained allegations based on illegally obtained evidence, but whether, putting aside all tainted allegations, the independent and lawful information stated in the affidavit suffices to show probable cause. . . . Judge Weinfield aptly stated the point in *United States* v. *Epstein,* 240 F. Supp. 80 (SDNY 1965):

"There is authority, and none to the contrary, that when a warrant issues upon an affidavit containing both proper and improper grounds, and the proper grounds—considered alone—are more than sufficient to support a finding of probable cause, inclusion of the improper grounds does not vitiate the entire affidavit and invalidate the warrant." *Id.,* at 82.

I know of no precedent holding to the contrary.

The application of this principle to the pen register extension orders is clear beyond doubt. The original pen register order was based on a showing of probable cause made prior to, and therefore undeniably independent of, the invalid wiretap. The affidavit supporting the first extension of the pen register order incorporated the allegations contained in the affidavit submitted for the original order and provided the additional untainted information that Giordano had sold heroin to a narcotics agent on October 17, 1970. The affidavit for the second extension of the pen register order is not included in the record, but there is no reason to doubt that it made a similar incorporation by reference of the earlier, untainted allegations. I would hold the evidence obtained under the first pen register extension order admissible and remand the case for determination of whether evidence obtained under the second extension should be admitted as well.

The basis for the majority's conclusion to the contrary is far from apparent. In the final footnote to its opinion, the Court states that the evidence obtained under the defective original wiretap order "should be considered a critical element in extending the pen register authority." The majority does not suggest, however, that the original pen register order was based on anything less than probable cause. Nor does it deny that the affidavit supporting the extension of the pen register authority fully incorporated the earlier untainted allegations. And, finally, the majority does not contradict the established principle that a warrant based on an affidavit containing tainted allegations may nevertheless be valid if the independent and lawful information stated in the affidavit shows probable cause. In light of these significant silences, the majority's bare assertion that the tainted evidence obtained under the original wiretap order was a "critical element" in the extension of the pen register authority is, to me, an unexplained conclusion—not a rationale.

Mapp v. Ohio

367 US 643, 81 S Ct 1648, 6 L Ed2d 1081 (1961)

All evidence obtained by searches and seizures in violation of the federal Constitution is inadmissible in a criminal trial in a state court.

MR. JUSTICE CLARK delivered the opinion of the Court.

On May 23, 1957, three Cleveland police officers arrived at appellant's [Dolree Mapp's] residence in that city pursuant to information that "a person [was] hiding out in the home, who was wanted for questioning in connection with a recent bombing, and that there was a large amount of policy paraphernalia being hidden in the home." Miss Mapp and her daughter by a former marriage lived on the top floor of the two-family dwelling. Upon their arrival at that house, the officers knocked on the door and demanded entrance but appellant, after telephoning her attorney, refused to admit them without a search warrant. They advised their headquarters of the situation and undertook a surveillance of the house.

The officers again sought entrance some three hours later when four or more additional officers arrived on the scene. When Miss Mapp did not come to the door immediately, at least one of the several doors to the house was forcibly opened and the policemen gained admittance. Meanwhile Miss Mapp's attorney arrived, but the officers, having secured their own entry, and continuing in their defiance of the law, would permit him neither to see Miss Mapp nor to enter the house. It appears that Miss Mapp was halfway down the stairs from the upper floor to the front door when the officers, in this highhanded manner, broke into the hall. She demanded to see the search warrant. A paper, claimed to be a warrant, was held up by one of the officers. She grabbed the "warrant" and placed it in her bosom. A struggle ensued in which the officers recovered the piece of paper and as a result of which they handcuffed appellant because she had been "belligerent" in resisting their official rescue of the "warrant" from her person. Running roughshod over appellant, a policeman "grabbed" her, "twisted [her] hand," and she "yelled [and] pleaded with him" because "it was hurting." Appellant, in handcuffs, was then forcibly taken upstairs to her bedroom where the officers searched a dresser, a chest of drawers, a closet and some suitcases. They also looked into a photo album and through personal papers belonging to the appellant. The search spread to the rest of the second floor including the child's bedroom, the living room, the kitchen and a dinette. The basement of the building and a trunk found therein were also searched. The obscene materials for possession of which she was ultimately convicted were discovered in the course of that widespread search.

At the trial no search warrant was produced by the prosecution, nor was the failure to produce one explained or accounted for. . . .

The State says that even if the search were made without authority, or otherwise unreasonably, it is not prevented from using the unconstitutionally seized evidence at trial, citing *Wolf* v. *Colorado,* 338 US 25 (1949), in which this Court did indeed hold "that in a prosecution in a State court for a State crime the Fourteenth Amendment does not forbid the admission of evidence obtained by an unreasonable search and seizure." At p. 33. On this appeal . . . it is urged once again that we review that holding.

Seventy-five years ago, in *Boyd* v. *United States,* 116 US 616, 630 (1886), considering the Fourth and Fifth Amendments as running "almost into each other" on the facts before it, this Court held that the doctrines of those Amendments

"apply to all invasions on the part of the government and its employees of the sanctity of a man's home and the privacies of life. It is not the breaking of his doors, and the rummaging of his drawers, that constitutes the essence of the offence; but it is the invasion of his indefeasible right of personal security, personal liberty and private property. . . ."

Concluding, the Court specifically referred to the use of the evidence there seized as "unconstitutional." At p. 638.

Less than 30 years after *Boyd,* this Court, in *Weeks* v. *United States,* 232 US 383 (1914), . . . dealing with the use of the evidence unconstitutionally seized, . . . concluded:

> "If letters and private documents can thus be seized and held and used in evidence against a citizen accused of an offense, the protection of the Fourth Amendment declaring his right to be secure against such searches and seizures is of no value, and, so far as those thus placed are concerned, might as well be stricken from the Constitution. The efforts of the courts and their officials to bring the guilty to punishment, praiseworthy as they are, are not to be aided by the sacrifice of those great principles established by years of endeavor and suffering which have resulted in their embodiment in the fundamental law of the land." At p. 393. . . .

. . . This Court has ever since required of federal law officers a strict adherence to that command which this Court has held to be a clear, specific, and constitutionally required—even if judicially implied—deterrent safeguard without insistence upon which the Fourth Amendment would have been reduced to "a form of words." Holmes, J., *Silverthorne Lumber Co.* v. *United States,* 251 US 385, 392 (1920). It meant, quite simply, that "conviction by means of unlawful seizures and enforced confessions . . . should find no sanction in the judgments of the courts . . . ," *Weeks* v. *United States, supra,* at 392, and that such evidence "shall not be used at all." *Silverthorne Lumber Co.* v. *United States, supra,* at 392.

There are in the cases of this Court some passing references to the *Weeks* rule as being one of evidence. But the plain and unequivocal language of *Weeks*—and its later paraphrase in *Wolf*—to the effect that the *Weeks* rule is of constitutional origin, remains entirely undisturbed. . . .

In 1949, 35 years after *Weeks* was announced, this Court, in *Wolf* v. *Colorado, supra,* again for the first time, discussed the effect of the Fourth Amendment upon the States through the operation of the Due Process Clause of the Fourteenth Amendment. It said:

> "[W]e have no hesitation in saying that were a State affirmatively to sanction such police incursion into privacy it would run counter to the guaranty of the Fourteenth Amendment." At p. 28.

Nevertheless, after declaring that the "security of one's privacy against arbitrary intrusion by the police" is "implicit in 'the concept of ordered liberty' and as such enforceable against the States through the Due Process Clause" . . . the Court decided that the *Weeks* exclusionary rule would not then be imposed upon the States as "an essential ingredient of the right." 338 US, at 27–29. The Court's reasons . . . were bottomed on factual considerations. . . .

Since the Fourth Amendment's right of privacy has been declared enforceable against the States through the Due Process Clause of the Fourteenth, it is enforceable against them by the same sanction of exclusion as is used against the Federal Government. Were it otherwise, then just as without the *Weeks* rule the assurance against unreasonable federal searches and seizures would be "a form of words,". . . so too, without that rule the freedom from state invasions of privacy would be so ephemeral and so neatly severed from its conceptual nexus with the freedom from all brutish means of coercing evidence as not to merit this Court's high regard as a freedom "implicit in the concept of ordered liberty.". . .

Moreover, our holding that the exclusionary rule is an essential part of both the Fourth and Fourteenth Amendments is not only the logical dictate of prior cases, but it also makes very good sense. There is no war between the Constitution and common sense. . . .

The judgment of the Supreme Court of Ohio is reversed and the cause remanded for further proceedings not inconsistent with this opinion.

Reversed and remanded.

[The concurring opinions of JUSTICES BLACK and DOUGLAS, and the memorandum of JUSTICE STEWART are omitted.]

MR. JUSTICE HARLAN, whom MR. JUSTICE FRANKFURTER and MR. JUSTICE WHITTAKER, join, dissenting. . . .

At the heart of the majority's opinion in this case is the following syllogism: (1) the rule excluding in federal criminal trials evidence which is the product of an illegal search and seizure is "part and parcel" of the Fourth Amendment; (2) *Wolf* held that the "privacy" assured against federal action by the Fourth Amendment is also protected against state action by the Fourteenth Amendment; and (3) it is therefore "logically and constitutionally necessary" that the *Weeks* exclusionary rule should also be enforced against the States.

This reasoning ultimately rests on the unsound premise that because *Wolf* carried into the States, as part of "the concept of ordered liberty" embodied in the Fourteenth Amendment, the principle of "privacy" underlying the Fourth Amendment (338 US, at 27), it must follow that whatever configurations of the Fourth Amendment have been developed in the particularizing federal precedents are likewise to be deemed a part of "ordered liberty," and as such are enforceable against the States. For me, this does not follow at all.

It cannot be too much emphasized that what was recognized in *Wolf* was not that the Fourth Amendment *as such* is enforceable against the States as a facet of due process, . . . a view of the Fourteenth Amendment which . . . has long since been discredited, but the principle of privacy "which is at the core of the Fourth Amendment." (*Id.,* at 27.) It would not be proper to expect or impose any precise equivalence, either as regards the scope of the right or the means of its implementation, between the requirements of the Fourth and Fourteenth Amendments. For the Fourth, unlike what was said in Wolf of the Fourteenth, does not state a general principle only; it is a particular command, having its setting in a pre-existing legal context on which both interpreting decisions and enabling statutes must at least build. . . .

[W]e are told that imposition of the *Weeks* rule on the States makes "very good sense," in that it will promote recognition by state and federal officials of their "mutual obligation to respect the same fundamental criteria" in their approach to law enforcement, and will avoid " 'needless conflict between state and federal courts.' " Indeed the majority now finds an incongruity in *Wolf's* discriminating perception between the demands of "ordered liberty" as respects the basic right of "privacy" and the means of securing it among the States. That perception, resting both on a sensitive regard for our federal system and a sound recognition of this Court's remoteness from particular state problems, is for me the strength of that decision.

An approach which regards the issue as one of achieving procedural symmetry or of serving administrative convenience surely disfigures the boundaries of this Court's functions in relation to the state and federal courts. . . .

A state conviction comes to us as the complete product of a sovereign judicial system. Typically a case will have been tried in a trial court, tested in some final appellate court, and will go no further. In the comparatively rare instance when a conviction is reviewed by us on due process grounds we deal then with a finished product in the creation of which we are allowed no hand, and our task, far from being one of over-all supervision, is, speaking generally, restricted to a determination of whether the prosecution was Constitutionally fair. The specifics of trial procedure, which in every mature legal system will vary greatly in detail, are within the sole competence of the States. I do not see how it can be said that a trial becomes unfair simply because a State determines the evidence may be considered by the trier of fact, regardless of how it was obtained, if it is relevant to the one issue with which the trial is concerned, the guilt or innocence of the accused. Of course, a court may use its procedures as an incidental means of pursuing other ends than the correct resolution of the controversies before it. Such indeed is the *Weeks* rule, but if a State does not choose to use its courts in this way, I do not believe that this Court is empowered to impose this much-debated procedure on local courts, however efficacious we may consider the *Weeks* rule to be as a means of securing Constitutional rights. . . .

I regret that I find so unwise in principle and so inexpedient in policy a decision motivated by the high purpose of increasing respect for Constitutional rights. But in the last analysis I think this Court can increase respect for the Constitution only if it rigidly respects the limitations which the Constitution places upon it, and respects as well the principles inherent in its own processes. In the present case I think we exceed both, and that our voice becomes only a voice of power, not of reason.

Note

Proposal by Chief Justice Burger. In a dissenting opinion in *Bivens* v. *Six Unknown Federal Narcotics Agents*, 403 US 388 (1971), the chief justice wrote:

This case has significance far beyond its facts and its holding. For more than 55 years this Court has enforced a rule under which evidence of undoubted reliability and probative value has been suppressed and excluded from criminal cases whenever it was obtained in violation of the Fourth Amendment. *Weeks* v. *United States*, 232 US 383 (1914); *Boyd* v. *United States*, 116 US 616, 633 (1886) (dictum). This rule was extended to the States in *Mapp* v. *Ohio*, 367 US 645 (1961). The rule has rested on a theory that suppression of evidence in these circumstances was imperative to deter law enforcement authorities from using improper methods to obtain evidence.

The deterrence theory underlying the suppression doctrine, or exclusionary rule, has a certain appeal in spite of the high price society pays for such a drastic remedy.

Notwithstanding its plausibility, many judges and lawyers and some of our most distinguished legal scholars have never quite been able to escape the force of Cardozo's statement of the doctrine's anomalous result:

"The criminal is to go free because the constable has blundered. . . . A room is searched against the law, and the body of a murdered man is found. . . . The privacy of the home has been infringed, and the murderer goes free." *People* v. *Defore,* 242 NY 13, 21, 23–24, 150 NE 585, 587, 588 (1926).

The plurality opinion in *Irvine* v. *California,* 347 US 128, 136 (1954), catalogued the doctrine's defects:

"Rejection of the evidence does nothing to punish the wrong-doing official, while it may, and likely will, release the wrong-doing defendant. It deprives society of its remedy against one lawbreaker because he has been pursued by another. It protects one against whom incriminating evidence is discovered, but does nothing to protect innocent persons who are the victims of illegal but fruitless searches." . . .

This evidentiary rule is unique to American jurisprudence. Although the English and Canadian legal systems are highly regarded, neither has adopted our rule. . . .

Some clear demonstration of the benefits and effectiveness of the exclusionary rule is required to justify it in view of the high price it extracts from society—the release of countless guilty criminals. . . . But there is no empirical evidence to support the claim that the rule actually deters illegal conduct of law enforcement officials. . . .

There are several reasons for this failure. The rule does not apply any direct sanction to the individual official whose illegal conduct results in the exclusion of evidence in a criminal trial. . . .

The suppression doctrine vaguely assumes that law enforcement is a monolithic governmental enterprise. . . . But the prosecutor who loses his case because of police misconduct is not an official in the police department; he can rarely set in motion any corrective action or administrative penalties. Moreover, he does not have control or direction over police procedures or police actions that lead to the exclusion of evidence. It is the rare exception when a prosecutor takes part in arrests, searches, or seizures so that he can guide police action. . . .

Instead of continuing to enforce the suppression doctrine inflexibly, rigidly, and mechanically, we should view it as one of the experimental steps in the great tradition of the common law and acknowledge its shortcomings. But in the same spirit we should be prepared to discontinue what the experience of over half a century has shown neither deters errant officers nor affords a remedy to the totally innocent victims of official misconduct.

I do not propose, however, that we abandon the suppression doctrine until some meaningful alternative can be developed. . . .

The problems of both error and deliberate misconduct by law enforcement officials call for a workable remedy. Private damage actions against individual police officers concededly have not adequately met this requirement. . . .

I conclude, therefore, that . . . Congress should develop an administrative or quasi-judicial remedy against the government itself to afford compensation and restitution for persons whose Fourth Amendment rights have been violated. The venerable doctrine of *respondeat superior* in our tort law provides an entirely appropriate conceptual basis for this remedy. If, for example, a security guard privately employed by a department store commits an assault or other tort on a customer such as an improper search, the victim has a simple and obvious remedy—an action for money damages against the guard's employer, the department store. . . . Such a statutory scheme would have the added advantage of providing some remedy to the completely innocent persons who are sometimes the victims of illegal police conduct—something that the suppression doctrine, of course, can never accomplish.

A simple structure would suffice. For example, Congress could enact a statute along the following lines:

(a) a waiver of sovereign immunity as to the illegal acts of law enforcement officials committed in the performance of assigned duties;

(b) the creation of a cause of action for damages sustained by any person aggrieved by conduct of governmental agents in violation of the Fourth Amendment or statutes regulating official conduct;

(c) the creation of a tribunal, quasi-judicial in nature or perhaps patterned after the United States Court of Claims, to adjudicate all claims under the statute;

(d) a provision that this statutory remedy is in lieu of the exclusion of evidence secured for use in criminal cases in violation of the Fourth Amendment; and

(e) a provision directing that no evidence, otherwise admissible, shall be excluded from any criminal proceeding because of violation of the Fourth Amendment. . . .

Adams v. Williams

407 US 143, 92 S Ct 1921, 32 L Ed2d 612 (1972)

A policeman making a reasonable investigatory stop may conduct a limited search for concealed weapons.

Mr. Justice Rehnquist delivered the opinion of the Court.

Respondent Robert Williams was convicted in a Connecticut state court of illegal possession of a handgun found during a "stop and frisk," as well as possession of heroin that was found during a full search incident to his weapons arrest. . . .

Police Sgt. John Connolly was alone early in the morning on car patrol duty in a high crime area of Bridgeport, Connecticut. At approximately 2:15 A.M. a person known to Sgt. Connolly approached his cruiser and informed him that an individual seated in a nearby vehicle was carrying narcotics and had a gun at his waist.

After calling for assistance on his car radio, Sgt. Connolly approached the vehicle to investigate the informant's report. Connolly tapped on the car window and asked the occupant, Robert Williams, to open the door. When Williams rolled down the window instead, the sergeant reached into the car and removed a fully loaded revolver from Williams' waistband. The gun had not been visible to Connolly from outside the car, but it was in precisely the place indicated by the informant. Williams was then arrested by Connolly for unlawful possession of the pistol. A search incident to that arrest was conducted after other officers arrived. They found substantial quantities of heroin on Williams' person and in the car, and they found a machete and a second revolver hidden in the automobile.

Respondent contends that the initial seizure of his pistol, upon which rested the later search and seizure of other weapons and narcotics, was not justified by the informant's tip to Sgt. Connolly. He claims that absent a more reliable informant, or some corroboration of the tip, the policeman's actions were unreasonable under the standards set forth in *Terry* v. *Ohio* [392 US 1].

In *Terry* this Court recognized that "a police officer may in appropriate circumstances and in an appropriate manner approach a person for the purpose of investigating possible criminal behavior even though there is no probable cause to make an arrest.". . . The Fourth Amendment does not require a policeman who lacks the precise level of information necessary for probable cause to arrest to simply shrug his shoulders and allow a crime to occur or a criminal to escape. On the contrary, *Terry* recognizes that it may be the essence of good police work to adopt an intermediate response. See *id.,* at 23. A brief stop of a suspicious individual, in order to determine his identity or to maintain the status quo momentarily while obtaining more information, may be most reasonable in light of the facts known to the officer at the time. . . .

The Court recognized in *Terry* that the policeman making a reasonable investigatory stop should not be denied the opportunity to protect himself from attack by a hostile suspect. "When an officer is justified in believing that the individual whose suspicious behavior he is investigating at close range is armed and presently dangerous to the officer or to others," he may conduct a limited protective search for concealed weapons. *Id.,* at 24. The purpose of this limited search is not to discover evidence of crime, but to allow the officer to pursue his investigation without fear of violence, and thus the frisk for weapons might be equally necessary and reasonable whether or not carrying a concealed weapon violated any applicable state law. So long as the officer is entitled to make a forcible stop and has reason to believe that the suspect is armed and dangerous, he may conduct a weapons search limited in scope to this protective purpose. *Id.,* at 30.

Applying these principles to the present case we believe that Sgt. Connolly acted justifiably in responding to his informant's tip. The informant was known to him personally and had provided him with information in the past. This is a stronger case than obtains in the case of an anonymous telephone tip. The informant here came forward personally to give information that was immediately verifiable at the scene. Indeed, under Connecticut law, the informant herself might have been subject to immediate arrest for making a false complaint had Sgt. Connolly's investigation proven the tip incorrect. Thus, while the Court's decisions indicate that this informant's unverified tip may have been insufficient for a narcotics arrest or search warrant, . . . the information carried enough indicia of reliability to justify the officer's forcible stop of Williams.

In reaching this conclusion, we reject respondent's argument that reasonable cause for a stop and frisk can only be based on the officer's personal observation, rather than on information supplied by another persons. Informants' tips, like all other clues and evidence coming to a policeman on the scene, may vary greatly in their value and reliability. One simple rule will not cover every situation. Some tips, completely lacking in indicia of reliability, would either warrant no police response or require further investigation before a forcible stop of a suspect would be authorized. But in some situations—for example, when the victim of a street crime seeks immediate police aid and gives a description of his assailant, or when a credible informant warns of a specific impending crime—the subtleties of the hearsay rule should not thwart an appropriate police response.

While properly investigating the activity of a person who was reported to be carrying narcotics and a concealed weapon and who was sitting alone in a car in a high crime area at 2:15 in the morning, Sgt. Connolly had ample reason to fear for his safety. When Williams rolled down his window, rather than complying with the policeman's request to step out of the car so that his movements could more easily be seen, the revolver allegedly at Williams' waist became an even greater threat. Under these circumstances the policeman's action in reaching to the spot where the gun was thought to be hidden constituted a limited intrusion designed to insure his safety, and we conclude that it was reasonable. The loaded gun seized as a result of this intrusion was therefore admissible at Williams' trial. . . .

Once Sgt. Connolly had found the gun precisely where the informant had predicted, probable cause existed to arrest Williams for unlawful possession of the weapon. Probable cause to arrest depends "upon whether, at the moment the arrest was made . . . the facts and circumstances within [the arresting officers'] knowledge and of which they had reasonably trustworthy information were sufficient to warrant a prudent man in believing that the [suspect] had committed or was committing an offense." *Beck* v. *Ohio,* 379 US 89, 91 (1964). In the present case the policeman found Williams in possession of a gun in precisely the place predicted by the informant. This tended to corroborate the reliability of the informant's further report of narcotics, and together with the surrounding circumstances certainly suggested no lawful explanation for possession of the gun. Probable cause does not require the same type of specific evidence of each element of the offense as would be needed to support a conviction. See *Draper* v. *United States,* 358 US 307, 311–312 (1959). Rather, the court will evaluate generally the circumstances at the time of the arrest to decide if the officer had probable cause for his action. . . . Under the circumstances surrounding Williams' possession of the gun seized by Sgt. Connolly, the arrest on the weapons charge was supported by probable cause, and the search of his person and of the car incident to that arrest was lawful. . . . The fruits of the search were therefore properly admitted at Williams' trial, and the Court of Appeals erred in reaching a contrary conclusion.

Reversed.

MR. JUSTICE MARSHALL, with whom MR. JUSTICE DOUGLAS joins, dissenting.

Four years have passed since we decided *Terry* v. *Ohio,* 392 US 1 (1968), and its companion cases, *Sibron* v. *New York* and *Peters* v. *New York,* 392 US 40 (1968). They were the first cases in which this Court explicitly recognized the concept of "stop and frisk" and squarely held that police officers may, under appropriate circumstances, stop and frisk persons suspected of criminal activity even though there is less than probable cause for an arrest. This case marks our first opportunity to give some flesh to the bones of *Terry et al.* Unfortunately, the flesh provided by today's decision cannot possibly be made to fit on *Terry's* skeletal framework.

"[T]he most basic constitutional rule in this area is that 'searches conducted outside the judicial process without prior approval by judge or magistrate, are *per se* unreasonable under the Fourth Amendment—subject only to a few specifically established and well-delineated exceptions.' The exceptions are 'jealously and carefully drawn,' and there must be 'a showing by those who seek exemption . . . that the exigencies of the situation make that course imperative.' ' The burden is on those seeking the exemption to show the need for it.' " *Coolidge* v. *New Hampshire,* 403 US 443, 454–455 (1971).

In *Terry* we said that "We do not retreat from our holdings that the police must, whenever practicable, obtain advance judicial approval of searches and seizures through the warrant procedure." 392 US, at 20. Yet, we upheld the stop and frisk in *Terry* because we recognized that the realities of on-the-street law enforcement require an officer to act at times on the basis of strong evidence, short of probable cause, that criminal activity is taking place and that the criminal is armed and dangerous. Hence, *Terry* stands only for the proposition that police officers have a "narrowly drawn authority to . . . search for weapons" without a warrant.

In today's decision the Court ignores the fact that *Terry* begrudgingly accepted the necessity for creating an exception from the warrant requirement of the Fourth Amendment and treats this case as if warrantless searches were the rule rather than the "narrowly drawn" exception. This decision betrays the careful balance that *Terry* sought to strike between a citizen's right to privacy and his government's responsibility for effective law enforcement and expands the concept of warrantless searches far beyond anything heretofore recognized as legitimate. I dissent.

[A dissenting opinion by JUSTICE BRENNAN is omitted here.]

B. COUNSEL

Introduction

"In all criminal prosecutions the accused shall . . . have the assistance of counsel for his defense," states the Sixth Amendment. While this specific provision was applicable to prosecutions in federal courts only, in the 1932 case of *Powell* v. *Alabama* (p. 444), the Court recognized that counsel was also required in state prosecutions by the due process clause of the Fourteenth Amendment in some cases. As explained in *Betts* v. *Brady,* 316 US 455 (1942), the phrase due process "formulates a concept less rigid and more fluid than those envisioned in other specific and particular provisions of the Bill of Rights. Its application is less a matter of rule. Asserted denial is to be tested by an appraisal of the totality of facts in a given case." This concept was overruled in *Gideon* v. *Wainwright,* 372 US 335 (1963), which held that "the Fourteenth Amendment requires appointment of counsel in a state court, just as the Sixth Amendment requires in a federal court." *Argersinger* v. *Hamlin,* 407 US 25 (1972), held that "absent a knowing and intelligent waiver, no person may be imprisoned for any offense, whether classified as petty, misdemeanor, or felony, unless he was represented by counsel at his trial."

Pretrial stage. *Escobedo* v. *Illinois,* 378 US 478 (1964), held inadmissible as evidence incriminating statements made by Escobedo at a police station before he was indicted, and *Miranda* v. *Arizona* (p. 448) clarified the "in custody interrogation" concept. *United States* v. *Wade,* 388 US 218 (1967), held that the "post-indictment lineup (unlike such preparatory steps as analyzing fingerprints and blood samples) was a critical prosecutive stage at which respondent was entitled to the aid of counsel." *Coleman* v. *Alabama,* 399 US 1 (1970), adhered to the right of counsel at "any pretrial confrontation"—in this case, identification in a lineup. Dissenting, Chief Justice Burger objected to "placing a premium on 'recent cases' rather than the language of the Constitution," and asked: "If the current mode of constitutional analysis sub-scribed to by this Court in recent cases requires that counsel be present at preliminary hearings, how can this be reconciled with the fact that the Constitution itself does not permit the assistance of counsel at the decidedly more 'critical' grand jury inquiry?"

Kirby v. *Illinois,* 406 US 682 (1972), held that the right to counsel did not apply to an identification made in a police station by the victim of a robbery when the defendant had been taken into custody but had not been indicted or formally charged with a crime. The Court confined the *Wade-Gilbert* per se exclusionary rule to cases that involve "points of time at or after the initiation of adversary judicial criminal proceedings." No attempt was made to distinguish *Escobedo* other than to say that "the Court has limited the holding of *Escobedo* to its own facts. . . . "

Harmless error. In *Milton* v. *Wainwright,* 407 US 371 (1972), the Court applied the doctrine of harmless error. Milton was accused of murdering his wife through a simulated accident. His lawyer advised him not to talk about the case. The state placed Langford, a police officer posing as a fellow prisoner, in the cell with Milton, and a day later this disguised officer elicited a confession which was admitted in evidence at the trial. Milton was convicted and sentenced to life imprisonment. Years later he sought release through habeas corpus. With three justices dissenting, the decision of the Court held:

> In initiating the present habeas corpus proceeding in the District Court, petitioner sought to have his conviction set aside on the ground that the statements he made to police officer Langford should not have been admitted against him. Our review of the record, however, leaves us with no reasonable doubt that the jury at petitioner's 1958 trial would have reached the same verdict without hearing Langford's testimony. The writ of habeas corpus has limited scope; the federal courts do not sit to re-try state cases *de novo* but rather to review for violation of federal constitutional standards. In that process we do not close our eyes to the reality of overwhelming evidence of guilt fairly established in the state court 15 years ago by use of evidence not challenged here; the use of the additional evidence challenged in this proceeding and arguably open to challenge was, beyond reasonable doubt, harmless.

Compare the distinction in *Donnelly* v. *DeChristoforo,* 416 US 637 (1974), between "ordinary trial error of a prosecutor and . . . egregious misconduct."

Fees. *James* v. *Strange,* 407 US 128 (1972), invalidated Kansas' recoupment statute which enabled the state to recover in subsequent civil proceedings legal defense fees from indigents provided with counsel by the court. The opinion, by Justice Powell, contains a summary of recent state attempts to recover such fees and is by no means a broadside condemnation of such attempts. "We note here . . . that the state interests represented by recoupment laws may prove important ones. Recoupment proceed-ings may protect the State from fraudulent concealment of assets and false assertion of indigency." Moreover, many states are hard pressed for public funds. The particular statute of Kansas was held void because it placed indigent defendant debtors in a class separate from other civil judgment debtors and subjected them to harsh treatment such as garnishment of their total wage. *Fuller* v. *Oregon,*   US   (1974), sus-tained the application of Oregon's recoupement statute to a person on probationary sentence.

Powell v. Alabama

287 US 45, 53 S Ct 55, 77 L Ed 158 (1932)

The right of the accused, at least in a capital case, to have the aid of counsel for his defense, which includes the right to have sufficient time to advise with counsel and to prepare a defense, is one of the fundamental rights guaranteed by the due process clause of the Fourteenth Amendment.

MR. JUSTICE SUTHERLAND delivered the opinion of the Court. . . .

The petitioners [Ozie Powell and other], hereinafter referred to as defendants, are negroes charged with the crime of rape, committed upon the persons of two white girls. The crime is said to have been committed on March 25, 1931. The indictment was returned in a state court of first instance on March 31, and the record recites that on the same day the defendants were arraigned and entered pleas of not guilty. There is a further recital to the effect that upon the arraignment they were represented by counsel. But no counsel had been employed, and aside from a statement made by the trial judge several days later during a colloquy immediately preceding the trial, the record does not disclose when, or under what circumstances, an appointment of counsel was made, or who was appointed. During the colloquy referred to, the trial judge, in response to question, said that he had appointed all the members of the bar for the purpose of arraigning the defendants and then of course anticipated that the members of the bar would continue to help the defendants if no counsel appeared. Upon the argument there both sides accepted that as a correct statement of the facts concerning the matter. . . .

April 6, six days after indictment, the trials began. When the first case was called, the court inquired whether the parties were ready for trial. The state's attorney replied that he was ready to proceed. No one answered for the defendants or appeared to represent or defend them. Mr. Roddy, a Tennessee lawyer not a member of the local bar, addressed the court, saying that he had not been employed, but that people who were interested had spoken to him about the case. He was asked by the court whether he intended to appear for the defendants, and answered that he would like to appear along with counsel that the court might appoint. The record then proceeds:

> "The Court: If you appear for these defendants, then I will not appoint counsel; if local counsel are willing to appear and assist you under the circumstances, all right, but I will not appoint them." . . .

It never has been doubted by this court, or any other so far as we know, that notice and hearing are preliminary steps essential to the passing of an enforceable judgment, and that they, together with a legally competent tribunal having jurisdiction of the case, constitute basic elements of the constitutional requirement of due process of law. . . .

What . . . does a hearing include? Historically and in practice, in our own country at least, it has always included the right to the aid of counsel when desired and provided by the party asserting the right. The right to be heard would be, in many cases, of little avail if it did not comprehend the right to be heard by counsel. Even the intelligent and educated layman has small and sometimes no skill in the science of law. He lacks both the skill and knowledge adequately to prepare his defense, even though he have a perfect one. He requires the guiding hand of counsel at every step in the proceedings against him. Without it, though he be not guilty, he faces the danger of conviction because he does not know how to establish his innocence. If that be true of men of intelligence, how much more true is it of the ignorant and illiterate, or those of feeble intellect. . . .

All that is necessary now to decide, as we do decide, is that in a capital case, where the defendant is unable to employ counsel, and is incapable adequately of making his own defense because of ignorance, feeble mindedness, illiteracy, or the like, it is the duty of the court, whether requested or not, to assign counsel for him as a necessary requisite of due process of law; and that duty is not discharged by an assignment at such a time or under such circumstances as to preclude the giving of effective aid in the preparation and trial of the case. . . .

Judgments reversed.

[JUSTICES BUTLER and MCREYNOLDS dissented.]

C. SELF-INCRIMINATION

"No person . . . shall be compelled in any criminal case to be a witness against himself" states the Fifth Amendment, and almost everyone in America knows something of the right to "take the Fifth." Under the Warren Court the prohibition against self-incrimination was incorporated as a limitation on the states—*Malloy* v. *Hogan,* 378 US 1 (1964)—and vastly expanded in scope. There has been some retraction under the Burger Court. For a scholarly study of the subject in historical perspective, see Otis H. Stephens, Jr., *The Supreme Court and Confessions of Guilt* (Knoxville, 1973).

Where Applicable

"The Amendment not only protects the individual against being involuntarily called as a witness against himself in a criminal prosecution but also privileges him not to answer official questions put to him in any other proceeding, civil or criminal, formal or informal, where the answers might incriminate him in future proceedings." *Lefkowitz* v. *Turley,* 414 US 70 (1973).

To Whom Applicable

The immunity against self-incrimination is a personal right that cannot be asserted for the protection of others. *Oklahoma Press Publishing Co.* v. *Walling,* 327 US 186 (1946), held that the privilege "gives no protection to corporations or their officers against the production of corporate records," and *United States* v. *White,* 322 US 694 (1944), held that books and papers kept "in a representative rather than a personal capacity cannot be the subject of the personal privilege against self-incrimination, even though production of the papers might tend to incriminate [their keeper] personally." Contrast the decisions in *Gibson* v. *Florida Legislative Committee,* 372 US 539 (1963); *Spevak* v. *Klein,* 385 US 511 (1967); and *United States* v. *Kordel,* 397 US 1 (1970). *Bellis* v. *United States,*   US   (1974), applied the *White* rule to the records of a dissolved law partnership kept by one of its former members.

Who decides?   *Hoffman* v. *United States,* 341 US 479 (1951), held that when a witness declines to answer a question on a plea of self-incrimination, "It is for the court to say whether his silence is justified," and this appears to be the general practice. However, in recent years the Supreme Court has veered toward the view of Chief Justice Marshall that the witness, who alone knows the answer, is the best judge of whether answering a question would incriminate him. Dissenting in *Malloy* v. *Hogan,* 378 US 1 (1964), Justice White wrote that "the Court has all but stated that a witness' invocation of the privilege to any question is to be automatically, and without more, accepted."

Immunity Technique

The government may value the testimony of a witness so highly that it is willing to grant him immunity from, as expressed in the Compulsory Testimony Act of 1893, being "prosecuted or subjected to any penalty or forfeiture for or on account of any transaction, matter or thing, concerning which he may testify. . . . " This technique has been approved by the Supreme Court, and a witness granted immunity who still refuses to answer may be punished for contempt. *Ullman* v. *United States,* 350 US 422 (1956). On the application of the immunity if accepted, see *Smith* v. *United States,* 337 US 137 (1949). For a listing of the dozens of Federal Witness Immunity Acts, see 72 Yale L. J. 1568, 1611–1612.

It had already been decided that the federal government could grant immunity from the use in state courts of evidence given by a witness under compulsion in a federal proceeding. On the same day on which the Court announced that the self-incrimination clause of the Fifth Amendment was incorporated into the Fourteenth, it announced in *Murphy* v. *Waterfront Commission,* 378 US 52 (1964), the following rule governing federal-state relations: "[W]e hold the constitutional rule to be that a state witness may not be compelled to give testimony which may be incriminating under federal law unless the compelled testimony and its fruits cannot be used in any manner by federal officials in connection with a criminal prosecution against him. We conclude, moreover, that in order to implement this constitutional rule and accommodate the interests of the State and Federal Governments in investigating and prosecuting crime, the Federal Government may be prohibited from making any such use of compelled testimony and its fruits. This exclusionary rule, while permitting the States to secure information necessary for effective law enforcement, leaves the witness and the Federal Government in substantially the same position as if the witness had claimed his privilege in the absence of a state grant of immunity."

Transactional versus use theory.   Under the "transaction" theory, to compel a witness to testify he must be given immunity from prosecution "for or on account of any transaction . . . concerning which he may testify." In essence, the witness' testimony must "operate as a pardon" for criminal conduct substantially related to the testimony.

Under the "use" theory, neither the compelled testimony nor its fruits may be used, but this does not prevent prosecution based upon independent sources of evidence.

In *Kastigar* v. *United States,* 406 US 941 (1972), the Court adopted the use theory. It held that . . .

> the United States can compel testimony from an unwilling witness who invokes the Fifth Amendment privilege against compulsory self-incrimination by conferring immunity, as provided by 18 USC § 6002, from use of the compelled testimony and evidence derived therefrom in subsequent criminal proceedings, as such immunity from use and derivative use is coextensive with the scope of the privilege and is sufficient to compel testimony over a claim of the privilege. Transactional immunity would afford broader protection than the Fifth Amendment privilege, and is not constitutionally required. In a subsequent criminal prosecution, the prosecution has the burden of proving affirmatively that evidence proposed to be used is derived from a legitimate source wholly independent of the compelled testimony.

Public Officers

The fact that a person is a public officer does not, of course, withdraw from him the constitutional protection against self-incrimination. But does the state have the right to discharge an employee because, claiming immunity under the Fifth Amendment, he refuses to answer questions? Two interests are usually in competition in such cases: the right of the individual to exercise his right to remain silent, and the right of the government to gain information from its employees. The Court has not followed the view of Holmes that every person has the right to refuse to answer questions but not a right to hold public office. In the 1960s it balanced the interests involved in individual cases with shifting results, much akin to the results in the security cases discussed in chapter 10. But having adopted the use theory of immunity in *Kastigar,* thus making it more expedient for the state to apply the immunity technique, in *Lefkowitz* v. *Turley,* 414 US 70 (1973), the Court indicated that it would give full protection of the self-incrimination clause to public officers. In holding void a New York statute which provided that persons who refused to waive immunity before a grand jury investigating public contracts should be disqualified for five years from contracting with the state, Justice White wrote:

> Although due regard for the Fifth Amendment forbids the State to compel incriminating answers from its employees and contractors that may be used against them in criminal proceedings, the Constitution permits that very testimony to be compelled if neither it nor its fruits are available for such use. *Kastigar* v. *United States, supra.* Furthermore, the accommodation between the interest of the State and the Fifth Amendment requires that the State have means at its disposal to secure testimony if immunity is supplied and testimony is still refused. This is recognized by the power of the courts to compel testimony, after a grant of immunity, by use of civil contempt and coerced imprisonment. . . . Also, given adequate immunity, the State may plainly insist that employees either answer questions under oath about the performance of their job or suffer the loss of employment. By like token, the State may insist that the architects involved in this case either respond to relevant inquiries about the performance of their contracts or suffer cancellation of current relationships and disqualification from contracting with public agencies for an appropriate time in the future. But

the State may not insist that appellees waive their Fifth Amendment privilege against self-incrimination and consent to the use of the fruits of the interrogation in any later proceedings brought against them. Rather, the State must recognize what our cases hold: that answers elicited upon the threat of the loss of employment are compelled and inadmissible in evidence. Hence, if answers are to be required in such circumstances States must offer to the witness whatever immunity is required to supplant the privilege and may not insist that the employee or contractor waive such immunity.

Procedure Relating to Confessions

Jackson v. *Denno,* 378 US 368 (1964), held that a defendant is denied due process of law if the issue of the voluntariness of his confession is submitted to the jury along with other issues, and a general verdict of guilty accepted. In invalidating the New York procedure, the Court explained:

> . . . If an issue of coercion is presented, the judge may not resolve conflicting evidence or arrive at his independent appraisal of the voluntariness of the confession, one way or the other. These matters he must leave to the jury.

This procedure has a significant impact upon the defendant's Fourteenth Amendment rights. In jurisdictions following the orthodox rule, under which the judge himself solely and finally determines the voluntariness of the confession, or those following the Massachusetts procedure, under which the jury passes on voluntariness only after the judge has fully and independently resolved the issue against the accused, the judge's conclusions are clearly evident from the record since he either admits the confession into evidence if it is voluntary or rejects it if involuntary. Moreover, his findings upon disputed issues of fact are expressly stated or may be ascertainable from the record. In contrast, the New York jury returns only a general verdict upon the ultimate question of guilt or innocence. It is impossible to discover whether the jury found the confession voluntary and relied upon it, or involuntary and supposedly ignored it. Nor is there any indication of how the jury resolved disputes in the evidence concerning the critical facts underlying the coercion issue. Indeed, there is nothing to show that these matters were resolved at all, one way or the other. . . .

A defendant objecting to the admission of a confession is entitled to a fair hearing in which both the underlying factual issues and the voluntariness of his confession are actually and reliably determined. . . .

Miranda v. Arizona

384 US 436, 86 S Ct 1602, 16 L Ed2d 694 (1966)

In criminal cases the prosecution cannot use confessions obtained after the accused is taken into custody unless adequate procedural safeguards are followed to insure that the accused's right not to confess is maintained.

[Ernest A. Miranda, age twenty-three, was picked up in Phoenix by police investigating a rape. He was placed in a line-up with four other Mexicans of approximately his age, height, and build. The complaining witness identified him as the man who had abducted and raped her. The police then took him to Interrogation Room No. 2 of the detective bureau, and within two hours his confession was reduced to writing. Miranda had completed only eight years of school. Near the date set for his trial, his defense counsel filed notice of intention to file a plea of insanity. After a hearing, the trial court found Miranda to be sane and ordered his case to proceed to trial. Over the objection of his cousel, Miranda's written confession was admitted into evidence, and the police officers were permitted to testify to his oral confession made during the interrogation. He was found guilty and sentenced to from twenty to thirty years imprisonment.

In a single opinion the United States Supreme Court reversed the conviction of Miranda and that of three persons in cases from other states involving similar legal issues.]

MR. CHIEF JUSTICE WARREN delivered the opinion of the Court.

The cases before us raise questions which go to the roots of our concepts of American criminal jurisprudence: the restraints society must observe consistent with the Federal Constitution in prosecuting individuals for crime. More specifically, we deal with the admissibility of statements obtained from an individual who is subjected to custodial police interrogation and the necessity for procedures which assure that the individual is accorded his privilege under the Fifth Amendment to the Constitution not to be compelled to incriminate himself. . . .

The constitutional issue we decide in each of these cases is the admissibility of statements obtained from a defendant questioned while in custody or otherwise deprived of his freedom of action in any significant way. In each, the defendant was questioned by police officers, detectives, or a prosecuting attorney in a room in which he was cut off from the outside world. In none of these cases was the defendant given a full and effective warning of his rights at the outset of the interrogation process. In all the cases, the questioning elicited oral admissions, and in three of them, signed statements as well which were admitted at their trials. They all thus share salient features—incommunicado interrogation of individuals in a police-dominated atmosphere, resulting in self-incriminating statements without full warnings of constitutional rights. . . .

In these cases, we might not find the defendants' statements to have been involuntary in traditional terms. Our concern for adequate safeguards to protect precious Fifth Amendment rights is, of course, not lessened in the slightest. In each of the cases, the defendant was thrust into an unfamiliar atmosphere and run through menacing police interrogation procedures. The potentiality for compulsion is forcefully apparent, for example, in *Miranda,* where the indigent Mexican defendant was a seriously disturbed individual with pronounced sexual fantasies, and in *Stewart,* in which the defendant was an indigent Los Angeles Negro who had dropped out of school in the sixth grade. To be sure, the records do not evince overt physical coercion or patent psychological ploys. The fact remains that in none of these cases did the officers undertake to afford appropriate safeguards at the outset of the interrogation to insure that the statements were truly the product of free choice. . . .

We sometimes forget how long it has taken to establish the privilege against self-incrimination, the sources from which it came and the fervor with which it was defended. Its roots go back into ancient times. . . .

Today . . . there can be no doubt that the Fifth Amendment privilege is available outside of criminal court proceedings and serves to protect persons in all settings in which their freedom of action is curtailed in any significant way from being compelled to incriminate themselves. We have concluded that without proper safeguards the process of in-custody interrogation of persons suspected or accused of crime contains inherently compelling pressures which work to undermine the individual's will to resist and to compel him to speak where he would not otherwise do so freely. In order to combat these pressures and to permit a full opportunity to exercise the privilege against self-incrimination, the accused must be adequately and effectively apprised of his rights and the exercise of those rights must be fully honored.

It is impossible for us to foresee the potential alternatives for protecting the privilege which might be devised by Congress or the States in the exercise of their creative rule-making capacities. Therefore we cannot say that the Constitution necessarily requires adherence to any particular solution for the inherent compulsions of the interrogation process as it is presently conducted. Our decision in no way creates a constitutional straitjacket which will handicap sound efforts at reform, nor is it intended to have this effect. We encourage Congress and the States to continue their laudable search for increasingly effective ways of protecting the rights of the individual while promoting efficient enforcement of our criminal laws. However, unless we are shown other procedures which are at least as effective in apprising accused persons of their right of silence and in assuring a continuous opportunity to exercise it, the following safeguards must be observed. . . .

. . . [W]hen an individual is take into custody or otherwise deprived of his freedom by the authorities in any significant way and is subjected to questioning, the privilege against self-incrimination is jeopardized. Procedural safeguards must be employed to protect the privilege, and unless other fully effective means are adopted to notify the person of his right of silence and to assure that the exercise of the right will be scrupulously honored, the following measures are required. He must be warned prior to any questioning that he has the right to remain silent, that anything he says can be used against him in a court of law, that he has the right to the presence of an attorney, and that if he cannot afford an attorney one will be appointed for him prior to any questioning if he so desires. Opportunity to exercise these rights must be afforded to him throughout the interrogation. After such warnings have been given, and such opportunity afforded him, the individual may knowingly and intelligently waive these rights and agree to answer questions or make a statement. But unless and until such warnings and waiver are demonstrated by the prosecution at trial, no evidence obtained as a result of interrogation can be used against him. . . .

MR. JUSTICE CLARKE, dissenting. . . .

The *ipse dixit* of the majority has no support in our cases. . . .

The rule prior to today . . . depended upon "a totality of circumstances evidencing an involuntary . . . admission of guilt." . . .

MR. JUSTICE HARLAN, whom MR. JUSTICE STEWART and MR. JUSTICE WHITE joint, dissenting.

I believer the decision of the Court represents poor constitutional law and entails harmful consequences for the country at large. How serious these consequences may prove to be only time can tell. But the basic flaws in the Court's justification seem to me readily apparent now once all sides of the problem are considered. . . .

MR. JUSTICE WHITE, with whom MR. JUSTICE HARLAN and MR. JUSTICE STEWART join, dissenting. . . .

First, we may inquire what are the textual and factual bases of this new fundamental rule. To reach the result announced on the ground it does, the Court must stay within the confines of the Fifth Amendment which forbids self-incrimination only if *compelled*. Hence the core of the Court's opinion is that because of the "compulsion inherent in custodial surroundings, no statement obtained from [a] defendant [in custody] can truly be the product of his free choice," . . . absent the use of adequate protective devices as described by the Court. However, the Court does not point to any sudden inrush of new knowledge requiring the rejection of 70 years' experience. . . . Insofar as appears from the Court's opinion, it has not examined a single transcript of any police interrogation, let alone the interrogation that took place in any one of these cases which it decides today. Judged by any of the standards for empirical investigation utilized in the social sciences the factual basis for the Court's premise is patently inadequate. . . .

Criticism of the Court's opinion, however, cannot stop with a demonstration that the factual and textual bases for the rule it propounds are, at best, less than compelling. Equally relevant is an assessment of the rule's consequences measured against community values. . . .

The obvious underpinning of the Court's decision is a deep-seated distrust of all confessions. . . . I see nothing wrong or immoral, and certainly nothing unconstitutional, in the police's asking a suspect whom they have reasonable cause to arrest whether or not he killed his wife or in confronting him with the evidence on which the arrest was based, at least where he has been plainly advised that he may remain completely silent, see *Escobedo* v. *Illinois*, 378 US 478, 499 (dissenting opinion). Until today, "the admissions or confessions of the prisoner, when voluntarily and freely made, have always ranked high in the scale of incriminating evidence." . . .

The most basic function of any government is to provide for the security of the individual and of his proptery. . . . These ends of society are served by the criminal laws which for the most part are aimed at the prevention of crime. Without the reasonably effective performance of the task of preventing private violence and retaliation, it is idle to talk about human dignity and civilized values. . . .

In some unknown number of cases the Court's rule will return a killer, a rapist or other criminal to the streets and to the environment which produced him, to repeat his crime whenever it pleases him. As a consequence, there will not be a gain, but a loss, in human dignity. . . .

Applying the traditional standards to the cases before the Court, I would hold these confessions voluntary. . . .

Notes

1. *Harris* v. *New York*, 401 US 222 (1971), held that a statement "inadmissible against a defendant in the prosecution's case in chief because of lack of the procedural safeguards required by *Miranda* . . . may, if its trustworthiness satisfies

legal standards, be used for impeachment purposes to attack the credibility of defendant's trial testimony." As Chief Justice Burger expressed it, "The shield provided by *Miranda* cannot be perverted into a license to use perjury by way of a defense, free from the risk of confrontation with prior inconsistent utterances. We hold, therefore, that petitioner's credibility was appropriately impeached by use of his earlier conflicting statements."

Justices Brennan, Douglas, and Marshall dissented. Justice Brennan wrote:

> The objective of deterring improper police conduct is only part of the larger objective of safeguarding the integrity of our adversary system. The "essential mainstay" of that system, *Miranda* v. *Arizona,* 384 US at 460, is the privilege against self-incrimination, which for that reason has occupied a central place in our jurisprudence since before the Nation's birth. Moreover, "we may view the historical development of the privilege as one which groped for the proper scope of governmental power over the citizen. . . . All these policies point to one overriding thought: the constitutional foundation underlying the privilege is the respect a government . . . must accord to the dignity and integrity of its citizens." *Ibid.* These values are plainly jeopardized if an exception against admission of tainted statements is made for those used for impeachment purposes. Moreover, it is monstrous that courts should aid or abet the law-breaking police officer. It is abiding truth that "[n]othing can destroy a government more quickly than its failure to observe its own laws, or worse, its disregard of the charter of its own existence." *Mapp* v. *Ohio,* 367 US 643, 659 (1961). Thus, even to the extent that *Miranda* was aimed at deterring police practices in disregard of the Constitution, I fear that today's holding will seriously undermine the achievement of that objective. The Court today tells the police that they may freely interrogate an accused incommunicado and without counsel and know that although any statement they obtain in violation of *Miranda* cannot be used on the State's direct case, it may be introduced if the defendant has the temerity to testify in his own defense. This goes far toward undoing much of the progress made in conforming police methods to the Constitution. I dissent.

2. *Lego* v. *Twomey,* 404 US 477 (1972), held that a trial judge could use a "preponderance of evidence" standard in passing upon the voluntariness of a confession, and that the accused had no right to have the voluntariness issue resolved by the judge also submitted to a jury for its separate consideration. Justices Brennan, Douglas, and Marshall dissented.

3. *Dukes* v. *Warden,* 406 US 250 (1972), held that a plea of guilty, negotiated in plea bargaining by defense attorney's partner, was not rendered involuntary by the fact that the defense attorney made disparaging remarks about Dukes in the trial of two co-defendants.

4. *Michigan* v. *Tucker,* 417 US 433 (1974), distinguished between (a) police conduct which infringes upon the constitutional right against compulsory self-incrimination and (b) the prophylactic rules set forth in *Miranda* to protect that right, and held admissible testimony by a witness whose identity was revealed by the defendant during custodial interrogation before he was advised of his right to appointed counsel. The custodial interrogation of Tucker took place before the

"*Miranda* rules" were announced by the Court, but it is debatable whether this was a decisive factor in the *Tucker* decision.

In a concurring opinion, Justice White wrote: "*Miranda* having been applied in this Court only to the exclusion of the defendant's own statements, I would not extend its prophylactic scope to bar the testimony of third persons even though they have been identified by means of admissions that are themselves inadmissible under *Miranda.*"

In the opinion of the Court, Justice Rehnquist wrote:

...[T]he Court in *Miranda,* for the first time, expressly declared that the Self-Incrimination Clause was applicable to state interrogations at a police station, and that a defendant's statements might be excluded at trial despite their voluntary character under traditional principles.

To supplement this new doctrine, and to help police officers conduct interrogations without facing a continued risk that valuable evidence would be lost, the Court in *Miranda* established a set of specific protective guidelines, now commonly known as the *Miranda* rules. The Court declared that "the prosecution may not use statements, whether exculpatory or inculpatory, stemming from custodial interrogation of the defendant unless it demonstrates the use of procedural safeguards effective to secure the privilege against self-incrimination." 384 US, at 444. A series of recommended "procedural safeguards" then followed. The Court in particular stated:

"Prior to any questioning, the person must be warned that he has the right to remain silent, that any statement he does make may be used as evidence against him, and that he has a right to the presence of an attorney, either retained or appointed." 384 US, at 444.

The Court said that the defendant, of course, could waive these rights, but that any waiver must have been made "voluntarily, knowingly and intelligently." 384 US, at 444.

The Court recognized that these procedural safeguards were not themselves rights protected by the Constitution but were instead measures to insure that the right against compulsory self-incrimination was protected. As the Court remarked:

"[W]e cannot say that the Constitution necessarily requires adherence to any particular solution for the inherent compulsions of the interrogation process as it is presently conducted." 384 US, at 467.

The suggested safeguards were not intended to "create a constitutional straightjacket," 384 US, at 467, but rather to provide practical reinforcement for the right against compulsory self-incrimination.

A comparison of the facts in this case with the historical circumstances underlying the privilege against compulsory self-incrimination strongly indicates that the police conduct here did not deprive respondent of his privilege against compulsory self-incrimination as such, but rather failed to make available to him the full measure of procedural safeguards associated with that right since *Miranda.* Certainly no one could contend that the interrogation faced by respondent bore any resemblance to the historical practices at which the right against compulsory self-incrimination was aimed. The District Court in this case noted that the police had "warned [respondent] that he had the right to remain silent," 352 F. Supp., at 267, and the record in this case clearly shows that respondent was informed that any evidence taken could be used against him. The record is also clear that respondent was asked whether he wanted an attorney and that he replied that he did not. Thus, his statements could hardly be termed involuntary as that term has been defined in the decisions of this Court.

Additionally, there were no legal sanctions, such as the threat of contempt, which could have been applied to respondent had he chosen to remain silent. He was simply not exposed to "the cruel trilemma of self-accusation, perjury, or contempt." *Murphy* v. *Waterfront Commission,* 378 US 52, 55 (1964).

Our determination that the interrogation in this case involved no compulsion sufficient to breach the right against compulsory self-incrimination does not mean there was not a disregard, albeit an inadvertent disregard, of the procedural rules later established in *Miranda.* The question for decision is how sweeping the judicially imposed consequences of this disregard shall be. This Court said in *Miranda* that statements taken in violation of the *Miranda* principles must not be used to prove the prosecution's case at trial. That requirement was fully complied with by the state court here; respondent's statements, claiming that he was with Henderson and then asleep during the time period of the crime were not admitted against him at trial. This Court has also said, in *Wong Sun* v. *United States,* 371 US 471 (1963), that the "fruits" of police conduct which actually infringed a defendant's Fourth Amendment rights must be suppressed. But we have already concluded that the police conduct at issue here did not abridge respondent's constitutional privilege against compulsory self-incrimination, but departed only from the prophylactic standards later laid down by this Court in *Miranda* to safeguard that privilege. Thus, in deciding whether Henderson's testimony must be excluded, there is no controlling precedent of this Court to guide us. We must therefore examine the matter as a question of principle.

Just as the law does not require that a defendant receive a perfect trial, only a fair one, it cannot realistically require that policemen investigating serious crimes make no errors whatsoever. The pressures of law enforcement and the vagaries of human nature would make such an expectation unrealistic. Before we penalize police error, therefore, we must consider whether the sanction serves a valid and useful purpose. . . .

The deterrent purpose of the exclusionary rule necessarily assumes that the police have engaged in willful, or at the very least, negligent conduct which has deprived the defendant of some right. By refusing to admit evidence gained as a result of such conduct, the courts hope to instill in those particular investigating officers, or in their future counterparts, a greater degree of care towards the right of an accused. Where the official action was pursued in complete good faith, however, the deterrence rationale loses much of its force.

California v. Byers

402 US 424, 91 S Ct 1535, 29 Ed2d 9 (1971)

Requiring a driver to stop and furnish his name and address after involvement in an automobile accident does not violate his privilege against self-incrimination.

MR. CHIEF JUSTICE BURGER announced the judgment of the Court and an opinion in which MR. JUSTICE STEWART, MR. JUSTICE WHITE, and MR. JUSTICE BLACKMUN join.

This case presents the narrow but important question of whether the constitutional privilege against compulsory self-incrimination is infringed by California's so-called "hit and run" statute which requires the driver of a motor vehicle involved in an accident to stop at the scene and give his name and address. . . .

(1)

Whenever the Court is confronted with the question of a compelled disclosure that has an incriminating potential, the judicial scrutiny is invariably a close one. Tension between the State's demand for disclosures and the protection of the right against self-incrimination is likely to give rise to serious questions. Inevitably these must be resolved in terms of balancing the public need on the one hand, and the individual claim to constitutional protections on the other; neither interest can be treated lightly.

An organized society imposes many burdens on its constituents. It commands the filing of tax returns for income; it requires producers and distributors of consumer goods to file informational reports on the manufacturing process and the content of products, on the wages, hours, and working conditions of employees. Those who borrow money on the public market or issue securities for sale to the public must file various information reports; industries must report periodically the volume and content of pollutants discharged into our waters and atmosphere. Comparable examples are legion.

In each of these situations there is some possibility of prosecution—often a very real one—for criminal offenses disclosed by or deriving from the information that the law compels a person to supply. Information revealed by these reports could well be "a link in the chain" of evidence leading to prosecution and conviction. But under our holdings the mere possibility of incrimination is insufficient to defeat the strong policies in favor of a disclosure called for by statutes like the one challenged here.

United States v. *Sullivan,* 274 US 259 (1927), shows that an application of the privilege to the California statute is not warranted. There a bottlegger was prosecuted for failure to file an income tax return. He claimed that the privilege against compulsory self-incrimination afforded him a complete defense because filing a return would have tended to incriminate him by revealing the unlawful source of his income. Speaking for the Court, Mr. Justice Holmes rejected this claim on the ground that it amounted to "an extreme if not an extravagant application of the Fifth Amendment." *Id.,* at 263-264. Sullivan's tax return, of course, increased his risk of prosecution and conviction for violation of the National Prohibition Act. But the Court had no difficulty in concluding that an extension of the privilege to cover that kind of mandatory report would have been unjustified. In order to invoke the privilege it is necessary to show that the compelled disclosures will themselves confront the claimant with "substantial hazards of self-incrimination."

The components of this requirement were articulated in *Albertson* v. *SACB,* 382 US 70 (1965), and later in *Marchetti* v. *United States,* 390 US 39 (1968), *Grosso* v. *United States,* 390 US 62 (1968), and *Haynes* v. *United States,* 390 US 85 (1968). In *Albertson* the Court held that an order requiring registration by individual members of a Communist organization violated the privilege. There *Sullivan* was distinguished:

> "In *Sullivan* the questions in the income tax return were neutral on their face and directed at the public at large, but here they are directed at a *highly selective group inherently suspect of criminal activities.* Petitioners' claims are not asserted in an *essentially noncriminal* and *regulatory area* of inquiry, but against an inquiry in an area permeated with criminal statutes, where response to any of the . . . questions in context might involve the petitioners in the admission of a crucial element of a crime." 382 US, at 79 (emphasis added).

Albertson was followed by *Marchetti* and *Grosso* where the Court held that the privilege afforded a complete defense to prosecutions for noncompliance with federal gambling tax and registration requirements. It was also followed in *Haynes* where petitioner had been prosecuted for failure to register a firearm as required by federal statute. In each of these cases the Court found that compliance with the statutory disclosure requirements would confront the petitioner with "substantial hazards of self-incrimination." *E.g., Marchetti* v. *United States,* 390 US, at 61.

In all of these cases the disclosures condemned were only those extracted from a "highly selective group inherently suspect of criminal activities" and the privilege was applied only in "an area permeated with criminal statutes"—not in "an essentially noncriminal and regulatory area of inquiry." . . .

Although the California Vehicle Code defines some criminal offenses, the statute is essentially regulatory, not criminal. . . .

The disclosure of inherently illegal activity is inherently risky. Our decisions in *Albertson* and the cases following illustrate that truism. But disclosures with respect to automobile accidents simply do not entail the kind of substantial risk of self-incrimination involved in *Marchetti, Grosso,* and *Haynes.* Furthermore, the statutory purpose is noncriminal and self-reporting is indispensable to its fulfillment.

(2)

Even if we were to view the statutory reporting requirement as incriminating in the traditional sense, in our view it would be the "extravagant" extension of the privilege Justice Holmes warned against to hold that it is testimonial in the Fifth Amendment sense. Compliance with § 20002(a) (1) requires two things: first, a driver involved in an accident is required to stop at the scene; second, he is required to give his name and address. The act of stopping is no more testimonial—indeed less so in some respects —than requiring a person in custody to stand or walk in a police lineup, to speak prescribed words, or to give samples of handwriting, fingerprints, or blood. *United States* v. *Wade,* 388 US 218, 221-223 (1967); *Schmerber* v. *California,* 384 US 757, 764 and n. 8 (1966). . . .

The judgment of the California Supreme Court is vacated and the case is remanded for further proceedings not inconsistent with this opinion.

Vacated and remanded.

Mr. Justice Harlan, concurring in the judgment. [Omitted here.]

Mr. Justice Black, with whom Mr. Justice Douglas and Mr. Justice Brennan join, dissenting.

Since the days of Chief Justice John Marshall this Court has been steadfastly committed to the principle that the Fifth Amendment's prohibition against compulsory self-incrimination forbids the Federal Government to compel a person to supply information which can be used as a "link in the chain of testimony" needed to prosecute him for a crime. . . .

The plurality opinion labors unsuccessfully to distinguish this case from our previous holdings enforcing the Fifth Amendment guarantee against compelled self-incrimination. . . . The plurality opinion . . . appears to suggest that those previous cases are not controlling because respondent Byers would not have subjected himself to a "substantial risk of self-incrimination" by stopping after the accident and providing his name and address as required by California law. . . . This suggestion can hardly be taken seriously. . . .

The plurality opinion also seeks to distinguish this case from our previous decisions on the ground that § 20002(a) (1) requires disclosure in an area not "permeated with criminal statutes" and because it is not aimed at a "highly selective group inherently suspect of criminal activities." Of course, these suggestions ignore the fact that *this particular respondent* would have run a serious risk of self-incrimination by complying with the disclosure statute. Furthermore, it is hardly accurate to suggest that the activity of driving an automobile in California is not "an area permeated with criminal statutes." *Ibid.* And it is unhelpful to say the statute is not aimed at an "inherently suspect" group because it applies to "all persons who drive automobiles in California." *Ibid.* The compelled disclosure is required of all persons who drive automobiles in California *who are involved in accidents causing property damage.* If this group is not "suspect" of illegal activities, it is difficult to find such a group. . . .

I also find unacceptable the alternative holding that the California statute is valid because the disclosures it requires are not "testimonial" (whatever that term may mean). *Ante,* at 431. Even assuming that the Fifth Amendment prohibits the State only from compelling a man to produce "testimonial" evidence against himself, the California requirement here is still unconstitutional. What evidence can possibly be more "testimonial" than a man's own statement that he is a person who has just been involved in an automobile accident inflicting property damage? . . .

MR. JUSTICE BRENNAN, with whom MR. JUSTICE DOUGLAS and MR. JUSTICE MARSHALL join, dissenting.

Although I have joined my Brother BLACK's opinion in this case, the importance of the issues involved and the wide range covered by the two opinions supporting the Court's judgment in this case make further comment desirable. Put briefly, one of the primary flaws of the plurality opinion is that it bears so little relationship to the case before us. Notwithstanding the fact that respondent was charged both with a violation of the California Vehicle Code which resulted in an accident, and with failing to report the accident and its surrounding circumstances as required by the statute under review, the plurality concludes, contrary to all three California courts below, that respondent was faced with no substantial hazard of self-incrimination under California law. My Brother HARLAN, by contrast, recognizes the inadequacy of any such conclusion. In his view, our task is to make the Bill of Rights "relevant to contemporary conditions" by simply not applying its provisions when we think the Constitution errs. *Ante,* at 454. In the context of the present case, this appears to mean that current technological progress enabling the Government more easily to use an individual's compelled statements against him in a criminal prosecution should be matched by frank judicial contraction of the privilege against self-incrimination lest the Government be hindered in using modern technology further to reduce individual privacy. . . .

D. TRIAL BY JURY

Introduction

"In all criminal prosecutions the accused shall enjoy the right to a speedy and public trial, by an impartial jury of the State and district wherein the crime shall have been committed, which district shall have been previously ascertained by law," states the Sixth Amendment. In addition, it will be recalled that Article III of the original Constitution provides that "The trial of all crimes, except in impeachment, shall be by jury; and such trial shall be held in the State where the said crime shall have been committed; but when not committed within any State, the trial shall be at such place or places as the Congress may by law have directed."

Prior to 1970 it was generally held that the jury trial guaranteed by the Constitution was the jury trial as known to the common law. The three essentials of such a trial were summarized in *Patton* v. *United States,* 281 US 276 (1930), as: "(1) that the jury shall consist of twelve men, neither more nor less; (2) that the jury should be in the presence of and under the superintendence of a judge having power to instruct them as to the law and advise them in respect of the facts; and (3) that the verdict should be unanimous." These elements remain in effect in the federal courts, at least by statute.

Duncan v. *Louisiana,* 391 US 145 (1968), held that "the Fourteenth Amendment guarantees a right of jury trial [in state courts] in all criminal cases which—were they to be tried in a federal court—would come within the Sixth Amendment's guarantee." Concurring in this decision, Justice Fortas wrote: "[A]lthough I agree with the decision of the Court, I cannot agree with the implication . . . that the tail must go with the hide: that when we hold, influenced by the Sixth Amendment, that 'due process' requires that the States accord the right of jury trial for all but petty offenses, we automatically import all the ancillary rules which have been or may hereafter be developed incidental to the right to jury trial in the federal courts. I see no reason whatever, for example, to assume that our decision today would require us to impose federal requirements such as unanimous verdicts or a jury of 12 upon the States."

In *Williams* v. *Florida,* 399 US 78 (1970), Williams was tried for robbery by a jury of six, found guilty, and sentenced to life imprisonment. Upon appeal, the Supreme Court upheld the judgment of the Florida court. It concluded that "the fact that the jury at common law was composed of precisely 12 is an historical accident, unnecessary to effect the purpose of the jury system and wholly without significance 'except to mystics.' . . . Legislatures may well have their own views about the relative value of the larger and smaller juries, and may conclude that, wholly apart from the jury's primary function, it is desirable to spread the collective responsibility for the determination of guilt among the larger group. In capital cases, for example, it appears that no State provides for less than 12 jurors. . . ." According to this decision, "the essential feature of a jury obviously lies in the interposition between the accused and his accusor of the common-sense judgment of a group of laymen, and in the community participation and shared responsibility which results from that group's determination of guilt or innocence."

Apodaca v. *Oregon,* 406 US 404 (1972), sustained conviction by less-than-unanimous jury verdicts. Four justices dissented. In his concurring opinion, Justice Powell wrote: "I concur in the plurality opinion . . . insofar as it concludes that a defendant in a state court may constitutionally be convicted by less than a unanimous verdict, but I am not in accord with a major premise upon which that judgment is based. Its premise is that the concept of jury trial, as applicable to the States under the Fourteenth Amendment, must be identical in every detail to the concept required in federal courts by the Sixth Amendment. I do not think that all of the elements of jury trial within the meaning of the Sixth Amendment are necessarily embodied in or incorporated into the Due Process Clause of the Fourteenth Amendment." This view, first expressed by Justice Fortas, has been the view also of Justices Harlan and Stewart and of Chief Justice Burger.

Exceptions to Requirement

The three types of criminal cases constituting exceptions to the requirement of trial by jury are petty offenses, military trials, and contempt of court.

1. *Petty offenses.* The term "petty" is applied to an offense not punishable by imprisonment for as long as six months. *Frank* v. *United States,* 395 US 147 (1969), held, however, that "A petty offender may be placed on probation for up to five years and, if the terms of probation are violated, he may then be imprisoned for six months. . . ."

2. *Military trials.* The right of trial by jury does not apply in military courts. Article I, Section 8 of the Constitution vests in Congress authority "to make rules for the government and regulation of the land and naval forces." The statutes in this field are codified in the Uniform Code of Military Justice, 10 USC § 801-934.

The Court of Military Appeals, composed of three civilian judges appointed by the president with senatorial confirmation, is the highest court in the military law establishment. Decisions of the military courts are not subject to review by the civilian courts, save on the question of jurisdiction.

Interesting recent cases dealing with the power of military tribunals include: *Ex parte Quirin,* 317 US 1 (sustaining the power of a military tribunal to try German saboteurs landed on our shores during war); *United States ex rel. Toth* v. *Quarles,* 350 US 11 (holding that military jurisdiction did not extend to a discharged soldier); and *Reid* v. *Covert,* 354 US 1 (holding that a military court could not try the wife of a soldier accompanying him abroad).

O'Callahan v. *Parker,* 395 US 258 (1969), held that members of the armed services are entitled to the benefit of indictment by grand jury and trial by jury in a civilian court for crimes that are not service connected. O'Callahan, an Army sergeant, while on an evening pass from his army post, broke into a hotel room, assaulted a girl, and attempted rape. City police apprehended him and delivered him to the military police. He was tried by court martial and convicted of housebreaking, assault, and attempted rape. Through habeas corpus proceedings, his case eventually reached the Supreme Court. It reversed the judgment of the military court on the ground that O'Callahan's alleged crimes were not service connected and hence were not within the jurisdiction of the military court.

Relford v. *Commandant,* 401 US 335 (1971), clarified somewhat the "service connected crime" concept. Relford, a corporal on active duty, was convicted by court marital of raping, on a military reservation within the period of a few weeks, three women, including the visiting fourteen-year-old sister of another serviceman and a waitress who worked at the post concession. Sustaining the conviction, the Supreme Court held that "a serviceman's crime against the person of an individual upon the base or against property on the base is 'service connected.' . . ."

3. *Contempt of court.* The use of a jury is not required in civil contempt proceedings, and traditionally it was not required in proceedings for criminal contempt, but, under recent holdings, a jury is required in criminal contempt proceedings wherein a penalty of imprisonment for more than six months is imposed. See *Cheff* v. *Schnackenberg,* 384 US 373 (1966).

Waiver

Trial by jury in criminal cases is usually thought of as a right of the defendant; however, *Singer* v. *United States,* 380 US 24 (1965), held that the defendant has no right to trial before a judge alone, and that the prosecutor may refuse to approve a waiver of jury trial.

Civil cases

In addition to the provisions requiring jury trial in criminal cases, the Constitution has a provision on jury trial in designated civil cases. Amendment VII reads: "In suits at common law, where the value in controversy shall exceed twenty dollars, the right of trial by jury shall be preserved, and no fact tried by a jury shall be otherwise re-examined in any court of the United States, than according to the rules of the common law."

The amendment uses the term "suits at common law" to designate suits in which legal rights are to be ascertained, as distinguished from suits designed to ascertain equitable rights. "In a just sense, the amendment then may well be construed to embrace all suits, which are not of equity and admiralty jurisdiction, whatever may be the peculiar form which they may assume to settle legal rights." *Parsons* v. *Bedford* (1880), quoted in *Ross* v. *Bernhard,* 396 US 531 (1970). *Pernell* v. *Southall Realty,* US   (1974), held that in an action to recover possession of real property, either party may demand trial by jury. For comments on equity jurisdiction, see page 48.

United States v. Barnett

376 US 681, 84 S Ct 984, 12 L Ed2d 23 (1964)

A person charged with criminal contempt of court has no constitutional right to trial by jury in cases where the punishment given does not exceed the maximum punishment for a petty crime.

MR. JUSTICE CLARK delivered the opinion of the Court.

This proceeding in criminal contempt was commenced by the United States upon the specific order, *sua sponte,* of the Court of Appeals for the Fifth Circuit. Ross R. Barnett, Governor of the State of Mississippi at the time this action arose, and Paul B. Johnson, Jr., Lieutenant Governor, stand charged with willfully disobeying certain restraining orders issued, or directed to be entered, by that court. Governor Barnett and Lieutenant Governor Johnson moved to dismiss, demanded a trial by jury and filed motions to sever and to strike various charges. The Court of Appeals, being evenly divided on the question of right to jury trial, has certified the question to this Court. . . . We pass only on the jury issue and decide that the alleged contemners are not entitled to a jury as a matter of right.

The proceeding is the aftermath of the efforts of James Meredith, a Negro, to attend the University of Mississippi. . . .

As we have said, the sole issue before us is whether the alleged contemners are entitled as a matter of right to a jury trial on the charges. We consider this issue without prejudice to any other contentions that have been interposed in the case and without any indication as to their merits.

The First Congress in the Judiciary Act of 1789 conferred on federal courts the power "to punish by fine or imprisonment, at the discretion of said courts, all contempts of authority in any cause or hearing before the same. . . ." 1 Stat 83. It is undisputed that this Act gave federal courts the discretionary power to punish for contempt as that power was known to the common law. *In re Savin,* 131 US 267, 275–276 (1889). In 1831, after the unsuccessful impeachment proceedings against Judge Peck, the Congress restricted the power of federal courts to inflict summary punishment for contempt to misbehavior "in the presence of the said courts, or so near thereto as to obstruct the administration of justice," misbehavior of court officers in official matters, and disobedience or resistance by any person to any lawful writ, process, order, rule, decree, or command of the courts. Act of March 2, 1831, c 99, 4 Stat 487, 488. These provisions are now codified in 18 USC § 401 without material difference. The Court of Appeals proceeded in this case under the authority of this section. . . .

[I]t is urged that those charged with criminal contempt have a constitutional right to a jury trial. This claim has been made and rejected here again and again. Only six years ago we held a full review of the issue in *Green v. United States,* 356 US 165 (1958). We held there that "[t]he statements of this Court in a long and unbroken line of decisions involving contempts ranging from misbehavior in court to disobedience of court orders established beyond peradventure that criminal contempts are not subject to jury trial as a matter of constitutional right." At 183. Nor can it be said with accuracy that these cases were based upon historical error. It has always been the law of the land, both state and federal, that the courts—except where specifically precluded by statute—have the power to proceed summarily in contempt matters. There were, of course, statutes enacted by some of the Colonies which provided trivial punishment in specific, but limited, instances. Some statutes concerned the contempt powers of only certain courts or minor judicial officers. Others concerned specific offenses such as swearing in the presence of officials or the failure of a witness or juror to answer a summons.

But it cannot be said that these statutes set a standard permitting exercise of the summary contempt power only for offenses classified as trivial. . . .[12]

Mr. Justice Black, with whom Mr. Justice Douglas joins, dissenting. . . .

I think that in denying a jury trial here the Court flies in the face of . . . two

---

12. However, our cases have indicated that . . . the severity of the penalty imposed . . . might entitle a defendant to the benefit of a jury trial. [Footnote by the Court.]

constitutional commands. My reasons for this belief were stated in *Green* v. *United States,* 356 US 165, 193 (dissenting opinion). . . . Unfortunately, as the Court's opinion points out, judges in the past despite these constitutional safeguards have claimed for themselves "inherent" power, acting without a jury and without other Bill of Rights safeguards, to punish for criminal contempt of court people whose conduct they find offensive. This means that one person has concentrated in himself the power to charge a man with a crime, prosecute him for it, conduct his trial, and then find him guilty. I do not agree that any such "inherent" power exists. Certainly no language in the Constitution permits it; in fact, it is expressly forbidden by the two constitutional commands for trial by jury. And of course the idea that persons charged with criminal offenses such as criminal contempt are not charged with "crimes" is a judicial fiction. As I said in Green, I think that this doctrine that a judge has "inherent" power to make himself prosecutor, judge and jury seriously encroaches upon the constitutional right to trial by jury and should be repudiated.

In *Green* the Court affirmed a three-year sentence imposed for criminal contempt. But now in note 12 of its opinion in the present case the Court has inserted an ambiguous statement which intimates that if a sentence of sufficient "severity" had already been imposed on these defendants, a majority of the Court would now overrule *Green* in part, by holding that if a criminal contempt charge is tried without allowing the defendant a jury trial, punishment is constitutionally limited to that customarily meted out for "petty offenses." I welcome this as a halting but hopeful step in the direction of ultimate judicial obedience to the doubly proclaimed constitutional command that all people charged with a crime, including those charged with criminal contempt must be given a trial with all the safeguards of the Bill of Rights, including indictment by grand jury and trial by jury. . . .

Mr. Justice Goldberg with whom The Chief Justice and Mr. Justice Douglas join, dissenting.

In response to the certified question, I would answer that defendants have both a statutory and a constitutional right to have their case tried by a jury. . . .

The Court, in denying defendants' constitutional claim to a jury trial, rests on the history of criminal contempts relied on in its past decisions. . . .

A review of the original sources convinces me, however, that the history relied on by the decisions of this Court does not justify the relatively recent practice of imposing *serious* punishment for criminal contempts without a trial by jury. My research, which is confirmed by the authorities cited in the Appendix to the opinion of the Court, suggests the following explanation as to why criminal contempts were generally tried without a jury at the time of the Constitution: the penalties then authorized and imposed for criminal contempts were generally minor; and the courts were authorized to impose minor criminal penalties without a trial by jury for a variety of trivial offenses including, but not limited to, criminal contempts. . . .

I wish to make it clear that I am not here concerned with, nor do I question, the power of the courts to compel compliance with their lawful orders by the imposition of conditional punishment—commonly referred to as civil contempt. In such cases, it may be said that "the defendant carries the keys to freedom in his willingness to comply with the court's directive. . . ." Nor am I here concerned with the imposition of the trivial punishments traditionally deemed sufficient for maintaining order in the courtroom. Cf. *Ungar* v. *Sarafite, ante,* p. 575. I am concerned solely with the imposition, without trial by jury, of fixed nontrivial punishments *after* compliance with the court's order has been secured.

Thus limited, criminal contempts are not essentially different from other "crimes" or "criminal prosecutions." In each case punishment is imposed for a past violation of a mandate of a coordinate organ of government: criminal contempt involves punishment for violation of an order of a court: "crime" involves punishment for a violation of a statute enacted by a legislature. I can see no greater need for certain and prompt punishment for the former than for the latter. . . .

Note

Civil Rights Act of 1964.   Section 1101 of this Act (Public Law 88–350) reads as follows:

> In any proceeding for criminal contempt arising under title II, III, IV, V, VI, or VII of this Act, the accused, upon demand therefor, shall be entitled to a trial by jury, which shall conform as near as may be to the practice in criminal cases. Upon conviction, the accused shall not be fined more than $1,000 or imprisoned for more than six months.
>
> This section shall not apply to contempts committed in the presence of the court, or so near thereto as to obstruct the administration of justice, nor to the misbehavior, misconduct, or disobedience of any officer of the court in respect to writs, orders, or process of the court. No person shall be convicted of criminal contempt hereunder unless the act or omission constituting such contempt shall have been intentional, as required in other cases of criminal contempt.
>
> Nor shall anything herein be construed to deprive courts of their power, by civil contempt proceedings, without a jury, to secure compliance with or to prevent obstruction of, as distinguished from punishment for violations of, any lawful writ, process, order, rule, decree, or command of the court in accordance with the prevailing usages of law and equity, including the power of detention.

E. TRIAL BY NEWS MEDIA

Introduction

The law is frequently faced with the problem of reconciling competing concepts, each valid within proper limits. One aspect of the competition between freedom of the press, on the one hand, and, on the other, the right of an accused to a fair trial was presented above (p. 276) under the heading "Contempt of Court." The aspect of the subject dealt with here is presented forcefully in the concurring opinion of Justice Frankfurter in *Irvin* v. *Dowd,* 366 US 717 (1960):

> Not a Term passes without this Court being importuned to review convictions, had in States throughout the country, in which substantial claims are made that a jury trial has been distorted because of inflammatory newspaper accounts—too often, as in this case, with the prosecutor's collaboration—exerting pressures upon potential jurors

before trial and even during the course of trial, thereby making it extremely difficult, if not impossible, to secure a jury capable of taking in, free of prepossessions, evidence submitted in open court. Indeed such extraneous influences, in violation of the decencies guaranteed by our Constitution, are sometimes so powerful that an accused is forced, as a practical matter, to forego trial by jury. . . . For one reason or another this Court does not undertake to review all such envenomed state prosecutions. But, again and again, such disregard of fundamental fairness is so flagrant that the Court is compelled, as it was only a week ago, to reverse a conviction in which prejudicial newspaper intrusion has poisoned the outcome. . . . This Court has not yet decided that the fair administration of criminal justice must be subordinated to another safeguard of our constitutional system—freedom of the press, properly conceived. The Court has not yet decided that, while convictions must be reversed and miscarriages of justice result because the minds of jurors or potential jurors were poisoned, the poisoner is constitutionally protected in plying his trade.

In *Billie Sol Estes* v. *Texas,* 381 US 532 (1965), the thesis was advanced "that the freedoms granted in the First Amendment extend a right to the news media to televise from the courtroom, and that to refuse to honor this privilege is to discriminate between the newspaper and television." The Court rejected the thesis on the ground that "Court proceedings are held for the solemn purpose of endeavoring to ascertain the truth which is the *sine qua non* of a fair trial" and that televising court proceedings was "inherently lacking in due process." For the majority of the Court, Mr. Justice Clark wrote:

As has been said, the chief function of our judicial machinery is to ascertain the truth. The use of television, however, cannot be said to contribute materially to this objective. Rather its use amounts to the injection of an irrelevant factor into court proceedings. In addition experience teaches that there are numerous situations in which it might cause actual unfairness—some so subtle as to defy detection by the accused or control by the judge. We enumerate some in summary:

1. The potential impact of television on the jurors is perhaps of the greatest significance. They are the nerve center of the fact-finding process. . . .

2. The quality of the testimony in criminal trials will often be impaired. The impact upon a witness of the knowledge that he is being viewed by a vast audience is simply incalculable. . . .

3. A major aspect of the problem is the additional responsibilities the presence of television places on the trial judge. His job is to make certain that the accused receives a fair trial. This most difficult task requires his undivided attention. Still when television comes into the courtroom he must also supervise it. . . .

4. Finally, we cannot ignore the impact of courtroom television on the defendant. Its presence is a form of mental—if not physical—harassment, resembling a police line-up or the third degree. . . .

It is said that the ever-advancing techniques of public communication and the adjustment of the public to its presence may bring about a change in the effect of telecasting upon the fairness of criminal trials. But we are not dealing here with future developments in the field of electronics. Our judgment cannot be rested on the hypothesis of tomorrow but must take the facts as they are presented today.

Justices Black, White, Stewart, and Brennan dissented.

In *Sheppard* v. *Maxwell* the Court suggested measures that should be taken by the trial judge to guard against prejudice to a defendant by news media. Contrast the recommendations of the American Bar Association's advisory committee (the Reardon Committee) of 1966 entitled *Fair Trial and Free Press* with those of the 1967 committee of the Bar of the City of New York (the Medina Committee) entitled *Freedom of the Press and Fair Trial.* See also Tennant Bryant, ed., *Free Press and Fair Trial* (New York, 1967) and Alfred Friendly and Ronald L. Goldfarb, *Crime and Publicity* (New York, 1967).

Sheppard v. Maxwell

384 US 333, 86 S Ct 1507, 16 L Ed2d 600 (1966)

It is a denial of due process for the judge to permit a trial to be conducted in the atmosphere of a Roman holiday for the news media.

MR. JUSTICE CLARK delivered the opinion of the Court.

This federal habeas corpus application involves the question whether Sheppard was deprived of a fair trial in his state conviction for the second-degree murder of his wife because of the trial judge's failure to protect Sheppard sufficiently from the massive, pervasive and prejudicial publicity that attended his prosecution. . . .

There can be no question about the nature of the publicity which surrounded Sheppard's trial. We agree, as did the Court of Appeals, with the findings in Judge Bell's opinion for the Ohio Supreme Court:

"Murder and mystery, society, sex and suspense were combined in this case in such a manner as to intrigue and captivate the public fancy to a degree perhaps unparalleled in recent annals. Throughout the preindictment investigation, the subsequent legal skirmishes and the nine-week trial, circulation-conscious editors catered to the insatiable interest of the American public in the bizarre. . . . In this atmosphere of a 'Roman holiday' for the news media, Sam Sheppard stood trial for his life. . . ."

Much of the material printed or broadcast during the trial was never heard from the witness stand, such as the charges that Sheppard had purposely impeded the murder investigation and must be guilty since he had hired a prominent criminal lawyer; that Sheppard was a perjurer; that he had sexual relations with numerous women; that his slain wife had characterized him as a "Jekyll-Hyde"; that he was "a bare-faced liar" because of his testimony as to police treatment; and, finally, that a woman convict claimed Sheppard to be the father of her illegitimate child. As the trial progressed, the newspapers summarized and interpreted the evidence, devoting particular attention to the material that incriminated Sheppard, and often drew unwarranted inferences from testimony. At one point, a front-page picture of Mrs. Sheppard's blood-stained pillow was published after being "doctored" to show more clearly an alleged imprint of a surgical instrument.

Nor is there doubt that this deluge of publicity reached at least some of the jury. On the only occasion that the jury was queried, two jurors admitted in open court to hearing the highly inflammatory charge that a prison inmate claimed Sheppard as the father of her illegitimate child. Despite the extent and nature of the publicity to which the jury was exposed during trial, the judge refused defense counsel's other requests that the jurors be asked whether they had read or heard specific prejudicial comment about the case, including the incidents we have previously summarized. In these circumstances, we can assume that some of this material reached members of the jury. . . .

The court's fundamental error is compounded by the holding that it lacked power to control the publicity about the trial. From the very inception of the proceedings the judge announced that neither he nor anyone else could restrict prejudicial news accounts. And he reiterated this view on numerous occasions. Since he viewed the news media as his target, the judge never considered other means that are often utilized to reduce the appearance of prejudicial material and to protect the jury from outside influence. We conclude that these procedures would have been sufficient to guarantee Sheppard a fair trial and so do not consider what sanctions might be available against a recalcitrant press nor the charges of bias now made against the state trial judge.

The carnival atmosphere at trial could easily have been avoided since the courtroom and courthouse premises are subject to the control of the court. As we stressed in *Estes*, the presence of the press at judicial proceedings must be limited when it is apparent that the accused might otherwise be prejudiced or disadvantaged. Bearing in mind the massive pretrial publicity, the judge should have adopted stricter rules governing the use of the courtroom by newsmen, as Sheppard's counsel requested. The number of reporters in the courtroom itself could have been limited at the first sign that their presence would disrupt the trial. They certainly should not have been placed inside the bar. Furthermore, the judge should have more closely regulated the conduct of newsmen in the courtroom. For instance, the judge belatedly asked them not to handle and photograph trial exhibits lying on the counsel table during recesses.

Secondly, the court should have insulated the witnesses. All of the newspapers and radio stations apparently interviewed prospective witnesses at will, and in many instances disclosed their testimony. A typical example was the publication of numerous statements by Susan Hayes, before her appearance in court, regarding her love affair with Sheppard. Although the witnesses were barred from the courtroom during the trial the full verbatim testimony was available to them in the press. . . .

Thirdly, the court should have made some effort to control the release of leads, information, and gossip to the press by police officers, witnesses, and the counsel for both sides. Much of the information thus disclosed was inaccurate, leading to groundless rumors and confusion. . . .

. . . [I]t is obvious that the judge should have . . . sought to alleviate this problem by imposing control over the statements made to the news media by counsel, witnesses, and especially the Coroner and police officers. The prosecution repeatedly made evidence available to the news media which was never offered in the trial. Much of the "evidence" disseminated in this fashion was clearly inadmissible. The exclusion of such evidence in court is rendered meaningless when news media make it available to the public. For example, the publicity about Sheppard's refusal to take a lie detector test came directly from police officers and the Coroner. The story that Sheppard had been called a "Jekyll-Hyde" personality by his wife was attributed to a prosecution witness. No such testimony was given. The further report that there was "a 'bombshell witness' on tap" who would testify as to Sheppard's "fiery temper" could only have emanated from the prosecution. Moreover, the newspapers described in detail clues that had been found by the police, but not put into the record.

The fact that many of the prejudicial news items can be traced to the prosecution, as well as the defense, aggravates the judge's failure to take any action. . . . Effective control of these sources—concededly within the court's power—might well have prevented the divulgence of inaccurate information, rumors, and accusations that made up much of the inflammatory publicity, at least after Sheppard's indictment.

More specifically, the trial court might well have proscribed extrajudicial statements by any lawyer, party, witness, or court official which divulged prejudicial matters, such as the refusal of Sheppard to submit to interrogation or take any lie detector tests; any statement made by Sheppard to officials; the identity of prospective witnesses or their probable testimony; any belief in guilt or innocence; or like statements concerning the merits of the case. See *State* v. *Van Duyne,* 43 NJ 369, 389, 204 A. 2d 841, 852 (1964), in which the court interpreted Canon 20 of the American Bar Association's Canons of Professional Ethics to prohibit such statements. Being advised of the great public interest in the case, the mass coverage of the press, and the potential prejudicial impact of publicity, the court could also have requested the appropriate city and county officials to promulgate a regulation with respect to dissemination of information about the case by their employees. In addition, reporters who wrote or broadcast prejudicial stories, could have been warned as to the impropriety of publishing material not introduced in the proceedings. The judge was put on notice of such events by defense counsel's complaint about the WHK broadcast on the second day of trial. . . . In this manner, Sheppard's right to a trial free from outside interference would have been given added protection without corresponding curtailment of the news media. Had the judge, the other officers of the court, and the police placed the interest of justice first, the news media would have soon learned to be content with the task of reporting the case as it unfolded in the courtroom—not pieced together from extrajudicial statements. . . .

Since the state trial judge did not fulfill his duty to protect Sheppard from the inherently prejudicial publicity which saturated the community and to control disruptive influences in the courtroom, we must reverse the denial of the habeas petition. The case is remanded to the District Court with instructions to issue the writ and order that Sheppard be released from custody unless the State puts him to its charges again within a reasonable time.

It is so ordered.

Mr. Justice Black dissents.

F. DOUBLE JEOPARDY

Introduction

The Fifth Amendment contains the clause, "nor shall any person be subject for the same offense to be twice put in jeopardy of life or limb." *Benton* v. *Maryland,* 395 US 784 (1969), incorporated this clause as a limitation on the states.

A person is in jeopardy "when he is put upon trial, before a court of competent jurisdiction upon an indictment or information which is sufficient in form and substance to sustain a confiction, and a jury has been empaneled and sworn to try him." T. M. Cooley, *Principles of Constitutional Law,* 3d ed. (Boston, 1898), p. 325. Once put on trial, an accused has a right to a verdict by the jury sworn to try him, and the government has no right to withdraw the charges because of insufficiency of evidence. If the verdict is for acquittal, the accused cannot again be tried for the same offense.

Two Sovereignties

While neither the national government nor a state government may twice put a person in jeopardy for the same offenses, a person may be punished by both governments for a single act which constitutes an offense under the laws of both. *United States* v. *Lanza,* 260 US 377 (1922). According to Chief Justice Taft, "We have two sovereignties, deriving power from different sources, capable of dealing with the same subject matter within the same territory." This principle was confirmed in *Bartkus* v. *Illinois,* 359 US 121 (1959), in which a person tried and acquitted in a federal court on a charge of robbing a Federal Savings and Loan Bank was subsequently convicted in an Illinois court under a robbery statute and sentenced to life imprisonment. The same year in *Abbate* v. *United States,* 359 US 187 (1959), the Court also confirmed the power of the United States to punish a person for an act already punished by a state. Abbate plead guilty to an Illinois indictment alleging conspiracy to dynamite telephone facilities and was sentenced to three months imprisonment. Later he was indicted, tried, and convicted in a federal District Court for conspiring to destroy communication facilities controlled by the United States in violation of a federal statute carrying a penalty fine of not more than $10,000 or imprisonment of not more than five years, or both.

While double punishment under the two sovereigns principle is possible, in practice it is uncommon. A week after the *Abbate* decision was announced, Attorney General Rogers stated in a press release (*New York Times,* 6 April 1959) that the federal power to prosecute a person for an offense already punished under a state law is "used sparingly" and only when the reasons are "compelling." Note also the holding in *Waller* v. *Florida,* 397 US 387 (1970), that "The State of Florida and its municipalities are not separate sovereign entities each entitled to impose punishment for the same alleged crime. . . ."

One Act, Several Offenses

A single act may constitute several offenses. For example, a person may commit the act of illegally transporting imported opium in an automobile driven at an excessive speed down a one-way street in the wrong direction. Three offenses are here involved, with different evidence needed for the proof of each. The Supreme Court has adopted no clear policy governing successive trials of the same defendant for offenses involved in a single transaction. However, *Ashe* v. *Swenson,* 397 US 436 (1970), applied the doctrine of collateral estoppel to prevent a second trial. "It means simply that when an issue of ultimate fact has once been determined by a valid and final judgment, that issue cannot again be litigated between the same parties in any future lawsuit" and is a rule applicable to both civil and criminal cases. In the *Ashe* case, a group of men playing poker were held up and robbed by four masked bandits. Ashe, thought to be one of the bandits, was tried for robbing Knight, one of the poker players. For lack of clear evidence of identity, Ashe was acquitted. Six weeks later he was again tried, this time for robbing Roberts, another of the poker players, convicted, and sentenced to thirty-five years imprisonment. The Supreme Court reversed the conviction, holding the second trial to have constituted double jeopardy.

Retrial upon Reversal of Conviction

In general, retrial after a conviction in the trial court has been reversed by an appellate court is not considered as double jeopardy. However, *Green* v. *United States,* 355 US 184 (1957), held that a person tried for murder and convicted in the second degree, could not, upon reversal of the judgment by an appellate court, be retried for murder in the first degree. *North Carolina* v. *Pearce,* 395 US 711 (1969), held that the state was not prevented, upon retrial of a case, from imposing a greater penalty than that imposed in the first trial. The *Green* case was distinguished on the ground that it involved a retrial for an offense of which the defendant had been acquitted. Dissenting, Justice Douglas held this to be "a matter of semantics." To him it was immaterial "whether the Legislature divides a crime into different degrees carrying different punishments or allows the court or jury to fix different punishments for the same crime."

Retrial after Mistrial

A mistrial resulting from a circumstance such as failure of the jury to reach a verdict is no bar to a retrial, but a mistrial caused by the prosecution usually is. *United States* v. *Jorn,* 400 US 470 (1971), held that the trial judge's abuse of discretion in discharging the jury in the early stages of a tax fraud case barred a retrial of the case.

The prosecution had sought to present as witnesses taxpayers whom Jorn had aided in preparing tax returns.

> After the first of these witnesses was called, but prior to the commencement of direct examination, defense counsel suggested that these witnesses be warned of their constitutional rights. The trial court agreed, and proceeded, in careful detail, to spell out the witness' right not to say anything that might be used in a subsequent criminal prosecution against him and his right, in the event of such a prosecution, to be represented by an attorney. The first witness expressed a willingness to testify and stated that he had been warned of his constitutional rights when the Internal Revenue Service first contacted him. The trial judge indicated, however, that he did not believe the witness had been given any warning at the time he was first contacted by the IRS, and refused to permit him to testify until he had consulted an attorney.
>
> The trial judge then asked the prosecuting attorney if his remaining four witnesses were similarly situated. The prosecutor responded that they had been warned of their rights by the IRS upon initial contact. The judge, expressing the view that any warnings that might have been given were probably inadequate, proceeded to discharge the jury. . . .

Justice Stewart, joined by Justices White and Blackmun, dissented because there was "no showing of an intent on the part of either the prosecutor or the judge to harass the defendant or to enhance the chances of conviction in a second trial."

A summary of the cases on the subject is contained in *Illinois* v. *Somerville,* 410 US 458 (1973). Somerville was indicted for theft. The case was called for trial and a jury impaneled and sworn. The next day, before any evidence had been presented, the prosecution discovered that the indictment failed to allege an intent to permanently deprive the owner of his property, a fatal defect, not subject to correction by amendment under Illinois law. Over the defense's objection, the trial judge granted a motion of mistrial. Somerville was later reindicted, tried, and convicted.

The United States Supreme Court sustained the action of the trial judge in granting the motion for mistrial. For the Court, Justice Rehnquist wrote:

> The fountainhead decision construing the Double Jeopardy Clause in the context of a declaration of mistrial over a defendant's objection is *United States* v. *Perez,* 9 Wheaton (22 US) 579 (1824). Mr. Justice Story, writing for a unanimous Court, set forth the standards for determining whether a retrial, following a declaration of a mistrial over a defendant's objection, constitutes double jeopardy within the meaning of the Fifth Amendment. In holding that the failure of the jury to agree on a verdict of either acquittal or conviction did not bar retrial of the defendant, Mr. Justice Story wrote:
>
> "We think, that in all cases of this nature, the law has invested Courts of Justice with the authority to discharge a jury from giving any verdict, whenever, in their opinion, taking all the circumstances into consideration, there is a manifest necessity for the act, or the ends of public justice would otherwise be defeated. They are to exercise a sound discretion on the subject; and it is impossible to define all the circumstances, which would render it proper to interfere. To be sure, the power ought to be used with the greatest caution under urgent circumstances, and for very plain and obvious cases; and, in capital cases especially, Courts should be extremely careful how they interfere with any of the chances of life, in favor of the prisoner. But, after all, they have the right to order the discharge, and the security which the public have for the faithful, sound and conscientious exercise of this discretion, rests, in this, as in other cases, upon the responsibility of the Judges, under their oaths of office." *Id.,* at 580.
>
> This formulation, consistently adhered to by this Court in subsequent decisions, abjures the application of any mechanical formula by which to judge the propriety of declaring a mistrial in the varying and often unique situations arising during the course of a criminal trial. The broad discretion reserved to the trial judge in such circumstances has been consistently reiterated in decisions of this Court. . . .
>
> The determination by the trial court to abort a criminal proceeding where jeopardy has attached is not one to be lightly undertaken, since the interest of the defendant in having his fate determined by the jury first impaneled is itself a weighty one. . . . Nor will the lack of demonstrable additional prejudice preclude the defendant's invocation of the double jeopardy bar in the absence of some important countervailing interest of proper judicial administration. . . . But where the declaration of a mistrial implements a reasonable state policy and aborts a proceeding that at best would have produced a verdict that could have been upset at will by one of the parties, the defendant's interest in proceeding to verdict is outweighed by the competing and equally legitimate demand for public justice. . . .

Justices Brennan, Douglas, Marshall, and White dissented. Justice White wrote:

> Although recognizing that "a criminal trial is, even in the best of circumstances, a complicated affair to manage," *id.,* the Court has not thought prosecutorial error sufficient excuse for not applying the Double Jeopardy Clause. In *Jorn,* for instance, the Court declared that "unquestionably an important factor to be considered is the need to hold litigants on both sides to standards of responsible professional conduct in the clash of an adversary criminal process" and cautioned, "The trial judge must recognize that lack of preparedness by the Government . . . directly implicates policies underpinning both the double jeopardy provision and the speedy trial guarantee." *Id.,* at 486. See also *id.,* at 487–488 (BURGER, C. J., concurring); *Downum* v. *United States,* 372 US, at 737. Here, the prosecutorial error, not the independent operation of a state procedural rule, necessitated the mistrial. Judged by the standards of *Downum* and *Jorn* I cannot find, in the words of the majority, an "important countervailing interest of proper judicial administration" in this case; I cannot find "manifest necessity" for a mistrial to compensate for prosecutorial mistake.

Blackledge v. *Perry,* 417 US 21 (1974), applied the principle that imposition of a penalty upon a defendant for pursuing a statutory right of appeal violates due process. Perry, a North Carolina prison inmate, had an altercation with another prisoner. He was charged with the misdemeanor of assault with a deadly weapon, tried, and convicted in the state district court. While Perry was appealing the conviction to the superior court, the prosecutor obtained an indictment based on the same conduct charging Perry with the felony of assault with intent to kill, to which he plead guilty. He later applied to a federal district court for a writ of habeas corpus, which was granted. Blackwell, the North Carolina warden involved, then appealed and lost in both the court of appeals and the Supreme Court. For the latter, Justice Stewart wrote:

> As in the District Court, Perry directs two independent constitutional attacks upon the conduct of the State in hailing him into court on the felony charge after he took an appeal from the misdemeanor conviction. First, he contends that the felony indictment in the Superior Court placed him in double jeopardy, since he had already been convicted on the lesser included misdemeanor charge in the District Court. Second, he urges that the indictment on the felony charge constituted a penalty for his exercising his statutory right to appeal, and thus contravened the Due Process Clause of the Fourteenth Amendment. We find it necessary to reach only the latter claim.
>
> Perry's due process arguments are derived substantially from *North Carolina* v. *Pearce,* 395 US 711, and its progeny. . . .
>
> The lesson that emerges from *Pearce, Colten,* and *Chaffin* is that the Due Process Clause is not offended by all possibilities of increased punishment upon retrial after appeal, but only by those that pose a realistic likelihood of "vindictiveness." Unlike the circumstances presented by those cases, however, in the situation here the central figure is not the judge or the jury, but the prosecutor. The question is whether the opportunities for vindictiveness in this situation are such as to impel the conclusion that due process of law requires a rule analogous to that of the *Pearce* case. We conclude that the answer must be in the affirmative.

United States v. Tateo

377 US 463, 84 S Ct 1587, 12 L Ed2d 448 (1964)

The prohibition against double jeopardy does not preclude the government from retrying a defendant whose conviction is set aside because of an error in the proceedings that led to conviction.

MR. JUSTICE HARLAN delivered the opinion of the Court.

This case presents the question whether a federal criminal defendant who has had his conviction overturned in collateral proceedings on the ground that a guilty plea entered by him during trial was not voluntary but induced in part by comments of the trial judge, may be tried again for the same crimes or is protected against such a prosecution by the Double Jeopardy Clause of the Fifth Amendment. We hold that under these circumstances retrial does not infringe the constitutional protection against double jeopardy.

On May 15, 1956, the respondent [Rocco] Tateo, and another were brought to trial before a jury on a five-court indictment charging bank robbery . . . ; kidnaping in connection with the robbery . . . ; taking and carrying away bank money . . . ; receiving and possessing stolen bank money . . .; and conspiracy . . . to commit some of these substantive offenses. On the fourth day of trial, the judge informed Tateo's counsel that if Tateo were found guilty by the jury he would impose a life sentence on the kidnaping charge and consecutive sentences on the other charges. Upon being told of the judge's position and advised by his counsel that the likelihood of conviction was great, Tateo pleaded guilty, as did his codefendant. Thereupon the jury was discharged; the kidnaping count was dismissed with the prosecution's consent; and Tateo was sentenced to a total of 22 years and 6 months imprisonment on the other counts.

In a later proceeding under 28 USC § 2255, another district judge (Judge Weinfeld) granted Tateo's motion to set aside the judgment of conviction and for a new trial, determining that the cumulative impact of the trial testimony, the trial judge's expressed view on punishment, and the strong advice given by his counsel rendered it doubtful that Tateo possessed the freedom of will necessary for a voluntary plea of guilty. . . .

After being reindicted on the kidnaping charge, Tateo was brought before a third district judge (Judge Tyler) for trial on that charge and the four bank robbery charges to which he had earlier pleaded guilty. Upon motions by the defense, Judge Tyler dismissed both the kidnaping count, now abandoned by the Government, and the other four counts. He reasoned that, since neither genuine consent nor an "exceptional circumstance" underlay the termination of the first trial and no "waiver" of the double jeopardy claim had been made by Tateo, the Government was precluded from retrying him. . . . The Government appealed, in accord with 18 USC § 3731, which permits direct appeal to this Court from a decision of a District Court sustaining a motion in bar before the defendant has been put in jeopardy. We noted probable jurisdiction. . . . For reasons given below, we reverse the judgment of the District Court.

The Fifth Amendment provides that no "person [shall] be subject for the same offence to be twice put in jeopardy of life or limb; . . . ." The principle that this provision does not preclude the Government retrying a defendant whose conviction is set aside because of an error in the proceedings leading to conviction is a well-established part of our constitutional jurisprudence. In this respect we differ from the practice obtaining in England. The rule in this country was explicitly stated in *United States* v. *Ball,* 163 US 662, 671–672, a case in which defendants were reindicted after this Court had found the original indictment to be defective. . . .

While different theories have been advanced to support the permissibility of retrial, of greater importance than the conceptual abstractions employed to explain the *Ball* principle are the implications of that principle for the sound administration of justice. Corresponding to the right of an accused to be given a fair trial is the societal interest in punishing one whose guilt is clear after he has obtained such a trial. It would be a high price indeed for society to pay were every accused granted immunity from punishment because of any defect sufficient to constitute reversible error in the proceedings leading to conviction. From the standpoint of a defendant, it is at least doubtful that appellate courts would be as zealous as they now are in protecting against the effects of improprieties at the trial or pretrial stage if they knew that reversal of a conviction would put the accused irrevocably beyond the reach of further prosecution. In reality, therefore, the practice of retrial serves defendants' rights as well as society's interest. The underlying purpose of permitting retrial is as much furthered by application of the rule to this case as it has been in cases previously decided.

Tateo contends that his situation must be distinguished from one in which an accused has been found guilty by a jury, since his involuntary plea of guilty deprived him of the opportunity to obtain a jury verdict of acquittal. We find this argument unconvincing. . . .

We conclude that this case falls squarely within the reasoning of Ball and subsequent cases allowing the Government to *retry* persons whose convictions have been overturned. The judgment below is therefore reversed and the case remanded to the District Court with instructions to reinstate the four bank robbery counts.

It is so ordered.

MR. JUSTICE GOLDBERG, with whom MR. JUSTICE BLACK and MR. JUSTICE DOUGLAS join, dissenting.

I would affirm the District Court's holding . . . that under our decision last term in *Downum* v. *United States,* 372 US 734, the Double Jeopardy Clause of the Fifth Amendment protects Tateo against reprosecution. . . .

In Downum, on the morning the case was called for trial both sides announced ready. A jury was selected, sworn, and instructed to return at 2 P.M. When it returned the prosecution asked that the jury be discharged because its key witness on two counts of the indictment was not present—a fact discovered by the prosecutor only during the noon recess. It was not contended that the failure to secure the attendance of this witness was in any way deliberate or based upon the prosecutor's conclusion that the impaneled jury was likely to acquit. Instead, the "jury first selected to try petitioner and sworn was discharged because a prosecution witness had not been served with a summons and because no other arrangements had been made to assure his presence." *Downum* v. *United States, supra,* at 737. In sustaining the claim of double jeopardy as to a retrial commenced two days later, this Court said:

"At times the valued right of a defendant to have his trial completed by the particular tribunal summoned to sit in judgment on him may be subordinated to the public interest —when there is an imperious necessity to do so. ... Differences have arisen as to the application of the principle. ... Harassment of an accused by successive prosecutions or declaration of a mistrial so as to afford the prosecution a more favorable opportunity to convict are examples when jeopardy attaches. ... But those extreme cases do not mark the limits of the guarantee. The discretion to discharge the jury before it has reached a verdict is to be exercised 'only in very extraordinary and striking circumstances,' to use the words of Mr. Justice Storey in *United States* v. *Coolidge*, 25 Fed Cas 622, 623. For the prohibition of the Double Jeopardy Clause is 'not against being twice punished, but against being twice put in jeopardy.' *United States* v. *Ball*, 163 US 662, 669." *Id.*, at 736. ...

The Court thus held that *Downum* could not be reprosecuted, since by virtue of prosecutorial neglect, he was denied his constitutional right to have the impaneled jury hear and decide his case. ...

I agree with my Brother DOUGLAS dissenting in *Gori* v. *United States*, 367 US, at 373 that: "The question is not ... whether a defendant is "to receive absolution for his crime. ... The policy of the Bill of Rights is to make rare indeed the occasions when the citizen can for the same offense be required to run the gantlet twice. The risk of judicial arbitrariness rests where, in my view, the Constitution puts it—on the Government." As in *Downum* I would "resolve any doubt 'in favor of the liberty of the citizen.' "

For these reasons, I dissent.

G. MISCELLANEOUS

Furman v. Georgia

408 US 238, 92 S Ct 2726, 33 L Ed2d 346 (1972)

The imposition of the death penalty in the three cases before the Court constitutes cruel and unusual punishment.

PER CURIAM.

Petitioner in No. 69-5003 was convicted of murder in Georgia and was sentenced to death pursuant to Ga. Code Ann. § 26-1005 (Supp. 1971) ... Petitioner in No. 69-5030 was convicted of rape in Georgia and was sentenced to death ... Petitioner in No. 69-5031 was convicted of rape in Texas and was sentenced to death ... *Certiorari* was granted limited to the following question: "Does the imposition and carrying out of the death penalty in [these cases] constitute cruel and unusual punishment in violation of the Eighth and Fourteenth Amendments?" ... The Court holds that the imposition and carrying out of the death penalty in these cases constitutes cruel and unusual punishment in violation of the Eighth and Fourteenth Amendments. The judgment in each case is therefore reversed insofar as it leaves undisturbed the death sentence imposed, and the cases are remanded for further proceedings.

So ordered.

MR. JUSTICE BRENNAN, concurring. [Omitted.]

MR. JUSTICE STEWART, concurring.

The penalty of death differs from all other forms of criminal punishment, not in degree but in kind. It is unique in its total irrevocability. It is unique in its rejection of rehabilitation of the convict as a basic purpose of criminal justice. And it is unique, finally, in its absolute renunciation of all that is embodied in our concept of humanity.

For these and other reasons, at least two of my Brothers [Brennan and Marshall] have concluded that the infliction of the death penalty is constitutionally impermissible in all circumstances under the Eighth and Fourteenth Amendments. Their case is a strong one. But I find it unnecessary to reach the ultimate question they would decide. . . .

The opinions of other Justices today have set out in admirable and thorough detail the origins and judicial history of the Eighth Amendment's guarantee against the infliction of cruel and unusual punishments, and the origin and judicial history of capital punishment. There is thus no need for me to review the historical materials here, and what I have to say can, therefore, be briefly stated.

Legislatures—state and federal—have sometimes specified that the penalty of death shall be the mandatory punishment for every person convicted of engaging in certain designated criminal conduct. Congress, for example, has provided that anyone convicted of acting as a spy for the enemy in time of war shall be put to death. The Rhode Island Legislature has ordained the death penalty for a life term prisoner who commits murder. Massachusetts has passed a law imposing the death penalty upon anyone convicted of murder in the commission of a forcible rape. An Ohio law imposes the mandatory penalty of death upon the assassin of the President of the United States or the Governor of a State.

If we were reviewing death sentences imposed under these or similar laws, we would be faced with the need to decide whether capital punishment is unconstitutional for all crimes and under all circumstances. We would need to decide whether a legislature—state or federal—could constitutionally determine that certain criminal conduct is so atrocious that society's interest in deterrence and retribution wholly outweighs any considerations of reform or rehabilitation of the perpetrator, and that despite the inconclusive empirical evidence, only the automatic penalty of death will provide maximum deterrence.

On that score I would say only that I cannot agree that retribution is a constitutionally impermissible ingredient in the imposition of punishment. The instinct for retribution is part of the nature of man, and channeling that instinct in the administration of criminal justice serves an important purpose in promoting the stability of a society governed by law. When people begin to believe that organized society is unwilling or unable to impose upon criminal offenders the punishment they "deserve," then there are sown the seeds of anarchy—of self-help, vigilante justice, and lynch law.

The constitutionality of capital punishment in the abstract is not, however, before us in these cases. For the Georgia and Texas legislatures have not provided that the death penalty shall be imposed upon all those who are found guilty of forcible rape. . . .

For these reasons I concur in the judgments of the Court.

MR. JUSTICE WHITE, concurring.

The facial constitutionality of statutes requiring the imposition of the death penalty for first degree murder, for more narrowly defined categories of murder or for rape would present quite different issues under the Eighth Amendment than are posed by the cases before us. In joining the Court's judgment, therefore, I do not at all intimate that the death penalty is unconstitutional *per se* or that there is no system of capital punishment that would comport with the Eighth Amendment. That question, ably argued by several of my Brethren, is not presented by these cases and need not be decided. . . .

I concur in the judgments of the Court.

MR. JUSTICE MARSHALL, concurring. [Omitted.]

MR. CHIEF JUSTICE BURGER, with whom MR. JUSTICE BLACKMAN, MR. JUSTICE POWELL, and MR. JUSTICE REHNQUIST join, dissenting.

At the outset it is important to note that only two members of the Court, MR. JUSTICE BRENNAN and MR. JUSTICE MARSHALL, have concluded that the Eighth Amendment prohibits capital punishment for all crimes and under all circumstances. MR. JUSTICE DOUGLAS has also determined that the death penalty contravenes the Eighth Amendment, although I do not read his opinion as necessarily requiring final abolition of the penalty. For the reasons set forth in . . . this opinion, I conclude that the constitutional prohibition against "cruel and unusual punishments" cannot be construed to bar the imposition of the punishment of death.

MR. JUSTICE STEWART and MR. JUSTICE WHITE have concluded that petitioners' death sentences must be set aside because prevailing sentencing practices do not comply with the Eighth Amendment. . . . I believe this approach fundamentally misconceives the nature of the Eighth Amendment guarantee and flies directly in the face of controlling authority of extremely recent vintage. . . .

Today the Court has not ruled that capital punishment is *per se* violative of the Eighth Amendment; nor has it ruled that the punishment is barred for any particular class or classes of crimes. The substantially similar concurring opinions of MR. JUSTICE STEWART and MR. JUSTICE WHITE, which are necessary to support the judgment setting aside petitioners' sentences, stop short of reaching the ultimate question. . . .

. . . The decisive grievance of the opinions . . . is that the present system of discretionary sentencing in capital cases has failed to produce evenhanded justice; the problem is not that too few have been sentenced to die, but that the selection process has followed no rational pattern. . . .

Since there is no majority of the Court on the ultimate issue presented in these cases, the future of capital punishment in this country has been left in an uncertain limbo. Rather than providing a final and unambiguous answer on the basic constitutional question, the collective impact of the majority's ruling is to demand an undetermined measure of change from the various state legislatures and the Congress. While I cannot endorse the process of decisionmaking that has yielded today's result and the restraints which that result imposes on legislative action, I am not altogether displeased that legislative bodies have been given the opportunity, and indeed unavoidable responsibility, to make a thorough re-evaluation of the entire subject of capital punishment. If today's opinions demonstrate nothing else, they starkly show that this is an area where legislatures can act far more effectively than courts.

Notes

1. *Desist* v. *United States,* 394 US 244 (1969), contains a summary of the cases dealing with the question of retroactive application of the new rules of criminal procedure promulgated by the Warren Court. See also *Jenkins* v. *Delaware,* 395 US 213 (1969), and *Chaffin* v. *Stynchcombe,* 412 US 17 (1973).

2. *Allen* v. *Illinois,* 397 US 337 (1970), held that through conduct so "disorderly, disruptive, and disrespectful of the court that his trial cannot be carried on with him in the courtroom," a defendant can lose his right to be present at his trial. Compare *Mayberry* v. *Pennsylvania,* 400 US 455 (1971), and *Johnson* v. *Mississippi,* 403 US 212 (1971).

3. *In re Gault,* 387 US 1 (1967), held that in a juvenile proceeding to determine "delinquency" which may lead to commitment to a state institution the basic elements of due process, including notice and hearing, the right to counsel, and the right to cross-examine witnesses, must be observed. *In re Winship,* 397 US 358 (1970), held that in such a proceeding "the constitutional safeguard of proof beyond a reasonable doubt" was applicable. However, *McKeiver* v. *Pennsylvania,* 403 US 528 (1971), held that trial by jury was not required.

4. *Jencks* v. *United States,* 353 US 657 (1957), held that in federal prosecutions the accused has the right to have produced in court reports from the files of the FBI containing statements made against him by a witness being used against him. *Palermo* v. *United States,* 360 US 343 (1959), modified the rule by holding that the trial judge could excise from such report security information not relevant to the testimony of the witness.

5. *Witherspoon* v. *Illinois,* 391 US 510 (1968), held that imposition of the death penalty by a "hanging jury" cannot be squared with the Constitution. "If the State had excluded only those prospective jurors who stated in advance of trial that they would not even consider returning a verdict of death, it could be argued that the resulting jury was simply 'neutral' with respect to penalty. But when it swept from the jury all who expressed conscientious or religious scruples against capital punishment and all who opposed it in principle, the State crossed the line of neutrality."

6. *Morrissey* v. *Brewer,* 408 US 471 (1972), spelled out the procedural requirements for the revocation of parole, as follows:

> Due process requires a reasonably prompt informal inquiry conducted by an impartial hearing officer near the place of the alleged parole violation or arrest to

determine if there is reasonable ground to believe that the arrested parolee has violated a parole condition. The parolee should receive prior notice of the inquiry, its purpose, and the alleged violations. The parolee may present relevant information and (absent security considerations) question adverse informants. The hearing officer shall digest the evidence on probable cause and state the reasons for holding the parolee for the parole board's decision.

At the revocation hearing, which must be conducted reasonably soon after the parolee's arrest, minimum due process requirements are: (a) written notice of the claimed violations of parole; (b) disclosure to the parolee of evidence against him; (c) opportunity to be heard in person and to present witnesses and documentary evidence; (d) the right to confront and cross-examine adverse witnesses (unless the hearing officer specifically finds good cause for not allowing confrontation); (e) a "neutral and detached" hearing body such as a traditional parole board, members of which need not be judicial officers or lawyers; and (f) a written statement by the factfinders as to the evidence relied on and reasons for revoking parole.

Chapter 13

Citizenship

A. ACQUISITION OF CITIZENSHIP

"All persons born or naturalized in the United States, and subject to the jurisdiction thereof, are citizens of the United States, and of the State wherein they reside," reads the Fourteenth Amendment. A leading case interpreting the meaning of this sentence is *United States* v. *Wong Kim Ark,* 169 US 649 (1898). Wong, a Chinese admittedly born in the United States, was refused admission by our immigration officials after a temporary visit to China. This action was based on the assumption that Wong was not a citizen of the United States because his parents, although domiciled in the United States, were subjects of the Emperor of China and ineligible to naturalization under the laws of the United States. The Supreme Court, however, ruled that Wong was a citizen of the United States. Mr. Justice Gray wrote:

> The fourteenth amendment affirms the ancient and fundamental rule of citizenship by birth within the territory, in the allegiance and under the protection of the country, including all children here born of resident aliens, with the exceptions or qualifications (as old as the rule itself) of children of foreign sovereigns or their ministers [but not consuls], or born on foreign public ships, or of enemies within and during a hostile occupation of part of our territory, and with the single additional exception of children of members of the Indian tribes owing direct allegiance to their several tribes. The amendment, in clear words and in manifest intent, includes the children born within the territory of the United States of all other persons, of whatever race or color, domiciled within the United States. Every citizen or subject of another country, while domiciled here, is within the allegiance and the protection, and consequently subject to the jurisdiction, of the United States. . . .

Citizenship by birth, as defined in the Constitution, cannot be restricted; yet Congress is free to expand citizenship by birth as it sees fit. Under the Immigration and

Nationality Act of 1952 (66 Stat 163), citizenship by birth is based on place of birth, on parentage, or on a combination of these two factors. For details, see Albert B. Saye et al., *Principles of American Government* (New York, 1974), pp. 132–46.

B.   LOSS OF CITIZENSHIP

Afroyim v. Rusk

387 US 253, 87 S Ct 1660, 18 L Ed2d 757 (1967)

Congress has no general power to take away an American citizen's citizenship without his consent.

MR. JUSTICE BLACK delivered the opinion of the Court.

Petitioner, born in Poland in 1893, immigrated to this country in 1912 and became a naturalized American citizen in 1926. He went to Israel in 1950, and 1951 he voluntarily voted in an election for the Israeli Knesset, the legislative body of Israel. In 1960, when he applied for renewal of his United States passport, the Department of State refused to grant it on the sole ground that he had lost his American citizenship by virtue of § 401 (e) of the Nationality Act of 1940 which provides that a United States citizen shall "lose" his citizenship if he votes "in a political election in a foreign state." Petitioner then brought this declaratory judgment action in federal district court. . . .

First we reject the idea expressed in *Perez* that, aside from the Fourteenth Amendment, Congress has any general power, express or implied, to take away an American citizen's citizenship without his assent. This power cannot, as *Perez* indicated, be sustained as an implied attribute of sovereignty possessed by all nations. . . .

. . . [A]ny doubt as to whether prior to the passage of the Fourteenth Amendment Congress had the power to deprive a person against his will of citizenship once obtained should have been removed by the unequivocal terms of the Amendment itself. It provides its own constitutional rule in language calculated completely to control the status of citizenship: "All persons born or naturalized in the United States . . . are citizens of the United States . . ." There is no indication in these words of fleeting citizenship, good at the moment it is acquired but subject to destruction by the Government at any time. Rather the Amendment can most reasonably be read as defining a citizenship which a citizen keeps unless he voluntarily relinquishes it. Once acquired, this Fourteenth Amendment citizenship was not to be shifted, canceled, or diluted at the will of the Federal Government, the States, or any other governmental unit. . . .

Because the legislative history of the Fourteenth Amendment and of the expatriation proposals which preceded and followed it, like most other legislative history, contains many statements from which conflicting inferences can be drawn, our holding might be unwarranted if it rested entirely or principally upon that legislative history. But it does not. Our holding we think is the only one that can stand in view of the language and the purpose of the Fourteenth Amendment, and our construction of that Amendment, we believe, comports more nearly than *Perez* with the principles of liberty and equal justice to all that the entire Fourteenth Amendment was adopted to guarantee. Citizenship is no light trifle to be jeopardized any moment Congress decides to do so under the name of one of its general or implied grants of power. In some instances, loss of citizenship can mean that a man is left without the protection of citizenship in any country in the world—as a man without a country. Citizenship in this Nation is a part of a cooperative affair. Its citizenry is the country and the country is its citizenry. The very nature of our free government makes it completely incongruous to have a rule of law under which a group of citizens temporarily in office can deprive another group of citizens of their citizenship. We hold that the Fourteenth Amendment was designed to, and does, protect every citizen of this Nation against a congressional forcible destruction of his citizenship, whatever his creed, color, or race. Our holding does no more than to give to this citizen that which is his own, a constitutional right to remain a citizen in a free country unless he voluntarily relinquishes that citizenship.

Perez v. *Brownell* is overruled. The judgment is

Reversed.

MR. JUSTICE HARLAN, whom MR. JUSTICE CLARK, MR. JUSTICE STEWART, and MR. JUSTICE WHITE join, dissenting. [Twenty-five pages omitted here.]

Notes

1. *Roger* v. *Bellei,* 401 US 815 (1971), sustained the constitutionality of § 301 (b) of the Immigration and Nationality Act of 1952 which provides that one who acquires United States citizenship by virtue of having been born abroad to parents, one of whom is a United States citizen, shall lose his citizenship unless he resides in this country continuously for five years between the ages of fourteen and twenty-eight. Such person does not come within the Fourteenth Amendment's definition of citizens as those "born or naturalized in the United States," and the residence requirement imposed by Congress is not unreasonable.

2. *Kawakita* v. *United States,* 343 US 725 (1957), recognized dual citizenship, in this case Japanese-American. Kawakita did not lose his Japanese citizenship by acquiring United States citizenship, nor did he lose United States citizenship by claiming privileges under his Japanese citizenship. "As we have said, dual citizenship presupposes rights of citizenship in each country. It could not exist if the assertion of rights or the assumption of liabilities of one were deemed inconsistent with the maintenance of the other. For example, when one has a dual citizenship, it is not necessarily inconsistent with his citizenship in one nation to use a passport proclaiming his citizenship in the other. . . . Hence the use by petitioner of a Japanese passport on his trip to China, his use of the Koseki entry to obtain work at the Ocyama camp, the bowing to the Emperor, and his acceptance of labor draft papers from the Japanese government might reasonably mean no more than acceptance of some of the incidents of Japanese citizenship made possible by his dual citizenship."

C. PRIVILEGES AND IMMUNITIES

National Citizenship

Slaughterhouse Cases

16 Wallace 36, 21 L Ed 394 (1873)

The privileges and immunities of citizens of the United States are those which arise out of the nature and essential character of the national government, the provisions of its Constitution, or its laws and treaties made in pursuance thereof.

MR. JUSTICE MILLER . . . delivered the opinion of the court.

These cases are brought here by writs of error to the Supreme Court of the State of Louisiana. They arise out of the efforts of the butchers of New Orleans to resist the Crescent City Livestock Landing and Slaughter-House Company in the exercise of certain powers conferred by the charter which created it, and which was granted by the legislature of that State. . . .

The statute thus assailed as unconstitutional was passed March 8th, 1869, and is entitled "An act to protect the health of the city of New Orleans, to locate the stock-landings and slaughter-houses, and to incorporate the Crescent City Live-Stock Landing and Slaughter-House Company."

The [statute] forbids the landing or slaughtering of animals whose flesh is intended for food, within the city of New Orleans and other parishes and boundaries named and defined, or the keeping or establishing any slaughter-houses or *abattoirs* within those limits except by the corporation thereby created, which is also limited to certain places afterwards mentioned. Suitable penalties are enacted for violations of this prohibition. . . .

The plaintiffs in error . . . allege that the statute is a violation of the Constitution of the United States in . . ..

That it abridges the privileges and immunities of citizens of the United States; . . .

This court is thus called upon for the first time to give construction to these articles. . . .

The first section of the fourteenth article, to which our attention is more specially invited, opens with a definition of citizenship—not only citizenship of the United States, but citizenship of the States. . . .

"All persons born or naturalized in the United States, and subject to the jurisdiction thereof, are citizens of the United States and of the State wherein they reside." . . .

[T]he distinction between citizenship of the United States and citizenship of a State is clearly recognized and established. Not only may a man be a citizen of the United States without being a citizen of a State, but an important element is necessary to convert the former into the latter. He must reside within the State to make him a citizen of it, but it is only necessary that he should be born or naturalized in the United States to be a citizen of the Union.

It is quite clear, then, that there is a citizenship of the United States, and a citizenship of a State, which are distinct from each other, and which depend upon different characteristics or circumstances in the individual.

We think this distinction and its explicit recognition in this amendment of great weight in this argument, because the next paragraph of this same section, which is the one mainly relied on by the plaintiffs in error, speaks only of privileges and immunities of citizens of the United States, and does not speak of those of citizens of the several States. . . .

The language is, "No State shall make or enforce any law which shall abridge the privileges or immunities of citizens of *the United States.*" It is a little remarkable, if this clause was intended as a protection to the citizen of a State against the legislative power of his own State, that the word citizen of the State should be left out when it is so carefully used, and used in contradistinction to citizens of the United States, in the very sentence which precedes it. It is too clear for argument that the change in phraseology was adopted understandingly and with a purpose. . . .

If, then, there is a difference between the privileges and immunities belonging to a citizen of the United States as such, and those belonging to the citizen of the State as such, the latter must rest for their security and protection where they have heretofore rested; for they are not embraced by this paragraph of the amendment.

The first occurrence of the words "privileges and immunities" in our constitutional history, is to be found in the fourth of the articles of the old Confederation. . . .

In the Constitution of the United States, which superseded the Articles of Confederation, the corresponding provision is found in section two of the fourth article, in the following words: "The citizens of each State shall be entitled to all the privileges and immunities of citizens of the several States." . . .

Fortunately we are not without judicial construction of this clause of the Constitution. The first and the leading case on the subject is that of *Corfield* v. *Coryell,* decided by Mr. Justice Washington in the Circuit Court for the District of Pennsylvania in 1823[1] . . .

Having shown that the privileges and immunities relied on in the argument are those which belong to citizens of the States as such, and that they are left to the State governments for security and protection, and not by this article placed under the special care of the Federal government, we may hold ourselves excused from defining the privileges and immunities of citizens of the United States which no State can abridge, until some case involving those privileges may make it necessary to do so.

But lest it should be said that no such privileges and immunities are to be found if those we have been considering are excluded, we venture to suggest some which owe their existence to the Federal government, its National character, its Constitution, or its laws.

One of these is well described in the case of *Crandall* v. *Nevada.* It is said to be the right of the citizen of this great country, protected by implied guarantees of its Constitution, "to come to the seat of government to assert any claim he may have upon that government, to transact any business he may have with it, to seek its protection, to

---

1. See below, page 485.

share its offices, to engage in administering its functions. He has the right of free access to its seaports, through which all operations of foreign commerce are conducted, to the subtreasuries, land offices, and courts of justice in the several States." . . .

Another privilege of a citizen of the United States is to demand the care and protection of the Federal government over his life, liberty, and property when on the high seas or within the jurisdiction of a foreign government. Of this there can be no doubt, nor that the right depends upon his character as a citizen of the United States. The right to peaceably assemble and petition for redress of grievances, the privilege of the writ of *habeas corpus,* are rights of citizen guaranteed by the Federal Constitution. The right to use the navigable waters of the United States, however they may penetrate the territory of the several States, all rights secured to our citizens by treaties with foreign nations, are dependent upon citizenship of the United States, and not citizenship of a State. One of these privileges is conferred by the very article under consideration. It is that a citizen of the United States can, of his own volition, become a citizen of any State of the Union by a *bona fide* residence therein, with the same rights as other citizens of that State. To these may be added the rights secured by the thirteenth and fifteenth articles of amendment, and by the other clause of the fourteenth, next to be considered.

But it is useless to pursue this branch of the inquiry, since we are of opinion that the rights claimed by these plaintiffs in error, if they have any existence, are not privileges and immunities of citizens of the United States within the meaning of the clause of the fourteenth amendment under consideration. . . .

The judgments of the Supreme Court of Louisiana in these cases are

Affirmed.

MR. JUSTICE FIELD, dissenting. . . .

The [Fourteenth] amendment does not attempt to confer any new privileges of immunities upon citizens, or to enumerate or define those already existing. It assumes that there are such privileges and immunities which belong of right to citizens as such, and ordains that they shall not be abridged by State legislation. If this inhibition has no reference to privileges and immunities of this character, but only refers, as held by the majority of the court in their opinion, to such privileges and immunities as were before its adoption specially designated in the Constitution or necessarily implied as belonging to citizens of the United States, it was a vain and idle enactment, which accomplished nothing, and most unnecessarily excited Congress and the people on its passage. With privileges and immunities thus designated or implied no State could ever have interfered by its laws, and no new constitutional provision was required to inhibit such interference. The supremacy of the Constitution and the laws of the United States always controlled any State legislation of that character. But if the amendment refers to the natural and inalienable rights which belong to all citizens, the inhibition has a profound significance and consequence.

What, then, are the privileges and immunities which are secured against abridgment by State legislation? . . .

The privileges and immunities designated are those *which of right belong to the citizens of all free governments.* Clearly among these must be placed the right to pursue a lawful employment in a lawful manner, without other restraint than such as equally affects all persons. . . .

I am authorized by the CHIEF JUSTICE, MR. JUSTICE SWAYNE, and MR. JUSTICE BRADLEY, to state that they concur with me in this dissenting opinion.

MR. JUSTICE BRADLEY, also [dissented]. . . .

Notes

1. *Subsequent history.*   The decision in the *Slaughterhouse Cases* has never been overruled, and, as a result, the privileges and immunities clause of the Constitution is of little significance in our constitutional law. In the forty-odd cases in which the contention has been advanced that a state law was in conflict with this clause, only once has the contention been sustained, and within five years this decision was overruled, *Colgate* v. *Harvey,* 296 US 404 (1935), reversed by *Madden* v. *Kentucky,* 309 US 83 (1940). See also 34 Illinois Law Review 998 (1940). Thus, while citizens of the United States enjoy many privileges and immunities, they enjoy few of these *because* they are citizens. All persons under the jurisdiction of the United States, regardless of citizenship, enjoy most of these privileges.

2. *Passports.*   *Kent* v. *Dulles,* 357 US 116 (1958), held that the right to travel abroad is "an important aspect of the citizen's 'liberty' " guaranteed by the due process clause of the Fifth Amendment. *Aptheker* v. *Secretary of State Rusk,* 378 US 500 (1964), held void Section 6 of the Subversive Activities Control Act of 1950 which made it unlawful for a member of a Communist organization to apply for or to use an American passport.
  Zemel v. *Rusk,* 381 US 1 (1965), held that the secretary of state had valid statutory authority to refuse to validate passports for travel to Cuba. Compare the holding in *United States* v. *Laub,* 385 US 475 (1967), that area restrictions upon the use of an otherwise valid passport were not criminally enforceable under existing statutes.

State Citizenship

Corfield v. Coryell

4 Wash CC 371, 6 Fed Cas 546
Circuit Court, ED Pennsylvania. April Term, 1823

A state may confine the use of fisheries within its territorial limits to its own citizens.

[Coryell found Corfield, a nonresident, raking oysters in Maurice River Cove, N.J. Acting as a prize master, he conducted Corfield's boat, the Hiram, to Leesburg and had it condemned. Corfield brought this action of trespass.]

WASHINGTON, Circuit Justice. The points reserved present for the consideration of the court many interesting and difficult questions, which will be examined in the shape of objections made by the plaintiff's counsel to the seizure of the Hiram, and the proceedings of the magistrates of Cumberland County, upon whose sentence the defendant rests his justification of the alleged trespass. These objections are,—

First. That the act of the legislature of New Jersey of the 9th of June 1820, under which this vessel, found engaged in taking oysters in Maurice River Cove by means of dredges, was seized, condemned, and sold, is repugnant to the constitution of the United States in the following particulars: ... To the second section of the fourth article, which declares, that the citizens of each state shall be entitled to all privileges and immunities of citizens in the several states. ...

The ... act of New Jersey delcares ... that it shall not be lawful for any person who is not, at the time, an actual inhabitant and resident of this state, to gather oysters in any of the rivers, bays, or waters in this state ... and every person so offending, shall forfeit $10 and shall also forfeit the vessel employed in the commission of such offence. ...

The inquiry is, what are the privileges and immunities of citizens in the several states? We feel no hesitation in confining these expressions to those privileges and immunities which are, in their nature, fundamental; which belong, of right, to the citizens of all free governments; and which have, at all times, been enjoyed by the citizens of the several states which compose this Union, from the time of their becoming free, independent, and sovereign. What these fundamental principles are, it would perhaps be more tedious than difficult to enumerate. They may, however, be all comprehended under the following general heads: Protection by the government; the enjoyment of life and liberty, with the right to acquire and possess property of every kind, and to pursue and obtain happiness and safety; subject nevertheless to such restraints as the government may justly prescribe for the general good of the whole. The right of a citizen of one state to pass through or to reside in any other state, for purposes of trade, agriculture, professional pursuits, or otherwise; to claim the benefit of the writ of habeas corpus; to institute and maintain actions of any kind in the courts of the state; to take, hold and dispose of property, either real or personal; and an exemption from higher taxes or impositions than are paid by the other citizens of the state; may be mentioned as some of the particular privileges and immunities of citizens, which are clearly embraced by the general description of privileges deemed to be fundamental: to which may be added, the elective franchise, as regulated and established by the laws or constitution of the state in which it is to be exercised. These, and many others which might be mentioned, are, strictly speaking, privileges and immunities, and the enjoyment of them by the citizens of each state, in every other state, was manifestly calculated (to use the expressions of the preamble of the corresponding provision in the old articles of confederation) "the better to secure and perpetuate mutual friendship and intercourse among the people of the different states of the Union." But we cannot accede to the counsel, that, under this provision of the constitution, the citizens of the several states are permitted to participate in all the rights which belong exclusively to the citizens of any other particular state, merely upon the ground that they are enjoyed by those citizens; much less, that in regulating the use of the common property of the citizens of such state, the legislature is bound to extend to the citizens of all the other states the same advantages as are secured to their own citizens. ...

The oyster beds belonging to a state may be abundantly sufficient for the use of the citizens of that state, but might be totally exhausted and destroyed if the legislature could not so regulate the use of them as to exclude the citizens of the other states from taking them, except under such limitations and restrictions as the laws may prescribe. . . .

Let judgment be entered for the defendant.

Notes

1. *Toomer* v. *Witsell*, 334 US 385 (1948). In this case a statute that imposed a $2500 license fee on nonresidents for each boat engaged in shrimp fishing in a three-mile belt off the South Carolina coast but only a $25 fee upon residents was held invalid. The Court found that the reasons advanced for the statute bore no reasonable relation to the high degree of discrimination practiced.

2. *Corporations.* The privileges and immunities clause of Article IV does not apply to aliens or to artificial "persons" such as corporations or partnerships. Except insofar as its action may burden interstate commerce, a state may refuse a corporation the right of doing business within its territory or impose conditions upon the exercise of this privilege. Thus an insurance company chartered under the laws of one state may be admitted to do business in another state only upon condition that it maintain local agents and grant them designated commissions, *Osborn* v. *Ozlin*, 310 US 53 (1940).

3. *Professions.* Whether this constitutional provision applies to those engaging in professions or trades that require special skills is not altogether clear. In *Graham* v. *Richardson*, 403 US 365 (1971), Justice Blackmun wrote:

> It is true that this Court on occasion has upheld state statutes that treat citizens and noncitizens differently, the ground for distinction having been that such laws were necessary to protect special interests of the State or its citizens. Thus, in *Traux* v. *Raich*, 239 US 33 (1915), the Court, in striking down an Arizona statute restricting the employment of aliens, emphasized that "[t]he discrimination defined by the act does not pertain to the regulation or distribution of the public domain, or of the common property or resources of the people of the State, the enjoyment of which may be limited to its citizens as against both aliens and the citizens of other States." 239 US, at 39–40. And in *Crane* v. *New York*, 239 US 195 (1915), the Court affirmed the judgment in *People* v. *Crane*, 214 NY 154, 108 NE 427 (1915), upholding a New York statute prohibiting the employment of aliens on public works projects. . . . On the same theory, the Court has upheld statutes that, in the absence of overriding treaties, limit the right of noncitizens to engage in exploitation of a State's natural resources, restrict the devolution of real porperty to aliens, or deny to aliens the right to acquire and own land.
> *Takahashi* v. *Fish & Game Comm'n* . . ., however, cast doubt on the continuing validity of the special public-interest doctrine in all contexts. . . .
> Whatever may be the contemporary vitality of the special public-interest doctrine in other contexts after *Takahashi*, we conclude that a State's desire to preserve limited welfare benefits for its own citizens is inadequate to justify Pennsylvania's making noncitizens ineligible for public assistance, and Arizona's restricting benefits to citizens

and longtime resident aliens. First, the special public interest doctrine was heavily grounded on the notion that "[w]hatever is a privilege, rather than a right, may be made dependent upon citizenship." *People* v. *Crane,* 214 NY, at 164. . . . But this Court now has rejected the concept that constitutional rights turn upon whether a governmental benefit is characterized as a "right" or as a "privilege." . . .

Supreme Court Justices

Note: The names of the Chief Justices are in boldface.

1.	**John Jay**	1789–1795
2.	**John Rutledge**[1]	
3.	William Cushing	1789–1810
4.	James Wilson	1789–1798
5.	John Blair	1789–1796
6.	James Iredell	1790–1799
7.	Thomas Johnson	1791–1793
8.	William Paterson	1793–1806
9.	Samuel Chase	1796–1811
10.	**Oliver Ellsworth**	1796–1800
11.	Bushrod Washington	1798–1829
12.	Alfred Moore	1799–1804
13.	**John Marshall**	1801–1835
14.	William Johnson	1804–1834
15.	Brockholst Livingston	1806–1823
16.	Thomas Todd	1807–1826
17.	Joseph Story	1811–1845
18.	Gabriel Duval	1811–1835
19.	Smith Thompson	1823–1843
20.	Robert Trimble	1826–1828
21.	John McLean	1829–1861

---

1. John Rutledge was appointed to the Supreme Court in 1789 but resigned without serving. In 1795 he was given a recess appointment as chief justice and served until his appointment was rejected by the Senate on December 15, 1795.

22.	Henry Baldwin	1830–1844
23.	James Moore Wayne	1835–1867
24.	**Roger Brooke Taney**	1836–1864
25.	Philip Pendleton Barbour	1836–1841
26.	John Catron	1837–1865
27.	John McKinley	1837–1852
28.	Peter Vivian Daniel	1841–1860
29.	Samuel Nelson	1845–1872
30.	Levi Woodbury	1845–1851
31.	Robert Cooper Grier	1846–1870
32.	Benjamin Robbins Curtis	1851–1857
33.	John Archibald Campbell	1853–1861
34.	Nathan Clifford	1858–1881
35.	Noah Haynes Swayne	1862–1881
36.	Samuel Freeman Miller	1862–1890
37.	David Davis	1862–1877
38.	Stephen Johnson Field	1863–1897
39.	**Salmon Portland Chase**	1864–1873
40.	William Strong	1870–1880
41.	Joseph P. Bradley	1870–1892
42.	Ward Hunt	1872–1882
43.	**Morrison Remick Waite**	1874–1888
44.	John Marshall Harlan	1877–1911
45.	William Burnham Woods	1880–1887
46.	Stanley Matthews	1881–1889
47.	Horace Gray	1881–1902
48.	Samuel Blatchford	1882–1893
49.	Lucius Quintus Cincinnatus Lamar	1888–1893
50.	**Melville Weston Fuller**	1888–1910
51.	David Josiah Brewer	1889–1910
52.	Henry Billings Brown	1890–1906
53.	George Shiras	1892–1903
54.	Howell Edmunds Jackson	1893–1895
55.	**Edward Douglass White**[2]	
56.	Rufus Wheeler Peckham	1895–1909
57.	Joseph McKenna	1898–1925
58.	Oliver Wendell Holmes	1902–1932
59.	William Rufus Day	1903–1922
60.	William Henry Moody	1906–1910
61.	Horace Harmon Lurton	1909–1914
62.	**Charles Evans Hughes**[3]	
63.	Willis Van Devanter	1910–1937
64.	Joseph Rucker Lamar	1910–1916
65.	Mahlon Pitney	1912–1922
66.	James Clark McReynolds	1914–1941
67.	Louis Dembitz Brandeis	1916–1939
68.	John Hessin Clarke	1916–1922
69.	**William Howard Taft**	1921–1930

2. White was associate justice, 1894–1910, and chief justice, 1910–1921.

3. Hughes was associate justice, 1910–1916, and chief justice, 1930–1941.

70. George Sutherland	1922–1938
71. Pierce Butler	1922–1939
72. Edward Terry Sanford	1923–1930
73. **Harlan Fiske Stone**[4]	
74. Owen Josephus Roberts	1930–1945
75. Benjamin Nathan Cardozo	1932–1938
76. Hugo Lafayette Black	1937–1971
77. Stanley Forman Reed	1938–1957
78. Felix Frankfurter	1939–1962
79. William Orville Douglas	1939–
80. Frank Murphy	1940–1949
81. James Francis Byrnes	1941–1942
82. Robert Hougwout Jackson	1941–1954
83. Wiley Blout Rutledge	1943–1949
84. Harold Hitz Burton	1945–1958
85. **Frederick Moore Vinson**	1946–1953
86. Thomas Campbell Clark	1949–1967
87. Sherman Minton	1949–1956
88. **Earl Warren**	1953–1969
89. John Marshall Harlan	1955–1971
90. William Joseph Brennan	1956–
91. Charles Evans Whittaker	1957–1962
92. Potter Stewart	1958–
93. Byron R. White	1962–
94. Arthur Joseph Goldberg	1962–1965
95. Abe Fortas	1965–1969
96. Thurgood Marshall	1967–
97. **Warren Earl Burger**	1969–
98. Harry A. Blackmun	1970–
99. Lewis F. Powell	1971–
100. William H. Rehnquist	1971–

4. Stone was associate justice, 1925–1941, and chief justice, 1941–1946.

Constitution of the United States

We the People of the United States, in order to form a more perfect Union, establish Justice, insure domestic Tranquility, provide for the common Defence, promote the general Welfare, and secure the Blessings of Liberty to ourselves and our Posterity, do ordain and establish this CONSTITUTION for the United States of America.

Article I

Sect. 1. All legislative powers herein granted shall be vested in a Congress of the United States, which shall consist of a Senate and House of Representatives.

Sect. 2. The House of Representatives shall be composed of members chosen every second year by the people of the several states, and the electors in each state shall have the qualifications requisite for electors of the most numerous branch of the state legislature.

No person shall be a representative who shall not have attained to the age of twenty-five years, and been seven years a citizen of the United States, and who shall not, when elected, be an inhabitant of that state in which he shall be chosen.

Representatives and direct taxes shall be apportioned among the several states which may be included within this Union, according to their respective numbers, which shall be determined by adding to the whole number of free persons, including those bound to service for a term of years, and excluding Indians not taxed, three-fifths of all other persons. The actual enumeration shall be made within three years after the first meeting of the Congress of the United States, and within every subsequent term of ten years, in such manner as they shall by law direct. The number of representatives shall not exceed one for every thirty thousand, but each state shall have at least

---

The text of the Constitution presented here is taken from the literal print in Senate Document No. 126, 83d Congress, 2d sess. Subsequent amendments have been added.

one representative; and until such enumeration shall be made, the state of New-Hampshire shall be entitled to chuse three, Massachusetts eight, Rhode-Island and Providence Plantations one, Connecticut five, New-York six, New-Jersey four, Pennsylvania eight, Delaware one, Maryland six, Virginia ten, North-Carolina five, South-Carolina five, and Georgia three.

When vacancies happen in the representation from any state, the Executive authority thereof shall issue writs of election to fill such vacancies.

The House of Representatives shall chuse their Speaker and other officers; and shall have the sole power of impeachment.

Sect. 3. The Senate of the United States shall be composed of two senators from each state, chosen by the legislature thereof, for six years; and each senator shall have one vote.

Immediately after they shall be assembled in consequence of the first election, they shall be divided as equally as may be into three classes. The seats of the senators of the first class shall be vacated at the expiration of the second year, of the second class at the expiration of the fourth year, and of the third class at the expiration of the sixth year, so that one-third may be chosen every second year; and if vacancies happen by resignation, or otherwise, during the recess of the legislature of any state, the Executive thereof may make temporary appointments until the next meeting of the legislature, which shall then fill such vacancies.

No person shall be a senator who shall not have attained to the age of thirty years, and been nine years a citizen of the United States, and who shall not, when elected, be an inhabitant of that state for which he shall be chosen.

The Vice-President of the United States shall be President of the senate, but shall have no vote, unless they be equally divided.

The Senate shall chuse their other officers, and also a President *pro tempore,* in the absence of the Vice-President, or when he shall exercise the office of President of the United States.

The Senate shall have the sole power to try all impeachments. When sitting for that purpose, they shall be on oath or affirmation. When the President of the United States is tried, the Chief Justice shall preside: And no person shall be convicted without the concurrence of two-thirds of the members present.

Judgment in cases of impeachment shall not extend further than to removal from office, and disqualification to hold and enjoy any office of honor, trust or profit under the United States; but the party convicted shall nevertheless be liable and subject to indictment, trial, judgment and punishment, according to law.

Sect. 4. The times, places and manner of holding elections for senators and representatives, shall be prescribed in each state by the legislature thereof: but the Congress may at any time by law make or alter such regulations, except as to the places of chusing Senators.

The Congress shall assemble at least once in every year, and such meeting shall be on the first Monday in December, unless they shall by law appoint a different day.

Sect. 5. Each house shall be the judge of the elections, returns and qualifications of its own members, and a majority of each shall constitute a quorum to do business; but a smaller number may adjourn from day to day, and may be authorised to compel the attendance of absent members, in such manner, and under such penalties as each house may provide.

Each house may determine the rules of its proceedings, punish its members for disorderly behaviour, and, with the concurrence of two-thirds, expel a member.

Each house shall keep a journal of its proceedings, and from time to time publish the same, excepting such parts as may in their judgment require secrecy; and the yeas and nays of the members of either house on any question shall, at the desire of one-fifth of those present, be entered on the journal.

Neither house, during the session of Congress, shall, without the consent of the other, adjourn for more than three days, nor to any other place than that in which the two houses shall be sitting.

Sect. 6. The senators and representatives shall receive a compensation for their services, to be ascertained by law, and paid out of the treasury of the United States. They shall in all cases, except treason, felony and breach of the peace, be privileged from arrest during their attendance at the session of their respective houses, and in going to and returning from the same; and for any speech or debate in either house, they shall not be questioned in any other place.

No senator or representative shall, during the time for which he was elected, be appointed to any civil office under the authority of the United States, which shall have been created, or the emoluments whereof shall have been encreased during such time; and no person holding any office under the United States, shall be a member of either house during his continuance in office.

Sect. 7.   All bills for raising revenue shall originate in the house of representatives; but the senate may propose or concur with amendments as on other bills.

Every bill which shall have passed the house of representatives and the senate, shall, before it become a law, be presented to the President of the United States; if he approve he shall sign it, but if not he shall return it, with his objections to that house in which it shall have originated, who shall enter the objections at large on their journal, and proceed to reconsider it. If after such reconsideration two-thirds of that house shall agree to pass the bill, it shall be sent, together with the objections, to the other house, by which it shall likewise be reconsidered, and if approved by two-thirds of that house, it shall become a law. But in all such cases the votes of both houses shall be determined by yeas and nays, and the names of the persons voting for and against the bill shall be entered on the journal of each house respectively. If any bill shall not be returned by the President within ten days (Sundays excepted) after it shall have been presented to him, the same shall be a law, in like manner as if he had signed it, unless the Congress by their adjournment prevent its return, in which case it shall not be a law.

Every order, resolution, or vote to which the concurrence of the Senate and House of Representatives may be necessary (except on a question of adjournment) shall be presented to the President of the United States; and before the same shall take effect, shall be approved by him, or, being disapproved by him, shall be re-passed by two-thirds of the Senate and House of Representatives, according to the rules and limitations prescribed in the case of a bill.

Sect. 8.   The Congress shall have power

To lay and collect taxes, duties, imposts and excises, to pay the debts and provide for the common defence and general welfare of the United States; but all duties, imposts and excises shall be uniform throughout the United States:

To borrow money on the credit of the United States:

To regulate commerce with foreign nations, and among the several states, and with the Indian tribes:

To establish an uniform rule of naturalization, and uniform laws on the subject of bankruptcies throughout the United States:

To coin money, regulate the value thereof, and of foreign coin, and fix the standard of weights and measures:

To provide for the punishment of counterfeiting the securities and current coin of the United States:

To establish post-offices and post-roads:

To promote the progress of science and useful arts, by securing for limited times to authors and inventors the exclusive right to their respective writings and discoveries:

To constitute tribunals inferior to the supreme court:

To define and punish piracies and felonies committed on the high seas, and offences against the law of nations:

To declare war, grant letters of marque and reprisal, and make rules concerning captures on land and water:

To raise and support armies, but no appropriation of money to that use shall be for a longer term than two years:

To provide and maintain a navy:

To make rules for the government and regulation of the land and naval forces:

To provide for calling forth the militia to execute the laws of the Union, suppress insurrections and repel invasions:

To provide for organizing, arming, and disciplining the militia, and for governing such part of them as may be employed in the service of the United States, reserving to the States respectively, the appointment of the officers, and the authority of training the militia according to the discipline prescribed by Congress:

To exercise exclusive legislation in all cases whatsoever, over such district (not exceeding ten miles square) as may, by cession of particular states, and the acceptance of Congress, become the seat of the government of the United States, and to exercise like authority over all places purchased by the consent of the legislature of the state in which the same shall be, for the erection of forts, magazines, arsenals, dock-yards, and other needful buildings:—And

To make all laws which shall be necessary and proper for carrying into execution the foregoing powers, and all other powers vested by this constitution in the government of the United States, or in any department or officer thereof.

Sect. 9.   The migration or importation of such persons as any of the states now existing shall think proper to admit, shall not be prohibited by the Congress prior to the year one thousand eight hundred and eight, but a tax or duty may be imposed on such importation, not exceeding ten dollars for each person.

The privilege of the writ of *habeas corpus* shall not be suspended, unless when in cases of rebellion or invasion the public safety may require it.

No bill of attainder or *ex post facto* law shall be passed.

No capitation, or other direct, tax shall be laid, unless in proportion to the *census* or enumeration herein before directed to be taken.

No tax or duty shall be laid on articles exported from any state. No preference shall be given by any regulation of commerce or revenue to the ports of one state over those of another; nor shall vessels bound to, or from, one state, be obliged to enter, clear, or pay duties in another.

No money shall be drawn from the treasury, but in consequence of appropriations made by law; and a regular statement and account of the receipts and expenditures of all public money shall be published from time to time.

No title of nobility shall be granted by the United States: And no person holding any office of profit or trust under them, shall, without the consent of the Congress, accept of any present, emolument, office, or title, of any kind whatever, from any king, prince or foreign state.

Sect. 10.   No state shall enter into any treaty, alliance, or confederation; grant letters of marque and reprisal; coin money; emit bills of credit; make any thing but gold and silver coin a tender in payment of debts; pass any bill of attainder, *ex post facto* law, or law impairing the obligation of contracts, or grant any title of nobility.

No state shall, without the consent of the Congress, lay any imposts or duties on imports or exports, except what may be absolutely necessary for executing its inspection laws; and the net produce of all duties and imposts, laid by any state on imports or exports, shall be for the use of the Treasury of the United States; and all such laws shall be subject to the revision and controul of the Congress. No state shall, without the consent of Congress, lay any duty of tonnage, keep troops, or ships of war in time of peace, enter into any agreement or compact with another state, or with a foreign power, or engage in war, unless actually invaded, or in such imminent danger as will not admit of delay.

Article II

Sect. 1.   The executive power shall be vested in a President of the United States of America. He shall hold his office during the term of four years, and, together with the Vice-President, chosen for the same term, be elected as follows:—

Each state shall appoint, in such manner as the legislature thereof may direct, a number of electors, equal to the whole number of senators and representatives to which the state may be entitled in the Congress: but no senator or representative, or person holding an office of trust or profit under the United States, shall be appointed an elector.

The electors shall meet in their respective states, and vote by ballot for two persons, of whom one at least shall not be an inhabitant of the same state with themselves. And they shall make a list of all the persons voted for, and of the number of votes for each; which list they shall sign and certify, and transmit sealed to the seat of the government of the United States, directed to the President of the Senate. The president of the Senate shall, in the presence of the Senate and House of Representatives, open all the certificates, and the votes shall then be counted. The person having the greatest number of votes shall be the President, if such number be a majority of the whole number of electors appointed; and if there be more than one who have such majority, and have an equal number of votes, then the House of Representatives shall immediately chuse by ballot one of them for President; and if no person have a majority, then from the five highest on the list the said House shall in like manner chuse the President. But in chusing the President, the votes shall be taken by states, the representation from each state having one vote; a quorum for this purpose shall consist of a member or members from two-thirds of the states, and a majority of all the states shall be necessary to a choice. In every case, after the choice of the President, the person having the greatest number of votes of the electors shall be the Vice-President. But if there should remain two or more who have equal votes, the Senate shall chuse from them by ballot the Vice-President.

The Congress may determine the time of chusing the electors, and the day on which they shall give their votes; which day shall be the same throughout the United States.

No person except a natural born citizen, or a citizen of the United States, at the time of the adoption of this constitution, shall be eligible to the office of President; neither shall any person be eligible to that office who shall not have attained to the age of thirty-five years, and been fourteen years a resident within the United States.

In case of the removal of the President from office, or of his death, resignation, or inability to discharge the powers and duties of the said office, the same shall devolve on the Vice-President, and the Congress may by law provide for the case of removal, death, resignation, or inability, both   the President and Vice-President, declaring what officer shall then act as President, and such officer shall act accordingly, until the disability be removed, or a President shall be elected.

The President shall, at stated times, receive for his services, a compensation, which shall neither be increased nor diminished during the period for which he shall have been elected, and he shall not receive within that period any other emolument from the United States, or any of them.

Before he enter on the execution of his office, he shall take the following oath or affirmation:
—
"I do solemnly swear (or affirm) that I will faithfully execute the office of President of the United States, and will to the best of my ability, preserve, protect and defend the constitution of the United States."

Sect. 2.   The President shall be commander in chief of the army and navy of the United States, and of the militia of the several states, when called into the actual service of the United States; he may require the opinion, in writing, of the principal officer in each of the executive departments, upon any subject relating to the duties of their respective offices, and he shall have power to grant reprieves and pardons for offences against the United States, except in cases of impeachment.

He shall have power, by and with the advice and consent of the Senate, to make treaties, provided two-thirds of the Senators present concur; and he shall nominate, and by and with the advice and consent of the Senate, shall appoint ambassadors, other public ministers and consuls, judges of the supreme court, and all other officers of the United States, whose appointments are not herein otherwise provided for, and which shall be established by law. But the Congress may by law vest the appointment of such inferior officers, as they think proper in the President alone, in the courts of law, or in the heads of departments.

The President shall have power to fill up all vacancies that may happen during the recess of the Senate, by granting commissions which shall expire at the end of their next Session.

Sect. 3. He shall from time to time give to the Congress information of the state of the union, and recommend to their consideration such measures as he shall judge necessary and expedient; he may, on extraordinary occasions, convene both houses, or either of them, and in case of disagreement between them, with respect to the time of adjournment, he may adjourn them to such time as he shall think proper; he shall receive ambassadors and other public ministers; he shall take care that the laws be faithfully executed, and shall commission all the officers of the United States.

Sect. 4. The president, vice-president and all civil officers of the United States shall be removed from office on impeachment for, and conviction of, treason, bribery, or other high crimes and misdemeanors.

Article III

Sect. 1. The judicial power of the United States shall be vested in one supreme court, and in such inferior courts as the Congress may from time to time ordain and establish. The judges, both of the supreme and inferior courts, shall hold their offices during good behaviour, and shall, at stated times, receive for their services, a compensation, which shall not be diminished during their continuance in office.

Sect. 2. The judicial power shall extend to all cases, in law and equity, arising under this constitution, the laws of the United States, and treaties made, or which shall be made, under their authority; to all cases affecting ambassadors, other public ministers and consuls; to all cases of admiralty and maritime jurisdiction; to controversies to which the United States shall be a party; to controversies between two or more states, between a state and citizens of another state, between citizens of different states, between citizens of the same state claiming lands under grants of different states, and between a state, or the citizens thereof, and foreign states, citizens or subjects.

In all cases affecting ambassadors, other public ministers and consuls, and those in which a state shall be party, the supreme court shall have original jurisdiction. In all the other cases before mentioned, the supreme court shall have appellate jurisdiction, both as to law and fact, with such exceptions, and under such regulations as the Congress shall make.

The trial of all crimes, except in cases of impeachment, shall be by jury; and such trial shall be held in the state where the said crimes shall have been committed; but when not committed within any state, the trial shall be at such place or places as the Congress may by law have directed.

Sect. 3. Treason against the United States, shall consist only in levying war against them, or in adhering to their enemies, giving them aid and comfort. No person shall be convicted of treason unless on the testimony of two witnesses to the same overt act, or on confession in open court.

The Congress shall have power to declare the punishment of treason, but no attainder of treason shall work corruption of blood, or forfeiture, except during the life of the person attainted.

ARTICLE IV

Sect. 1.   Full faith and credit shall be given in each state to the public acts, records and judicial proceedings of every other state. And the Congress may by general laws prescribe the manner in which such acts, records and proceedings shall be proved, and the effect thereof.

Sect. 2.   The citizens of each state shall be entitled to all privileges and immunities of citizens in the several states.

A person charged in any state with treason, felony, or other crime, who shall flee from justice, and be found in another state, shall, on demand of the executive authority of the state from which he fled, be delivered up, to be removed to the state having jurisdiction of the crime.

No person held to service or labour in one state, under the laws thereof, escaping into another, shall, in consequence of any law or regulation therein, be discharged from such service or labour, but shall be delivered up on claim of the party to whom such service or labour may be due.

Sect. 3.   New states may be admitted by the Congress into this union; but no new state shall be formed or erected within the jurisdiction of any other state; nor any state be formed by the junction of two or more states, or parts of states, without the consent of the legislatures of the states concerned as well as of the Congress.

The Congress shall have power to dispose of and make all needful rules and regulations respecting the territory or other property belonging to the United States; and nothing in this constitution shall be so construed as to prejudice any claims of the United States, or of any particular state.

Sect. 4.   The United States shall guarantee to every state in this union a Republican form of government, and shall protect each of them against invasion; and on application of the legislature, or of the executive (when the legislature cannot be convened) against domestic violence.

ARTICLE V

The Congress, whenever two-thirds of both Houses shall deem it necessary, shall propose amendments to this constitution, or, on the application of the legislatures of two-thirds of the several states, shall call a convention for proposing amendments, which, in either case, shall be valid to all intents and purposes, as part of this constitution, when ratified by the legislatures of three-fourths of the several states, or by conventions in three-fourths thereof, as the one or the other mode of ratification may be proposed by the Congress: Provided, that no amendment which may be made prior to the year one thousand eight hundred and eight shall in any manner affect the first and fourth clauses in the ninth section of the first article; and that no state, without its consent, shall be deprived of its equal suffrage in the Senate.

ARTICLE VI

All debts contracted and engagements entered into, before the adoption of this constitution, shall be as valid against the United States under this constitution, as under the confederation.

This constitution, and the laws of the United States which shall be made in pursuance thereof; and all treaties made, or which shall be made, under the authority of the United States, shall be the supreme law of the land; and the judges in every state shall be bound thereby, any thing in the constitution or laws of any state to the contrary notwithstanding.

The senators and representatives before mentioned, and the members of the several state legislatures, and all executive and judicial officers, both of the United States and of the several states, shall be bound by oath or affirmation, to support this constitution; but no religious test shall ever be required as a qualification to any office or public trust under the United States.

ARTICLE VII

The ratification of the conventions of nine states, shall be sufficient for the establishmentof this constitution between the states so ratifying the same.

DONE in Convention, by the unanimous consent of the States present, the seventeenth day of September, in the year of our Lord one thousand seven hundred and eighty-seven, and of the Independence of the United States of America the twelfth. In witness whereof we have hereunto subscribed our Names.

GEORGE WASHINGTON, President,
And Deputy from VIRGINIA,

NEW-HAMPSHIRE.	John Langdon, Nicholas Gilman.
MASSACHUSETTS.	Nathaniel Gorham, Rufus King.
CONNECTICUT.	William Samuel Johnson, Roger Sherman.
NEW-YORK.	Alexander Hamilton.
NEW-JERSEY.	William Livingston, David Brearly, William Paterson, Jonathan Dayton.
PENNSYLVANIA.	Benjamin Franklin, Thomas Mifflin, Robert Morris, George Clymer, Thomas Fitzsimons, Jared Ingersoll, James Wilson, Gouverneur Morris.
DELAWARE.	George Read, Gunning Bedford, Junior, John Dickinson, Richard Bassett, Jacob Broom.
MARYLAND.	James M'Henry, Daniel of St. Tho. Jenifer, Daniel Carrol.
VIRGINIA.	John Blair, James Madison, Junior.
NORTH-CAROLINA.	William Blount, Richard Dobbs Spaight, Hugh Williamson, John Rutledge.
SOUTH-CAROLINA.	Charles Cotesworth Pinckney, Charles Pinckney, Pierce Butler.
GEORGIA.	William Few, Abraham Baldwin.

Attest. WILLIAM JACKSON, *Secretary.*

AMENDMENTS

I.   Congress shall make no law respecting an establishment of religion, or prohibiting the free exercise thereof; or abridging the freedom of speech, or of the press; or the right of the people peaceably to assemble, and to petition the Government for a redress of grievances.

II.   A well-regulated militia, being necessary to the security of a free State, the right of the people to keep and bear arms, shall not be infringed.

III.   No soldier shall, in time of peace be quartered in any house, without the consent of the owner, nor in time of war, but in a manner to be prescribed by law.

IV.   The right of the people to be secure in their persons, houses, papers, and effects, against unreasonable searches and seizures, shall not be violated, and no warrants shall issue, but upon probable cause, supported by oath or affirmation, and particularly describing the place to be searched, and the persons or things to be seized.

V.   No person shall be held to answer for a capital, or otherwise infamous crime, unless on a presentment or indictment of a grand jury, except in cases arising in the land or naval forces, or in the militia, when in actual service in time of war or public danger; nor shall any person be subject for the same offence to be twice put in jeopardy of life or limb; nor shall be compelled in any criminal case to be a witness against himself, nor be deprived of life, liberty, or property, without due process of law; nor shall private property be taken for public use, without just compensation.

VI.   In all criminal prosecutions, the accused shall enjoy the right to a speedy and public trial, by an impartial jury of the State and district wherein the crime shall have been committed, which district shall have been previously ascertained by law, and to be informed of the nature and cause of the accusation; to be confronted with the witnesses against him; to have compulsory process for obtaining witnesses in his favor, and to have the assistance of counsel for his defence.

VII.   In suits at common law, where the value in controversy shall exceed twenty dollars, the right of trial by jury shall be preserved, and no fact tried by a jury, shall be otherwise reexamined in any court of the United States, than according to the rules of the common law.

VIII.   Excessive bail shall not be required, nor excessive fines imposed, nor cruel and unusual punishments inflicted.

IX.   The enumeration in the Constitution, of certain rights, shall not be construed to deny or disparage others retained by the people.

X.   The powers not delegated to the United States by the Constitution, nor prohibited by it to the States, are reserved to the States respectively, or to the people.[1]

XI.   The judicial power of the United States shall not be construed to extend to any suit in law or equity, commenced or prosecuted against one of the United States by citizens of another State, or by citizens or subjects of any foreign state.[2]

XII.   The electors shall meet in their respective States, and vote by ballot for President and Vice-President, one of whom, at least, shall not be an inhabitant of the same State with themselves; they shall name in their ballots the person voted for as President, and in distinct ballots the person voted for as Vice-President, and they shall make distinct lists of all persons voted for as President, and of all persons voted for as Vice-President, and of the number of votes for each, which lists they shall sign and certify, and transmit, sealed, to the seat of the government of the United States, directed to the President of the Senate. The President of the Senate shall, in the presence of the Senate and House of Representatives, open all the certificates, and the votes shall then be counted. The person having the greatest number of votes for President, shall be the President, if such number be a majority of the whole number of electors appointed; and if no person have such majority, then from the persons having the highest numbers not exceeding three

---

1. The first ten amendments took effect December 15, 1791.

2. Proclaimed January 8, 1798.

on the list of those voted for as President, the House of Representatives shall choose immediately, by ballot, the President. But in choosing the President, the votes shall be taken by States, the representation from each State having one vote; a quorum for this purpose shall consist of a member or members from two-thirds of the States, and a majority of all the States shall be necessary to a choice. And if the House of Representatives shall not choose a President whenever the right of choice shall devolve upon them, before the fourth day of March[3] next following, then the Vice-President shall act as President, as in the case of the death or other constitutional disability of the President. The person having the greatest number of votes as Vice-President, shall be the Vice-President, if such number be a majority of the whole number of electors appointed, and if no person have a majority, then from the two highest numbers on the list, the Senate shall choose the Vice-President; a quorum for the purpose shall consist of two-thirds of the whole number of Senators, and a majority of the whole number shall be necessary to a choice. But no person constitutionally ineligible to the office of President shall be eligible to that of Vice-President of the United States.[4]

XIII. Section 1. Neither slavery nor involuntary servitude, except as a punishment for crime whereof the party shall have been duly convicted shall exist within the United States, or any place subject to their jurisdiction.

Section 2. Congress shall have power to enforce this article by appropriate legislation.[5]

XIV. Section 1. All persons born or naturalized in the United States, and subject to the jurisdiction thereof, are citizens of the United States and of the State wherein they reside. No State shall make or enforce any law which shall abridge the privileges or immunities of citizens of the United States; nor shall any State deprive any person of life, liberty, or property, without due process of law; nor deny to any person within its jurisdiction the equal protection of the laws.

Section 2. Representatives shall be apportioned among the several States according to their respective numbers, counting the whole number of persons in each State, excluding Indians not taxed. But when the right to vote at any election for the choice of electors for President and Vice-President of the United States, Representatives in Congress, the executive and judicial officers of a State, or the members of the legislature thereof, is denied to any of the male inhabitants of such State, being twenty-one years of age, and citizens of the United States, or in any way abridged, except for participation in rebellion, or other crime, the basis of representation therein shall be reduced in the proportion which the number of such male citizens shall bear to the whole number of male citizens twenty-one years of age in such State.

Section 3. No person shall be a Senator or Representative in Congress, or elector of President and Vice-President, or hold any office, civil or military, under the United States, or under any State, who, having previously taken an oath, as a member of Congress, or as an officer of the United States, or as a member of any State legislature, or as an executive or judicial officer of any State, to support the Constitution of the United States, shall have engaged in insurrection or rebellion against the same, or given aid or comfort to the enemies thereof. But Congress may be a vote of two-thirds of each house, remove such disability.

Section 4. The validity of the public debt of the United States, authorized by law, including debts incurred for payment of pensions and bounties for services in suppressing insurrection or rebellion, shall not be questioned. But neither the United States nor any State shall assume or pay any debt or obligation incurred in aid of insurrection or rebellion against the United States, or any claim for the loss or emancipation of any slave; but all such debts, obligations and claims shall be held illegal and void.

---

3. Superseded by Amendment XX.

4. Proclaimed September 25, 1804.

5. Proclaimed December 18, 1865.

Section 5.   The Congress shall have power to enforce, by appropriate legislation, the provisions of this article.[6]

XV.   Section 1.   The right of citizens of the United States to vote shall not be denied or abridged by the United States or by any State on account of race, color, or previous condition of servitude.

Section 2.   The Congress shall have power to enforce this article by appropriate legislation.[7]

XVI.   The Congress shall have power to lay and collect taxes on incomes, from whatever source derived, without apportionment among the several States, and without regard to any census or enumeration.[8]

XVII.   The Senate of the United States shall be composed of two Senators from each State, elected by the people thereof, for six years; and each Senator shall have one vote. The electors in each State shall have the qualifications requisite for electors of the most numerous branch of the State legislature.

When vacancies happen in the representation of any State in the Senate, the executive authority of such State shall issue writs of election to fill such vacancies: Provided, That the legislature of any State may empower the executive thereof to make temporary appointments until the people fill the vacancies by election as the legislature may direct.

This amendment shall not be so construed as to affect the election or term of any Senator chosen before it becomes valid as part of the Constitution.[9]

XVIII.   Section 1.   After one year from the ratification of this article the manufacture, sale, or transportation of intoxicating liquors within, the importation thereof into, or the exportation thereof from the United States and all territory subject to the jurisdiction thereof for beverage purposes is hereby prohibited.

Section 2.   The Congress and the several States shall have concurrent power to enforce this article by appropriate legislation.

Section 3.   This article shall be inoperative unless it shall have been ratified as an amendment to the Constitution by the legislatures of the several States, as provided in the Constitution, within seven years from the date of the submission hereof to the States by the Congress.[10]

XIX.   The right of citizens of the United States to vote shall not be denied or abridged by the United States or by any State on account of sex.

Congress shall have power to enforce this article by appropriate legislation.[11]

XX.   Section 1.   The terms of the President and Vice-President shall end at noon on the 20th day of January, and the terms of Senators and Representatives at noon on the 3rd day of January, of the years in which such terms would have ended if this article had not been ratified; and the terms of their successors shall then begin.

Section 2.   The Congress shall assemble at least once in every year, and such meeting shall begin at noon on the 3rd day of January, unless they shall by law appoint a different day.

Section 3.   If, at the time fixed for the beginning of the term of the President, the President-elect shall have died, the Vice-President-elect shall become President. If a President shall not have been chosen before the time fixed for the beginning of his term, or if the President-elect shall have failed to qualify, then the Vice-President-elect shall act as President until a President shall have qualified; and the Congress may by law provide for the case wherein neither a President-

---

6. Proclaimed July 28, 1868.

7. Proclaimed March 30, 1870.

8. Proclaimed February 25, 1913.

9. Proclaimed May 31, 1913.

10. Proclaimed January 29, 1919; rescinded by Amendment XXI.

11. Proclaimed August 26, 1920.

elect nor a Vice-President-elect shall have qualified, declaring who shall then act as President, or the manner in which one who is to act shall be selected, and such person shall act accordingly until a President or Vice-President shall have qualified.

Section 4. The Congress may by law provide for the case of the death of any of the persons from whom the House of Representatives may choose a President whenever the right of choice shall have devolved upon them, and for the case of the death of any of the persons from whom the Senate may choose a Vice-President whenever the right of choice shall have devolved upon them.

Section 5. Sections 1 and 2 shall take effect on the 15th day of October following the ratification of this article.

Section 6. This article shall be inoperative unless it shall have been ratified as an amendment to the Constitution by the legislatures of three-fourths of the several States within seven years from the date of its submission.[12]

XXI. Section 1. The eighteenth article of amendment to the Constitution of the United States is hereby repealed.

Section 2. The transportation or importation into any State, Territory, or possession of the United States for delivery or use therein of intoxicating liquors, in violation of the laws thereof, is hereby prohibited.

Section 3. This article shall be inoperative unless it shall have been ratified as an amendment to the Constitution by conventions in the several States, as provided in the Constitution, within seven years from the date of the submission hereof to the States by the Congress.[13]

XXII. Section 1. No person shall be elected to the office of the President more than twice, and no person who has held the office of President, or acted as President, for more than two years of a term to which some other person was elected President shall be elected to the office of the President more than once. But this Article shall not apply to any person holding the office of President when this article was proposed by the Congress, and shall not prevent any person who may be holding the office of President, or acting as President, during the term within which this Article becomes operative from holding the office of President or acting as President during the remainder of such term.

Section 2. This article shall be inoperative unless it shall have been ratified as an amendment to the Constitution by the legislatures of three-fourths of the several States within seven years from the date of its submission to the States by the Congress.[14]

XXIII. Section 1. The District constituting the seat of Government of the United States shall appoint in such manner as the Congress may direct:

A number of electors of President and Vice-President equal to the whole number of Senators and Representatives in Congress to which the District would be entitled if it were a State, but in no event more than the least populous State; they shall be in addition to those appointed by the States, but they shall be considered, for the purposes of the election of President and Vice-President, to be electors appointed by a State; and they shall meet in the District and perform such duties as provided by the twelfth article of amendment.

Section 2. The Congress shall have power to enforce this article by appropriate legislation.[15]

XXIV. Section 1. The right of citizens of the United States to vote in any primary or other election for President or Vice-President, for electors for President or Vice-President or for Senators or Representatives in Congress, shall not be denied or abridged by the United States or any State by reason of failure to pay any poll tax or other tax.

---

12. Proclaimed February 6, 1933.

13. Proclaimed December 5, 1933.

14. Certified as adopted by the Administrator of General Services on March 1, 1951 [16 FR 2019].

15. Certified April 3, 1961.

Section 2.   The Congress shall have power to enforce this article by appropriate legislation.[16]

XXV.   Section 1.   In case of the removal of the President from office or of his death or resignation, the Vice President shall become President.

Section 2.   Whenever there is a vacancy in the office of the Vice-President, the President shall nominate a Vice-President who shall take office upon confirmation by a majority vote of both Houses of Congress.

Section 3.   Whenever the President transmits to the President pro tempore of the Senate and the Speaker of the House of Representatives his written declaration that he is unable to discharge the powers and duties of his office, and until he transmits to them a written declaration to the contrary, such powers and duties shall be discharged by the Vice-President as Acting President.

Section 4.   Whenever the Vice-President and a majority of either the principal officers of the executive departments or of such other body as Congress may by law provide, transmit to the President pro tempore of the Senate and the Speaker of the House of Representatives their written declaration that the President is unable to discharge the powers and duties of his office, the Vice-President shall immediately assume the powers and duties of the office as Acting President.

Thereafter, when the President transmits to the President pro tempore of the Senate and the Speaker of the House of Representatives his written declaration that no inability exists, he shall resume the powers and duties of his office unless the Vice-President and a majority of either the principal officers of the executive departments or of such other body as Congress may by law provide, transmit within four days to the President pro tempore of the Senate and the Speaker of the House of Representatives their written declaration that the President is unable to discharge the powers and duties of his office. Thereupon Congress shall decide the issue, assembling within forty-eight hours for that purpose if not in session. If the Congress, within twenty-one days after receipt of the latter written declaration, or, if Congress is not in session, within twenty-one days after Congress is required to assemble, determines by two-thirds vote of both Houses that the President is unable to discharge the powers and duties of his office, the Vice-President shall continue to discharge the same as Acting President; otherwise, the President shall resume the powers and duties of his office.[17]

XXVI.   Section 1.   The right of citizens of the United States, who are eighteen years of age or older, to vote shall not be denied or abridged by the United States or by any State on account of age.

Section 2.   The Congress shall have power to enforce this article by appropriate legislation.[18]

---

16. Certified February 5, 1964.

17. Certified February 23, 1967.

18. Certified July 7, 1971.

Index

Abortions, 364
Abstention, 170
Administrative inspection, 428
Administrative Office of the U.S. Courts, 14
Advisory opinions, 19
Airlines, 153
Alienage, 389
Amish religion, 238–41
Amnesty, 79
Appointments, 74
Apportionment, 398
Assimilative Crime Act, 169
Atomic Energy Commission, 167
Automobiles, 426

Baconsfield, 221
Bakers, 354
Ballots, 405
Bartenders, 369
Baseball, 46
Bible reading, 247
Bill of attainder, 184
Blockade, 70
Bond elections, 414
Busing, 383

Captive audience, 332
Cases and controversies, 20
Cash registers, 144
Certiorari, 11
Chain stores, 368
Child Labor Tax Law, 111
Church property, 232
Citizenship, 479
Civil rights acts, 90–91
Cohabitation, 387
Coke, Sir Edward, 31
Comity, 173
Commerce, regulation of, 87, 93–108, 125–41
Confessions, 448
Confidentiality, 60
Congress, 81–123
Conscientious objectors, 231
Constitution, 493
Contempt of court, 276, 460
Contraceptives, 361
Contract clause, 188
Corporations, 368, 487
Corwin, Edward S., 55
Counsel, 442
Court of Claims, 52

Courts of Appeals, 9
Criminal procedure, 425
Currency exchanges, 369

Death penalty, 474
Declaratory judgments, 19
De facto segregation, 384
Delegation of power, 83–84
Demonstrations, 332
District courts, 7
District of Columbia, schools, 381
Diversity of citizenship, 8
Double jeopardy, 467
Draft cards, 324
Drummers, 149
Due process of law, 339

Effect of unconstitutional statute, 27
Elections, 414
Electronic surveillance, 430
Emergency Price Control Act, 40
Employment tests, 122
Enclaves, 169, 411
Enforcement of decisions, 28
Equal Pay Act, 397
Equal protection, 365ff
Equity, 48
Escheat, 44
Establishment of religion, 228, 242
Executive agreements, 67
Exports, 144
Ex post facto laws, 186

Federal courts, history of, 6–7
Federal enclave, 169, 411
Federalism, 87
Fees, 443
Fighting words, 274
Fiscal powers, 88, 108, 125
Flag desecration, 322
Flag salute, 237
Forced disclosure, 292
Foreign relations, 64
Freedom of choice, 383
Freedom of religion, 201, 227
Freedom of speech, 253
Frisk, 427, 439
Full faith and credit, 173

Georgia Railroad Co., 194
Girard College, 217

Government bonds, 167
Government employees, 310
Grandfather clauses, 386
Gross sales tax, 156–62

Habeas corpus, 41, 171–72, 179–84
Handbills, 327
Harmless error, 443
Hatch Act, 314
Hawaiian Organic Act, 181
Help-wanted ads, 291
Higher education, 382
Highways, 123

Identification card, 285
Illegitimacy, 391
Immunity of executive officers, 85
Immunity technique, 446
Impact of decisions, 28
Impeachment, 5
Implied powers, 91
Imports, 141
Incorporation theory, 203–7
Indigents, 416–23
Intergovernmental taxation, 163–68
International law, 46–48
Interstate agreements, 173
Investigations, 84–86

Japanese, 72
Judges, election of, 403
Judicial review, 15–38
Juries, 388
Jury trial, 457
Justices, list of, 489
Juvenile courts, 477

Ku Klux Klan Act, 214

Law applied, 41
Legislative courts, 13
Legislature, 81–123
Libel, 271
Liquor, 128, 131
Literacy test, 115–16
Lottery, 194
Loyalty oaths, 306

Mail, 428
Membership lists, 292
Military powers, 70

Military trials, 459
Milk, 135
Minimum wage, 358
Miranda rules, 453
Miscegenation, 387
Montesquieu, 82
Mormon Church, 234
Motion pictures, 283
Motor vehicles, 155
Mudguards, 135

National Industrial Recovery Act, 84
Nationality, 389
Natural resources, 128
News media, 463
Newsmen, 301

Obscenity, 263, 283
Occupation of field, 138
Omnibus Crime Control Act, 41, 431
Open housing, 119, 223
Original package, 141

Parades, 332
Pardons, 77
Parks, 221
Parole, 477
Passports, 68, 485
Pearl Harbor, 181
Peddlers, 150
Petty offenses, 459
Pickets, 326
Plea bargaining, 452
Pledge of allegiance, 237
Police power, 194
Political questions, 29
Poll tax, 403
Poor persons, 416, 423
Postal inspection, 428
Preemption, 138–41
Pregnancy, 340
President, 53–79
Previous restraint, 280
Price fixing, 137
Prince Edward County, 382
Prisoners, 318
Privacy, 423
Private club, 224
Privileges and immunities, 482
Professions, 487
Property rights, 369

Property taxes, 167
Pupil assignment laws, 382

Race, 377
Reapportionment, 398
Recreational facilities, 224
Registration, 407
Released time, 344
Religion, freedom of, 201, 227
Religious tests, 200
Removal from state courts, 8
Removal power, 74–77
Rendition, 172
Residence, 407
Restrictive covenants, 211
Retroactive laws, 188
Retroactive rules, 477
Right to contract, 354
Right to reply, 291
Right to work laws, 360

Sales taxes, 152, 166
School finance, 371
Searches and seizures, 425
Security programs, 308
Sedition, 253
Segregation, 377
Self-incrimination, 445
Separability, 28
Separation of powers, 82–83
Service connected crimes, 459
Service tax, 155
Sex, 394
Sit-ins, 215, 217–21
Smith Act, 255, 260
Soldiers, 316
Sound amplifiers, 332
Special prosecutor, 77
Speech and Debate Clause, 82
Standing to sue, 23
State action concept, 208
Statutes invalidated, 35
Steel mills, 58
Stewardship theory, 55
Student rights, 310
Suits against states, 48
Sunday closing laws, 230
Supreme Court, 9–13
Suspect classifications, 377
Swimming pools, 223
Symbolic speech, 322

Three-judge cases, 9
Tobacco, 140
Trains, 127
Transportation media, 127
Travel right, 419
Treason, 198
Treaties, 88
Trial by jury, 457
Trucks, 133, 155

Unemployment tax, 113
Use tax, 150, 153

Vietnam, 72
Voting rights, 117, 386, 398

Warrants, 426
Warren, Charles, 37
Water vessels, 156
Watergate, 55, 60–63, 77
Welfare, 419
White primary, 386
Wilson, Woodrow, 84
Wiretapping, 430
Women's rights, 394

Yazoo land fraud, 190
Yellow-dog contracts, 356

Zoning, 364